Windows Phone 7 Game Development

Adam Dawes

Apress®

Windows Phone 7 Game Development

President and Publisher: Paul Manning
Lead Editors: Mark Beckner, Ewan Buckingham
Technical Reviewer: Don Sorcinelli
Editorial Board: Steve Anglin, Mark Beckner, Ewan Buckingham, Gary Cornell, Jonathan Gennick, Jonathan Hassell, Michelle Lowman, Matthew Moodie, Duncan Parkes, Jeffrey Pepper, Frank Pohlmann, Douglas Pundick, Ben Renow-Clarke, Dominic Shakeshaft, Matt Wade, Tom Welsh
Coordinating Editor: Mary Tobin
Copy Editor: Nancy Sixsmith
Compositor: MacPS, LLC
Indexer: Brenda Miller
Artist: April Milne
Cover Designer: Anna Ishchenko

Distributed to the book trade worldwide by Springer Science+Business Media, LLC., 233 Spring Street, 6th Floor, New York, NY 10013. Phone 1-800-SPRINGER, fax (201) 348-4505, e-mail orders-ny@springer-sbm.com, or visit www.springeronline.com.

For information on translations, please e-mail rights@apress.com, or visit www.apress.com.

Apress and friends of ED books may be purchased in bulk for academic, corporate, or promotional use. eBook versions and licenses are also available for most titles. For more information, reference our Special Bulk Sales–eBook Licensing web page at www.apress.com/info/bulksales.

The information in this book is distributed on an "as is" basis, without warranty. Although every precaution has been taken in the preparation of this work, neither the author(s) nor Apress shall have any liability to any person or entity with respect to any loss or damage caused or alleged to be caused directly or indirectly by the information contained in this work.

The source code for this book is available to readers at www.apress.com.

For Ritu and Kieran.

Contents at a Glance

Contents

About the Author

 **Adam Dawes** is a software developer and systems architect working at a cutting-edge online service development company.

He has been a compulsive programmer since the age of four, when he was first introduced to a monochrome Commodore PET. The love affair has continued through three subsequent decades, flourishing through the days of the 8-bit dinosaurs to today's era of multicore processors and pocket supercomputers.

A constant throughout Adam's career has been his fondness for computer games. From the very first time *Nightmare Park* displayed its devious maze of pathways in green symbols back in 1980, he has been a games player across a variety of genres and styles. These days, he spends his spare time playing the latest 3D titles on his PC, or enjoying some of the classics in his stand-up arcade machine or sit-in cockpit driving cabinet. Creating his own games has always been a hobby and, while he has no intention of becoming part of the professional games industry, he has a lot of fun developing his own titles.

Adam lives with his wife Ritu and son Kieran in southeast England. His web site is at www.adamdawes.com (all his finished projects can be downloaded there) and he can be emailed at adam@adamdawes.com. He would particularly like to see the results of your own game development projects.

About the Technical Reviewer

■ **Don Sorcinelli** has been involved with planning, developing, and deploying enterprise applications for over 15 years. His involvement in these processes expanded to include the PDA platforms starting in the late 1990s. He is currently a Product Engineer focused on Mobile Device Management solutions.

Don frequently presents on Windows Mobile topics for users, developers, and IT professionals. As a result, he was awarded Most Valuable Professional status for Windows Mobile Devices by Microsoft Corporation in January 2004 for his work with the Windows Mobile community.

Currently, Don is co-manager of the Boston/New England Windows Mobile User and Developer Group, and webmaster of BostonPocketPC.com (http://www.bostonpocketpc.com). He can be contacted at donsorcinelli@bostonpocketpc.com.

Acknowledgments

I must start by thanking my parents for all the opportunities they gave me when I was growing up and for encouraging my computer habit from a very young age.

Thank you to everyone at Apress for their assistance in getting this book written and delivered; in particular to Mark Beckner for allowing me the opportunity in the first place, to Mary Tobin for her tireless assistance and encouragement, and to Nancy Sixsmith for making the book much more readable and for putting up with correcting the same grammatical errors over and over again.

I owe thanks, too, to Don Sorcinelli for his invaluable input throughout the whole book, and to Mike Ormond for arranging for me to get my hands on a real live Windows Phone 7 device during the writing of the book.

And finally, of course, thanks without end to my wife Ritu and my son Kieran, for their constant encouragement and for tolerating my shutting myself in my study and writing every evening and weekend. I'll be spending much more time with you both now, I promise!

Introduction

This Goal of This Book

Gaming on the move has become very popular during recent years. With the arrival of the Nintendo Gameboy, people realized that they could take their games out and about with them, and as technology has become more sophisticated these games have grown, too. They now encompass complex game mechanics, advanced 2D and 3D graphics, and engrossing stories and game worlds that the player can literally become lost in.

Alongside this phenomenon is the explosion in popularity of mobile communication devices. Nearly everyone carries a phone with them every time they leave the house. These devices have become much more than just phones, however; they provide contact management, e-mail, web browsing, satellite navigation, and entertainment.

Writing games for mobile devices allows both these trends to be brought together into the same place. It is very easy for people to "pick up and play" a game on their mobile device as they always have it in their pocket—whether they are progressing through a sprawling role-playing game on a train or simply want the few minutes of casual diversion that mobile gaming can provide while waiting for an appointment.

Windows Phone 7 Game Development aims to bring you the knowledge and techniques that you will need to create your own games for devices running the Microsoft's powerful Windows Phone 7 operating system. Starting with the basics of the platform and its development environment, and progressing through to advanced topics such as 3D graphics, it will guide you step by step toward creating a simple and manageable environment into which you can write your own mobile games and distribute them to the world for fun or profit. Example projects are provided to demonstrate all the techniques discussed and are ideal as a basis for experimentation.

Both of the application environments supported by Windows Phone 7 are addressed, exploring how games can be produced in the dedicated gaming environment, XNA, and also in the more general-purpose and user-interface-driven Silverlight.

Who This Book Is For

This book is written for those who are already familiar with programming one of the two main managed Visual Studio languages: C# or Visual Basic.NET. It is assumed that you already have a grasp of the fundamentals of programming and are familiar with using the environment for PC-based application development. This is not an introduction to programming or to Visual Studio itself.

You will, however, be given a complete guide to setting up the development environment for Windows Phone 7 programming, getting your first programs to compile, and interactively debugging your games as they run either on the Windows Phone 7 emulator included with the phone's free software development kit or on a real device.

In order to develop software for your device, you will need to use the Visual Studio 2010 development environment. If you already have Visual Studio 2010, you can integrate the Windows Phone 7 development tools into your existing environment; if you do not have it, you can obtain Visual

Studio 2010 Express for Windows Phone free of charge via a simple download from the Microsoft web site.

Although most of the projects in the book can be developed using the provided emulator, it is strongly recommended that you also have access to a real device to test your games.

The examples in this book are all written using C#, the only development language fully supported for Windows Phone 7 development. Developers who are more familiar with VB.NET should find that the language code and concepts translate over to C# fairly easily, so this should not present too much of a barrier to entry.

Chapter Overview

The following is a brief description of each chapter. The chapters tend to build on one another, so it is recommended that you read them in sequence to avoid knowledge gaps in later chapters.

Chapter 1 introduces Windows Phone 7 and using the Visual Studio 2010 development environment to create Windows Phone 7 games and applications. It explains how to set up simple .NET projects running against the emulator and real devices, explores debugging techniques, and begins to look at the two application environments: XNA and Silverlight.

Chapter 2 dives into XNA, exploring in detail the structure of XNA projects, the approach to displaying and updating graphics, how *sprites* can be used to create complex 2D graphics output, and how to work with fonts and text.

Chapter 3 takes the concepts explored so far and builds them into a simple reusable game framework that simplifies many of the tedious elements of setting up a game project. This allows you to focus on the game itself rather than getting weighed down with object management. This chapter also introduces the first of the example game projects in this book: *Cosmic Rocks*.

Chapter 4 covers the subject of user input. All sorts of input devices are available on Windows Phone 7 devices, from touch screens and keyboards through to accelerometers, and they are explored in detail to show how they can be used to allow your games to be controlled.

Chapter 5 turns up the volume and reveals the options for game audio. Covering simple sound effects to MP3 music playback, everything you need to know about sound for your games can be found here.

Chapter 6 begins to explore rendering with vertices and matrices instead of using sprites. Matrix transformations are uncovered and explained so that graphics can be rotated, scaled, and translated; and concepts such as texture mapping, blending, and alpha effects in this environment are explored.

Chapter 7 lifts the XNA feature set up into the third dimension, explaining how to create 3D game worlds. Subjects covered include perspective and orthographic projections, the depth buffer, and lighting so that your scenes really come to life.

Chapter 8 continues the exploration of XNA in the third dimension and introduces a number of useful new rendering features. These features include importing 3D objects from third-party modeling packages, moving and manipulating the camera within a game world, using particle effects, creating background imagery with sky boxes, applying fog to a 3D scene, and using XNA's Effect objects to add new features and capabilities to your game.

Chapter 9 provides some useful reusable components that can be used in any game. A simple mechanism for loading and saving user settings and a high-score table implementation are provided to allow you to focus on writing your game rather than having to reinvent these features yourself.

Chapter 10 exposes the Windows Phone 7 application life cycle and *tombstoning*, an essential topic that you will need to get to grips with so that your game can live side by side with other applications that the user chooses to open on their device.

Chapter 11 moves away from XNA and begins to explore Windows Phone 7's other application environment: Silverlight. While not specifically geared around games, Silverlight still has plenty of capabilities and great potential for game development. This chapter introduces the environment and explores how it is used.

Chapter 12 takes a more detailed look at the controls that are available for use in Silverlight projects, and also explores topics such as page navigation, orientation, and full-screen mode.

Chapter 13 focuses on game development in Silverlight, building a simple but flexible sprite control, and covering topics such as hardware acceleration, storyboard animation, game timing, and user input. It also begins development of this book's second example game project: *Diamond Lines*.

Chapter 14 steps through a series of additional Silverlight topics, exploring subjects including navigation through the different stages of a game, music and sound effects, game settings, high-score tables, and Silverlight's view of the application life cycle.

Chapter 15 sets up shop inside the Windows Phone Marketplace. This is the outlet that you need to use to distribute your game to the rest of the world, and possibly make some money from it, too. The chapter contains a guide to the Marketplace submission requirements, as well as tips on testing your game, managing versions, creating trial versions, and promoting your game to encourage people to try it.

Chapter 16 brings things to a close by stepping back from the phone and looking at how both XNA and Silverlight games can be brought to life on other platforms. XNA games can be played on Windows PCs (as well as the Xbox 360), and Silverlight games can be run in a variety of web browsers. This chapter shows you how to painlessly convert your games so that they run in these environments.

PART 1

■■■

The Beginning

CHAPTER 1

■ ■ ■

Windows Phone and .NET

It is a genuine pleasure to develop software for Windows Phone 7 devices using Visual Studio .NET.

Microsoft's latest version of its mobile operating system provides a very different environment from the versions that came before it. Virtually everything about Windows Phone is new to the mobile platform: it includes an entirely redesigned user interface, implements the powerful XNA audio/visual libraries for high-performance gaming, and has standard high-specification hardware requirements that all devices are obliged to meet.

There is one key element of Windows Phone that has stayed essentially the same as the platforms that preceded it: the use of the .NET programming environment to create games and applications. This brings with it some exceedingly powerful and flexible programming languages and one of the best development environments available anywhere.

The development platform for Microsoft's mobile devices has advanced substantially over the last decade. During the early years of the original Windows Mobile/Pocket PC operating system, programming involved using the suite of eMbedded Visual tools. They came supporting two different languages: eMbedded Visual Basic and eMbedded Visual C++.

eMbedded Visual Basic was based on the same technologies as Visual Basic for Applications (VBA). It was similar in a number of ways to Visual Basic 6 (VB6), the desktop version of VB that was current at the time, but had many shortcomings, such as the lack of strongly typed variables and poor object orientation features. Programs were written using a stand-alone integrated development environment (IDE), which had its own peculiarities and different ways of working than VB6.

eMbedded Visual C++ presented more of a challenge because of differences not only in the IDE but also in the code. Although established C++ programmers would no doubt have managed to pick up this language without too many problems, those who were less well versed in the intricacies of C++ might have found the amount of new information they needed to learn a significant barrier to entry.

All this changed with the release of Visual Studio .NET and the .NET Compact Framework (.NET CF). .NET CF provides a set of class libraries that are parallel to the desktop .NET Framework. The libraries are not identical because parts of the full .NET Framework functionality are missing from .NET CF. However, a substantial set of identical functionality does exist, and any programmer who is comfortable developing C# or VB .NET applications for Windows will be instantly at home developing against .NET CF, too.

Windows Phone development uses the very latest Visual Studio 2010. The IDE has made advances in a number of ways since that of the earlier versions of Visual Studio, but best of all, Microsoft has chosen to release an "Express" version of Visual Studio that supports Windows Phone development completely free of charge. Although there are charges and fees involved in some areas of development and in distribution of finished applications (as we will see later in this book when we discuss this subject in more detail), these are generally fairly modest and do not create the barriers to entry that having to purchase the full versions of Visual Studio presented in the past.

The Windows Phone development environment also integrates into the full versions of Visual Studio seamlessly if you have such a version already installed.

On Windows Phone devices, all applications are written using managed .NET code. The Silverlight and XNA runtime libraries are preinstalled on the device, so no awkward installation is required of your end users. Finished games and applications are distributed through a central Marketplace operated by Microsoft, which has support for useful features such as update notifications, trial versions, and protection against piracy.

A major advantage of developing for Windows Phone using Visual Studio .NET is that the exact same IDE is used as for desktop Windows development. There is no need to learn the details or keyboard shortcuts of a new IDE; instead, you will be working within the environment you are already used to, which includes all your user interface tweaks and preferences changes. Developing an application for Windows Phone is simply a question of creating a different project type.

Programming within Visual Studio .NET also means that the Windows Phone developer can take advantage of the maturity of the Visual Studio.NET development environment. Microsoft has spent many years improving the user interfaces and functionality of Visual Studio, and countless versions and releases have cumulated in an extremely powerful and user-friendly studio for application design, development, and debugging. All this is at your disposal when developing Windows Phone games and applications.

The Framework also retains much of the power of its desktop cousin, including extensive object orientation features, strong variable typing, generics, flexible collections, and powerful XML processing functions.

Finally, the use of .NET, Silverlight, and XNA means that there are great opportunities for cross-platform development with only a small amount of additional effort. Silverlight games can be modified to run in the browser on a desktop PC, and XNA games can be made to run on a PC or Xbox 360 in addition to the phone.

In this chapter, we will take a closer look at the .NET Framework, at setting up and using Visual Studio, and at creating your first simple Windows Phone application. We will also examine some of the options that are available for game development.

Looking Closely at Visual Studio Development for Windows Phone

Let's start by taking a look at the versions of Visual Studio that we can use for developing software for Windows Phone.

We can develop either using Visual Studio 2010 Express for Windows Phone, which is available free of charge, or by using one of the full versions of Visual Studio. Both products will produce the same resulting games and applications. Visual Studio 2010 has system requirements that necessitate a reasonably modern PC, running either Windows Vista with Service Pack 2 or Windows 7. Both x86 and x64 versions of the operating system can be used, but the Starter Editions of Windows are not supported. A DirectX 10 or later graphics card with a WDDM 1.1 driver is required for developing games using XNA. In practice, this requirement will be met by most graphics cards from the last couple of years, although many mobile graphics chips present in laptop computers might lack these capabilities.

There is no support for developing for Windows Phone in earlier versions of Visual Studio. The good news is that Visual Studio 2010 will install side by side with earlier versions of Visual Studio without causing any problems, so if you need to keep Visual Studio 2005 or 2008 on your PC, you can.

Language Choices

.NET development offers the choice of a number of different languages including C#, VB, and C++. Currently, however, only C# is supported for Windows Phone development. Microsoft is promising support for VB in the near future, so check the latest version of the development environment if you want to use VB for your development.

If you are already familiar with VB, you should find that both reading and writing C# will come naturally with a little practice. In this book we will focus on C# for all of our samples and example code.

IDE Features

As would be expected from Visual Studio, a number of very useful features are available to help develop and debug Windows Phone applications.

Emulators

Visual Studio offers a Windows Phone emulator to help test and debug your programs. Although it is essential to use a real device regularly during your application development process to ensure that everything works properly on actual hardware, being able to use the emulator for general coding and testing is extremely useful. A screenshot of the Windows Phone emulator is shown in Figure 1–1.

Figure 1–1. Windows Phone emulator

The emulator offers a full implementation of the physical device and is capable of running genuine Windows Phone applications. It offers access to a number of features of the device, including the ability to simulate networking, screen rotation, and touch screen input using the mouse cursor. (In fact, if you are developing on a Windows 7 computer with a touch-enabled screen, you can perform touch and multitouch operations on the emulator by touching your PC screen.)

Running your application in an emulator is as simple as can be: just select to use the emulator within the Visual Studio IDE and start your application. The emulator will appear, and your program will run.

When we fire up the emulator shortly, note that it takes a little while to initialize itself. This would get frustrating very quickly when you are in a repeat modify/compile/test cycle, but the emulator can be left running in the background when you stop your code from executing and will then resume much more quickly the next time you begin a debug session. When the emulator's Close button is clicked, it will prompt for confirmation that the emulator is really no longer required, which is very useful protection against accidentally closing the window without actually meaning to.

Silverlight Page Designer

A fully featured page designer is available to lay out windows and controls for use within Silverlight programs. The designer goes as far as to display an image of the device around the edge of your page to help visualize its appearance.

Silverlight pages can be created and modified by either using the designer or by editing the underlying eXtensible Application Markup Language (XAML, which is generally pronounced "zammal"). We will look at XAML and the Silverlight page designer in a great deal more detail later in this book. Visual Studio will display both the designer and the XAML editor as side-by-side panels within the IDE, as shown in Figure 1–2, and any change made to either will be immediately reflected in the corresponding panel. This provides a very flexible mechanism for page design, allowing each panel to work together to perform their actions more efficiently.

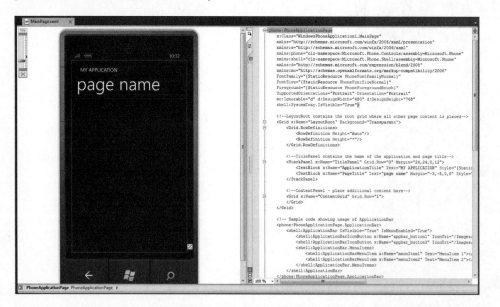

Figure 1–2. The Silverlight page editor showing the designer and page source together

Breakpoints

Another extremely useful tool is Visual Studio's breakpoint feature. No doubt familiar to any desktop developer, breakpoints are fully supported for Windows Phone development, too, and can be used both when running against the emulator and against a physical device. It can be extremely useful to break into your code, examine your variables, and step through the instructions while watching the results on a real device on the desk next to you.

Debug Output

Access to the Visual Studio Output window is available from Windows Phone applications running inside the IDE. Text can be written to the Output window at any time, allowing you to easily keep track of what your program is doing. Pairing this with the ability to have two independent screens (your PC screen and your mobile device screen) makes this tool particularly powerful.

Windows Phone Platform

One of the major changes that Microsoft has made for Windows Phone, as compared with the previous Windows Mobile platform, concerns hardware requirements.

The huge diversity of hardware could provide quite a barrier for entry for Windows Mobile. Devices all had different screen resolutions, different hardware buttons, and a fairly substantial range of other internal hardware. Writing games and applications that worked across the entire set of devices could result in a considerable amount of additional effort, whereas saving time by not addressing all these platforms could exclude a significant proportion of the potential customer base from being able to use the application.

This has been tackled head on in Windows Phone by requiring a very rigid set of hardware requirements. It will be interesting to see how they evolve as time passes and technology evolves, but for the time being you can depend upon this hardware platform being present in all Windows Phone devices.

Let's take a look at what we can expect.

Screen Hardware

To begin with, all Windows Phone devices will have a screen with a Wide VGA (WVGA) resolution (480 pixels across by 800 pixels tall), which will greatly simplify the task of ensuring that games and applications properly fit on the screen without having to stretch, shrink, or leave large areas of the screen unused.

Microsoft has stated that future devices might use a Half VGA (HVGA) resolution of 480 pixels by 320 pixels, but at the time of writing no such devices have been announced.

All Windows Phone7 devices will have capacitive touch screens. Capacitive screens tend to be much more durable than the resistive screens used in many older devices and tend to be more sensitive. They also offer support for multitouch input, which is generally not available on resistive devices. The main disadvantage of capacitive screens is that they require interaction from a conductive source (such as a finger) and they don't work with a stylus (although special capacitive styluses are available if you hunt around). The design of the Windows Phone operating system is based around touch input rather than stylus input, a decision that is consistent with most smartphone platforms and operating systems currently in production.

Windows Phone devices will support multitouch, with a minimum of four distinct points able to be tracked at once. This opens up some interesting possibilities for gaming, and we'll be looking at how to use multitouch in games later on in this book.

An important consideration when designing a game for a mobile platform is that the screen orientation can be rotated when compared to that of a desktop PC, resulting in a screen that is tall rather than wide. This benefits some types of games (Tetris-style games, for example), but can be problematic for others. Fortunately, Windows Phone 7 has extremely good support for rotating into landscape orientations, so you can take advantage of whichever screen layout best suits your game.

Hardware Buttons

One of the details that Microsoft has been very strict about for devices running its new operating system is hardware buttons. All devices must have exactly three buttons on the front of the device: a Back button, a Windows button, and a Search button.

Having consistency over the available buttons is good for developers as it means that we don't have to worry about lots of combinations of control mechanisms. However, this limited set of buttons means that there will be no directional pad available, which is a pity because they are very useful as a game input device.

Instead we can use the touch screen for input, and there are lots of clever and creative ways that this can be done, from designing games that the user interacts with by touching objects on the screen to displaying movement buttons at the bottom of the screen for the user to press.

These rigid requirements don't rule out the possibility of a device manufacturer including a hardware keyboard with the device, however, and this is likely to be a common feature among Windows Phone 7 devices. Keyboards can be implemented either as a slide-out panel behind the screen or below the screen in a similar style to BlackBerry devices. The presence of a keyboard opens up the opportunities for the player to control your game, but in most cases it would be sensible to avoid making this a necessity for your game to avoid excluding a large proportion of your audience.

Processors

The Windows Phone 7 platform specification states that all devices must be equipped with at least a 1GHz processor. This should result in excellent performance across all devices.

You should expect processor speeds to increase as the platform evolves, so it is important to cater for devices that are running at faster speeds than this, but as a minimum it does mean that a significant amount of processing power will be available on all devices.

Graphics Hardware

One of the problems that developers on the Windows Mobile platform faced was in the choice of a graphics application programming interface (API). It was uncommon for Windows Mobile devices to have hardware acceleration, which meant that the only graphics API available across all devices was the Graphics Device Interface (GDI), which was very lacking both in terms of features and performance.

This problem can be put firmly in the past with Windows Phone. The graphics API for high-performance games is XNA, a powerful library based around the DirectX technology that has been powering desktop PC games for the last decade. The phone implementation isn't quite as powerful as on the desktop, but it still has very impressive capabilities for a mobile device.

Alongside the API is hardware graphics acceleration, which the phone needs to create fast-moving, complex two-dimensional and three-dimensional scenes without bringing the device to its knees. Because it will be included as standard in all devices, the opportunities for gaming are immense.

Location and Orientation

Also standard on all devices will be an accelerometer and a Global Positioning System (GPS) receiver.

The accelerometer can be very useful for game developers. It allows the device to detect which way up it is being held and can sense in detail any movement that results in the device being rotated. This provides an excellent input control mechanism, allowing players to influence what is happening on the screen by physically moving their phones.

Probably of less interest for gaming is the GPS functionality. When appropriate line-of-sight reception has been established with the GPS satellites, the device can detect where in the world it is located. This opens opportunities for making games that revolve around the player's whereabouts, but the scope for this in gaming is likely to be limited.

Cooperation with the Device

Let's not forget an extremely important fact: your game is running on other people's phones and personal organizers. They will place more importance on tasks such as answering a phone call or responding to a calendar reminder alert than in continuing to play your game.

Running applications have limited control over what happens when other features of the device become active. An application that loses focus will be closed down, regardless of whether the user was finished with it.

These terminated applications can be resumed at a later time, and the operating system will indicate that they are being relaunched rather than restarted from scratch. To ensure that users don't lose their progress in a game, we can take care to behave nicely under these conditions: we can save the game state to the device prior to exiting so that it can be automatically restored the next time the game starts and automatically pause when the game resumes to allow the user time to adjust to what is going on. People will appreciate details like these.

This kind of feature often becomes invisible when it works well but is much more likely to be very visible when it *doesn't* work. Make sure that you take these unexpected interactions into consideration.

Using Visual Studio for Windows Phone Development

Let's take a look now at the steps required to begin development of Windows Phone games and applications.

Installing Visual Studio

Installing Visual Studio for Windows Phone development is very easy. If you do not already have a full version of Visual Studio installed, you can visit http://create.msdn.com to download Visual Studio 2010 Express for Windows Phone. This is a free, complete, and fully functional development environment that will provide all the tools needed for you to develop your games.

If you already have a full version of Visual Studio 2010 installed, the same download will allow you to add support for Windows Phone projects to your existing installation. The setup application will detect the presence of Visual Studio 2010 when it is launched, and will download just the components that are required, based on your current system configuration.

Once the installation is complete, Visual Studio 2010 can be launched, and the new project types for Windows Phone development will appear. Figure 1–3 shows the New Project window from Visual Studio 2010 Express for Windows Phone, containing just the Silverlight and XNA project template.

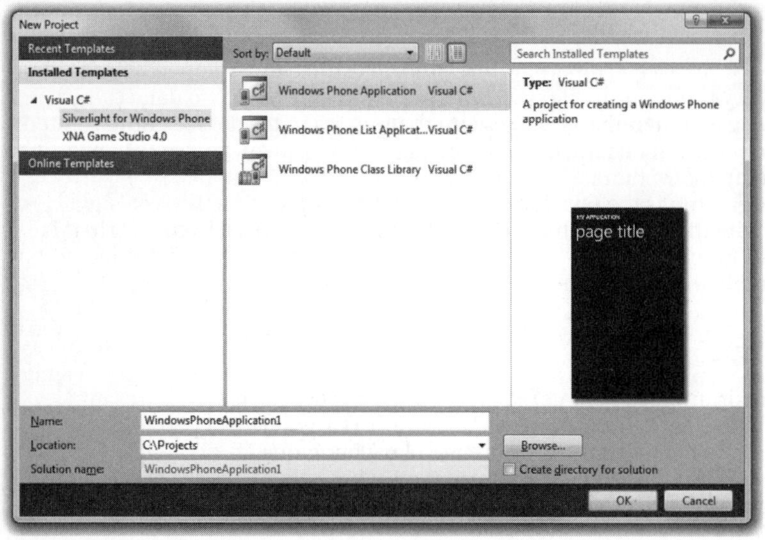

Figure 1–3. Creating a new project in Visual Studio 2010 Express for Windows Phone

Figure 1–4 shows the same window in Visual Studio 2010 Professional with the Windows Phone development tools installed.

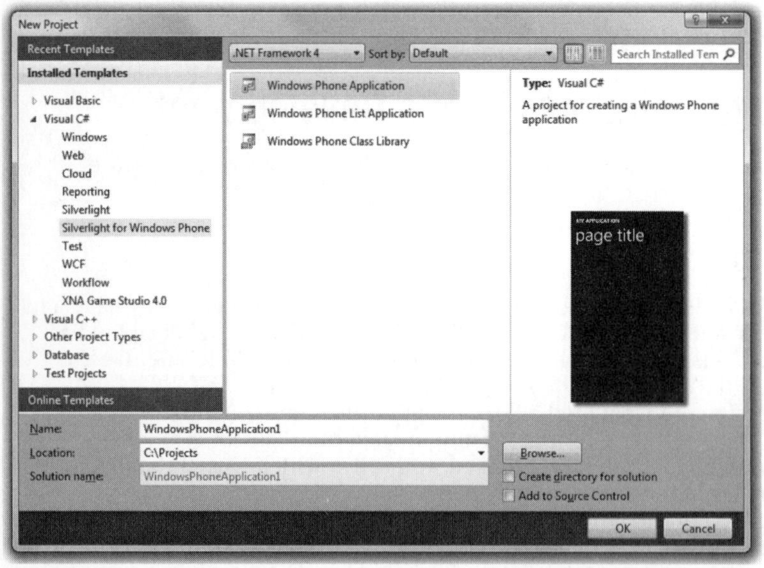

Figure 1–4. Creating a new project in Visual Studio 2010 Professional

Once everything is installed as required, we are ready to begin.

Creating a Windows Phone Project

With tools all in place, it is time to finally create a simple Windows Phone application and take a look at how we interact with both the emulators and real devices. We will create a simple Silverlight application for this purpose.

To begin, select File ➤ New ➤ Project within Visual Studio, and choose the Visual C# item within the list of Installed Templates, followed by the Silverlight for Windows Phone template. The panel to the right will display the available Silverlight templates that can be used to create a new project. Select the Windows Phone Application item.

Above the templates is a drop-down list that allows the .NET Framework version to be selected. For Windows Phone development we will always leave this set to .NET Framework 4.

At the bottom of the window, select a project directory and enter a project name (or accept the default name of WindowsPhoneApplication1 if you wish). Unless you have a particular preference for using separate directories for the solution and project files, uncheck the Create directory for solution check box to keep the directory structure a little tidier.

Once everything is ready, click the OK button to create the project. After a few seconds, the new project will open within the Visual Studio IDE.

Project Templates

A number of different templates are provided by Visual Studio for your new project. Each of these will result in a different initial project for you to start working on, as follows:

- *Silverlight/Windows Phone Application*: This is the main project template for creating Silverlight applications. When we build games using Silverlight later in this book, this is the template we will use to create them.

- *Silverlight/Windows Phone List Application*: This template creates another near-empty Silverlight project, but with a scrollable item list initially present within the main page. This can be a useful shortcut if your user interface takes this form.

- *Silverlight/Windows Phone Class Library*: In order to create a class library that can be used by other Silverlight projects, use this template. Note that Silverlight class libraries cannot be used by XNA projects.

- *XNA Game Studio 4.0/Windows Phone Game*: This is the template to select to create a new XNA game project. We will use this template when we begin creating our first XNA projects in Chapter 2.

- *XNA Game Studio 4.0/Windows Phone Game Library*: Just as with the corresponding Silverlight template, this template creates a class library that can be used by other XNA projects. XNA class libraries cannot be used by Silverlight projects.

It is not possible to change the project type once the project has been created. If you find that you need to change the project once you have started developing it, you will need to create a new project of the required type and copy in all of the existing code files.

Designing a Page

Now, we are ready to make some minor changes to your test application's default page. The page is named MainPage.xaml inside Solution Explorer and should open automatically when the project is created.

On the left half of the page editor window is the page designer and preview area. On the right half is the XAML code for the page. If you want, you can change the orientation of the divide by clicking the Horizontal Split or Vertical Split buttons at the bottom or right of the dividing bar between the two. The two parts can also be quickly swapped over by clicking the Swap Panes button, also located inside the divider. The designer panel also contains a useful zoom slider that allows you to focus more closely on the page design for detailed layout work if required.

Notice that the page is very, well, black. There is actually a good reason for this, and it is something that you'll notice across many of the Windows Phone applications. Windows Phone devices commonly use organic light emitting diode (OLED) screens for display; they provide a sharp image and are highly responsive to updates, but consume more power when they emit more light. Having a black background therefore results in lower power consumption, which is always a good thing for a mobile device.

For the purposes of this simple application, we will simply place a Button control onto the page and get it to display a message when clicked. The Button is added from the toolbox exactly as it would be for a desktop application: click the Button icon in the Toolbox panel and then draw it into the empty region in the center area of the page. The result can be seen in Figure 1–5.

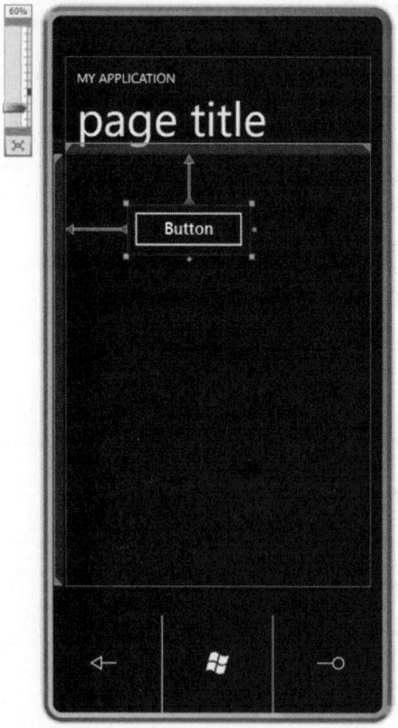

Figure 1–5. Windows Phone Silverlight page designer

Once you have added your Button, take a look at its properties in the Properties window (see Figure 1–6). If you are used to creating Silverlight applications outside of the Windows Phone environment, everything should look very familiar: all the normal Silverlight properties should be present and correct. If you have worked only with Windows Forms in the past, many of these properties might be unfamiliar, but there should also be some whose purpose is obvious. Once again, we'll look into many of these properties in much greater detail in the Silverlight chapters later in this book.

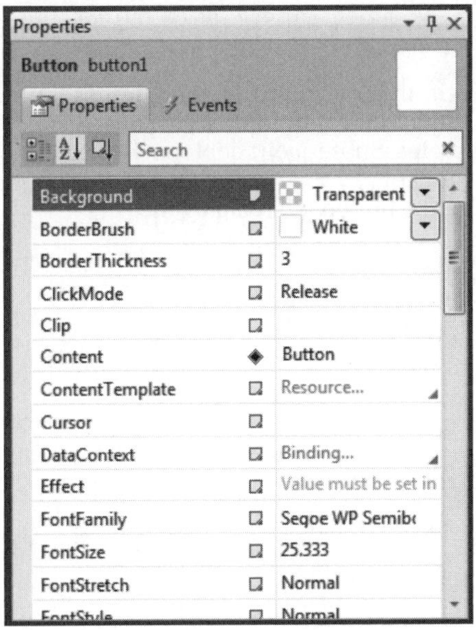

Figure 1–6. *The Button's properties*

■ **TIP** If the Properties window is not open, it can be opened by selecting the View/Properties Window item from Visual Studio's main menus. Under the default key mappings, it can also be opened by pressing F4 on the keyboard.

Double-click the button to open the code designer and create the button's `Click` event handler. This will display the "code behind" file for the page, which is where the C# code is developed. In Solution Explorer you will see that the `MainPage.xaml` item has expanded to reveal `MainPage.xaml.cs` contained within. These two files are analogous to the form design and form code files that are present when working with Windows Forms.

The code within `MainPage.xaml.cs` should look just as you would expect when developing a desktop application. At this stage, it should be clear how much similarity there is within the Visual Studio IDE between desktop and Windows Phone application development.

Complete the implementation of the `button1_Click` procedure, as shown in Listing 1–1, so that it simply displays a `MessageBox`.

Listing 1–1. The button1_Click procedure

```
private void button1_Click(object sender, RoutedEventArgs e)
{
    System.Diagnostics.Debug.WriteLine("Debug text");
}
```

Running the Application

We are now ready to compile and run the project. Press F5 to begin the process. After compilation (and assuming that there are no errors!), Visual Studio launches the emulator. As mentioned earlier, this can take a little while to open, so be patient while this task completes. Subsequent deployments to the emulator will go much more quickly if the emulator is already running.

Once this is all complete, your program will launch. Clicking the button will display the MessageBox, as you would expect (see Figure 1–7).

Figure 1–7. The test application in action

To stop the program, click the Stop Debugging button in Visual Studio. The IDE will return to edit mode, and your program will close on the emulator. The emulator will keep running, ready for any additional programs that you start.

Another way to stop the program is to click the Back button on the emulator. The default behavior when this button is clicked is to close the application and return to the phone's main page (although this behavior can be overridden, as we will see later on). This process will also return the IDE to edit mode. The fact that the Back button actually closes the application instead of simply putting it into the background is important, as we will need to hook into this if we want to allow the application to retain its state when it restarts.

Running on a Real Device

You will no doubt be pleased to hear that running your application on a real device is no more difficult than running it within an emulator, and it provides an extremely similar experience. There are a few steps that you will need to go through before you can begin working with the device, however. Let's take a look at the details now.

Registering the Device

Before you can deploy applications to a device, you must first have a Windows Phone developer account. These accounts are not free, though they are relatively inexpensive (currently priced at $99 per year, though this might change in the future). You will need this account before you can publish any of your finished games into the Windows Phone Marketplace, anyway, so there is not really any way to avoid this charge, even if you develop entirely on the emulator.

You can sign up for an account at the http://create.msdn.com web site. You will be required to prove your identity to Microsoft as part of this process and will receive e-mail notification telling you how to do this. The process might take a couple of days from start to finish.

Besides providing your personal details, you will also be able to provide banking details so that you can be paid for applications that you create and sell in the Marketplace.

Once your account is registered and active, the next step is to set the device up to connect to your PC. First, plug the device in and allow Windows to set up its drivers. This should be a completely automatic process.

Next you will need to install the latest Zune client software. An up-to-date version of this software is essential, so if you have an older version already installed, you will need to upgrade. This application is used for all data transfer and synchronization between the phone and your PC, and will need to be running all the time that you are working with the device. Without this, you will receive an error from Visual Studio when you attempt to deploy.

Once the Zune software has launched, you have to sign in to your Marketplace account, which allows the software to identify that you have registered for development and will unlock the deployment facility that Visual Studio needs to use to transfer your games and applications to the device. The device confirmation screens then appear, as shown in Figure 1–8, allowing you to set up the device for use with your PC.

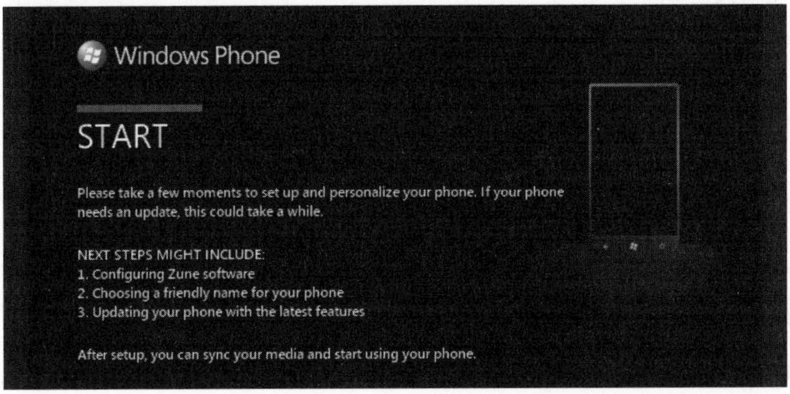

Figure 1–8. Configuring the device inside the Zune software for use with the PC

The final step in setting up the device is to run the Windows Phone Developer Registration application on the PC. This is part of the Windows Phone Software Development Kit, and can be found in the Start menu inside All Programs/Windows Phone Developer Tools. When launched, the application displays a screen like the one shown in Figure 1–9.

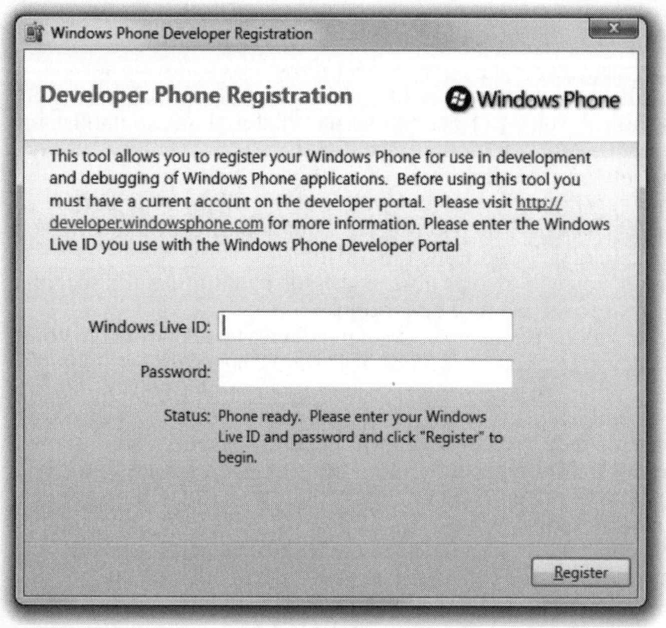

Figure 1–9. The Windows Phone Developer Registration application

You need to enter the username and password of your developer account and then click the Register button. After a few seconds, you should be notified that the phone was successfully registered. At this point you are finally ready to begin working with your phone in Visual Studio.

These steps only need to be performed once for each device that you use.

Deploying to the Device from Visual Studio

Now we are ready to deploy our project to the device from inside Visual Studio.

First, with the Zune software running in the background on your PC, connect your device to the PC and ensure that it is recognized by Windows. Once everything is ready, choose to deploy your application to the device rather than the emulator. This is done by dropping down the Device combo box in the toolbar and selecting Windows Phone 7 Device, as shown in Figure 1–10. When you next start your program, Visual Studio will connect to the device and then install and launch the application executable.

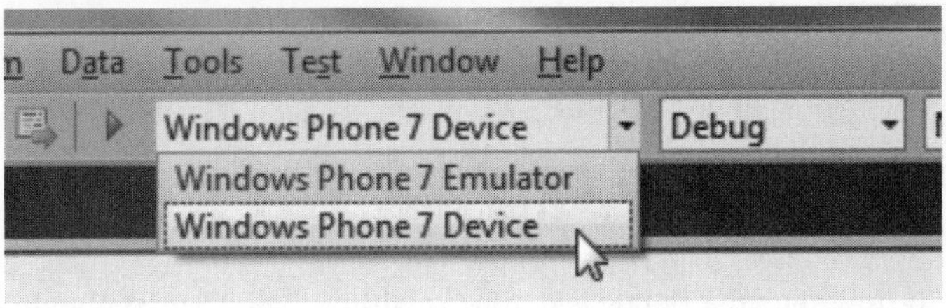

Figure 1–10. Choosing to launch the application on a physical device

---

■ **NOTE** For deployment to succeed, the phone must be switched on, and the lock screen must not be displayed. If these conditions are not met, a deployment error will occur, although Visual Studio usually provides good feedback about what the problem is to help you figure out how to proceed.

Unsurprisingly, the project running on the phone looks and behaves just as it did in the emulator. Congratulations, you have written and deployed your first Windows Phone application!

Debugging

Now that you have a simple application written and working, let's take a closer look at some of the debugging features that are available.

The powerful debugging tools that can be used within the Visual Studio IDE make development systems from the past look extremely primitive in comparison. We can use all these tools for Windows Phone development, making tracking down problems simple.

Breakpoints

First, try setting a breakpoint on the line of code containing the MessageBox function call. Launch the program (on a real device or the emulator), and click the button within the page. As you would expect, the breakpoint triggers just as it would on a desktop application.

From here, you can explore all the usual attributes of your application: the call stack, object property windows, visualizers, and immediate window commands. Everything is present and working.

The one useful feature that is not available, however, is "edit and continue." Unfortunately, because the application is actually running outside of Visual Studio's controlled environment, such changes cannot be applied at runtime and will need to be held back until the IDE returns to edit mode.

Debug Output

At any stage within your application you can display text in Visual Studio's Output window. This is done in just the same way as for a desktop application—by using the System.Diagnostics.Debug object. To test this, modify the button click handler as shown in Listing 1–2.

Listing 1–2. Writing text to the Debug Output window

```
private void button1_Click(object sender, RoutedEventArgs e)
{
    System.Diagnostics.Debug.WriteLine("Debug text");
    MessageBox.Show("Hello Windows Phone!", "Testing", MessageBoxButton.OK);
}
```

Each time you click the button, you will now see your debug text appear within the IDE, as shown in Figure 1–11.

Figure 1–11. Debug text appearing in the Debug Output window

■ **TIP** If the Output window is not displayed, it can be opened by selecting View/Output from Visual Studio's menu. If the Output window is open but no text is appearing, ensure that the "Show output from" combo box in the window toolbar is set to Debug, as shown in Figure 1–11.

Getting Help

Sooner or later you will run into a development problem that you cannot solve on your own. A number of great resources at your disposal can provide insight and inspiration to keep you moving. Here are some of them.

MSDN

As you would expect from one of Microsoft's products, comprehensive and detailed documentation is available for all aspects of Windows Phone development and the .NET CF. Provided you have it installed, MSDN is an excellent source of help and is never farther away than a quick press of the F1 key.

Search Engines

The Web is, as ever, an indispensable fountain of information. When searching, try to accompany your search phrase with "windows phone" or "windows phone 7" (including the quotation marks).

Microsoft's Windows Phone Developer Center

The Developer Center can be found at the following URL:

```
http://create.msdn.com/
```

The site hosts a large variety of articles, development tips, frequently asked questions, and code samples. Also of particular interest is the Forums link, which leads to a number of very active message forums. There's a good chance that someone will be able to offer you some assistance.

Community Sites

Some excellent community sites have built up around the XNA and Silverlight technologies used on Windows Phone 7, and they are a good place to read and ask questions if you need assistance.

For XNA, you can visit http://creators.xna.com for one such community. For Silverlight, http://www.silverlight.net provides similar resources. Besides their forums, both sites are packed with information and downloads, and are well worth visiting.

Windows Phone Game Development

We've spent a lot of time discussing development in general, but we have not yet looked at game development. We will start preparing to actually write a game in the next chapter, but let's conclude this overview of Windows Phone software development by thinking about what types of games we can create and the technologies available to create them.

Suitable Games

Although the power of the Windows Phone graphics hardware might not be approaching that of dedicated PC graphics cards, it is nonetheless very capable for a mobile device. Coupled with the lower screen resolution of the phone compared to that of a typical PC monitor, very impressive 3D graphical displays should be well within your reach.

Not everything has to reach into the third dimension, however. Two-dimensional games can be extremely enjoyable and rewarding to play, too. We can do great things with the more laid-back game genres such as strategy, role playing, and puzzle games. Well-crafted games such as these can become extremely popular because the immediate "switch on and play" nature of the device is ideal for people who have only a few spare minutes to dedicate to gaming before real life gets in the way. This type of game is well suited to the phone and has a potentially large audience.

Board and card games are examples of other styles that are easily accessible to a wide audience, and they convert well to handheld devices. In particular, the ability to physically drag cards around the game with a finger leads to a satisfying feeling of involvement.

Novelty games have recently become popular on other platforms such as the iPhone, allowing users to create and distort photographs of their friends, to create sound effects in response to interactions with the device, and a variety of other unusual things. If you have creative flair and imagination to spare, this could be an interesting area to explore!

Selecting an Application Framework

One of the first decisions that you need to make when you begin programming a game is which application framework to use: XNA or Silverlight.

XNA

XNA is the framework of choice for anything involving 3D graphics, full-screen graphical effects, or large numbers of moving objects. The graphical approach of XNA relies on completely redrawing the whole screen every frame (30 times per second or more), and it's just as easy to redraw things in different positions as it is to redraw them unmoved.

The whole architecture of an XNA game application is based around rapid and continuous updates of the graphics onscreen. We have full access to all the device features, including the use of the multitouch screen, accelerometer, and sound and music output.

Silverlight

For games that require a little less graphical grunt, Silverlight is a very capable environment for game development. Ideal for puzzle games and other games that don't require dozens of constantly moving objects, Silverlight's graphical capabilities still provide features such as transparency, scaling, and rotation of graphics—all of which are very useful for games.

Games that require a rich graphical user interface (GUI) are likely to be obvious candidates for Silverlight. Its page design capabilities are highly flexible, offering everything from labels to fully working web browser controls—unlike XNA, which has no built-in user interface features at all and requires everything to be manually programmed.

As with XNA, the device features are all available in Silverlight, including the multitouch display and accelerometer. Unlike XNA, Silverlight is event-driven, so your coding model will generally be responding to event calls rather than polling the device state.

Silverlight is also much better at displaying text than XNA. Whereas XNA relies on bitmap representations of fonts (which become blocky and are distorted if they are drawn too large), Silverlight uses vector-based fonts, allowing them to be zoomed without any such distortion.

A nice side effect of developing for Silverlight is that games can, with some work, be converted to run on a PC within a web browser. This can be very useful for helping to promote your game—instead of just telling your audience about it, you can actually let them play it immediately at the click of a button.

Welcome to the World of Windows Phone Development

This concludes our overview of the .NET CF development process. I hope you are enthusiastic and excited about the opportunities of developing for the Windows Phone platform.

Please spend a little time experimenting with the capabilities of the environment and the .NET CF libraries. We will look at exactly what we can do with .NET CF in much more detail in the following chapters, but for now, do get comfortable with building and launching applications.

PART 2

XNA

CHAPTER 2

■ ■ ■

Getting Started with XNA

For the next few chapters, we will look at the XNA environment and learn all we need to know to use it for displaying graphics, reading user input, and playing music and sound effects. XNA is in some ways a more straightforward approach to games programming than Silverlight, offering a very draw-things-to-the-screen approach to its graphics rendering, rather than Silverlight's somewhat more complex control hierarchies. Its entire focus is on games and game programming, whereas Silverlight is a general-purpose graphical interface rather than a gaming engine. XNA also takes full advantage of the graphical hardware acceleration built into the device, whereas Silverlight performs a lot more of its processing using the CPU instead.

In this chapter, we will focus on some of the fundamental mechanics of XNA and drawing graphics in 2D. These are important even if you wish to focus on 3D games because the underlying program structure is identical. Even in 3D applications, you are likely to want to use some 2D graphics as well to present status information or text to the user, so it is important to have a good understanding of XNA's capabilities in this area. We'll look at how these principles begin to build into a proper game in Chapter 3.

What Is XNA?

In the world of desktop development, DirectX has for many years been the Microsoft graphical API. It is very powerful with excellent support for all sorts of 2D and 3D graphical effects, and when paired with a capable graphics card can produce breathtaking scenes and animations.

For many generations of DirectX, the API was really accessible only by developing in C or C++. All the library information was made available to these languages, and, although it was theoretically possible to access them from Visual Basic 6, and later from the .NET languages, it was a significant amount of work to actually do so.

With the introduction of DirectX 9 in 2002, Microsoft provided a set of .NET libraries known as Managed DirectX (MDX). This finally gave a proper supported interface for .NET developers to use to access the DirectX features.

Before MDX was established, however, Microsoft changed direction and released a replacement set of technologies called XNA (it officially stands for XNA's Not Acronymed in case you were curious—I expect you wish you hadn't asked now!). XNA also offers a fully managed interface, available from any .NET language, and wraps around DirectX functionality. It also allows cross-platform development, initially supporting Windows and the Xbox 360, adding the Zune portable media player, and now finally providing support for Windows Phone 7, too.

For the most part, the functionality available on Windows Phone 7 is the same as for the Windows and Xbox versions. The only significant feature missing is the ability to program shaders. Shaders are a cut-down programming language that allow for custom processing of graphics as they are being calculated and displayed to the screen, and are typically used for effects such as blurring, lighting, reflections, and so on. Despite the lack of programmable shader support in Windows Phone, a set of predefined shader functions are provided and can be used in XNA games, as we will see later on.

The version of XNA used for Windows Phone 7 development is version 4.0, which is being released for Windows and Xbox at the same time as it is for the phone. XNA 4.0 contains changes to some of its libraries that are incompatible with earlier versions. It is important to bear this in mind when asking or searching for help on the Internet to avoid confusion if you should encounter one of these changes.

That's enough of the history lesson; let's move on and get some coding underway.

Your First XNA Project

Our first project will be very basic: simply displaying a moving graphic on the screen. We can use this as an opportunity to see some of the basic functions of an XNA game and to look at the development environment that XNA games all use.

In the following sections, we will build up this first XNA project. If you wish to look at the finished source code, you will find it in Chapter 2's FirstXNAProject folder in the download accompanying this book.

Creating the Project

To get things started, fire up Visual Studio 2010 and select to create a new XNA Game Studio 4 Windows Phone Game project, as shown in Figure 2–1. Give it a name and optionally uncheck the "Create directory for solution" box (Visual Studio creates a lot of nested directories if this is checked); then click OK to create the project.

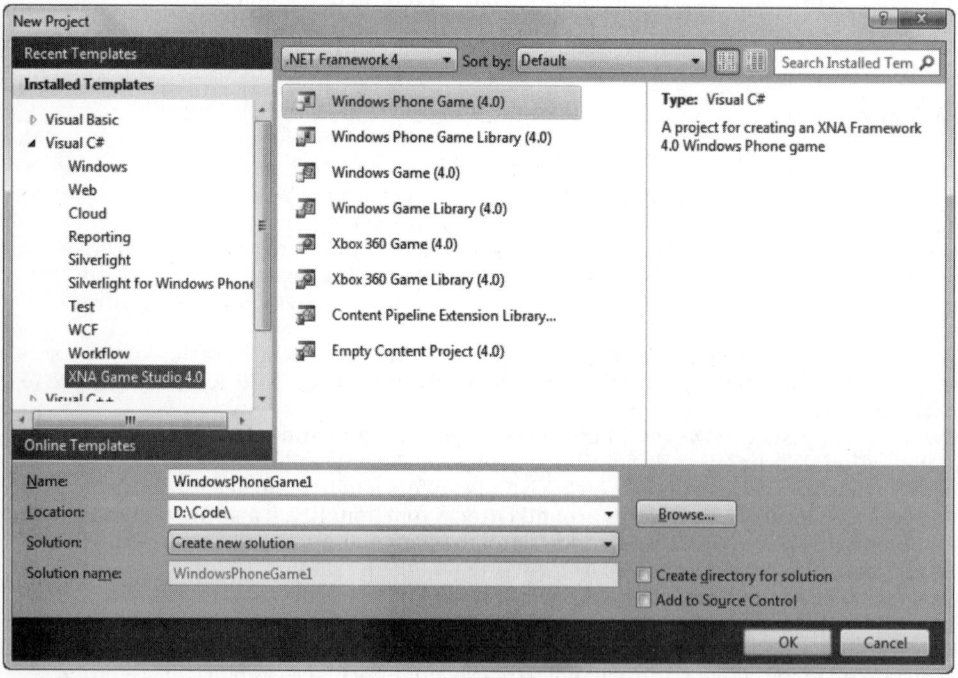

Figure 2–1. Creating a new Windows Phone Game XNA project

The project will be created by Visual Studio and opened in the IDE. The initial window that you will be presented with after this is completed is the code window for the Game1.cs file, which, as you will see, already contains a fair amount of code.

You can, in fact, run the project without doing anything more. The emulator will launch, and after its initialization is complete (you may need to be a little patient), the game will start. It doesn't do very much; it just displays an empty blue screen.

The blue screen is actually of some use, though: seeing the screen turn blue tells you that the program actually is running and is managing to render to the screen. Having a default that isn't black lets you know that the project is operating normally and hasn't just crashed with a blank screen.

Now let's put something on the screen other than just a solid color.

Adding Some Content

Click the Stop Debugging button in Visual Studio to return your project to edit mode. Right-click the Content project node; select Add and then Existing Item, as shown in Figure 2–2.

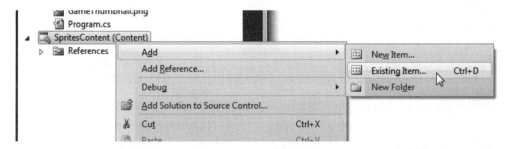

Figure 2–2. Adding an existing item to the Content project

In the file browser window that appears, choose a graphic file that you wish to display on the screen. Try to pick something that will actually fit on the screen; if you want to use the smiley face graphic that is shown in the following example, you can find it in the Content folder for the FirstXNAProject example in the source code that accompanies this book.

■ **TIP** Visual Studio will automatically copy any content files that you select into the Content project's directory, if they are not already present there. This means that there is no need to manually copy files into this folder before selecting them, nor is there a need to keep the files in their selected locations on your hard drive after they have been added.

Once this has been done, the graphic file will appear within the Content project inside Solution Explorer, as shown in Figure 2–3.

Figure 2–3. *The Content project with a graphic file added*

Displaying the Graphic

With our graphic in place, we can now amend the code to display it on the screen. This is very simple and consists only of modifications to Game1.cs, so ensure that it is open in the code editor.

First of all, we need to add a class-level object into which our graphic image will be stored. The object type for this is Texture2D, and so we declare it, as shown in Listing 2–1, just below the existing spriteBatch declaration.

Listing 2–1. *Declaring the Texture2D object for the graphic*

```
private Texture2D _smileyTexture;
```

■ **NOTE** As a naming convention in this book, private class fields will be prefixed with an underscore. All fields will be defined as being private, with internal or public properties added to access them if required.

The next step required is to load the graphic into the variable that we have created. This is performed in the class's LoadContent procedure, which you'll find about halfway through the source code. In addition to the existing code, we load the texture by calling the Content.Load function, as shown in Listing 2–2.

Listing 2–2. *Loading the graphic file into the Texture2D object*

```
/// <summary>
/// LoadContent will be called once per game and is the place to load
/// all of your content.
/// </summary>
protected override void LoadContent()
{
    // Create a new SpriteBatch, which can be used to draw textures.
    spriteBatch = new SpriteBatch(GraphicsDevice);

    // Use this.Content to load your game content here
    _smileyTexture = Content.Load<Texture2D>("SmileyFace");
}
```

The Content.Load function uses .NET's *generics* feature to allow us to specify its return type. In this case, we want it to return a Texture2D object, and so we specify this type in the angle brackets in the function call. We then pass the parameter SmileyFace. Note that this doesn't exactly match the file name that we added to the Content project because the file extension is missing. The reason for this is that the Content project automatically assigns an *asset name* to each file that is added, defaulting this to the file name without its extension. You can see this by selecting the graphic file in the Content project and examining its properties, as shown in Figure 2–4. The Asset Name property is editable and can be modified if you wish.

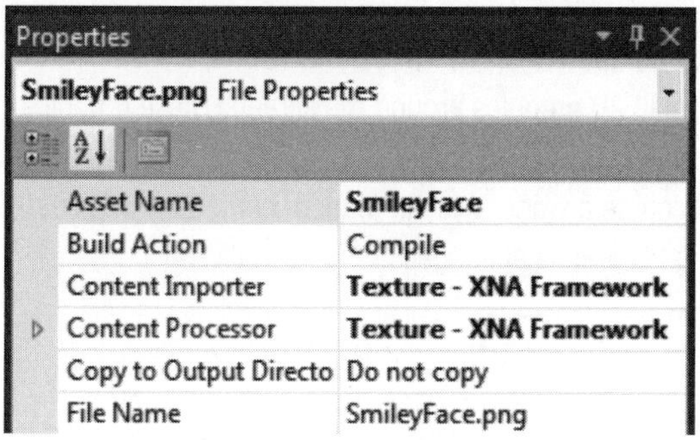

Figure 2–4. The properties for the graphic file in the Content project

The project is now loading the graphic, and so the final step is to display it on the screen. This is achieved by adding a few new lines of code to the Draw function at the bottom of the source listing. The modified function is shown in Listing 2–3.

Listing 2–3. Drawing the graphic file to the screen

```
/// <summary>
/// This is called when the game should draw itself.
/// </summary>
/// <param name="gameTime">Provides a snapshot of timing values.</param>
protected override void Draw(GameTime gameTime)
{
    // Clear the background
    GraphicsDevice.Clear(Color.CornflowerBlue);

    // Set the position for the sprite
    Vector2 position = new Vector2(100, 100);

    // Begin a sprite batch
    spriteBatch.Begin();
    // Draw the sprite
    spriteBatch.Draw(_smileyTexture, position, Color.White);
    // End the sprite batch
    spriteBatch.End();

    // Let the base class do its work
    base.Draw(gameTime);
}
```

We first declare a position for the graphic using a Vector2 structure. This structure is very important in XNA and we'll look at it in more detail later on. Then we use the spriteBatch object that the default code created for us to begin drawing a series of graphics to the screen. The spriteBatch object is then used once again to actually draw the graphic, specifying the graphic that we wish to draw, the position to draw it at, and the color to draw. The color is specified as white in this case; we will look at the behavior of this parameter shortly. Once the image is drawn, we call the spriteBatch.End method to tell XNA that we have finished drawing.

■ **NOTE** The use of the word *sprite* dates back to the old 8-bit computers of the 1970s and 1980s, whose graphical capabilities were generally limited to moving only small 2D graphics around the screen. These graphics were given the name *sprites* in reference to their ability to make lively movements, as compared with background images that were usually static. Hardware capabilities are of course a world away in modern computer graphics, but the term has stuck around as a way of referring to moving 2D graphical images.

You may also notice the call to GraphicsDevice.Clear in this listing, passing in the parameter Color.CornflourBlue. It is this line of code that is responsible for the blue background when the project is running. You can change this color to anything you wish if you tire of the default color.

Finally, we need to set the display into portrait orientation. This is achieved by adding the code shown in Listing 2–4 to the Game1 class constructor. We will discuss orientation and back buffer sizes in more detail in the Other Graphics Options section near the end of this chapter, so don't worry too much about what these lines are doing for the moment.

Listing 2–4. Setting the back buffer size and orientation

```
// Set backbuffer size and orientation
graphics.PreferredBackBufferWidth = 480;
graphics.PreferredBackBufferHeight = 800;
```

Once the code has been added to your project, run it; if all is well you should see your graphic presented on the screen, as shown in Figure 2–5.

Figure 2–5. Displaying the graphic on the phone screen

This is obviously a trivial example (although one we will build on), but it hopefully demonstrates the tiny amount of effort required to get a graphic to display on the screen.

Moving the Graphic

Static images aren't too interesting, so let's make the graphic move. At the moment, we are specifying its position within the Draw procedure by passing a Vector2 structure initialized with the values 100 and 100. These two values are the x and y positions at which the graphic will be drawn, and represent its top-left corner. This position is known as a *coordinate*.

When coordinates are written down, they are enclosed within parentheses inside which the two values are placed, separated by a comma. The first value is the x coordinate, and the second is the y coordinate. For example, (20, 50) represents a coordinate with an x position of 20 and a y position of 50.

The coordinate system used by XNA sprites starts from (0, 0) at the top-left corner of the screen. It then extends across the screen's width and height so that the point at the bottom-right corner of the screen is (Window.ClientBounds.Width - 1, Window.ClientBounds.Height - 1). All sprite coordinates are measured in pixels.

To make the sprite move, we just need to remember its coordinate from one draw to the next and modify its values so that the sprite's position changes. We can do this very easily. First we will declare another class-level variable to store the sprite position, as shown in Listing 2–5.

Listing 2–5. Declaring a variable to hold the position of the graphic

```
private Vector2 _smileyPosition;
```

Next we need to provide an initial position for the graphic. The default uninitialized Vector2 object has a coordinate of (0, 0), corresponding to the top-left corner of the screen. Because our game window doesn't actually quite fill the screen (the top section is currently being used by the operating system to display status information), this is in fact outside the bounds of our game display and will result in the graphic being partly obscured by the status bar.

We will continue to use the coordinate (100, 100) as our initial position. We have a couple of options for setting it, one of which is to specify the position as part of the variable declaration in Listing 2–5. It may be useful to be able to reset the position later on, however, so we will create a new procedure called ResetGame and set the coordinate here, as shown in Listing 2–6.

Listing 2–6. Setting the initial position for the smiley graphic

```
/// <summary>
/// Reset the game to its default state
/// </summary>
private void ResetGame()
{
    // Set the initial smiley position
    _smileyPosition = new Vector2(100, 100);
}
```

To get this code to run, we will call the ResetGame procedure from the existing Initialize procedure that was generated automatically when the project was created. The modified procedure is shown in Listing 2–7.

Listing 2–7. Calling the ResetGame procedure

```
/// <summary>
/// Allows the game to perform any initialization it needs to before starting to run.
/// This is where it can query for any required services and load any non-graphic
/// related content.  Calling base.Initialize will enumerate through any components
/// and initialize them as well.
```

```
/// </summary>
protected override void Initialize()
{
    // Reset the game
    ResetGame();

    base.Initialize();
}
```

The Draw code now needs to be modified to use the new position variable. This is achieved by removing the Vector2 position variable, and instead using the _smileyPosition variable, as shown in Listing 2–8.

Listing 2–8. Drawing the sprite from the class-level variable

```
// Draw the sprite
spriteBatch.Draw(_smileyTexture, _smileyPosition, Color.White);
```

Finally, we need to change the position stored in the _smileyPosition variable so that the graphic actually moves. Although it would be easy to do this in the Draw code, this wouldn't be the appropriate place to make this change; the Draw function should be entirely focused on the drawing operation alone and not on updating the game variables. Instead we use the Update procedure, which once again was added when the project was created, to make these variable changes. Listing 2–9 shows a simple Update implementation that moves the smiley face toward the bottom of the screen and resets its position back to the top once the bottom is reached.

Listing 2–9. The Update procedure, modified to update our graphic position

```
/// <summary>
/// Allows the game to run logic such as updating the world,
/// checking for collisions, gathering input, and playing audio.
/// </summary>
/// <param name="gameTime">Provides a snapshot of timing values.</param>
protected override void Update(GameTime gameTime)
{
    // Allows the game to exit
    if (GamePad.GetState(PlayerIndex.One).Buttons.Back == ButtonState.Pressed)
        this.Exit();

    // Update the game state
    _smileyPosition.Y += 5;
    if (_smileyPosition.Y >= Window.ClientBounds.Bottom) _smileyPosition.Y = 0;

    base.Update(gameTime);
}
```

If you now run the project again you should find that the graphic moves down the screen, wrapping back around to the top after it leaves the bottom.

The separation of updating the game and drawing the game is something that you will see across all our XNA samples and is something you should try to stick to in your own projects. There is nothing physically stopping you from updating the game variables in the Draw function (nor, in fact, from drawing in the Update function), but both for readability and also to ensure that your game works in the way XNA expects, it is strongly advised to keep the appropriate functionality in each of these two procedures.

Examining the Solution in More Detail

Before we press on with making further modifications to the code, let's take a quick step back and look a little more closely at the solution and its contents. As you have already seen, your solution contains two projects, rather than the one you might have initially expected. Before we get to the reason for the second project (the Content project), let's look in a little more detail at the main game project.

The Game Project

An example of the files present in a new game project can be seen in Figure 2–6.

Figure 2–6. *The default files contained within a new XNA project*

The Properties and References sections of the project will no doubt be familiar (and serve exactly the same purpose as in any other project you may work on). The rest of the items within the project deserve a little more explanation, however, so let's take a look at each of them.

First is the Content References item, which allows the project to read content (such as graphics, sound effects, or music files) that it needs to use in order to run the game. If you expand the Content References tree node, you'll see that it references the Content project (named SpritesContent in the example shown) that has also been created within your solution. We will examine the reason for having a separate Content project (and some of the things that you can do with it) later in this chapter.

Next is Background.png. This 173 x 173 pixel image provides a large graphic for your game, which will be present if the user pins it to the start screen. You should make sure that it provides an attractive and identifiable image of your game.

This is followed by Game.ico, a 32 x 32 pixel icon that will be used by your game executable when it is compiled. It defaults to an image of an Xbox controller. You will almost certainly want to change this for any finished game to help it stand out from the crowd.

Following this is the Game1.cs file that we have open in the code editor. We will be looking at this in much more detail during this and the following chapters.

GameThumbnail.png is next; it is a 64 x 64 pixel icon used when your game is displayed in the full application list and in the Windows Phone Marketplace (a topic we will discuss toward the end of the book). The default image for this looks like a dark-gray blob, but actually provides a shaded background into which you can draw your own imagery to help make your game identifiable. This

31

image should be essentially the same as that from Background.png so the user can recognize the game in both the start screen and the application list.

Finally we arrive at Program.cs. If you open it in the code editor, you will see that it contains content similar to that shown in Listing 2–10.

Listing 2–10. *The default content of the Program.cs file*

```
using System;

namespace Sprites
{
#if WINDOWS || XBOX
    static class Program
    {
        /// <summary>
        /// The main entry point for the application.
        /// </summary>
        static void Main(string[] args)
        {
            using (Game1 game = new Game1())
            {
                game.Run();
            }
        }
    }
#endif
}
```

The code is simple: creating an instance of the Game1 class that has been provided for us and calling its Run method. But before the Program class is defined within this source file, a compiler directive tells Visual Studio to build the class only if the WINDOWS or XBOX constants have been defined. For Windows Phone development, neither of these constants is defined (the constant WINDOWS_PHONE is defined instead). The end result is that this class won't be defined for Windows Phone XNA games.

Instead, XNA looks for the first class it can find that inherits from Microsoft.Xna.Framework.Game, which is the case for the Game1.cs that was created in our project. If you have multiple classes that inherit from Microsoft.Xna.Framework.Game, Visual Studio will raise a compilation error. You can actually resolve this by selecting a specific game class in the Project Properties window, but in practical terms there is little reason to have multiple game classes within the same project.

You will notice from the set of files present in the project that there are no forms or files representing any other user interface classes. XNA does not use anything analogous to forms, instead relying purely on graphics being rendered through program code.

The Content Project

Something else that may have been unexpected when you created the XNA project is the presence of the Content project. This project, which is initially empty, has the sole purpose of containing all the external data files (graphics, sound files, 3D models and so on) that you wish to use within your game.

So why is this created as a separate project? There are several reasons why it is useful:

- The main reason is for performance. Our test project has a single graphic file, but full games can contain dozens of content files. Each time the project is compiled, all these files need to be processed by XNA in order to put them into a form that it can use. The content tends to be modified fairly infrequently, but the program code is modified in virtually every build. Putting the content into a separate project means that the processing of this content need only be performed each time the content actually changes, speeding up compile time for all the rest of the compilations.

- Another benefit of a Content project is that it allows you to separate the content for different hardware targets. You may well want to use larger graphics on an Xbox version of a game than on a Windows Phone version, and maybe even larger still for high-end PC versions. Using separate Content projects allows you to create a project for each and keep the same code in your main game project.

- If you have content that you wish to share between multiple games (a company logo, for example), it can be placed into a separate Content project and referenced by each of the game projects. Changes made to this Content project will then be reflected in all the games.

The way in which the game accesses the content is very simple. In the Game1 constructor of the game project we have been working on, you will find the line of code shown in Listing 2–11.

Listing 2–11. Setting the RootDirectory property of the Content object

```
Content.RootDirectory = "Content";
```

The value of "Content" that is set corresponds to the Content Root Directory property of the Content project, which you will find in the Properties window when the Content project's main node is selected in Solution Explorer, as shown in Figure 2–7. This is also shown in brackets after the project name. If you do decide to add multiple Content projects to your solution, ensure that each has a different Content Root Directory so that XNA knows where it can find each referenced asset.

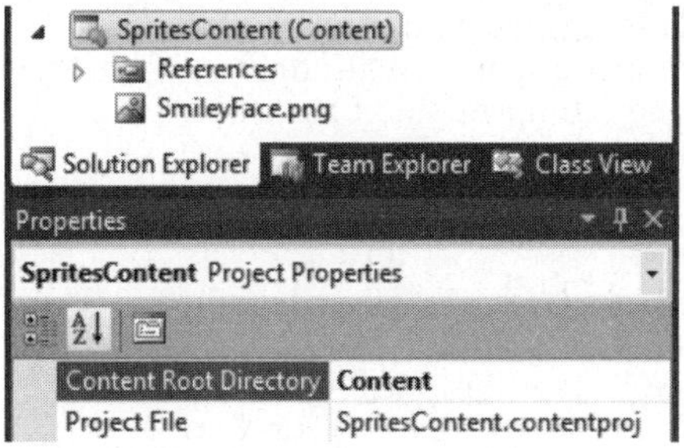

Figure 2–7. The Content project's Content Root Directory property

Once the RootDirectory property has been set, you can access assets within that directory just by specifying their asset name, as we have seen already. If you wish to divide your assets into groups (perhaps by type, graphics, sounds, music, and so on), you can create subdirectories within your Content project by right-clicking the main project node and selecting Add / New Folder. When you place assets into these folders, you can access them either by setting the RootDirectory to include the subdirectory name or by including the directory name when calling the Content.Load function, as shown in Listing 2–12.

Listing 2–12. Loading Content from a subdirectory

```
_smileyTexture = Content.Load<Texture2D>("Graphics/SmileyFace");
```

■ **TIP** If you use multiple Content projects, you can forego setting the `RootDirectory` property altogether and instead specify the Content project's root directory name as part of the path provided to `Content.Load`.

Sprites in Detail

You have now seen how easy it is to draw a simple graphic to the screen, but sprites have a few more tricks in store. Let's examine some of the other properties and abilities of XNA sprites.

Supported Graphic Formats

We have a choice of graphic file formats to use when loading images for use within our games. Some are distinctly better than others. Here is a summary of the main formats that can be used:

- *BMP* (bitmap) files have a simple structure internally and are, therefore, easy for graphics libraries to interact with. One of the reasons for this simplicity is that they do not employ any form of compression at all. For this reason, BMP files can be huge in terms of file size compared with the other graphics formats that are available. BMP files do not offer any form of transparency. There are no compelling reasons to use BMP files, so please avoid using them wherever possible.

- *PNG* (Portable Network Graphics) files, as used for the smiley face image in the previous example, are the most recently developed file format supported by XNA. They can store graphics using the full 24-bit color palette and are additionally able to support alpha (transparency) information. They compress their content to reduce the size of the graphic file. This compression is *lossless*, so no degradation of the image occurs as a result. For nonphotographic images, this is the file format that I recommend.

- *JPG* (a contraction of *JPEG*, the Joint Photographic Experts Group that developed the format) files revolutionized the Web and have been an enabling technology in a range of other areas too, such as digital cameras. The format's strength is its ability to hugely compress images to file sizes that are dramatically smaller than their uncompressed originals, far more so than the PNG format is able to offer. The problem with this, however, is that JPG uses a *lossy* compression technique: after decompressing the image, you don't get back exactly what you started with. Compressed JPGs quickly start to exhibit graphics distortions, and this is most strongly apparent with graphics that contain highly contrasting areas of color, such as those within a computer game often do. JPG files can be useful for reducing the size of photographic images, but are not well suited to hand-drawn game graphics. Even with photographs, be careful not to compress the image to a point where distortion begins to appear.

One familiar graphic format that you may notice is absent from the list is the *GIF* (Graphics Interchange Format) file. XNA does not support GIF files. This is not really much of a loss because PNG files can do almost everything that GIF files can do, have better compression, support more colors (24-bit color as opposed to GIF's 8-bit color), and have proper alpha support. If you have a GIF file that you wish to use, convert it to a PNG file and use it in that format instead.

Scaling

In the earlier example we drew the sprite at its original size. XNA can *scale* the sprite as we draw it, changing its size to make it smaller or larger. It can scale either *uniformly* (the sprite scales equally along the x and y axes) or *non-uniformly* (the x and y axes scale differently, stretching or squashing the image).

Using a Uniform Scaling Factor

There are several overloads of the SpriteBatch.Draw method that support scaling in various different ways. The first and simplest of these allows us to specify the amount of scaling that should be applied to the sprite. The sprite width and height is multiplied by the provided value to determine the finished size, so passing a value of 1 will leave the sprite size unchanged, 2 will double it, and so on.

■ **NOTE** Passing a scale value of 0 will cause the width and height to be multiplied by 0, with the result that your sprite will vanish completely. This is particularly important to remember when you aren't actually taking advantage of scaling but are using the other features of the Draw methods instead. Remember that to draw your sprite at its normal size, you need to pass 1 as the scale factor.

The version of Draw that we use to access this scale parameter takes quite a few more parameters than the version we used earlier, as shown in Listing 2–13.

Listing 2–13. Rendering a sprite with scaling

```
spriteBatch.Draw(_smileyTexture, new Vector2(100, 100), null, Color.White, 0,
                            Vector2.Zero, 3.0f, SpriteEffects.None, 0.0f);
```

From left to right, the parameters are as follows:

- The sprite graphic texture to render (as before).

- The position to render at (as before).

- The area of the sprite texture to render (we will look at this parameter in more detail in the "Partial Image Rendering" section in a moment). Passing null tells XNA to render the entire image.

- The render color (as before). We'll look at this parameter in the "Colorization" section coming up shortly.

- The rotation angle. This is explained further in the next section.

- The image origin. We'll discuss this soon.

- The scaling factor. At last—this is where we tell XNA how much to enlarge or shrink the image.

- Sprite effects. We'll look at these shortly.

- Layer depth. This will be covered in a moment, too.

As you can see, this is quite a lot of extra data to specify, but as shown it is easy to pass values that result in these parameters having no effect.

In addition to the scaling factor, the origin parameter also has an effect on scaling. Listing 2–13 shows this passed as Vector2.Zero, which produces a coordinate of (0, 0). The origin has two immediate effects: it specifies which point within the image is actually being specified by the position parameter and it controls the point around which scaling takes place.

Let's begin with the first effect. When we discussed rendering sprites back in the example project, we saw that the position parameter set the top-left corner of the rendered sprite. If we use the origin parameter, this allows us to control the location within the image that is actually set by position. For example, if we set the origin to new Vector2(10, 20), the point 10 pixels across the image and 20 pixels down the image would appear exactly at the location specified by position.

This may not sound very useful, but it becomes more important when the second effect is considered because the origin point within the image also becomes the center of image scaling. As the image is scaled up or down, the origin point will stay in exactly the same place, while the rest of the image scales around it.

This can be seen in Figure 2–8, in which the dot indicates the origin of the differently scaled rectangular sprites. In the image on the left, the origin is set at (0, 0), so the sprites scale down and to the right. The middle image has the origin in the center of the rectangle, causing the sprite to keep the same center point as the rectangle is enlarged and reduced. The final image shows the origin at the bottom-right corner of the sprite, causing it to scale up and to the left. In all three images, the position parameter was passed as the same location.

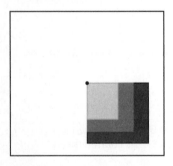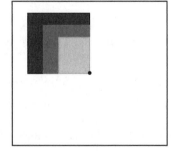

Figure 2–8. Scaling with different origins

It is also possible to scale with a negative factor, which will cause the image to be mirrored horizontally and vertically about the origin point.

Using a Non-uniform Scaling Factor

The Draw call in Listing 2–13 allows just a single value to be passed for the scaling factor, which means that it only supports uniform scaling. Non-uniform scaling is no harder to achieve, however: we just substitute a Vector2 structure in place of the float that we used before. The Vector2 x value will represent the scaling on the horizontal axis, and its y value will represent the scaling on the vertical axis.

An example non-uniform scale using this approach is shown in Listing 2–14. This listing doubles the width of the sprite and halves its height.

Listing 2–14. Rendering a sprite with non-uniform scaling

```
spriteBatch.Draw(_smileyTexture, new Vector2(100, 100), null, Color.White, 0,
                 Vector2.Zero, new Vector2(2.0f, 0.5f), SpriteEffects.None, 0.0f);
```

The origin parameter behaves in exactly the same way when using this approach as it did for uniform scaling.

Using a Destination Rectangle

The final method for scaling a sprite uses a slightly different approach. Instead of specifying the position, an origin, and a scale factor, we instead define the overall rectangle into which the sprite is to be rendered.

Listing 2–15 shows a call to the Draw method that scales a sprite in this way. The top-left corner of the rendered sprite is at the coordinate (50, 50) and it has a width of 300 pixels and a height of 500 pixels. This puts the bottom-right corner at the coordinate (350, 550).

Listing 2–15. Rendering a sprite to fill a defined rectangle

```
spriteBatch.Draw(_smileyTexture, new Rectangle(50, 50, 300, 500), Color.White);
```

Exactly which of these scaling approaches works best for you will depend on the way in which you are using the sprite. Sometimes it is best to use a scaling factor (particularly if you want the sprite to grow or shrink in size as the game progresses), although other times a destination rectangle may be the easier approach. Make sure you consider all the options to avoid creating unnecessary work for yourself.

Rotation

Sprites also have the ability to be smoothly rotated to any angle you wish. The angle is specified by using either of the Draw calls shown in Listing 2–13 or 2–14, passing the angle for the appropriate parameter.

The angle is measured clockwise in radians, meaning that an angle of 0 is the right way up, PI / 2 is rotated a quarter of the way around to the right, PI is upside down, and 3 PI / 2 is rotated three-quarters of the way around.

Personally, I find working in radians quite unnatural and I much prefer working in degrees. XNA is here to help with this because it offers a very useful class named MathHelper, which is full of static functions to assist with graphics-related mathematical functions. One such function is ToRadians, which converts the supplied degrees angle into radians. Using this with the Draw function's rotation parameter makes providing the angle much easier.

Just as with scaling, the point around which the image rotates can be controlled using the origin parameter. Set this to the center of the sprite image to rotate on the spot or provide a different origin for off-center rotation. The origin can be completely outside the sprite area if you wish.

Listing 2–16 shows a call to Draw that rotates a sprite by 45 degrees around its center. The output from this call can be seen in Figure 2–9.

Listing 2–16. Drawing a sprite rotated around its center

```
spriteBatch.Draw(_smileyTexture, new Vector2(100, 100), null, Color.White,
                MathHelper.ToRadians(45),
                new Vector2(_smileyTexture.Width / 2, _smileyTexture.Height / 2),
                1.0f, SpriteEffects.None, 0.0f);
```

Figure 2–9. Rotating a sprite

Tinting

Throughout all the calls to Draw, we have passed through a Color parameter, and in each case it has been Color.White. We can pass different colors instead of white to tint the graphic that is being drawn. If we pass Color.Blue, the sprite will be shaded in blue, for example.

A very useful application of this feature is to allow a single graphic to be drawn in lots of different colors, without having to add all the different colored graphics individually into the Content project. If the source image is provided in grayscale, the tint can be used to display this in whatever color we want. You can see this in action in the TintedSprites example project, an image from which is shown in Figure 2–10 (though this obviously looks better in color!).

To understand just how the tinting works (and what kind of results you can expect from it), we need to discuss how colors are represented in computer graphics.

In XNA there are two ways that we can specify a color to use:

- Using one of the named color values from Microsoft.Xna.Framework.Color

- Specifying the individual levels of red, green, and blue that will make up the color

A large range of named colors is provided, from standard colors such as Black and Blue to those with more extravagant names including the sublime PapayaWhip and the unmistakable BlanchedAlmond. This list of named colors is actually the full list of X11 colors, which also form the predefined named colors used for HTML and Cascading Style Sheets (CSS). For further information about these colors, see the Wikipedia page at http://en.wikipedia.org/wiki/Web_colors where a full list and an example of each can be seen.

Figure 2–10. *Tinted sprites*

Alternatively, colors may be specified by providing the levels of red, green, and blue intensity (the additive primary colors) that are required to form the required color. Each of these is specified independently and ranges from 0 (no intensity) to 255 (full intensity). For example, creating a color with its red component set to 255 and its green and blue components set to 0 will result in a pure red. By varying the intensity of each color, all the available shades that the device is able to display can be created.

■ **NOTE** There are various different models in which colors can be specified. In printing, the most common model is the CMYK model. CMYK is an abbreviation for "cyan, magenta, yellow, and key-black." Cyan, magenta, and yellow are the primary **subtractive colors**—so named because, when additional color is applied, they reduce the amount of light that is reflected and result in a darker color. The model that is most commonly used in computer devices is RGB, an abbreviation for "red, green, and blue." Red, green, and blue are the primary **additive colors**, which result in an increased amount of light when the colors are mixed together (so that, in fact, mixing all three results in white light). The .NET framework supports color specifications using the RGB model.

To create a color from red, green, and blue intensity levels, create a new Color structure and pass the intensity levels into its constructor. There are actually two ways in which the intensity levels can be specified: either as integer values from 0 to 255 as described, or as float values from 0 to 1. Exactly which of these approaches you prefer is up to you; they are functionally equivalent. Listing 2–17 shows an example of creating two identical Color structures, one using integer values and the other using floats.

Listing 2–17. Creating colors from red, green, and blue intensity levels

```
Color myColor1 = new Color(255, 128, 0);
Color myColor2 = new Color(1.0f, 0.5f, 0.0f);
```

Because we can specify 256 levels of each of the three color components, we can create colors from a total palette of 16,777,216 different colors (256 x 256 x 256 = 16,777,216). This is the same color depth as used on virtually all modern desktop PC displays. Because each of the three color components requires 8 bits of data (to store a value from 0 to 255), this is known as 24-bit color.

So how does all this apply to tinting? In order to apply a tint, XNA first reads the color of each pixel from the image using the float representation, using a value between 0 and 1 for each of the red, green, and blue components. It then obtains the tint color using the same float representation. The corresponding values for red, green, and blue are then multiplied together, and the resulting value is the color that is actually displayed on the screen.

Because the color white has RGB values of (1, 1, 1), the result of using white as a tint is that each pixel color component is multiplied by 1—in other words it is not changed, and the image is rendered untinted. If we used a tint color of black, which has RGB values (0, 0, 0), all the pixel color components would be multiplied by 0, resulting in the sprite appearing totally black. By using tint colors that have different levels of red, green, and blue—for example, orange has the RGB value (1, 0.5, 0)—we can cause the sprite to be tinted toward whatever color we wish.

Note that if the source image is not grayscale, however, it may not tint in the way you necessarily want. For example, if you have a sprite that consists of strips of red, green, and blue color, and you tint it using a solid blue color, the areas of red and green will turn completely black (because the intensity levels for red and green in the blue tint are 0). This is why a grayscale image is often the best to use when tinting.

Partial Image Rendering

Sprites can draw just a subsection of their images, too. One of the main uses for this is for animation: multiple animation frames can be placed into a single image, and then individual frames can be rendered to the screen in sequence to animate the sprite.

An example of how this can be used is in the AnimationFrames project. Its Content project contains a single image, Radar.png, which can be seen in Figure 2–11.

Figure 2–11. The frames of the radar animation placed into a single graphic file

As this figure shows, there are eight individual images contained within the file. Each has exactly the same width (75 pixels), so we can draw any frame by locating its left edge and then drawing a section of the image that is 75 pixels wide. To find the edge, we take the animation frame number (from 0 to 7) and multiple it by the frame width (75 pixels). Frame 0 therefore has a left edge of 0 pixels, frame 1 a left edge of 75 pixels, frame 2 a left edge of 150 pixels, and so on.

Drawing a section of the image is easy and is achieved by passing a Rectangle structure to the sourceRectangle property of Draw. This defines the left and top corner of the rectangle within the source image, and also the width and height to copy. The code that performs the frame drawing in the AnimationFrames project is shown in Listing 2–18.

Listing 2–18. Rendering a sprite using a source rectangle

```
_spriteBatch.Draw(_radarTexture, new Vector2(100, 100),
                  new Rectangle(_animationFrame * 75, 0, 75, 75), Color.White);
```

Although it is not shown in Listing 2–18, it is possible to combine the use of a source rectangle with scaling and rotation because all the versions of the Draw method that allow these operations to be specified also accept a sourceRectangle parameter. In fact, we have been passing this in all the examples using these techniques, except that we passed null to indicate that we wanted the whole image to be drawn rather than a subsection.

Layer Depth

If overlapping sprites are rendered using any of the code samples so far, each will be rendered in front of the sprites already on the screen. Sometimes you need to order the sprites in a particular way so that some sprites appear in front of other sprites.

XNA provides an easy way to implement this. Some of the Draw overloads accept a float parameter called layerDepth, and we can pass a value for this between 0 and 1 to control which sprites appear in front of others. A value of 0 puts the sprite right at the front, whereas a value of 1 puts it right at the back.

The only catch to this is that layerDepth processing is disabled by default. To enable it, we need to pass some additional parameters to the SpriteBatch.Begin call. The parameter that switches this on is the sortMode parameter, which we will set to SpriteSortMode.BackToFront. It instructs XNA to draw the objects at the back first and then work toward the front, allowing each sprite to draw over the top of the sprites behind. When this parameter is passed, Begin also requires a value for its blendState parameter; we will pass BlendState.AlphaBlend, which is the default for this property when the overload of Draw with no parameters is used.

Listing 2–19 shows this effect in operation. Although the sprites are drawn from left to right (which would normally result in the rightmost sprite appearing in the front), we are specifying layerDepth values that put the leftmost sprite in front and the rightmost sprite at the back. You can find the full code for this in the LayerDepth example project.

Listing 2–19. Drawing sprites with layerDepth sorting enabled

```
// Begin a sprite batch with BackToFront sorting enabled
_spriteBatch.Begin(SpriteSortMode.BackToFront, BlendState.AlphaBlend);
// Draw some sprites with different layerDepth values
_spriteBatch.Draw(_smileyTexture, new Vector2(100, 100), null, Color.White, 0.0f,
                               Vector2.Zero, 1.0f, SpriteEffects.None, 0.0f);
_spriteBatch.Draw(_smileyTexture, new Vector2(140, 100), null, Color.White, 0.0f,
                               Vector2.Zero, 1.0f, SpriteEffects.None, 0.5f);
_spriteBatch.Draw(_smileyTexture, new Vector2(180, 100), null, Color.White, 0.0f,
                               Vector2.Zero, 1.0f, SpriteEffects.None, 1.0f);
// End the sprite batch
_spriteBatch.End();
```

The end result is shown in Figure 2–12.

Figure 2–12. Sprites rendered left to right with layerDepth sorting enabled

Sprite Transparency

The smiley face texture we have been using is circular, but sprites are always rectangular. Why is it then that we don't end up with a rectangular box drawn around the edge of the sprite?

The reason is that we are using an image with transparency information. Without this, the sprite would be drawn completely to the edges of its draw rectangle. Figure 2–13 shows an example of drawing the smiley face texture without any transparency. As you can see, it's not exactly the effect we want to achieve in most cases.

Figure 2–13. Drawing the smiley face sprite with no transparency information

We have two techniques at our disposal for making transparent sections within our sprites: color keys and alpha channels. Let's take a look at each of these techniques. Examples of both techniques can be found within the Transparency example project.

■ **NOTE** JPEG images are not recommended for use with either of these transparency techniques. JPEG's lossy compression means that colors are not stored accurately enough for color key transparency, and the information required for alpha channels is not supported by JPEG images. If you wish to use transparency, you will need to stick with PNG image files instead.

Color Key Transparency

A color key provides the simplest mechanism for making areas of your sprite transparent, but it is less flexible than the alpha channel approach that we will discuss in a moment. A color key identifies a particular pixel color within your image that will be treated as transparent. Any and all pixels that exactly match the specified color will become completely transparent when your sprite is rendered, whereas all other pixels will be completely opaque.

By convention, the color *fuchsia* is by default used as the color key. This has full intensity of red and blue, and none of green, and is, by any other name, purple. This has been chosen as it is a relatively infrequently used color within computer graphics.

The ColorKey.png image in the Transparency example's Content project is set up to use a color key. As you will see when you run the project, the sprite is drawn as if it were circular, and all the rest of the rectangular sprite area is left untouched when the sprite is drawn.

But why has XNA decided to use the color key? And how could we use a different color as the color key if we needed to use fuchsia in our graphic? The answer to these questions can be found in the Properties window for the ColorKey.png file within the Content project. If you expand the Content Processor property, you will find that hiding inside are properties named Color Key Enabled and Color Key Color, as shown in Figure 2–14. These default to True and 255, 0, 255, 255, respectively (the Color Key Color values represent the red, green, blue and alpha values of the transparent color). If you wish to disable the color key or change the key color, modify these properties as required.

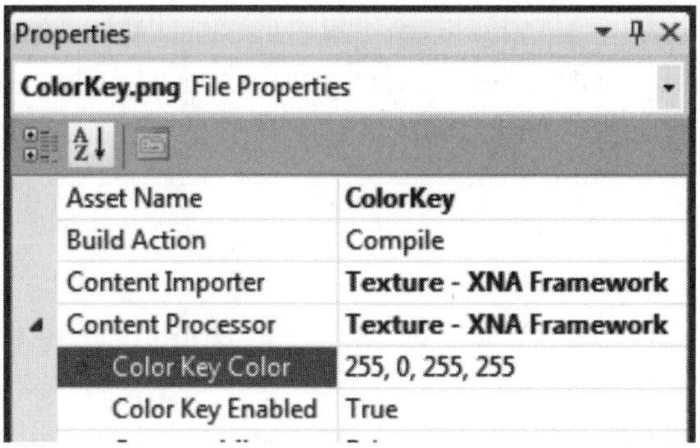

Figure 2–14. The Color Key properties inside the Content project

Alpha Channel Transparency

Color key transparency is a quick and simple method, but it is binary: pixels are either fully transparent or fully opaque. Sometimes we want more control than that, allowing individual pixels in the image to have different degrees of transparency. We can achieve this using an *alpha channel*.

As already discussed, each pixel color within an image is made from varying the intensity of red, green, and blue. PNG images are able to store one final additional value alongside each pixel: the alpha value. This also ranges from 0 to 255, where 0 represents a fully transparent pixel (which will actually be completely invisible when drawn to the screen) and 255 (which represents a fully opaque pixel). The values in between form a smooth gradiation of transparency levels.

Although the end results of using an alpha channel are usually superior to those from color keyed graphics, the amount of effort required to set up the graphic can be much greater. For more information on how to use alpha channels in your graphics package of choice, please consult its documentation.

■ **TIP** Most well-featured graphics packages allow you to work on an image's alpha channel. If you are looking for a flexible and powerful image editor on a budget, try the freeware application Paint.NET. Visit the web site at `http://www.getpaint.net/` to download. Paint.NET has full alpha channel support, although it can take a while to get the hang of using it.

For images with alpha channels, there is no need to set up any properties within the Content project: XNA will automatically recognize and use the alpha data within the image. The `Transparency` example project displays two instances of a graphic with an alpha channel. The color data in the graphic is in fact completely white, but the alpha data contains a radial fade from opaque in the image center to fully transparent at the edges.

The project randomly changes the background color every few seconds. Note how the alpha channel images blend in with the background, taking on its color in their semitransparent regions. You can also see how the two overlapping images blend with one another rather than erasing the pixels of the sprite in the background.

■ **TIP** Alpha channels can, of course, be used when tinting sprites, too. Try changing the color of one of the alpha channel sprites from `Color.White` to `Color.Blue`, for example, and see how the sprites now appear when the project is run.

Alpha Tinting

Now that we have discussed alpha channels and transparency, we can revisit the sprite tinting feature that we discussed a few pages back.

You may recall that we could define a color for tinting by specifying the red, green, and blue intensity levels. But hold on; if PNG images can store alpha information as well as color information, can we use alpha values for tinting?

Well yes, we can. A further overload of the `Color` constructor allows an alpha value to be specified alongside the red, green, and blue values. If we set our `SpriteBatch` object up in the appropriate way and pass the alpha value as something other than 255 (or 1.0f, if you prefer the float-based version), the sprite will be drawn semitransparently. This can be used to smoothly fade objects in or out of the display, or to provide ghostly shadow effects in your games.

To use this effect, we first need to specify a different parameter when calling the `SpriteBatch.Begin` method. Pass the value of `BlendState.NonPremultiplied` for the `blendState` parameter. There are various methods that XNA uses to blend new graphics with those already on the screen, and this is the one that allows us to draw new sprites with varying levels of transparency.

Then it is simply a matter of providing an alpha level in your `Color` object: 0 for fully transparent; 255 for fully opaque. Listing 2–20 creates a series of smiley faces that are fully transparent on the left to opaque on the right. The results are shown in Figure 2–15.

Listing 2–20. Drawing sprites with alpha tinting

```
// Begin a sprite batch with nonpremultiplied blending
_spriteBatch.Begin(SpriteSortMode.Deferred, BlendState.NonPremultiplied);
// Draw some sprites with different alpha tints
for (int i = 0; i < 20; i++)
{
    _spriteBatch.Draw(_smileyTexture, new Vector2(I * 20, 100),
                                    new Color(255, 255, 255, i * 12));
}
// End the sprite batch
_spriteBatch.End();
```

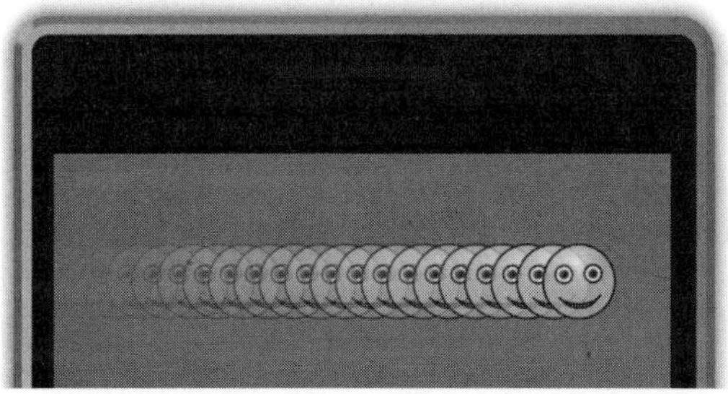

Figure 2–15. Varying levels of alpha in the sprite color

The example shown in Figure 2–15 can be found in the `AlphaTinting` project in the accompanying download.

Useful Sprite Effects

Besides drawing individual graphics on the screen, there are various other useful effects that we can perform by using sprites. Let's take a look at a few of these effects: background images, fading to black, and fading between images.

Setting a Background Image

Games with solid color backgrounds can look a bit dull, but we can liven things up by drawing a single sprite that precisely fills the background of the game area. Because the sprite results in the entire screen being redrawn, there is no need for the `Draw` code to clear the graphics device, which saves a little bit of graphics processing time.

The background is then drawn by specifying a render rectangle rather than a sprite position and ensuring that the rectangle fills the entire screen. We can actually obtain such a rectangle from XNA very easily by querying the `Game.Window.ClientBounds` property. This returns a `Rectangle` structure that corresponds with the dimensions and position of the game window.

Provided that we draw the background first (or use a `layerDepth` value that ensures it appears behind everything else), this will draw the background texture to fill the screen and allow all our other graphics to appear on top. The code to achieve this is shown in Listing 2–21.

Listing 2–21. Using a sprite to create a background image

```
protected override void Draw(GameTime gameTime)
{
    // No need to clear as we are redrawing the entire screen with our background image
    //GraphicsDevice.Clear(Color.CornflowerBlue);

    // Begin the spriteBatch
    _spriteBatch.Begin();
    // Draw the background image
    _spriteBatch.Draw(_backgroundTexture, this.Window.ClientBounds, Color.White);
    // Draw the smiley face
    _spriteBatch.Draw(_smileyTexture, _smileyPosition, Color.White);
    // End the spriteBatch
    _spriteBatch.End();

    base.Draw(gameTime);
}
```

This can be seen in action in the BackgroundImage example project. Note that we use a JPEG image for the background because it is a photograph, which reduces the size of the compiled application—just make sure that the picture is of the same aspect ratio as the screen (tall and thin) so that it isn't distorted when it is displayed. Figure 2–16 shows the output from this project.

Figure 2–16. Rendering on top of a background image

Fading to Black

A common and useful effect seen on TV and in films is the *fade to black,* which simply involves fading away everything on the screen to blackness. This is great for scene transitions because it allows the content of the entire screen to be updated without any jarring movement. It can add a layer of presentational sparkle to games, too, perhaps fading from the title screen into the game or fading between one level and the next.

We can implement a fade to black very easily by first drawing all the content on the screen and then rendering a full-screen sprite over the top, colored black and with variable alpha intensity. To fade to black, we start with an alpha value of 0 (transparent), at which point the sprite will be invisible, and fade to 255 (opaque), at which point the sprite will completely obscure everything on the screen. Once we reach this point, the rest of the scene can be changed in whatever way is appropriate, and the alpha level faded back toward zero to fade the scene into visibility again.

Because the texture we need for the sprite is just a solid color, we can actually create the texture in code rather than having to add an image to the Content project. We can create a new texture by specifying the device on which we will render it (a reference to which is stored in the Game class's GraphicsDevice property) along with its width and height. We can create the texture with a width and height of just 1 pixel because XNA will happily stretch it to whatever size we want.

Perhaps surprisingly, we will tell XNA to make the texture's only pixel white rather than black because we can tint it black when we draw it. Setting the texture up this way means that we could also tint it any other color should we wish: fading to white, green, or powder blue as suits our game.

First then, let's look at the code that creates the texture, which can be seen in Listing 2–22. This is extracted from the project's LoadContent method. It creates the Texture2D object and then calls its SetData method to pass in the colors for the texture pixels. If the texture were larger, this would set a pixel for each provided array element, working horizontally across each row from left to right and then vertically from top to bottom. Our array has just a single element to match the pixels in the texture.

Listing 2–22. Creating the fader texture

```
// Create the texture for our fader sprite with a size of 1 x 1 pixel
_faderTexture = new Texture2D(GraphicsDevice, 1, 1);
// Create an array of colors for the texture -- just one color
// as the texture consists of only one pixel
Color[] faderColors = new Color[] {Color.White};
// Set the color data into the texture
_faderTexture.SetData<Color>(faderColors);
```

The texture is then used in the Draw method, as shown in Listing 2–23. In this example, we draw a number of smiley faces onto the background and then draw the fader in front. The alpha level for the fader is stored in a class variable named _faderAlpha, which is faded between 0 and 255 in the Update method.

Listing 2–23. Drawing the fader texture

```
protected override void Draw(GameTime gameTime)
{
    GraphicsDevice.Clear(Color.CornflowerBlue);

    // Begin the spriteBatch
    _spriteBatch.Begin(SpriteSortMode.Deferred, BlendState.NonPremultiplied);

    // Draw the smiley face sprites
    for (int i = 0; i < _smileyPositions.Length; i++)
    {
        _spriteBatch.Draw(_smileyTexture, _smileyPositions[i], Color.White);
    }

    // Draw the fader
    _spriteBatch.Draw(_faderTexture, this.Window.ClientBounds,
```

```
                                        new Color(0, 0, 0, _faderAlpha));

        // End the spriteBatch
        _spriteBatch.End();

        base.Draw(gameTime);
    }
```

Each time the fader reaches maximum opacity, the positions of the smiley faces are all updated, but we never see them move because they are always obscured when this takes place. For the full code and to see this running, take a look at the FadeToBlack example project.

Fading between Images

Similar to the fade to black effect is the fading between images effect. It is essentially the same technique, but it uses two sprites containing images rather than one sprite containing solid color. By using a series of images, slideshow effects can be set up, providing a very pleasant transition between each pair of images.

The effect can be seen in the FadeBetweenImages example project. Although XNA provides a beautiful smooth transition between the images, unfortunately a picture doesn't speak 1,000 words in this case because it doesn't look very impressive at all on paper—it needs to be seen in motion.

We can take a quick look at the code, though. We set up an array of three different background textures and load them in the LoadContent method. To make the fade work, we store the index through the array of the current background image (which is the image that will be fading away) in the _backgroundImageIndex variable and the fader image (which is the image that will be fading into view) in the _faderImageIndex variable. These are initially given the values 0 and 1, respectively.

The Draw method, shown in Listing 2–24, should look very similar because it's just like the previous listing. Note that the tint color is now white rather than black so it shows in its normal colors.

Listing 2–24. Drawing the fading images

```
    protected override void Draw(GameTime gameTime)
    {
        // No need to clear as we are drawing a full-screen image
        //GraphicsDevice.Clear(Color.CornflowerBlue);

        // Begin the spriteBatch
        _spriteBatch.Begin(SpriteSortMode.Deferred, BlendState.NonPremultiplied);
        // Draw the background image
        _spriteBatch.Draw(_backgroundTextures[_backgroundImageIndex],
                                        this.Window.ClientBounds, Color.White);
        // Draw the fader
        _spriteBatch.Draw(_backgroundTextures[_faderImageIndex], this.Window.ClientBounds,
                                        new Color(255, 255, 255, _faderAlpha));
        // End the spriteBatch
        _spriteBatch.End();

        base.Draw(gameTime);
    }
```

The Update code simply increments the value of _faderAlpha, waiting for it to exceed 255. When this happens, it is reset back to 0, and the image index variables are incremented. We use the % modulus operator to automatically reset the index variables back to 0 once they reach the defined image count.

The fade can, of course, be made faster by adding a greater value to _faderAlpha; to slow it down, the variable could be converted to a float and a fractional value added. The relevant part of the code is in Listing 2–25.

Listing 2–25. The Update code to fade between the series of images

```
// Increment the opacity of the fader
_faderAlpha += 1;
// Has it reached full opacity?
if (_faderAlpha > 255)
{
    // Yes, so reset to zero and move to the next pair of images
    _faderAlpha = 0;
    _backgroundImageIndex = (_backgroundImageIndex + 1) % IMAGE_COUNT;
    _faderImageIndex = (_faderImageIndex + 1) % IMAGE_COUNT;
}
```

Displaying Text

Most games need to display text while they are running, providing everything from the player's score through to menus and game information pages. XNA provides a very easy-to-use mechanism for showing text on the screen, so let's see what it can do and how we use it.

Font Support

Fonts can cause all sorts of problem with regard to licensing. The vast majority of fonts that are included with Windows or can be downloaded from the Internet have license terms attached that prevent you from redistributing them in your own games.

Fortunately, Microsoft has helped us out by licensing a number of fonts that can be used and distributed in your Windows Phone games without any threat of legal action. We will therefore concentrate on how these particular fonts can be used in your games.

The available fonts are summarized in Table 2–1.

Table 2–1. Fonts licensed for use in Windows Phone games

Name	Example	Variations
Andy	Windows Phone 7 Game Development	Bold
Jing Jing	WINDOWS PHONE 7 GAME DEVELOPMENT	Regular
Kootenay	Windows Phone 7 Game Development	Regular
Lindsey	Windows Phone 7 Game Development	Regular
Miramonte	Windows Phone 7 Game Development	Regular, Bold

Name	Example	Variations
Moire	Windows Phone 7 Game Development	Light, Regular, Bold, ExtraBold
Motorwerk	*WINDOWS PHONE 7 GAME DEVELOPMENT*	Regular
News Gothic	Windows Phone 7 Game Development	Regular, Bold
OCR A Extended	Windows Phone 7 Game Development	Regular
Pericles	WINDOWS PHONE 7 GAME DEVELOPMENT	Light, Regular
Pescadero	Windows Phone 7 Game Development	Regular, Bold
Quartz MS	WINDOWS PHONE 7 GAME DEVELOPMENT	Regular
Segoe Keycaps	Windows Phone 7 Game Development	Regular
Segoe Print	Windows Phone 7 Game Development	Regular, Bold
Segoe UI Mono	Windows Phone 7 Game Development	Regular, Bold
Wasco Sans	Windows Phone 7 Game Development	Regular, Italic, Bold, Bold Italic

As you can see, there are some diverse typefaces present. Note that some of them (Jing Jing, Motorwerk, Quartz MS) have no lowercase letters; they have display capitals instead, while Pericles uses small versions of its capital letters instead of lowercase letters.

The Variations column in the table shows the different font variations that are fully supported within the fonts. To use the Regular, Bold, or Italic versions, place the required word into the Style element within the .spritefont file. For Wasco Sans' Bold Italic, use Bold, Italic as the style. For the other variations (Light or ExtraBold), suffix the variation to the font name (for example, Moire ExtraBold) and leave the Style element set to Regular. Fonts that do not show bold or italic variations can still be set to be bold or italicized by setting the Style element as required, but they will be programmatically converted into the requested version rather than using a design from the font definition itself and so might not look quite as good.

If you do want to use other fonts, you can easily do so, but please do be careful that you have the appropriate permission first. There are freely licensed fonts around if you search for them on the Internet, but check the license terms carefully!

Creating SpriteFont Objects

Before we can display any text, we must first embed the font into our program. XNA and Visual Studio between them take all the pain out of doing this, and it can be mostly achieved with just a few mouse clicks.

Just like all the image resources we have been using, the font is added into the Content project. To add a font, right-click the main Content project node and select to Add a New Item. Select the SpriteFont template in the Add New Item window and give the font a name—it's a good idea to name it after the font that you plan to use, as shown in Figure 2–17.

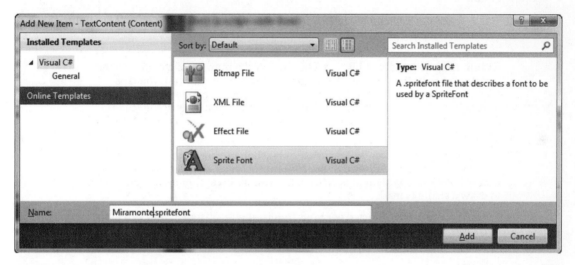

Figure 2–17. Adding a spritefont file to the Content project

Once the font has been added, a .spritefont file will appear. This is an XML document that describes to the compiler the details of the font that is to be used. When the Content project compiles, it reads the font from disk and converts it into a bitmap image to embed in your project. It is this image of the font rather than the font itself that is therefore used by your program. The .spritefont file describes how this bitmap is to be constructed.

There isn't all that much within the file to change; the available items are as follows:

- FontName provides the name of the font to embed. Set it to one of the XNA licensed fonts mentioned in the previous section or to any other font installed in Windows that you are licensed to use.

- Size sets the size of the font to be used to generate the bitmap. If you choose a large value, a higher-quality bitmap will be generated, but it will require a lot more space and memory to process, which is particularly wasteful if the font doesn't need to be displayed in large sizes. Smaller values lower the resource requirements, but result in blocky text appearing if the font is rendered larger than its default size. You will need to find a balance between size and appearance when setting this. The size is specified in *points* rather than in pixels; due to the way points are handled by XNA, you can find the approximate pixel size by adding one-third to the point size (a point size of 12 will result in a pixel size of 16 pixels).

- Spacing sets the number of pixels that will be left as a horizontal gap between each rendered character. Increasing it above 0 can make the text look very spaced out, so use with caution.

- UseKerning controls whether font kerning is used. *Kerning* is the process whereby characters are moved closer together if it can be achieved without the characters colliding. For example, the letters "AV" can be positioned so that the boxes containing each letter overlap, without the letters themselves touching. Kerning generally produces much more natural-looking text, so should usually be left enabled.

- Style allows the font style to be set to Regular, Bold, or Italic (it can also be set to Bold, Italic to combine these two styles).

- CharacterRegions provides one or more ranges of characters to be included within the generated font bitmap. The smaller the number of characters, the smaller the resulting bitmap. If, for example, you knew that you would be including only uppercase letters in your game, you could omit the lowercase letters from the font and thus reduce the resource requirements. Multiple CharacterRegion elements can be included in the outer CharacterRegions element if required.

- DefaultCharacter optionally provides a placeholder character that will be used any time a text string is printed that contains characters outside of the defined CharacterRegions. Without this, XNA will throw an exception if any such attempt to draw a string is made.

With the .spritefont file configured per your requirements, Visual Studio will automatically build the bitmap font each time the Content project is compiled.

Displaying Text

Our font is built and so we are ready to print with it to the screen. This is straightforward and painless, and involves first loading the font from the Content project, just as we did with our sprite textures.

This is achieved by once again calling the Content.Load method from within our game's LoadContent procedure, but indicating this time that we want it to return a SpriteFont object, as shown in Listing 2–26.

Listing 2–26. Loading the spritefont whose asset name is Miramonte

```
// Load the spritefont
_fontMiramonte = Content.Load<SpriteFont>("Miramonte");
```

To print the text to the screen we once again use the SpriteBatch object, calling its other method for drawing: DrawString. A number of overloads for this are available, but essentially they are all the same except that some accept a String parameter, whereas others accept a StringBuilder, some expect parameters to control rotation and uniform scaling, and yet others allow non-uniform scaling.

The simplest version, which is shown in Listing 2–27, simply prints the text at the coordinate (100, 100) in white text.

Listing 2–27. Using DrawString to display text to the screen

```
_spriteBatch.Begin();
_spriteBatch.DrawString(_fontMiramonte, "Hello world", new Vector2(100, 100),
                                                      Color.White);
_spriteBatch.End();
```

The text appears on the screen just as you would expect (see Figure 2–18). The specified coordinate refers to the top-left corner of the displayed text.

Figure 2–18. Displaying text on the screen using DrawString

All the other features available to sprites are available to spritefonts too, allowing us to display text in different colors (including with variable alpha levels to allow text to fade in and out of display), rotated to different angles, or scaled to whatever size is required. The syntax for drawing text with these effects applied is essentially just the same as for drawing sprites.

We also have the ability to specify an origin for the text. When we drew sprites, we could easily identify the width and height of the sprite by querying the Width and Height properties of the Texture2D object used to provide the sprite image. But for text, the size will be different for every string we draw depending on the string being displayed.

To overcome this, the SpriteFont object provides a very useful function called MeasureString. When the function is passed the text to be displayed, it returns a Vector2 structure with the required text width stored in its X property and the text height in its Y property. This allows us to easily determine the dimensions of the rendered string, and this value can be used as the basis of calculating DrawString Origin parameter. Finding the center point is especially easy because the Vector2 can be multiplied or divided by a scalar value, resulting in its X and Y values being multiplied or divided by the provided value. The center point can thus be obtained by simply dividing the result from MeasureString by 2.

■ **TIP** XNA can include line breaks within strings, both when drawing and measuring. Insert them into a string in C# using the \n character sequence.

Listing 2–28 shows an extract from the Text example project that does something a little more exciting-looking than the simple "Hello world" text. It measures a text string so that it can determine its center point and then uses it to draw a series of text strings to the same position on the screen, with each string a little larger, further rotated, and more faded than the last.

Listing 2–28. A text-based graphical effect using rotation, scaling, and alpha blending

```
// Calculate the size of the text
textString = "Text in XNA!";
textsize = _fontMiramonte.MeasureString(textString);
// Draw it lots of times
for (int i = 25; i >= 0; i--)
{
    // For the final iteration, use black text;
    // otherwise use white text with gradually increasing alpha levels
    if (i > 0)
    {
        textcolor = new Color(255, 255, 255, 255 - i * 10);
    }
    else
    {
        textcolor = Color.Black;
    }
    // Draw our text with its origin at the middle of the screen and
    // in the center of the text, rotated and scaled based on the
    // iteration number.
    _spriteBatch.DrawString(_fontMiramonte, textString, new Vector2(240, 400),
            textcolor, MathHelper.ToRadians (_angle * ((i + 5) * 0.1f)),
            textsize / 2, 1 + (i / 7.0f), SpriteEffects.None, 0);
}
```

The code actually loops backward so that the most faded/rotated/enlarged text is displayed first; each additional iteration draws a more focused version on top of it. The color is finally set to black for the very last iteration to make the text easier to read.

The DrawString call may look a bit complex, but if we break it down it's really very simple. We specify the spritefont to use, the text to write, and the position of the text origin, which is hard-coded at (240, 400) for simplicity in this example. After the color, we then provide the rotation angle, which is modified for each iteration so that each piece of text appears at a slightly different angle. The origin is specified next, simply by passing the textsize value retrieved from MeasureString, divided by 2 so that we obtain its center point. Finally we specify the scale, also set to change for each iteration, the SpriteEffect (which can be used to flip text upside down or back to front), and the layer depth.

Once this is all put together, the output is as shown in Figure 2–19. This can also be seen in action in the Text example project, which is another example that looks much better in motion than in a static screenshot.

Figure 2–19. Rotated, scaled, and alpha blended text

Although the display of text is a basic requirement, XNA nevertheless provides a variety of options to make its display interesting and flexible.

Other Graphics Options

We've now covered most of the fundamental options available for 2D rendering, but there are a few important details still left to look at, so let's run through these now.

Rendering in Full Screen Mode

All the examples so far have operated in so-called *windowed* mode, which in the context of Windows Phone simply means that the status bar is visible at the top of the screen. In many instances users may prefer to have this available because it gives them a window into the phone: they can see their battery level, their signal reception level, and so on. Some games may benefit from having the game run in *full screen* mode, however, with this bar hidden. It is usually polite to offer a configuration option so that this mode can be configured per user preference.

Setting full screen mode is easy; just add the line of code shown in Listing 2–29 to your Game class's constructor:

Listing 2–29. Starting up in full screen mode

```
// Set the graphics device manager into full screen mode
_graphics.IsFullScreen = true;
```

If you wish to change the full screen state of your game at a later time, the easiest way is to call the GraphicsDeviceManager's ToggleFullScreen method. You can check the current state at any time by reading back the IsFullScreen property value.

Supporting Portrait and Landscape Orientations

All the examples that we have looked at in this chapter used portrait orientation for displaying their graphics. This is the orientation that the user is likely to be using for general-purpose interaction with the device, and if your game works well in this orientation it is a good idea to allow your game to run in this arrangement.

If your game would benefit from a landscape orientation, however, this is easy to implement. In fact, the default behavior of XNA is to present the game in landscape mode.

Windows Phone 7 devices have special hardware present to support orientation, which means that they cost absolutely no processing time whatsoever.

Let's look at the options for supporting different orientations within your games.

Using Portrait Orientation

To set a game to run in portrait mode, we can set the width and height of the back buffer in the game class constructor so that its height is greater than its width. We can set the width to 480 and the height to 800 to match the device resolution, as shown in Listing 2–30.

Listing 2–30. Setting the back buffer for portrait orientation

```
// Display using portrait orientation
_graphics.PreferredBackBufferWidth = 480;
_graphics.PreferredBackBufferHeight = 800;
```

With this configuration active, the game will always appear in portrait mode, regardless of how the device is physically rotated. You can test rotation on the emulator by clicking the rotate buttons that appear to the right of the device window and see how the graphics on the screen respond. With the game running in portrait mode, the graphics will display sideways when the device is in a landscape orientation.

You can see this in effect by running the Orientation sample project. This also displays the name of the orientation that the device is currently using, the size of the back buffer, and the size of the game window. Notice that they do not change when the device is rotated.

Using Landscape Orientation

To operate your game in landscape orientation, don't specify any preferred back buffer size in the class constructor; the game will default to landscape mode. Try commenting out the back buffer configuration in the Orientation project and run it to see the results.

If you leave the device or the emulator in portrait orientation, the display will appear sideways because the game is now supporting *only* landscape orientations. Note that if you switch the device over between being rotated to the left and to the right, it automatically rotates the screen content to match. The Current orientation display from the program will switch between LandscapeLeft and LandscapeRight as you do this.

The game itself doesn't need to know anything about such a rotation because the screen size is absolutely unchanged.

Allowing Landscape and Portrait Orientations

You may wish to support your game in both landscape and portrait orientations. Doing so is easy to accomplish from the point of view of the phone, but may introduce additional work into your game because you will probably need to resize or reposition your game elements to fit into the new window dimensions.

To enable all possible orientations, comment out the code that sets the preferred back buffer size and replace it with the code shown in Listing 2–31.

Listing 2–31. Allowing landscape and portrait orientations

```
// Allow portrait and both landscape rotations
_graphics.SupportedOrientations = DisplayOrientation.Portrait |
                    DisplayOrientation.LandscapeLeft |
                    DisplayOrientation.LandscapeRight;
```

If you run the project now, you will find that it automatically adjusts to whatever orientation the device is held in.

One important point is the way that the Window size and Back buffer size values are reported by the example project. The window size remains completely unaffected by the rotation because at heart the device is always operating in portrait mode, so this is the size that it considers its window to be. The back buffer size (retrieved from the BackBufferWidth and BackBufferHeight properties of the _graphics.GraphicsDevice.PresentationParameters object) always reflects the dimensions of the window as it is actually being rendered. If you are supporting rotation, be careful to read the buffer size in the correct way.

You can, of course, provide any set of orientations that you wish for the SupportedOrientations property. Setting it to just DisplayOrientation.LandscapeLeft would prevent portrait or landscape-right orientations from being displayed. Generally if you are allowing landscape orientation, you should allow both modes so that users can hold the device in whichever way they are comfortable with.

To change the supported orientations after the game has started, set the SupportedOrientations property as needed and then call the _graphics.ApplyChanges method. The updated orientations will become immediately effective.

If you need to detect the orientation changing so that you can update your game accordingly, the easiest way to do it is to subscribe to the game window's OrientationChanged event. This is fired each time the orientation changes, and the new orientation can be retrieved from the Window.CurrentOrientation property. The Orientation example project uses this event to display the new orientation to the debug window each time it changes.

Graphic Scaling

Compared with modern game consoles, Windows Phone 7 devices are fairly low-powered in terms of graphical capability, despite the hardware that they have at their disposal. Yet they still run at a fairly high resolution: 480 x 800 pixels is a substantial amount of screen data to update.

In many cases, the hardware will be entirely capable of handling this, but when the graphic updates are more intense the phone may struggle. To assist with this scenario, the device has a hardware image scaler built in, which enables XNA to render at any size that it likes, allowing the scaler to increase the size of the rendered graphics so that they fill the screen. Just as with rotation, special hardware is present to perform this task, so it takes no processor time whatsoever. The scaler smoothes the graphics as it processes them, so it avoids displaying pixelated graphics. The scaler is particularly effective with fast-moving graphics, which further helps to disguise the scaling that is taking place.

To use the scaler, we just set the preferred back buffer size in the game constructor to whatever size we need. If the game is running in portrait mode, we can scale everything to twice its size by using the code shown in Listing 2–32. Note that the size provided here is exactly half the actual screen size. This means that we can render into the screen area 240 pixels wide by 400 pixels high (instead of the normal 480 x 800 pixels) and still have it fill the screen. This is one-quarter of the volume of pixels, resulting in a lot less work for the device to do.

Listing 2–32. Double-size scaling in portrait mode

```
// Scale up by 2x
_graphics.PreferredBackBufferWidth = 240;
_graphics.PreferredBackBufferHeight = 400;
```

If your game is using landscape mode, set the preferred back buffer size so that the width is greater than the height, as shown in Listing 2–33. This is the correct approach if using both landscape and portrait modes via the SupportedOrientations property too: XNA will automatically swap the back buffer width and height when switching into portrait mode, so always provide the buffer size with the dimensions that will be used for the landscape display orientation.

Listing 2–33. Double-size scaling in landscape mode

```
// Scale up by 2x
_graphics.PreferredBackBufferWidth = 400;
_graphics.PreferredBackBufferHeight = 240;
```

The scaler can also work with smaller resolutions than this if desired, but the more dramatic the scaling, the more pixelated and distorted the final image will be.

To change the scaling after the game has started, set the preferred back buffer size as required, just as we have seen in the constructor, and then call the _graphics.ApplyChanges method. The scaler will immediately start or stop work as required.

Suppressing Drawing

The update/draw loop that XNA employs is generally very good for presenting a game to the screen and offers great opportunities for rich-looking graphic updates. But sometimes the graphics being drawn to the screen aren't actually moving at all. XNA is unaware of this, however, and continues to clear and repaint the same identical scene frame after frame, using the CPU and graphics hardware in the process and wasting the battery as a result.

These is, however, a way to indicate to XNA that it doesn't need to redraw the screen and can just re-present the most recently drawn screen. This is achieved simply by calling the Game class's SuppressDraw method from within the Update function.

A simple approach to managing this is to create a bool variable within Update called objectsMoved, initially set to false. As soon as your Update code causes anything to happen that needs the screen to be redrawn, it sets this variable to true. At the end of the function, the code can then check this variable and call SuppressDraw if it still contains its initial false value.

Experiment and Play with XNA

In this chapter, we have covered a lot of XNA's capabilities for 2D rendering. In the next chapter, we will build on these capabilities and start to develop a model for flexible game development.

Please feel free to spend some time experimenting with what you have learned so far. You already have lots of useful and flexible graphical techniques under your belt, and the more familiar and comfortable you can get with these the better. Try out using some of these effects and see what you can produce yourself.

CHAPTER 3

■■■

Creating a Game Framework

We have covered a lot of the technology foundations so far, and you have a good understanding of the functions required for displaying 2D content to the screen. Now it is time to start organizing and structuring what you have learned.

It would be very easy to launch into our first game at this point, but instead of diving straight in, we will take a rather more planned approach.

In this chapter, we will begin the creation of a *game framework*, an object structure that we will build upon when writing games. The framework will be able to simplify the code that we write for each game, speeding up development time and allowing us to focus on the game rather than getting caught up in fiddly technical details. We can address all these details in the framework just once and then we don't have to worry about them when we are developing.

Designing the Game Framework

XNA's Game class already provides a flexible engine for initializing and driving the game. What it doesn't offer is any built-in mechanism for managing the *game objects* that we want to display and manipulate inside the game.

The examples that we have been looking at have provided mechanisms for moving small numbers of sprites, but any real game needs to track significantly more objects than this. Instead of building all the objects into the game on an ad hoc basis, we will build the framework inside which the objects can be managed.

These objects will be used for all elements of the game that we need to draw: they will be the falling tiles in a game of *Tetris*; the ghosts, dots, and player in *Pac Man*; and all the spaceships and bullets in *Space Invaders*. Objects will know various things about themselves (such as where they are on the screen) and will allow us to manage a consistent and simple mechanism for moving and rendering efficiently. Providing a simple and flexible implementation for game objects is the primary area that we will address in the design and construction of the game framework.

We will take advantage of the .NET object orientation features in the design of the framework. We will create an abstract base class that supports a core set of functions that will be generally useful in any of our game objects. We will then derive another abstract class from this and set up this derived class to provide support specifically for 2D sprite-based game objects that we can create using the techniques in the last chapter. In Chapter 6, we will derive another class for 3D objects, allowing us to keep a significant part of the functionality and methodology that we have discussed and developed along the way.

All these classes will be placed into a separate Game Library project named GameFramework, which will allow us to reuse them between projects without having to reimplement them or share source files. Instead, we will just add a reference to the framework library, and its classes will be immediately available.

Let's take a look at the classes in the framework. You can find its code by opening the `MultipleGameObjects` project from this chapter's example code.

The GameObjectBase Class

The first class is the `GameObjectBase` class, an abstract class from which all our game object classes will ultimately be derived. The functionality within `GameObjectBase` is limited, but we can declare collections of game objects by using this class without initially needing to know any more details about which types of objects we are going to store.

The actual functionality within the class is very limited. In the class constructor, we take a `Game` object as a parameter. You might recall that the XNA games that we write all have their main class derived from the `Game` class, so storing it provides a mechanism that allows code within this class and any derived class to access the main `Game` object. The constructor is shown in Listing 3–1.

Listing 3–1. The GameObjectBase class constructor

```
/// <summary>
/// Constructor for the object
/// </summary>
/// <param name="game">A reference to the XNA Game class inside which the object
/// resides</param>
public GameObjectBase(Microsoft.Xna.Framework.Game game)
{
    Game = game;
}
```

In addition to the constructor, we define a single method, `Update`, which will be used to update the state of the object. It accepts a `GameTime` object as a parameter so that timing information can be extracted, just like the `Update` method in the main `Game` class. The function does nothing more than increment a variable, `UpdateCount`, so that we can tell how many updates have taken place; its code can be seen in Listing 3–2. Our derived classes will override this function, however, so that they can perform the actual updates of their corresponding game objects.

Listing 3–2. The Update function

```
/// <summary>
/// Update the object state
/// </summary>
/// <param name="gameTime"></param>
public virtual void Update(GameTime gameTime)
{
    // Increment the UpdateCount
    UpdateCount += 1;
}
```

The SpriteObject Class

Derived from `GameObjectBase` is the `SpriteObject` class (see Figure 3–1). This is a concrete class (not abstract) in which we will add all the basic functionality that we might want to use to position and draw our sprites. In its basic form, the class is capable of maintaining a sprite's position, scaling, rotation, and origin, a texture for it to render with, a color to tint with, a source rectangle for partial texture rendering (if required), and a layer depth to help define the order in which the sprites should be rendered.

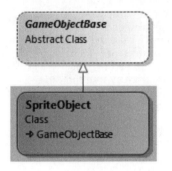

Figure 3–1. The SpriteObject's position in the framework project

It doesn't contain any object logic, however: it knows nothing about how to move or change any of its properties. This logic will be added by deriving further classes from SpriteObject, as we will see shortly. Such derived classes are generally what we will use when we build our games, but if a simple static sprite is all that is required, instances of SpriteObject can be created and added to the game.

Various different constructor overloads are provided to allow the calling code to easily set some of the common properties of the class. The signatures for each of these are shown in Listing 3–3 (the bodies of the functions are omitted for brevity because they are simply setting the provided parameter values into the class properties).

Listing 3–3. The available constructors for the SpriteObject class

```
public SpriteObject(Game game)

public SpriteObject(Game game, Vector2 position)

public SpriteObject(Game game, Vector2 position, Texture2D texture)
```

The class offers a lot of additional properties to allow us to control the position and appearance of the sprite, however, as follows:

- SpriteTexture stores a reference to a texture that can be used to render the sprite. The default implementation of the Draw method (which we will discuss in a moment) will use this texture to draw the sprite, though this behavior can be overridden if required.

- PositionX and PositionY store the sprite's position as float variables, whereas the Position property represents the same position as a Vector2. Any of them can be set or retrieved, though they update the same internal variables so setting PositionX or PositionY will have an immediate effect on the return value from Position, and vice versa. The reason they are stored as floats as well as a Vector2 is that Vector2 is a structure rather than a class, so when we read the Position property we are actually given a copy of the underlying structure. This copy's properties cannot be modified, and Visual Studio will give an error if, for example, you attempted to assign a value to Property.X. So instead we expose the individual coordinates for modification and interrogation, and the Vector2 structure for passing into functions that expect a value of this type.

- OriginX, OriginY, and Origin store the sprite's origin coordinate, using a pair of floats and a Vector2 structure just as for the Position properties in the previous paragraph. The default origin is the coordinate (0, 0).

- Angle stores the angle of rotation in radians, defaulting to 0.

- ScaleX and ScaleY are float values that allow for uniform or non-uniform scaling to be applied to the sprite. In addition to this, the Scale property represents the same values as a Vector2 structure.

- SourceRect is a Rectangle structure with which we can define a subregion of the sprite's texture that is to be rendered. If the structure is "empty" (its values are all zero), this feature will be ignored, and the whole texture will be rendered. Its default state is to be empty.

- SpriteColor allows tinting and alpha levels to be applied to the sprite. It defaults to Color.White, with full intensity alpha.

- LayerDepth stores a float value that will be used for setting the rendering order of the sprite if the appropriate mode is set when calling the SpriteBatch.Begin method, as described in the previous chapter.

As you can see, the object allows virtually all the basic sprite state to be stored and maintained. Creating an instance of this class (or a class derived from it) allows a good deal of flexibility for displaying the sprite without needing any further variables to be defined. That greatly simplifies the repetitive code that we would otherwise need to write to store all this information.

In addition to storing the sprite state, we also add a virtual function called Draw. Just like the Draw method in the XNA main Game class, we expect a GameTime object as a parameter, but we also require a SpriteBatch object to be passed in. Because this class is dedicated entirely to drawing sprites, it makes sense to expect a SpriteBatch, and we need access to one so that we can call its Draw method to display our sprite to the screen.

The default behavior of the SpriteObject.Draw method is to draw the configured sprite to the screen. It can do this only if it has a valid SpriteTexture, so this is checked first. After that, one of two different calls is made to SpriteBatch.Draw, depending on whether a SourceRect has been specified. The code for the Draw function is shown in Listing 3–4.

Listing 3–4. The SpriteObject class Draw function

```
public virtual void Draw(GameTime gameTime, SpriteBatch spriteBatch)
{
    // Do we have a texture? If not then there is nothing to draw...
    if (SpriteTexture != null)
    {
```

```
        // Has a source rectangle been set?
        if (SourceRect.IsEmpty)
        {
            // No, so draw the entire sprite texture
            spriteBatch.Draw(SpriteTexture, Position, null, SpriteColor, Angle,
                                Origin, Scale, SpriteEffects.None, LayerDepth);
        }
        else
        {
            // Yes, so just draw the specified SourceRect
            spriteBatch.Draw(SpriteTexture, Position, SourceRect, SpriteColor, Angle,
                                Origin, Scale, SpriteEffects.None, LayerDepth);
        }
    }
}
```

Other classes that derive from SpriteObject can, of course, override the Draw method and supplement or entirely replace the default functionality as needed.

A final property present within the class can be used to help determine the area on the screen in which the sprite is being drawn. BoundingBox calculates this by looking at the sprite's position, its origin, the texture size, and the current scale. These are factored into a Rectangle structure that can then be used for simple collision checks, for example. The code for this function is shown in Listing 3–5.

Listing 3–5. Calculating the sprite's bounding box

```
public virtual Rectangle BoundingBox
{
    get
    {
        Rectangle result;
        Vector2 spritesize;

        if (SourceRect.IsEmpty)
        {
            // The size is that of the whole texture
            spritesize = new Vector2(SpriteTexture.Width, SpriteTexture.Height);
        }
        else
        {
            // The size is that of the rectangle
            spritesize = new Vector2(SourceRect.Width, SourceRect.Height);
        }

        // Build a rectangle whose position and size matches that of the sprite
        // (taking scaling into account for the size)
        result = new Rectangle((int)PositionX, (int)PositionY,
                        (int)(spritesize.X * ScaleX), (int)(spritesize.Y * ScaleY));

        // Offset the sprite by the origin
        result.Offset((int)(-OriginX * ScaleX), (int)(-OriginY * ScaleY));

        // Return the finished rectangle
        return result;
    }
}
```

The code first determines the size of the texture being displayed, which is the width and height of the whole texture, or the size defined by the SourceRect property if it has been set. It then creates its Rectangle structure by using the sprite position for the Left and Top values and the calculated texture size for its Width and Height. The texture size is scaled as appropriate to ensure that the resulting rectangle matches the size of the texture displayed on the screen.

The rectangle is then offset by the origin position. The further the origin moves toward the right, the further the sprite itself moves to the left, and so we subtract the origin position from the rectangle's top-left corner. Once again, this is scaled as appropriate.

The finished rectangle is then returned.

■ **CAUTION** This function works well for many sprites, but those that have been rotated will not produce the expected results. The code does not take rotation into account, and so rotated sprites—and particularly those that are not square in shape—will protrude outside of the bounding box. If your sprites need more sophisticated bounding box calculation, this will need to be implemented in your derived game object classes.

The TextObject Class

So we have a simple way of representing a sprite, but it would be very useful to have a corresponding mechanism for representing text. We achieve this by creating the TextObject class. Because text shares many of the same features as sprites (a position, origin, color, rotation, scaling, and more) we derive TextObject from SpriteObject as shown in Figure 3–2, allowing us to take advantage of all the SpriteObject properties.

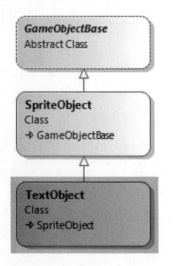

Figure 3–2. The TextObject position in the framework project

The constructors available to this class are more text-oriented and are shown in Listing 3–6.

Listing 3–6. The available constructors for the TextObject class

```
public TextObject(Game game)

public TextObject(Game game, Vector2 position)

public TextObject(Game game, Vector2 position, SpriteFont font)

public TextObject(Game game, Vector2 position, SpriteFont font, String text)

public TextObject(Game game, Vector2 position, SpriteFont font, String text,
                TextAlignment horizontalAlignment, TextAlignment verticalAlignment)
```

All the SpriteObject properties are relevant to TextObject except for SpriteTexture (we need a font instead of a texture) and SourceRect (which has no relevance to rendering text). We will ignore these, and instead add a couple of new properties of our own:

- Font stores a reference to a SpriteFont object that will be used to render the text.

- Text stores a text string to be displayed.

- HorizontalAlignment and VerticalAlignment offer the creator of the object a simple way of automatically aligning the text around its position.

All four of these properties are backed by a private class variable rather than being autoimplemented using the { get; set; } syntax. This allows us to hook into their set code and perform some additional processing relating to text alignment, an example of which is shown in Listing 3–7.

Listing 3–7. The implementation of the Text property

```
public String Text
{
    get { return _text; }
    set
    {
        // Has the text changed from whatever we already have stored?
        if (_text != value)
        {
            // Yes, so store the new text and recalculate the origin if needed
            _text = value;
            CalculateAlignmentOrigin();
        }
    }
}
```

In each of the properties, if the code detects that a changed value has been provided, it calls into a function named CalculateAlignmentOrigin. This function examines the content of the HorizontalAlignment and VerticalAlignment properties, and if either is set to a value other than Manual, it automatically calculates a new Origin coordinate by calling the SpriteFont.MeasureString function (as detailed in the previous chapter). This allows the object creator to instruct the text to be left- or right-aligned, or for it to be centered (and the same options are available for vertical alignment, too). With the alignment properties set, this alignment will continue to be automatically applied whenever an update to the object is made. Alternatively, either or both of the alignment properties can be set to Manual (which is also their default), in which case the Origin coordinate can be set explicitly by the game.

Next we have the Draw method. TextObject overrides it and replaces the SpriteObject implementation completely, rendering text rather than a texture. The implementation is very simple and is shown in Listing 3–8.

Listing 3–8. The TextObject Draw method

```
public override void Draw(GameTime gameTime, SpriteBatch spriteBatch)
{
    // Do we have a font? And some text? If not then there is nothing to draw...
    if (Font != null && Text != null && Text.Length > 0)
    {
        // Draw the text
        spriteBatch.DrawString(Font, Text, Position, SpriteColor, Angle, Origin, Scale,
                                            SpriteEffects.None, LayerDepth);
    }
}
```

Finally, the class overrides the BoundingBox function to return a box calculated from the measured text size instead of from the texture size (because we don't use a texture in the TextObject class).

Just as with the SpriteObject class, the TextObject class gives us an easy-to-use mechanism for representing all the possible properties of a piece of text that is to be displayed within a game. Game-specific classes can derive from TextObject if they want to perform their own custom processing (they might override the Update method, for example, to change the content or positioning of the text), or alternatively it might be directly instantiated if nothing else is required for display.

The GameHost Class

The next framework class is the GameHost class. This class holds collections of various objects that we will want to use in our games, specifically Dictionary objects containing textures and fonts, and a List of the actual game objects. The game objects are stored in a list containing objects of type GameObjectBase, which allows us to store within it the derived SpriteObject and TextObject game objects that we have so far discussed, as well as any game-specific classes that derive from any one of these.

The class also contains some simple methods that we can call to save having to write boilerplate functions in the main project's Game class.

The GameHost position within the framework is shown in Figure 3–3. It derives from the Microsoft.XNA.Framework.Game class (from which all actual game projects must derive a single class). This means that in our game projects we can derive the main game class from GameFramework.GameHost instead of from Microsoft.XNA.Framework.Game. As a result, we get all the functionality of the XNA Game class and all the functionality added into GameHost.

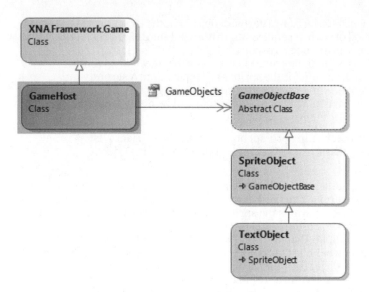

Figure 3–3. The GameHost class position in the framework project

The object collections are accessed by the following properties:

- Textures stores a dictionary of Texture2D objects. Any stored texture can be easily retrieved via its named dictionary key.

- Fonts performs the same function for SpriteFont objects.

- GameObjects is the list into which all the game's active objects will be placed. This is defined as a generic collection of GameObjectBase objects.

In many cases, we can add game objects to the class and then simply allow them to carry out their own tasks until one encounters a circumstance that requires us to interact with it. For example, in an *Asteroids* game we can simply set each asteroid object to move around the screen and then pretty much forget about them until one happens to collide with a bullet or the player's ship. When we detect that this has happened, we will process the asteroid as required. There is no reason to track the asteroids other than by having them present in the GameObjects list.

For other objects, however, we might need to be more proactive. The player's spaceship, for example, will need direct modification from the game so that it can respond to player input. To keep track of this, a separate reference to the game object will need to be stored in the game itself. The same applies for text objects whose values need to be updated (for the player score, for example).

Once the game is initialized and running, two additional methods are available to simplify the code in the main game class:

- UpdateAll loops through all the items in the GameObjects list and calls the Update method on each one. This function can be called from the main game class's Update method to keep everything moving forward.

- DrawSprites identifies all SpriteObject (and derived) objects in the GameObjects list and calls the Draw method of each. It requires an initialized SpriteBatch object to be passed in, and it is the calling code's responsibility to call its Begin and End methods. Keeping the call to Begin in the game class means that it can be given whatever parameters are appropriate for the sprite batch operation. A second overload draws only the sprites with a specified texture. This might be useful for some games, but is provided particularly for a reason that will be discussed in the "Benchmarking and Performance" section later in this chapter.

- DrawText identifies all TextObject (and derived) objects in the GameObjects list and calls the Draw method for them, just as DrawSprites does for SpriteObject game objects.

DrawSprites and DrawText are essentially provided simply for convenience and need not be used if additional functionality is required. If several sprite batches are needed with different parameters, for example, and the DrawSprites overload that separates the sprites by texture is not sufficiently flexible, the game class can simply implement its own custom version of this function.

The code within UpdateAll is more complex than a simple for each loop and it is worth some further exploration, so let's take a look at what it is doing. The reason for its complexity is that, when .NET is iterating through a collection, GameObjects in this case, the collection is not allowed to be modified in any way. Attempting to add an object to, or remove an object from, the collection will result in an immediate exception because, if the order of the object is changed in any way, .NET cannot ensure that it hasn't skipped over or double-processed any of the objects.

A simple way in which we could have worked around this would be to call the collection's ToArray method and iterate over this instead of the collection, as shown in Listing 3–9.

Listing 3–9. A simple but flawed approach to iterating over the objects while still allowing collection modifications

```
foreach (GameObjectBase obj in GameObjects.ToArray())
{
    obj.Update(gameTime);
}
```

This appears to work very well and meets our objectives: all the objects are updated and each can perform any modification to the collection that it wants. It has a flaw, however: every time the loop is prepared, it creates another array of object pointers and as a result consumes a little extra memory. This might not sound important, but the method is being called 30 times per second and might be processing hundreds of objects. This quickly runs into noticeable amounts of memory being used: 30 updates per second with 100 objects requiring 4 bytes per object pointer results in 12,000 bytes allocated per second.

When memory is being allocated this quickly on a device running .NET Compact Framework (CF), the garbage collection ends up triggering on a frequent basis. Each time this happens, the application briefly pauses while the process executes. This is not likely to be noticed in an e-mail or diary application, but in a fast-running game it will really attract the user's attention in an unpleasant way.

We therefore want to try to minimize the amount of memory that is allocated within the game loop. To solve this within the GameHost, a private array of GameObjects is declared at class level, as shown in Listing 3–10. We will use this array over and over again, minimizing memory allocation as far as possible.

Listing 3–10. The class-level _objectArray variable

```
public class GameHost : Microsoft.Xna.Framework.Game
{

    //-------------------------------------------------------------------------------
    // Class variables

    private GameObjectBase[] _objectArray;

    [...]
```

This array initially starts off uninitialized. The UpdateAll function first checks for this state; when found, it creates the array with enough space to hold all the current known objects in the GameObjects collection, plus space for 20 percent more. Allowing a little extra like this means that we don't need to reallocate the array every time a new object is added. If there are fewer than 20 objects in the game, it allocates a minimum of 20 to prevent reallocation each time a new object is added with low object numbers (adding 20 percent to 4 objects results in still only 4 objects after rounding).

If UpdateAll instead finds that the array has been previously created, it checks its capacity against the current game object count. If the object count fits within the array, it leaves the array alone. On the other hand, if the object count is now too large for the array, it reallocates the array by creating a new object collection, once again providing space for 20 percent more objects than are currently present.

This ensures that the array starts at a reasonable size and increases in stages rather than one object at a time. The old arrays that are discarded will be garbage-collected in time, but will be small in number and so won't waste large amounts of memory.

The opening section of UpdateAll that performs the steps discussed so far can be seen in Listing 3–11.

Listing 3–11. The beginning of the UpdateAll function, allocating space in the _objectArray variable

```
public virtual void UpdateAll(GameTime gameTime)
{
    int i;
    int objectCount;

    // First build our array of objects.
    // We will iterate across this rather than across the actual GameObjects
    // collection so that the collection can be modified by the game objects'
    // Update code.
    // First of all, do we have an array?
    if (_objectArray == null)
    {
        // No, so allocate it.
        // Allocate 20% more objects than we currently have, or 20 objects,
        // whichever is more
        _objectArray = new GameObjectBase[
                                (int)MathHelper.Max(20, GameObjects.Count * 1.2f) ];
    }
    else if (GameObjects.Count > _objectArray.Length)
    {
        // The number of game objects has exceeded the array size.
        // Reallocate the array, adding 20% free space for further expansion.
        _objectArray = new GameObjectBase[(int)(GameObjects.Count * 1.2f)];
    }
```

With the array created at an appropriate size, UpdateAll now populates it. This takes place for every update because we cannot tell at a high level whether the objects have been manipulated (checking the object count would not be sufficient as objects might have been removed and inserted in equal numbers). This might seem wasteful, but is really just assigning object pointers and so is extremely quick to execute.

There is another important thing that we need to do with the array, and that is to release any references we have to objects that have been removed from the GameObjects collection. Without this, our array could potentially keep them alive for extended periods within the elements past the end of our main object loop, even though nothing is actually using them any more. Releasing them ensures that their memory can be freed the next time garbage collection runs.

Removing these references is simply a matter of setting the array elements to null for all objects other than those in the GameObjects collection. As we are looping through the array to tell each object to update, it is easy to just continue looping to the end of the array setting the elements that we are not using to null. This will release all the expired object references.

The array population section of UpdateAll is shown in Listing 3–12.

Listing 3–12. Copying the current game object references into _objectArray and removing expired object references

```
// Store the current object count for performance
objectCount = GameObjects.Count;

// Transfer the object references into the array
for (i = 0; i < _objectArray.Length; i++)
{
    // Is there an active object at this position in the GameObjects collection?
    if (i < objectCount)
    {
        // Yes, so copy it to the array
        _objectArray[i] = GameObjects[i];
    }
    else
    {
        // No, so clear any reference stored at this index position
        _objectArray[i] = null;
    }
}
```

With the array populated, we can now iterate through the array and tell each object to update. The GameObjects collection is not being iterated, and so the objects are free to manipulate it in any way they want without exceptions occurring.

We know how many objects we actually have to process because we already queried the GameObjects.Count property and stored it in the objectCount variable. Remember that we can't rely on the array length for this because we are allocating space for additional objects. The stored object count value has an additional use in the update loop: because the GameObjects collection might be modified during the loop (which would affect the result returned by the Count property), we cannot rely on the value being stable while the updates are processing.

Once we know how many objects to process, it is then just a matter of calling the Update method for each. The remainder of the UpdateAll function is shown in Listing 3–13.

Listing 3–13. Updating the game objects

```
        // Loop for each element within the array
        for (i = 0; i < objectCount; i++)
        {
            // Update the object at this array position
            _objectArray[i].Update(gameTime);
        }
    }
}
```

When the number of game objects is static, the array will persist without any reallocations from one update to the next. Each time the number of objects is allocated past the current maximum, a reallocation will occur, but the frequency of these reallocations will be limited by the addition of the 20 percent buffer for additional objects. Once the game's actual maximum is reached, no further allocations will take place at all. The only overhead for all this is two simple loops through the array, one to copy references from the GameObjects collection, and the other to draw the objects and remove expired object references. In return, we gain complete flexibility to manipulate the set of objects from within each object's Update code.

The GameHelper Class

Finally there is the GameHelper class, a place into which generally useful functions can be added (similar to XNA's own MathHelper class). The class is declared as static, so it cannot be instantiated.

For the moment, the class just contains a number of functions relating to random numbers. It hosts an instance of a Random object and exposes several overloads of a function called RandomNext, each of which returns a random number. There are two reasons for having these functions:

- They provide our game code with immediate access to random numbers (a common requirement for game development) without needing to instantiate its own Random instance.

- They add some useful overloads that return random float values, either between zero and a specified upper limit, or between an arbitrary lower and upper limit. They can be extremely useful when randomizing game objects because they use float variables for nearly all their properties.

We will add further functionality to this class (and indeed to the whole framework) as we progress through the following chapters.

Using the Game Framework

The MultipleGameObjects example project shows a simple example of using the game framework to display a number of moving sprites on the screen with minimal code required in the derived Game class.

The project creates a number of colored box objects that move toward the bottom of the screen while rotating, a number of colored ball objects that bounce around the screen (and squash against the edges when they hit), and a text object that displays a message in the middle of the screen. An image of the project can be seen in Figure 3–4.

Figure 3–4. The results of the MultipleGameObjects example project

Let's take a look at how the project has been put together.

Referencing the GameFramework Project

Before the game framework classes can be accessed, we need to add a reference to the GameFramework project from the main game project. Assuming that the GameFramework project is already part of the current Solution, this is simply a matter of right-clicking the main game project node in Solution Explorer, selecting Add Reference, and then picking the GameFramework project from the Projects tab of the Add Reference dialog, as shown in Figure 3–5.

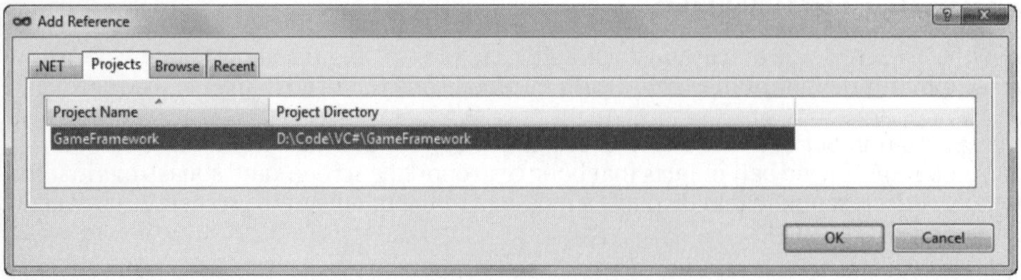

Figure 3–5. Adding a reference to the GameFramework project

If the GameFramework project is not a part of your solution, you can either add it or add a reference to GameFramework.dll by using the Browse tab in the Add Reference window.

Setting Inheritance for the Main Game Class

We already know that a Windows Phone XNA game project must contain exactly one class that derives from Microsoft.Xna.Framework.Game, and by default Visual Studio creates new XNA projects with one such class present.

In order to use the game framework, we must change the inheritance of this class so that it instead derives from GameFramework.GameHost, as shown in Listing 3–14.

Listing 3–14. The declaration of a game class using the game framework

```
/// <summary>
/// This is the main type for your game
/// </summary>
public class MultipleObjectsGame : GameFramework.GameHost
{
```

Creating Derived SpriteObject Classes

Now that we are set up to use the 17.200 game framework, we can start writing code to use it. In the MultipleGameObjects example, there are two classes that derive from the game framework's SpriteObject: BoxObject and BallObject. Each of these contains all the logic required for that object to update and draw itself.

The BoxObject Class

BoxObject is the more straightforward of the two derived object classes. Its constructor is shown in Listing 3–15.

Listing 3–15. The constructor for the BoxObject class

```
    internal BoxObject(MultipleObjectsGame game, Texture2D texture)
        : base(game, Vector2.Zero, texture)
{

    // Store a strongly-typed reference to the game
    _game = game;

    // Set a random position
    PositionX = GameHelper.RandomNext(0, _game.Window.ClientBounds.Width);
    PositionY = GameHelper.RandomNext(0, _game.Window.ClientBounds.Height);

    // Set the origin
    Origin = new Vector2(texture.Width, texture.Height) / 2;

    // Set a random color
    SpriteColor = new Color(GameHelper.RandomNext(0, 256),
                GameHelper.RandomNext(0, 256), GameHelper.RandomNext(0, 256));

    // Set a random movement speed for the box
```

```
    _moveSpeed = GameHelper.RandomNext(2.0f) + 2;

    // Set a random rotation speed for the box
    _rotateSpeed = GameHelper.RandomNext(-5.0f, 5.0f);
}
```

It accepts parameters that are relevant for the box, namely a reference to the MultipleGameObjects game class and the texture to display in the box. After storing the game class reference, the constructor randomizes the object ready for display on the screen.

This process consists of setting random values for the PositionX, PositionY, and SpriteColor properties (all of which are provided by the SpriteObject base class). It also sets the Origin property to be at the center of the sprite, calculated by halving the width and height of the provided texture.

Once the base class properties have been set, the constructor code also generates random values for its own class-specific variables. These values are _moveSpeed, a variable that controls how fast the box moves, and _rotateSpeed, which controls how fast it rotates. These values will be used each time the sprite updates and will be added to the PositionY and Angle properties, respectively. The GameHelper class is used to generate random float values for both of these. Note that the rotation speed can be either positive or negative, which means that the box can rotate either clockwise or counterclockwise.

Along with the functionality inherited from the SpriteObject class, this is already sufficient to display the colored box in a random position, but it won't yet move in any way. Movement is implemented by overriding the Update method, as shown in Listing 3–16.

Listing 3–16. The Update method for the BoxObject class

```
public override void Update(GameTime gameTime)
{
    // Allow the base class to do any work it needs
    base.Update(gameTime);

    // Update the position of the box
    PositionY += _moveSpeed;
    // If we pass the bottom of the window, reset back to the top
    if (BoundingBox.Top > _game.Window.ClientBounds.Bottom)
    {
        PositionY = -SpriteTexture.Height;
    }

    // Rotate the box
    Angle += MathHelper.ToRadians(_rotateSpeed);
}
```

This is all very simple: the movement speed is first added to the PositionY property to update the sprite position. The position is then checked to see whether the sprite has passed the bottom of the screen. This is the case if its BoundingBox.Top is below the bottom of the window, at which point the sprite's position is reset back to the top. It is set so that its position is actually above the top of the screen so that it doesn't "pop" into view.

The Angle property is then updated according to the rotation speed. Note that we use the MathHelper.ToRadians function when rotating, which means that the _rotateSpeed variable is storing degrees rather than radians. It doesn't really matter which unit you use, but you should stick to the same unit throughout all of your game to avoid confusion.

Note that there is no need for any other code within the class, including any to perform drawing, because this is all provided by the SpriteObject base class. All the class needs to concern itself with is the simple task of moving itself.

The BallObject Class

The BallObject implementation is slightly more complex, but only slightly. Instead of simply moving down the screen, the balls need to bounce off the screen edges, obey gravity (or an approximation thereof), and "wobble" when they hit the edges of the screen, as if they were made of rubber.

To make the ball move in this way, we need to store the direction in which it is moving (its velocity). In order to know an object's velocity, we need to know both the direction in which it is moving and the speed with which it is traveling. There are two methods in which we can describe an object's velocity: either by storing its direction (as an angle from 0 to 360 degrees) and its speed of movement in that direction, or by storing its speed as a value along each of the axes: x and y.

The first of these methods provides for a simulation of movement that is closer to how things move in reality, and, in many scenarios, this will be an appropriate system to use. For the sake of simplicity in our example, however, we will use the second method. This simply tracks the x and y distance that we want to move the object each time it updates. To bounce an object off the side of the screen, we can simply negate the speed in that particular axis: if we are adding a value of 5 to the x position and we hit the right side of the screen, we then start subtracting 5 to move to the left again. Subtracting 5 is the same as adding –5, so changing the x speed from 5 to –5 will reverse the direction on that axis. Exactly the same function applies to the y axis. The calculation is illustrated in Figure 3–6.

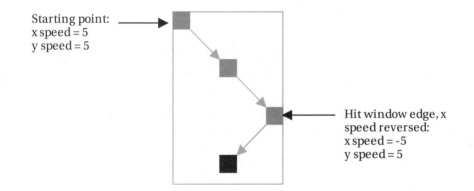

Starting point:
x speed = 5
y speed = 5

Hit window edge, x
speed reversed:
x speed = -5
y speed = 5

Figure 3–6. *The motion of a bouncing ball, as controlled using x and y axis speeds*

Just as with the box class, we implement all this inside the derived game object. We use several class-level variables to support this:

- _xadd and _yadd keep track of the ball's velocity in each of the two axes of movement.

- _wobble tracks the amount that the ball is wobbling (where zero is not at all, and greater values indicate higher wobble levels).

The _xadd variable is set in the constructor along with some of the inherited sprite properties, as shown in Listing 3–17. The _yadd and _wobble variables are left with their default values of 0; they will be modified in the Update method, as we will see in a moment.

Listing 3–17. The constructor for the BallObject class

```
internal BallObject(MultipleObjectsGame game, Texture2D texture)
    : base(game, Vector2.Zero, texture)
{
    // Store a strongly-typed reference to the game
    _game = game;

    // Set a random position
    PositionX = GameHelper.RandomNext(0, _game.Window.ClientBounds.Width);
    PositionY = GameHelper.RandomNext(0, _game.Window.ClientBounds.Height);

    // Set the origin
    Origin = new Vector2(texture.Width, texture.Height) / 2;

    // Set a random color
    SpriteColor = new Color(GameHelper.RandomNext(0, 256),
                    GameHelper.RandomNext(0, 256), GameHelper.RandomNext(0, 256));

    // Set a horizontal movement speed for the box
    _xadd = GameHelper.RandomNext(-5.0f, 5.0f);
}
```

As with the box, the rest of the class code is contained within the Update method. To make the ball move, we first add the velocity in each axis to the corresponding position, detecting collisions with the left, right, and bottom edges of the screen as described at the start of this section. The beginning of the Update method, which handles these changes, is shown in Listing 3–18.

Listing 3–18. Part of the ball's Update method: moving the ball and bouncing from the screen edges

```
public override void Update(GameTime gameTime)
{
    // Allow the base class to do any work it needs
    base.Update(gameTime);

    // Update the position of the ball
    PositionX += _xadd;
    PositionY += _yadd;

    // If we reach the side of the window, reverse the x velocity so that the ball
    // bounces back
    if (PositionX < OriginX)
    {
        // Reset back to the left edge
        PositionX = OriginX;
        // Reverse the x velocity
        _xadd = -_xadd;
        // Add to the wobble
        _wobble += Math.Abs(_xadd);
    }
    if (PositionX > _game.Window.ClientBounds.Width - OriginX)
    {
        // Reset back to the right edge
```

```
            PositionX = _game.Window.ClientBounds.Width - OriginX;
            // Reverse the x velocity
            _xadd = -_xadd;
            // Add to the wobble
            _wobble += Math.Abs(_xadd);
        }

        // If we reach the bottom of the window, reverse the y velocity so that the ball
        // bounces upwards
        if (PositionY >= _game.Window.ClientBounds.Bottom - OriginY)
        {
            // Reset back to the bottom of the window
            PositionY = _game.Window.ClientBounds.Bottom - OriginY;
            // Reverse the y-velocity
            _yadd = -_yadd; // +0.3f;
            // Add to the wobble
            _wobble += Math.Abs(_yadd);
        }
        else
        {
            // Increase the y velocity to simulate gravity
            _yadd += 0.3f;
        }
```

The ball's position is checked against the screen edges by taking the origin values into account because the origin is set to be at the center of the ball. If the OriginX value is 20, the ball has hit the left edge of the window if the PositionX value falls below 20. The same applies to the right edge, where its OriginX value is subtracted from the window width to determine the maximum permitted PositionX value; and to the bottom edge, where its OriginY is subtracted from the window's Bottom position.

If the ball hasn't hit the bottom edge, we add a small amount to the _yadd variable, as seen in the final line of code in Listing 3–18. This is the all-important update that simulates gravity. For every update, the ball moves downward a little more than it did the previous update. If the ball is moving upward, this erodes its upward momentum until it eventually starts to fall downward again. Changing the amount that is added to _yadd each update will increase or decrease the intensity of the simulated gravity.

The remainder of the update code deals with the ball's wobble. As you can also see in Listing 3–18, the _wobble variable is increased each time the ball bounces by adding the corresponding velocity. This means that the harder the ball hits into the window edge, the more it wobbles. The Math.Abs function is used to ensure that the wobble value increases even if the velocity contains a negative value.

The wobble is implemented by updating the ball's scale properties. We use a sine wave to make the ball oscillate between being thinner and fatter than normal, and offset it so that when it is at its thinnest on the x axis it is also at its fattest on the y axis, and vice versa. This provides a pleasing rubbery visual effect.

Listing 3–19 shows the rest of the Update function, containing the wobble code. If the wobble level is zero, it ensures that the scaling is reset by assigning a unit vector to the Scale property. Otherwise, it uses the UpdateCount property from GameObjectBase as a mechanism for moving through the sine values. The WobbleSpeed constant controls how rapidly the ball oscillates, and WobbleIntensity controls how much it squashes the ball. Try altering these values and see the effect that it has on the balls.

Finally, the wobble level is gradually decreased with each update and checked to stop it falling below 0 or getting too high (at which point it looks silly).

Listing 3–19. The remaining Update method code: making the ball wobble

```
    // Is there any wobble?
    if (_wobble == 0)
    {
        // No, so reset the scale
        Scale = Vector2.One;
    }
    else
    {
        const float WobbleSpeed = 20.0f;
        const float WobbleIntensity = 0.015f;

        // Yes, so calculate the scaling on the x and y axes
        ScaleX = (float)Math.Sin(MathHelper.ToRadians(UpdateCount * WobbleSpeed))
                                        * _wobble * WobbleIntensity + 1;
        ScaleY = (float)Math.Sin(MathHelper.ToRadians(UpdateCount * WobbleSpeed + 180.0f))
                                        * _wobble * WobbleIntensity + 1;
        // Reduce the wobble level
        _wobble -= 0.2f;
        // Don't allow the wobble to fall below zero or to rise too high
        if (_wobble < 0) _wobble = 0;
        if (_wobble > 50) _wobble = 50;
    }
}
```

Adding Game Objects to the Game Host

Let's focus now on the game class, which is named `MultipleObjectsGame` in the example project. Instead of deriving from `Microsoft.Xna.Framework.Game`, it derives from `GameFramework.GameHost`, so it picks up all the functionality that the `GameHost` class offers.

In `LoadContent`, the textures and fonts are loaded in the same way as in the previous examples, but this time they are added into the appropriate `GameHost` collections, as shown in Listing 3–20.

Listing 3–20. Loading game resources into the Host object

```
    protected override void LoadContent()
    {
        // Create a new SpriteBatch, which can be used to draw textures.
        _spriteBatch = new SpriteBatch(GraphicsDevice);

        // Load the object textures into the textures dictionary
        Textures.Add("Ball", this.Content.Load<Texture2D>("Ball"));
        Textures.Add("Box", this.Content.Load<Texture2D>("Box"));

        // Load fonts
        Fonts.Add("Kootenay", this.Content.Load<SpriteFont>("Kootenay"));

        // Reset the game
        ResetGame();
    }
```

The final line of code in LoadContent calls into a new function named ResetGame, in which we create the objects that will do the work when the game is running; its code is shown in Listing 3–21.

Listing 3–21. Resetting the game

```
private void ResetGame()
{
    TextObject message;

    // Remove any existing objects
    GameObjects.Clear();

    // Add 10 boxes and 10 calls
    for (int i = 0; i < 10; i++)
    {
        GameObjects.Add(new BoxObject(this, Textures["Box"]));
        GameObjects.Add(new BallObject(this, Textures["Ball"]));
    }

    // Add some text
    message = new TextObject(this, Fonts["Kootenay"], new Vector2(240, 400),
                "Windows Phone 7 Game Development",
                TextObject.TextAlignment.Center, TextObject.TextAlignment.Center);
    message.SpriteColor = Color.DarkBlue;
    message.Scale = new Vector2(1.0f, 1.5f);
    GameObjects.Add(message);
}
```

ResetGame first removes any objects that might have been added to the game host earlier on. Although this will never happen in our example because the game is reset only once, in a proper game this could be called each time the player runs out of lives in order to prepare a new game. To stop the previous game from leaving debris behind, we would need to remove those objects that the previous game had been using.

The game then loops to add ten boxes and ten balls to the game host. These are created using the derived game object classes that we have been discussing over the last few pages. It also adds a TextObject instance to display the writing in the middle of the screen. No custom functionality is needed for this object, so the TextObject class is instantiated directly.

All that is left is to implement the Update and Draw functions, both of which can be seen in Listing 3–22. As you can see, these are absolutely trivial, just telling the game host to perform the required updates and drawing.

Listing 3–22. Updating and drawing the game

```
protected override void Update(GameTime gameTime)
{
    // Allows the game to exit
    if (GamePad.GetState(PlayerIndex.One).Buttons.Back == ButtonState.Pressed)
        this.Exit();

    // Update all the game objects
    UpdateAll(gameTime);

    base.Update(gameTime);
}
```

```
protected override void Draw(GameTime gameTime)
{
    GraphicsDevice.Clear(Color.Wheat);

    // Begin the spritebatch
    _spriteBatch.Begin();
    // Draw the sprites
    DrawSprites(gameTime, _spriteBatch);
    // Draw the text
    DrawText(gameTime, _spriteBatch);
    // End the spritebatch
    _spriteBatch.End();

    base.Draw(gameTime);
}
```

The small amount of code presented in this section is all that is needed to get the game example running. Please spend a little time getting comfortable with the general approach used here: the framework classes, the derived game object classes, and the code within the game class. We will build on these principles throughout the rest of the book, so it is important that you become comfortable with how they fit together.

The framework is very lightweight in nature, essentially just allowing us to easily organize and access the objects that we want to work with. It is deliberately unobtrusive and transparent so that it doesn't get in the way of your game code, allowing you instead to simply focus on the game rather than the mechanics of managing your objects.

Because of the code present in the GameHost.UpdateAll function for transferring the game object collection into an array for processing (as discussed in "The GameHost Class" earlier in this chapter), game objects can also add objects to the game during their Update calls. If, for example, a sprite detects that it has landed in water and wants to create a splash, it can add objects for the water droplets at the point at which its movement into the water is being processed, which makes for a much more readable project overall.

Removing Objects from the Game Host

So we can add objects to the game, but how do we remove them?

The game (in its Update method) has full access to the GameObjects collection within GameHost. If it determines that an object is no longer needed, it can simply remove the object from the list.

Just as game objects can add further objects in their Update method, so they can remove objects too. If an object determines that it is no longer needed, it can simply remove itself from the collection and it will receive no further calls to Update or Draw. This includes the ability for an object to remove itself if it needs to.

Overriding Object Properties

The example derived game object classes that we have looked at all declared additional properties to define their custom behavior (the downward movement speed for the box, the x and y axis velocities, and wobble for the ball) and used them in their Update methods to set their properties to affect how they are drawn.

In many cases, this will be the most appropriate way to control the presentation of the object, but there is an alternative mechanism that in other cases might result in simpler code.

All the basic properties in the SpriteObject class are defined as being virtual. This covers the sprite's texture, position coordinates, origin coordinates, angle, scale values, source rectangle, color and layer depth, but excludes the Vector2-typed properties (Position, Origin, and Scale) because they are just based around the underlying float values. By default, they simply store and return the provided value. Because they are virtual, however, the properties can be overridden in the derived classes, and the way that they work can be modified.

For example, we could create a moon object that orbited a planet object, and override its PositionX and PositionY properties to allow them to calculate their positions on demand, based on the position of the planet and its rotation angle instead of having to calculate this in the Update method. Overriding the properties in this way guarantees that the position is up to date and accurate, even if the planet's position has changed since the moon's last Update call.

This scenario is demonstrated in the OrbitingSprites example project, an image from which is shown in Figure 3–7. It defines two sprite object classes, PlanetObject and MoonObject, and then creates a couple of planet instances with some moons orbiting them. Just to demonstrate the flexibility of this environment, it also creates a moon that orbits around one of the other moons. This scenario might be physically unlikely in the real universe but it works well for demonstration purposes!

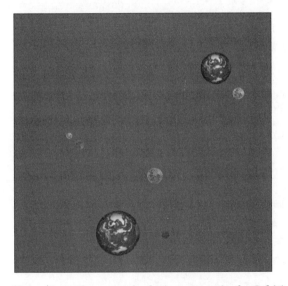

Figure 3–7. Planets and orbiting moons in the OrbitingSprites project

Within PlanetObject we just set up a simple horizontal bounce movement pattern so that the planets gradually move back and forth across the screen. (You have already seen this code in earlier parts of this chapter.)

MoonObject is where the interesting code resides. Its constructor includes parameters to define the moon's target object (around which it will orbit), its orbital speed, the distance at which it will orbit its target, and its size. The target object, speed, and distance are stored in variables defined for the moon, whereas the rest of the properties are passed through to the base class.

The moon class has no Update code at all. Instead, its movement relies on the position of the target object and on the UpdateCount property implemented within the GameObjectBase class. The position of the moon is calculated on demand when its PositionX and PositionY properties are queried. The implementation is shown in Listing 3–23.

Listing 3–23. The position property overrides for the moon object

```
/// <summary>
/// Calculate the x position of the moon
/// </summary>
public override float PositionX
{
    get
    {
        return _targetObject.PositionX + (float)Math.Sin(UpdateCount * _speed) * _distance;
    }
}

/// <summary>
/// Calculate the y position of the moon
/// </summary>
public override float PositionY
{
    get
    {
        return _targetObject.PositionY + (float)Math.Cos(UpdateCount * _speed) * _distance;
    }
}
```

The properties read the position of the target object and then use the Sin and Cos functions to return the positions of a circle that orbits this initial position. The UpdateCount value is multiplied by _speed variable to allow the moon to orbit at a defined rate, and the return values from Sin and Cos (which will always range between -1 and 1) are multiplied by the _distance variable to set the distance at which the moon is positioned from its target.

■ **NOTE** As shown in Listing 3–23, it is quite possible to override just the get part of a property. Because the PositionX and PositionY properties in the MoonObject class make no use of the underlying value, we can simply ignore the set part and allow any attempts to access it to fall through to the base class.

MoonObject also uses the same technique, but overrides the Angle property to make each moon slowly rotate as it orbits around its target sprite.

The game objects are added to the game in the LoadContent method, as shown in Listing 3–24. First a planet is instantiated and added to the GameObjects collection. A moon is then created and passed to the planet as its target object. This is then repeated for the second planet, which is given three moons. The last of those moons gets its own moon, too; because the moon can orbit any object, it doesn't matter whether it is a planet or another moon that it targets (and indeed, this moon-of-a-moon could itself be given a moon, and so on). With this object configuration in place, the simulation runs and produces this comparatively complex set of object movements with an extremely small amount of game code required.

Listing 3–24. Initializing the objects for the OrbitingSprites project

```
protected override void LoadContent()
{
    PlanetObject planet;
    MoonObject moon;

    // Create a new SpriteBatch, which can be used to draw textures.
    _spriteBatch = new SpriteBatch(GraphicsDevice);

    Textures.Add("Planet", Content.Load<Texture2D>("Planet"));
    Textures.Add("Moon", Content.Load<Texture2D>("Moon"));

    // Add a planet...
    planet = new PlanetObject(this, new Vector2(150, 200),
                                    Textures["Planet"], 0.7f);
    GameObjects.Add(planet);
    // ...and give it a moon
    GameObjects.Add(new MoonObject(this, Textures["Moon"],
                                    planet, 0.02f, 60, 0.3f, Color.White));

    // Add another planet...
    planet = new PlanetObject(this, new Vector2(300, 500),
                                    Textures["Planet"], 1.0f);
    GameObjects.Add(planet);
    // ...and give it some moons
    GameObjects.Add(new MoonObject(this, Textures["Moon"],
                                    planet, 0.04f, 90, 0.2f, Color.OrangeRed));
    GameObjects.Add(new MoonObject(this, Textures["Moon"],
                                    planet, 0.025f,130, 0.4f, Color.PaleGreen));
    moon = new MoonObject(this, Textures["Moon"],
                                    planet, 0.01f, 180, 0.25f, Color.Silver);
    GameObjects.Add(moon);
    // Add a moon to the moon
    GameObjects.Add(new MoonObject(this, Textures["Moon"],
                                    moon, 0.1f, 25, 0.15f, Color.White));
}
```

Benchmarking and Performance

None of the example projects that we've used so far has created large volumes of objects, so their performance has all been very good, animating smoothly on the phone. Real games are likely to be much more complex and will result in substantially more objects being drawn to the screen during each update.

To allow us to monitor how the game is performing, it is very useful to use a *benchmark*. This is a measurement of how well the game is performing and allows us to see how many frames of animation are being displayed per second while the game is running.

In the constructor of the Game class, we tell XNA the frame rate that we would ideally like it to run at. This defaults for Windows Phone projects to 1/30th of a second, as shown in Listing 3–25.

Listing 3–25. Setting the target frame rate

```
// Frame rate is 30 fps by default for Windows Phone.
TargetElapsedTime = TimeSpan.FromSeconds(1.0f / 30);
```

In theory, this means that we will receive 30 calls to Update per second and 30 corresponding calls to Draw per second. This might well be the case with small numbers of objects in motion, but how about if there are thousands of them? Or tens of thousands? A benchmark will allow us to see exactly how the game performs under these conditions.

Another more important use for the benchmark is to allow us to spot unexpected low levels of performance and provide us with an opportunity to identify and resolve them to improve the way that a game runs. We will look at an example of such a problem later in this section and see what can be done to resolve it.

The BenchmarkObject Class

To easily obtain frame rate information in any game we develop, another class is present within the GameFramework project: BenchmarkObject. Because the task of this class is essentially to display some text (containing the benchmark information we are trying to obtain), it is derived from the TextObject class.

The class needs to be able to count the number of calls to Update and Draw that occur each second. On a periodic basis (once per second is usually sufficient), we should determine exactly how much time has passed since our last measurement, and how many updates and draws have taken place. The count of the updates and draws can then be divided by the elapsed time to calculate the count per second.

The GameObject base class already counts the number of updates in its UpdateCount property, so the benchmark class doesn't need to do that. It doesn't count the number of calls to Draw, however, so the benchmark class creates a class-level variable named _drawCount and adds 1 to this each time its Draw method is called.

In order to tell how many calls have occurred since the last time the frame rate was calculated, the class also stores the previous draw and update counts. The newly elapsed counts can then be obtained by subtracting the last counts from the current counts. The class-level variables _lastDrawCount and _lastUpdateCount are defined for this purpose.

Finally we need to know when the frame rate was last measured so that we can determine the time period during which the new updates and draws have occurred. This is stored in the class-level _lastUpdateMilliseconds property. The full set of variables is shown in Listing 3–26.

Listing 3–26. The class-level variables required by BenchmarkObject

```
//-------------------------------------------------------------------------------
// Class variables
private double _lastUpdateMilliseconds;
private int _drawCount;
private int _lastDrawCount;
private int _lastUpdateCount;
```

This gives us everything we need to measure the frame rate. First, the Draw method is overridden to update the draw count. The frame rate calculation is then performed in the Update method, as shown in Listing 3–27.

Listing 3–27. The BenchmarkObject Update method

```
override void Update(GameTime gameTime)
{
    StringBuilder message = new StringBuilder();
    int newDrawCount;
    int newUpdateCount;
    double newElapsedTime;

    // Allow the base class to do its stuff
    base.Update(gameTime);

    // Has 1 second passed since we last updated the text?
    if (gameTime.TotalGameTime.TotalMilliseconds > _lastUpdateMilliseconds + 1000)
    {
        // Find how many frames have been drawn within the last second
        newDrawCount = _drawCount - _lastDrawCount;
        // Find how many updates have taken place within the last second
        newUpdateCount = UpdateCount - _lastUpdateCount;
        // Find out exactly how much time has passed
        newElapsedTime = gameTime.TotalGameTime.TotalMilliseconds -
                                            _lastUpdateMilliseconds;

        // Build a message to display the details and set it into the Text property
        message.AppendLine("Object count: " + Game.GameObjects.Count.ToString());
        message.AppendLine("Frames per second: " +
                ((float)newDrawCount / newElapsedTime * 1000).ToString("0.0"));
        message.AppendLine("Updates per second: " +
                ((float)newUpdateCount / newElapsedTime * 1000).ToString("0.0"));
        Text = message.ToString();

        // Update the counters for use the next time we calculate
        _lastUpdateMilliseconds = gameTime.TotalGameTime.TotalMilliseconds;
        _lastDrawCount = _drawCount;
        _lastUpdateCount = UpdateCount;
    }
}
```

The code refreshes the frame rate only once per second, detected by comparing the current total game time's elapsed milliseconds against the value stored in _lastUpdateMilliseconds. If a second has elapsed, the number of new calls to the Draw and Update methods are determined, the exact amount of time elapsed is calculated, and everything is built into a string for display onscreen. All the current values are then stored in the class variables for use the next time the frame rate is updated.

Using BenchmarkObject

BenchmarkObject can easily be used in any project by simply adding an instance of it to the GameObjects collection. Its constructor expects a font, position, and text color to be provided, but because it is derived from TextObject it can also be scaled or rotated if needed.

The Benchmark example project shows this in action, and its output can be seen in Figure 3–8. The example, which is based on the same game objects as in the OrbitingSprites example from earlier in this chapter, is initially set to draw ten planets, each of which has a moon.

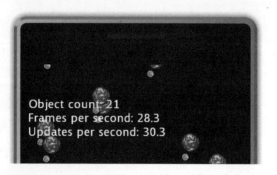

Figure 3–8. The text displayed by BenchmarkObject

As Figure 3–8 shows, there are 21 game objects (10 planets, 10 moons, and the benchmark object), and the game is achieving 28.3 drawn frames per second and 30.3 updates per second.

Performance Considerations

Now that we can monitor the performance of our game, let's take a look at some of the things that can cause it to slow down and then determine some approaches to resolving these problems.

Texture Loading

What happens if we increase the number of planets significantly, perhaps to 1000? This is easily tested by modifying the PlanetCount constant at the top of the BenchmarkGame.cs source file. Give it a try and see what happens.

The result is a dramatic drop in the frames per second, as shown in Figure 3–9. It now displays a mere 5.9 frames drawn per second.

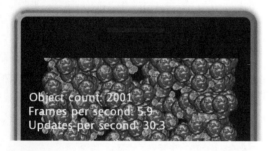

Figure 3–9. The benchmark results with 1000 planets

> ■ **NOTE** This benchmark shows up an important feature of the XNA engine: although the frame rate has dropped all the way down to 5.9 frames per second, the updates per second still stay exactly as they were with just 10 planets. This is because XNA is detecting that the game is running slowly due to the amount of time the sprites are taking to draw, and as a result is calling the game's Draw method less frequently. It prioritizes calls to Update so that the game logic runs at full speed even though the rendering does not. This ensures that the game runs at the same speed across all devices and regardless of processor power being drained by other applications on the phone.

So this large frame rate drop is disappointing, but perhaps that is all the device has the power to draw? There are a large number of sprites after all. In fact, the sprite count is not the actual cause of the frame rate dropping. The cause is the order in which the sprites are being drawn.

Each time XNA draws a sprite, it must pass the texture for the sprite to the graphics hardware ready for it to draw. Most of the information needed to draw a sprite will fit into just a few bytes of data (its position, rotation, scaling, and so on don't need very much memory to describe), but compared with the sprite location, the texture is comparatively huge. It is therefore in our interest to minimize the amount of texture information that is passed to the graphics hardware.

Once a texture has been loaded into the hardware it can be used over and over again without needing to be reloaded, but when another texture is loaded, the original texture is discarded. If you recall, the way we set up the moons and planets in the game was by first adding a planet object and then adding the corresponding moon object. This means that planets and moons are alternating in the GameObjects collection. Every single sprite we draw needs a new texture to be loaded: first the planet texture, then the moon, then the planet again, right through to the end of the sprite batch. In total we end up loading 2000 textures in this configuration. No wonder the game slowed down.

There are various ways to address this problem. The first is to sort the objects in the GameObjects list so that they are ordered by texture. To try out this approach, modify the Benchmark project's LoadContent method so that it calls into AddPlanets_InBlocks instead of AddPlanets_Interleaved. This adds exactly the same number of objects (and the benchmark display will confirm this), but as 1000 planets followed by 1000 moons. If you run this again, you will see that the frame rate has now nearly doubled. In this configuration, XNA has to load only two textures rather than 2000, requiring just one load each of the planet texture and then the moon texture.

> ■ **CAUTION** If you try this out on both the emulator and on a real device, you will find that the device performance is not nearly as good as that of the emulator. The emulator doesn't cap its frame rate or anything similar, and as a result can display far more updates per second than an actual phone. It is important to performance test your game on real hardware as you are writing it to avoid unpleasant surprises later on.

In a real game, however, it is impractical to expect the objects to always be ordered by their textures. As objects are added and removed through the course of the game, the object collection will naturally become scrambled. There are two additional approaches that we can take to deal with this performance problem: one provided by XNA and one by the game framework.

The XNA approach involves modifying the parameters that we send to the SpriteBatch object when calling its Begin method. Most of our examples have not passed any parameters at all, although we have passed the SpriteSortMode.BackToFront value so that the sprites' LayerDepths are observed.

One of the other sort modes is SpriteSortMode.Texture. In this mode, the LayerDepth is ignored, but instead the sprites are, as you might expect, sorted by their textures. Modify the example project so that it once again adds the sprites interleaved rather than in blocks, and then take a look at its Draw method. You will find three different versions of the sprite batch code: comment out the current version 1 and uncomment version 2.

Despite having added the sprites in alternating order, the frame rate is still high just as it was when we added the sprites in blocks. This has also resulted in just two texture loads for all the sprites.

There are some drawbacks to this approach, however. Most obviously, we have lost control of exactly which sprites are drawn first; as evidence you will see that the moons have disappeared behind the planets and the benchmark text has disappeared behind everything. In addition, using the Texture sort mode means that we cannot use the LayerDepth feature at all.

In many cases, these drawbacks will be of no significance and this approach will work fine. If you need to regain some of the control of the rendering process, use the second approach.

The GameHost.DrawSprites method that we have been calling actually has another overload that allows a texture to be passed in as a parameter. When this version is used, only sprites that use the supplied texture will be drawn; all others will be completely ignored. This allows us to draw the sprites grouped by texture, but to also be in control of which textures are processed first.

If you comment out version 2 of the Draw code and instead uncomment version 3, you will see this approach in action. The moons are now rendered in front of the planets, and the benchmark text is in front of everything.

However, none of these approaches gives the exact same rendering of the planets and the moons that we started with, in which each moon went in front of the planets defined earlier in the GameObjects list and behind any planets defined after. Some effects cannot be achieved when sprite ordering is in place and for which there is no alternative but to repeatedly load the same textures into the graphics hardware. The important thing is to be aware of this performance bottleneck and to reduce or eliminate it wherever possible.

In most cases, the performance degradation will not be as significant as in this example. Use the BenchmarkObject to help you to identify drops in frame rate as soon as they occur so that you can focus your efforts to track them down as quickly as possible.

Creating and Destroying Objects

You are probably aware of the .NET garbage collection feature. Once in a while, .NET will reach a trigger point that instructs it to search all its memory space, looking for objects that are no longer in use. They are marked as unneeded and then the remaining active objects are reorganized so that they use the system memory efficiently. This process stops memory from becoming fragmented and ensures that the application doesn't run out of space to create new objects.

This has many benefits, primarily by simplifying the creation of objects and removing any need to free up memory once those objects are no longer needed. The disadvantage is that, when .NET does decide to perform a garbage collection operation, it can have a noticeable effect on your game. We therefore need to try to reduce the amount of garbage that we create as far as possible.

We already discussed an approach to this in the GameHost class's Update method earlier in this chapter. The number one rule is to try to avoid creating temporary object instances while the game is running. There will, of course, be instances where it is essential (all our game objects are object instances after all!), but we should keep our eyes open for instances that can be avoided and remove them wherever possible.

■ **NOTE** Due to the way that .NET manages its memory, we need to worry about garbage collection only when using objects. A structure (struct) has its memory allocated in a different way that does not result in garbage being generated. It is therefore perfectly okay to create new Vector2, Rectangle, and Color structures, as well as any other struct-based data structure.

You will see examples of this efficient use of object allocation within the default content created when a new XNA project is created. The SpriteBatch object is declared at class level even though it is only used within the Draw method. Declaring it at class level means that it can be instantiated just once for the entire game run, whereas declaring it in Draw would result in a new object being created every time the sprites were drawn.

Using for and foreach Loops

The foreach syntax is extremely useful and in many cases faster to operate than a regular for loop when using collections because moving from one item to the next steps just one element forward through a linked list of objects. On the other hand, accessing collection object by index requires the whole of the collection to be traversed up to the point where the requested object is reached.

But in Windows Phone 7 XNA games, there is a potential drawback with foreach loops, which means that they need a little extra consideration. These loops create an iterator object and use it to step through the collection items. For certain types of collection, when the loop finishes, the iterator object is discarded and ends up on the pile of objects ready for garbage collection. As discussed in the previous section, this process will increase the frequency of the garbage collection operation and cause the game performance to suffer.

The collection types that suffer this problem are all nongeneric collections and the generic Collection<T> object. For code inside your game loop (anywhere inside the Update or Draw methods), you should either avoid using these collection types or iterate through them with a for loop instead of a foreach loop. It is fine to use foreach for arrays and all other generic collection types, however.

Also be aware that when you do use for loops, if you include a method or property call for the end condition of the loop, your compiled code will call into it for every iteration of the loop. It is, therefore, a good idea to read the collection size into a local variable prior to entering the loop and use it in your for loop instead. You can see this in the GameHost.Update method back in Listing 3–12: the GameObjects.Count value is read into a local variable, and the variable is used in the loop rather than the collection property.

Game in Focus: Cosmic Rocks (Part I)

At the end of this and the next couple of chapters, we will start to build the material that we have covered into a simple game. The game, which is called *Cosmic Rocks*, is essentially an *Asteroids* clone.

In this chapter, we will cover the basic game design and implement the sprite processing into the game engine. We haven't yet discussed user input (which is covered in the next chapter), so the game won't be interactive yet, but you will see the beginnings of a playable game lurking at the end of this chapter.

All the code and resources for the game can be found in the CosmicRocksPartI example project.

Designing the Game

The game design for *Cosmic Rocks* is pretty straightforward. The player will control a small spaceship that will initially be placed in the middle of the screen. By tapping a point on the screen, the spaceship will turn to face that location and will fire a plasma bolt. By holding a point on the screen, the spaceship will thrust toward that point. It will continue to accelerate for as long as the touch point is held, after which it will gradually begin to slow down again.

Alongside the player's ship there will be a number of cosmic space rocks that drift aimlessly across the screen. If one of these rocks makes contact with the player's ship, the ship explodes, and the player loses a life. The player can shoot plasma bolts at the rocks, however. Shooting the initial rocks will cause them to divide into two smaller rocks. Shooting these rocks will cause them to divide once again into even smaller rocks. These smallest rocks can then be shot to completely destroy them.

The player's ship will be invulnerable for a brief period when it first enters play. The invulnerability will last until a point is reached in which no asteroids are within a small area around the ship to prevent it from being immediately destroyed as soon as it appears.

The edges of the screen wrap around, so anything moving off the left side of the screen will reappear on the right, and the same for the top and bottom edges. This ensures that all objects remain in play no matter where they end up.

When all the rocks have been destroyed, the player will progress to the next level, which will contain one more cosmic rock than the previous level, ensuring that the difficulty steadily increases.

The game continues until the player has lost all his lives.

Creating the Graphics

If you are intending to create professional games, it is definitely advisable to ensure that you have someone on hand who can create professional-looking graphics (unless you have graphical talent as well as being a programmer!). I am no graphic artist, but I like to take advantage of materials around me and use them within my games whenever possible.

To this end, I created three images for my cosmic rocks by taking photographs of pebbles from my garden with a digital camera. With a little bit of a touch-up in a paint package, the photographs produced quite acceptable results. The rocks can be seen in Figure 3–10.

Figure 3–10. A parade of cosmic rocks

Note that these rocks are roughly circular in shape, which will help with collision detection in a moment.

The player's spaceship required a little more thought, but I eventually found a suitable object at the bottom of my son's toy box. The resulting ship image is shown in Figure 3–11.

Figure 3–11. The rocks' nemesis: the player spaceship

With the graphics ready, they can be slotted into the game itself.

Creating the Game Objects

At this stage, the game object classes within the game are all very simple. We need a class for the rocks, another for the player's ship, one for handling explosions, and a fourth for each of the stars that will be displayed in the background to liven up the screen a little. Let's look at the content of each.

The RockObject Class

The rocks have one aim in life: to drift in a single direction until they hit something. In the examples we looked at earlier, we tracked movement by storing a value that was added to the objects' x and y coordinates each time the game was updated. For the rocks we will use a slightly different approach.

We will store the direction in which the rock will move as a Vector2, in a class-level variable named _direction. The movement direction is completely random, so we initialize both the variable's X and Y properties with a random value between -1 and 1. This will allow the rock to potentially move in any direction at all.

However, we want all the rocks to move at a consistent speed. One rock might emerge with a Vector2 containing the values (1, 1), whereas another might emerge with the values (0.01, 0.01). Clearly the former will be moving very much more quickly than the latter. To resolve this discrepancy, we can *normalize* the vector, which ensures that the length of the vector (the distance between the origin at (0, 0) and the position defined within the vector) is exactly 1. As a result, moving the rock as defined by the _direction vector will always result in the same movement speed, regardless of the angle in which the rock is moving. The code required to set up this vector, taken from the RockObject class's InitializeRock function, is shown in Listing 3–28.

Listing 3–28. Setting the rock's direction of movement

```
// Create a random direction for the rock. Ensure that it doesn't have zero
// as the direction on both the x and y axes
do
{
    _direction = new Vector2(GameHelper.RandomNext(-1.0f, 1.0f),
                             GameHelper.RandomNext(-1.0f, 1.0f));
} while (_direction == Vector2.Zero);
```

```
// Normalize the movement vector so that it is exactly 1 unit in length
_direction.Normalize();
```

The constructor sets a random position for the rock, sets its origin to its center, and then calls InitializeRock to set the rest of the rock properties. We separate these out from the constructor because, when a rock is damaged and splits into two, we will reuse the existing instance for one of the two new rocks. This cuts down on the number of new objects that need to be created, helping reduce the garbage collection frequency.

In the constructor, we also take a parameter named generation, which helps us track how many more times the rock can split before it is finally destroyed. The initial rocks will be given the value 2 for this, and each time the rock is damaged the value will be decreased by 1. If this value is then found to still be zero or above, the rock will split into two smaller rocks; if it has fallen below zero, the rock will be completely destroyed instead.

InitializeRock sets all the operational parameters of the rock. It scales the rock as specified by the size parameter, generates a random rotation speed (which is purely cosmetic and has no actual effect on the game), and generates a random direction and speed for the rock to move. The speed is stored in the class-level _moveSpeed variable.

To update the rock, all that is needed is for its angle to be updated and its new position to be calculated. The position update is worth a little exploration because it demonstrates some useful features of the Vector2. The position is calculated as shown in Listing 3–29.

Listing 3–29. Updating the rock's position

```
// Update the position of the rock
Position += _direction * _moveSpeed;
```

As you can see, it multiplies the _direction vector by the movement speed and then adds this to the Position. This process looks simple enough, but don't forget that Position and _direction are both Vector2 structures, not simple values. The reason we can do this is because Vector2 provides all sorts of additional functionality that is very useful for games programming.

When a vector is multiplied by a scalar value, such as when it is multiplied by the movement speed, all its elements will be individually multiplied by the value. For example, multiplying a vector of (5, 7) by 3 results in a new vector containing the values (15, 21).

Adding two vectors together results in a new vector in which the corresponding elements in each of the source vectors are added together. For example, adding the vector (5, 7) to the vector (3, 10) results in the vector (8, 17).

Both addition and multiplication can be performed with negative values and work exactly as you would expect. Vectors can also be subtracted from one another.

This very simple line of code therefore moves the rock in the direction and the speed that we have defined.

Once its position has been set, it is checked against the window boundaries to see whether it needs to wrap to the opposite side.

The rock's Draw code does nothing more than the SpriteObject, so this method is not overridden within the RockObject class.

Finally with this class is the DamageRock function, which will be called each time the rock is damaged. When the game code progresses a little further, we will call it when one of the player's bullets hits a rock. At the moment, however, the only thing that will cause this function to be called is a collision with the player's ship.

DamageRock first checks the generation value. If it is already 0, the rock has been destroyed and it is removed from the GameObjects list. Otherwise, the code splits the rock into two, which is done by reinitializing the current rock at a slightly smaller size (calculated by multiplying the current size by

0.7 for a 30 percent size reduction). The code then creates a second rock with exactly the same parameters, sets its position to match its own, and adds the new rock to the game.

The game adds five rocks to the GameObjects list in its ResetGame function. We don't need to do anything more to track them because we can loop through the object collection hunting for them. Because there could be many rock objects in play at once, this is the simplest way to manage them. Each rock gets a random texture from the three available, which is purely cosmetic and has no bearing on the behavior of the rock.

The SpaceshipObject Class

The player's spaceship is obviously a very important part of the game, but at this stage it is lacking some important functions: we haven't looked at how the user can interact with the device yet (this is coming up in the next chapter), so there is no way for us to control the ship. Instead it is a bit of a sitting duck, motionless in the middle of the screen watching nervously as the huge lumps of rock hurtle past it.

We still have some interesting functionality to add, however. Even though the ship cannot move, it can still react to a collision with any rock that might happen to crash into it. This means we have to be able to determine whether a rock is touching the ship and, if one is, to explode in a fiery ball of destruction.

Let's deal with the collision detection first. This process is handled in the HasCollided function, which returns a reference to any object that has collided with the ship, or null if no collision was detected. The only thing we need to worry about colliding with is a rock, so the code loops through all the game objects looking for objects that are of type RockObject. For each one found, the game performs some further checks to detect collisions.

The quickest but least accurate check is to see whether the bounding boxes of the ship and the rock intersect. If they do, there might possibly (but not necessarily) be a collision; if they do not, then the ship and the rock have definitely not collided. Figure 3–12 demonstrates some scenarios that this test might encounter.

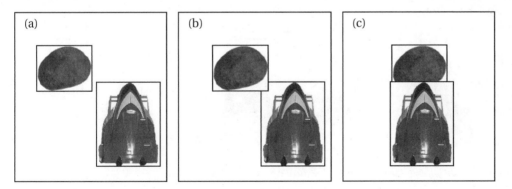

Figure 3–12. Collision scenarios for the bounding box intersection check

Figure 3–12(a) shows a scenario in which the bounding box can quickly and easily determine that the ship and rock have not collided. Their bounding boxes do not intersect, so it is impossible for the two to be touching each other.

Figure 3–12(b) and Figure 3–12(c) both pass the intersection check, although in 3–12 (b) they are clearly not actually touching. If the bounding boxes do intersect, we need to perform an additional check to gain some additional accuracy. This more accurate check is a little more computationally expensive, so the simple bounding box check saves us from having to calculate it for the majority of the collision checks.

We can get a more accurate test by calculating the actual distance between the position of the rock and the position of the spaceship. This calculation will effectively place a circular collision region around the rock (all the space up to the distance we specify from the origin) and another circular region around the spaceship. Of course, neither of them is exactly circular so this won't be pixel perfect, but it will be good enough for our purposes here.

XNA gives us a nice easy mechanism for finding the distance between two points. To calculate this manually, we would need to use Pythagoras's theorem, but XNA saves us the effort of having to get out our old schoolbooks by providing the shared Vector2.Distance function. When this function is passed two Vector2 structures, it calculates the distance between the two.

■ **TIP** If you simply need to compare two distances to find out which is larger without actually needing to know what those distances are, use the Vector2.DistanceSquared function. This function performs the same Pythagoras calculation, but doesn't square-root the answer at the end. It therefore produces a value that is useful only for comparison purposes, but is much faster to calculate.

So we can tell how far apart the two objects are, but how close must they get before they are treated as being in collision? If the distance is less than the radius of the collision circle of each of the objects added together, they have collided. The radius is calculated as the width of the texture divided by 2 and then multiplied by the scale of the object. The relationship between the object radii and the distance between them can be seen in Figure 3–13.

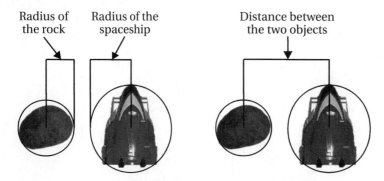

Figure 3–13. The radius of each object and the distance between them

The distance check is illustrated in Figure 3–14, which shows the same three scenarios as before. In Figure 3–14(b), the sprites can now be seen not to be colliding, even though their bounding boxes overlap. In Figure 3–14(c), the sprites are colliding because the distance between them has fallen below their combined radius values.

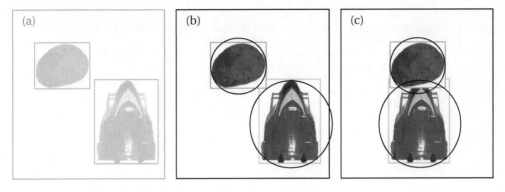

Figure 3–14. *Collision scenarios for the object distance check*

The HasCollided code that performs these checks is shown in Listing 3–30. Observe that all the checks we have discussed are performed: first the bounding box intersection is checked using the Rectangle.Intersects function and then the sizes of the objects are compared to their distance as calculated by Vector2.Distance. Wherever possible, values are calculated just once rather than repeatedly evaluated within the loop; examples of this are the spaceship bounding box (stored in shipBox) and the ship radius (stored in shipSize).

Listing 3–30. *Checking for collisions between the player's ship and the rocks*

```
internal SpriteObject HasCollided()
{
    int objectCount;
    GameObjectBase gameObj;
    SpriteObject spriteObj;
    Rectangle shipBox;
    float shipSize;
    float objectSize;
    float objectDistance;

    // Retrieve the ship's bounding rectangle.
    shipBox = BoundingBox;

    // Calculate the distance from the center of the ship to the
    // edge of its bounding circle.
    shipSize = SpriteTexture.Width / 2.0f * ScaleX;

    objectCount = _game.GameObjects.Count;
    for (int i = 0; i < objectCount; i++)
    {
        // Get a reference to the object at this position
        gameObj = _game.GameObjects[i];
        // Is this a space rock?
        if (gameObj is RockObject)
        {
            // It is... Does its bounding rectangle intersect with the spaceship?
            spriteObj = (SpriteObject)gameObj;
            if (spriteObj.BoundingBox.Intersects(shipBox))
```

```
                    {
                        // It does.. See if the distance is small enough for them to collide.
                        // First calculate the size of the object
                        objectSize = spriteObj.SpriteTexture.Width / 2.0f * spriteObj.ScaleX;
                        // Find the distance between the two points
                        objectDistance = Vector2.Distance(Position, spriteObj.Position);
                        // Is this less than the combined object sizes?
                        if (objectDistance < shipSize + objectSize)
                        {
                            // Yes, so we have collided
                            return spriteObj;
                        }
                    }
                }
            }
        }

        // The ship hasn't hit anything
        return null;
    }
```

With the capability to detect whether the ship has hit a rock, the spaceship's Update method can ensure that such a collision receives an appropriate response. It first determines whether the ship is already in the process of exploding. This will be the case when the ExplosionUpdateCount value is greater than zero. If so, the value is reduced by 1 so that the ship progresses toward resurrection on its next life.

If the ship is not exploding, the HasCollided function is used to check for collisions. If a RockObject is returned, its DamageRock method is called to break it into two (it hit something hard, after all, so it's only fair to expect that it would be damaged in the collision, too). The code then calls the Explode function to destroy the spaceship.

In Explode we do two things: set the initial ExplosionUpdateCount value so that the ship is out of action for a small period of time and create a cloud of particles to represent the explosion within the game (the ParticleObject is described in the next section). When the game is finished, we will also decrease the player's remaining lives in this function.

This is all straightforward stuff, but we will add 150 particle objects to the game to display the explosion. They will be active only for a couple of seconds and will then no longer be required. This action will, of course, leave a large number of unused objects, which will then all be garbage-collected, and more will be added every time the player explodes. Is there a way that we could reduce these wasted objects?

The strategy that we will employ is to keep the expired particle objects alive and reuse them the next time an explosion takes place. When a particle's time runs out, instead of removing it from the GameObjects list we simply set a flag, IsActive, to false to indicate that it is no longer needed. The next time we need some particles we can hunt down all the inactive particles and reuse them, saving us from having to create any more. Only if insufficient inactive particles can be found will further objects be created.

This process is handled in the main game class's GetParticleObjects function, which is called from the spaceship's Explode method.

A benchmark object is set up, ready for use within the project, but is commented out by default. If you enable it by uncommenting the line at the end of the ResetGame function, you will see that the object count increases the first time the player ship explodes, but the subsequent explosions require no further particles to be created.

The main game class creates a single instance of SpaceshipObject and stores the reference in its _playerShip class variable. Because the game will need to access this later on to apply the player's input to the game, we need to ensure that we can easily find this object. Keeping a separate reference is much faster than hunting through the GameObjects collection looking for it every time it needs to be interacted with.

The ParticleObject Class

Particles are just small fragments of material that will drift in space for some reason. They might be the debris from an explosion, a cloud of dust from a rock being split in half, or the exhaust emission from the player's ship once we have implemented thruster controls.

They all exhibit pretty much the same functionality, however: they move through space in a particular direction and gradually fade away to nothing and disappear.

The ParticleObject class has been created to handle all these particles. It can be instantiated and set on its way and then forgotten about; once it fades away to nothing it will become inactive and wait to be recycled, as discussed in the previous section.

The class contains properties to keep track of its movement direction and speed, as we have seen in other classes. It also stores an inertia value, which is multiplied by the speed each time it updates. Setting this value to 1.0 results in no inertia at all; the particle will keep moving forever. Lower values will cause the particle to slow down as it moves. Don't set this value too low—a value of 0.9 already causes the particle to stop moving after a very short distance. Values between 0.9 and 1.0 are probably most useful.

The particles also track an Intensity, which is used as their SpriteColor alpha value, and an IntensityFadeAmount. The fade amount is subtracted from the intensity at each update, and once the intensity reaches zero the particle is made inactive.

All the properties are set to their initial or randomized states in the ResetProperties method. This can be called either after a new instance is created or when an instance is being recycled to ensure that it is in a default state. The properties can then be updated as required for the task at hand.

The StarObject Class

The final class in the game so far is the StarObject, which is a very simple object that simply displays a star as a gently flickering dot. There is nothing too remarkable about this class, so we won't examine it in any more detail here.

Running the Game

Because all the objects know how to behave and how to react to significant events that take place, there is very little to do in the game class so far. The ResetGame function adds a number of stars, some rocks, and the player ship to the game; and the Draw function draws everything one texture at a time.

Although the game is not yet playable, it is still fun to watch the rocks crashing into the spaceship and to see the ship explode in a shower of particles. If you are patient enough, you will see that, once a rock has divided in two twice, the remaining tiny rocks will disappear completely if they collide with the player, just as we need.

An image of the game is shown in Figure 3–15.

Figure 3–15. The Cosmic Rocks *game so far*

At the end of the next chapter, we will add interactivity into the game so that the player can shoot and move the spaceship.

Creating XNA Games

I hope that this chapter has given you an idea of the huge power and flexibility that we can obtain from XNA and from the game framework that we have created. With very small amounts of code you can create rich and complex environments with objects that behave in interesting ways and can interact with one another.

Feel free to play with what we have created so far and build some game projects of your own. With a little time you should begin to feel very comfortable with creating new projects and getting your game objects to behave in whatever way you want.

In the next chapter, we will allow the player to get in touch with our game world by processing inputs to the device.

CHAPTER 4

■ ■ ■

User Input

We've given XNA plenty of opportunity to tell us what it is thinking. Now let's even things up and let it know what's going on inside our human brains. Input is, of course, an essential part of any game and will add interactivity and excitement to our projects.

Microsoft has made some fairly strict decisions about the inputs that can be featured on Windows Phone 7 devices. All devices will have a touch screen and this will naturally form the primary input mechanism that we will use for gaming. The screens all support multitouch and are required to be able to track a minimum of four simultaneous touch points.

In terms of buttons, devices must have exactly three front-facing buttons: a Back button, a Windows button, and a Search button. They all have predefined expected roles, and we must observe them if we want our application to be approved for publication. We cannot do anything at all in response to the Windows or Search buttons being pressed, and can in fact expect our game to disappear from view when either of them is used. The only button we can legitimately hook into is the Back button. If we are in a subscreen of a game (for example, an options page or a highscore table), this button must return to the previous game page (the main game). Otherwise, the game must exit when this button is pressed.

We do have some other inputs available to us, however. The most useful of them for gaming is the accelerometer, which lets us work out exactly which way up the device is being held. This has lots of interesting uses for gaming. In this chapter, we'll examine these input mechanisms and explore how they can be used to control the games that you create.

Using the Touch Screen

All touch input from the screen is obtained using a class within XNA called TouchPanel. This provides two mechanisms with which input information can be obtained: raw touch point data and the Gestures API.

The raw touch point data provides a collection of all current input points on the screen ready to be interpreted in whichever way the program desires. Each touch point identifies whether its touch is new, moved, or released; and allows its previous coordinate to be obtained if appropriate, but nothing more is provided. It is therefore up to the application to interpret this data and handle it as appropriate for the game.

The advantage of the touch point data is that it gives us the most flexible access to multitouch inputs. It also offers the most straightforward method for reading simple input if nothing more complex is required.

The Gestures API recognizes a series of types of input that the user might want to use, such as tap, double tap, or drag. By telling XNA which gestures we are interested in, it will look for these movement patterns and report back to us whatever it finds.

This greatly simplifies many types of input that would be more difficult to recognize and manage using the raw touch point data. The main disadvantage of using gestures is that they are primarily single-touch in nature (with the exception of the *pinch* gesture which uses two touch points). If you need to be able to gain full access to multiple simultaneous input points, the raw touch point data might be more suitable.

Let's look at how each of these systems is used in detail.

Reading Raw Touch Data

When reading the current touch points from the screen, we *poll* for information: we make a call out to the device and ask it for its current state.

This is in contrast with the way you might be used to obtaining data in desktop applications (and indeed it is in contrast with how we will obtain input data in Silverlight applications when we get to them later in the book), which tends to be event driven: each time the operating system detects that something has happened, it queues up an event.

Event-driven systems tend not to "miss" any events, whereas polling systems can skip inputs if they happen too quickly. If the user taps the screen so quickly that the input state is not polled while the screen contact is made, the button press will be missed entirely.

The advantage of polling, however, is that it is fast, easy to use, and provides information at exactly the point where we need it. When you want to see if your player should shoot, you simply check to see if a screen location is currently being touched. This check can take place anywhere in your game code rather than having to be placed within an event handler.

To read the touch points, we simply call the TouchPanel.GetState function. It returns a TouchCollection, inside which we will find a TouchLocation object for each touch point that is currently active. If the collection is empty, the user is not currently touching the screen. If multiple location objects are present, multiple touches are active simultaneously.

Listing 4–1 shows a simple piece of code in a game class's Update method that reads the current touch points and displays the number of touch points returned to the debug window.

Listing 4–1. Retrieving the current TouchPanel state

```
protected override void Update(GameTime gameTime)
{
    // Allows the game to exit
    if (GamePad.GetState(PlayerIndex.One).Buttons.Back == ButtonState.Pressed)
        this.Exit();

    // Get the current screen touch points
    TouchCollection touches = TouchPanel.GetState();
    // Output the touch count to the debug window
    System.Diagnostics.Debug.WriteLine("Touch count: " + touches.Count.ToString());

    base.Update(gameTime);
}
```

When developing with the Windows Phone emulator, you can, of course, simulate touching the screen by clicking the emulator window with the mouse cursor. If you are running Windows 7 and have a touch-sensitive monitor, the emulator has full support for genuine touch input—including multitouch if your monitor is capable of supporting it. However if you lack a multitouch monitor, it is very hard to develop multitouch applications within the emulator, and using a real device is the only way to properly test your game in this case.

The Life and Times of a Touch Point

When the user touches the screen, we find a TouchLocation object in the collection returned by TouchPanel.GetState. Contained within this location object are the following properties:

- Id returns a unique identification value for this touch point. As long as the user maintains contact with the screen, location objects with the same Id value will continue to be sent to the application. Each time a new touch is established, a new Id value will be generated. This is very useful for multitouch input because it helps tell which point is which, but for single-touch input we can ignore it.

- Position is a Vector2 structure inside which the touch point coordinate is stored.

- State stores a value that helps us determine whether the touch point is new or has been released by the user.

When the state is polled when a new touch point has been established, the State of that touch point will be set to the enumeration value TouchLocationState.Pressed. If you are interested only in when contact is established, check for this state in your location objects. This is the equivalent of a MouseDown event in a WinForms environment.

When the state is polled and a previously reported touch point is still active, its state will be set to Moved. Note that it doesn't matter whether the point actually *has* moved or not, this state simply means that this is an established touch point that is still present. You will see how we can determine whether it really has moved in a moment.

Finally when the state is polled and a previously reported touch point has been released, it will be present within the touch collection for one final time with a state of Released. This will always be present once the touch point is released, so you can rely on the fact that every Pressed point will have a corresponding Released state. If the screen is tapped very quickly, it is entirely possible to see a point go straight from Pressed to Released without any Moved states in between.

■ **NOTE** Because XNA ensures that all released points are reported, it is theoretically possible for there to be more points within the TouchCollection than the device is actually able to read. If four touch points were in contact with the screen during one poll, and all four had been released and retouched during the next poll, the collection would contain eight points (four with a State of Released and four more with a State of Pressed).

Finding a Touch Point's Previous Location

For TouchLocation objects whose State is Moved, we can ask the TouchLocation for the point's previous location by calling its TryGetPreviousLocation method. This will return a Boolean value of true if a previous position is available or false if it is not (which should be the case only if the State value is Pressed). The method also expects a TouchLocation to be passed as an output parameter, and into this the touch point's previous location will be placed.

Listing 4–2 shows a simple Update function that displays the state, current position, and previous position of the first detected touch point.

Listing 4–2. Retrieving a touch point's previous location

```
protected override void Update(GameTime gameTime)
{
    // Allows the game to exit
    if (GamePad.GetState(PlayerIndex.One).Buttons.Back == ButtonState.Pressed)
        this.Exit();

    // Get the current screen touch points
    TouchCollection touches = TouchPanel.GetState();
    // Is there an active touch point?
    if (touches.Count >= 1)
    {
        // Read the previous location
        TouchLocation prevLocation;
        bool prevAvailable = touches[0].TryGetPreviousLocation(out prevLocation);
        // Output current and previous information to the debug window
        System.Diagnostics.Debug.WriteLine("Position: " + touches[0].Position.ToString()
                    + " Previous position: " + prevLocation.Position.ToString());
    }

    base.Update(gameTime);
}
```

Note that TryGetPreviousLocation gives back a TouchLocation object, not a Vector2, so we can interrogate its other properties, too. It gives access to its State property, which allows a touch point to tell whether it is receiving its first Move state (this will be the case if its previous location's state is Pressed). It is not possible to obtain additional historical information by further calling TryGetPreviousLocation on the previous location object: it will always return false.

If you want to experiment with this, take a look at the TouchPanelDemo example project. This project provides a simple TouchPanel display that places a circular object at the position of each detected touch point. It supports multitouch input and will display the first touch point in white, the second in red, the third in blue, and the fourth in green. Any additional touch points will display in white. When the touch point is released, the circle will fade away into nothing.

All the while this is running, information about the first returned touch point will be written to the debug window. This includes the point's Id, State, Position, and previous Position. From this information you will be able to see the sequence of State values that are returned, see the previous Position for each touch point, and observe the behavior of the previous Position for Pressed and Released touch points.

Touch Panel Capabilities

If you need to know how many simultaneous touch points are available, you can ask the TouchPanel for this information. Its GetCapabilities method returns a TouchPanelCapabilities object, from which the MaximumTouchCount property can be queried.

All devices are required to support a minimum of four touch points, so anything you write should be able to rely on being able to read this many points at once. In practice, this number is probably quite sufficient for most games.

The only other useful capability property is the IsConnected property, which tells you whether a touch panel is currently connected to the device. For Windows Phone 7 games, it will always return true, but the property might return other values for XNA games running on other platforms (Windows or an Xbox 360, for example).

Working with Rotated and Scaled Screens

It's very useful being able to read the touch screen coordinate, but what happens if the game is running in a landscape orientation? Do we need to swap over the x and y coordinate values to find out where the touch point is relative to our game coordinates?

You will be pleased to find that the answer is no; XNA automatically takes care of this for us. We don't need to pay any attention at all to screen orientation because the screen coordinates will be translated into the same coordinate system that we are using for rendering.

Taking this concept even further, XNA does exactly the same thing when scaling is in effect. If the back buffer is set to a size of 240 x 400, for example, the touch point coordinates will be automatically scaled into exactly the same range. No special processing is required for these configurations at all.

Try changing the back buffer size in the TouchPanelDemo game class constructor to experiment. You will see that both rotated and scaled output provides correspondingly rotated and scaled input values. This is a very useful feature that greatly simplifies working with touch coordinates under these conditions.

Reading Input Using the Touch Gestures

TouchPanel.GetState returns simple information about how the user is touching the screen; in many cases, this information will be perfectly sufficient for games that you might want to write. TouchPanel offers an alternative high-level way to read input, however, called *Gestures*.

The Gestures API recognizes a series of common movement types that the user might make when touching the screen and reports them back by telling you what type of movement has been detected as well as the relevant screen coordinates for the movement.

The recognized gestures are as follows:

- Tap: The user has briefly pressed and released contact with the screen.

- DoubleTap: The user has quickly tapped the screen twice in the same location.

- Hold: The user has made sustained contact with the same point on the screen for a small period of time.

- VerticalDrag: The user is holding contact with the screen and moving the touch point vertically.

- HorizontalDrag: The user is holding contact with the screen and moving the touch point horizontally.

- FreeDrag: The user is holding contact and moving the touch point around the screen in any direction.

- DragComplete: Indicates that a previous VerticalDrag, HorizontalDrag, or FreeDrag has concluded, and contact with the screen has been released.

- Flick: The user has moved a contact point across the screen and released contact while still moving.

- Pinch: Two simultaneous touch points have been established and moved on the screen.

- PinchComplete: Indicates that a previous Pinch has concluded, and contact with the screen has been released.

This list contains some very useful input mechanisms that your user will no doubt be familiar with. Using them saves a lot of effort tracking previous positions and touch points, and allows the gestures system to do all the work for us.

■ **NOTE** The Gestures API is currently implemented only in XNA for Windows Phone. If you intend to port your game to the Windows or Xbox 360 platforms in the future, you will need to find an alternative way of reading input for those platforms.

Let's look at the Gestures API and each of the supported gesture types in more detail and see exactly how they all work and how they can be used.

Enabling the Gestures

Before you can use gestures you must tell XNA which of the gestures you are interested in being notified about. It is potentially able to track all of them at once, but it is likely that certain gestures are going to be unwanted in any given situation. Enabling only those gestures that you need improves the performance of the gesture recognition engine and also reduces the chance that a gesture will not be interpreted in the way that you need.

All the gestures are disabled by default. Attempting to read gesture information in this state will result in an exception.

To enable the appropriate gestures, logically OR together the required values from the GestureType enumeration and then provide the result to the TouchPanel.EnabledGestures property. For example, the code in Listing 4–3 enables the tap, hold, and free drag gestures.

Listing 4–3. Enabling gestures required for the game

```
// Enable the gestures that we want to be able to respond to
TouchPanel.EnabledGestures = GestureType.Tap | GestureType. Hold |
                                               GestureType.FreeDrag;
```

The enabled gestures can be set or changed at any stage in your game. If you find that you are moving from the main game into a different area of functionality (such as an options screen or a high-score table) and you need to change the gestures that are to be processed, simply reassign the EnabledGestures property as needed.

Processing Gestures

Once the required gestures have been enabled, you can begin waiting for them to occur in your game's Update function. Unlike reading the raw touch data, gesture information is fed via a queue, and it is important that this queue is fully processed and emptied each update. Without this it is possible for old events to be picked up and processed some time after they actually took place, giving your game a slow and laggy sensation.

To check to see whether there are any gestures in the queue, query the TouchPanel.IsGestureAvailable property. This can be used as part of a while loop to ensure that all waiting gesture objects within the queue are processed.

If IsGestureAvailable returns true, the next gesture can be read (and removed) from the queue by calling the TouchPanel.ReadGesture function. This returns a GestureSample object containing all the required details about the gesture. Some of the useful properties of this object include the following:

- GestureType: This property indicates which of the enabled gestures has resulted in the creation of this object. It will contain a value from the same GestureType enumeration that was used to enable the gestures, and can be checked with a switch statement or similar construct to process each gesture in the appropriate way.

- Position: A Vector2 that contains the location on the screen at which the gesture occurred.

- Position2: For the Pinch gesture, this property contains the position of the second touch point.

- Delta: A Vector2 containing the distance that the touch point has moved since the gesture was last measured.

- Delta2: For the Pinch gesture, this property contains the delta of the second touch point.

A typical loop to process the gesture queue might look something like the code shown in Listing 4–4.

Listing 4–4. Processing and clearing the gestures queue

```
while (TouchPanel.IsGestureAvailable)
{
    // Read the next gesture
    GestureSample gesture = TouchPanel.ReadGesture();

    switch (gesture.GestureType)
    {
        case GestureType.Tap: Shoot(gesture.Position); break;
        case GestureType.FreeDrag: Move(gesture.Position); break;
    }
}
```

Tap and DoubleTap

The Tap gesture fires when you briefly touch and release the screen without moving the touch point. The DoubleTap gesture fires when you quickly touch, release, and then touch the screen again without any movement taking place. If both of these gestures are enabled, a Tap and DoubleTap gesture will be reported in quick succession.

Note that repeat rapid taps of the screen are not quite as responsive through the Gestures API as they are by reading the raw touch information. If you need to be very responsive to lots of individual screen taps, you might find raw touch data more appropriate.

Hold

The Hold gesture fires after stationary contact has been maintained for a brief period of time (about a second).

If the touch point moves too far from the initial contact position, the hold gesture will not fire. This means that, although it is quite possible for a Hold to fire after a Tap or DoubleTap, it is less likely after one of the drag gestures.

VerticalDrag, HorizontalDrag and FreeDrag

The three drag gestures can be used independently or together, though using FreeDrag at the same time as one of the axis-aligned drags can be awkward because once XNA has decided the direction of movement, it doesn't change. Beginning a horizontal drag and then moving vertically will continue to be reported as a horizontal drag. For this reason, it is generally better to stick to either axis-aligned drags or free drags, but not mix the two.

In addition to reporting the position within the returned GestureSample object, XNA also returns the Delta of the movement—the distance that the touch point has moved on the x and y axes since the last measurement. This can be useful if you want to scroll objects on the screen because it is generally more useful than the actual touch position itself. For VerticalDrag and HorizontalDrag, only the relevant axis value of the Delta structure will be populated; the other axis value will always contain 0.

Once a drag has started, it will continually report the touch position each time it moves. Unlike when reading raw input, no gesture data will be added to the queue if the touch point is stationary. When the touch point is released and the drag terminates, a DragComplete gesture type will be reported.

Flick

Flick gestures are triggered when the user releases contact with the screen while still moving the touch point. This tends to be useful for initiating *kinetic scrolling*, in which objects continue moving after touch is released in the direction that the user had been moving. We will look at how you can implement this in your games in the "Initiating Object Motion" section later in this chapter.

To tell how fast and in which direction the flick occurred, read the GestureSample.Delta property. Unlike drag gestures, however, this property contains the movement distance for each axis measured in pixels per second, rather than pixels since the previous position measurement.

To scale this to pixels per update to retain the existing motion, we can multiply the Delta vector by the length of time of each update, which we can retrieve from the TargetElapsedTime property. The scaled delta value calculation is shown in Listing 4–5.

Listing 4–5. Scaling the Flick delta to represent pixels-per-Update rather than pixels-per-second

```
Vector2 deltaPerUpdate = gesture.Delta * (float)TargetElapsedTime.TotalSeconds;
```

One piece of information that we unfortunately do not get from the Flick gesture is the position from which it is being flicked, which is instead always returned as the coordinate (0, 0). To determine where the flick originated, we therefore need to remember the position of a previous gesture, and the only gestures that will reliably provide this information are the drag gestures. It is therefore likely that you will need to have a drag gesture enabled for this purpose.

Pinch

When the user makes contact with the screen with two fingers at once, a Pinch gesture will be initiated and will report on the position of both touch points for the duration of the contact with the screen. As with the drag gestures, updates will be provided only if one or both of the touch points has actually moved.

XNA will ensure that the same point is reported in each of its position and delta properties (Position, Position2, Delta, and Delta2), so you don't need to worry about them swapping over unexpectedly.

Once either of the contacts with the screen ends, a PinchComplete gesture is added to the queue to indicate that no further updates from this gesture will be sent. If the remaining touch point continues to be held, it will initiate a new gesture once it begins to move.

Just as with multitouch data from the raw touch API, testing pinch gestures on the emulator is impossible unless you have a suitable touch screen and Windows 7. This gesture is therefore best tested on a real device.

Working with Rotated and Scaled Screens

Just as with the raw touch data coordinates, positions from the Gestures API are automatically updated to match the rotation and scaling that is active on the screen, so no special processing is required if these features are in use.

Experimenting with the Gestures API

The GesturesDemo example project will help you experiment with all the gestures we have discussed in this section. It is similar to the TouchPanelDemo from the previous section, but uses different icons for each of the recognized gestures. The icons are shown in Figure 4–1.

| Tap | Double Tap | Hold | Vertical Drag | Horizontal Drag | Free Drag | Flick | Pinch (1ˢᵗ point) | Pinch (2ⁿᵈ point) |

Figure 4–1. The icons used for the different gesture types in the GesturesDemo project

---

■ **NOTE** This project deliberately displays the icons a little above and to the left of the actual touch point so that they can be seen when touching a real phone (otherwise they appear directly beneath your fingers and are impossible to see). This looks a little odd in the emulator, however, as their positions don't directly correspond to the mouse cursor position, so don't be surprised by this.

By default, the project is set to recognize the Tap, DoubleTap, FreeDrag, Flick and Hold gestures. Try enabling and disabling each of the gesture types and experiment with the movement patterns needed to initiate each. You can also use this as a simple way to see how the gestures relate to one another (for example, try enabling all three of the drag gestures and see how XNA decides which one to use).

Sprite Hit Testing

A very common requirement for games will be to tell whether the player has touched one of the objects onscreen. We know where the objects all are and we know the point that the user has touched, so how can we tell if they coincide?

There are several approaches that we can use, each with different characteristics. Some of the different mechanisms that can be used are the following:

- Checking against the sprite bounding box. This is very simple and quick, but as we saw in the last chapter it doesn't take rotation into account and is therefore not very accurate. For sprites that have not been rotated, this is the best approach to use.

- Rectangular hit tests are similar to the bounding box test but properly take the sprite rotation into account. This test requires a little more calculation, but can accurately reflect whether the point falls within the rendered sprite rectangle.

- Elliptical hit tests are good for sprites whose shape is essentially round. They perform a test by finding the distance from the touch point to the center of the sprite and checking whether this is within the area of the ellipse.

Let's see how each of these approaches can be implemented.

Bounding Box Hit Tests

The easiest but least flexible mechanism for detecting whether a sprite has been touched is to see whether the sprite's bounding box contains the touch point. This can be achieved as shown in Listing 4–6.

Listing 4–6. A simple hit test using the bounding box

```
bool IsPointInObject (Vector2 point)
{
    Rectangle bbox;

    // Retrieve the bounding box
    bbox = BoundingBox;

    // See whether the box contains the point
    return bbox.Contains((int)point.X, (int)point.Y);
}
```

The Rectangle structure conveniently performs this check for us, though it is really just a simple matter of checking that the x coordinate falls between the rectangle's left and right edges, and that the y coordinate falls between the top and bottom edges.

As the BoundingBox property already takes notice of scaling and custom sprite origins, this is all that we need to do for this simple check. If we need to be able to work with rotated rectangles, though, we need something a little more sophisticated...

Rectangular Hit Tests

There are various ways that we could test a point within a rotated rectangle. The easiest to conceptualize is taking the four corners of the rectangle and seeing whether the point falls inside them. However, there are simpler and more efficient ways to achieve this in code.

A more efficient way to achieve this is to imagine that we have rotated the rectangle back around its origin until its angle is zero, and correspondingly rotate the test point by the same angle. Once we have done this, we can simply perform a simple aligned rectangle check, just as we did in Listing 4–6.

In Figure 4–2, two images are shown of some test points and a rectangle. The rectangle has been scaled so that it is longer along its x axis, and rotated by about 15 degrees. Looking at Figure 4–2(a), it is obvious visually that test point 1 is within the rectangle, and test point 2 is not. In order for our code to determine this, we imagine rotating the sprite back until its angle is 0, and we rotate the two points by exactly the same amount. Of course, we don't actually draw it like this or even update the sprite's properties; we just perform the calculations that would be required for this rotation. If we *were* to draw the rotation, we would end up with the arrangement shown in Figure 4–2(b).

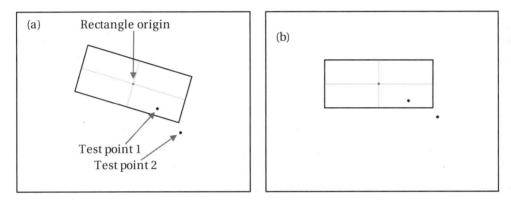

Figure 4–2. Testing hit points against a rotated scaled sprite

Having arranged the points as shown in Figure 4–2(b), we can now perform a simple check to see whether each point is within the left-right and top-bottom boundaries, just as we did with the bounding box test. This is a very simple calculation and gives us exactly the results we are looking for.

The code to perform this check is fairly straightforward. The main focus of the calculation is to perform the rotation of the test point around the rectangle's origin. We don't need to actually perform any calculation on the rectangle at all; we just need to rotate the points and then check them against the rectangle's unrotated width and height, which is already returned to us from the BoundingBox property.

When we rotate a point in space, it always rotates around the *origin*—the point at coordinate (0, 0). If we want to rotate around the rectangle's origin, we therefore need to find the distance from the rectangle origin to the test point. The calculation can then be performed in coordinates relative to the rectangle, not the screen.

We can do this simply by subtracting the origin position from the test point position, as shown in Figure 4–3. In Figure 4–3(a), we see the coordinates specified as screen coordinates—the actual pixel position on the screen that forms the origin of the rectangle and the user's touch points. In Figure 4–3(b), these coordinates are specified relative to the rectangle origin. As you can see, this has simply subtracted 200 from the x values and 100 from the y values because they are the rectangle's origin coordinate.

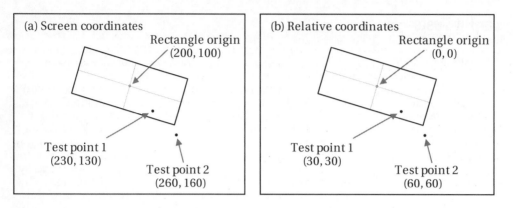

Figure 4–3. Finding the touch coordinates relative to the rectangle's origin

These modified coordinates are considered as being in *object space* rather than in the normal *screen space* as they are now measured against the object (the rectangle) rather than the screen. We can now rotate these points around the origin, and as long as we remember that we are measuring their position in object space rather than screen space, we will find the new positions that we saw in Figure 4–2(b).

■ **NOTE** If at any time we want to map the coordinates back into screen space, all we need to do is re-add the rectangle's origin that we have subtracted. If we move a point to object space (by subtracting the object's origin coordinate), rotate it, and then move it back to screen space (by re-adding the object's origin coordinate), we will have rotated around the object's origin even though it is not at the screen's origin coordinate.

Having obtained the coordinate in object space, we now need to rotate it to match the rectangle's angle. The rectangle in the figures we have been looking at is rotated 15 degrees in a clockwise direction. As you can see in Figure 4–2(b), to reset the rectangle back to its original angle we therefore need to rotate it back by the same angle—in other words 15 degrees counterclockwise. We can achieve this by negating the rotation angle.

The calculation to rotate a point around the origin is as follows:

$$x' = x \cos \theta - v \sin \theta$$
$$v' = x \sin \theta + v \cos \theta$$

The code to perform this calculation is shown in Listing 4–7.

Listing 4–7. Rotating the point variable to calculate the new rotatedPoint variable

```
// Rotate the point by the negative angle sprite angle to cancel out the sprite rotation
rotatedPoint.X = (float)(Math.Cos(-Angle) * point.X - Math.Sin(-Angle) * point.Y);
rotatedPoint.Y = (float)(Math.Sin(-Angle) * point.X + Math.Cos(-Angle) * point.Y);
```

Now we have the coordinate relative to the unrotated object's origin. We can therefore simply move the bounding box into object space (by once again subtracting the rectangle position) and then see whether the point is contained within the bounding box. If so, the point is a hit; if not, it is a miss.

Table 4–1 shows the calculations that we have described for each of the touch points shown in Figure 4–3. The sprite in question is 64 x 64 pixels and has been scaled to be double its normal width, resulting in a rectangle of 128 x 64 pixels.

Table 4–1. Calculation steps to determine whether a test point is within a rotated scaled rectangle

	Test Point 1	Test Point 2
Screen coordinate	(230, 130)	(260, 160)
Object-space coordinate	(30, 30)	(60, 60)
Rotated coordinate	(36.7, 21.2)	(73.5, 42.4)
Rectangle top-left/bottom-right in object coordinates	(-64, -32) / (64, 32)	
Point contained within rectangle	Yes	No

As this table shows, the rotated test point 1 coordinate is inside the rectangle's object coordinates (its x coordinate of 36.7 is between the rectangle x extent of -64 to 64, and its y coordinate of 21.2 is within the rectangle y extent of -32 to 32), and the rotated test point 2 coordinate is not.

The complete function to perform this calculation is shown in Listing 4–8. This code is taken from the `SpriteObject` class, and so has direct access to the sprite's properties.

Listing 4–8. Checking a test point to see whether it is within a rotated and scaled sprite rectangle

```
protected bool IsPointInObject_RectangleTest(Vector2 point)
{
    Rectangle bbox;
    float width;
    float height;
    Vector2 rotatedPoint = Vector2.Zero;

    // Retrieve the sprite's bounding box
    bbox = BoundingBox;

    // If no rotation is applied, we can simply check against the bounding box
    if (Angle == 0) return bbox.Contains((int)point.X, (int)point.Y);

    // Get the sprite width and height
    width = bbox.Width;
    height = bbox.Height;

    // Subtract the sprite position to retrieve the test point in
    // object space rather than in screen space
    point -= Position;

    // Rotate the point by the negative angle of the sprite to cancel out the sprite
```

```
    // rotation
    rotatedPoint.X = (float)(Math.Cos(-Angle) * point.X - Math.Sin(-Angle) * point.Y);
    rotatedPoint.Y = (float)(Math.Sin(-Angle) * point.X + Math.Cos(-Angle) * point.Y);

    // Move the bounding box to object space too
    bbox.Offset((int)-PositionX, (int)-PositionY);

    // Does the bounding box contain the rotated sprite?
    return bbox.Contains((int)rotatedPoint.X, (int)rotatedPoint.Y);
}
```

Elliptical Hit Tests

Although rectangular hit tests are appropriate in some cases, in others it might be useful to test against a round sprite shape. To facilitate this, we can perform an elliptical hit test.

The ellipse that will be tested will completely fill the rectangular region occupied by the sprite, as shown in Figure 4–4.

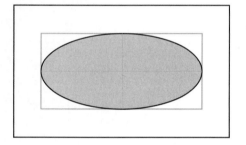

Figure 4–4. The elliptical test region contained within a rectangular sprite

Of course, ellipses, unlike circles, are affected by rotation, so we need to take this into account when working out whether a test point falls inside the ellipse. In Figure 4–5(a), we can see a rotated ellipse whose scale is such that its width is twice its height. Also marked in the figure are two test points, the first of which is within the ellipse, whereas the second is not (though it is within the bounds of the sprite rectangle).

The approach that we take to determine whether the points are within the ellipse starts off the same as that used for the rectangle: performing the calculation to rotate the points and the ellipse back to an angle of zero. Once that has been done we can ignore the rotation and concentrate just on the elliptical shape. Again, we don't actually draw the sprite with the angle reset to zero or update the sprite's properties; we just perform the calculations that would be required for this rotation. If we were to draw the rotation, we would end up with the arrangement shown in Figure 4–5(b).

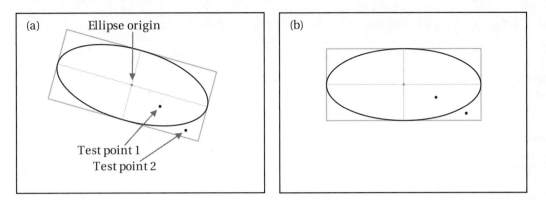

Figure 4–5. Elliptical hit tests against a rotated scaled sprite

Having obtained the coordinates relative to an unrotated ellipse, we can now determine whether the points are within the ellipse or not. For a circle this would be easy: we would find the radius of the circle and we would find the distance from the test point to the center of the circle. If the point distance is less than the radius, the point is inside the circle.

For an ellipse, this process is more complex, however. An ellipse doesn't have a radius because the distance from its center to its edge varies as the edge is traversed.

Fortunately, there is a very easy way to resolve this. We know how the sprite has been scaled, so we can divide the width of the ellipse by the scaled sprite width, and divide the height of the ellipse by the scaled sprite height. This will result in a new ellipse that is exactly one unit wide and one unit high. The size is less important than the fact that this resulting size is now that of a circle (with a radius of 0.5) rather than an ellipse, meaning that we can perform calculations against it very easily. Instead of scaling the sprite in this way, we can scale the test point and then see whether its distance from the circle center is less than 0.5. If so, the point is a hit; otherwise, it's a miss.

The steps required for the whole procedure are as follows; they are just like the steps for the rectangular hit test:

- Move the touch point to be in object space rather than in screen space.

- Rotate the point back by the sprite rotation angle.

- Move the point to be relative to the center of the ellipse.

- Divide the point's x position by the ellipse width and its y position by the ellipse height to scale down relative to a unit-width circle.

- Test the point distance from the circle center to see whether it is within the circle's radius of 0.5.

Table 4–2 shows each of these calculations for each of the touch points shown in Figure 4–5. The sprite in question is 64 x 64 pixels and has been scaled to be double its normal width, resulting in an ellipse with a width of 128 pixels and a height of 64 pixels. Its center (and origin) is at the coordinate (200, 100).

Table 4–2. *Calculation steps to determine whether a test point is within a rotated scaled ellipse*

	Test Point 1	Test Point 2
Screen coordinate	(224, 117)	(248, 134)
Object-space coordinate	(24, 17)	(48, 34)
Rotated coordinate	(27.6, 10.2)	(55.2, 20.4)
Ellipse width/height	128 pixels by 64 pixels	
Rotated coordinate scaled by width and height	(0.216, 0.159)	(0.432, 0.318)
Distance from circle center at (0, 0)	0.268	0.536
Point contained within rectangle (distance <= 0.5)	Yes	No

As this table shows, the test point 1 coordinate is inside the ellipse (its calculated distance is less than 0.5), and the test point 2 coordinate is not.

The complete function to perform this calculation is shown in Listing 4–9. This code is taken from the SpriteObject class, so it has direct access to the sprite's properties.

Listing 4–9. *Checking a test point to see if it is within a rotated and scaled sprite ellipse*

```
protected bool IsPointInObject_EllipseTest(Microsoft.Xna.Framework.Vector2 point)
{
    Rectangle bbox;
    Vector2 rotatedPoint = Vector2.Zero;

    // Retrieve the basic sprite bounding box
    bbox = BoundingBox;

    // Subtract the ellipse's top-left position from the test point so that the test
    // point is relative to the origin position rather than relative to the screen
    point -= Position;

    // Rotate the point by the negative angle of the sprite to cancel out the sprite
    // rotation
    rotatedPoint.X = (float)(Math.Cos(-Angle) * point.X - Math.Sin(-Angle) * point.Y);
    rotatedPoint.Y = (float)(Math.Sin(-Angle) * point.X + Math.Cos(-Angle) * point.Y);

    // Add back the origin point multiplied by the scale.
    // This will put us in the top-left corner of the bounding box.
    rotatedPoint += Origin * Scale;
    // Subtract the bounding box midpoint from each axis.
    // This will put us in the center of the ellipse.
    rotatedPoint -= new Vector2(bbox.Width / 2, bbox.Height / 2);

    // Divide the point by the width and height of the bounding box.
    // This will result in values between -0.5 and +0.5 on each axis for
```

```
// positions within the bounding box. As both axes are then on the same
// scale we can check the distance from the center point as a circle,
// without having to worry about elliptical shapes.
rotatedPoint /= new Vector2(bbox.Width, bbox.Height);

// See if the distance from the origin to the point is <= 0.5
// (the radius of a unit-size circle). If so, we are within the ellipse.
return (rotatedPoint.Length() <= 0.5f);
}
```

Building the Hit Tests into the Game Framework

Checking touch points against game objects to see whether they have been selected is an operation that will be common to many games. To save each game from having to reimplement this logic, we will build these checks into the game framework.

This procedure starts off as an abstract function in GameObjectBase called IsPointInObject, as shown in Listing 4–10. It expects a Vector2 parameter to identify the position on the screen to test and returns a boolean value indicating whether that point is contained within the object.

Listing 4–10. The abstract declaration for IsPointInObject contained inside GameObjectBase

```
/// <summary>
/// Determine whether the specified position is contained within the object
/// </summary>
public abstract bool IsPointInObject(Vector2 point);
```

To implement the IsPointInObject function for sprites, it is overridden within SpriteObject. We will enable our sprites to support testing against both the rectangular and elliptical tests that we have described, and to allow the game to specify which type of test to use a new property is added to the class, named AutoHitTestMode. The property is given the AutoHitTestModes enumeration as its type, allowing either Rectangle or Ellipse to be selected.

The SpriteObject implementation of IsPointInObject checks to see which of these hit modes is selected and then calls into either IsPointInObject_RectangleTest (as shown in Listing 4–8) or IsPointInObject_EllipseTest (as shown in Listing 4–9). Any game object can thus have its AutoHitTestMode property set at initialization and can then simply test points by calling the IsPointInObject function.

For sprites that need to perform some alternative or more complex processing when checking for hit points (perhaps just as simple as only allowing a hit to take place under certain conditions or perhaps implementing entirely new region calculations), the IsPointInObject can be further overridden in derived game object classes.

Retrieving the Objects at a Hit Location

Another common function will be to identify the sprites that are contained in a specific location or the frontmost sprite at a specific location. Once again, we can add functions for both of these operations to the GameHost class.

The first, GetSpritesAtPoint, loops through all the game objects looking for those that can be found at the specified position. These are added to an array and returned to the calling procedure. The code for this function is shown in Listing 4–11.

Listing 4–11. Finding all the objects at a specified position

```
public SpriteObject[] GetSpritesAtPoint(Vector2 testPosition)
{
    SpriteObject spriteObj;
    SpriteObject[] hits = new SpriteObject[GameObjects.Count];
    int hitCount = 0;

    // Loop for all of the SelectableSpriteObjects
    foreach (GameObjectBase obj in GameObjects)
    {
        // Is this a SpriteObject?
        if (obj is SpriteObject)
        {
            // Yes... Cast it to a SelectableSpriteObject
            spriteObj = (SpriteObject)obj;
            // Is the point in the object?
            if (spriteObj.IsPointInObject(testPosition))
            {
                // Add to the array
                hits[hitCount] = spriteObj;
                hitCount += 1;
            }
        }
    }

    // Trim the empty space from the end of the array
    Array.Resize(ref hits, hitCount);

    return hits;
}
```

The second function, GetSpriteAtPoint, returns just a single sprite and attempts to find the frontmost sprite at the specified location. It does this by keeping track of the LayerDepth value for each matching sprite. When subsequent sprites are ready to be checked, they are compared against the LayerDepth of the previous matching sprite and ignored if the value is higher (remember that lower values appear in front of higher values).

If LayerDepth values are found to be equal, the check is still made, and the later sprite will supersede the earlier sprite if it also matches the hit point. Because XNA will normally draw sprites in the order requested when LayerDepth values match, later objects in the GameObjects collection will appear in front of earlier objects with a matching depth. This check therefore allows us to find the frontmost object even if LayerDepths are not being used.

The GetSpriteAtPoint function is shown in Listing 4–12.

Listing 4–12. Finding the frontmost sprite at a specified position

```
public SpriteObject GetSpriteAtPoint(Vector2 testPosition)
{
    SpriteObject spriteObj;
    SpriteObject ret = null;
    float lowestLayerDepth = float.MaxValue;

    // Loop for all of the SelectableSpriteObjects
```

```
        foreach (GameObjectBase obj in GameObjects)
        {
            // Is this a SpriteObject?
            if (obj is SpriteObject)
            {
                // Yes... Cast it to a SelectableSpriteObject
                spriteObj = (SpriteObject)obj;
                // Is its layerdepth the same or lower than the lowest we have seen so far?
                // If not, previously encountered objects are in front of this one
                // and so we have no need to check it.
                if (spriteObj.LayerDepth <= lowestLayerDepth)
                {
                    // Is the point in the object?
                    if (spriteObj.IsPointInObject(testPosition))
                    {
                        // Mark this as the current frontmost object
                        // and remember its layerdepth for future checks
                        ret = spriteObj;
                        lowestLayerDepth = spriteObj.LayerDepth;
                    }
                }
            }
        }

        return ret;
}
```

Hit Testing Example Projects

Two example projects demonstrating the hit test functionality can be found in the downloads for this chapter. The first, HitTesting, provides a demonstration of the accuracy of the hit testing functions that we have added to the SpriteObject class. A screenshot from this project can be seen in Figure 4–6.

Figure 4–6. A sample image from the HitTesting project

This example project creates a number of randomly positioned sprites, some of which have a square texture, whereas others have a circular texture. The sprites are rotated and scaled such that they form rectangles and ellipses. The objects can be touched to select them; all the objects that fall under the touch position will be selected and highlighted in red.

The image in Figure 4–6 is taken from the emulator, and the mouse cursor can be seen selecting some of the shapes that are displayed. The emulator is a great way to accurately explore the edges of the shapes because the mouse cursor is much more precise than a finger on a real device touch screen. You will see that the object really is selected only when it is touched inside its displayed shape and that the algorithms we are using for hit testing work exactly as required.

Inside the HitTestingGame.Update method you will find that there are actually two possible calls to object selection functions, one of which is in use (calling SelectAllMatches); the other is commented out (calling SelectFrontmost). SelectAllMatches finds all the objects at the touch point using the GetSpritesAtPoint function and selects all of them, whereas SelectFrontmost uses GetSpriteAtPoint and selects just the one sprite returned (if there is one).

Try swapping these over so that SelectFrontmost is called instead. You will find now that it is always the object in front that is selected when multiple objects overlap, as described in the previous section.

The project defines a new game object class called SelectableSpriteObject and adds to the basic SpriteObject functionality a new boolean property called Selected. It also overrides the SpriteColor property and returns a red color when the sprite is selected or the underlying sprite color if it is not. This simple class provides a useful mechanism for selecting sprites and visually indicating which are selected. We will use this same approach in the "Initiating Object Motion" section coming up in a moment.

The second example project, Balloons, turns the hit testing into a simple interactive game. Colored balloons gently float up the screen, and the player must pop them by touching them. This can be quite relaxing until too many balloons start to reach the top of the screen, at which point trying to pop them all becomes somewhat more frantic! A screenshot from the project is shown in Figure 4–7.

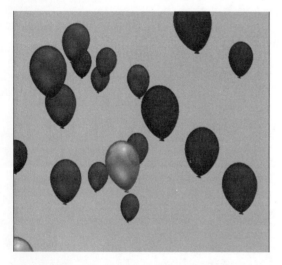

Figure 4–7. A sample image from the Balloons project

This project brings together a number of the things that you have learned during this and the previous chapters: it uses tinting to display the balloons in different colors, layer depths to render the balloons so that the smaller (more distant) balloons appear behind the larger (closer) balloons, raw TouchPanel input to determine when and where the user has touched the screen, and the GetSpriteAtPoint function to determine the frontmost balloon each time the screen is touched (this time using the layer depth to ensure that the frontmost balloon is selected).

This project has very little code and was very quick to put together, but it forms the basis of what could be an enjoyable game with a little more work.

Initiating Object Motion

You should now feel comfortable with reading user input from the touch screen. Before we finish examining screen input, let's discuss a couple of common movement patterns that you might want to include in your games: dragging and flicking.

Dragging Objects

The code required to drag objects is very straightforward. If a touch point is held, we simply need to find the movement distance between its current and previous locations and add it to the position of the objects that are being dragged.

The first part of dragging some objects is to allow them to be selected. Sometimes the selection will be a separate input from the drag (where the objects are tapped and then dragged afterward), but in most cases a drag will include object selection when contact with the screen is first established.

This is easy to do when using raw input as we can look for a TouchLocation.State value of Pressed. When it is detected, the object selection can be established ready for the objects to be dragged.

If we are using gestures, though, we have a problem: there is no gesture that is triggered when contact is first established with the screen. The tap gesture fires only when contact is released, and the drag gestures fire only once the touch point has moved far enough to be considered as actually dragging. So how do we perform the object selection?

The answer is to once again use raw input for this. Raw input and gestures can be mixed together so that the initial screen contact for object selection comes from raw input, and the dragging comes from a gesture.

Once the objects are selected, we can update them in response to the touch point moving around the screen. When using gestures, we simply look for one of the drag gestures and read out the Delta property of the GestureSample object. This contains the distance that the touch point has moved on each axis, which is exactly what we need.

■ **TIP** Don't forget that the HorizontalDrag and VerticalDrag gestures will provide only delta values for the appropriate axis. There is no need to cancel out or ignore the other movement axis because XNA takes care of this automatically.

To calculate the delta using raw input, we obtain the previous touch position using the TryGetPreviousLocation function and subtract that position from the current position. The result is the movement distance. The code for this is shown in Listing 4–13.

Listing 4–13. Calculating the drag delta when using raw touch input

```
if (touches[0].State == TouchLocationState.Moved)
{
    // Drag the objects. Make sure we have a previous position
    TouchLocation previousPosition;
    if (touches[0].TryGetPreviousLocation(out previousPosition))
    {
        // Calculate the movement delta
        Vector2 delta = touches[0].Position - previousPosition.Position;
        ProcessDrag(delta);
    }
}
```

Whichever method we used to calculate the delta, we now simply add the delta value to the position of all the selected sprites. They will then follow the touch location as it is moved around the screen.

Two example projects are provided to demonstrate this: DragAndFlick is a gesture-based implementation, whereas DragAndFlickRaw achieves the same effect using raw touch data. Both projects contain a SelectableSpriteObject class based on the one from the HitTesting project and contain identical functions for selecting the sprites at a point (SelectAllMatches), deselecting the sprites (DeselectAllObjects), and dragging the selected objects (ProcessDrag). There are some additional properties present, but we will look at them in the next section.

Try running both of the examples and see how they work. You'll notice that they don't feel exactly the same, even though they do essentially the same thing. The gesture-based project has a delay between when you move the touch point and when the objects actually respond to the movement. The reason for this is that the gesture system waits for the touch point to move a small distance before it considers a drag gesture to have started. As a result, it feels a little less responsive.

The raw touch input assumes that all movement is part of a drag, so there is no delay at all. As a result, it feels a lot more responsive. Bear this difference in mind when considering the input options that are available when you are coding your games.

Flicking Objects

With the object movement under our control, it is sometimes useful to allow the user to *flick* or *throw* them across the screen. This is often known as *kinetic* movement, and it consists of retaining the velocity at which the object is moving when the touch point is released and continuing to move the object in the same direction, gradually decreasing the speed to simulate friction.

To control the movement of the object, some new code has been added to the SelectableSpriteObject class. This code consists of a new Vector2 property called KineticVelocity, which tracks the direction and speed of movement; a float property called KineticFriction, which controls how strong the friction effect is (as a value between 0 and 1), and an Update override that applies the movement and the friction.

The Update code simply adds the velocity to the position, and then multiplies the velocity by the friction value. This function is shown in Listing 4–14. Notice how it uses the MathHelper.Clamp function to ensure that the friction is always kept between 0 and 1 (values outside of this range would cause the object to accelerate, which is probably undesirable, though perhaps it might be useful in one of your games!).

Listing 4–14. Updating the SelectableSpriteObject to allow it to observe kinetic movement

```
public override void Update(GameTime gameTime)
{
    base.Update(gameTime);

    // Is the movement vector non-zero?
    if (KineticVelocity != Vector2.Zero)
    {
        // Yes, so add the vector to the position
        Position += KineticVelocity;
        // Ensure that the friction value is within range
        KineticFriction = MathHelper.Clamp(KineticFriction, 0, 1);
        // Apply 'friction' to the vector so that movement slows and stops
        KineticVelocity *= KineticFriction;
    }
}
```

With the help of this code, the objects can respond to being flicked, so now we need to establish how to provide them with an initial KineticVelocity in response to the user flicking them. The example projects both contain a function called ProcessFlick, which accepts a delta vector as a parameter and provides it to all the selected objects.

To calculate this flick delta using the gesture input system is very easy. We have already looked at the Flick gesture and seen how to translate its pixels-per-second Delta value into pixels-per-update. We can do this now and provide the resulting Vector2 value to the ProcessFlick function, as shown in Listing 4–15.

Listing 4–15. Initiating object flicking using gesture inputs

```
while (TouchPanel.IsGestureAvailable)
{
    GestureSample gesture = TouchPanel.ReadGesture();
    switch (gesture.GestureType)
    {
        case GestureType.Flick:
            // The object has been flicked
            ProcessFlick(gesture.Delta * (float)TargetElapsedTime.TotalSeconds);
            break;
        [... handle other gestures here ...]
    }
}
```

Unfortunately, using raw input is a little more work. If we calculate the delta of just the final movement, we end up with a fairly unpredictable delta value because people tend to involuntarily alter their finger movement speed as they release contact with the screen. This is coupled with the fact that the Released state always reports the same position as the final Moved state, meaning that it alone doesn't provide us with any delta information at all.

To more accurately monitor the movement delta, we will build an array containing a small number of delta vectors (five is sufficient), and will add to the end of this array each time we process a Moved touch state. At the point of touch release, we can then calculate the average across the whole array and use it as our final movement delta.

This is implemented using three functions: ClearMovementQueue, AddDeltaToMovementQueue, and GetAverageMovementDelta. The first of these clears the array by setting all its elements to have coordinates of float.MinValue. We can look for this value when later processing the array and ignore any elements that have not been updated. ClearMovementQueue is called each time a new touch point is established with the screen.

AddDeltaToMovementQueue shifts all existing array elements down by one position and adds the provided delta to the end, as shown in Listing 4–16. This ensures that we always have the most recent delta values contained within the array, with older values being discarded. AddDeltaToMovementQueue is called each time we receive a touch point update with a state of Moved, with the delta vector calculated as described in the previous section.

Listing 4–16. Adding new delta values to the movement queue

```
private void AddDeltaToMovementQueue(Vector2 delta)
{
    // Move everything one place up the queue
    for (int i = 0; i < _movementQueue.Length - 1; i++)
    {
        _movementQueue[i] = _movementQueue[i + 1];
    }
    // Add the new delta value to the end
    _movementQueue[_movementQueue.Length - 1] = delta;
}
```

Finally, the GetAverageMovementDelta calculates the average of the values stored within the array, as shown in Listing 4–17. Any items whose values are still set to float.MinValue are ignored. The returned vector is ready to be passed into the ProcessFlick function. Of course, the movement array is storing deltas in distance-per-update format, so we have no need to divide by the update interval as we did for gestures. GetAverageMovementDelta is called (along with ProcessFlick) when a touch point is detected with a state of Released.

Listing 4–17. Calculating the average of the last five delta values

```
private Vector2 GetAverageMovementDelta()
{
    Vector2 totalDelta = Vector2.Zero;
    int totalDeltaPoints = 0;

    for (int i = 0; i < _movementQueue.Length; i++)
    {
        // Is there something in the queue at this index?
        if (_movementQueue[i].X > float.MinValue)
        {
            // Add to the totalMovement
            totalDelta += _movementQueue[i];
            // Increment to the number of points added
            totalDeltaPoints += 1;
        }
    }
    // Divide the accumulated vector by the number of elements
    // to retrieve the average
    return (totalDelta / totalDeltaPoints);
}
```

The main Update loop for the raw input example is shown in Listing 4–18. You will see here the situations that cause it to deselect objects, select objects, and reset the movement queue (when a new touch point is made), drag the objects and add their deltas to the movement queue (when an existing touch point is moved), and calculate the average and process the object flick (when a touch point is released).

Listing 4–18. The update code for selecting, dragging, and flicking objects using raw touch data

```
// Get the raw touch input
TouchCollection touches = TouchPanel.GetState();
// Is there a touch?
if (touches.Count > 0)
{
    // What is the state of the first touch point?
    switch (touches[0].State)
    {
        case TouchLocationState.Pressed:
            // New touch so select the objects at this position.
            // First clear all existing selections
            DeselectAllObjects();
            // The select all touched sprites
            SelectAllMatches(touches[0].Position);
            // Clear the movement queue
            ClearMovementQueue();
            break;
        case TouchLocationState.Moved:
            // Drag the objects. Make sure we have a previous position
            TouchLocation previousPosition;
            if (touches[0].TryGetPreviousLocation(out previousPosition))
            {
                // Calculate the movement delta
                Vector2 delta = touches[0].Position - previousPosition.Position;
                ProcessDrag(delta);
                // Add the delta to the movement queue
                AddDeltaToMovementQueue(delta);
            }
            break;
        case TouchLocationState.Released:
            // Flick the objects by the average queue delta
            ProcessFlick(GetAverageMovementDelta());
            break;
    }
}
```

Try flicking the objects in each of the two DragAndFlick projects. The behavior of this operation is much more consistent between the two than it was for dragging. Also try experimenting with different friction values and see how this affects the motion of the objects when they are flicked.

Finger-Friendly Gaming

When designing the input mechanisms for your game, always be aware that people will use their fingers to control things. Unlike stylus input that was commonly used on earlier generations of mobile devices, fingers are inherently inaccurate when it comes to selecting from small areas on the screen.

With a little planning, you can help the user to have a comfortable experience despite this limitation; without any planning, you can turn your game into an exercise in frustration! If you have lots of objects that can be selected in a small area, give some thought to how you can help the user to select the object they actually desire rather than having them continually miss their target.

One option is to allow users to hold their finger on the screen and slide around to select an object rather than simply tapping an object. As they slide their finger, a representation of the selected object can be displayed nearby to highlight the current selection (which, of course, will be obscured by the finger). Once users have reached the correct place, they can release contact, happy that they have picked the object they desired.

Another possibility is to magnify the area of the screen surrounding the touch point, making all the objects appear larger. Users can then easily select the object they want, at which point the magnified area disappears.

Finger-friendly input options don't need to involve a lot of additional work, especially if they are planned and implemented early in a game's development, and it is definitely a good idea to avoid putting off your target audience with fiddly and unpredictable input mechanisms wherever possible.

Reading the Keyboard and Text Input

There are two different areas where we might consider reading some form of keyboard input from the user: for controlling a game (by using the cursor keys, for example) and for text input (perhaps to enter a name in a high-score table).

The first of these requires the presence of a hardware keyboard. Keyboards can make a huge difference to some applications such as when taking notes or writing e-mail, and they can be useful for gaming, too.

Some of your users will have such a keyboard, and others (probably the majority) will not. For this reason, it is strongly advised not to make having a hardware keyboard a requirement of your game. By all means allow the keyboard to enhance the gaming experience, but please do ensure that it still works for those users who have only a touch screen for control.

For text input, users can type on a hardware keyboard if they have one, or use the onscreen keyboard known as the Soft Input Panel (SIP) if they do not. The methods both produce the same end result from the perspective of your game: it can ask for some text input, which it receives from the user. Exactly how the user enters it is not something that your game needs to worry about.

Let's take a look at how to interact with hardware keyboards and how to get the user to enter some text into your game.

Using a Hardware Keyboard

Just as XNA provides the TouchPanel object to allow us to read input from the touch screen, it also provides the Keyboard object to allow keyboard input to be read. It provides a single method, GetState, which provides a snapshot of the current keyboard activity. Just as with the TouchPanel, this object allows us to poll the keyboard state rather than use an event-based model such as the one you might be familiar with if you have spent time in WinForms development.

GetState returns a KeyboardState object from which we can read whatever information we need to control a game. There are three methods that can be called on the KeyboardState object:

- GetPressedKeys returns an array of Keys values from which the complete set of current pressed keys can be read. If you want to allow a large range of keys to be used (such as to read the input when the user is typing, for example), this is probably the best method for querying the keyboard. Note that the array contains simple keycodes and nothing more: no information about pressed or released states is contained within this data.

- IsKeyDown returns a boolean indicating whether a specific key (provided as a parameter) is currently pressed down.

- IsKeyUp is the reverse of IsKeyDown, checking to see whether a specific key is not currently pressed.

All these functions operate using the XNA-provided Keys enumeration. This enumeration includes a huge range of keys that might potentially be pressed, even though some of them won't exist on any given target device. The alphabetical characters have values in the enumeration with names from A to Z; because the enumeration deals only with pressed keys rather than typed characters, there is no provision for lowercase letters. The numeric digits are represented by the names D0 to D9 (enumerations do not allow names starting with digits, so a prefix had to be applied to these items to make their names valid). The cursor keys are represented by the values named Up, Down, Left, and Right.

■ **TIP** If you are unsure about which enumeration item corresponds to a key on the keyboard, add some code to your Update function that waits for GetPressedKeys to return one or more items and then set a breakpoint when this condition is met. You can then interrogate the contents of the Keys array to see which keycode has been returned.

Direct Keyboard Polling

The example project KeyboardInput provides a very simple implementation of moving a sprite around the screen using the cursor keys. The code to perform this, taken from the Update function, is shown in Listing 4–19.

Listing 4–19. Using the keyboard to move a sprite

```
// Move the sprite?
if (Keyboard.GetState().IsKeyDown(Keys.Up)) sprite.PositionY -= 2;
if (Keyboard.GetState().IsKeyDown(Keys.Down)) sprite.PositionY += 2;
if (Keyboard.GetState().IsKeyDown(Keys.Left)) sprite.PositionX -= 2;
if (Keyboard.GetState().IsKeyDown(Keys.Right)) sprite.PositionX += 2;
```

If you are lucky enough to have a device with a hardware keyboard, you can try the example and see how it responds. If you don't have such a device, you can use the emulator to experiment instead. But you will notice something that seems to be a bit of a problem here: pressing the cursor keys in the emulator has no effect; the sprite doesn't move at all.

The reason for this is that the emulator disables keyboard input by default. There are three keys that can be pressed on the PC keyboard to change this: the Page Up key will enable keyboard input, Page Down will disable it, and the Pause/Break key will toggle its enabled state. By default, keyboard input is disabled.

Press the Page Up key and then try the cursor keys again. The sprite should spring into life (if it doesn't, click within the screen area of the emulator and try pressing Page Up again). Knowing how to enable the keyboard is useful in other areas within the emulator, too—it makes it much easier to use the web browser, for example!

Polling for input in this way is ideal for games. There is no *keyboard repeat delay* between the first report of a key being pressed and subsequent reports for the same key, and no *repeat speed* to worry about that would cause delays between reports of a held key even after the initial delay had expired. Polling gives us a true and accurate picture of each key state every time we ask for it.

It also allows us to easily check for multiple keys pressed together. If you try pressing multiple cursor keys, you will see that the sprite is happy to move diagonally. This is perfect for gaming, in which pressing multiple keys together is a common requirement.

Checking for Key Pressed and Key Released States

If you need to monitor for the point in time where the user has just pressed or released a key, XNA's Keyboard object doesn't provide any information to this effect for you to use. It is easy to work this out with a little extra code, however.

Once the keyboard state has been read, the returned KeyboardState structure keeps its values even after the keyboard state has moved on. By keeping a copy of the previous state and comparing it with the current state, we can tell when a key has been pressed or released: if it was up last time but is down now, the key has just been pressed; if it was down last time but is up now, it has just been released.

We can easily use this approach to look for individual keys or can loop through the array returned from GetPressedKeys in order to look for all keys that were pressed or released since the last update. Listing 4–20 shows how details of all pressed and released keys can be printed to the Debug window. This code can also be found within the KeyboardInput example project.

Listing 4–20. Checking for pressed and released keys

```
// Read the current keyboard state
currentKeyState = Keyboard.GetState();

// Check for pressed/released keys.
// Loop for each possible pressed key (those that are pressed this update)
Keys[] keys = currentKeyState.GetPressedKeys();
for (int i = 0; i < keys.Length; i++)
{
    // Was this key up during the last update?
    if (_lastKeyState.IsKeyUp(keys[i]))
    {
        // Yes, so this key has been pressed
        System.Diagnostics.Debug.WriteLine("Pressed: " + keys[i].ToString());
    }
}
// Loop for each possible released key (those that were pressed last update)
keys = _lastKeyState.GetPressedKeys();
for (int i = 0; i < keys.Length; i++)
{
    // Is this key now up?
    if (currentKeyState.IsKeyUp(keys[i]))
    {
        // Yes, so this key has been released
        System.Diagnostics.Debug.WriteLine("Released: " + keys[i].ToString());
    }
}

// Store the state for the next loop
_lastKeyState = currentKeyState;
```

There are two important things to remember when monitoring for pressed and released keys. First, you must check them during every single update if you want to avoid missing key state updates. Second, you should query the keyboard state only once per update and should store this retrieved state data away for use during the next update. Without following this approach, the state might change between the individual calls to GetState resulting in key state changes being overwritten and lost.

Prompting the User to Enter Text

The Keyboard object provides a simple way to read the keyboard for controlling a game, but if you want your user to enter text it is generally not the best approach. The two main reasons are that it takes quite a lot of code to process all the keyboard state changes to build up the user's text string, and (more importantly) that users without keyboards will be completely unable to enter any text at all.

We can prompt the user to enter text using the SIP, which resolves both of the issues with reading the keyboard directly: the code is simple to develop and use, and the onscreen keyboard means that users relying on the touch screen for text entry can still continue to play your game. An example of this input dialog can be found in the SoftInputPanel example project.

To initiate text entry, we use the XNA Guide class and call its static BeginShowKeyboardInput method. This will cause the screen to be taken over by a text input box with the SIP displayed for touch screen users. We can provide a title for the input dialog, a message for the user, and a default value to display within the text input area. A screenshot of the input screen can be seen in Figure 4–8.

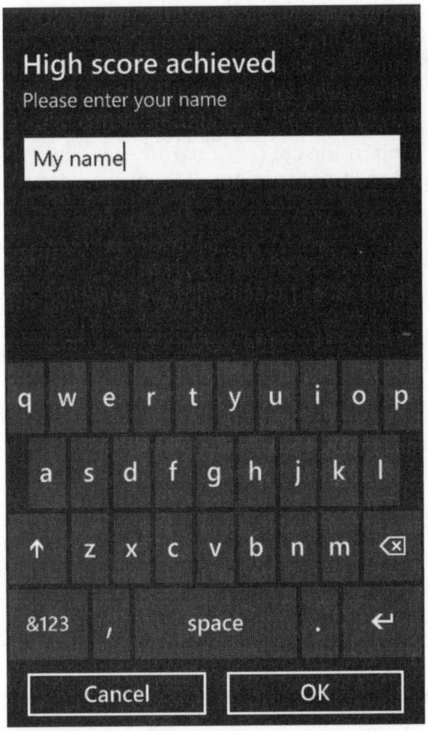

Figure 4–8. Entering text using the SIP

The code required to initiate the input panel shown in Figure 4–8 is shown in Listing 4–21. It first ensures that the keyboard is not already visible and then opens the input window for the user to use.

Listing 4–21. Displaying the text entry dialog window

```
// Make sure the input dialog is not already visible
if (!(Guide.IsVisible))
{
    // Show the input dialog to get text from the user
    Guide.BeginShowKeyboardInput(PlayerIndex.One, "High score achieved",
                    "Please enter your name", "My name", InputCallback, null)
}
```

From left to right, the parameters for BeginShowKeyboardInput are as follows:

- player. This is the number of the player for whom the dialog is to be displayed. Because we have only single-player support on the phone, this will always be set to PlayerIndex.One.

- title. The title will be displayed at the top of the input dialog.

- description. The description will be shown below the title in smaller text.

- defaultText. An initial value to display in the input field.

- callback. The address of a function that will be called once the input dialog is complete.

- state. A user-provided object for the input dialog. This can be passed as null.

When the input dialog completes (by the user entering some text and clicking the OK button, or by clicking the Cancel button), XNA will call into the function specified in the callback parameter. This function must be declared with void return type, and with a single parameter of type IAsyncResult.

When the function is called, it can read the user-entered string by calling the Guide.EndShowKeyboardInput method, passing in the IAsyncResult object. This will return either a string containing the entered string or null if the input dialog was canceled. Listing 4–22 shows the implementation of the callback function from the SoftInputPanel example.

Listing 4–22. A callback function for the text entry dialog window

```
void InputCallback(IAsyncResult result)
{
    string sipContent = Guide.EndShowKeyboardInput(result);

    // Did we get some input from the user?
    if (sipContent != null)
    {
        // Store it in the text object
        ((TextObject)GameObjects[0]).Text = "Your name is " + sipContent;
    }
    else
    {
        // The SIP was canceled
        ((TextObject)GameObjects[0]).Text = "Name entry was canceled.";
    }
}
```

One thing to be aware of when using the input dialog is that it is not synchronous. You might expect that your game will stop running while the dialog is open, but this is not the case: the game continues to run in the background the whole time.

There might be some useful aspects to this—for example, it will allow you to keep your music and sound effects generating (a subject we will be covering in the next chapter). In terms of the game, however, you might want to have this pause while the dialog is open.

We can achieve this very easily by checking the Guide.IsVisible property (which you already saw in Listing 4–21). If this returns true, skip updating the game objects or any other game logic during that call to Update. Once the function returns false, the dialog has closed, and updates can be resumed once again.

Reading the Accelerometer

An *accelerometer* is a device contained within the phone that can report the device's current orientation or position. In other words, it can tell if the device is lying flat on a desk, being held upright, rotated onto its side, or is in any position in between. Accelerometers have become common in mobile devices over the last couple of years and are a required component of all Windows Phone 7 devices, so they can be used in games as another interesting input device.

This information presents all sorts of opportunities for games. If we can tell the angle of the device, we can use it as a control mechanism. Instead of touching the screen or pressing a button to move objects on the screen, the player can simply tilt the device in whatever direction is needed to affect the gameplay.

In this section we will investigate how to read and interpret the data from the Windows Phone 7 device accelerometer. The code presented here can be found in the Accelerometer example project, an image from which is shown in Figure 4–9.

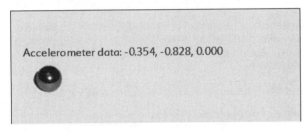

Figure 4–9. Rolling a ball around the screen using the accelerometer

Initializing the Accelerometer

The classes that provide access to the accelerometer are not actually part of XNA, but are instead provided via one of the standard Windows Phone 7 libraries: Microsoft.Devices.Sensors. In order to access it, you must first add a reference to it.

Once the reference has been added, we can add a using directive, as shown in Listing 4–23, to save having to fully qualify the namespace each time we want to refer to the sensor classes.

Listing 4–23. Adding a using directive for the Microsoft.Devices.Sensors namespace

```
using Microsoft.Devices.Sensors;
```

Next we declare a class-level variable to hold an instance of the Accelerometer object, as shown in Listing 4–24. This will be created during initialization and will remain for the duration of the game.

Listing 4–24. Declaring a class variable to hold the Accelerometer object instance

```
private Accelerometer _accelerometer;
```

With these code sections in place, we can now instantiate and initialize the Accelerometer object inside the game's Initialize method. The code required for this is shown in Listing 4–25. After creating an instance, the code adds an event handler for the accelerometer's ReadingChanged event. Unlike touch panel and keyboard input, the accelerometer provides data updates using an event rather than allowing us to poll it. In the event we can store the most recent reading, however, and then query this on demand whenever we want, which gives just the same effect from the perspective of our game code.

Once the object has been created and set up, we call its Start method so that it begins feeding information to us.

Listing 4–25. Instantiating and initializing the accelerometer object

```
// Instantiate the accelerometer
_accelerometer = new Accelerometer();
// Add an event handler
_accelerometer.ReadingChanged += AccelerometerReadingChanged;
// Start the accelerometer
_accelerometer.Start();
```

Finally we need to provide the AccelerometerReadingChanged event handler that we provided to the accelerometer object. This is very simple and is shown in Listing 4–26. The accelerometer provides three values, consisting of a reading for the X, Y, and Z axes. These are stored into a Vector3 structure stored in the class-level variable _accelerometerData.

Listing 4–26. Storing the data from the accelerometer each time it provides an updated reading.

```
void AccelerometerReadingChanged(object sender, AccelerometerReadingEventArgs e)
{
    AccelerometerData = new Vector3((float)e.X, (float)e.Y, (float)e.Z);
}
```

■ **NOTE** The Vector3 structure is very similar to the Vector2 structure that we've been using during the last few chapters, except that it stores an additional Z component to represent the third dimension. We will be using Vector3 structures a lot more in the next chapter once we start working with 3D graphics.

Using the Accelerometer Data

We can now read the x, y, and z axis readings from the accelerometer. Together they provide a reading of the acceleration of the device relative to freefall. What exactly does that mean?

First, let's look at the vector itself. It contains three properties that can be used to interrogate the device orientation: X, Y, and Z. Each of them is a float value that represents the movement of the device in the real world in the appropriate axis. If the device is lying flat and face up on a table, the values returned for the vector will be approximately as follows:

```
X = 0, Y = 0, Z = -1
```

The value -1 represents the full force of gravity applied along the appropriate axis. The x axis represents the direction between the left and right edges of the device, the y axis the direction between the top and bottom of the device, and the z axis the direction between the front and back of the device. As gravity is pulling the device toward its back while it lies flat on the table, the accelerometer shows a value of -1 on the z axis (-1 on this axis represents the back of the device, whereas +1 represents the front of the device, and this is what would appear if the device were put face down on the table).

This z value reading is very useful because it means we always get a movement reading relative to the force of gravity, even when the device is not in motion. By working out which of the x, y, and z axes the reading applies to, we can therefore work out which way up the device is.

As you've seen, with the device face up, we get a negative reading on the z axis. With the device upright, the accelerometer returns a value of -1 on the y axis (and upright but upside down, it returns the opposite value, 1). Turn the device on its side and you'll get a value between -1 and 1 on the x axis, depending on which way the device has rotated. All orientations between these extremes return values spread across the three axes.

Because our screen is only two-dimensional, we can for the most part ignore the value on the z axis. We can instead read out the x and y values and apply them as acceleration to objects in the game. When the device is flat on the desk, x and y are 0, so our objects don't move at all. Tip the device up, and the x and y values change based on the tilt angle, providing acceleration for our objects—the steeper the tilt, the faster the acceleration.

The Accelerometer project in the accompanying downloads includes all the code required to move a ball around on the screen under control of the accelerometer. It also displays the vector values on the screen, so you can easily see the data coming back from the accelerometer as you change the orientation of your device.

The project contains a single game object: BallObject, which is mostly just the same as the objects we have looked at in earlier projects. The ball offers a Velocity vector, and in its Update method it adds this to the ball position, bouncing if the edges of the screen are hit.

The one new addition is the use of the accelerometer data within the Update code. It retrieves the data from the game class, adds the accelerometer's x axis reading to its horizontal velocity and subtracts its y axis reading from its vertical velocity, as shown in Listing 4–27. This is what makes the ball move in response to the device being rotated. As you can see, we observe only the x and y axis readings because the z axis doesn't do anything useful in this 2D environment.

Listing 4–27. Applying the accelerometer data to the ball velocity

```
// Add the accelerometer vector to the velocity
Velocity += new Vector2(_game.AccelerometerData.X, -_game.AccelerometerData.Y);
```

You now have all the code that is required to simulate a ball rolling around a virtual desktop. Try running the project on a device and see how the ball reacts to the device being tilted. Observe the way the ball moves faster when the device is tilted at a steeper angle.

There are a couple of additional things to be aware of when using the accelerometer. First, unlike touch input, the returned vector is not automatically rotated to match the orientation of the screen. The values will be completely unaffected by rotating the device, so you will have to compensate for this in your game code if your game plays in a non-portrait orientation.

Second, if your game has been configured to allow multiple orientations (as we discussed back in Chapter 2), XNA will automatically rotate your display whenever it detects that the device has been rotated to a different orientation. This might be useful for non-accelerometer-based games, but if the screen flips upside down every time the player tries to roll a ball toward the top of the screen, it will quickly become very annoying. To cure this, ensure that you explicitly specify a single supported orientation when working with the accelerometer.

Simulating the Accelerometer in the Emulator

If you want to work with an accelerometer in the Windows Phone 7 emulator, there is an obvious problem: the emulator has no access to an accelerometer so always returns a vector containing the values (0, 0, -1). This makes it very hard to test your game unless on a real device.

There have been various clever workarounds for this problem suggested on the Internet (including hooking a Nintendo Wii controller up to the PC and using its accelerometer), but they involve a fairly considerable amount of effort to get working. We can take advantage of a couple of much simpler options: use the touch screen to simulate accelerometer data or use the keyboard to simulate rotation of the device.

Either way, we want to ensure that this happens only when running on the emulator, not on a real device. Microsoft has provided a way to determine whether we are running in the emulator, and it can be accessed by adding a reference to the Microsoft.Phone DLL. Once this has been added, we can query the Microsoft.Devices.Environment.DeviceType property, which will return either Device or Emulator as appropriate.

Having determined that we are running in the emulator, we can now apply either of the two accelerometer simulation methods described. The first of these, using the touch screen, is shown in Listing 4–28. It calculates the position of the touch point across the width and height of the screen and uses this position to derive a value for the AccelerometerData vector. It sets just the x and y axis values, leaving the z value set permanently at 0.

Listing 4–28. Simulating the accelerometer using touch screen input

```
void AccelerometerReadingChanged(object sender, AccelerometerReadingEventArgs e)
{
    if (Microsoft.Devices.Environment.DeviceType == Microsoft.Devices.DeviceType.Device)
    {
        AccelerometerData = new Vector3((float)e.X, (float)e.Y, (float)e.Z);
    }
    else
    {
        // Use the touch screen to simulate the accelerometer
        float x, y;
        TouchCollection touches;
        touches = TouchPanel.GetState();
        if (touches.Count > 0)
        {
            x = (touches[0].Position.X - Window.ClientBounds.Width / 2)
                                        / (Window.ClientBounds.Width / 2);
            y = -(touches[0].Position.Y - Window.ClientBounds.Height / 2)
                                        / (Window.ClientBounds.Height / 2);
            AccelerometerData = new Vector3(x, y, 0);
```

```
        }
    }
}
```

This code provides an intuitive method for providing simulated accelerometer data, but has the problem that it requires touch screen interaction, which could interfere with other parts of your game that rely on the touch screen. The second method avoids this problem by using the keyboard cursor keys. They are much less likely to be used in a game and so reduce the likelihood of interference.

The problem with using the cursor keys like this is that it is much harder to keep track of which way the simulated accelerometer vector is pointing. For this reason it is very useful to add a text object to the game and use it to display the content of the AccelerometerData property on the screen. You can then refer to this in order to get your bearings. The keyboard-based simulation code is shown in Listing 4–29.

Listing 4–29. Simulating the accelerometer using touch keyboard input

```
void AccelerometerReadingChanged(object sender, AccelerometerReadingEventArgs e)
{
    if (Microsoft.Devices.Environment.DeviceType == Microsoft.Devices.DeviceType.Device)
    {
        AccelerometerData = new Vector3((float)e.X, (float)e.Y, (float)e.Z);
    }
    else
    {
        // Use the cursor keys on the keyboard to simulate the accelerometer
        Vector3 accData = AccelerometerData;
        if (Keyboard.GetState().IsKeyDown(Keys.Left)) accData.X -= 0.05f;
        if (Keyboard.GetState().IsKeyDown(Keys.Right)) accData.X += 0.05f;
        if (Keyboard.GetState().IsKeyDown(Keys.Up)) accData.Y += 0.05f;
        if (Keyboard.GetState().IsKeyDown(Keys.Down)) accData.Y -= 0.05f;
        // Ensure that the data stays within valid bounds of -1 to 1 on each axis
        accData.X = MathHelper.Clamp(accData.X, -1, 1);
        accData.Y = MathHelper.Clamp(accData.Y, -1, 1);
        // Put the vector back into the AccelerometerData property
        AccelerometerData = accData;
    }
    // Display the accelerometer data in a text object
    _accText.Text = "Accelerometer data: " + AccelerometerData.X.ToString("0.000")
                    + ", " + AccelerometerData.Y.ToString("0.000")
                    + ", " + AccelerometerData.Z.ToString("0.000");
}
```

Both of these mechanisms are present in the Accelerometer example project, though the keyboard mechanism is commented out. Try swapping between them to see how each one feels.

Game in Focus: Cosmic Rocks (Part II)

So now that we are comfortable with all the options for reading input from the user, let's use them to add to the *Cosmic Rocks* game that we started building in the last chapter. The rest of this chapter will focus on using input techniques to turn the project into an actual playable game.

There are three actions that we need to be able to support: shooting in a specified direction, firing the ship thrusters to move the spaceship forward, and hitting the hyperspace button to randomly transport the player to another location on the screen.

There are various touch-based mechanisms that we could use to implement these actions. It would seem sensible to make tapping the screen the instruction for the spaceship to shoot. Thrusting has various options, which include allowing the user to drag the ship or to hold a point on the screen to indicate that the ship should fly toward that position. Hyperspace needs to be easily accessible, but not interfere with either of the other controls.

After some experimentation, the following controls were found to be the most natural-feeling:

- *Shoot*: Tap the screen. The spaceship will rotate toward the touch point and shoot.

- *Thrust*: Hold contact with the screen. The spaceship will rotate toward the touch point and thrust forward.

- *Hyperspace*: Pinch the screen. Using multitouch allows a clear indication of the player's intention without having to worry about distinguishing hyperspace requests from moving or shooting.

Let's see how each of these controls is implemented and then build the rest of the game. There's quite a lot of new code involved, and not all of it is featured here for space reasons. The full project can be found in the CosmicRocksPartII example project from the accompanying downloads for this chapter.

Making the Player's Ship Shoot

Tapping the screen actually causes two things to happen: the ship will begin to rotate to face the tapped position and it will shoot a "bullet" (or an energy bolt or whatever we decide to make it). It will shoot in whichever direction it is facing at the time the screen is tapped, which might not be toward the touch point, but repeated taps of the screen will ultimately get the bullets going in the direction the player wants.

As we observed back in the gestures discussion, using the Tap gesture is not quite as responsive as using raw touch data because it misses some of the user's touches. Because it is important for our game to feel as responsive as possible, we will bypass gestures and use raw touch data instead. We can easily tell that the user has touched the screen by waiting for a touch point with a state of Pressed.

The code that takes care of this can be found within the SpaceshipObject.Update method, and the relevant portion of it is shown in Listing 4–30.

Listing 4–30. Detecting and handling taps on the screen

```
// Is the player tapping the screen?
TouchCollection tc = TouchPanel.GetState();
if (tc.Count == 1)
{
    // Has the first touch point just been touched?
    if (tc[0].State == TouchLocationState.Pressed)
    {
        // Yes, so rotate to this position and fire
        RotateToFacePoint(tc[0].Position);
        // Shoot a bullet in the current direction
        FireBullet();
        // Note the time so we can detect held contact
        _holdTime = DateTime.Now;
    }
}
```

■ **NOTE** We are reading input values in the SpaceshipObject class because this is where we need to actually process it. You can process input wherever you like, but you need to ensure that all TouchPanel inputs are retrieved just once per update, and all gestures are processed just once per update, too. Reading either of these more than once per update will result in inputs being retrieved in one place but not the other, which can be very confusing to track down and debug.

On detection of a new touch, it calls two functions: RotateToFacePoint and FireBullet. It also puts the time into a class variable called _holdTime, but you'll look at that in more detail when we discuss ship movement in the next section.

Each of the two called functions is simple in concept, but deserve a little more exploration about its implementation.

Rotating the Ship to Face a Point

To rotate to face a particular angle, we need to use some trigonometry. For those of you not of a mathematical persuasion, don't panic! This really isn't too complicated, thanks in part to some of the functionality provided by XNA.

In order to rotate to a point, we first need to find the distance of the point from the spaceship's own position. We have a Vector2 for the spaceship and another for the touch point, so to find the distance we can simply subtract the spaceship position from the touch point. This is the first thing that the RotateToFacePoint function does, the beginning of which is shown in Listing 4–31. If it finds that the touch point is exactly the same as the spaceship position, it returns without doing anything because there is no real way to know which direction we should turn toward in order to look exactly at ourselves.

Listing 4–31. Finding the direction of the touch point relative to the spaceship position

```
private void RotateToFacePoint(Vector2 point)
{
    // Find the angle between the spaceship and the specified point.
    // First find the position of the point relative to the position of the spaceship
    point -= Position;

    // If the point is exactly on the spaceship, ignore the touch
    if (point == Vector2.Zero) return;
```

Now we are ready to find the angle toward which we need to face. Before doing this, the code ensures that the current sprite Angle property is greater or equal to 0 radians, and less than 2 PI radians (360 degrees). The reason is that we can actually end up rotating outside of this range, as you will see shortly.

Once this has been established, the sprite angle is converted into degrees. Personally I find working in radians quite uncomfortable and I much prefer degrees, so this makes the code much easier to understand. There is, of course, a small performance hit for performing this conversion, so if you can work in radians (or convert your code back to using radians once you have it working), it will run a little faster as a result.

Now for the trigonometry. XNA provides a Math class function called Atan2, which returns the angle through which we need to rotate from 0 radians in order to face the specified point—exactly what we need. Because we are now storing the touch point in object space, we can simply find the angle needed to face the point and we are there—well, nearly, anyway. To keep things using the same measurements, we convert the return value from Atan2 into degrees. The code is shown in Listing 4–32.

Listing 4–32. Finding the angle required to face the touch point

```
// Ensure that the current angle is between 0 and 2 PI
while (Angle < 0) { Angle += MathHelper.TwoPi; }
while (Angle > MathHelper.TwoPi) { Angle -= MathHelper.TwoPi; }
// Get the current angle in degrees
float angleDegrees;
angleDegrees = MathHelper.ToDegrees(Angle);

// Calculate the angle between the ship and the touch point, convert to degrees
float targetAngleDegrees;
targetAngleDegrees = MathHelper.ToDegrees((float)Math.Atan2(point.Y, point.X));
```

We have a little more work to do, however. XNA considers 0 degrees to point straight upward, and we generally expect it to range from 0 to 360 degrees. Atan2 returns an angle in the range of -180 to 180 degrees, however, with 0 degrees pointing to the left instead of up.

To map this angle into the same space that XNA uses, we can first add 90 to the angle we have calculated. This puts the 0 degree angle pointing up again, and results in a range of -90 to 270 degrees. To get back to the positive degree range, we check to see whether the value is less than 0, and add 360 if it is. This finally results in an XNA-aligned angle in the range of 0 to 360. Listing 4–33 contains the calculations for this.

Listing 4–33. Aligning the Atan2 angle with the angle system used by XNA

```
// XNA puts 0 degrees upwards, whereas Atan2 returns it facing left, so add 90
// degrees to rotate the Atan2 value into alignment with XNA
targetAngleDegrees += 90;
// Atan2 returns values between -180 and +180, so having added 90 degrees we now
// have a value in the range -90 to +270. In case we are less than zero, add
// 360 to get an angle in the range 0 to 360.
if (targetAngleDegrees < 0) targetAngleDegrees += 360;
```

So do we now have an angle that we can turn to face? Well, yes we do, but making the spaceship jump immediately toward the touch point feels very unnatural. It is much nicer to get it to rotate toward the touch point, so let's transition from the current angle to the target angle.

To do this we will simply check to see whether the target angle is less than or greater than the current sprite angle. If they are not equal, we will move the sprite angle toward the target angle until they meet, at which point we have finished rotating.

There is a final complication here, however. If the current spaceship angle is at 350 degrees, and the calculated target angle is at 10 degrees, the approach that we have just discussed will cause the spaceship to rotate all the way around through 340 degrees in a counterclockwise direction, whereas it would be much more efficient for it to rotate just 20 degrees clockwise. This is illustrated in Figure 4–10. In practice, having the ship rotate like this is very jarring and will be very frustrating for the player who asked for only a minor rotation!

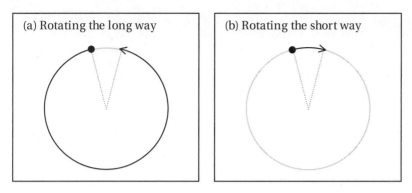

Figure 4–10. The long and the short way to rotate across the 0 degree boundary

To prevent this from happening, we will check to see whether the target angle is more than 180 degrees away from the current spaceship angle. If it is over 180 degrees above the spaceship angle, we subtract 360 from the target angle so that the spaceship rotates the other way (which will be less than 180 degrees and is thus the shorter angle). If it is over 180 degrees below the spaceship angle, we do the reverse and add 360 degrees to the target angle.

These will ensure that we always take the short route to the desired angle. It might also result in a target angle that is above 360 degrees or below 0 degrees, however. This itself doesn't cause any problems, but is the reason we ensure that the Angle value is between 0 and 2 PI back in Listing 4–32.

Listing 4–34 shows the remainder of the RotateToFacePoint function. Once the target angle has been calculated as described, it is converted back to radians and stored in the class-level _targetAngle variable.

Listing 4–34. Ensuring that the rotation always takes the short route, and storing the target angle ready for use

```
// Is the target angle over 180 degrees less than the current angle?
if (targetAngleDegrees < angleDegrees - 180)
{
    // Yes, so instead of rotating the whole way around to the left,
    // rotate the smaller distance to the right instead.
    targetAngleDegrees += 360;
}
// Is the target angle over 180 degrees more than the current angle?
if (targetAngleDegrees > angleDegrees + 180)
{
    // Yes, so instead of rotating the whole way around to the right,
    // rotate the smaller distance to the left instead.
    targetAngleDegrees -= 360;
}

// Store the calculated angle, converted back to radians
_targetAngle = MathHelper.ToRadians(targetAngleDegrees);
}
```

The end result of this is that the target angle has been calculated, taking the current angle into account, but the spaceship hasn't actually rotated at all. The rotation is performed in the SpaceshipObject.Update function, as shown in Listing 4–35. It rotates by 20 percent of the remaining angle difference, with the result that it rotates quickly at first and then more slowly as it approaches the desired angle. This gives a pleasingly smooth movement without too much delay getting to the target angle, even if the rotation is large.

Listing 4–35. Rotating the spaceship toward the target angle

```
// Rotate towards the target angle
if (Angle != _targetAngle)
{
    Angle += (_targetAngle - Angle) * 0.2f;
}
```

Firing a Bullet

The second function of tapping the screen is to fire a bullet. This is fairly simple to implement. We need a sprite that will initially appear at the same position and angle as the spaceship and will travel in the direction that the spaceship is facing.

The bullets are implemented in a new game object class, BulletObject. In addition to the standard SpriteObject properties, it also stores a movement vector that will be added to the position each update, and keeps track of the number of times the bullet has moved so that it can expire after it has traveled a certain distance.

To avoid having to create and destroy bullet objects each time one is fired or expired, we use the same approach as described for the ParticleObject in the previous chapter: we keep all the bullet objects that we create and mark them as inactive when they are no longer required. When a new object is required, we first look for an existing inactive object and create a new one only if no existing object can be found.

For this reason, all the volatile properties of the bullet are initialized in a function named InitializeBullet rather than in the class constructor because the constructor cannot be used when a bullet object is recycled.

InitializeBullet expects the bullet position and angle to be passed as its parameters. They are placed directly into its Position and Angle properties. It then needs to calculate its movement vector so that the bullet travels forward each update. This is easily calculated from the bullet angle using some more basic trigonometry: the Sine of the angle will provide the distance to move horizontally, whereas the Cosine will return the vertical distance. The code to perform this initialization is shown in Listing 4–36.

Listing 4–36. Initializing a bullet object

```
internal void InitializeBullet(Vector2 Position, float Angle)
{
    // Initialize the bullet properties
    this.Position = Position;
    this.Angle = Angle;

    // Calculate the velocity vector for the bullet
    _velocity = new Vector2((float)Math.Sin(Angle), -(float)Math.Cos(Angle));

    // Mark the bullet as active
    IsActive = true;
    // Reset its update count
    _updates = 0;
}
```

Updating the bullet requires a few simple tasks. First, the _velocity vector is added to the sprite position (it is actually multiplied by 10 to make the bullet move faster). Then the position is checked against the edge of the window and moved to the opposite edge if it goes off the screen. The _updates count is incremented, and if it reaches the lifetime of the bullet (defined as 40 updates), it is expired by setting its IsActive property to false.

Finally, the bullet position is checked against each of the rocks. This is similar to the spaceship collision detection described in the last chapter, but is actually a little easier: because the bullet is very small, we can consider it as being just a single point rather than a rectangle. The collision check is therefore simply a matter of seeing whether the distance from the rock position to the bullet position is less than the rock size. The CheckForCollision function is shown in Listing 4–37.

Listing 4–37. Checking to see if the bullet object has collided with a rock

```
private void CheckForCollision()
{
    int objectCount;
    GameObjectBase gameObj;
    RockObject rockObj;
    float rockSize;
    float rockDistance;

    // Loop backwards through the rocks as we may modify the collection when a rock is
    // destroyed
    objectCount = _game.GameObjects.Count;
    for (int i = objectCount - 1; i >= 0;  i--)
    {
        // Get a reference to the object at this position
        gameObj = _game.GameObjects[i];
        // Is this a space rock?
        if (gameObj is RockObject)
        {
            // It is... Does its bounding rectangle contain the bullet position?
            rockObj = (RockObject)gameObj;
            if (rockObj.BoundingBox.Contains((int)Position.X, (int)Position.Y))
            {
                // It does.. See if the distance is small enough for them to collide.
                // First calculate the size of the object
                rockSize = rockObj.SpriteTexture.Width / 2.0f * rockObj.ScaleX;
                // Find the distance between the two points
                rockDistance = Vector2.Distance(Position, rockObj.Position);
                // Is the distance less than the rock size?
                if (rockDistance < rockSize)
                {
                    // Yes, so we have hit the rock
                    rockObj.DamageRock();
                    // Destroy the bullet
                    IsActive = false;
                }
            }
        }
    }
}
```

Note how the loop across the game objects runs backward; this is because we can remove rock objects from the collection when they are destroyed. This leads to a reduction in the collection size, which means that accessing the elements at the end would result in an out of bounds index. Looping backward ensures that the rocks we remove will always affect the indexes of only the objects that we have already processed, removing the need to worry about this situation.

The BulletObject class now contains all the code it needs to be initialized, to move, to collide with rocks, and to expire when it has traveled a set distance. All that is left is the code to create the bullet in response to the player tapping the screen.

This is handled in the SpaceshipObject.FireBullet function, shown in Listing 4–38. It tries to retrieve a bullet object using the GetBulletObject function (which we will examine in a moment); if one is obtained, it calls its InitializeBullet function as already detailed in Listing 4–36.

Listing 4–38. Firing a bullet from the player's ship

```
private void FireBullet()
{
    BulletObject bulletObj;

    // Try to obtain a bullet object to shoot
    bulletObj = GetBulletObject();
    // Did we find one?
    if (bulletObj == null)
    {
        // No, so we can't shoot at the moment
        return;
    }

    // Initialize the bullet with our own position and angle
    bulletObj.InitializeBullet(Position, Angle);
}
```

GetBulletObject uses exactly the same approach that we saw for obtaining ParticleObject instances in the previous chapter: it looks for an existing bullet object whose IsActive value is false. If one is found, it is returned. If no such object is found, it creates a new object. However, to make the game a little more challenging, we allow the player to have only four bullets active at any time. If these bullets are already present, GetBulletObject returns null to prevent any further bullets from being fired. The code for this function is shown in Listing 4–39.

Listing 4–39. Finding or creating a bullet object for the player to fire

```
private BulletObject GetBulletObject()
{
    int objectCount;
    int bulletCount = 0;
    GameObjectBase gameObj;
    BulletObject bulletObj = null;

    // Look for an inactive bullet
    objectCount = _game.GameObjects.Count;
    for (int i = 0; i < objectCount; i++)
    {
        // Get a reference to the object at this position
        gameObj = _game.GameObjects[i];
        // Is this object a bullet?
```

```
        if (gameObj is BulletObject)
        {
            // Count the number of bullets found
            bulletCount += 1;
            // Is it inactive?
            if (((BulletObject)gameObj).IsActive == false)
            {
                // Yes, so re-use this bullet
                return (BulletObject)gameObj;
            }
        }
    }

    // Did we find a bullet?
    if (bulletObj == null)
    {
        // No, do we have capacity to add a new bullet?
        if (bulletCount < MaxBullets)
        {
            // Yes, so create a new bullet
            bulletObj = new BulletObject(_game, _game.Textures["Bullet"]);
            _game.GameObjects.Add(bulletObj);
            return bulletObj;
        }
    }

    // No more bullets available
    return null;
}
```

Making the Player's Ship Move

When the player holds a point on the screen for a brief period, we will use that as the signal that the ship should fire its thrusters and move toward the point the user is touching. This gives a simple and intuitive mechanism for moving the ship around the screen.

We could have used the Hold gesture to initiate this, but it has a drawback in this situation: the time between initiating the hold and the Hold gesture triggering is too long—about a second, which is just too slow for a fast-moving game such as this one.

Instead, *Cosmic Rocks* uses the raw touch API to implement its own version of the hold gesture. The process is actually very simple:

- When a touch point with a state of Pressed is received, it stores the current time in a class-level variable.

- Each time the touch point returns a state of Moved, the current time is compared to the stored time. If sufficient time has elapsed between the two, the touch point is considered as being held and the thrust processing is executed.

The code from SpaceshipObject.Update required to perform this (which also includes the bullet firing check from the previous section) is shown in Listing 4–40. The code waits for 300 milliseconds (0.3 seconds) before it starts thrusting the ship. This figure seems to work well; increasing it makes the thrust control unresponsive, whereas lowering it makes it possible for the user to accidentally thrust when they were intending only to shoot.

Listing 4–40. Detecting a held touch point using raw touch data

```
// Is the player tapping the screen?
TouchCollection tc = TouchPanel.GetState();
if (tc.Count == 1)
{
    // Has the first touch point just been touched?
    if (tc[0].State == TouchLocationState.Pressed)
    {
        // Yes, so rotate to this position and fire
        RotateToFacePoint(tc[0].Position);
        // Shoot a bullet in the current direction
        FireBullet();
        // Note the time so we can detect held contact
        _holdTime = DateTime.Now;
    }
    if (tc[0].State == TouchLocationState.Moved)
    {
        // Has sufficient time passed to start thrusting?
        if (DateTime.Now.Subtract(_holdTime).TotalMilliseconds > 300)
        {
            // Yes, so thrust towards this position
            RotateToFacePoint(tc[0].Position);
            Thrust();
        }
    }
}
```

Once the hold is established, the code calls into a function called Thrust to initiate the movement of the spaceship. This is achieved in just the same method as for initializing the bullet: the ship's Angle is used to determine a movement vector. This vector is then added to the ship's existing velocity so that its existing movement is taken into account, too. This means that continuing to thrust in the same direction will cause the ship to accelerate, whereas thrusting in the opposite direction to movement will cause it to slow down and eventually stop.

The Thrust code is shown in Listing 4–41. In the game it also adds some particle objects to represent the thruster exhaust, but this is omitted from the listing here for brevity.

Listing 4–41. Thrusting—adding to the ship's velocity

```
private void Thrust()
{
    Vector2 shipFacing;

    // Calculate the vector towards which the ship is facing
    shipFacing = new Vector2((float)Math.Sin(Angle), -(float)Math.Cos(Angle));
    // Scale down and add to the velocity
    _velocity += shipFacing / 10;
}
```

The _velocity is applied in the SpaceshipObject.Update code, just as it has been for the bullets and rocks. Note that we don't apply any kind of friction to the spaceship; it is floating in a vacuum after all, so once the player has started moving it is quite a challenge to stop again!

Implementing Hyperspace

The final input control left to handle is for hyperspace. Hyperspace can be used as a last resort emergency measure when the player cannot escape from the approaching rocks. It makes the playership disappear for a few seconds before reappearing at a random location somewhere on the screen. This can be a life saver, but it can also cause the ship to reappear right on top of a rock so it needs to be used with caution.

We use the Pinch gesture as a trigger for hyperspace. This is easily accessed by the player, but is not something that is likely to be triggered accidentally.

Because using multitouch on the device emulator presents a problem in most development environments, we will also provide a keyboard function to trigger the hyperspace. This is unlikely to be useful on a real device, but makes testing much easier. Pressing H (for *hyperspace*) will be the trigger used to test in the emulator.

The input processing code relating to hyperspace is shown in Listing 4–42, taken from SpaceshipObject.Update.

Listing 4–42. Checking the user input for hyperspace

```
// Is the player pinching?
while (TouchPanel.IsGestureAvailable)
{
    GestureSample gesture = TouchPanel.ReadGesture();
    switch (gesture.GestureType)
    {
        case GestureType.Pinch:
            Hyperspace();
            break;
    }
}
// Did the player press 'H' on the keyboard?
// (Allows us to hyperspace on the emulator with no multitouch)
if (Keyboard.GetState().IsKeyDown(Keys.H)) Hyperspace();
```

Hyperspacing is implemented using two class-level variables: _hyperspaceZoom and _hyperspaceZoomAdd. Normally these are both set to zero, but when hyperspace is active the _hyperspaceZoomAdd variable is set to a value that is added to _hyperspaceZoom each update. While _hyperspaceZoom is greater than zero, the ship is in hyperspace.

Once _hyperspaceZoom reaches a certain level, _hyperspaceZoomAdd is negated so that it starts reducing the value of _hyperspaceZoom back toward zero. Once it reaches zero, the hyperspace is finished: both variables are set back to zero, and the spaceship update process returns to its normal state.

The Hyperspace function, shown in Listing 4–43, therefore simply sets the _hyperspaceZoomAdd variable to have a value of 5.

Listing 4–43. Initiating hyperspace

```
private void Hyperspace()
{
    // Initiate the hyperspace by setting the zoom add
    _hyperspaceZoomAdd = 5;
}
```

In Update, the code checks to see whether the _hyperspaceZoomAdd value is non-zero. If so, it is applied as has been described. When _hyperspaceZoom reaches its maximum level (defined in the listing as 150), the spaceship is put into a random new position, and _hyperspaceZoomAdd is negated. When _hyperspaceZoom reaches zero, the hyperspace variables are set to zero. The spaceship velocity is also cancelled, meaning that hyperspace is the one thing that can completely stop the ship from moving.

Note that the hyperspace processing code returns from the Update function at the end. This stops all other processing of the spaceship (movement, input controls, and so on) while hyperspacing is active.

Also note that all touch gestures are read and discarded before returning; this is important because without this they will queue up and all be processed together when the hyperspace has finished. If the gesture system reports a number of Pinch gestures in response to the user's initial input, it will result in the ship going into hyperspace over and over again until the whole queue is empty. Discarding the queued gestures ensures that these extra gesture reports will have no effect.

The relevant Update code is shown in Listing 4–44.

Listing 4–44. Updating the hyperspace variables

```
// Are we hyperspacing?
if (_hyperspaceZoomAdd != 0)
{
    // Add to the zoom
    _hyperspaceZoom += _hyperspaceZoomAdd;

    // Have we reached maximum zoom?
    if (_hyperspaceZoom >= 150)
    {
        // Yes, so move to the new location
        // Start to zoom back out
        _hyperspaceZoomAdd = -_hyperspaceZoomAdd;
        // Set a random new position
        PositionX = GameHelper.RandomNext(0,
                        _game.Window.ClientBounds.Width - SpriteTexture.Width)
                        + SpriteTexture.Width / 2;

        PositionY = GameHelper.RandomNext(0,
                        _game.Window.ClientBounds.Height - SpriteTexture.Height)
                        + SpriteTexture.Height / 2;
    }

            // Have we finished hyperspacing?
            if (_hyperspaceZoom <= 0)
            {
                // Yes, so cancel the hyperspace variables
                _hyperspaceZoom = 0;
                _hyperspaceZoomAdd = 0;
                // Stop movement
                _velocity = Vector2.Zero;
            }           // Discard any queued gestures and then return
            while (TouchPanel.IsGestureAvailable) { TouchPanel.ReadGesture(); }
            // Don't allow any other updates while hyperspacing
            return;
}
```

Finally, to indicate visually that hyperspace is in effect, we increase the scale of the ship and fade out its alpha across the duration of the hyperspace processing. This is achieved by overriding the ScaleX, ScaleY, and SpriteColor properties. The scale properties increase the return value based on the contents of the _hyperspaceZoom variable, whereas SpriteColor reduces the alpha level toward zero.

Because the _hyperspaceZoom value is 0 when not hyperspacing, these property overrides will have no effect unless the hyperspace is active. The overrides are shown in Listing 4–45.

Listing 4–45. Overriding the scale and color properties to indicate the progress through hyperspace

```
// If the player is hyperspacing, zoom the spaceship to indicate this
public override float ScaleX
{
    get { return base.ScaleX + (_hyperspaceZoom * 0.02f); }
}
// If the player is hyperspacing, zoom the spaceship to indicate this
public override float ScaleY
{
    get { return base.ScaleX + (_hyperspaceZoom * 0.02f); }
}

// If the player is hyperspacing, fade out the spaceship to indicate this
public override Color SpriteColor
{
    get
    {
        Color ret = base.SpriteColor;
        ret.A = (byte)MathHelper.Clamp(255 - _hyperspaceZoom * 2.5f, 0, 255);
        return ret;
    }
}
```

Considering Input Design

In this chapter, we have looked at all the different mechanisms that you have at your disposal when dealing with user interaction with your game.

The limited standard control mechanisms available to Windows Phone 7 devices mean that some thought might be needed to set up the input approach for your game. With no buttons or directional pad, some types of game can be a challenge to implement, whereas other game types will hugely benefit from the presence of the touch screen. The accelerometer is also useful as an input and can be used either in isolation or alongside the touch screen.

Before you start working on a game you should have a clear idea of how you expect the user to interact with it. These ideas might change during development, of course, but it is important to consider them before starting to try to avoid unexpected input problems once you have invested time in your game.

Cosmic Rocks is now looking and playing like a real game, and hopefully you are already finding it fun to play. It is, of course, still missing some important elements, such as moving to new levels, a score, and player lives. We could implement them with a little effort, but there is one other thing that it is missing that we haven't explored at all yet: sound. It will be the subject of the next chapter.

CHAPTER 5

■ ■ ■

Sounding Out with Game Audio

Our worlds have been very quiet so far; apart from the occasional sound of the screen being tapped, everything has moved in complete silence. That's no way for a game to be, so in this chapter, we'll make some noise by adding sound effects and music to our games.

Game audio plays a significant role in the experience that a player has when playing a game. A game with little or no sound feels hollow and empty, whereas distinctive and characteristic sound effects and music can really draw a player into the game and make it a much more absorbing event.

Mobile devices typically have less opportunity to impress in this regard than desktop PCs or game consoles because they are usually limited to smaller speakers, whereas PCs or consoles might well be hooked up to powerful surround sound systems. Headphones are likely to be commonly used with mobile devices, however, and they can provide very effective sound to your players.

Regardless of the way that the device is producing sound, you should still ensure that your games sound as good as possible. In this chapter, we'll explore just how you can go about achieving that goal.

Sound Effects and Music

XNA makes a distinction between two types of sound that it can play: sound effects and music. Sound effects are ideal for sounds that correspond to the actions taking place within your game, while music can be played on a loop in the background to accompany your game the whole time it is playing.

Each of these has certain requirements that must be taken into account, and various options that can affect the sound playback.

Let's start with looking at sound effects.

Playing Sound Effects

XNA provides a fair amount of flexibility for playing sound effects inside your games. It can play multiple sounds simultaneously (including multiple instances of the same sound) and offers control over volume levels, stereo panning, and pitch shifting. It can loop sounds or play them just once and also offers controls to allow sounds to be paused and resumed.

Note that sound effects are really intended just for sounds that take place as your game is playing. Microsoft's certification requirements (that your games will be required to meet when you want to distribute them through the Windows Phone Marketplace, as we will discuss in Chapter 15) stipulate that sound effects are not to be used for playing background music.

Adding Sound Effects to your Project

Sound effects are created as part of the Content project, as has been the case with all the other resource data (textures and sprite fonts) that we used in previous chapters. They are added in just the same way: by right-clicking the main Content project node inside Solution Explorer and then selecting Add / Existing Item. The sound file can then be located and added to the project.

You will see after adding a sound file that the content item's Content Importer is set to WAV Audio File, and the Content Processor is set to Sound Effect, as shown in Figure 5–1.

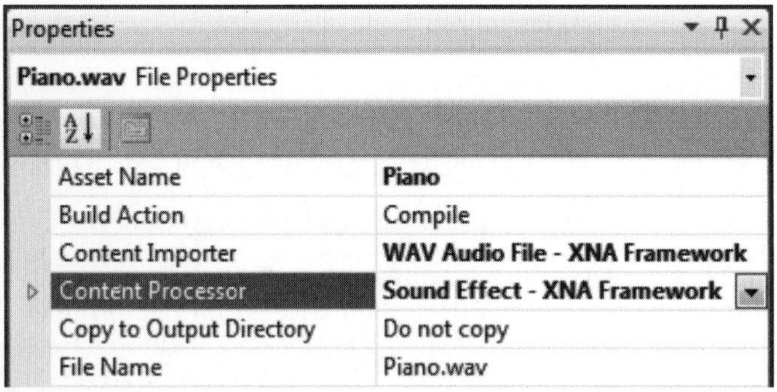

Figure 5–1. The properties for a WAV file added to an XNA Content project

All sound effects must be created from WAV files. WAV (short for Waveform Audio File Format) files are one of the oldest sound formats used by Microsoft. They usually store sound in an uncompressed format, making them easy to read and write, but result in large file sizes.

On desktop PCs, WAV files have largely been replaced by formats offering higher levels of compression such as MP3, but XNA unfortunately cannot use MP3 files for sound effects (though it does use them for background music, as you will see later in this chapter). As a result, we find ourselves with no choice but to use WAV files for our sounds.

■ **NOTE** It is possible to use MP3 or WMA files as sound effects by adding them and then changing the Content Processor from the initial value of Song back to Sound Effect (refer to Figure 5–1). Although this change will provide access to the sound from within your game, unfortunately during compilation the Sound Effect content processor will silently convert your MP3 or WMA file into a WAV file for the compiled game, resulting in the same large file that would have resulted from adding a WAV file in the first place.

Once the file has been added, we are ready to load it into our game. Once again, this is handled in the same way as with other resources that we have loaded from the Content project: using the Content.Load method. Listing 5–1 shows a piece of code that declares a SoundEffect object and loads it from the Content project. Just as before, we provide the Load method with the type of object that is being loaded.

Listing 5–1. Loading a sound effect from the Content project

```
SoundEffect mySound;
mySound = Content.Load<SoundEffect>("Piano");
```

■ **NOTE** The desktop versions of XNA can take advantage of an application called *XACT* (which is short for *cross-platform audio creation tool*), which can organize sound effects for easier playback within a game. XACT is only supported for Windows and Xbox360 XNA games, however, so cannot be used for Windows Phone 7 games.

Playing the Sound Effects

With a sound effect loaded, we are now ready to play it by simply calling the Play method of the SoundEffect object.

Two overloads of this method are available. The first takes no parameters and simply plays the sound at full volume. The second overload provides some additional control, allowing us to provide values for the volume level, the pitch, and the stereo panning of the sample:

- Volume is a float that specifies the playback volume level from 0 (silent) to 1 (full volume).

- Pitch is a float that controls the frequency of the sound playback. It is specified as a value between -1 (an octave lower than its native pitch) through 0 (its native pitch) to 1 (an octave higher than its native pitch). Values outside of this range will result in an exception, so if you need to play a sound using a larger range of pitches, you will need to load multiple differently pitched samples into your game.

- Pan is a float that controls the stereo position of the played sound. Values range from -1 (fully to the left) through 0 (centered) to 1 (fully right).

■ **NOTE** Sound effect volume is always played relative to the volume setting of the device, so a volume level of 1 actually means to play at the configured device volume level. When using the emulator, you can press F9 to increase the device volume level or press F10 to decrease it. Press the key repeatedly to reach full volume or to silence the emulated device.

Play is asynchronous and returns to your game immediately, leaving the sound playing in the background. If you call Play again before an earlier call has completed, the new sound will play alongside the older sound. Options to stop the earlier sound are provided via the SoundEffectInstance object, which we'll discuss in a moment.

Integrating Sound Effects into the Game Framework

Just as we have added GameFramework support for textures and fonts, so we will add support for sound effects too. This support is implemented using another Dictionary within the GameHost class, this time named SoundEffects. The declaration of the dictionary is shown in Listing 5–2.

Listing 5–2. The SoundEffects dictionary present within the GameFramework.GameHost class

```
// A dictionary of loaded sound effects.
public Dictionary<string, SoundEffect> SoundEffects { get; set; }
```

We can then use the dictionary to load sound effects in the same way as we do for textures and fonts, and can access the dictionary items anywhere within the game.

The SoundEffects example project that accompanies this chapter shows how sound effects can be loaded into the game engine and then played back. It loads four different samples (named EnergySound, Piano, MagicSpell, and Motorbike) and divides the screen into four regions to allow each to be played. Experiment with the project and with playing multiple sounds together.

The example project also sets the sound effect's panning based on the horizontal position of the screen tap. Tapping the left side of the screen will pan to the left; tapping the right will pan to the right.

Try experimenting with changing the source code to produce different volume levels and different pitches, too.

Sound Effect Instances

Calling the Play method on a SoundEffect object provides a very easy way to get a sound playing, and in many cases this will be sufficient. For gunfire, explosions, player achievement sounds and all sorts of other one-off effects, this is likely to be all that you need.

In other places, however, you might find that a greater level of control is needed over the sounds that you play. The ability to loop a sound, for example, can be very useful, but the functions provided by the SoundEffect class alone cannot offer this ability. The main reason is that we would have no way to stop the sound; we don't obtain a sound ID value or anything similar, so once several sounds were active we would be unable to tell the class which one it should stop.

This problem is resolved by the inclusion of the SoundEffectInstance class. Instances of this class are created by calling the CreateInstance method of a SoundEffect object.

SoundEffectInstance objects are very similar to SoundEffect objects, with the following key differences:

- Each instance can play only one sound at a time. Calling Play multiple times will have no effect. To play multiple sounds simultaneously using sound effect instances, multiple instance objects would need to be created from the underlying SoundEffect.

- The Volume, Pitch, and Pan of an instance are specified using class properties rather than as parameters to the Play method. This allows the properties to be easily altered after the sound has started playing.

- SoundEffectInstance objects contain a property named IsLooped that can be set to true to instruct the sound to loop.

- In addition to the Play method, effect instances also have methods to Pause and Stop the sound. They don't need to be used at all if the sound is not looping, but if it is looping one or other will likely be useful to stop the sound from playing. Pause will remember how much of the sound has been played and will resume from this point the next time Play is called. Stop will reset the sound so that it plays from the beginning when Play is next called. To find out whether a sound effect instance is stopped, paused, or playing, query its State property.

The SoundEffectInstances example project demonstrates the use of this class. It looks just the same as the SoundEffects example, but works in a different way. When you press and hold your finger on one of the sound panels, the sound will play and will loop endlessly. When you release your finger, the sound will pause. When the panel is touched again, playback resumes from where it left off (this is most noticeable with the Piano and Motorbike sounds). This behavior couldn't have been accomplished with just the SoundEffect class.

Additionally, if you slide your finger to the left and right as the sound is playing, the pitch of the sound will change in response. Once again, only the SoundEffectInstance allows this change to be made because the SoundEffect class only allows the pitch (as well as the volume and panning) to be set when the sound playback is first initiated.

The code that plays, repitches, and pauses the sounds, taken from the example project's Update method, is shown in Listing 5–3.

Listing 5–3. Playing, setting the pitch, and pausing SoundEffectInstances

```
TouchCollection tc = TouchPanel.GetState();
if (tc.Count > 0)
{
    // Find the region of the screen that has been touched
    screenRegion = (int)(tc[0].Position.Y * 4 / Window.ClientBounds.Height);
    // Ensure we have a region between 0 and 3
    if (screenRegion >= 0 && screenRegion <= 3)
    {
        // What type of touch event do we have?
        switch (tc[0].State)
        {
            case TouchLocationState.Pressed:
                // Set the pitch based on the horizontal touch position
                _soundInstances[screenRegion].Pitch =
                        (tc[0].Position.X / this.Window.ClientBounds.Width) * 2 - 1;
                // Start the sound for this region
                _soundInstances[screenRegion].Play();
                break;
            case TouchLocationState.Moved:
                // Is the sound for this region currently playing?
                if (_soundInstances[screenRegion].State == SoundState.Playing)
                {
                    // Yes, so set the pitch based on the horizontal touch position
                    _soundInstances[screenRegion].Pitch =
                        (tc[0].Position.X / this.Window.ClientBounds.Width) * 2 - 1;
                }

                break;
            case TouchLocationState.Released:
                // Pause all of the sounds
                for (int i = 0; i < _soundInstances.Length; i++)
                {
```

```
                    _soundInstances[i].Pause();
                }
                break;
        }
    }
}
```

Try changing the code when the touch point is released so that it calls the `Stop` method of the `SoundEffectInstance` objects rather than `Pause`. You will then see that each time the sound is played, it restarts from the beginning rather than resuming from where it was interrupted.

Other Sound Effect Properties

Among the other properties exposed by the `SoundEffect` class are two that we will briefly look at.

The first is the `Duration` property, which returns a `TimeSpan` indicating exactly how long the sample will take to play at its default pitch. This property can be useful for queueing up sounds to play one after another.

The second is the `MasterVolume` property, which is actually a static property called against the `SoundEffect` class rather than on an instance. It controls the overall volume of all sound effects, subsequently played or already playing, so it is a great way to fade up or down the sound from or to silence.

Just like the volume of individual sounds, `MasterVolume` is set in the range of 0 (silence) to 1 (full volume, based on the current device volume level). It defaults to 1.

Obtaining Sound Effects for your Game

Although you might want to create your own sound effects, there are many thousands available on the Internet that you can use in your game instead. It is generally much easier to get hold of quality sounds this way because you can search through the libraries playing each sound you find until you locate one that will fit into your game.

The main issue to be aware of with downloaded sounds is licensing. Just as with everything else in life, it is hard to find good things for free—particularly if you intend to sell your game. An organization called Creative Commons has made this particular area easier to deal with, however, and this is extremely helpful for getting good sound effects.

A number of different Creative Commons licenses are available, many of which permit the material that they cover to be used in free or commercial products, and some of which also allow modifications to be made to the licensed items. The only general requirement is that you include attribution for the source of the material in your game. So if you include the details of the sound author and a link to the site from which it was downloaded, all such licensed sounds can be freely used within your games. Do check the license of each individual sound that you want to use, however, because some licenses forbid commercial use.

A couple of great sites for finding Creative Commons licensed sound effects are the following:

- http://www.freesound.org

- http://www.soundbible.com

Both of these sites clearly describe the license applied to each sound and have search facilities and online previews of each sound in their database. Many other sound sites exist, too, and can be found via your search engine of choice.

Selecting a sound can be tricky, and it is essential to try out each sound that you like and see how it fits in with the game environment. Sometimes sounds that initially seem ideal just don't work well inside a game, so spend some time experimenting to get things sounding just right. Don't forget that altering the volume or pitch can help with getting your sounds to fit in, too.

To manipulate sounds that you have downloaded or to convert them between different formats, a sound editing application is essential. This application will let you cut out or exclude sections of a sound, fade its volume up or down, add echo and distortion, and do dozens of other useful things.

Lots of commercial applications are available for this task, but if you are looking to keep your costs down, a free application called Audacity is well worth a look. It has a large range of sound processing effects, has flexible editing features, and supports saving to numerous file formats (including WAV and MP3). Visit audacity.sourceforge.net to download a copy.

An Interactive Example

Recall the Balloons project that we created in Chapter 4 to illustrate mapping input coordinates to objects on the screen. To bring a little more life to the example, an updated version of Balloons is included with this chapter with some sound effects added.

Three different popping sounds are included to make the sound a little more varied, and as each sound is played it is also given a slightly randomized pitch as well as being panned to match the balloon position on the screen. This makes for an entirely more satisfying balloon-popping experience!

Playing Music

We have already discussed the fact that the SoundEffect class is not to be used for playing music, but that doesn't mean that we can't provide backing tracks for our games. XNA provides separate functionality for playing music, but in the context of Windows Phone 7 there are some things that we need to be aware of in order for our game to meet Microsoft's certification requirements.

Let's look at how (and when) you can play music within your games.

To Play or Not To Play

The certification requirement complication for Windows Phone 7 games revolves around the fact that one of the other primary uses for the device is as a media player. The operating system has a flexible media library that allows music and other audio content to be played on the device, even when the media library has been moved to the background.

As a result, it is entirely possible that, when the user launches your game, music is already playing in the background. Microsoft has decided that this existing music should take priority over your game music and that you must not stop it from playing without either directly asking the user for permission (by displaying a dialog box, for example, asking if the user wants to play the game music instead of the current audio track) or by providing a configuration option that allows it to be configured on a more permanent basis (in which case the option must default to not interrupting the existing media playback). Without observing this requirement, your game will be rejected when you submit it to the Windows Phone Marketplace.

We will look at how to perform this check (and how to pause the background music if appropriate) in a moment, but for now please bear in mind the need to do this.

Note that this check applies only to playing music with the MediaPlayer class, which is the class that provides access to the music player functionality. Sound effect playback is permitted even if the device is already playing music, so no special checking needs to be performed for sound effects. The certification requirements state that sound effect objects should not be used for playing background music, however, so this isn't a way to bypass the requirement.

Adding Music to your Project

Music is also added to the Content project. Unlike sound effects, music is expected to be in either MP3 or WMA format. This is a good thing because such formats produce much smaller files than WAV files due to the way they are compressed. Because music is likely to be much longer in duration than a sound effect, having compression applied is essential for keeping the size of your finished game under control.

MP3 files have taken over the world during the last decade and must surely form one of the most widely known file formats in existence. Sound files encoded using MP3 are compressed using a lossy compression algorithm. Although this means that there is some degradation of the audio when it is played back (just as there is a loss of image quality with JPG images), in most cases the quality loss is virtually or completely unnoticeable.

MP3 can compress audio data to different degrees, and the higher the compression the greater the quality loss on playback. The compression level is set when the MP3 is created by specifying a bit rate, which controls how many kilobits of data can be used to store each second of compressed audio. Compressing files at a bit rate of 128 kilobits per second will typically reduce CD quality audio to about 9 percent of its original file size—a massive saving.

Windows Media Audio (WMA) files are similar in approach to MP3s, also using a proprietary Microsoft compress to provide lossy compression (although a lossless variation is available). Microsoft claims that WMA files can be created that have the same quality level as an MP3 while using only half the storage space, though there are those who dispute this claim. Nevertheless, it is still a capable format and certainly worth considering as a format for your game music.

■ **NOTE** Audacity is capable of exporting sounds in both MP3 and WMA format.

When you add a music file to the content, the properties show the Content Processor as Song, as shown in Figure 5–2.

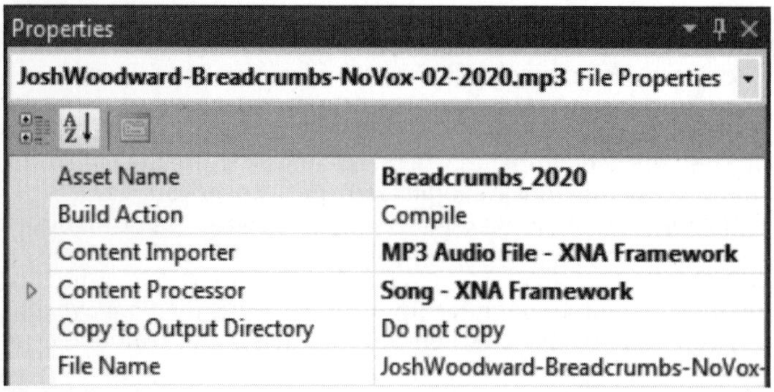

Figure 5–2. The properties for an MP3 file added to an XNA Content project

"Song" is in fact the term that XNA uses to refer to a piece of music, and its class names reflect this. To load a song, we use the Song class along with the usual Content.Load call. In the game framework, we store a collection of songs within the GameHost class inside a Dictionary named Songs. Listing 5–4 shows the instruction within a project's LoadContent function that loads a song into the framework.

Listing 5–4. Loading a song into the game framework from the Content project

```
// Load our song
Songs.Add("2020", Content.Load<Song>("Breadcrumbs_2020"));
```

Playing the Music

Playing a song is very easy: just call the static `MediaPlayer.Play` function, passing in the `Song` object that you have loaded. Only one song can play at a time; trying to play a second song will stop the first song from playing.

However, we have the tricky issue of whether we are allowed to play music or not because, if the device is already playing background music, we must leave it alone.

This is determined using the `MediaPlayer.GameHasControl` property. If it returns `true`, we have full access to playing music; if it returns `false`, there is music already playing; and unless the user has explicitly confirmed that they want for our game to take control, we must allow it to continue. Listing 5–5 shows some code from the `LoadContent` function of the `BackgroundMusic` example project that accompanies this chapter. If it detects that media are already playing, it doesn't even attempt to load the song; otherwise, the song is loaded and played.

Listing 5–5. Checking whether the game is allowed to play music and then loading and starting playback

```
// Load songs
if (MediaPlayer.GameHasControl)
{
    // Load our song
    Songs.Add("2020", Content.Load<Song>("Breadcrumbs_2020"));

    // Play the song, repeating
    MediaPlayer.IsRepeating = true;
    MediaPlayer.Play(Songs["2020"]);
}
```

Assuming that we can play our music, there is a number of other methods and properties that we can access from the `MediaPlayer` class to affect the way in which the music plays:

- `Pause` and `Stop` can be used to halt playback. Just as with sound effects, `Pause` will remember the position at which the song was paused, allowing it to be later resumed; whereas `Stop` will discard the position. Either way, you can call the `Resume` method to start the song playing again.

- `IsMuted` and `Volume` provide control over the playback volume. `IsMuted` is a boolean property that will completely silence the song without pausing it, while `Volume` allows the playback volume to be faded between silence (0.0) and the current device volume (1.0).

- `IsRepeating` allows you to set the song to loop endlessly. This looping is often very useful for games because they tend to have background music that plays repeatedly the whole time the game is running. There is a slight issue with repeating music to be aware of, however, as we will discuss in a moment.

- `PlayPosition` returns a `TimeSpan` object detailing the current playback time through the song. This can be used to create a playback time display, as will be demonstrated shortly.

Each loaded Song object also has a series of interesting-looking properties that might be interrogated. Unfortunately, it turns out that they aren't too useful after all. Properties are available to provide information on the song's Album, Artist, and Genre, among other things, but when songs are read from a game's Content project, none of them is populated even if the information is present inside the MP3 file. These properties are instead used to access data on songs contained within the device's media library.

One useful property that we can read from the Song is its Duration, which also returns a TimeSpan, this time containing the length of the song. We can use this alongside the MediaLibrary.PlayPosition for our playback time display. The BackgroundMusic example project displays such a timer and generates its text as shown in Listing 5–6. An example of the display it produces is shown in Figure 5–3.

Listing 5–6. Displaying the current position and duration of a song

```
// Are we playing a song?
if (MediaPlayer.GameHasControl)
{
    // Yes, so read the position and duraction
    currentPosition = MediaPlayer.PlayPosition;
    duration = Songs["2020"].Duration;
    // Display the details in our text object
    TextObject positionText = (TextObject)GameObjects[0];
    positionText.Text = "Song position: "
                + new DateTime(currentPosition.Ticks).ToString("mm:ss") + "/"
                + new DateTime(duration.Ticks).ToString("mm:ss");
}
```

Song position: 00:11/00:23

Figure 5–3. The display from the BackgroundMusic example project

This is nearly all you need to know about playing music, but there is one other thing that you should be aware of, and it is a rather annoying feature of XNA's media playback functionality. When you set a song to loop, there is a very slight pause between the song finishing and restarting. If your song fades to silence at the end, it will be unnoticeable, but if you try to loop the song so that it restarts seamlessly, this pause can be quite noticeable.

Although there is nothing you can do to eliminate the pause, you can make a minor adjustment to the song to slightly reduce its impact. The pause can be irritating on two levels: it enforces a brief moment of silence and it results in the music playback being thrown slightly off-beat. This second problem can be very distracting indeed.

To eliminate the timing problem, edit your music file and trim about one-tenth of a second from the end. Then save it and use this modified version in your game. The pause will then be offset by a corresponding gap in the music track, allowing the beat to continue uninterrupted.

Game in Focus: Cosmic Rocks (Part III)

We could certainly enhance *Cosmic Rocks* by adding some sound effects, so let's do so now.

After giving some thought to the aspects of the game that could use sound effects, the following list emerged:

- A laser gun sound for when the player fires. It needs to avoid being overpowering because it will be played a lot of times.

- A white noise sound for when the player is thrusting.

- A sound for hyperspace.

- A substantial explosion for when the player's ship is destroyed,

- A smaller explosion for when a rock is damaged. Once again, this is a very frequent sound, so it needs to be much quieter than the player explosion.

I spent some time searching through the Creative Commons sound effect sites; after a little hunting, I managed to find a set of samples that I think work very well. All the sounds and the attribution information can be found within the Content project of the CosmicRocksPartIII project that accompanies this chapter. The attribution information is contained within the Attribution.txt file, also included in the Content project. In a finished game, this information would need to be included somewhere inside the game itself (perhaps in an "About" or "Credits" screen, but we've not developed one of them yet, so this will suffice for the time being).

For the most part, the integration of the sound is very straightforward: at the appropriate trigger points (the spaceship's FireBullet, Hyperspace, and Explode functions and the rocks' DamageRock function), the game simply needs to call the Play method of the appropriate sound effect.

The only sound that is a little more complex is that of the thruster. It is implemented using a looping sound effect, so a SoundEffectInstance object is used. This is declared as a class-level variable within the SpaceshipObject class and is named _thrusterSound.

Two simple functions are present within the spaceship code to support this: StartThrusterSound and StopThrusterSound. When the game detects that the screen has been touched long enough for thrusting to begin, it calls the first of these functions to start the sound; when contact is released, it calls the second function to stop it again.

The only minor complication is that, when the spaceship explodes or enters hyperspace, the thrust is cancelled immediately, without waiting for the player to release contact with the screen. To stop the thruster sound from continuing to play when these events occur, the Explode and Hyperspace functions both call into StopThrusterSound. Remember when you are writing your own games to keep track of looping sounds so that they can be carefully controlled.

One final feature worth noting is the sound of the player's ship exploding. The sound effect used for this is already quite a deep bassy sound, but when the ship explodes, the game actually starts two instances of the sound. The first is played at the default pitch, but the second has a very small random variation to its pitch. These two sounds interfere with one another in a pleasing way when they are played, giving the impression of even more depth to the produced sound. This combination provides a satisfying auditory output for an event as significant as the player losing a life.

Make Some Noise

Sound and music form an important part of a game experience. Carefully crafted sound effects and background music can really bring the game to life and help the player to connect with the action that is taking place on the screen. It is well worth investing some time and effort into choosing the sounds that you include with your game.

Don't overlook the possibility that your player will want to completely disable all of the game sound, however. There are many environments (such as in an office) where someone might want to have a quick play of your game, but doesn't want to have sound unexpectedly blasting from their device. Be considerate and provide players with an option to switch the sound off quickly and easily should they want to do so.

■ ■ ■

CHAPTER 6

Drawing with Vertices and Matrices

For the next few chapters we will begin to move away from the two-dimensional graphics that we have been using so far and enter the brave new world of the third dimension. Before we get too far, however, there are some new concepts and approaches that you need to become familiar with.

A New Approach to Drawing

Three-dimensional rendering introduces a variety of new challenges: 3D graphics are rendered as models rather than as simple bitmaps, our brains need to shift into a different gear to keep track of movement in and out of the screen, and we have an entirely different way of telling XNA where we want to draw things on the screen.

We will examine some of these changes in this chapter so that you can fully understand the environment in which you need to work in order to draw 3D graphics. This chapter doesn't get too involved in the actual 3D rendering; we'll cover that in Chapter 7, but everything contained here is essential to know in order to be able to effectively use XNA's 3D rendering technology.

Let's start by discussing some of the features of the 3D rendering environment.

Matrix-Based Positioning

All the graphics that we have rendered in the chapters up to this point have been based around *sprites*. They were configured by using a series of simple properties to define their position, rotation, scaling, and coloring. This gave us a simple mechanism for putting sprites wherever we needed them.

As we prepare to render 3D graphics, we leave this approach behind for the time being (though don't forget it entirely because we can use sprites and 3D graphics together, as discussed in Chapter 8). Instead, we use a system based around *matrices*.

Matrices allow us to encode a series of movements and transformations into a compact structure that can then be applied to the graphics that we want to draw. Most of the calculations required to do this are conveniently wrapped up in handy XNA functions, so we don't need to get too involved in their inner workings.

Just like anything else, it might take a little time to become accustomed to thinking with matrix transformations, but once you do you will find them a very useful tool. In fact, you might ultimately decide that you prefer them to XNA's sprite rendering approach.

Abstract Coordinate System

When we render in 3D, XNA generally uses an abstract coordinate system rather than a pixel-based coordinate system like the one used for sprite rendering, meaning that we are not concerned with pixels. Although this might sound like a disadvantage at first, freeing ourselves from pixel coordinates actually turns out to be rather useful.

When we initialize XNA, we can tell it the dimensions of the screen and the coordinate system will scale to match. Moving a graphic object a certain distance to the right, therefore, moves the same distance regardless of the back buffer size. As a result, should we decide to use a smaller buffer to increase performance, none of the rendering code needs to change (as it did when we were rendering sprites).

■ **NOTE** 3D rendering with a pixel-based coordinate system is also an option if you want. This will be discussed in the "Orthographic Projection" section in Chapter 7.

After all the time we have spent with sprites, getting to grips with the 3D coordinate system requires a slight twist of the brain. First of all, the coordinate (0, 0) is generally right in the center of the screen rather than in the top-left corner. Second, movement along the positive y axis will travel up the screen, as opposed to down for sprites. It can be a nuisance having to keep these two conflicting coordinate systems in your brain, but once you are in the frame of mind for one system over the other, it should be easy to remember which way is up.

Because we are now using a 3D graphical environment, we actually need to add a third element to our coordinates. The coordinate values we have looked at in the past have been in the form of (x, y), representing the specified distances along the x and y axes. 3D coordinates are in the form (x, y, z), providing values in the z axis as well as the x and y axes. The z axis represents movement into or out of the screen—literally the third dimension. Positive values on the z axis result in movement toward the player, negative values result in movement into the screen.

Drawing Primitives

When it comes to drawing graphics, XNA is actually not able to draw anything more complex than triangles. This might at first seem very restrictive, but in fact, it is not as you will see when we start to use it in some example projects.

The reason we can create more complex scenes is partly because much more complex shapes can be created by putting lots of triangles together (for example, a rectangle is just two triangles joined along their long edge) and partly because we can put graphic images onto the triangles. As a simple example, we can display graphics that work along very similar lines to the sprites from earlier chapters by simply rendering a rectangle with a graphic displayed across it.

When we are drawing, we refer to each triangle as a *surface*. The points that form the triangle are called *vertices*. Figure 6–1 shows two triangular surfaces created using four vertices. Two of the vertices are shared between the triangles.

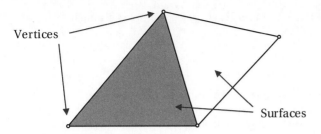

Figure 6–1. Vertices and surfaces used in XNA rendering

The vertices themselves are not actually displayed by XNA, just the surfaces that they define; the vertices are shown in Figure 6–1 just to clarify what they are.

The only primitives available other than triangles are lines.

Textures

Just as we used Texture2D objects to provide graphics for our sprites, so we can use them to fill the triangles that we are rendering. We have a lot of flexibility to use textures within our applications—much more so than we had with sprites. We can take small rectangular sections just as we did with sprites, or we can stretch textures in a variety of different ways across the shapes that we draw. We'll look at some of the tricks and techniques that we can use when texturing in the "Applying Textures" section later in this chapter.

XNA is a State Engine

Whereas, with sprite rendering, each individual call to draw graphics provided all the information needed for drawing to take place, the approach for 3D rendering is slightly different. XNA maintains lots of *state* values for things such as which texture is currently being used for rendering, whether transparency is enabled, whether lighting is switched on, and so on.

In order for our rendering to appear as we expect, each of these states must be set prior to the rendering call. Once a state has been set, it will stay with its value until we decide to change it again.

■ **NOTE** All this actually applies to sprite rendering, too, except that the sprite engine always sets the state values according to the parameters passed to the SpriteBatch.Draw and DrawString methods. Under the covers, the rendering of sprites is using exactly the same approach described in this chapter.

Creating our First Vertex Rendering Project

Before we get into too much more detail, let's see what is involved in setting up a simple project that uses the new rendering approach. Some of the code that we will work through here will be unfamiliar and we will gloss over some of it for the time being just so that we can get some code running. All this will be explained in much more detail during the rest of this and the following chapters.

The full source code for this project can be found in the ColoredSquare example accompanying this chapter.

Setting Up the Environment

We start off by creating a new XNA project, exactly as we have always done. For simplicity, we will work in isolation of the game framework at the moment, so don't worry about adding a reference to it or changing the game class derivation; it can continue to derive from Microsoft.Xna.Framework.Game for this example.

We need to add some class-level variables to the game class to manage the scene that we wish to render. The required declarations are shown in Listing 6–1.

Listing 6–1. Variables required for the scene to be rendered

```
private BasicEffect _effect;
private VertexPositionColor[] _vertices = new VertexPositionColor[4];
```

Next we need to set up these variables ready for them to be used by XNA. The code required for this is added to the Initialize function.

The first thing we do here is set up the *projection matrix*. This is something that we will discuss in more detail in the next chapter, but for the moment we can consider its main task as being to set up the abstract coordinate system. As you can see in Listing 6–2, the screen's aspect ratio is determined by dividing the viewport width by its height, and this ratio is one of the values used to initialize the matrix. This ensures that objects remain square when drawn on the screen.

Listing 6–2. The beginning of the Initialize function, creating the projection matrix

```
protected override void Initialize()
{
    // Calculate the screen aspect ratio
    float aspectRatio =
            (float)GraphicsDevice.Viewport.Width / GraphicsDevice.Viewport.Height;
    // Create a projection matrix
    Matrix projection = Matrix.CreatePerspectiveFieldOfView(MathHelper.ToRadians(45),
                                                    aspectRatio, 0.1f, 1000.0f);
```

Note how the matrix is being initialized by calling one of the shared methods of the Matrix structure. There are dozens of such methods that allow us to create all kinds of matrices, as you will see as we progress.

The next step is to create the *view matrix*. This can be likened to a camera within the scene, and controls which objects rendered are visible and where they appear on the screen. Our example project's view matrix is created as shown in Listing 6–3. Once again, this will be discussed in more detail later.

Listing 6–3. Initializing the view matrix

```
// Calculate a view matrix (where we are looking from and to)
Matrix view = Matrix.CreateLookAt(new Vector3(0, 0, 10), Vector3.Zero, Vector3.Up);
```

Now we need to create an *effect* object to tell XNA how it should render our graphics to the screen. All rendering needs an effect of some kind, and several are provided for the Windows Phone 7 implementation of XNA. We'll look at some of the interesting things that they can achieve in Chapter 8, but for the time being we will use the BasicEffect to allow us to render without doing anything fancy.

The effect object is passed a reference to our graphics device when it is instantiated, and we then set a series of properties to control how it will behave. These are some of the state values that were discussed at the beginning of this chapter. Listing 6–4 shows the creation and initialization of the effect object. Note that among the values passed are the projection and view matrices that we have just constructed.

Listing 6–4. Creating and initializing the effect object

```
_effect = new BasicEffect(GraphicsDevice);
_effect.LightingEnabled = false;
_effect.TextureEnabled = false;
_effect.VertexColorEnabled = true;
_effect.Projection = projection;
_effect.View = view;
_effect.World = Matrix.Identity;
```

The environment is now fully initialized. We don't yet have anything to draw, however, so we need to take care of this before we can render anything.

As mentioned earlier, XNA expects us to define our objects using vertices. It can then use them to construct the solid triangles that form the graphics we see on the screen.

Vertices can hold various pieces of information. They will always hold a position, but in addition to that they might contain color information, texture information, and other data that affects the way they are drawn. XNA provides some built-in configurations for common vertex structures, and the one we will use here is called VertexPositionColor. As its name implies, it stores position and color information, and nothing more.

We will get our example to draw a simple square on the screen. To tell XNA about the square, we must set up an array of vertex objects, telling it the position and color of each. Figure 6–2 shows the vertices that we will be using to form this square. The coordinate (0, 0, 0) is right in the middle of the square, and it extends 2 units across the x and y axes (from -1 to 1 on each axis). Note that the z coordinate is left at 0 for all the vertices so that the square remains flat.

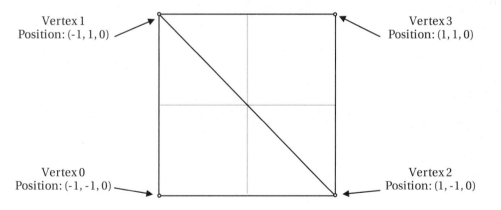

Vertex 1
Position: (-1, 1, 0)

Vertex 3
Position: (1, 1, 0)

Vertex 0
Position: (-1, -1, 0)

Vertex 2
Position: (1, -1, 0)

Figure 6–2. The vertices for the square that we will be rendering

The vertices are constructed within the program code by setting their coordinates into the _vertices array that we declared back in Listing 6–1. The code is shown in Listing 6–5.

Listing 6–5. Setting the vertex positions to form a square

```
_vertices[0].Position = new Vector3(-1, -1, 0);
_vertices[1].Position = new Vector3(-1, 1, 0);
_vertices[2].Position = new Vector3(1, -1, 0);
_vertices[3].Position = new Vector3(1, 1, 0);
```

Just as we used Vector2 structures for providing positions for sprites, so we now use Vector3 structures to declare positions in three-dimensional space.

The final part of our initialization is to provide a color for each vertex. This will produce an attractive effect when it is rendered—and also one that we could not easily achieve using sprites without having to generate a texture containing the different colors. The remaining vertex initialization, and the conclusion of the Initialize function, is shown in Listing 6–6.

Listing 6–6. Setting the vertex colors

```
_vertices[0].Color = Color.Red;
_vertices[1].Color = Color.White;
_vertices[2].Color = Color.Blue;
_vertices[3].Color = Color.Green;

base.Initialize();
}
```

Rendering the Object

Everything is fully initialized now and we're ready to draw the square to the screen. Because we are only using vertex colors without textures, there is nothing to read in the LoadContent function, so we can leave this alone. We have nothing to update at the moment, either, so let's move straight on to the Draw function.

The screen is cleared (to CornflowerBlue once again) as it was for sprites, but the approach we take to drawing now is very different. Instead of the SpriteBatch object, we use the BasicEffect that we created earlier to manage the drawing for us.

Each effect can contain one or more *techniques*. These are the specific rendering operations that are contained within the effect—the effect acting as a container for one or more techniques. Each of the effects provided with XNA for Windows Phone 7 contains just a single technique, so we don't need to pay much attention to this. We will just use the default technique that the effect provides for us.

Finally, each technique contains one or more passes that perform the actual rendering to the screen. If the rendering of an effect needs to perform multiple updates to the content of the screen in order to render, there will be multiple passes returned from the technique, each of which will need to be drawn. BasicEffect uses only one pass, but just for good form we will set our code to loop for all passes that might be returned from the effect, to save confusion later on when we do encounter multiple-pass effects.

Bearing all that in mind, the code required to render the square is shown in Listing 6–7. Once the pass has been determined, its Apply method is called to tell XNA to activate it. The code then calls DrawUserPrimitives, telling it the type of primitive that it is rendering, and passing various details about what to draw. The parameters for the DrawUserPrimitives function are as follows:

- primitiveType contains the type of primitive that we wish to draw. In this case, we draw a TriangleStrip. The available primitives will be discussed in the next section.

- vertexData allows us to pass the array of vertices that we have defined.

- vertexOffset is a value that allows us to start considering the vertices at a position within the array other than its start. We are not using this, so we just pass 0.

- primitiveCount is the number of primitives that we are drawing. As we specified that XNA should draw triangles, setting this to 2 means to draw 2 triangles. Remember that this is counting primitives, not vertices.

The code for the Draw function is shown in Listing 6–7.

Listing 6–7. Drawing the colored square

```
protected override void Draw(GameTime gameTime)
{
    GraphicsDevice.Clear(Color.CornflowerBlue);

    foreach (EffectPass pass in _effect.CurrentTechnique.Passes)
    {
        // Apply the pass
        pass.Apply();
        // Draw the square
        GraphicsDevice.DrawUserPrimitives(PrimitiveType.TriangleStrip, _vertices, 0, 2);
    }

    base.Draw(gameTime);
}
```

The resulting graphic can be seen in Figure 6–3.

Figure 6–3. The rendered output from the ColoredSquare example

Notice how XNA has handled the colors within the rendered square. Each vertex is colored exactly as we had requested, but between them XNA performs a smooth fade between the colors. This is known as *color interpolation* and is something that you will see again in the future: any vertex parameters such as colors that differ from one vertex to the next will result in a smooth fade as XNA renders between them. This can be very useful and attractive, as this example demonstrates.

Moving the Object

The section titled "Understanding Matrix Transformations" later in this chapter will fully cover the approach to moving our objects, but to make things a little more interesting than a static square, let's take a quick preview and get our square to spin around on the screen.

To achieve this, we first need to track the rotation angle. We will do this by adding a class-level float variable named _angle, and will update it by 5 degrees each update, as shown in Listing 6–8.

Listing 6–8. Updating the angle of the square

```
protected override void Update(GameTime gameTime)
{
    // Allows the game to exit
    if (GamePad.GetState(PlayerIndex.One).Buttons.Back == ButtonState.Pressed)
        this.Exit();

    _angle += MathHelper.ToRadians(5);

    base.Update(gameTime);
}
```

To apply the angle to the square, we need to update the world matrix (full details of which will be provided in the "Understanding Matrix Transformations" section). Because we want to rotate the square, we need to give it a rotation matrix. XNA's Matrix class provides various methods for creating such a matrix, and the one we will select for our example is the CreateRotationZ function. This function accepts a single parameter (the rotation angle) and returns a matrix ready for us to use.

The updated code to draw the square with rotation is shown in Listing 6–9.

Listing 6–9. Rotating and drawing the colored square

```
protected override void Draw(GameTime gameTime)
{
    GraphicsDevice.Clear(Color.CornflowerBlue);

    // Set the world matrix so that the square rotates
    _effect.World = Matrix.CreateRotationZ(_angle);

    foreach (EffectPass pass in _effect.CurrentTechnique.Passes)
    {
        // Apply the pass
        pass.Apply();
        // Draw the square
        GraphicsDevice.DrawUserPrimitives(PrimitiveType.TriangleStrip, _vertices, 0, 2);
    }

    base.Draw(gameTime);
}
```

Note that the call to DrawUserPrimitives that is actually drawing the square is completely unchanged; it is the state of the effect that is causing the object to rotate, not the instruction to draw. This is clearly different to the approach we used with sprite-based rendering.

Adding some Sparkle

Of course, this rotating square only scratches the surface of what we can achieve with XNA. Let's make a simple change to the project that results in a dramatic and attractive enhancement to the displayed graphics.

If we modify the Draw code so that it is as shown in Listing 6–10, we will see that it has a significant effect on the graphics that are drawn to the screen, as shown in Figure 6–4. The code for this can be found in the NestedSquares example project.

Listing 6–10. *Rendering the square in the NestedSquares example project.*

```
protected override void Draw(GameTime gameTime)
{
    GraphicsDevice.Clear(Color.CornflowerBlue);

    // Reset the world matrix
    _effect.World = Matrix.Identity;

    // Loop for each square
    for (int i = 0; i < 20; i++)
    {
        foreach (EffectPass pass in _effect.CurrentTechnique.Passes)
        {
            // Apply a further rotation
            _effect.World = Matrix.CreateRotationZ(_angle) * _effect.World;
            // Scale the object so that it is shown slightly smaller
            _effect.World = Matrix.CreateScale(0.85f) * _effect.World;

            // Apply the pass
            pass.Apply();
            // Draw the square
            GraphicsDevice.DrawUserPrimitives
                              (PrimitiveType.TriangleStrip, _vertices, 0, 2);
        }
    }

    base.Draw(gameTime);
}
```

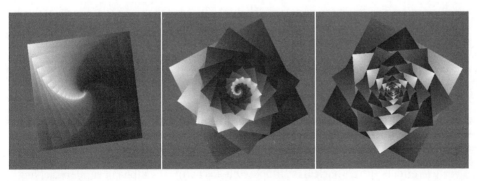

Figure 6–4. *The rendered output from the NestedSquares example*

The screen shots sadly don't do justice to the effect project in operation; it is much better in motion than in still images, but this gives an idea of the patterns that this tiny piece of code is able to generate.

All that the loop is doing is drawing 20 shapes instead of one, each of which is slightly smaller than the last and rotated to a different angle. The scale and rotate operations are cumulative, meaning that, although the first (largest) square is rotated by the angle specified in _angle, the second square is rotated by double this angle, the third by three times the angle, and so on.

Tinting Objects

One of the useful features we explored when using sprites is the ability to tint the sprite into a different color. The same facility is available when rendering objects using vertices, too.

The effect object has a property named DiffuseColor, which allows the tint color to be set. This property defaults to white, which leaves the colors of our objects unchanged, but can be modified to any color that we desire. The color is applied to our vertex colors just as it was for sprites: it takes the red, green, and blue values of each vertex color and represents them as a value between 0 and 1. Each of them is then multiplied by the corresponding color element within DiffuseColor, and the resulting values used for the final vertex color.

Setting DiffuseColor to black will therefore result in all vertex colors becoming black, too. Setting DiffuseColor to red will remove all green and blue color information from the vertices, resulting in just the red color elements surviving.

Unlike the color properties we have seen so far, however, DiffuseColor is implemented as a Vector3 structure rather than as a Color. Each of the three elements within the Vector3 relates to one of the color elements in a color: the x element stores the amount of red, the y element stores the amount of green, and the z element stores the amount of blue. All three of these measure color using a float value in the range of 0 to 1, rather than an integer from 0 to 255.

To make our lives easier, the XNA developers have taken into account the need to translate color values between the Color structure and the Vector3 structure and have provided built-in functions to accomplish this.

To convert a Color into a Vector3, simply call its ToVector3 method. The resulting vector values will match those of the color. A simple example of this can be seen in Listing 6–11.

Listing 6–11. Converting a Color structure into a Vector3

```
Vector3 myColorVector;
myColorVector = Color.PeachPuff.ToVector3();
```

To convert a Vector3 into a Color, create a new Color and pass the Vector3 as a parameter to its constructor. This will produce a color whose values match that of the vector. A simple example of this is shown in Listing 6–12.

Listing 6–12. Converting a Vector3 structure into a Color

```
Vector3 myColorVector = new Vector3(1.0f, 0.8f, 0.2f);
Color myColor;
myColor = new Color(myColorVector);
```

Try modifying the NestedSquares example project so that the effect's DiffuseColor is set prior to rendering the squares in the Draw method and see the effect that it has on the generated graphics.

Being a Vector3, however, this gives no opportunity to set an alpha value. When we tinted sprites, alpha values were also available and allowed us to fade the transparency of the sprites that were being rendered. In the vertex-rendering approach, it is still possible to change the alpha of rendered objects, but this is controlled using a separate property. This will be discussed in the "Object Transparency" section later in this chapter.

Understanding Matrix Transformations

Let's take a closer look at what is happening when we move the shape that we are drawing.

Within XNA, the position at which we will draw graphics is tracked using the *world matrix*. A matrix is a set of values, arranged in rows and columns, which can be applied to the coordinates of our vertices in order to move them around on the screen.

By combining multiple matrices, movement operations can be grouped together. For example, we might want to move an object 1 unit to the right and then rotate it by 45 degrees. To do this, we start with an empty matrix, apply the movement matrix, and then the rotation matrix. The resulting matrix can be used to transform any vertex coordinate so that it moves 1 unit to the right and rotates by 45 degrees. There is no need to separately apply the movement and rotation to each vertex because the transformation matrix will perform both steps in one calculation.

This allows for transformations to be built up into greater and greater levels of complexity, but doesn't make calculating the point onscreen at which each vertex will be drawn any more difficult or processor-intensive.

Exactly how these matrices are created, manipulated, and applied is not something that we will cover in any detail in this book. There are plenty of online references that will explain this subject in further detail; for example, see http://en.wikipedia.org/wiki/Matrix_(mathematics) for information on what a matrix is, how matrices and constructed, and how arithmetic operations are performed; and http://tinyurl.com/matrixtransform to read about how matrix transformations work at a mathematical level.

We will discuss how matrix transformations are actually used in practical terms. Though the numerical representations of transformations might be somewhat abstract, visualizing what each transformation will do is somewhat easier.

Setting the Identity Matrix

We have already discussed the fact that XNA maintains state for lots of properties that affect how it will render to the screen, and that one of these is the world matrix. Each time we begin drawing, a world matrix of some description will already be set, usually from a previous call to Draw, and we won't necessarily have any idea what it contains. We should therefore always ensure that the world matrix is set prior to performing any drawing.

In order to reset this matrix to its initial state, we set the matrix to a preset set of values called the *identity matrix*. This ensures that any rendering that takes place will initially be centered at the origin—at coordinate (0, 0, 0)—and will not be rotated or scaled at all.

We can obtain an identity matrix at any time from the static Matrix.Identity property. To render objects without any transformation, set it as the effect's world matrix prior to applying the effect passes. You can see this being used at the beginning of Listing 6–10.

A square with a width and height of one unit can be seen in Figure 6–5 after the identity matrix has been applied. It is directly centered on the origin of the coordinate system.

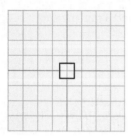

Figure 6–5. *A unit square rendered after a call to LoadIdentity*

Applying Translation Transformations

In the terminology of matrix transformations, moving an object along one or more of the axes is called a *translation*. The shape, size, and angle of the object are entirely unchanged; the object is just moved left or right, up or down, and in or out of the world to a new position.

Figure 6–6 shows the effect of a translation matrix. The image on the left shows the unit square in position after the identity matrix has been loaded; the image on the right shows the same square after it has been translated 3 units in the x axis and –2 units in the y axis. (For simplicity, we will ignore the z axis for the moment, but transformation along the z axis is achieved in exactly the same way as for the x and y axes.)

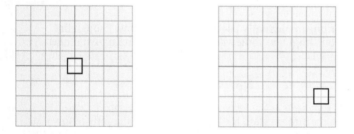

Figure 6–6. *Translation of a square along the x and y axes*

To obtain a translation matrix, call the static `Matrix.CreateTranslation` function. This function has a couple of overloads: the first requires three parameters (the translation distance for the x, y, and z axes, respectively); the second accepts a single `Vector3` parameter.

Both of them have their uses depending on the way you want to specify your movement. The `Vector3` approach is very handy because it allows a movement path to be stored (just as we did in two dimensions for the rocks in the *Cosmic Rocks* examples from the previous chapters) and easily transformed into a translation matrix.

■ **NOTE** The `Matrix.CreateTranslation` function has two different calling styles: one that returns its generated matrix as a return value from the function, and another that returns the matrix in an output parameter. All the other matrix generation functions share these two approaches. Feel free to use whichever you are more comfortable with, but in the text of this book we will use the versions that return matrices as their return values.

Applying Rotation Transformations

We can also rotate the objects that we draw. Objects can be rotated around any of the three axes, as shown in Figure 6–7.

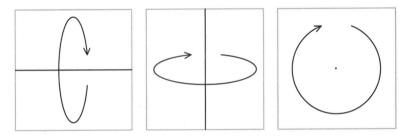

Figure 6–7. Rotations around the x, y, and z axes

Rotation around the x axis is around a horizontal line drawn across the screen. If you held a sheet of paper in front of you so that you were looking directly at the flat face of the paper, rotation on the x axis would rotate the paper so that the bottom edge was brought toward you and the top edge away, resulting in you looking at the paper's front edge.

Rotation on the y axis is exactly the same, but rotating around a vertical line.

Z axis rotation is around a line that traces a path into and out of the screen. This is the axis of rotation that we have used in the `ColoredSquare` and `NestedSquares` example projects.

To obtain a matrix to rotate around one of these axes, call one of the following static functions:

- `Matrix.CreateRotationX` to rotate around the x axis
- `Matrix.CreateRotationY` to rotate around the y axis
- `Matrix.CreateRotationZ` to rotate around the z axis

All three functions require the rotation angle to be passed as a parameter (in radians).

■ **NOTE** Rotating around the z axis will result in counterclockwise rotation. To rotate clockwise, simply negate the rotation angle.

Rotation around other axes can also be achieved by using the `Matrix.CreateFromAxisAngle` function. It requires two parameters: an *axis vector* defining the line around which the rotation is to take place and the rotation angle.

To calculate the axis vector, imagine the rotation axis as a line that passes through the origin point at (0, 0, 0). Then determine a point that is on that line and provide its coordinate as the values for the vector.

For example, if we want to rotate around a line that slopes upward at a 45-degree angle, we can visualize it passing through the origin point, as shown in Figure 6–8. The figure shows a point that has been selected on the line at coordinate (2, 2, 0), though any point on the line would be fine. This coordinate forms the values for the axis vector.

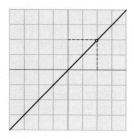

Figure 6–8. Calculating a rotation vector

One important detail must be taken into account for the axis vector, however: it must be normalized. If it is not, the objects will warp and distort as they rotate around it. Listing 6–13 provides an example of using the `CreateFromAxisAngle` function to rotate around the line from Figure 6–8.

Listing 6–13. Rotating around an arbitrary axis

```
Vector3 axisVector = new Vector3(2, 2, 0);
axisVector.Normalize();
_effect.World = Matrix.CreateFromAxisAngle(axisVector, _angle);
```

Applying Scaling Transformations

The last of the transformations that we will be working with for the time being is for scaling the objects that we render. Scaling matrices can be either *uniform*, in which case the object scales by the same amount on all three axes; or *non-uniform*, in which case each axis scales by a different amount.

Figure 6–9 shows an object in its identity location on the left, with a uniform scale of 2.0 in the middle, and then on the right with a scale of 4.0 on the x axis and 0.5 on the y axis.

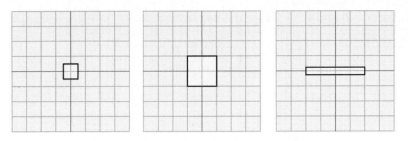

Figure 6–9. Scaling transformations

To obtain a scaling matrix, call the static `Matrix.CreateScale` function. It has three calling methods: it can be passed a single `float` to perform a uniform scale, it can be passed three `floats` to perform a non-uniform scale with the values provided for the x, y, and z axes; or it can be passed a `Vector3` containing the values for non-uniform scaling.

Passing a scale value of 0 for any of the axes will squash the shape on that axis so that it is completely flat. It can be easy to accidentally pass this when you had intended to leave the scaling unchanged for an axis; for any axis that you want to leave unchanged when scaling, pass a value of 1.

Negative scale values are also permitted. These will cause the object to flip over so that the vertices appear on the opposite side of the negatively scaled axis.

Applying Multiple Transformations

To apply a single transformation to our objects, we can simply obtain the required matrix and set it into the effect's `World` matrix property. We have already seen several examples of this.

Any practical application of matrix transformations will quickly find that setting the matrix for just a single transformation is insufficient, however. If we need to perform multiple transformations at once (for example, perhaps we need to move the object to another point within the world and then rotate it), we need some way to combine these transformations together.

Fortunately, matrix transformations are perfectly suited to this task. We can combine two or more transformations by simply multiplying the matrices together. The resulting matrix will contain the effects of both of the input matrices.

The different types of translation can have an effect on each other that might not at first be obvious, so let's first look at the effects of applying multiple transformations. We will then come back to look at how they are implemented in code.

Rotating Objects

When we rotate an object, we actually rotate its entire coordinate system because we are transforming the entire world, not just the object itself. If the identity matrix is loaded, the world coordinates are reset so that the origin point (0, 0, 0) is in the center, and no scaling or rotation is applied. Once we begin to transform this matrix, the coordinate system moves around accordingly.

Objects always move relative to the transformed coordinate system, not to the identity coordinate system. This means that, if we rotate an object by 45 degrees around the z axis and then translate it along the y axis, it will actually move diagonally onscreen rather than vertically. The rotation has changed the direction of the axes within the world coordinate system.

The effects of this rotation can be seen in Figure 6–10. On the left is the usual unit square at the identity position. In the middle, we rotate it by 45 degrees around the z axis (counterclockwise). The pale lines show the x and y axes in the identity coordinate system, whereas the darker diagonal lines show the x and y axes for the transformed world coordinate system. On the right, we translate it along its y axis. Observe that it has moved diagonally relative to the identity coordinates, though it has followed the transformed world y axis. Also note that the world coordinate system follows the translation, too. The coordinate (0, 0, 0) moves along with the translations that are applied to the world matrix.

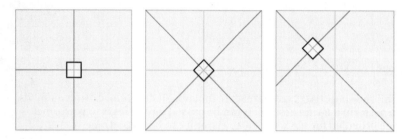

Figure 6–10. Rotation and translation in the world coordinate system

This sequence of updates brings us to another important feature of matrix transformations: the order in which they are applied is significant. In Figure 6–10, we first rotated and then translated our object. If we instead translate and then rotate it, the coordinate system for the translation would still be aligned with the identity coordinate system, so the movement on the screen would be vertical. This is shown in Figure 6–11, which contains exactly the same transformations but performed with the translation before the rotation.

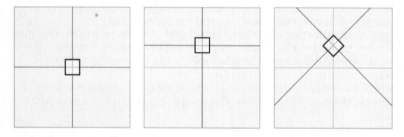

Figure 6–11. Translation before rotation

As you can see, the object ends up in a different place if we translate it first.

This is actually very easy to visualize. Imagine that you are standing in place of the square object in these diagrams. You are initially standing at the origin of the identity coordinate system, looking along the positive y axis (up the screen).

You then decide to rotate 45 degrees counterclockwise, just as in Figure 6–10. You are still facing straight ahead of your body, but relative to the identity coordinates, you are now looking diagonally. If you now take a few paces forward, you are walking diagonally in terms of the identity coordinates but straight ahead in terms of your own position within the world.

If you hold your arms out to the sides, they will be pointing along the x axis relative to your position but are once again at a diagonal angle relative to the identity coordinates.

Any time you want to visualize the transformations that you are applying, think of this same scenario and apply each transformation in sequence to yourself in the world. It should then be easy to see the sequence of transformations that you need to apply to get from one place to another. (It gets slightly harder to visualize in three dimensions, but just imagine you have wings or a jet-pack.)

Hopefully, this makes the effects of cumulative transformations clear. Always remember that, when you transform an object, the transformation will be relative to the existing transformed coordinates, not to those of the identity coordinate system.

Scaling Objects

When we scale an object, the transformation once again has an effect on the world coordinate system. If we scale an object so that its size doubles, a movement of one unit in the x axis in the transformed world coordinate system will correspond to a movement of two units relative to the identity coordinate system.

If you simply want to draw an object at a different size but without affecting its position, remember to perform the scale transformation after all the translations have been completed to avoid affecting the movement distances.

Applying Multiple Transformations in XNA

So we know that multiple transformations can be combined by multiplying them together, so let's see some sample code to achieve this in XNA.

The first transformation that we want to use can be obtained directly by calling the appropriate static Matrix function. From that point on, subsequent transformations must be obtained and multiplied by the existing calculated matrix.

To translate an object two units along the y axis and then rotate it by a specified angle, we would use the code shown in Listing 6–14. It causes the object to rotate on the spot a short distance away from the center of the screen.

Listing 6–14. Multiple transformations: translation and then rotation

```
// First translate...
_effect.World = Matrix.CreateTranslation(0, 2, 0);
// ...then rotate
_effect.World = Matrix.CreateRotationZ(_angle) * _effect.World;
```

Notice the order of multiplication: the new transformation is on the left of the multiplication symbol, and the existing matrix is on the right. Unlike multiplication of simple numbers, matrix multiplication is not commutative, which is why the order of transformations is significant. If we multiply matrix A by matrix B, we will get results different from multiplying matrix B by matrix A.

We can swap the order of these transformations so that we first rotate and then translate along the (rotated) y axis, as shown in Listing 6–15.

Listing 6–15. Multiple transformations: rotation and then translation

```
// First rotate...
_effect.World = Matrix.CreateRotationZ(_angle);
// ...then rotate
_effect.World = Matrix.CreateTranslation(0, 2, 0) * _effect.World;
```

Even though we are generating the same matrices with the same parameter, the resulting behavior is different. Instead of spinning on the spot, the object now rotates around a circular path, centered at the identity origin and with a radius of two units (because this is the distance that the object was translated).

Try plugging each of them into the ColoredSquare project in place of the existing matrix code to see their effects.

We are not limited to using transformation types just once within a transformation sequence, of course, and some movement paths will require the same transformation to be applied repeatedly at different stages of the calculation.

For example, let's get the object to trace a circle as in Listing 6–15, but this time the circle will be away from the identity origin, and the object itself will remain "upright" without rotating at all. This is achieved using the transformations shown in Listing 6–16.

Listing 6–16. Repeatedly transforming to achieve a more complex movement path

```
// First translate to the center of the circular path
_effect.World = Matrix.CreateTranslation(0, 3, 0);
// Rotate the object towards the current position on the circular path
_effect.World = Matrix.CreateRotationZ(_angle) * _effect.World;
// Translate to the edge of the circle
_effect.World = Matrix.CreateTranslation(0, 2, 0) * _effect.World;
// ...then rotate back to an upright position
_effect.World = Matrix.CreateRotationZ(-_angle) * _effect.World;
```

This time the circular path is centered at (0, 3, 0) because we translate to here before rotating. Then the object is rotated toward the point on the circle at which it will be rendered. The object is then translated to the edge of the circle; as the translation is two units along the (rotated) y axis, this will be the radius of the circle. Finally, to keep the object upright, it is rotated back by its angle. This cancels out the rotation that was applied in the original rotation. The original rotation therefore results in having an effect on the position of the object but not its final angle.

As you can see, this entire series of events is eventually contained in the single _effect.World matrix. There is no limit to the number of calculations that can be accumulated into a single matrix in this way.

Specifying Vertex Positions

You might recall that, when we looked at the ColoredSquare example back in Listing 6–5, the code defined the square's vertices by specifying four vertices with coordinates at (–1, –1, 0), (1, –1, 0), (–1, 1, 0), (1, 1, 0). These coordinates are, of course, interpreted relative to the world matrix, not the identity coordinate system.

When we use transformations to manipulate the world matrix, this resulting matrix is applied to each individual vertex when rendering, which causes the object to actually move onscreen. Because the coordinate system has been moved, rotated, and scaled relative to the world, all the vertex positions are transformed in exactly the same way. We can, therefore, define any shape we like using these vertex coordinates, and it will move around the screen as specified by our matrix transformations.

Drawing Multiple Objects at Different Positions

The example code in the projects we have looked at has always set the world matrix before looping through the effect passes and calling the Apply method on each. This is important because it is the world matrix that is present at the point of calling Apply that will be used for the subsequently rendered objects.

If you want to draw multiple objects within the same call to Draw (as you will undoubtedly want to!), you need to ensure that a call to the effect pass's Apply is made after each object's world matrix is set into the effect. Any changes made to the world matrix after this will be ignored.

There are two sequences with which this can be implemented. The first is to loop for the effect passes for each object, repeating the loop for each subsequent object. The second is to loop through the passes just once, applying each one multiple times and drawing each object after its matrix has been applied.

The first of these approaches can be seen in Listing 6–17. The effect loop is present twice, once for each of the objects being rendered. Each effect pass is applied once per loop.

Listing 6–17. Drawing multiple objects with an effect pass loop per object

```
// Draw the first object
foreach (EffectPass pass in _effect.CurrentTechnique.Passes)
{
    // Set the world matrix
    _effect.World = Matrix.CreateRotationZ(_angle);
    // Apply the pass and draw
    pass.Apply();
    GraphicsDevice.DrawUserPrimitives
                        (PrimitiveType.TriangleStrip, _vertices, 0, 2);
}

// Draw the second object
foreach (EffectPass pass in _effect.CurrentTechnique.Passes)
{
    // Set the world matrix
    _effect.World = Matrix.CreateRotationZ(_angle * 2);
    // Apply and draw
    pass.Apply();
    GraphicsDevice.DrawUserPrimitives
                        (PrimitiveType.TriangleStrip, _vertices, 0, 2);
}
```

The second approach is shown in Listing 6–18. It loops through the effect passes just once, but applies each one multiple times (once per object being rendered).

Listing 6–18. Drawing multiple objects with a single effect pass loop

```
// Draw the objects
foreach (EffectPass pass in _effect.CurrentTechnique.Passes)
{
    // Set the world matrix for the first object
    _effect.World = Matrix.CreateRotationZ(_angle);
    // Apply the pass and draw
    pass.Apply();
    GraphicsDevice.DrawUserPrimitives
                        (PrimitiveType.TriangleStrip, _vertices, 0, 2);

    // Set the world matrix for the second object
    _effect.World = Matrix.CreateRotationZ(_angle * 2);
    // Apply the pass and draw
    pass.Apply();
    GraphicsDevice.DrawUserPrimitives
                        (PrimitiveType.TriangleStrip, _vertices, 0, 2);
}
```

These code samples produce exactly the same visual results. The one you use is entirely up to you; you might find that one approach or another better fits in with the object structure that you are rendering. The important thing to remember is that the pass.Apply method needs to be called each time an updated world matrix needs to be observed.

There is one area where the two approaches will result in a performance difference, however. When we begin to apply textures to our objects (which we will examine in the "Applying Textures" section later in this chapter), we will need to pass the texture graphics to the graphics hardware each time we draw an object. Moving the graphic around in memory is a relatively expensive process because graphic files can be quite large.

We can therefore optimize our rendering by loading each texture into the graphics hardware just once and then drawing all objects that use that texture together. The next texture can then be loaded and its objects drawn. This way, we load each texture only once per draw, rather than potentially once per object.

The second rendering approach, shown in Listing 6–18, is potentially less efficient for textured objects. If we have multiple passes in our effect and each of the objects rendered has a different texture, we will end up alternating between the two textures. The first approach in Listing 6–17 deals with the object in its entirety before moving on to the next object, allowing its texture to be used by all the passes without needing it to be reloaded.

Drawing Primitives

All the drawing in our examples has been handled by making a call to the GraphicsDevice.DrawUserPrimitives function. The first parameter passed to this function, the primitiveType parameter, has always been PrimitiveType.TriangleStrip. There are several values that we can pass here, so let's take a look at each and discuss what they do and how they are used.

Drawing Lines

There are two different mechanisms provided for drawing lines on the screen: PrimitiveType.LineList and PrimitiveType.LineStrip.

LineList will work through the supplied vertices, taking each pair as the beginning and end coordinate of a line. The lines do not need to be connected (and indeed, if they are it might be more efficient to use the LineStrip drawing mode). The DrawUserPrimitive primitiveCount parameter specifies how many lines are to be drawn. Because each line requires two vertices, the vertex array must contain at least twice the number of entries as the specified primitive count.

Figure 6–12 shows the lines drawn between four vertices using the LineList mode primitive type, and a primitive count of 2.

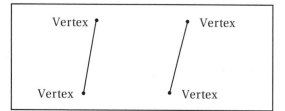

Figure 6–12. Drawing lines with the LineList primitive type

LineStrip is similar, but instead of working through pairs of vertices, it takes each new vertex and draws a line between it and the previous vertex. The result is a line drawn between all the specified vertices, as shown in Figure 6–13. The first line requires two vertices, but each subsequent line requires just one more. As a result, the vertex array must contain at least primitiveCount + 1 elements.

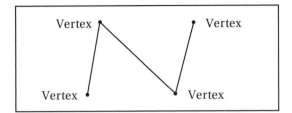

Figure 6–13. *Drawing lines with the LineStrip primitive type*

XNA does not offer a line drawing mode that automatically reconnects the final vertex back to the first vertex (to create a *line loop*). If such rendering is required, a final additional vertex will need to be added to the end of the LineStrip whose position matches that of the first vertex.

You can easily see the effects of drawing lines by modifying the ColoredSquare project to use the line primitive types instead of its existing TriangleStrip type. Notice how the vertex colors are still observed when drawing lines, and the line color fades between the color of each connected vertex.

There is no facility for setting the width of the line: all lines will be drawn with single-pixel thickness. If you need to draw lines thicker than this, you will need to simulate lines by drawing long thin rectangles formed from a pair of triangles instead.

Drawing Triangles

The remaining drawing primitives provide two different methods for creating triangles. Triangles are by far the most common type of object drawn in XNA, so these primitive types will become very familiar. The available triangle primitive modes are PrimitiveType.TriangleList and PrimitiveType.TriangleStrip.

The TriangleList primitive takes each set of three vertices as an individual triangle, allowing multiple isolated triangles to be drawn. Figure 6–14 shows how six vertices are used to build two triangles using this mode. Because each triangle requires three vertices, the vertex array must contain at least three times the number of entries as the specified primitive count.

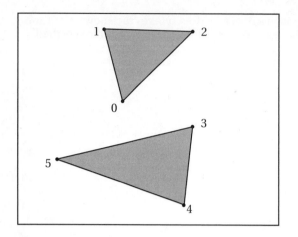

Figure 6–14. *Drawing triangles with the TriangleList primitive type*

The `TriangleStrip` primitive reuses vertices within the vertex array to create multiple triangles, each of which shares an edge with the previous triangle. The first three vertices are used to create the first triangle; after that, the next triangle is formed by removing the earliest vertex in the triangle and replacing it with the next vertex. The first triangle is, therefore, formed from vertices 0, 1, and 2; the second triangle from vertices 1, 2, and 3; the third triangle from vertices 2, 3, and 4; and so on.

As long as you can arrange your triangles so that they share their edges in this way, the triangle strip is a very efficient way of drawing because the shared vertices need to be transformed only once even though they are used by as many as three different triangles.

Figure 6–15 shows an example using the `TriangleStrip` to join a series of vertices. The first triangle requires three vertices, but each subsequent triangle requires just one more. As a result, the vertex array must contain at least `primitiveCount + 2` elements.

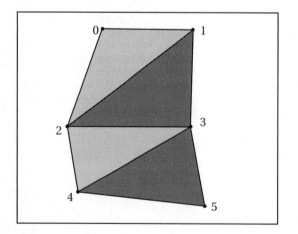

Figure 6–15. *Drawing triangles with the TriangleStrip primitive type*

The TriangleStrip mode is perfectly suited for drawing squares and rectangles because they are formed from two triangles that share an edge. As more complex objects are encountered, however, the ability to model them using triangle strips soon becomes difficult or impossible, and for them a triangle list will be required instead.

If you have used earlier versions of XNA or are familiar with DirectX or OpenGL, you might be expecting to find a further primitive type known as a *triangle fan*. It defines a series of triangles that all share a single vertex, allowing that vertex to be calculated just once for the entire object. Support for triangle fans was removed in XNA version 4.0 (as used on Windows Phone 7), so this primitive type is no longer available for use.

When you are defining your triangles, you will need to be aware of XNA's *hidden surface culling*. This is a feature that prevents it from having to draw unnecessary triangles. We'll discuss this in more detail in the "Hidden Surface Culling" section in the next chapter, but for now just be aware that you need to ensure that the vertices of your triangle are defined so that they are in clockwise order when you look at the triangle front on. You will observe that both of the triangles shown in Figure 6–14 are defined in this way.

For triangle strips, however, this would appear to present a problem: as each triangle shares its vertices with the previous triangle, the points alternate between clockwise and counterclockwise order. This can be seen in Figure 6–15: the first triangle (consisting of vertices 0, 1, and 2) is defined in clockwise order, but the second (vertices 1, 2, and 3) is counterclockwise. XNA realizes this and takes it into account automatically; the important thing is to ensure that the *first* triangle in a triangle strip is defined in a clockwise direction.

Drawing Points

Unlike earlier versions of XNA, support for drawing points (individual pixels) to the screen using vertices has been removed. To simulate drawing points, you will need to instead draw very small triangles, rectangles or lines.

Generally point drawing is of limited use anyway, so this will hopefully not present too much of a problem for your games.

Applying Textures

Colored shapes are all very nice, but they're not generally what we need when we are creating a game. For our games, we want to be able to display graphics onscreen. How do we do this with XNA when rendering with vertices?

Fortunately, it is very easy to do so. First, we need to load a texture and then we tell XNA to display that texture on the triangles that it draws. The following sections show how this is done.

Loading Graphics

Even though we can render 3D objects when we render with vertices, the graphics that we apply to them are still 2D bitmap graphics. The graphics are wrapped around the 3D objects as if they were stickers that we are applying to a solid object.

Textures are therefore added to the Content project and loaded ready for use by our 3D objects using the exact same code as we used when loading textures for sprites.

Alpha channels and color keys can still be used with textures just as they were with sprites, but there is a wide range of different ways that we can process them. These will be discussed in the "Using Transparency and Alpha Blending" section later in this chapter.

Setting the Active Texture

When we are ready to render with our texture, we first need to instruct XNA to use the texture. Just as with the other state properties inside XNA, it will remember the specified texture until we tell it to use a different texture. The code in Listing 6–19 tells XNA to use our loaded texture for subsequent textured objects.

Listing 6–19. Loading and activating a texture

```
// Load our texture
_texture = Content.Load<Texture2D>("Grapes");
// Set it as the active texture within our effect
_effect.Texture = _texture;
```

Applying the Texture to an Object

When we rendered triangles using colored vertices, we specified a color for each vertex. Now that we are rendering with textures, we instead tell each vertex to map to a point within the texture instead.

You will recall that sprite rendering allowed us to render either the entire texture across the surface of the sprite or a subsection of the texture. When we render using vertex buffers we can also render subsections of the texture, although we achieve this in a different way. We can also distort or stretch the texture in a variety of ways that were not available to sprites.

Just as coordinates on the screen are measured using axes called x and y, textures have axes called u and v. The u axis covers the distance across the width of a texture, whereas the v axis covers the distance across its height.

■ **NOTE** If you are familiar with OpenGL, you might expect the texture axes to be called *s* and *t*. Although XNA uses the letters *u* and *v* instead, the function and purpose of these axes are identical to the axes in OpenGL.

Regardless of the resolution of the graphic that has been loaded, the u and v coordinates will scale from 0 to 1, where 0 represents the left edge of the u axis and the top edge of the v axis, and 1 represents the right edge of the u axis and the bottom edge of the v axis, as shown in Figure 6–16. This is a very useful feature because it lets you switch between high- and low-resolution textures without needing to modify your code in any way.

Figure 6–16. The u and v axes for texture coordinates

When we want to draw using texture mapping, we provide a (u, v) coordinate for each vertex that tells it the position within the texture that should be applied at that vertex. Just as colors are interpolated between the vertices of rendered objects, so too are texture coordinates. The area inside the triangle formed by the texture coordinates will be stretched to fill the triangle formed onscreen by the vertex coordinates. This can be seen in Figure 6–17, which shows a triangle along with its vertex coordinates, the positions of those coordinates on a texture, and the resulting textured triangle.

Figure 6–17. A triangle and its texture coordinates, their positions on a texture, and the resulting textured triangle

Although the vertices are specified in three dimensions and therefore contain three values per vertex, texture coordinates are reading from a 2D image. So we provide just two values per vertex: the u and v coordinates for that vertex to use. They are provided to each vertex in a Vector2 structure. Because the Vector2 uses X and Y for its property names, we will use the X property to store the texture's u value and the Y property to store the texture's v value. The value is stored in the TextureCoordinate property of each vertex.

But hold on—the vertex structure that we have been using doesn't have a TextureCoordinate property! This is because we have been using the VertexPositionColor vertex structure, which (as its name suggests) can only store a position and a color for each vertex. To store texture coordinates, we need to switch to a different structure that supports texture information. We will use the VertexPositionTexture structure, which stores position and texture information.

■ **NOTE** You could alternatively use the VertexPositionColorTexture structure, which has properties for both colors and texture coordinates. This will allow a texture and per-vertex colors to be used together.

In the TexturedSquare example project, you will see that the _vertices array has been modified to use this new structure, as shown in Listing 6–20.

Listing 6–20. The _vertices array using the VertexPositionTexture structure

```
private VertexPositionTexture[] _vertices = new VertexPositionTexture[4];
```

To draw a square so that it displays the entire texture mapped on it, we specify u and v coordinates of (0, 1) for the bottom-left corner; (1, 1) for the bottom-right corner; (0, 0) for the top-left corner; and (1, 0) for the top-right corner. Each of these coordinates is specified for the vertex's TextureCoordinate property. Listing 6–21 contains the code required to initialize the vertex positions and texture coordinates for such a texture mapped square object.

Listing 6–21. Creating a square from two triangles and displaying an entire texture on its surface

```
_vertices[0].Position = new Vector3(-1, -1, 0);
_vertices[1].Position = new Vector3(-1, 1, 0);
_vertices[2].Position = new Vector3(1, -1, 0);
_vertices[3].Position = new Vector3(1, 1, 0);

_vertices[0].TextureCoordinate = new Vector2(0, 1);
_vertices[1].TextureCoordinate = new Vector2(0, 0);
_vertices[2].TextureCoordinate = new Vector2(1, 1);
_vertices[3].TextureCoordinate = new Vector2(1, 0);
```

Alternatively, we can specify just a section of the texture that we want to map. Remember that the physical vertex coordinates are completely unaffected by this; all we are doing is specifying the area of the texture that will be applied to the object. If we provide texture coordinates that cover only a smaller portion of the texture image, this portion will be stretched to fit the shape being drawn.

Figure 6–18 shows an example of using a subsection of the texture in this way. The texture coordinates span from 0 to 0.5 along both the u and v axes.

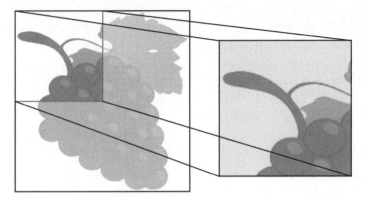

Figure 6–18. *Mapping a section of the source texture into a rendered square*

Another feature of the texture coordinates is that they are not restricted to staying within the range of 0 to 1. If we specify coordinates outside of this range, we can get the texture to repeat within our rendered graphics. Figure 6–19 shows a square object rendered with values from 0 to 3 on the u axis and 0 to 2 on the v axis. This might not be so useful when our texture is a bunch of grapes, but if you use a texture that tiles seamlessly (maybe a pattern of bricks or a stone texture), this can be a very handy way of filling the entire body of the object with a relatively small source image repeated over and over again.

Figure 6–19. *Wrapping the texture*

Preparing the Effect for Texture Mapping

The final thing we need to do is tell the XNA effect that we want it to use texture mapping. In the earlier examples, we told the effect to observe the vertex coloring by setting its VertexColorEnabled property to true. This time we will set it to false and instead set its TextureEnabled property to true. The complete effect initialization code for texturing is shown in Listing 6–22.

Listing 6–22. Configuring the effect for texture mapping

```
_effect = new BasicEffect(GraphicsDevice);
_effect.LightingEnabled = false;
_effect.VertexColorEnabled = false;
_effect.TextureEnabled = true;
_effect.Projection = projection;
_effect.View = view;
_effect.World = Matrix.Identity;
```

■ **NOTE** If you want to use the VertexPositionColorTexture structure to combine texturing and coloring, you will, of course, need to set both the VertexColorEnabled and TextureEnabled properties to true.

Our Draw code remains entirely unchanged. Because we have set the state of the effect object to use textures and provided a reference to a texture we have loaded, and we have provided texture coordinates for each vertex, XNA will automatically apply the texture to the object when it draws.

The TexturedSquare example project contains all the code needed to get this up and running; an image from the running example is shown in Figure 6–20. Try experimenting with the texture coordinates to get a feel for how they work. Some things that you can try to achieve with these are the following:

- Provide a texture coordinate range that spans only part of the texture (for example, ranging from 0 to 0.5 instead of from 0 to 1) and observe how the texture is stretched across the square.

- Provide texture coordinates outside of the range of 0 to 1 (for example, 0 to 3) and observe how the texture is squashed and repeated across the square.

- Provide coordinates that don't correlate with the position of the vertex and observe how the texture is distorted and stretched to fit within the rendered object.

Figure 6–20. The output from the TexturedSquare example project

Configuring the Sampler State

When XNA renders your texture, it queries a set of values known as the *sampler state* in order to fine-tune the resulting graphics. There are a couple of properties that we might want to change within the sampler state to alter the way in which the textures are processed.

Updating the Sampler State

The sampler state data can be read from the SamplerStates property of the GraphicsDevice object. This actually returns a collection of SamplerState objects, but the object at index 0 is the one that XNA will use for rendering.

However, the properties of this object are all read-only once the object has been attached to a GraphicsDevice (which it has by the time we can query it), and attempting to set one will result in an exception being thrown.

To change the sampler state properties, we must instead create a new SamplerState object, set its properties, and then set it into the SamplerStates collection. Listing 6–23 shows how this is achieved.

Listing 6–23. Providing a new SamplerState object for XNA

```
// Create a new SamplerState object
SamplerState samplerstate = new SamplerState();
// Set its properties as required...
// (set properties here)
// Give the object to XNA
GraphicsDevice.SamplerStates[0] = samplerstate;
```

The SamplerState class also provides a series of static properties that return preinitialized SamplerState objects in various configurations. If one of them matches your needs, you can set it directly into the SamplerState collection without having to instantiate and configure it yourself. The available preconfigured sampler states are AnisotropicClamp, AnisotropicWrap, LinearClamp, LinearWrap, PointClamp, PointWrap. The purpose of each of these will become clear once you have read through the following sections.

It is important to remember not to create new SamplerState objects during each Update or Draw because this will quickly cause garbage collection problems as we discussed earlier. If you need to use multiple sampler states within your drawing code, create them all once during initialization and just reuse these existing objects when drawing.

Texture Addressing Modes

The first SamplerState properties that we might want to set are the *texture address mode* properties. Back in Figure 6–19 we saw a texture with a coordinate range that causes the texture to be repeated across the object when the texture coordinates exceed the range of 0 to 1. This is known as Wrap mode, and it is the default behavior of XNA.

There are two other modes available, however: Clamp and Mirror. The Clamp mode tells XNA to observe texture coordinates only in the range 0 to 1. Any texture coordinate that falls outside of that range will be *clamped* back into the range (in other words, all values greater than 1 will be treated as if they were 1, and values less than 0 will be treated as if they were 0).

The primary effect is that the texture will not wrap within the rendered object. The secondary effect is that any texture coordinate that does fall outside of the 0 to 1 range will stretch out the pixel at that texture boundary for the whole of the clamped area. In other words, setting a horizontal texture coordinate range of 0 to 2 with clamping would display the texture as normal in the left half of the rendered object, and would then stretch the pixels from the right edge of the texture image across the whole of the right half of the rendered object.

The same texture coordinates shown in Figure 6–19 are shown again in Figure 6–21 with a `Clamp` address mode active.

Figure 6–21. *Drawing a texture with Clamp addressing*

The final mode, `Mirror`, works very much like `Wrap`, except that every alternate repeat will be flipped back to front (on the u axis) or upside down (on the v axis). The same texture can once again be seen in Figure 6–22 with `Mirror` addressing active.

Figure 6–22. *Drawing a texture with Mirror addressing*

The addressing modes can be set independently for each axis, so if you want you can mirror horizontally and wrap vertically. The horizontal address mode is set using the `RenderState.AddressU` property, and the vertical address mode is set using the `RenderState.AddressV` property.

Texture Filtering

The other sampler state property that we might want to set is the Filter property. This specifies the mechanism with which XNA will enlarge and shrink textures as it renders them to the screen. Three options are available: Linear, Point, and Anisotropic.

The Point filter is primarily noticeable when enlarging textures so that they are rendered at greater than their native size. When XNA uses a point filter, it determines for each pixel rendered on the screen which of the underlying texture pixels most closely matches in position. This texture pixel color is then directly displayed on the screen. The result is that the resulting graphic becomes very pixelated and blocky, reminiscent of early 3D games before dedicated graphics hardware became commonplace.

The Linear filter (which is active by default) is a little clever when it comes to enlarging textures. Instead of directly mapping texture pixels onto the screen, it blends together the surrounding pixels to approximate a smooth blend of the underlying texture pixels. This is not magic, of course, and the image will quickly become blurry, but it generally provides a substantially better result than the Point filter.

Figure 6–23 shows the textured square from in the earlier example projects, but greatly zoomed in. On the left it is rendered with a point filter and on the right with a linear filter.

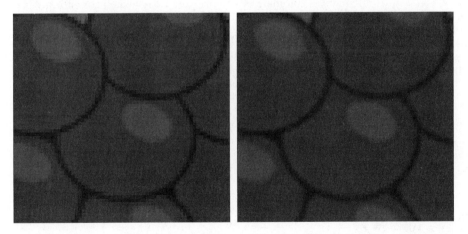

Figure 6–23. The SamplerState's Point filter on the left and its Linear filter on the right

The final filter, Anisotropic, comes into play when textures are being rendered so they stretch off into the distance of the screen. The perspective transformation (which we will examine in the next chapter) will result in the texture in the distance appearing much smaller than the texture in the foreground.

Linear filtering can cause noticeable visual artifacts to appear on texture that are rotated in this way. They are particularly noticeable when the texture is moving toward the player because it would be on the road in a racing game, for example. Using an anisotropic filter in this environment would provide the same general results as the linear filter, but with these texturing artifacts lessened so as to be much less apparent.

Supported Texture Image Formats

XNA is happy to apply any of its supported image types to your objects, so textures can be provided in BMP, PNG, and JPG formats. However, due to the way that the graphics hardware handles textures, you will find under some conditions your texture pixel width and height must exactly match a power of 2 (1, 2, 4, 8, 16, 32, 64, 128, 256, and so on).

The images do not need to be square, so you can, for example, use a texture that is 32 x 256 pixels, but for maximum flexibility they must observe these restrictions.

Images with sizes that are not powers of 2 can still be used in XNA provided that the texture address mode on the appropriate axes is set to Clamp, as described in the previous section. This will allow the texture to be displayed, but it means that wrapping and mirroring the texture cannot be supported on that axis.

If you want to use other texture address modes, and your texture dimensions are not powers of 2, you have a couple of options available.

First, you can enlarge or shrink your texture using a graphics editing application so that its dimensions are powers of 2. The easiest way to handle this is to stretch (or shrink) the graphic to fit the new dimensions. This gives you the greatest degree of control over the final image size and the way in which your graphic is manipulated to fit within its new space.

The second option is to get Visual Studio to automatically resize your image when compiling. This is by far the easiest approach, but does reduce the amount of control you have over the process. In many cases this will be quite sufficient, however.

To instruct Visual Studio to resize the image for you, edit the properties of the image within the Content project. Inside the Content Processor section you will find a property called Resize to Power of Two, as can be seen in Figure 6–24. Simply set this to True, and the image will be expanded to the next power of 2 on each axis when the content project is compiled.

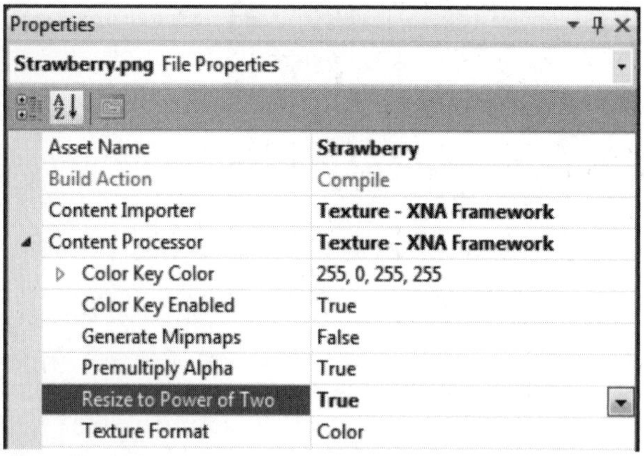

Figure 6–24. Setting an image to be automatically resized to a power of 2

Using Different Textures Within the Same Draw Call

In the TexturedSquare project, the single texture is set into the effect's Texture property as soon as it is loaded, and this stays active for the entire duration of the project.

In any real game it is highly likely that you will need multiple textures so that different objects can be drawn with different appearances on the screen.

This is easy to achieve. Once all the textures have been loaded, each one can be activated as needed within the Draw function by setting the effect's Texture property before applying the passes of the effect.

As mentioned earlier, setting the active texture is one of the most expensive things you can do in terms of performance, and so you should try to batch up your drawing so that all objects for each texture are drawn together. Avoiding setting the texture unnecessarily within each draw will help to ensure that your game performs the best it can.

The MultipleTextures example project demonstrates drawing two objects together, each with a different texture. The code from its Draw function is shown in Listing 6–24.

Listing 6–24. Drawing multiple objects, each using different textures

```
// Activate the first texture
_effect.Texture = _texture1;
// Apply a transformation to move and rotate the object
_effect.World = Matrix.CreateRotationZ(_angle);
_effect.World = Matrix.CreateTranslation(0, 1.2f, 0) * _effect.World;
foreach (EffectPass pass in _effect.CurrentTechnique.Passes)
{
    // Apply the pass
    pass.Apply();
    // Draw the square
    GraphicsDevice.DrawUserPrimitives(PrimitiveType.TriangleStrip, _vertices, 0, 2);
}

// Activate the second texture
_effect.Texture = _texture2;
// Apply a transformation to move and rotate the object
_effect.World = Matrix.CreateRotationZ(_angle);
_effect.World = Matrix.CreateTranslation(0, -1.2f, 0) * _effect.World;
foreach (EffectPass pass in _effect.CurrentTechnique.Passes)
{
    // Apply the pass
    pass.Apply();
    // Draw the square
    GraphicsDevice.DrawUserPrimitives(PrimitiveType.TriangleStrip, _vertices, 0, 2);
}
```

Using Transparency and Alpha Blending

XNA offers us support for dealing with transparency when we render our graphics. We can achieve various effects with this, such as removing transparent parts of an image or drawing an image so that it is semitransparent, allowing the graphics behind to show through. This is known as *alpha blending*.

The examples we have looked at so far in this chapter have rendered images with solid black backgrounds. As you will see, alpha blending allows us to remove this and observe the alpha channel within the texture, just as we did for sprites in the earlier chapters.

In this section we'll look at the available alpha blending options and learn how you can customize them for your games.

Enabling and Disabling Alpha Blending

In order to take advantage of alpha blending, we need to instruct XNA to use a *blend state* object. This contains information that XNA will use to determine exactly how to mix the pixels of the objects that it is drawing with the pixels that are already present on the screen.

This might be as simple as determining whether to completely replace an existing pixel or leave it with its current color, or it might involve a blend of the existing pixel and the pixel from the rendered object.

The active BlendState object can be found in the GraphicsDevice.BlendState property. The object can be interrogated, but its properties cannot be updated: just like the SamplerState objects we saw in the last section, a BlendState object's properties all become read-only once it has been set into the GraphicsDevice.

To alter the active BlendState, we must create a new BlendState object, configure its properties, and only then pass it to the GraphicsDevice, as can be seen in Listing 6–25. Once again, it is important to avoid doing this inside your Update or Draw functions: any required BlendState objects should instead be created just once during initialization and then reused as and when needed.

Listing 6–25. Creating and activating a new BlendState object

```
// Create a new BlendState object
BlendState blendState = new BlendState();
// Set blend state object properties
// ...
// Set the object into the GraphicsDevice
GraphicsDevice.BlendState = blendState;
```

To disable alpha blending, the BlendState property should be set to BlendState.Opaque, as shown in Listing 6–26. There are two reasons why it is very important to remember to disable alpha blending as soon as you have finished with it. First, alpha blending has a higher processing overhead on the graphics hardware than opaque rendering because it needs to consider the pixels already on the screen as well as those being rendered. Second, having blending active when you are not expecting it to be can produce very confusing results in your game, causing objects to become transparent or even disappear.

Listing 6–26. Disabling alpha blending

```
// Switch to the Opaque blend state
GraphicsDevice.BlendState = BlendState.Opaque;
```

XNA's Built-In Blend States

There are some transparency effects that are more frequently used within games than others, and to simplify using these effects XNA provides a series of static objects whose properties reflect this. Before we get into the complexities of how alpha blending actually works, let's take a look at some of these states and describe the purpose and use of each. We will look at how the blend states work under the covers later in this section.

Throughout this section we will describe colors and alpha values as float values rather than as integers. This means that they will always be in the range of 0 to 1, rather than 0 to 255. The reason for this will become apparent later in the section.

You can experiment with these blend states by opening the AlphaBlending example project and changing the state that is set at the end of the Initialize function.

Opaque

The BlendState.Opaque reference that we saw in Listing 6–26 is not an enumeration as it might at first appear, but is in fact one of the built-in blend state objects. Opaque is a static property on the BlendState class that returns a BlendState object configured with alpha blending disabled.

This is the default blend state that is active when your XNA game launches, and is therefore the state that we have been using so far through this chapter.

With opaque blending active, every pixel rendered from the source texture will be written to the screen so that it entirely replaces the content that is already present.

Figure 6–25 shows the Grapes texture rendered using the opaque blend mode.

Figure 6–25. Overlapping textures rendered with the Opaque blend state

AlphaBlend

A particularly useful blend state is AlphaBlend, which is actually the mode that we were using with sprites when an alpha channel or a color key was present. This mode reads the alpha value from the source texture and uses it to determine how opaque the pixel should be when rendered on top of the existing graphics.

Pixels whose alpha values are 0.0 within the texture will be rendered entirely transparent (invisible). Pixels whose alpha values are 1.0 are rendered entirely opaque. Alpha values between them will result in varying levels of semitransparency. This is therefore ideal for textures that contain an alpha channel or color key because it allows them to be rendered with sections that are partially or completely transparent.

Figure 6–26 shows the Grapes textures once again, this time rendered with the AlphaBlend blend state.

Figure 6–26. Overlapping textures rendered with the AlphaBlend blend state

Additive

Setting the blend state to `BlendState.Additive` applies another blend that takes into account the existing graphics that have already been displayed on the screen and also the alpha information contained within the texture being rendered.

This time, however, the colors of the pixels being rendered are added to the colors on the screen, rather than replacing them. Colors are added by taking their individual red, green, and blue color elements, multiplying them by the texture's alpha value to make them observe the texture transparency information, and then finally adding them to the existing red, green, and blue color values already present on the screen. This might well result in some of the elements exceeding their maximum level of 1.0. When this happens, they are clamped to 1.0.

If, for example, the screen were filled with a dark green color whose RGB values are (0.0, 0.5, 0.0), and we render a solid red texture with RGB values (1.0, 0.0, 0.0) and full alpha (1.0), the resulting calculation would be as follows:

$$\text{Red}_{new} = (\text{Red}_{source} \times \text{Alpha}) + \text{Red}_{dest} = (1.0 \times 1.0) + 0.0 = 1.0$$
$$\text{Green}_{new} = (\text{Green}_{source} \times \text{Alpha}) + \text{Green}_{dest} = (0.0 \times 1.0) + 0.5 = 0.5$$
$$\text{Blue}_{new} = (\text{Blue}_{source} \times \text{Alpha}) + \text{Blue}_{dest} = (0.0 \times 1.0) + 0.0 = 0.0$$

The resulting color will have RGB values (1.0, 0.5, 0.0)—an orange color. If we had a yellow color already on the screen (1.0, 1.0, 0.0) and we rendered a purple texture (1.0, 0.0, 1.0) with an alpha value of 0.5, the final color would be calculated as follows:

$$\text{Red}_{new} = (\text{Red}_{source} \times \text{Alpha}) + \text{Red}_{dest} = (1.0 \times 0.5) + 1.0 = 1.5$$
$$\text{Green}_{new} = (\text{Green}_{source} \times \text{Alpha}) + \text{Green}_{dest} = (0.0 \times 0.5) + 1.0 = 1.0$$
$$\text{Blue}_{new} = (\text{Blue}_{source} \times \text{Alpha}) + \text{Blue}_{dest} = (1.0 \times 0.5) + 0.0 = 0.5$$

The resulting color would be (1.0, 1.0, 0.5) as the red value would be clamped at 1.0. This is a pale yellow color.

Because additive blending is adding two colors together, repeated rendering of the same area on the screen pushes the color toward full red, green, and blue intensity. If the colors being mixed contain elements of all three color components, the color will tend toward white.

■ **TIP** Additive blending is ideally suited for making explosion effects. The explosion of the spaceship in the *Cosmic Rocks* examples we saw in earlier chapters uses additive blending for just such a purpose.

Figure 6–27 shows the grape textures rendered with additive blending. The color of the background is being retained and mixed with the texture as it is drawn, resulting in a blue tinge across everything, and cyan leaves on the grapes as the texture's green color and the screen's blue color are mixed together.

Figure 6–27. Overlapping textures rendered with the Additive blend state

Creating Custom Blend States

Although the built-in blend states will be appropriate in many situations, sometimes it is useful to be able to further customize the blend state that XNA uses. There is an enormous number of combinations of blend states that can be created, and they are defined using three properties of the `BlendState` object: `ColorBlendFunction`, `ColorSourceBlend`, and `ColorDestinationBlend`.

They are matched by three similar properties that refer to the alpha channel: `AlphaBlendFunction`, `AlphaSourceBlend`, and `AlphaDestinationBlend`. On Windows and Xbox platforms they can be set independently of the color properties to create even more combinations of blending operations, but on Windows Phone 7 they must exactly match the corresponding color properties or XNA will throw an exception.

The way in which blending is performed using these properties is consistent and understandable on a mathematical level, but can sometimes require a little experimentation to achieve the desired effect. As we saw with the Additive blend, a calculation is performed against the individual red, green, and blue components of the source and destination colors in order to obtain the final color that will appear on the screen.

The calculation is as follows:

(source color x `ColorSourceBlend`) `ColorBlendFunction` (destination color x `ColorDestinationBlend`)

For each pixel that XNA renders to the screen, it first takes the red, green, blue, and alpha elements of the source color (the color of the pixel being rendered from the texture) and multiplies them by the corresponding elements from the ColorSourceBlend value. It then repeats this with the color of the pixel already present on the screen, multiplying it by the ColorDestinationBlend elements.

With these two colors calculated, they are combined using the appropriate ColorBlendFunction.

We will look at all the available options for them in a moment, but before we do that let's pick a simple example to demonstrate this calculation.

One of the available blend types is Blend.One, which provides the value 1.0 for each of the red, green, blue, and alpha color elements. Another factor is Blend.Zero, which provides the value 0.0 for each color component. Finally we have a blend function named BlendFunction.Add which simply adds the source and the destination color element values together.

If we use Blend.One as the source blend, Blend.Zero as the destination blend, and BlendFunction.Add as the blend function, the color for each pixel is calculated as follows:

$$Red_{new} = (Red_{source} \times 1.0) + (Red_{dest} \times 0.0)$$
$$Green_{new} = (Green_{source} \times 1.0) + (Green_{dest} \times 0.0)$$
$$Blue_{new} = (Blue_{source} \times 1.0) + (Blue_{dest} \times 0.0)$$

As you can see, the end result if these blending parameters are used is that the object is rendered absolutely opaque; no blending takes place at all. The output colors calculated are exactly the same as the source colors, with the existing destination color completely ignored. This is in fact the configuration that is provided by the BlendState.Opaque object. The code to configure this blend state is shown in Listing 6–27.

Listing 6–27. Manually configuring a BlendState object for opaque blending

```
// Create a new BlendState object
BlendState blendState = new BlendState();

// Set the color blend properties
blendState.ColorBlendFunction = BlendFunction.Add;
blendState.ColorSourceBlend = Blend.One;
blendState.ColorDestinationBlend = Blend.Zero;

// Copy the color blend properties to the alpha blend properties
blendState.AlphaBlendFunction = blendState.ColorBlendFunction;
blendState.AlphaSourceBlend = blendState.ColorSourceBlend;
blendState.AlphaDestinationBlend = blendState.ColorDestinationBlend;

// Set the object into the GraphicsDevice
GraphicsDevice.BlendState = blendState;
```

■ **NOTE** The initial configuration of a newly instantiated BlendState object is exactly the same as that of the built-in BlendState.Opaque object.

Let's take a look at a different pair of blend types. We will use Blend.SourceAlpha for the source blend and combine it with Blend.InverseSourceAlpha for the destination. SourceAlpha provides the source color's alpha value, whereas InverseSourceAlpha provides the source color's alpha subtracted from 1 (so a source alpha of 1 becomes 0, a source of 0 becomes 1, a source of 0.2 becomes 0.8, and so on). Using BlendFunction.Add once again, the output color of each pixel is therefore calculated as follows:

$$Red_{new} = (Red_{source} \times Alpha_{source}) + (Red_{dest} \times (1 - Alpha_{source}))$$
$$Green_{new} = (Green_{source} \times Alpha_{source}) + (Green_{dest} \times (1 - Alpha_{source}))$$
$$Blue_{new} = (Blue_{source} \times Alpha_{source}) + (Blue_{dest} \times (1 - Alpha_{source}))$$

Think for a moment about the results of this calculation. If the source alpha is 1 (opaque), the calculation will take the entire source color (because it is being multiplied by 1) and none of the destination color (because it is being multiplied by 0). The result will be that the pixel is rendered opaque.

If, on the other hand, the source alpha is 0 (transparent), the calculation will take none of the source color (as this is being multiplied by 0) and all the destination color (because it is being multiplied by 1). The result will be that the pixel is rendered entirely transparent.

Alpha values that fall between 0 and 1 will provide a gradual transition between transparent and opaque. This is exactly the effect that we need for rendering textures onto the screen so that they observe the image's alpha channel.

The available Blend enumeration values are shown in Table 6–1. The Values column uses the characters R, G, B, and A to refer to the red, green, blue, and alpha color components; and adds a subscript of s or d to identify whether this relates to the source or destination color.

Table 6–1. Blend Types

Blend	Description	Values
One	All color elements are set to 1	$(1, 1, 1, 1)$
Zero	All color elements are set to 0	$(0, 0, 0, 0)$
SourceColor	The color elements of the pixel in the source texture	(R_s, G_s, B_s, A_s)
InverseSourceColor	The inverse color elements of the pixel in the source texture (each subtracted from 1)	$(1 - R_s, 1 - G_s, 1 - B_s, 1 - A_s)$
SourceAlpha	The alpha value of the pixel in the source texture	(A_s, A_s, A_s, A_s)
InverseSourceAlpha	The inverse alpha value of the pixel in the source texture	$(1 - A_s, 1 - A_s, 1 - A_s, 1 - A_s)$
DestinationColor	The color elements of the pixel currently displayed on the screen	(R_d, G_d, B_d, A_d)
InverseDestinationColor	The inverse color elements of the pixel currently displayed on the screen	$(1 - R_d, 1 - G_d, 1 - B_d, 1 - A_d)$
DestinationAlpha	The alpha value of the pixel currently displayed on the screen	(A_d, A_d, A_d, A_d)

Blend	Description	Values
InverseDestinationAlpha	The inverse alpha value of the pixel currently displayed on the screen	$(1 - A_d, 1 - A_d, 1 - A_d, 1 - A_d)$
BlendFactor	The color elements of the graphic device's BlendFactor color	$(R_{blendfactor}, G_{blendfactor}, B_{blendfactor}, A_{blendfactor})$
InverseBlendFactor	The inverse color elements of the blend factor color	$(1 - R_{blendfactor}, 1 - G_{blendfactor}, 1 - B_{blendfactor}, 1 - A_{blendfactor})$
SourceAlphaSaturation	Either the source alpha or the inverse of the destination alpha, whichever is less	$(f, f, f, 1)$, where f is the calculation $\max(A_s, 1 - A_d)$

The ColorBlendFunction can be set to any of the values shown in Table 6–2. Remember that each of them operates on the red, green, blue, and alpha values independently to calculate the final color.

Table 6–2. Blending Functions

BlendFunction	Description
Add	The color is calculated by adding the source and destination colors: `Output = (source color * source blend) + (dest color * dest blend)`
Subtract	The color is calculated by subtracting the destination color from the source: `Output = (source color * source blend) - (dest color * dest blend)`
ReverseSubtract	The color is calculated by subtracting the source color from the destination: `Output = (dest color * dest blend) - (source color * source blend)`
Min	The color is calculated by finding the lesser value from the source and destination colors: `Output = Min( (source color * source blend), (dest color * dest blend) )` When using Min on Windows Phone 7, the source and destination blend functions must both be set to Blend.One, or XNA will throw an exception.
Max	The color is calculated by finding the greater value from the source and destination colors: `Output = Max( (source color * source blend), (dest color * dest blend) )` When using Max on Windows Phone 7, the source and destination blend functions must both be set to Blend.One, or XNA will throw an exception.

A huge range of effects can be obtained using different combinations of these functions and blendtypes. Try experimenting with them inside the AlphaBlending example project to see some of the results that you can obtain.

■ **NOTE** You might recall that we passed BlendState objects into the BlendState parameter SpriteBatch.Begin function in our 2D examples in the earlier chapters. These are exactly the same BlendState objects that we are using here. Now that you have a greater understanding of how they work, you can apply that knowledge to your sprite rendering, too.

Object Transparency

One very useful rendering feature that we've not yet seen support for in this section is the ability to fade an entire object between opaque and transparent. With sprite rendering, this could be controlled using the alpha component of the sprite tint, but as you saw in the "Tinting Objects" section earlier in this chapter, no such element is available for tinting when rendering vertices.

The reason is simply because the alpha value is stored in a separate property. Each Effect object (including BasicEffect) has an Alpha property that can be given a value between 0 (invisible) and 1 (opaque). All the source alpha values within the object will be multiplied by this to generate the value for the SourceAlpha blend. Providing your blend state observes the source alpha, you can therefore use the Alpha property to fade your objects between opaque and transparent and still observe the alpha information stored in your textures.

Handling Orientations

We discussed support for different orientations back in Chapter 2, and everything we looked at before still applies when rendering with vertices and matrices, but there is an additional step that we need to take into account to make things work properly.

The OrientationSupport example project demonstrates the problem that we need to address—and its solution. If you start the project running with the device or emulator in portrait mode, you will see that it displays three textured squares just as in the alpha blending example, except that this time they rotate back and forth so that they stay essentially upright. This will allow us to ensure that the graphics are being kept the right way up and are not appearing sideways.

The initial display from the project is just as we would expect, with the squares arranged vertically above one another. The project is configured to support all three of the Windows Phone 7 orientations, however, so now rotate the device or the emulator so that it is in a landscape orientation.

XNA correctly rotates the screen so that the graphics remain upright (the grapes are still the right way up, and the objects are still arranged vertically within the new orientation). However, the objects are no longer square: they are instead very squashed, as can be seen in Figure 6–28.

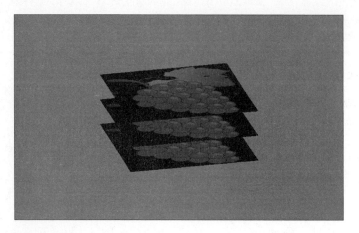

Figure 6–28. *Distorted objects after switching into landscape orientation*

To find the reason for this, we need to look all the way back to Listing 6–2. This is where we calculated the aspect ratio for the screen by dividing the back buffer width by its height. For a portrait screen, this calculation is 480 / 800, which equals 0.6. For a landscape screen, however, the calculation is 800 / 480, which results in 1.666. Because XNA is still rendering with the original portrait aspect ratio, it continues after rotation to render with the belief that the screen width is 6/10 of its height, which it no longer is.

To address the problem, we simply need to recalculate the aspect ratio when the orientation changes. We can add a handler for the Window.OrientationChanged event in the game class's constructor, as shown in Listing 6–28.

Listing 6–28. Handling the window's OrientationChanged event

```
// Add a handler to update projection matrix if the orientation changes
Window.OrientationChanged += new EventHandler<EventArgs>(Window_OrientationChanged);
```

The implementation of the OrientationChanged event is shown in Listing 6–29. This does result in a small amount of code duplication as the Initialize function also sets the projection matrix, so you might want to separate this out into a separate function that can be called from each of these two locations. For simplicity, we will duplicate the code in this example.

Listing 6–29. Updating the projection matrix when the screen orientation changes

```
void Window_OrientationChanged(object sender, EventArgs e)
{
    // Calculate the new screen aspect ratio
    float aspectRatio =
            (float)GraphicsDevice.Viewport.Width / GraphicsDevice.Viewport.Height;
    // Create a projection matrix
    Matrix projection = Matrix.CreatePerspectiveFieldOfView(MathHelper.ToRadians(45),
                                                    aspectRatio, 0.1f, 1000.0f);

    // Set the matrix into the effect
    _effect.Projection = projection;
}
```

This block of code is initially commented out in the OrientationSupport example project, which is why the graphics appeared distorted after the orientation was changed. Uncomment the code and then run the project again. This time you will see that the behavior after rotation from portrait to landscape is quite different: the objects are no longer distorted, and the scene "zooms out" so that the amount of vertical space that is displayed on the screen is the same in landscape orientation as it was in portrait. This can be seen in Figure 6–29.

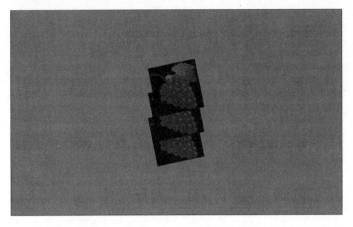

Figure 6–29. Landscape orientation with the aspect ratio correctly recalculated

Although the objects appear smaller than they were, the code to render them and the transformations that are applied are completely unchanged; it is just the projection matrix that has caused the change in appearance.

Graphic Scaling

If you want to use a smaller back buffer and take advantage of Windows Phone 7's automatic scaling, this is exceedingly easy using vertex and matrix rendering. Whereas when we were drawing with sprites we had to take into account that the sprites all appeared larger when they were rendered into a smaller back buffer, no such issues occur at all with the new approach.

You can see this for yourself by modifying the buffer size in any of the example projects. Try setting them to half their native size (in a portrait orientation, set the width to 240 pixels and the height to 480). The project will appear with its graphics in exactly the same positions and proportions as they were with the original buffer size. They will, of course, appear a little jagged due to the zooming, but with fast-moving scenes this can be much harder to spot.

Integration into the Game Framework

Just as we added support for sprite and text rendering into the game framework project, so we will add support for matrix-based rendering. This allows us to continue the simple object-based approach that we have used in the previous chapters and apply it to the new rendering techniques that we have learned in this chapter. All the code in this section can be found inside the GameFrameworkExample project that accompanies this chapter.

Sprites have a fairly limited set of operations that can be performed, so it was easy to wrap up a significant amount of their functionality in the game framework's SpriteObject class. When we render with matrices, there are many more variables to take into account, such as the flexibility of specifying the object's transformation matrix, the different primitives that can be rendered, and the different types of effect (BasicEffect is just one of several effects that are available, as you will see in Chapter 8).

As a result, the game framework's support for matrix rendering is a little less comprehensive than it was for sprite rendering. It provides the features that are most likely to be useful and then allows the individual object classes to use or ignore them as they see fit. They are present in a new class: MatrixObjectBase.

The MatrixObjectBase Class

MatrixObjectBase is an abstract class that derives from GameObjectBase (see Figure 6–30). It provides useful properties and functions that we might want to use within our derived game object classes (though in many cases they will be insufficient in isolation and will require additional object-specific properties to be added to the derived classes).

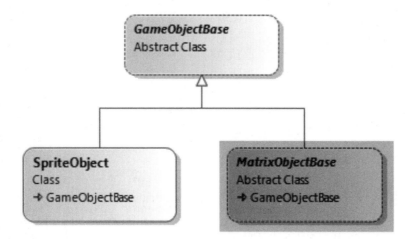

Figure 6–30. The MatrixObjectBase class's position within the framework project

The first content that is present in the class is a range of properties that can be used to control how instances of derived classes will be rendered. The properties contained within the class are as follows:

- ObjectTexture: a reference to a texture that will be used when rendering the object (or null if no texture is required). Defaults to null.

- Transformation: a matrix that defines the transformation to use when rendering the object. This will normally be set during the object's Update call and then used as the world matrix when rendering from the Draw call.

- Position, PositionX, PositionY, and Position Z: a 3D position for the object, represented both as a Vector3 and a series of floats (though they share the same underlying storage, so modifying the vector will affect the float values, and vice versa). Defaults to (0, 0, 0).

- Angle, AngleX, AngleY, and AngleZ: three angles that can be used to track rotation of the object around each axis. The Angle property sets or returns the same values as a Vector3. Defaults to (0, 0, 0).

- Scale, ScaleX, ScaleY, and ScaleZ: the scaling factors for each axis, available as a Vector3 or as three float values. Defaults to (1, 1, 1).

- ObjectColor: just as with sprites, this allows the color and alpha for the object to be specified. The red, green, and blue components will be passed into the effect object's DiffuseColor property, and its alpha component will be used to determine a value for the effect's Alpha property.

Object Transformation

The general approach when rendering objects is to calculate their transformation matrix during the call to each object's Update method, and then use that calculated matrix in its Draw method. Let's take a look at how the transformation is calculated.

There is clearly some overlap between the class's position properties: Transformation is used to store the calculated transformation for the object; whereas the Position, Angle, and Scale properties each make up a part of that transformation. Transformations can be much more complex than simply applying a translation, rotate, and scale matrix, however, because many transformations might need to be applied in an appropriate sequence to achieve the final matrix to use for rendering.

To allow us to achieve a balance between simplicity and flexibility, the class offers a few different approaches for calculating the Transformation matrix.

The first approach is to fully calculate the transformation matrix within the derived class. Essentially this requires the derived Update code to simply place the required matrix into the Transformation property ready to be read back during rendering.

It can do this by multiplying matrices together as we saw in earlier examples in this chapter. It can also take advantage of two simple functions within MatrixObjectBase: SetIdentity and ApplyTransformation.

SetIdentity simply loads the identity matrix into the Transformation property, as shown in Listing 6–30.

Listing 6–30. The SetIdentity function implementation

```
protected void SetIdentity()
{
    Transformation = Matrix.Identity;
}
```

ApplyTransformation takes a transformation matrix as a parameter and multiplies it with the existing Transformation matrix, as shown in Listing 6–31.

Listing 6–31. The ApplyTransformation function implementation

```
protected void ApplyTransformation(Matrix newTransformation)
{
    Transformation = newTransformation * Transformation;
}
```

These are clearly very simple and are almost unnecessary, but they allow simple step-by-step transformations to be applied in an Update function. Listing 6–32 shows an example of such an Update function from a derived class in a game project (it can actually be found in the

GameFrameworkExample.TexturedSquareObject class in the example project). This code resets the object transformation to the identity matrix, rotates by the angle stored in the AngleZ property, scales the matrix as per the object's Scale vector, and then translates according to the object's Position. At each stage, the resulting matrix is updated in the Transformation property.

Listing 6–32. Applying a series of transformations using the ApplyTransformation function

```
// Calculate the transformation matrix
SetIdentity();
ApplyTransformation(Matrix.CreateRotationZ(AngleZ));
ApplyTransformation(Matrix.CreateScale(Scale));
ApplyTransformation(Matrix.CreateTranslation(Position));
```

Listing 6–33 achieves the exact same result using direct matrix multiplications instead of the SetIdentity and ApplyTransformation functions.

Listing 6–33. Applying a series of transformations using direct matrix multiplication

```
Transformation = Matrix.CreateRotationZ(AngleZ);
Transformation = Matrix.CreateScale(Scale) * Transformation;
Transformation = Matrix.CreateTranslation(Position) * Transformation;
```

■ **NOTE** If you have experience of programming using OpenGL, the approach that specifies a sequence of transformations shown in Listing 6–32 will probably feel more comfortable because it approximates the approach used by OpenGL to specify its world transformation. Both approaches are functionally identical, though, so use whichever you prefer.

Note that, although these code samples have used some of the standard properties (AngleZ, Scale, and Position), nothing else within the class is taking any notice of them. In this example, they are being used simply as handy places to store information about the location of the object, but they have no further meaning to the class.

The second approach that we can use is to get MatrixObjectBase to apply all the transformation properties automatically. When we do this, it will perform the following steps, in this order:

1. Translate the object according to its Position vector.

2. Rotate the object around the x axis according to its AngleX value.

3. Rotate the object around the y axis according to its AngleY value.

4. Rotate the object around the z axis according to its AngleZ value.

5. Scale the object according to its Scale vector.

The code that performs these transformations is shown in Listing 6–34.

Listing 6–34. The MatrixObjectBase.ApplyStandardTransformations function

```
protected void ApplyStandardTransformations()
{
    Matrix result;

    // First obtain the object's underlying transformation
    result = Transformation;

    // Apply the object position if any of the coordinates are non-zero
    if (PositionX != 0 || PositionY != 0 || PositionZ != 0)
    {
        // Yes, so apply the position to the current transformation
        result = Matrix.CreateTranslation(Position) * result;
    }

    // Rotate the object if any of the angles are non-zero
    if (AngleX != 0) result = Matrix.CreateRotationX(AngleX) * result;
    if (AngleY != 0) result = Matrix.CreateRotationY(AngleY) * result;
    if (AngleZ != 0) result = Matrix.CreateRotationZ(AngleZ) * result;

    // Scale the object if any of the scale values are set to a value other than 1
    if (ScaleX != 1 || ScaleY != 1 || ScaleZ != 1)
    {
        // Yes, so apply the Scale to the current transformation
        result = Matrix.CreateScale(Scale) * result;
    }

    // Store the final calculated matrix
    Transformation = result;
}
```

Sometimes this set of steps will be quite sufficient for a game object, in which case no further processing is required. Listing 6–35 shows how to apply these steps to the object to calculate its transformation matrix. Note that these steps are applied in addition to the existing transformation, so it is important to remember to call SetIdentity first so that they are applied to an identity matrix rather than to any matrix left over from a previous update.

Listing 6–35. Applying the standard transformations to an object

```
// Calculate the transformation matrix
SetIdentity();
ApplyStandardTransformations();
```

Finally, a combination of these two approaches can be used, mixing both custom transformations and the standard transformations together. The transformation matrix can be set both before or after the standard transformations are applied so that customized behavior can be achieved. Listing 6–36 first offsets the object position to the left by one unit and then applies the standard transformations and then translates one unit along the (potentially rotated) y axis.

Listing 6–36. Mixing custom and standard transformations

```
SetIdentity();
ApplyTransformation(Matrix.CreateTranslation(-1, 0, 0));
ApplyStandardTransformations();
ApplyTransformation(Matrix.CreateTranslation(0, 1, 0));
```

Generally, however, it is best to stick to simple transformations prior to calling
`ApplyStandardTransformations` and no further transformations afterward. Because the standard
transformations are not listed step by step within the code as all the other transformations are, it can
be confusing to visualize exactly what happens during the `ApplyStandardTransformations` function call,
so mix the two approaches with caution.

Object Rendering

With the transformation matrix for the object calculated, the object can now be drawn. As with sprite
rendering, this is achieved using a method named `Draw`, but this time it is passed an `Effect` object
instead of a `SpriteBatch`. The function is declared as an abstract function, as shown in Listing 6–37,
because it has no default implementation, but must be overridden in each derived class.

Listing 6–37. The declaration of the MatrixObjectBase.Draw function

```
public abstract void Draw(GameTime gameTime, Effect effect);
```

When a class overrides this, it is its responsibility to perform the required steps to draw the object
to the screen. Some of this will vary from one class to another, but there are some properties of the
effect that can be looked after by `MatrixObjectBase`. They are handled within a function called
`PrepareEffect`.

The `PrepareEffect` function ensures that the appropriate texture is set into the effect, that the
texturing is enabled or disabled as required, that the `DiffuseColor` and `Alpha` properties are set
according to the `ObjectColor` value, and that the calculated `Transformation` is set. Once all these are in
place, the object is ready for rendering. Listing 6–38 shows the implementation of the `PrepareEffect`
function.

Listing 6–38. Preparing an effect ready for rendering

```
protected void PrepareEffect(BasicEffect effect)
{
    // Do we have a texture? Set the effect as required
    if (ObjectTexture == null)
    {
        // No texture so disable texturing
        effect.TextureEnabled = false;
    }
    else
    {
        // Enable texturing and set the texture into the effect
        effect.TextureEnabled = true;
        if (ObjectTexture != effect.Texture) effect.Texture = ObjectTexture;
    }

    // Set the color and alpha
    effect.DiffuseColor = ObjectColor.ToVector3();
```

```
    effect.Alpha = (float)ObjectColor.A / 255.0f;

    // Apply the transformation matrix
    effect.World = Transformation;

    // Now the effect is ready for the derived class to actually draw the object
}
```

This can then be easily used within a derived class to set the required effect properties before rendering. Listing 6–39 shows another piece of code from the TexturedSquareObject example class, this time for the Draw function.

Listing 6–39. Drawing an object in a derived class

```
public override void Draw(Microsoft.Xna.Framework.GameTime gameTime, Effect effect)
{
    // Prepare the effect for drawing
    PrepareEffect(effect);

    // Draw the object
    foreach (EffectPass pass in effect.CurrentTechnique.Passes)
    {
        // Apply the pass
        pass.Apply();
        // Draw the square
        effect.GraphicsDevice.DrawUserPrimitives(PrimitiveType.TriangleStrip,
                                                        _vertices, 0, 2);
    }
}
```

This should all be looking very familiar. If you examine the TexturedSquareObject class as a whole, you will see that it has very little code present, but it still manages to render our textured object to the screen.

There is, of course, no strict requirement to call PrepareEffect, and this work could instead be carried out directly within the derived class if necessary.

Updates to the GameHost Class

The game framework's GameHost class needs a small enhancement to support rendering matrix objects. This takes the form of the DrawObjects function.

DrawObjects performs the same task for matrix-based objects as DrawSprites performs for sprites: it draws all the objects in the game, potentially filtering them by a specified texture for performance reasons. However, we have a slight additional complexity for objects: not all of them actually *have* a texture. We need to be able to distinguish between drawing all the objects (ignoring textures completely) and drawing the objects for which the texture is null.

We achieve this by creating two public overloads, one that takes a texture as a parameter and draws only objects that use that texture, and one that doesn't take a texture parameter and draws all the objects. Internally, each of these calls into a third (private) overload that expects to be explicitly told whether to filter on textures or not. This allows it to look for objects whose ObjectTexture value is null and draw them alone should this be required.

The code for these functions is shown in Listing 6–40.

Listing 6–40. The DrawObjects function overloads in the GameHost class

```
/// <summary>
/// Call the Draw method on all matrix objects in the game
/// </summary>
public virtual void DrawObjects(GameTime gameTime, Effect effect)
{
    DrawObjects(gameTime, effect, false, null);
}


/// <summary>
/// Call the Draw method on all matrix objects in the game that use
/// the specified texture. Pass as null to draw only objects that do
/// not have a texture specified at all.
/// </summary>
public virtual void DrawObjects(GameTime gameTime, Effect effect,
                                        Texture2D restrictToTexture)
{
    DrawObjects(gameTime, effect, true, restrictToTexture);
}


/// <summary>
/// Draw the specified objects
/// </summary>
private void DrawObjects(GameTime gameTime, Effect effect, bool specifiedTextureOnly,
                                        Texture2D restrictToTexture)
{
    GameObjectBase obj;
    int objectCount;

    // Draw each matrix-based object
    objectCount = _objectArray.Length;
    for (int i = 0; i < objectCount; i++)
    {
        obj = _objectArray[i];
        // Is this a matrix object?
        if (obj is MatrixObjectBase)
        {
            // Does this object use the required texture?
            if (specifiedTextureOnly == false ||
                        ((MatrixObjectBase)obj).ObjectTexture == restrictToTexture)
            {
                ((MatrixObjectBase)obj).Draw(gameTime, effect);
            }
        }
    }
}
```

Using the Game Framework for Matrix Rendering

The game framework is now all ready to use for rendering our objects, so how is it used in a game project?

This is very easy, as can be seen in the GameFrameworkExampleGame class in the example project. All the class-level variables have been removed except for the BasicEffect variable, and the Initialize function has been reduced in size so that it simply creates and initializes this effect object.

LoadContent now loads its textures into the Textures collection that we've used throughout all the sprite examples. At the end, it calls ResetGame to create the game's objects. ResetGame, shown in Listing 6–41, simply adds some instances of the game project's TexturedSquareObject class to the GameObjects collection.

Listing 6–41. Resetting the example project

```
private void ResetGame()
{
    // Clear any existing objects
    GameObjects.Clear();

    // Add some new game objects
    GameObjects.Add(new TexturedSquareObject(this, new Vector3(0, 0.6f, 0),
                                        Textures["Grapes"], 2.0f));
    GameObjects.Add(new TexturedSquareObject(this, new Vector3(0, -0.6f, 0),
                                        Textures["Strawberry"], 2.0f));
}
```

Finally we call UpdateAll from the game's Update function and DrawObjects from the game's Draw function. That's all that is needed.

Enter the Matrix

This chapter has provided a tour through a whole new way of rendering in XNA, using matrix transformations and vertices. If you haven't encountered this approach before, it might seem like a lot of extra work to achieve similar results to those that were already accessible just using sprites.

The real power of this new approach is still ahead of us, however. The examples in this chapter have remained mainly in two dimensions, but matrix transformations and vertex declarations are the gateway into the third dimension, opening up an enormous number of new opportunities for gaming on Windows Phone 7 devices.

All the techniques that you have learned here operate in 3D, too, so, once you feel comfortable with the material that we have covered, prepare yourself for the next chapter, in which you will step into a new world of graphical rendering.

CHAPTER 7

■■■

The World of 3D Graphics

Three-dimensional graphics have completely revolutionized computer games over the last decade. For some time before this, it was obvious that 3D games were going to be big, with games such as DOOM creating moving images the likes of which had never been seen before.

When dedicated 3D graphics hardware began to appear back in the late 1990s, graphics were transformed even more, moving away from the blocky and grainy images that players had become accustomed to and replacing them with smooth textures, dynamic lighting, and enormous levels of detail. Game worlds really started to look like real worlds.

Mobile graphics hardware, even in dedicated devices such as Sony's PlayStation Portable, are trailing a fair distance behind the power of modern PC graphics hardware, and this applies to the hardware within Windows Phone 7 devices, too. The phone's capabilities are still quite sufficient to create very impressive 3D scenes and games, and the platform is perfectly capable of providing dynamic and complex 3D gaming opportunities for your audience.

This chapter examines how to bring the third dimension to life.

Perspective Projection

The vast majority of 3D games use a *perspective projection* to display their graphics. Just as in the real world, this projection simulates the application of perspective to objects rendered within the game, so that objects that are farther away appear smaller than objects that are closer.

In addition to this obvious size effect, the more subtle effects of perspective are picked up intuitively by the brain and add a substantial feeling of depth to the rendered scene. The sides of a cube will very slightly narrow due to the effects of perspective as they increase in distance from the viewer, allowing the brain to automatically determine the exact position in which the cube is situated.

The Viewing Frustum

When we use a perspective projection in XNA, we create as part of the Effect object initialization a three-dimensional volume known as a *viewing frustum*. The shape of the frustum is that of a rectangular cone with its tip cut off. A demonstration of such a frustum is shown in Figure 7-1.

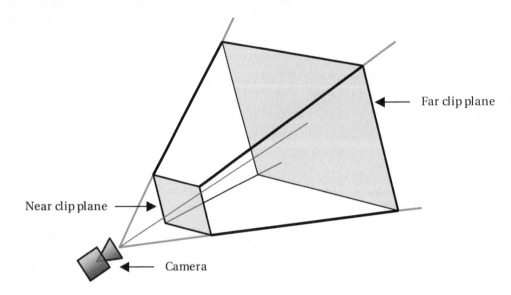

Figure 7–1. A diagram showing a 3D viewing frustum

The frustum can be visualized in the real world by imagining yourself looking through a window. Outside the window you can see the ground and various objects. The farther away into the distance you look, the wider the area that you can see. Objects that are too far to the side, above, or below will be hidden by the window frame.

Objects that fall inside the volume described by the frustum are visible to the camera (and would be visible through the window). Objects that fall outside the frustum volumes are hidden from the camera (and would not be able to be seen through the window).

The near and far clip planes are also taken into account when deciding whether objects are visible. Objects nearer to the camera than the near clip plane are deemed to be too close and are excluded from rendering. Similarly, objects farther than the far clip plane are too far away to be seen and are once again excluded.

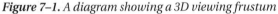

■ **NOTE** When we specify an object's z position (its distance into the screen), the negative z axis represents movement away from the player and into the screen: as an object's z coordinate decreases, so it moves farther away. When we specify the distance of the near and far clip planes, however, they are specified purely as distances from the camera and are therefore positive values.

When XNA transforms the objects that fall inside the frustum from the 3D space in which we have defined our world into the 2D space that is actually presented on the screen, it takes into account how much of the width and height of the frustum is filled by any particular object. An object will occupy a greater proportion of the frustum when it is positioned toward the near clip plane than it will at the far clip plane (see Figures 7–2 and 7–3). Figure 7–2 shows two identically sized objects within the viewing frustum. Figure 7–3 shows the same scene after the perspective projection has taken place to transform the scene into two dimensions for display on the screen. Note that the object at the near clip plane appears substantially larger than the one at the far clip plane.

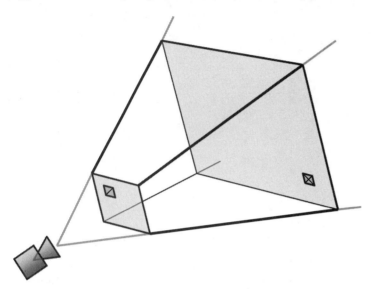

Figure 7–2. Two identically sized objects in the viewing frustum shown in 3D space

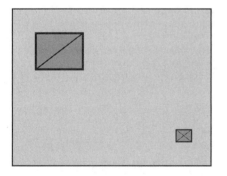

Figure 7–3. The same two objects after perspective projection into 2D

In addition to the clip planes, the frustum is defined by two more pieces of information: the viewing angle and the aspect ratio.

The *viewing angle* defines the angle, in degrees, between the camera and the upper edge of the frustum (the angle on the y axis). Changing this angle will make the overall shape of the frustum expand or compress, causing the apparent reduction in size of objects farther away to be increased or decreased.

Figure 7–4 shows two viewing frustums from the side: the first with a viewing angle of 45 degrees; the second with 22.5 degrees. The distance of the near and far clip planes is the same in both cases.

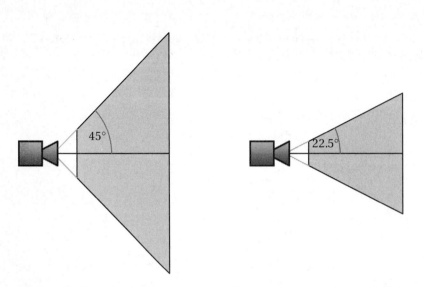

Figure 7–4. Two viewing frustums, one with a 45-degree viewing angle (left) and one with a 22.5-degree angle (right)

Consider how objects that fall into these two frustums will be projected. On the left, objects can deviate further from the center of the frustum and still be seen by the camera. Objects that are farther away will become rapidly smaller as their size relative to the extent of the frustum becomes less and less. On the right, objects farther from the center will leave the frustum more quickly and so will disappear off the edge of the screen. Distant objects will appear larger than with the first frustum as they occupy a greater proportion of the frustum's area.

Exactly what you should specify for the viewing angle will potentially vary from one game to the next. An angle of 45 degrees is usually a safe value. Setting the angle too low can make it appear that everything is closer to the player than it really is, which can result in the game feeling uncomfortable to play.

■ **TIP** Some interesting effects can be achieved by varying the viewing angle at strategic times within the game. For example, you could provide a transition between two scenes by rapidly decreasing the viewing angle down to zero, switching the scene, and then increasing the angle back to its original value. This process will cause everything in the center of the screen to appear to zoom toward the player and then zoom back again after the scene change. "Slow-motion" effects can often be accentuated by slightly reducing the viewing angle while they are active.

The second piece of information that the viewing frustum requires is the *aspect ratio*, which is calculated by dividing the display width by its height. The aspect ratio allows the viewing angle on the x axis to be calculated by XNA in response to the explicit angle that we provided for the y axis. The aspect ratio, together with the viewing angle and the distance of the clip planes, provides everything that is needed to fully describe the frustum.

Defining the Viewing Frustum in XNA

XNA actually performs the perspective transformation with the use of another matrix. You might recall that in the Initialize function of the example classes from Chapter 6, the code shown in Listing 7–1 is present to set up the default projection matrix.

Listing 7–1. Creating the viewing frustum matrix

```
// Calculate the screen aspect ratio
float aspectRatio =
        (float)GraphicsDevice.Viewport.Width / GraphicsDevice.Viewport.Height;
// Create a projection matrix
Matrix projection = Matrix.CreatePerspectiveFieldOfView(MathHelper.ToRadians(45),
                                            aspectRatio, 0.1f, 1000.0f);
```

You should be able to spot all the information that we have discussed as being required for the viewing frustum. The work of generating the projection matrix is performed by the static Matrix.CreatePerspectiveFieldOfView function. The parameters that it expects to be passed are as follows, in the following order:

- fieldOfView: the viewing angle for the projection

- aspectRatio: the aspect ratio of the display width/height

- nearPlaneDistance: the near clipping plane distance

- farPlaneDistance: the far clipping plane distance

In Listing 7–1, a viewing angle of 45 degrees is specified, along with the aspect ratio calculated from the game's ViewPort, and near and far clipping planes of 0.1 and 1000, respectively.

When rendering, XNA first calculates the positions of all the object vertices in 3D space and then uses the projection matrix to transform them into 2D coordinates to display on the screen.

If you want to change the viewing angle (or any of the other properties of the frustum), you can simply set a new projection matrix into the effect's Projection property before rendering your objects.

The Perspective example project in this chapter's accompanying download shows how objects move when a perspective projection is applied. The code is very simple; it creates a number of objects with random x, y, and z coordinates. Each time the objects update, they add to their PositionZ value, moving them closer to the screen. When they get to a value of 0, they add 100 to move them back into the distance. A screenshot from the demo can be seen in Figure 7–5.

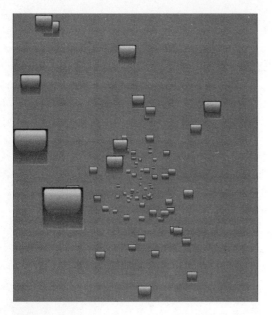

Figure 7–5. The Perspective project showing same-sized objects at different distances

Rendering 3D Objects

Moving objects around our 3D game world is great, but we need to be able to create 3D objects too; so far, we've worked just with flat rectangles. This section discusses how solid objects can be created.

The objects that we have been drawing up to this point have defined four vertices, all with a z value of zero, and used a triangle strip to combine them into the rendered shape. When we move into three-dimensional objects, we probably can't use triangle strips. Every triangle of a triangle strip shares an edge with the previous triangle, and with 3D objects we will very quickly find that we can't draw objects in this way. Instead, we will use a list of individual triangles, which gives us the flexibility to draw whatever triangle we need wherever we need it.

Defining a 3D Object

To start with we will define our 3D object by manually providing all its vertex coordinates. This is fairly straightforward for simple shapes, but does quickly become impractical once we want to move on to more complicated objects. We'll use a simple cube for the time being, however, and will look at how complicated geometry can be constructed in the "Importing Geometry" section in the next chapter.

A cube consists of six square faces and eight vertices. As each square needs to be rendered as two triangles, we end up with a total of 12 triangles to draw, as shown in Figure 7–6.

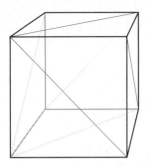

Figure 7–6. *The triangles required to build a 3D cube*

Because we will draw individual triangles rather than use a triangle strip, we need to specify each triangle coordinate individually. This means that when two triangles share a single coordinate, we actually need to specify the coordinate twice, once for each of the triangles. As a result, we have to provide a total of 36 vertices, three for each triangle. Because there are only eight distinct vertices forming the cube, this respecification of vertices is quite wasteful and requires XNA to perform the same calculations over and over again. We will look at a more efficient rendering method in the "Vertex and Index Buffers" section coming up shortly.

To build the vertices of the cube, we simply declare an array of vertices and add to it sets of three values, representing the vertices of each of the triangles. The coordinates for the front face of a unit-size cube can be seen in Listing 7–2. Note that the z coordinate in each coordinate is 0.5, meaning that it extends half a unit toward the viewpoint.

Listing 7–2. *Defining the front face of a cube*

```
// Create and initialize the vertices
_vertices = new VertexPositionColor[6];

// Set the vertex positions for a unit size cube.
int i = 0;
// Front face...
_vertices[i++].Position = new Vector3(-0.5f, -0.5f, 0.5f);
_vertices[i++].Position = new Vector3(-0.5f, 0.5f, 0.5f);
_vertices[i++].Position = new Vector3(0.5f, -0.5f, 0.5f);
_vertices[i++].Position = new Vector3(0.5f, -0.5f, 0.5f);
_vertices[i++].Position = new Vector3(-0.5f, 0.5f, 0.5f);
_vertices[i++].Position = new Vector3(0.5f, 0.5f, 0.5f);
```

Plotting out these coordinates shows that we have indeed formed a square that will form the front face of the cube, as shown in Figure 7–7.

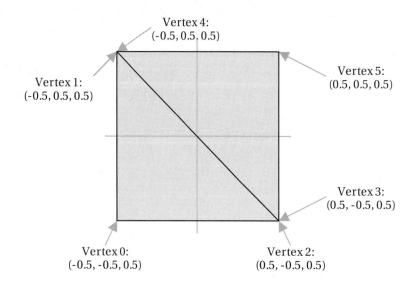

Vertex 4:
(-0.5, 0.5, 0.5)

Vertex 1:
(-0.5, 0.5, 0.5)

Vertex 5:
(0.5, 0.5, 0.5)

Vertex 3:
(0.5, -0.5, 0.5)

Vertex 0:
(-0.5, -0.5, 0.5)

Vertex 2:
(0.5, -0.5, 0.5)

Figure 7–7. The vertices forming the front face of the cube

The array is extended to cover all the faces of the cube, extending into the 3D space by using positive and negative values for the z positions. The full array is not included here because it is fairly large and not particularly interesting, but it can be seen in full inside the `CubeObject.BuildVertices` function in the `ColoredCubes` example project. The code in this function also sets the vertices for each face to be a different color to make the cube look nicer.

■ **TIP** The `CubeObject` class declares its array of vertices as `static`, so only a single instance of the array exists and is shared by all instances of the `CubeObject` class. Because the contents of this array are identical for every class instance, declaring the array in this way means that .NET allocates memory for the vertices only once for the whole application instead of once per cube object, saving some precious memory.

With all the vertices defined, the object can be rendered using exactly the same code used for flat objects. The result is shown in Figure 7–8.

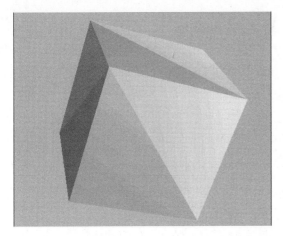

Figure 7–8. The cube resulting from the set of 3D vertices

Fundamentally, that is all there is to it! If you run the ColoredCubes example project, you will see how this basic object can be easily reused within the game engine to create a much more visually exciting scene, as shown in Figure 7–9. This example creates 100 cubes, gives each a random angle and position, and then rotates them around the y axis, resulting in a swirling tornado of colored blocks.

Figure 7–9. The ColoredCubes example project

The Depth Buffer

Something you might have observed in both the Perspective and ColoredCubes examples is that the objects nearer the camera all appear in front of the objects farther away. When we displayed our graphics using sprites, we had to put in some effort to provide a LayerDepth value for each sprite in order to facilitate depth sorting like this. There is no equivalent functionality in these 3D projects, though, and yet the objects still all appear in the right places. Why does this happen?

The answer is that XNA has a built-in mechanism for ensuring that objects in the front of the scene automatically hide any objects that fall behind them. This happens regardless of the order in which objects are drawn: objects drawn behind existing objects can still be partially (or totally) obscured even though they might be rendered after the object in front.

XNA achieves this effect by using a feature known as the *depth buffer*. It can be enabled or disabled, and is enabled by default. When rendering simple 2D graphics, the depth buffer might be unnecessary, but in 3D scenes it is almost certain to be required.

Just as the color of each rendered pixel is written into a graphical buffer for display on the screen, so the distance into the screen of each rendered pixel is written into a corresponding depth buffer when the buffer is enabled. For each individual pixel that it is about to render, XNA checks the depth of the pixel against the depth already stored in the buffer. If it finds that the new pixel is farther away than the pixel already in the buffer, the new pixel is not rendered to the screen; otherwise, the pixel is rendered and the depth buffer updated to remember the new depth of the pixel.

This per-pixel depth checking can be clearly seen in the DepthBuffer example project, shown in Figure 7–10. This figure displays two rotating cubes, positioned so that they intersect one another; and below them a third cube, squashed to form a "floor." Observe the behavior when the cubes intersect one another: at every single pixel position, the frontmost cube surface is always displayed.

Figure 7–10. The effect of the depth buffer on intersecting objects

The way that intersecting objects are handled can be very useful. For example, if you want to draw a landscape scene with water such as lakes or an ocean, the ground can be drawn in its entirety (the parts that are above the water level and also those that are below) and then a single semitransparent flat plane can be drawn at the water level across the entire scene. Only those parts of the scene that are below the water level will be affected by the water plane, providing a reasonably convincing approximation of water with very little complexity or processor cost.

Enabling and Disabling the Depth Buffer

Most of the time when you are rendering objects in your game, you will want the depth buffer to be available and active. Without it, distant objects will appear in front of nearer objects, destroying the illusion of the 3D world that you are trying to render.

On some occasions, however, you might want to render without updating the depth buffer. Examples include rendering background scenery that should never obscure any of the other graphics rendered and objects that are rendered in front of a scene to provide overlay content such as status bars or health displays.

The depth buffer can be temporarily disabled by setting the GraphicsDevice.DepthStencilState property to DepthStencilState.None. After this property has been set, graphics that are rendered will entirely ignore the depth buffer, neither observing values that are stored in it nor updating the values when new objects are rendered. To restore the normal behavior of the depth buffer, set the property back to its default value: DepthStencilState.Default.

You can see the effect of disabling the depth buffer by inserting the code from Listing 7–3 at the end of the LoadContent function in the Perspective example project.

Listing 7–3. Disabling the depth buffer

```
// Disable the depth buffer
GraphicsDevice.DepthStencilState = DepthStencilState.None;
```

Once the depth buffer has been disabled, you will find that the objects appear in the order that they are rendered rather than being sorted by their depth. This can be seen in Figure 7–11, in which some of the smaller, more distant shapes are clearly being displayed in front of the larger closer objects.

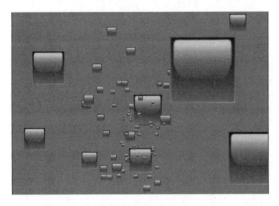

Figure 7–11. The Perspective project with the depth buffer disabled

---

■ **NOTE** If you want to *entirely* disable the depth buffer, you can set the _graphics.PreferredDepthStencilFormat property to DepthFormat.None in your game class constructor. This setting will initialize the graphics device without creating a depth buffer, which can save you some memory and processing overhead if you have no need for it.

There is another mode that can be set for the depth buffer: read-only mode. In this mode, XNA will observe the values in the depth buffer when rendering objects and will use it to prevent objects from being drawn if they are behind existing objects, but the depth buffer will not be updated in response to rendered objects.

This mode might seem like an unlikely feature to need, but it has various uses. One such use is for drawing *particles* in a 3D scene. We'll discuss particles in more detail in the next chapter, but they can be used for creating effects such as sparks, fire, and smoke. Although it is important that these correctly appear behind objects in the scene, we need to ensure that they don't obscure one another or else they won't display correctly.

XNA can be set to use a read-only depth buffer by setting the `GraphicsDevice.DepthStencilState` property to `DepthStencilState.DepthRead`. Don't forget to set it back to `DepthStencilState.Default` once you are finished with this mode.

Clearing the Depth Buffer

In some situations you might want to clear the values stored in the depth buffer. This might be the case if you are drawing two scenes, one in front of the other, and want to prevent each one from interfering with the other. The first scene can be drawn (with the depth buffer active and working), the depth buffer then cleared, and the second scene then drawn. The depth data from the first scene will not interfere with the second scene at all.

To clear the depth buffer, we can call the `GraphicsDevice.Clear` method, just as we do at the start of the game's `Draw` function, but instead of simply passing a color we pass some additional parameters that tell it to clear only the depth buffer, not the graphics that have been rendered. The code for clearing the depth buffer can be seen in Listing 7–4.

Listing 7–4. Clearing the depth buffer

```
GraphicsDevice.Clear(ClearOptions.DepthBuffer, Color.White, 1, 0);
```

Because the `Clear` method's first parameter is set to `ClearOptions.DepthBuffer`, only the depth buffer will be affected. We still have to pass a color (which will be ignored) and a stencil value (which we are not using), but the value 1 passed for the depth buffer tells XNA to set the buffer so that the depths are all considered as being at the very back of the viewing frustum. Subsequently drawn objects will therefore appear in front of this far depth and will not be obscured by previously drawn objects.

Rendering Transparent Objects with the Depth Buffer

The depth buffer might not work exactly as you expect when it comes to drawing semitransparent objects. Although XNA's alpha blending feature can merge together objects that are being drawn with those already on the screen, the depth buffer can store only a single depth for each pixel. This means that, if you draw a semitransparent object and then draw an object behind it, the object behind will be completely eliminated by the depth buffer, even though the first object was transparent.

There are several approaches that can be employed to handle this. The first is to draw all your transparent objects so that those in the back of your scene are rendered first. This will ensure that objects in the front do not obscure those behind.

The second approach is to draw all your opaque objects first and then switch the depth buffer into `DepthRead` mode before drawing the transparent objects. This way the transparent objects will not obscure anything subsequently drawn behind them.

The final option is to use the `AlphaTest` effect (instead of the `BasicEffect` that we have been using so far), which can update the depth buffer only for pixels that match certain conditions in terms of their calculated alpha values. We will examine this effect in more detail in the next chapter.

Exactly which of these approaches is best will depend on what your game is drawing. Bear this limitation in mind when creating transparent objects in 3D space.

Hidden Surface Culling

When we draw solid opaque objects such as cubes, the inside of the cube is completely obscured from view. XNA is unaware of this, however, and would potentially continue drawing the inside faces of the cube. This is a waste of processing power because it would unnecessarily compare and update the inside faces with the depth buffer, and if the faces at the back are processed before those at the front it would also actually render them, only to subsequently draw over them completely with the outer faces of the cube.

You probably won't be surprised to hear that XNA has a solution for this problem—and it's nice and easy to use, too.

XNA can work out whether each triangle is facing toward us (as the front face of the cube is) or away from us (as the back face of the cube is). It does this based on how the triangle is actually rendered, not just how its vertices were defined, so that, as a triangle rotates, the direction in which it is facing will change. Those triangles that are found to be facing away from us are *culled* and are not considered for inclusion in the depth or color buffers, saving all the work that would otherwise have been involved in checking and updating them.

In order for XNA to be able to determine the direction in which the triangles are facing, we need to give our triangle vertices to it in a particular way. When we define the triangles, we ensure that, when the front of the triangle is facing toward us, the vertices are provided such that they appear in a clockwise direction. Figure 7–12 shows two triangles, one whose vertices are defined in clockwise order (on the left) and the other in counterclockwise order.

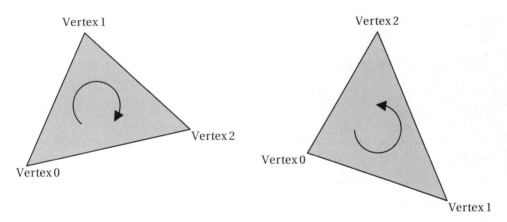

Figure 7–12. Triangles with vertices defined in clockwise (left) and counterclockwise (right) order

Given these two triangles to render, XNA will by default display the one on the left, not the one on the right. If we rotate them around so that their backs are toward us, the triangle on the left would not display, and the triangle on the right would appear.

■ **NOTE** Remember that the vertices must appear in clockwise order *when the triangle is facing you*. When we define a cube, the rear face is initially facing away from us, so the triangles would appear to be in counterclockwise order instead. If the cube were rotated around so that the back face was oriented toward us, the vertices would then appear to be clockwise, as we need them to be.

If you look back at the vertices defined for the front face of the cube in Figure 7–7, you will see that both of the triangles have their vertices defined in clockwise order. This is by design, of course. With our triangles specified correctly, XNA will automatically ignore those triangles that face away from us.

The HiddenSurfaceCulling project draws yet another cube, but this time it omits the final triangle from the cube (it tells DrawUserPrimitives to draw 11 triangles instead of 12), resulting in a triangular hole. We can look through this hole to the interior of the cube to see exactly what XNA is drawing for the reverse sides of the cube triangles.

If you run this project, you will see that the orange side of the cube that contains the missing triangle shows nothing behind it whatsoever (see Figure 7–13). Clearly, XNA shows the triangles only when they are actually facing toward us.

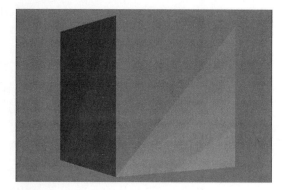

Figure 7–13. The rear faces of the cube's triangles have been culled.

Sometimes it is useful to draw the rear surfaces of triangles, too. If you have objects that are completely flat and need to be viewed from in front or behind, or if you have objects that are hollow and whose interior can be seen, we can configure XNA to render both surfaces of each triangle.

To instruct XNA to render in this way, we need to disable surface culling. Culling is controlled by the GraphicsDevice.RasterizerState.CullMode property, which accepts one of these values: CullCounterClockwiseFace (the default), CullClockwiseFace (the reverse; culls faces that are defined in clockwise order), or None (the value we need here; none of the faces is culled).

Just as with the BlendState and SamplerState objects we saw in the last chapter, the RasterizerState object's properties all become read-only once the object has been set into the GraphicsDevice. We therefore can't update the properties of the existing object. Instead, we create a new object, configure it as required, and then set the whole object into the GraphicsDevice, as shown in Listing 7–5.

Listing 7–5. Disabling hidden surface culling

```
// Create and activate a new RasterizerState with a different cull mode.
RasterizerState rs = new RasterizerState();
rs.CullMode = CullMode.None;
GraphicsDevice.RasterizerState = rs;
```

You will find this code present but commented out within the HiddenSurfaceCulling project's Initialize function. Uncomment it so that it becomes active and then run the project again. Now you will find when the orange face is toward you that you can see through the missing triangle into the fully rendered interior of the cube, as shown in Figure 7–14.

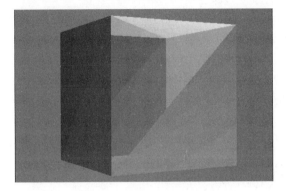

Figure 7–14. The rear faces of the cube's triangles have not been culled.

The important thing to remember with hidden surface culling disabled is that the interior faces are being calculated and compared against the depth buffer even when they are completely hidden from view. When hidden surface culling was enabled, the interior faces were discarded immediately as XNA knew that they faced away and therefore didn't need to be checked against the depth buffer at all.

The final culling mode, culling clockwise faces, can be useful if you are importing model files (as we will learn to do in the next chapter) that have been defined with their faces counterclockwise instead of clockwise. Some modeling applications will define triangles in this way, and this is in fact the default culling mechanism used by OpenGL. The easiest way to deal with such objects is to swap the culling mode.

When the culling mode doesn't match the order with which the vertices have been defined, XNA will render just the inside of the object, hiding all the triangles that face toward you. This can result in potentially useful effects, though they can be visually disorientating. Try modifying the example project code so that it culls clockwise faces and running it again. You will now see the inside of the cube, as shown in Figure 7–15.

Figure 7–15. The front faces of the cube's triangles have been culled.

Vertex and Index Buffers

We're making good progress in our journey into 3D rendering, but there are some inefficiencies in the approach that we have used so far that it would be wise to address before we go any further. These can be addressed by using two new constructs: *vertex buffers* and *index buffers*. Let's take a look and see what they can do for us and how they are used.

All the techniques discussed in this section can be seen in the VertexAndIndexBuffers example project. This project adds three cubes to the scene, one of each of the techniques that we are about to explore.

Using Vertex Buffers

In all the examples we have used so far, we have called the DrawUserPrimitives function to render our objects, passing it an array of vertices containing the object geometry. This works just fine, but is not the most efficient way of rendering. In order for the graphics hardware to use the vertex data, all the vertices must be transferred into the graphics memory. Just as we saw with repeated texture copying in earlier chapters, this data transfer can have a negative impact on performance.

We can address this performance issue by using a *vertex buffer*, which allows the vertex data to reside permanently within the graphics hardware. The advantage of this approach is that we can switch between vertex buffers with much less overhead than copying vertex data arrays.

A cube defined using a vertex buffer can be found in the VertexBufferCubeObject class. There are only a couple of differences between this class and the cube classes that we have looked at previously. First of all, a new static class-level variable has been defined of type VertexBuffer and with the name _vertexBuffer. When the class finds that the vertices have not been initialized, it creates them as before, but then also uses them to initialize the vertex buffer, as shown in Listing 7–6.

Listing 7–6. Creating and initializing a VertexBuffer object

```
// Have we already built the cube vertex array in a previous instance?
if (_vertices == null)
{
    // No, so build them now
    BuildVertices();
    // Create a vertex buffer
```

```
_vertexBuffer = new VertexBuffer(game.GraphicsDevice,
            typeof(VertexPositionColor), _vertices.Length, BufferUsage.WriteOnly);
    _vertexBuffer.SetData(_vertices);
}
```

The parameters passed to the VertexBuffer constructor are as follows, in this order:

- graphicsDevice: the graphics device to which this vertex buffer will be rendered
- vertexType: the type of vertex being added to the buffer
- vertexCount: the number of vertices to be added to the buffer
- usage: special usage flags

Most of these parameters should be self-explanatory. We know the vertex count because we've already built an array of vertices, so we can simply read the array size for the vertexCount parameter. The usage parameter needs a little additional explanation, however. It can be passed as either None or WriteOnly. The first of these options allows the vertex data to be retrieved at a later time (using the VertexBuffer.GetData function), but results in less efficient usage of the buffer in the graphics hardware. The WriteOnly option optimizes the buffer memory usage, but makes it impossible to read the vertex data back. It is unusual to need to read the data back (in this example, we have it in a separate array, anyway), so unless you need to read the data from the buffer, you should always specify WriteOnly.

This object creation results in an initialized but empty vertex buffer. The vertex data is copied into it by calling the SetData function, passing the vertex array as a parameter.

The buffer is now ready for use, and to render it we need to make some small changes to the object's Draw function. Prior to drawing we must tell the graphics device which vertex buffer it should render. Only a single vertex buffer can be set at any time, so it must be specified before the drawing instruction is executed. The buffer is set into the device, as shown in Listing 7–7.

Listing 7–7. Setting a vertex buffer into the graphics device

```
// Set the active vertex buffer
effect.GraphicsDevice.SetVertexBuffer(_vertexBuffer);
```

To render with the active vertex buffer, we use a different drawing method. Previously we had been calling DrawUserPrimitives and passing in the vertex array as a parameter. To render using a vertex buffer, we instead call DrawPrimitives. No vertex data needs to be passed because the vertex buffer from the graphics device will be used. We just need to tell XNA the primitive type, the start vertex, and the primitive count, just as we did before. The code to render the vertex buffer is shown in Listing 7–8.

Listing 7–8. Drawing the active vertex buffer

```
// Draw the object
foreach (EffectPass pass in effect.CurrentTechnique.Passes)
{
    // Apply the pass
    pass.Apply();
    // Draw the object using the active vertex buffer
    effect.GraphicsDevice.DrawPrimitives(PrimitiveType.TriangleList, 0, 12);
}
```

Other than these changes, the code and approach is identical to the examples we have already used.

Using Indexed Vertices

In order to draw the cube shown in the previous examples, we have had to provide the same vertex coordinates to XNA multiple times. As we discussed earlier, a cube has 8 vertices, and yet in our examples we are creating our vertex array with 36 vertices in it, 6 for each face (consisting of 3 vertices for each of the 2 triangles used to draw the face).

This configuration of vertices is, of course, quite wasteful in terms of processing resources because we are calculating the exact same vertex position many times.

XNA provides an alternative mechanism for providing the list of vertices that allows the number of repeated identical coordinates to be reduced. Instead of creating each vertex independently of the others, we can instead provide a list of just the unique vertices and then separately tell XNA how to join them together to make the triangles that it is to render. The list of vertex numbers that specifies how to join the vertices is simply stored as an array of numbers.

Consider again the front face of the cube that we saw in Figure 7–7. If we were to specify just the unique vertices, the vertex count would be reduced from the previous six to four. The four vertices are shown in Figure 7–16.

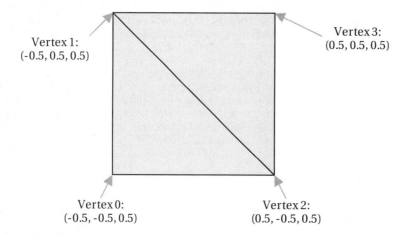

Vertex 1:
(-0.5, 0.5, 0.5)

Vertex 3:
(0.5, 0.5, 0.5)

Vertex 0:
(-0.5, -0.5, 0.5)

Vertex 2:
(0.5, -0.5, 0.5)

Figure 7–16. Specifying just the unique coordinates for the front face of the cube

Although this new set of coordinates allows the vertices to be defined, we no longer have the information required to join them together to form the rendered triangles. At this point, the index array makes an entrance. To draw the front face, we need two triangles, and the vertex indices for each are as follows:

- First triangle: 0, 1, 2

- Second triangle: 2, 1, 3

Just as before, the triangle is formed by specifying its vertices in clockwise order so that hidden surface culling can hide the triangles when they are facing away from the viewer.

The only additional complexity with this approach is that vertices do not only store a position; they also store colors, texture coordinates, and other information (as we will see in the next chapter). Just because two vertices share the same location, it doesn't necessarily mean that they are identical.

Each vertex position in our cube will be part of three different faces (because each corner of the cube has three squares attached to it), and each face in our example is a different color. We will therefore need to repeat the vertices for each face, even though they are in the same position, because they have different colors.

This still allows us to reduce the vertex count from the original 36 (6 vertices per face x 6 faces) to a much more efficient 24 (4 vertices per face x 6 faces). The two redundant vertices within each square face are eliminated, reducing the vertex count by one-third.

As a result, the code required to build the vertex array now needs only to specify the unique indexes. The beginning of the code to generate these vertices, from the IndexedCubeObject class, can be seen in Listing 7–9. Compare this code to the code in Listing 7–2, and you will see that the repeated vertices are no longer present.

Listing 7–9. Specifying vertex data for indexed rendering

```
// Set the vertex positions for a unit size cube.
i = 0;
// Front face...
_vertices[i++].Position = new Vector3(-0.5f, -0.5f, 0.5f);
_vertices[i++].Position = new Vector3(-0.5f, 0.5f, 0.5f);
_vertices[i++].Position = new Vector3(0.5f, -0.5f, 0.5f);
_vertices[i++].Position = new Vector3(0.5f, 0.5f, 0.5f);
```

In order to join the vertices together, we need to build the array of indices. XNA allows them to be stored either as an array of short values (permitting a maximum of 32767 vertices), or as an array of int values (with a maximum vertex count exceeding 2 billion), but on Windows Phone only short values are supported. This vertex limit still allows for very complex objects and is unlikely to present any practical limitation; it also saves memory by requiring two bytes per index instead of four.

For rendering a triangle list as we are, the array needs to be given sets of three indices in order to identify the three vertices for each triangle. The BuildIndices function sets them all up, and a small section can be seen in Listing 7–10. The resulting data is stored in the static class-level _indices array.

Listing 7–10. The start of the index array creation

```
private void BuildIndices()
{
    int i;

    // Create and initialize the indices
    _indices = new short[36];

    // Set the indices for the cube
    i = 0;
    // Front face...
    _indices[i++] = 0;
    _indices[i++] = 1;
    _indices[i++] = 2;
    _indices[i++] = 2;
    _indices[i++] = 1;
    _indices[i++] = 3;
    // Back face...
    _indices[i++] = 4;
    _indices[i++] = 5;
    _indices[i++] = 6;
    _indices[i++] = 5;
    _indices[i++] = 7;
    _indices[i++] = 6;
```

Note that we store 36 elements in the array: 6 faces x 2 triangles x 3 vertices = 36 elements in total. The first triangle is formed from the vertices at positions 0, 1, and 2; and the second triangle from the vertices at positions 2, 1, and 3—exactly as described in Figure 7–16. The array then continues to form another triangle from vertices 4, 5, 6; and another from vertices 5, 7, 6, and so on for all the triangles in the cube.

This is clearly quite a lot more work to set up than simply providing the stand-alone list of vertices, and in many cases the benefit of this approach will be negligible. In more complex objects, it can provide a noticeable performance boost, however. This indexed rendering approach can be taken advantage of without having to enter pages and pages of index numbers when geometry is read from external model files (as we will see in the next chapter) and also if you should write code that programmatically generates vertex coordinates and indices.

To render the cube using the index data, we call the DrawUserIndexedPrimitives function in the Draw function rather than DrawUserPrimitives. In addition to the DrawUserPrimitives parameters, this call also expects the index array to be provided and an offset through the index array from which it should start processing (which we will pass as 0 to specify that it should be processed from the beginning). The code for this call is shown in Listing 7–11.

Listing 7–11. Rendering the cube using the index array

```
// Draw the object
foreach (EffectPass pass in effect.CurrentTechnique.Passes)
{
    // Apply the pass
    pass.Apply();
    // Draw the object using the active vertex buffer
    effect.GraphicsDevice.DrawUserIndexedPrimitives(PrimitiveType.TriangleList,
                          _vertices, 0, _vertices.Length, _indices, 0, 12);
}
```

This approach results in unnecessary processing of identical vertices to be eliminated in the rendered object.

Using Vertex Buffers and Indexing Together

Vertex buffers and indexing provide optimizations to the way in which our objects are calculated, and to get the best of both worlds we can use them both at the same time. When we render an indexed vertex buffer, the vertex buffer itself is created exactly as we have already seen, but the indexes are specified in a slightly different way. Instead of storing them just as an array, we instead place the array data into an IndexBuffer object.

This combined approach can be seen in the VertexAndIndexBufferCubeObject class. The vertex and index data is created exactly as it was for indexed rendering, with the reduced number of vertices (24 instead of 36) and the index array joining them together into the finished object. In the class constructor, both of these arrays are set into buffer objects, as shown in Listing 7–12.

Listing 7–12. Creating a vertex buffer and an index buffer

```
// Have we already built the cube vertex array in a previous instance?
if (_vertices == null)
{
    // No, so build them now
    BuildVertices();
    // Create a vertex buffer
    _vertexBuffer = new VertexBuffer(game.GraphicsDevice,
```

```
                typeof(VertexPositionColor), _vertices.Length, BufferUsage.WriteOnly);
    _vertexBuffer.SetData(_vertices);

    // Create the index array
    BuildIndices();
    // Create an index buffer
    _indexBuffer = new IndexBuffer(game.GraphicsDevice, typeof(short),
                                    _indices.Length, BufferUsage.WriteOnly);
    _indexBuffer.SetData(_indices);
}
```

The parameters required when creating the index buffer are as follows:

- graphicsDevice: the graphics device to which this index buffer will be rendered
- type: the type used for each index array element (short or int)
- indexCount: the number of indices to be added to the buffer
- usage: special usage flags—None or WriteOnly, just as with the vertex buffer

This object creation sets up everything that is required to render the indexed vertex buffer. To actually draw it, we need to tweak the Draw function again.

Just as with the vertex buffer example, we need to provide the vertex buffer to the graphics device using the SetVertexBuffer function. Additionally, we now need to provide the index buffer into the graphics device's Indices property.

With these objects set in place, we render this time by calling the DrawIndexedPrimitive function. No vertex or index data needs to be passed because the function reads both of these from the objects set into the graphics device. Listing 7–13 shows the complete code to draw the cube using this approach.

Listing 7–13. Drawing indexed vertices from a vertex buffer

```
public override void Draw(Microsoft.Xna.Framework.GameTime gameTime, Effect effect)
{
    // Prepare the effect for drawing
    PrepareEffect(effect);

    // Set the active vertex and index buffer
    effect.GraphicsDevice.SetVertexBuffer(_vertexBuffer);
    effect.GraphicsDevice.Indices = _indexBuffer;

    // Draw the object
    foreach (EffectPass pass in effect.CurrentTechnique.Passes)
    {
        // Apply the pass
        pass.Apply();
        // Draw the object using the active vertex buffer
        effect.GraphicsDevice.DrawIndexedPrimitives(PrimitiveType.TriangleList, 0, 0,
                                            _vertices.Length, 0, 12);
    }
}
```

This approach provides the greatest efficiency for rendering in XNA because it reduces the calculation of redundant vertices and prevents unnecessary copying of vertex data within the device memory.

Lighting

Up to this point, all the colors used in our examples have been directly specified within our program code. This gives us a high level of control over the appearance of the graphics, but leads to a flat and cartoony look to the graphics. To add a further degree of realism to the objects that we render, we can use XNA's lighting features.

This section examines the lighting capabilities and explores how they can be used within our games.

Lights and Materials

XNA offers the facility to place up to three different lights into the game world and use these to illuminate the objects that are rendered. When lighting is switched on, the way in which objects are colored is altered from the behavior we have seen so far. XNA applies lighting to our objects by calculating the amount and color of light that falls onto each vertex and actually adjusts the vertex colors based on the result of this.

The outcome is that we can generate highly dynamic and realistic-looking shading on our objects. The minor downside is that because XNA implements lighting by taking control of coloring the object vertices, we can't specify vertex colors ourselves. We can still apply textures to our objects just as before, but vertex colors cannot be used.

Although we are no longer able to directly color vertices, we can still use different colors within a texture to provide coloring to different sections of our objects, so this is not necessarily as big a problem as it might at first sound.

Additionally, the DiffuseColor property can still be used to change the overall color of the objects being rendered. This is also known as the *material color* as it defines the color of the object. This works alongside the colors of lights that we place within the scene, allowing colors of lights and objects to be set independently. This provides a fair degree of flexibility with regard to how our objects are lit.

The following sections will discuss how lights and materials can be used within our game worlds.

Types of Illumination

A number of different types of illumination are available to shine onto our objects. Any or all of the illumination types can be applied to XNA's lighting model, and the color of each type of illumination can be specified independently.

Let's take a look at each of the illumination types that a light can use.

Ambient Light

The simplest type of light is *ambient light*, which is light that comes from all directions at once and falls equally on to all parts of each object rendered. It is completely flat in intensity, leaving no bright or dark areas on the objects that it illuminates.

In the real world, the closest analogy to ambient light is the light that is reflected from all the objects in the environment. If you are in a room with a single light source, those areas of the room that are not in direct line of sight from the bulb still receive some light from their surroundings. This is the illumination that ambient light seeks to simulate.

When an ambient light is present, all vertices will be equally lit by the appropriate ambient light level.

An example object illuminated with ambient light can be seen in Figure 7–17. The figure shows a 3D cylinder with a medium-intensity ambient light applied and no other lighting. Note how the object appears just as a silhouette: no variation of light intensity can be seen anywhere within the object.

Figure 7–17. A cylinder illuminated with an ambient light source

XNA's default ambient light is black, meaning that no ambient light appears within the rendered scene at all.

Diffuse Light

Diffuse light is reflected by an object based on how the object is angled toward the light source. If an object is rotated so that its faces are directly toward the light source, the faces will radiate the light with a high intensity. As they rotate away from the light, the intensity fades away.

The light is radiated equally in all directions, so the viewpoint from which the object is seen has no effect on the intensity of the lit surfaces. This is how an object with a matte surface would behave in the real world, as opposed to a reflective surface that would reflect more or less light depending upon the observation viewpoint.

An example object illuminated with diffuse light can be seen in Figure 7–18. The figure shows the same cylinder with a bright diffuse light situated directly to its right. Note that the object illumination increases as the object surface becomes more directly angled toward the light source.

Figure 7–18. A cylinder illuminated with a diffuse light source

Specular Light

Specular light is also reflected by an object based upon its angle with regard to the light source, but this type of illumination radiates light more like a mirror: light is reflected from the surface based on the angle of the surface relative to the viewer and light source.

If the light source is in the same location as the viewpoint, and a surface also faces directly toward the viewpoint, the specular light will radiate intensely. As soon as the surface rotates away from the viewpoint, the specular light will rapidly fall away. If the viewpoint and light source are in different locations, those faces that are angled directly between the two will radiate light most brightly, just as a mirror would.

This behavior allows objects to be given a "shine" or "highlight" that can make for very realistic looking objects.

An example object illuminated with specular light can be seen in Figure 7–19. The image shows the same cylinder with a bright specular light situated directly to its right. Note that the object illumination increases as the angle of the cylinder reflects our viewpoint toward the light, where the surface of the cylinder is at about a 45-degree angle from the viewpoint. As the surface deviates from this angle, the light intensity rapidly drops away.

Figure 7–19. A cylinder illuminated with a specular light source

Material Properties

Just as lights emit different types and intensities of light, so can objects reflect different types of light in different colors. For example, a red object in the real world is red because it reflects any red light that falls upon it, and absorbs the green and blue light.

In XNA we can set the color and intensity of light reflected from each individual object by setting the object *material*. Just as each light can have different colors for ambient, diffuse, and specular light, so we can define the intensity and color that objects reflect for each different type of light.

Let's take a look at the different material properties and then we will examine exactly how lights and materials interact with each other.

Diffuse Material

As the material's ambient property controls the amount of ambient light reflected, so its diffuse property controls the amount of diffuse light reflected. This can be set to white to reflect all the light that reaches the object, or it can be changed in order to absorb and reflect different elements of the color instead.

We have already discussed the diffuse material in the "Tinting Objects" section in the last chapter.

Specular Material

The material's specular color controls the amount of specular light that is reflected from the object. Setting the material's specular color to white will reflect all specular light that arrives at the object, whereas setting it to black will absorb and therefore completely disable the specular element of the light, preventing any shine effects from displaying on the object.

In addition to controlling how much of the specular light is reflected, XNA also offers control over the focus of the specular highlight. Low specular power values (values up to around 4 or 5) will result in a very soft specular component, reflecting lots of light back. As the value increases, the specular light becomes more and more focused, requiring faces to be angled more directly toward the light source before any reflection is made. There is no specific upper limit for the specular power value, but as it begins to reach into the hundreds, its effect becomes so slight that the specular light effects begin to disappear.

Emissive Material

The final material property allows us to set an *emissive color*. This property is used to specify a color that is then simulated as originating from the object, allowing it to have its own illumination independently of that of the lights around it.

Normally if an object has no light shining on it, it will appear completely black, but emissive colors allow the basic object color to be set even when it is not illuminated by any light at all.

It should be noted, however, that rendering an object with an emissive color set does not make the object into a light source itself. It will not add any light to the rest of the scene or cause any other objects to be illuminated in any way.

Light and Material Interaction

Now that you understand the role of light in a 3D scene and how it affects game objects, how do these lights and materials actually interact together?

A fairly simple calculation is used to determine the level of light for each vertex that is rendered. The engine first calculates the amount of diffuse light to apply to the object by multiplying each of the red, green, and blue diffuse values for the light (which range from 0 to 1) by the corresponding red, green, and blue diffuse values for the material (also ranging from 0 to 1). The resulting values are used to form the final diffuse color level for the object.

Let's look at an example. If we have a midlevel gray diffuse light with (red, green, blue) values of (0.5, 0.5, 0.5) and an object that has a blue diffuse material with color (0.7, 0.2, 0.2), the color components are multiplied as follows:

- *Red*: 0.5 x 0.7 = 0.35

- *Green*: 0.5 x 0.2 = 0.1

- *Blue*: 0.5 x 0.2 = 0.1

The resulting diffuse color for the object is therefore (0.35, 0.1, 0.1).

Consider another example in which we have a pure red diffuse light with color (1, 0, 0) and a pure green diffuse material with color (0, 1, 0). The calculation for this would be the following:

- *Red*: 1 x 0 = 0

- *Green*: 0 x 1 = 0

- *Blue*: 0 x 0 = 0

The resulting color is therefore (0, 0, 0): black. Shining a green light onto a red object results in all the green light being absorbed, so the object is not illuminated at all.

Once the final diffuse light has been calculated as shown, the same calculation is repeated for the specular light. The ambient light is then multiplied by the diffuse material to create a third calculated color, and a fourth and final color is derived from the emissive material color.

The red, green, and blue components of these four colors are then simply added together to produce the final color of light that will be applied to the object. If any of the color components exceed their upper limit of 1, they are clamped at this value and treated as being equal to 1.

Using Multiple Lights

We are not limited to having a single light active within our rendered scene. Up to a maximum of three available lights can be switched on when an object is rendered to provide light of different color and in different directions.

If an object is rendered with more than one light active, the final color for the object is calculated as explained a moment ago in the "Light and Material Interaction" section for each individual light. The color components for the individual lights are then all added together to provide a final color for the object being rendered.

This behavior means that it is possible for colors to become oversaturated if lots of different lights are present at once. Some thought and attention might be required to ensure that light sources don't cause objects to be flooded with so much light that they are overwhelmed by it.

Reusing Lights

An important feature to remember when using lights is that they are observed only at the moment at which an object is rendered. After an object render has been called, the lights that were active can be reconfigured, moved, enabled, or disabled in whatever way you want for the next object, and these changes will have no effect at all on those objects already rendered.

Lights do not need to affect all objects in the game world as lights in the real world would; they can be configured to apply only to specific game objects if needed.

■ **TIP** Also remember that you can switch the entire lighting feature on and off partway through rendering if you want. It is quite acceptable to draw a series of objects with lighting enabled, disable lighting, and draw further objects without any lighting effects at all so that vertex colors can be used.

Types of Light Source

Most 3D graphics APIs support multiple different types of light; they normally include directional lights, point lights, and spotlights. Each of these changes the way that the reflection of the light is calculated on each object that it illuminates.

XNA can also support these different types of light, but due to the limitations of the lighting model in the Windows Phone 7 implementation of XNA, only one light type is actually supported: the directional light.

Directional lights shine light in a single direction equally across an entire scene. They do not have a position, but rather are treated as being infinitely far away from the scene. The rays of light are parallel to each other.

The closest analogy in the real world is sunlight. Although the sun clearly does actually have a position, it is so far away that the light it emits is to all intents and purposes coming from the entire sky rather than from a single point.

Figure 7–20 shows the way in which a directional light shines on objects rendered within a 3D scene. Note that the light has direction but does not have a position: the rays shown are all parallel and do not converge on any specific location.

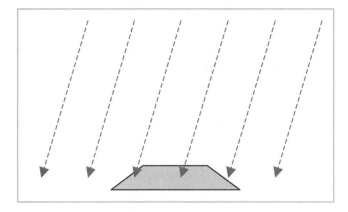

Figure 7–20. *Light rays from a directional light source*

How XNA Calculates Light Reflections

The explanations we have looked at for each light revolve to a significant degree around determining whether each triangle in a rendered object is facing toward or away from a light. Triangles that are at the appropriate angle relative to the light will be illuminated brightly, whereas triangles facing away from the light will become darker or not be illuminated at all.

How does XNA tell whether a triangle is facing toward a light or not? There's nothing magical about this; in fact, the answer is rather basic: we have to tell XNA the direction in which each triangle is facing.

We do this just once when we create our object. When the object is rotating or moving in the game world, XNA will use this information and apply all the object transformations to the direction in which the triangle is facing, just as it does to the position of the vertices. The object lighting will therefore be automatically and dynamically calculated as each object or light moves within the scene.

Describing a Triangle's Face Direction

To tell XNA the direction in which each triangle is facing, we provide a Vector3 value known as a *normal*. A normal describes a line that is pointing in a direction perpendicular to the front of the triangle. Figure 7–21 shows a single triangle with its normal. The triangle itself is completely flat with its surface pointing directly upward. The normal, which is represented by a dashed arrow, therefore points upward, too.

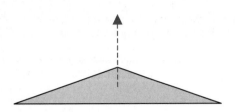

Figure 7–21. A triangle and its normal

In Figure 7–22, a solid shape is shown with its normals. Each side of the cube faces in a different direction, and once again dashed arrows are used to indicate the direction of the normal from each side.

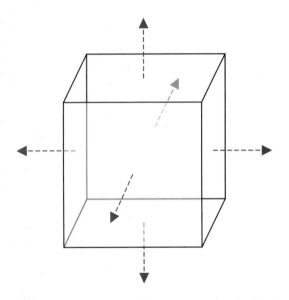

Figure 7–22. A cube and the normals of each of its faces

To describe each normal, we use a different type of vertex object: VertexPositionNormalTexture. In addition to the Position and TextureCoordinate vectors that we explored already, this object contains an additional vector called Normal. This vector allows the three different values (for the x, y, and z axes) to describe the distance along each axis that would need to be travelled to move along the line of the normal.

For the triangles on top of the cube whose faces point directly upward, the normal vector would be (0, 1, 0). This vector shows that to travel along the line of the normal, we would move zero units along the x and z axes, and 1 unit along the positive y axis; in other words, we would move directly upward. The opposite face that points downward would have a normal vector of (0, -1, 0). Moving in the direction of this vector would move us along the negative y axis.

Similarly, the triangles on the right edge of the cube have a normal vector of (1, 0, 0), and the triangles at the back of the cube (facing away from us) have a normal vector of (0, 0, -1).

We need to provide these normal vectors to XNA for it to use when our object is being rendered. We only need to provide the vectors for when the object is in its default untransformed position. As the object is rotated within the scene, XNA will recalculate its resulting normal vectors automatically.

Notice that the normals we have discussed all have a length of 1 unit. This is important because XNA takes the normal length into account when performing its lighting calculations, and normal vectors that are longer or shorter than this might cause the reflected light to become brighter or darker. Vectors with a length of 1 unit are known as *normalized* vectors, whereas those with longer or shorter lengths are *unnormalized* vectors.

Once XNA knows the direction each triangle is facing, it can work out whether they face toward or away from the scene's lights and so determine how much light to provide for the triangle.

Calculating Normals

Although working out normal vectors is easy when they are aligned directly along the x, y, or z axis, they can be much more difficult to work out in your head when the triangle faces in a direction away from these axes. Calculating the normals manually for these triangles would be both tedious and prone to errors.

Fortunately, we are using a computer (albeit one that fits in your pocket), so we can get it to calculate the normals for us automatically.

There are all sorts of mathematical operations that can be calculated on vectors (and there are lots of books and online references that will cover this subject in immense detail if you want to investigate it further) and we can use one of these called a *cross product* to calculate the normal for us.

We will now briefly look at the calculation performed by the cross product, to understand what it does. Don't worry if you find the arithmetic complex or off-putting, however, for as you will see in a moment, XNA has support for doing all this built in to its Vector3 structure, so we don't have to calculate any of this manually. The explanation here simply describes what is going on under the covers.

To perform a cross product calculation, we need to find two vectors that lay along the surface of our triangle. They are easy to calculate because we can simply find the difference in position between the vertices of the triangle. For the purposes of this example, we will call these vectors a and b.

Consider the triangle shown in Figure 7–23. It is oriented so that its surface points directly upward (to keep the example simple!) and has vertex coordinates as shown.

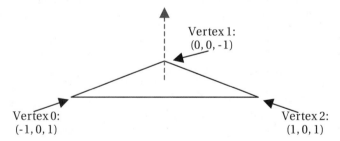

Figure 7–23. The vertices of a triangle ready for normal calculation

Note that the triangle vertices are, as always, defined in clockwise order. This is important to our calculation; if they were defined in counterclockwise order, the normal we calculate would be facing in the opposite direction (downward in this case).

To calculate the two vectors that we need, we subtract the coordinates of vertex 1 from vertex 2 for the first vector, and subtract the coordinates of vertex 0 from vertex 1 for the second vector, as follows:

- Vector a: Vertex 2 − Vertex 1 = (1 − 0, 0 − 0, 1 − -1) = (1, 0, 2)

- Vector b: Vertex 1 − Vertex 0 = (0 − -1, 0 − 0, -1 − 1) = (1, 0, -2)

As you can see, these do indeed represent the distances from each vertex to the next. To move from vertex 1 to vertex 2, we would need to move 1 unit along the x axis, 0 units on the y axis, and 2 units on the z axis. To move from vertex 0 to vertex 1, we would need to move 1 unit on the x axis, 0 units on the y axis and -2 units along the z axis.

To perform the cross product operation, we need to perform the following calculations on vectors a and b. These will produce the normal vector n:

- $n.x = (a.y \times b.z) - (a.z \times b.y)$

- $n.y = (a.z \times b.x) - (a.x \times b.z)$

- $n.z = (a.x \times b.y) - (a.y \times b.x)$

Let's substitute in the values for our vectors and see the results:

- $n.x = (0 \times -2) - (2 \times 0) = 0 - 0 = 0$

- $n.y = (2 \times 1) - (1 \times -2) = 2 - -2 = 4$

- $n.z = (1 \times 0) - (0 \times 1) = 0 - 0 = 0$

The resulting vector n is therefore calculated as (0, 4, 0). This does indeed describe a line in the positive y axis, directly upward, exactly as we had hoped. The same calculation can be performed for any triangle regardless of its vertex locations.

So having seen what the cross product calculation actually does, let's make things a little simpler and take a look at how XNA can do this work for us. We still need to calculate the vectors a and b, but XNA will allow us to simply subtract one vertex position from another to calculate these. With the a and b vectors prepared, we can pass them to the static Vector3.Cross function, and it will return the normal. The code required to perform all of this is shown in Listing 7–14, which uses the same triangle as we used for our manual calculations.

Listing 7–14. Calculating the normal for a triangle

```
// Create three  vertices for our triangle
Vector3 vertex0 = new Vector3(-1, 0, 1);
Vector3 vertex1 = new Vector3(0, 0, -1);
Vector3 vertex2 = new Vector3(1, 0, 1);

// Calculate the a and b vectors by subtracting the vertices from one another
Vector3 vectora = vertex2 - vertex1;
Vector3 vectorb = vertex1 - vertex0;

// Calculate the normal as the cross product of the two vectors
Vector3 normal = Vector3.Cross(vectora, vectorb);

// Display the normal to the debug window
System.Diagnostics.Debug.WriteLine(normal.ToString());
```

Hopefully that should be a bit easier to understand! The output that is displayed by the code is the vector (0, 4, 0), exactly as with our manual calculations.

The normal vector we have calculated is not normalized, however; its length is 4 rather than 1. XNA's Vector3 structure has a Normalize method that we can call to easily normalize the value however, so we can just let XNA do it for us. The code shown in Listing 7–15 can be added after the call to Vector3.Cross from Listing 7–14 to normalize the vector.

Listing 7–15. Normalizing the normal vector

```
normal.Normalize();
```

The resulting normalized vector is (0, 1, 0)—a unit-length vector pointing directly upward. Perfect.

We will look at implementing all this in our program code in the section entitled "Programmatic Calculation of Normals," coming up shortly.

Surface Normals and Vertex Normals

We have so far considered normals as applying to each face in our 3D object. In actual fact, it is not the faces that we apply normals to but the individual vertices that form the face. It is the vertices for which XNA calculates the color based on its lighting equations, and it then applies this to the whole triangle by interpolating the colors between the vertices just as we have manually interpolated colors ourselves by providing vertex colors.

This gives us an opportunity to perform a very useful lighting trick. We can provide different normals for the vertices of a single triangle. XNA will then consider each vertex of the triangle to be facing in a different direction and will interpolate the light directions across the surface of the triangle.

Consider the triangles in Figure 7–24. They are shown as thick lines, representing the triangles viewed edge-on. The long dashed arrows show the normals that have been applied for each of the vertices within the triangles. Note that for each triangle, the normals are pointing in different directions (they point slightly away from one another).

The shorter dashed arrows show the effective normals within the interior of the triangles due to interpolation. They smoothly transition from one normal to the next, giving the impression that the surface of the object when viewed face on is perfectly smooth, whereas in fact it is created from just five flat faces.

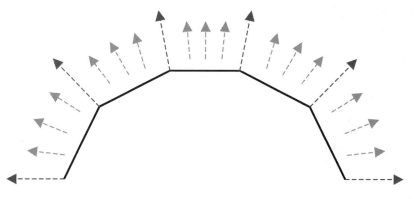

Figure 7–24. Interpolated vertex normals

An example of normal interpolation in practice can be seen in Figure 7–25. The two images shown are both of the same cylinder, rendered using a number of flat surfaces. The individual surfaces can be clearly seen in the image on the left, which uses the same normals for all vertices within each face. On the right, the vertex normals are modified so that they differ from one side of the face to the other (exactly as we did in Figure 12-20). Note that the appearance of this cylinder is entirely smooth, even though it is formed from the exact same faces as the image on the left.

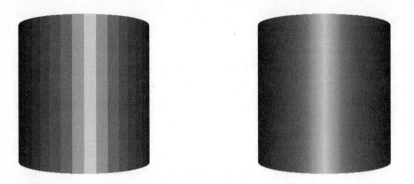

Figure 7–25. A cylinder with normals applied to each whole face (left) and to individual vertices (right)

Adding Lighting to Games

So that's the theory; now let's take a look at how we implement lighting in our game code. All the code in this section can be found in the Lighting example project that accompanies this chapter. A screenshot from the project is shown in Figure 7–26.

Figure 7–26. An illuminated cube and a cylinder rendered by the Lighting example project

Enabling and Disabling Lighting

The first thing that is needed is to tell the BasicEffect object that we want to use lighting. Without this, all light features will be disabled and ignored, as has been the case in our example projects up until now.

Lighting is enabled by simply setting the LightingEnabled property to true when initializing the effect, as shown in Listing 7–16.

Listing 7–16. Enabling XNA's lighting feature

```
_effect.LightingEnabled = true;
```

Lighting can, of course, be disabled by setting this back to false. This property can be updated anywhere within your game; it isn't restricted just to the Initialize function.

Light Configuration

Once the lighting system has been switched on, the next step is to configure the lights. We have three directional lights at our disposal, exposed via the DirectionalLight0, DirectionalLight1, and DirectionalLight2 properties of the BasicEffect object. Each of these lights has the following properties that can be used to configure its behavior:

- DiffuseColor: the diffuse color of the light. Defaults to white.

- Direction: a Vector3 structure indicating the direction in which the light is pointing. Defaults to (0, -1, 0), straight downward.

- Enabled: a bool indicating whether this light is switched on or off.

- SpecularColor: the specular color of the light. Defaults to black to disable specular lighting.

■ **NOTE** All the light colors are represented as Vector3 structures. Remember that you can convert a Color to a Vector3 by calling its ToVector3 method.

The default configuration of the lights is for light 0 to be enabled and the other two lights to be disabled. As the lights point downward by default, this configuration creates an effect similar to the sun shining from directly overhead.

Updating the light settings is very easy because the parameters can be freely updated. To change a light's direction or its colors, or to switch it on and off, simply set the properties as required before rendering your objects.

The code in Listing 7–17 configures light 0 so that it is directed along the negative z axis. As the user's viewpoint is also looking along the negative z axis in our examples so far, this configuration results in the light illuminating the objects from the camera position.

Listing 7–17. Configuring a white light to shine along the negative z axis

```
_effect.DirectionalLight0.Enabled = true;
_effect.DirectionalLight0.Direction = new Vector3(0, 0, -1);
_effect.DirectionalLight0.DiffuseColor = Color.White.ToVector3();
```

For the light itself, this code is all that is required to light up the objects within our scene. However, we haven't done anything to set the normals for our objects yet. Continuing to use the cube from our previous examples, we first modify the class to use the VertexPositionNormalTexture structure for its vertices. After setting the vertex positions as we always have, we now need to set the normal for each vertex. For a cube, the normals all point directly along the x, y, or z axis and so it is easy to set these up manually. Listing 7–18 shows the beginning of the code to perform this task, taken from the Lighting project's CubeObject class.

Listing 7–18. Setting the cube's vertex normals

```
// Set the vertex normals
i = 0;
// Front face...
_vertices[i++].Normal = new Vector3(0, 0, 1);
_vertices[i++].Normal = new Vector3(0, 0, 1);
_vertices[i++].Normal = new Vector3(0, 0, 1);
_vertices[i++].Normal = new Vector3(0, 0, 1);
_vertices[i++].Normal = new Vector3(0, 0, 1);
_vertices[i++].Normal = new Vector3(0, 0, 1);
// Back face...
_vertices[i++].Normal = new Vector3(0, 0, -1);
_vertices[i++].Normal = new Vector3(0, 0, -1);
_vertices[i++].Normal = new Vector3(0, 0, -1);
_vertices[i++].Normal = new Vector3(0, 0, -1);
_vertices[i++].Normal = new Vector3(0, 0, -1);
_vertices[i++].Normal = new Vector3(0, 0, -1);
// ... and so on for the remaining faces ...
```

The cube's class is otherwise unchanged. Running the project displays a cube as shown in Figure 7–27. You can see that each face of the cube has its own color, determined by the light calculation that we have already explored.

Figure 7–27. A cube lit using a directional light

Try experimenting with the light and material colors to see how they interact. The light color is set in the project's Initialize function (refer to Listing 7–17), whereas the object material is set against each individual object in its ObjectColor property. The cube in the example project is added by the ResetGame function, and its color can be modified here.

As additional lights are enabled, XNA has additional work to do to calculate the light for each vertex within the rendered objects. For this reason it is important to disable lights when they are not required. Lighting is a relatively inexpensive calculation, so feel free to get your lights set up exactly how you need them for your game.

Ambient Light

To use an ambient light, simply set the `BasicEffect.AmbientLight` property to the required color. All the objects rendered will take the ambient light into account.

Specular Light

Specular lighting is calculated both from the specular color of the active lights and from the specular material color. As the material colors are specific to each object, we will create new properties in the game framework's `MatrixObjectBase` class to support specular color for each individual object.

The new properties, `SpecularColor` (of type `Color`) and `SpecularPower` (of type `float`), mirror the properties within the `BasicEffect` that control the specular material. These can then be set within each object to control its specular lighting settings.

To apply the specular lighting, the `MatrixObjectBase.PrepareEffect` is modified to pass the object's values into the `BasicEffect` object's `SpecularColor` and `SpecularPower` properties.

Specular light generally looks at its best when it is white. By all means, experiment with colored specular light, but the effects might not always be natural-looking.

Figure 7–28 shows another cube with a white specular light and a specular power of 10. You can enable this in the example project by uncommenting the lines in ResetGame that set the two new specular lighting properties. Notice how shiny the cube looks compared with the one without specular lighting. One of the reasons for this shininess is that specular light affects each vertex differently, even if all the vertices of a face point in exactly the same direction. This effect results in a much more dynamic appearance on the rendered objects.

Figure 7–28. *A cube lit using a directional light and specular lighting*

Try experimenting with the specular power and see the results. As the power value increases into the tens and hundreds, the cube starts to reflect specular light only when its faces get closer and closer toward the light source as the specular effect becomes more and more tightly focused.

There is one additional `BasicEffect` property that has an effect on specular lighting: `PreferPerPixelLighting`. This property defaults to `false`, which results in the specular component of the lighting model being calculated for each vertex, as we have already discussed. On objects that have large triangles (and therefore have areas of the object where there are no vertices nearby), this can result in some visual artifacts that can detract from the otherwise very attractive looking specular lighting.

The first of these problems can be seen in the left image of Figure 7–29. The image shows a cube that is facing nearly directly toward the camera and the light source, but is slightly rotated so that the rightmost corner is the only one that is reflecting the specular light. As you can see, the light has a very angular look caused by the fact that only four vertices are being used to display the entire face of the cube. The interpolation is inaccurate due to this small number of color points.

The image on the right is of the exact same object and lighting configuration, except that PreferPerPixelLighting has been switched on. This property instructs XNA to calculate the specular lighting for each individual pixel that it renders, rather than just for the vertices. As will be clearly seen, the reflection looks much better: the angular lines have all disappeared, leaving a perfect round highlight in its place.

Figure 7–29. Two cubes, without (left) and with (right) per pixel lighting enabled

The second problem with specular lighting also occurs on objects with large triangles, but primarily affects specular light that is very tightly focused. Figure 7–30 shows two images of a cube that is directly facing toward the camera and the light source. The specular power has been set to 1000 for a very focused effect. Because the effect is so small, it doesn't reach any of the vertices at all. As a result, the specular light has no impact on the face. On the right is the same scene with per pixel lighting enabled. As each pixel then has its specular light individually calculated, the specular light effect clearly appears within the face.

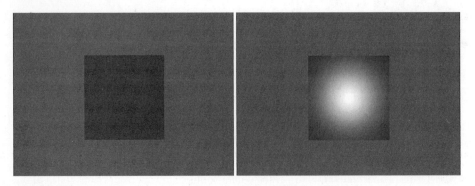

Figure 7–30. Two cubes, without and with per pixel lighting enabled with a high specular focus

Of course, as you might expect, there is a downside to per pixel lighting. Because the specular component needs to be calculated for each individual pixel as opposed to each vertex, it has a much higher processing requirement. Consider the cubes in Figure 7–30: the visible face consists of more than 30,000 pixels, as compared with only 6 vertices.

Per pixel lighting should therefore be used sparingly. If you have an object that is not using specular light, has no large faces, has a low specular power, or doesn't exhibit either of the problems discussed here, you will probably find a performance benefit from leaving it disabled. Experiment and find which setting provides the best balance between appearance and performance for your game.

Emissive Light

The emissive light for rendered objects is also most usefully set for each individual object, so we will add a new property for this to the MatrixObjectBase class just as we did for the specular material color.

The EmissiveColor property (of type Color) can then be set within each object to control its emissive lighting settings and is applied in the MatrixObjectBase.PrepareEffect, which passes its value into the BasicEffect object's EmissiveColor property.

The Standard Lighting Rig

The lighting properties of the BasicEffect object give you a great deal of freedom to set up your lighting system in whatever way you want, but XNA has one additional feature that you might find useful in your games: the *standard lighting rig*.

I will allow Shawn Hargreaves, one of the Microsoft's XNA Framework developers, to explain with the following text from his blog (which, incidentally, is a fantastically useful resource for XNA programming and can be found at http://blogs.msdn.com/b/shawnhar/):

> *Many years ago photographers discovered that a single light was not enough to make their subjects look good. Instead, they use three.*
>
> *The* key light *is the brightest, and provides the main illumination and shadows. This will typically be positioned to match a real light source such as an overhead lamp, a window, or the sun for an outdoor scene.*
>
> *The* fill light *is dimmer, and usually angled at 90 degrees to the key. This is used to soften the shadows, adding shading and definition to areas that would otherwise be solid black.*
>
> *Finally, the* back light *is positioned behind the character, facing toward the camera. This illuminates only the silhouette edges, helping the character stand out against the background.*

Because this is potentially a very useful light configuration, it can be applied to your 3D game world by simply calling the BasicEffect.EnableDefaultLighting function. In practice, it might provide a useful set of lights, it might provide a useful basis but require a little subsequent modification, or it might not be suitable for your game at all. Give it a try and see what kind of results it provides; you might just like it.

Programmatic Calculation of Normals

Earlier in this section, we explored the calculations required to automatically calculate the normals for a triangle within a 3D object. As a final lighting-related addition to the game framework, let's add a function that will calculate the normals automatically.

This will be relatively basic, and will operate within the following restrictions:

- It will only generate normals that are the same for all vertices of a triangle, so no smoothing using normal interpolation will be supported.

- It will assume that each vertex will be either used only once or that all of its uses will have the same vertex normal. The code could potentially be enhanced to average out multiple uses of the same vertex, but this enhancement is left as an exercise for the reader. When we begin importing geometry in the next chapter, you will see that this might not be as valuable an enhancement as it currently appears.

- It will support only triangle lists.

As we have two different ways of rendering triangles (a simple list of triangles or using vertex indices), we will create two corresponding functions that process data in these two formats. To reduce the amount of code, we will set the two functions up so that one simply calls into the other, allowing all the calculation to be put into just a single function.

The easiest way to implement this efficient code approach is to get the version that takes a simple list of triangles (without vertex indices) to build a corresponding index array. Once this is done, the vertices and the fabricated indices can be passed into the other function to calculate on its behalf.

Generating indices for an unindexed triangle list is very simple: each triangle is formed from the next three vertices in the list, so the indices are just a sequence of incremental numbers. The first triangle is formed from indices 0, 1, and 2; the second triangle from indices 3, 4, and 5; the third from indices 6, 7, and 8; and so on.

The code for the function that handles unindexed vertices, named CalculateVertexNormals and added to the MatrixObjectBase class, can be seen in Listing 7–19. It creates an array for the indices whose length is equal to the number of vertices. The array is then filled with sequential numbers starting from 0, and the vertices and constructed indices array are passed into a second overload of the same function to actually generate the normals, which we will examine in a moment.

Listing 7–19. Generating indices for an unindexed triangle list

```
public void CalculateVertexNormals(VertexPositionNormalTexture[] vertices)
{
    short[] indices;
    short i;

    // Build an array that allows us to treat the vertices as if they were indexed.
    // As the triangles are drawn sequentially, the indexes are actually just
    // an increasing sequence of numbers: the first triangle is formed from
    // vertices 0, 1 and 2, the second triangle from vertices 3, 4 and 5, etc.

    // First create the array with an element for each vertex
    indices = new short[vertices.Length];

    // Then set the elements within the array so that each contains
    // the next sequential vertex index
    for (i = 0; i < indices.Length; i++)
    {
        indices[i] = i;
    }

    // Finally delegate to the other overload to do the work
    CalculateVertexNormals(vertices, indices);
}
```

The second overload of the function accepts two parameters: the vertex array and the index array. This version of the function would be used directly if you are working with indexed vertices, or will otherwise be called from the code in Listing 7–19 if the vertices are unindexed.

The second overload works through the vertices in the array, using the indices to determine which vertices are used to form each triangle within the object. Once the vertices of each triangle have been determined, their vectors are calculated and stored in the va and vb variables. Their cross product is then calculated in order to determine the triangle's normal, and the resulting vector is normalized. The normal vector is then written into all three of the vertices that formed the triangle. This is all exactly as per the processes we discussed in the "Calculating Normals" section earlier in this chapter.

Note that as we are updating the vertex array that was passed in as a parameter; there is no need to return anything from this function. The normals will be written "in place" into the existing vertices.

The code to calculate the normals is shown in Listing 7–20.

Listing 7–20. Calculating the normals for an indexed triangle list

```
public void CalculateVertexNormals(VertexPositionNormalTexture[] vertices,
                                                          short[] indices)
{
    // Vectors to describe the relationships between the vertices of the triangle
    // being processed
    Vector3 vectora;
    Vector3 vectorb;
    // The resulting normal vector
    Vector3 normal;

    // Loop for each triangle (each triangle uses three indices)
    for (int index = 0; index < indices.Length; index += 3)
    {
        // Create the a and b vectors from the vertex positions
        // First the a vector from vertices 2 and 1
        vectora = vertices[index + 2].Position - vertices[index + 1].Position;
        // Next the b vector from vertices 1 and 0
        vectorb = vertices[index + 1].Position - vertices[index + 0].Position;

        // Calculate the normal as the cross product of the two vectors
        normal = Vector3.Cross(vectora, vectorb);

        // Normalize the normal
        normal.Normalize();

        // Write the normal back into all three of the triangle vertices
        vertices[index].Normal = normal;
        vertices[index+1].Normal = normal;
        vertices[index+2].Normal = normal;
    }
}
```

This function can simply be called after the vertex positions for an object have been calculated. If you look at the CubeObject class in the Lighting example project, you will find that this can be used in place of the code that manually provides the normals. Try commenting out all the BuildVertices code that sets the vertex normals (from the "Set the vertex normals" comment on to the end of the function) and instead enable the call to CalculateVertexNormals. The end result is identical, but with a lot less code and a lot less effort.

Orthographic Projection

Right at the start of this chapter we looked at the perspective projection matrix, and we have used this for all the subsequent exploration of 3D graphics. XNA offers another projection matrix that can be useful in certain game environments, however, called an *orthographic projection*.

Whereas the perspective projection causes objects farther away from the camera to become smaller, an orthographic projection does not: distant objects appear at exactly the same size as near objects. This is clearly an unrealistic representation of the real world and unsuitable for any game that tries to present a lifelike approximation of a 3D environment, but it does have two specific uses.

The first of these uses is for isometric 3D games. They are generally tile-based games viewed such that the camera is rotated around and elevated from its default position. Isometric viewpoints were common in pseudo-3D games before hardware acceleration become popular. Some famous games that have used this style of 3D graphics include *Q*bert*, *Zaxxon*, *Knight Lore*, *Marble Madness*, *Populous*, and (more recently) *Civilization III* and *Diablo II*. Isometric games are less common these days, but do still make occasional appearances, particularly as role playing and strategy games.

The second thing that orthographic projections are useful for is creating a pixel-aligned coordinate system. Clearly with perspective projections, moving an object one unit along the x or y axis might cause it to move a different number of physical pixels along that axis, depending on how near or far the object is from the camera. Because distance makes no difference in orthographic projections, a coordinate system can be set up that exactly matches the pixels on the screen, making precise pixel-based movement much easier.

Despite their different appearance, all other aspects of 3D rendering that we have explored still hold true with orthographic projection: hidden surfaces will still be removed, objects will still be lit, and transformations and rotations will still operate exactly as with perspective projection (though rotations can look a little strange without perspective: the brain thinks they are distorting and stretching because no equivalent transformation exists in the real world).

The Viewing Frustum

The shape of an orthographic viewing frustum is simply a cuboid area, such as the one shown in Figure 7–31.

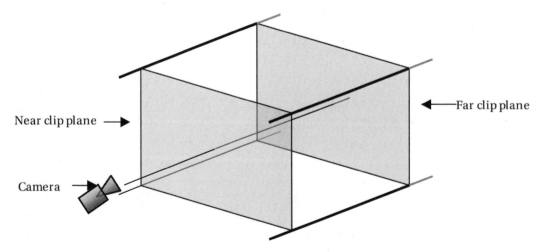

Figure 7–31. A diagram showing a 3D orthographic viewing frustum

Just as with a perspective projection, we still have a near and far clip plane, and objects that are rendered will still be checked to ensure that they fall within this region. Despite objects not growing or shrinking as their depth changes within a scene, the depth buffer is still used and will ensure that objects with a higher z value will appear in front objects with a lower z value.

The reason why depth has no effect on the object size is that objects at the far clip plane occupy exactly the same proportion of the plane as objects on the near clip plane. If you look back at Figure 7–2, you will see two objects, one near and one far, contained within a perspective viewing frustum, and then in Figure 7–3 the projected outcome on the screen of those two shapes. Let's repeat these with an orthographic viewing frustum. Figure 7–32 shows the objects within the frustum, one at the near clip plane and one at the far clip plane just as before.

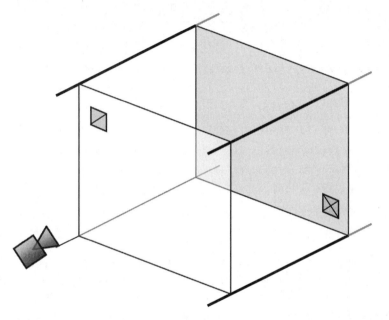

Figure 7–32. *Two identically sized objects in the viewing frustum shown in 3D space*

When these objects are transformed by the orthographic projection, they continue to appear at the same size, as can be seen in Figure 7–33. The proportion of the clip plane filled by the shapes is the same in both cases, and so they are not enlarged or shrunk at all.

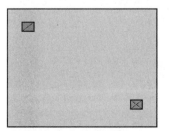

Figure 7–33. *The same two objects after orthographic projection into 2D*

When we set up an orthographic projection, we simply tell it how many units we want it to use across the x and y axis. It will automatically stretch the rendered objects to fit within this defined set of coordinates. If the ratio of the axes does not match that of the screen, we can end up with objects becoming distorted as they are rendered. For example, if we used a range of -1 to +1 for both the x and y axes and displayed it on a 480 x 800 pixel screen, a 1-unit-square object would appear with a width of 240 pixels and a height of 400 pixels. It is clearly not square! For this reason, we generally still use the aspect ratio in our own calculations when setting the orthographic scale.

There is no need for a viewing angle to be specified for this projection because the angle is always parallel.

Defining the Orthographic Viewing Frustum in XNA

Just as XNA provided a useful function for creating projection matrices, so it provides another for orthographic projections—two, in fact, as you will see.

The first of these functions is the static `Matrix.CreateOrthographic` function. This expects the following four parameters:

- `width`: the number of units to display across the projection. The center point will always be 0, so providing a width of 4 will result in a frustum that extends from -2 to +2 across the x axis.

- `height`: the number of units to display vertically for the projection. Just as with the `width`, the center point will always be 0.

- `zNearPlane`: the near clipping plane distance.

- `zFarPlane`: the far clipping plane distance.

■ **TIP** Because distance has no effect on the sizing of objects, it is quite acceptable to set a near clipping plane with a negative distance, allowing objects that are effectively behind the camera to still be rendered. This configuration allows a coordinate system to be created where the value 0 is the center of all the 3D axes, which can simplify the object positional calculations.

Listing 7–21 shows an example orthographic projection matrix being created. Its vertical size is set at 16 units, and the horizontal size is calculated from the aspect ratio to display the appropriate amount to keep the coordinate system square.

Listing 7–21. Calculating the normals for an indexed triangle list

```
// Calculate the screen aspect ratio
float aspectRatio =
            (float)GraphicsDevice.Viewport.Width / GraphicsDevice.Viewport.Height;
// Create a projection matrix
Matrix projection = Matrix.CreateOrthographic(16 * aspectRatio, 16, 0, 100.0f);
```

Let's take a look at a couple of applications of orthographic projection.

Isometric Projection

To obtain an isometric projection, we simply need to set the orthographic projection up as described and then rotate the camera so that it looks upon the scene from an angle, instead of straight on.

The effects of this camera rotation can be seen in Figure 7–34. The two images both display a unit-size cube with an orthographic projection. On the left, the camera is looking directly along the negative z axis, so only the front face of the cube can be seen. On the right, the camera has been moved so that it looks from the point (1, 1, 1) toward the origin point (0, 0, 0). As a result, the cube is now seen with its corner facing toward the camera. Note that the cube's front face (lit in medium gray) is now appearing at the bottom left of the cube; this should help you to visualize how the camera position has moved.

Figure 7–34. Direct orthographic projection and rotated orthographic projection

The code required to set the camera into this position is shown in Listing 7–22. This replaces the previous calculation of the view matrix in the game's Initialize function.

Listing 7–22. Setting the camera position for an isometric projection

```
// Calculate a view matrix (where we are looking from and to) for isometric projection
Matrix view = Matrix.CreateLookAt(new Vector3(1, 1, 1), Vector3.Zero, Vector3.Up);
```

With the camera so positioned, the world axes are shifted so that they are no longer aligned with the screen axis. Moving an object along the positive x axis will now cause it to move to the right and down on the screen. Moving an object along the positive z axis will cause it to move left and down on the screen, and the positive y axis will move up on the screen.

These positional effects can be seen in Figure 7–35. The cube labeled A is at position (0, 0, 0), the cube labeled B is at position (0, 1, 0), the cube labeled C is at position (0, 0, 1), and the cube labeled D is at position (2, 0, 0).

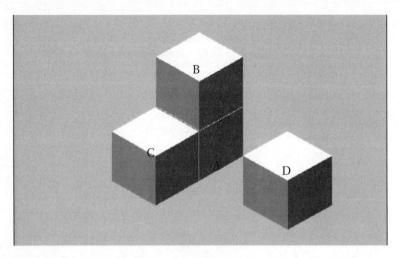

Figure 7–35. *Objects in different positions with an isometric projection.*

An example of using an isometric projection can be seen in the Isometric project accompanying this chapter. It sets up a grid of unit-size cubes along the x and z planes, and then scales them along the y axis to make them increase and decrease in height. An image from the project can be seen in Figure 7–36.

Figure 7–36. *The Isometric example project*

Using an isometric view of an orthographic projection will be useful in only a minority of games, but for those that do need it, XNA's rich 3D features create a powerful environment for displaying such graphical environments.

Pixel-Aligned Projection

We can also use orthographic projections to align the coordinate system exactly to the pixels on the screen. This is generally useful only for 2D rendering, and in many cases will be more easily achieved by simply using XNA's sprite technology instead. As you have seen by now, however, there are features that the 3D rendering environment offers that sprites cannot achieve, such as powerful matrix-based positioning and flexible lighting.

To set up a pixel-aligned projection, we simply need to provide the actual viewport width and height when creating the matrix, as shown in Listing 7–23. Given a width of 480 and a height of 800, this configuration will create a coordinate system ranging from position (-240, -400) in the screen's bottom-left corner to position (240, 400) in its top-right corner.

Listing 7–23. Creating a pixel-aligned orthographic projection matrix

```
// Create a pixel-aligned orthographic projection
Matrix projection = Matrix.CreateOrthographic(GraphicsDevice.Viewport.Width,
                                    GraphicsDevice.Viewport.Height, 0, 100);
```

This works fine, but has put the origin (0, 0) coordinate in the center of the screen. Normally when working with 2D coordinate systems (such as the one used by XNA's sprites), the origin is in the top-left corner, and the positive y axis points toward the bottom of the screen. We can replicate this same system by using a different projection matrix creation function: CreateOrthographicOffCenter.

This function expects six parameters to be passed, as follows and in this order:

- left: the coordinate to use to represent the left edge of the screen

- right: the coordinate for the right edge of the screen

- bottom: the coordinate for the bottom edge of the screen

- top: the coordinate for the top edge of the screen

- zNearPlane: the near clipping plane distance

- zFarPlane: the far clipping plane distance

Any values can be passed for the left, right, bottom, and top coordinates, so we can set the left and top values to be zero, and the right and bottom to be the viewport width and height, respectively. Listing 7–24 shows an example of setting the projection up in this way.

Listing 7–24. Creating an off-center pixel-aligned orthographic projection matrix

```
// Create a pixel-aligned orthographic projection with its origin in the top-left
// of the screen.
Matrix projection = Matrix.CreateOrthographicOffCenter
                             (0, GraphicsDevice.Viewport.Width,
                              GraphicsDevice.Viewport.Height, 0,
                              -100, 100);
```

If you wanted to put the origin (0, 0) coordinate to the bottom left instead, simply swap the bottom and top parameters and the whole display will flip vertically to achieve this.

Mastering the 3D World

Moving out of the realm of flat 2D graphics and into the depths of 3D is undeniably a big step. All sorts of additional challenges appear both in terms of code complexity and graphical modeling. XNA does provide a sound and flexible technology base to build on, and the rewards of 3D game programming can be great for players and developers alike.

Once you are happy and comfortable with the concepts and the code that we have discussed in this chapter, the next chapter will introduce you to a number of additional techniques that you can use in XNA to help bring your games to life.

■ ■ ■

CHAPTER 8

Further 3D Features and Techniques

In this chapter, you will extend your knowledge of XNA and take the features and capabilities of your code up to the next level. When you finish working through this chapter, you will be able to import 3D models from an external modeling application and use a number of additional XNA features to add life to your games.

Importing Geometry

In Chapter 7, we used two different methods for defining 3D objects in our XNA programs. The first required us to manually define a big array of vertex coordinates. This might be workable for simple objects such as cubes (though it is fairly tedious even for that!), but when we move on to more complex objects such as treasure chests or spaceships, it quickly becomes unrealistic. The second approach used mathematical formulae to create shapes for us (the cylinder from the Lighting example project). This is useful for regular geometric shapes, but once again it is unlikely to be of value for real-world game objects.

The solution is to use a 3D modeling application. Modeling applications are third-party software products that provide a rich (and often rather complex) user interface that is specifically designed to allow 3D models to be constructed.

In addition to creating the geometry, most modeling applications also allow textures to be mapped on to the objects that they build and will provide the resulting texture coordinates. They might also allow vertex normals to be calculated and stored as part of the object.

All this sounds wonderful, but unfortunately there is a bewildering array of formats into which 3D object definitions can be saved, and not all are easy to read.

Many such products can be used to create geometry files that can be used by our XNA games. These range from free products such as the open source Blender (visit www.blender.org for details) to costly commercial applications such as Autodesk's 3ds Max (see www.autodesk.com for more information), and many others in between. Wikipedia has a large list of 3D modeling applications at http://en.wikipedia.org/wiki/3D_computer_graphics_software, where you might be able to find other packages that suit your requirements.

The good news is that there is a modeling application available that is free to download, relatively easy to use, and (with a bit of creative tweaking) can save to a file format that you can easily read. This application is Google's *SketchUp*.

SketchUp

SketchUp was originally created by a company called @Last Software, with the design goal of creating a 3D modeling application that was just as easy to use as a pen and paper. As such, its user interface was considerably easier to learn than that of many other competing applications.

Some years later, @Last Software enhanced SketchUp so it could create 3D building models for Google Earth. Shortly after this, Google acquired the company and rebranded SketchUp as one of its own applications. You can visit www.sketchup.com to download a copy for yourself.

The new Google SketchUp is available in two different versions: SketchUp and SketchUp Pro. The basic SketchUp version is freely available and contains a huge amount of functionality. The Pro version adds even more features, including support for reading and writing a larger range of 3D file formats.

Unfortunately, the free version doesn't export to a file format that we can easily use within our XNA applications. There is a clever workaround, however, which we will look at shortly.

Creating 3D Objects in SketchUp

Even the easiest 3D modeling applications can be complex to use. The challenge of interactively describing a 3D world using 2D input and output devices that we have available to use (the mouse, keyboard, and monitor) is always going to make this requirement difficult to fulfill.

Despite SketchUp's relative ease of use, there is still a lot to learn to become proficient in using it, and a full guide to how to use it is beyond the scope of this book. Don't let this discourage you, though, because SketchUp also has an immense amount of help and guidance available online, including manuals, tutorials, walkthroughs, and video guides. All these can be accessed from the links presented when SketchUp is first launched.

In order to work with imported geometry in this chapter, we will create a simple object in SketchUp that will be subsequently read into an example project by the game engine. The following paragraphs define how a very simple model of a house was created. They are not intended as a step-by-step guide to using SketchUp, but merely provide information about the sequence of operations that could be used to create such a model. The model itself is included with the example projects, so you don't need to re-create it for yourself.

When SketchUp is launched (for reference, this book is written against SketchUp version 8), it prompts us to select a Template. Select one of the two Simple Template options (Meters or Feet and Inches, as you prefer) and then click Start using SketchUp to launch its main user interface. By default, SketchUp adds an image of a person to the empty scene to help put the scene's scale into perspective. The figure can be deleted to make way for the 3D object.

Our object can now be constructed in the empty scene. The first few steps toward this are shown in Figure 8–1. A rectangle is first drawn along the x/z plane to form the base of the house, as shown in Figure 8–1(a). The rectangle is then extruded using the Push/Pull tool to form a box, as shown in Figure 8–1(b). The Line tool is then used to create a line across the center of the top face of the box, as shown in Figure 8–1(c).

Once the top face has been divided in two, the line that was drawn can be moved around, and all the faces connected to it will move accordingly. Moving the line directly upward therefore creates a rudimentary but satisfactory roof shape, as shown in Figure 8–1(d). The basic geometry of the house is complete at this point.

Of course, we will almost certainly want to apply textures to our objects to complement the structure that we have created, and we will do just that now to make the house look more realistic. SketchUp has a set of tools for adding textures to objects, and its online help will provide everything you need to know to get familiar with them.

In Figure 8–1(e), a texture has been applied to the front face of the house. Figure 8–1(f) shows the finished house object, with textures applied to all the faces in the object.

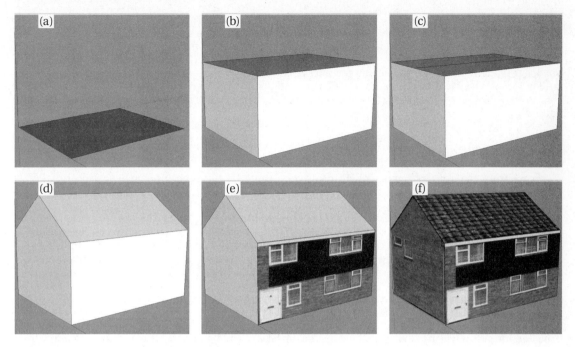

Figure 8–1. *The steps required to build a simple 3D house object in Google SketchUp*

As you might be able to tell, 3D modeling abilities are not among my strengths! Rest assured that XNA can handle much more complex objects than the simple example object presented here.

SketchUp and XNA are both capable of using multiple textures within a single object, so you can import multiple graphic files into the workspace and apply them all as needed. Don't forget, though, that textures can use significant resources in a game, so you should wherever possible try to keep the texture count as low as you can.

One simple approach that reduces the number of textures as far as possible is to place all the graphics for your object into a single texture image, and apply subsections of the image to the model's faces rather than applying the entire image. This is the approach that has been taken with the house shown here: the front, sides, and roof are all contained within a single texture image, as shown in Figure 8–2.

Figure 8–2. *The texture graphic used for the 3D house object*

As the graphic shows, the house texture has been divided into three sections: the left third of the texture contains the graphic for the roof, while the remaining area is split into a graphic for the side of the house and another for the front. Putting all the required texture information into a single graphic file in this way simplifies both the design of the object and the rendering. Using a single graphic makes rendering more efficient as the graphics hardware can process the whole object in a single step and it doesn't need to move as many textures around inside the device's memory.

With the object completed, it can be saved to a SketchUp .skp file in case it needs to be retrieved later on.

Exporting 3D Geometry

Unfortunately, the free version of SketchUp has very limited options when it comes to exporting its objects. The two formats natively supported are Collada (.dae) files and Google Earth (.kmz) files.

We could potentially write code to import either of these formats into our XNA games, but a far preferable solution is to find a way to create .x geometry files.

The .x geometry file format was introduced as part of Microsoft's DirectX many years ago and continues to be supported within both DirectX and XNA today. XNA has native support for reading .x files, just as it does for images and sound files, and in fact provides a very easy-to-use programming interface that allows us to save a huge amount of work in terms of reading and processing the geometry file.

So how do we get SketchUp to save its models in .x format? Unfortunately, neither the free nor Pro versions of SketchUp supports this file format.

The good news is that enterprising programmers on the Internet have managed to persuade the free version of SketchUp to export its objects in a variety of other geometry file formats, including .x format. SketchUp provides a programming interface, accessed using the Ruby programming language and able to query all the information about the object that is currently being worked on. A Ruby script has been created by a developer named Fernando Zanini that uses this interface to create .x files from the free version of SketchUp. You can visit http://tinyurl.com/skp2x to download the script or find it in the downloadable content for this chapter in the Resources/3DRadExporter.rbs file. The script works with older versions of SketchUp, too, from version 6 onward.

To install the exporter into SketchUp, close the application and then copy 3DRadExported.rbs into SketchUp's PlugIns directory (which can be found by default at C:\Program Files\Google\Google SketchUp 8\Plugins). Restart SketchUp, and a new 3D Rad menu item should appear under its PlugIns menu, under which is a long list of different export options, as shown in Figure 8–3.

The option that we are primarily interested in is the "Export as generic DirectX file" option. When this option is selected, it will prompt you to select a location and file name for your .x file. You can save it directly into your Content product directory if you want. The exporter will automatically save all the required textures into the same location.

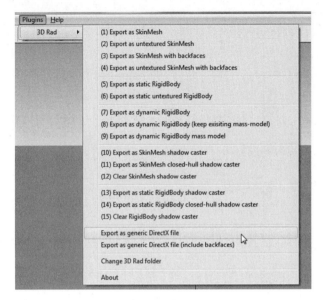

Figure 8–3. The 3D Rad Plugins options inside SketchUp

■ **CAUTION** Don't forget to save your objects into SketchUp's native .skp file format, too. An exported .x file is ideal for loading into your game, but SketchUp can't read data back from it.

Importing Saved Geometry into XNA Projects

Adding the saved object into a project for use within a game is very easy: simply add the .x file to your Content project just as you would for any other content resource. Just add the .x file; there is no need to add any of the textures that it uses. The ImportingGeometry example project has been created using the house model described in the previous section.

■ **TIP** If you want to add the textures into the Content project so that you can see them in Solution Explorer, add them and set their Build Action property to None in the Properties window. This will instruct the compilation process to ignore them, but they can still be manipulated or added to source code control via the Visual Studio IDE.

The Properties for the .x model's Content Processor contains several useful options that you might want to configure before using your object, as can be seen in Figure 8–4. When the project is being compiled, Visual Studio converts the .x file into a format that it can more easily use for rendering, and at this stage it can perform some basic transformations on the object geometry.

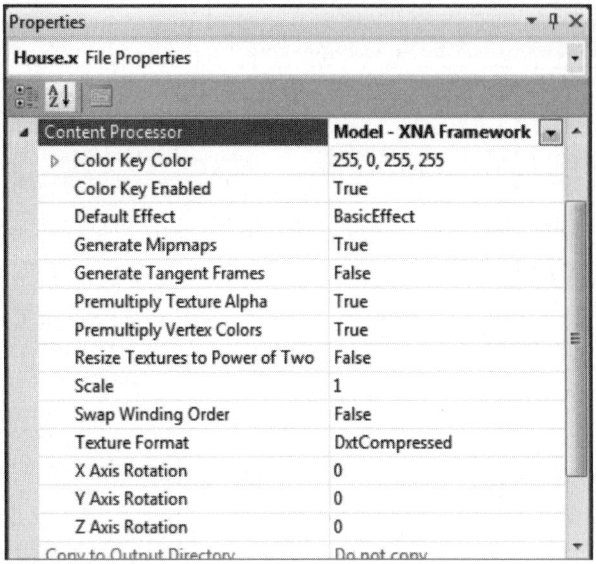

Figure 8–4. Properties for the Model Content Processor

The first of these properties is Scale. It is very common for objects to be created with wildly different geometry scales, which can end up with objects that are entirely the wrong sizes. This could of course be adjusted by scaling the object within the game, but it adds additional complexity to the matrix transformations, particularly if the object actually needs to change scale while the game is running.

This scaling requirement can be simplified by setting the Scale property, allowing the vertices to be scaled during compilation. The value entered is a numeric value, and as such, only uniform scaling is supported through this property. If you need to scale non-uniformly, you will still need to use a scaling transformation matrix to achieve it.

It is also fairly common when importing an object to find that the coordinate system used for the model is different to that used by XNA, resulting in models that are upside down or otherwise rotated from the way you want them to be. The three Axis Rotation properties can be used to rotate them back to the desired angle. Positive or negative values can be entered, but note that they are entered here in degrees, not radians, as normally used by XNA.

We discussed hidden surface culling in Chapter 7, and also mentioned that some other graphics APIs such as OpenGL display counterclockwise triangles instead of the clockwise triangles used by XNA. If you find that one of your models appears to be rendering inside out, showing you the internal surfaces instead of the external surfaces, you can set the Swap Winding Order property to True. This will instruct XNA to rearrange the vertices of each triangle so that they are in the opposite direction to that defined within the model.

The final properties that we'll touch on here for the moment are the Resize Textures to Power of Two property and the two Color Key properties. They are applied to the textures that are used by the model and are identical in function to the properties of the Texture Content Processor with the same names.

To load the model into your application, simply call the Content.Load method, just as we have for all the other types of data stored within the Content project. The object type to specify for the call is Model. A simple example of loading the house model is shown in Listing 8–1.

Listing 8–1. Loading a model into an XNA game

```
myModel = Content.Load<Model>("House");
```

Loading a model automatically handles loading all the textures required by the model, so there is no need to load them separately.

Rendering Imported Geometry

How do we render the geometry that we have loaded in our games? The answer, as you might hope, is fairly straightforward, though there are some complexities that we will have to deal with.

The Model object ultimately contains a series of VertexBuffer and IndexBuffer objects, and these are what we will be using to draw the object to the screen. Unlike the simple cube example from the last chapter, however, it is very possible that the model will consist of multiple sets of triangles that all need to be drawn together to form the complete object. For this reason, the model object contains a hierarchy of collections, as shown in Figure 8–5, which must be navigated in order to obtain the vertex data to be drawn.

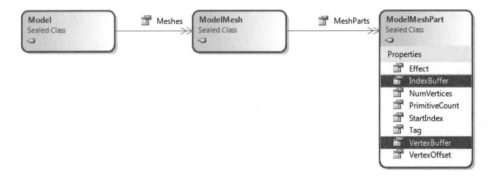

Figure 8–5. The Model, ModelMesh, and ModelMeshPart class hierarchy

Contained within the model object is a property named Meshes, which provides a collection of ModelMesh objects. Each ModelMesh represents a group of triangles that are to be rendered in a single position within the object.

The reason for having multiple model mesh objects is that Model objects are able to store geometry that contains complex hierarchies of parts. Imagine, for example, that you wanted to render a model of a helicopter. There are three primary parts to a helicopter model: the main body, the rotor above the body, and the tail rotor. Both of the rotors can move, relative to the helicopter, in order for them to be able to rotate. They are clearly part of the helicopter, but they cannot be rendered purely using the helicopter's transformation matrix.

XNA allows each of these separate pieces of the model, called *bones* in XNA's terminology, to be individually transformed. This is the reason why the model is stored and rendered in multiple pieces. We won't be going into any further detail about bones and how to use them in this book, but there are plenty of references on the Internet that you should be able to find with a search engine that will give you more information if you want to investigate this subject further.

Contained within the ModelMesh object is yet another collection, this time of ModelMeshPart objects and obtained from the property named MeshParts. Model mesh parts are subsections of the model mesh that collected together contain the geometry of the whole part. The reason for dividing model meshes into separate parts in this way is that each part might have parameters that differ from the other parts, such as the texture. If multiple textures are used within a model, this is the way different textures can be activated and individually rendered.

Within the ModelMeshPart class we finally find where the IndexBuffer and VertexBuffer have been hiding away. Alongside them are several other properties that are essential for us to be able to render the mesh part: VertexOffset is required when the vertex buffer is set into XNA using the SetVertexBuffer function; and NumVertices, StartIndex, and PrimitiveCount are all required by the DrawIndexedPrimitives function.

There are two different methods that we can use to draw the model. The first requires us to loop through each of the mesh parts, telling each one to draw itself using its own Effect object.

These Effect objects are provided by the model so we do not have to create them, but of course they don't know anything about the environment that we have set up. In order for the mesh part to render correctly to the screen, we need to give it the world, view, and projection matrices that it is to use. The easiest way to obtain them is from our own class-level BasicEffect, as defined within our main game class.

A sample piece of code that performs this task is shown in Listing 8–2. In this code, the ObjectModel variable contains the Model being rendered, the effect variable is the class-level BasicEffect, preconfigured with all the matrices required for rendering, and the mesheffect object is used to iterate through each of the Effect objects provided by the model.

Listing 8–2. Drawing a model using its component ModelMesh objects

```
// Build an array of the absolute bone transformation matrices
Matrix[] boneTransforms = new Matrix[ObjectModel.Bones.Count];
ObjectModel.CopyAbsoluteBoneTransformsTo(boneTransforms);

// Loop for each of the meshes within the model
foreach (ModelMesh mesh in ObjectModel.Meshes)
{
    // Initialize each of the effects within the mesh
    foreach (BasicEffect mesheffect in mesh.Effects)
    {
        mesheffect.World = boneTransforms[mesh.ParentBone.Index] * effect.World;
        mesheffect.View = effect.View;
        mesheffect.Projection = effect.Projection;
    }
    // Draw the mesh (including all of its meshparts)
    mesh.Draw();
}
```

■ **NOTE** Besides drawing the model, this code also handles the positions of the bones within the model. The call to CopyAbsoluteBoneTransformsTo populates an array with all the final positions for each bone, taking the bone hierarchy into account. These transformations are then combined with the active World matrix to determine the final position for each bone. Because our model does not include bones, the transformations will have no effect at all, but the code is present for compatibility with more complex models.

The code does everything that is needed to get the object appearing on the screen, but it has a drawback: because the Effect objects being used for rendering the model are not the Effect that we have created and configured in our main game class, none of our Effect property values is present in the model's effect objects. As the code in Listing 8–2 shows, the Effect transformation matrices need to be individually copied from our effect into the model's effect objects.

While setting these matrices gets the model appearing in the correct place onscreen, there are lots of other properties that are not being copied here, and will therefore be ignored by the rendered object. These properties include the lighting properties, diffuse and emissive colors, the alpha value, and more.

The alternative therefore is for us to render the model using our own Effect object. This already contains all the properties that we need the model to observe, so we don't need to worry about processing any of them within the rendering code. We can simply loop through the mesh parts, rendering each directly.

There is one critical piece of information that the model's Effect objects contain that our own Effect object does not: the texture to use for each mesh part. The code from Listing 8–2 draws the object fully textured, even though there is no mention of texturing anywhere within the code. We can read the texture out of the model's effects and use it in our own Effect to ensure that the correct texture is applied for each part of the model.

Having done this, the code can then use the information provided by the ModelMeshPart objects to set up the vertex and index buffers, and then draw them. The code to render in this way is shown in Listing 8–3.

Listing 8–3. Drawing a model using our Effect object

```
Matrix initialWorld;
Matrix[] boneTransforms;

// Store the initial world matrix
initialWorld = effect.World;

// Build an array of the absolute bone transformation matrices
boneTransforms = new Matrix[ObjectModel.Bones.Count];
ObjectModel.CopyAbsoluteBoneTransformsTo(boneTransforms);

// Loop for each mesh
foreach (ModelMesh mesh in ObjectModel.Meshes)
{
    // Update the world matrix to account for the position of this bone
    effect.World = boneTransforms[mesh.ParentBone.Index] * effect.World;

    // Loop for each mesh part
    foreach (ModelMeshPart meshpart in mesh.MeshParts)
    {
        // Set the texture for this meshpart
        SetEffectTexture(effect, ((BasicEffect)meshpart.Effect).Texture);
        // Set the vertex and index buffers
        effect.GraphicsDevice.SetVertexBuffer(meshpart.VertexBuffer,
                                                    meshpart.VertexOffset);
        effect.GraphicsDevice.Indices = meshpart.IndexBuffer;

        // Draw the mesh part
        foreach (EffectPass pass in effect.CurrentTechnique.Passes)
        {
            // Apply the pass
            pass.Apply();
```

```
            // Draw this meshpart
            effect.GraphicsDevice.DrawIndexedPrimitives(PrimitiveType.TriangleList,
                            0, 0, meshpart.NumVertices,
                            meshpart.StartIndex, meshpart.PrimitiveCount);
        }
    }
}

    // Restore the initial world matrix
    effect.World = initialWorld;
```

There are several points of interest in this code. Some of the processing is the same as in Listing 8–2: we retrieve the array of absolute bone transforms and then we loop through the model's Meshes collection. Within each mesh, we no longer have to update the effect properties because we are using our own Effect this time. It is already configured with all the required matrices and its other properties such as lighting, material, and so on. The one thing we do need to do, however, is observe the bone position. We do this by taking a copy of the original World matrix prior to the loop and multiplying this by the bone position for each mesh.

The effect is now ready to render the mesh, so we begin to process each of its parts. The first thing we do for each part is to interrogate its own Effect object to read out the texture that it needs. We pass this, along with our own Effect object, into a procedure called SetEffectTexture. This is a simple function that places the provided Texture2D into the supplied Effect, provided that it is not already present.

With the texture set as needed, the code then sets the mesh part's VertexBuffer and IndexBuffer into the graphics device. This prepares it for indexed rendering as described in the previous chapter. To save XNA from having to process unnecessary vertices, each part provides a VertexOffset. Vertices before this will be ignored by XNA, saving some processing time.

At last the mesh part is ready to render. Just as we always have, we then loop for each EffectPass, rendering the indexed triangle list into each pass. Note that all the details that DrawIndexedPrimitive needs to render are provided by the mesh part, so this is really very straightforward.

Finally, having completed all the loops, the initial World matrix is restored back into our Effect, overwriting any bone transformation that might have been left in place. This stops unexpected transformations from creeping into the rendering process.

Although the code shown in Listing 8–3 isn't especially complicated, it is a little bulky and it would be ideal if we could avoid having to repeat it for each object in our game. Fortunately, the game framework will help us out with this once again, so let's see how we can integrate model rendering into the functionality that we have already added.

Adding Support into the Game Framework

Just as we have with the other content resource that we have worked with, we will simplify the task of working with models by allowing them to be loaded into the game framework. These models are added into the GameHost class as a Dictionary of Model objects. All the models that we need can therefore be loaded into the dictionary in the game's LoadContent method, ready to be accessed when they are needed for drawing to the screen.

We could leave it at that as far as the game framework is concerned, but we can make our lives a little easier by adding another abstract base class set up for the purpose of rendering models. This class is named MatrixModelObject and is derived from the MatrixObjectBase class, as shown in Figure 8–6.

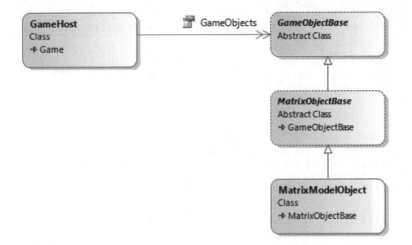

Figure 8–6. The MatrixModelObject's position within the game framework class hierarchy

Inheriting from MatrixObjectBase means that we immediately pick up all the matrix-based rendering properties, and on top of these we can add some further properties and methods specifically for dealing with models. The class is a concrete (nonabstract) class, however, and can be either directly instantiated and added into the GameObjects collection, or inherited from to create customized classes with additional game-specific functionality.

The derived class's properties are as follows:

- ObjectModel: a reference to a Model object that will be rendered by this class.

- ObjectTexture: this property is declared by the MatrixObjectBase class, but is overridden by MatrixModelObject so that, if it is queried without a texture ever having been explicitly provided, it attempts to read from the model's textures instead. Once a texture has been set into this property, it will take precedence and be returned in place of the model texture, and will also cause the model to be rendered using the provided texture.

The following methods are present in the class:

- DrawModel: this is essentially the same code as shown in Listing 8–3, and will draw the loaded model using the provided Effect object. It first ensures that an ObjectModel has been provided, and returns without doing anything if no such object is present. Additionally, if a texture has been explicitly provided for the object using the ObjectTexture property, this will be used instead of the textures from the model, allowing for simple customization of the model textures.

- Update: the standard Update method is overloaded so that the Effect properties can be applied prior to drawing the object. This can be overloaded as normal and the object properties updated as required.

- Draw: the standard Draw method is overloaded and set by default to first call PrepareEffect to load all the object settings and then call DrawModel to render the loaded model. As this will be the exact behavior required for many objects, implementing this in the base class removes the need for the derived class to have to implement its own Draw override.

The new class can be seen working in the ImportingGeometry example project. Once again, the code contained here is very straightforward, taking advantage of the game framework to manage all the more complex aspects of updating and presenting the game. In this project, a derived class named ImportedObject is created simply so that it can change its rotation angles during each call to Update.

The Google SketchUp 3D Warehouse

Being as focused on content as it is, Google offers a further service alongside the SketchUp application that allows users to upload 3D models that it has created and shares them with the rest of the world.

The service is called 3D Warehouse, and contains tens of thousands of models in .skp format ready for immediate download into SketchUp. Visit http://sketchup.google.com/3dwarehouse to find the front page of the 3D warehouse. A page of search results can be seen in Figure 8–7.

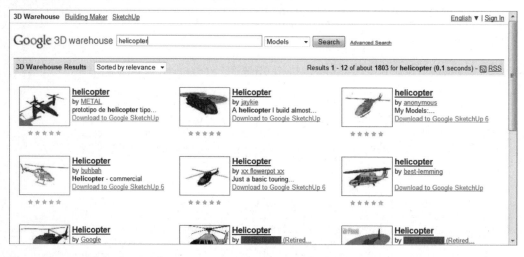

Figure 8–7. Google's 3D Warehouse

SketchUp isn't designed just for creating game models, however: it can also create extremely intricate 3D scenes and objects that would be far too complex to calculate and display in real time using Windows Phone 7's graphic capabilities. If you decide to search the 3D Warehouse for objects for inclusion within a game, it is important to try to find *low polygon* objects; that is, objects that have been designed with fast rendering in mind by reducing the number of triangles that are needed.

Objects that use small numbers of textures are preferable, too, and some complex geometry will cause problems for the .x exporter, so you'll need to try the models out in your code and see how they look before you get too attached to them.

The other important aspect of 3D Warehouse is that the objects within it are not in the public domain, but are instead all owned by their authors. If you find a good object, you should contact the author to get permission to use it in your game.

Importing Other File Formats

In addition to .x files, XNA is also capable of natively working with Autodesk .fbx files. Other file formats, such as 3D Studio's .3ds format and the popular .obj format, are not supported.

There are several ways that model definitions in other formats might be used within XNA. The first is to import them into SketchUp (or another modeling application that is able to save geometry to .x or .fbx files) and then save them for use within XNA.

A second option is to create your own geometry imported code. If you can read the file format, you can read the file and work through its content, building vertex and index buffers along the way. Depending on the complexity of the file format and the capabilities that you need to support, this process might be a very labor-intensive solution to the problem, however.

Finally, the XNA community has released a number of additional content importers and processors, some of which are targeted at 3D model files. A list of them can be found at http://tinyurl.com/xnamodelfiles, though their integration into Visual Studio is beyond the scope of this book.

Working with the Camera

If you have ever used a video camera, you know that the most dynamic scenes will have movement from the camera as well as from the actors within the scene. In many games, the ability to manipulate the camera is just as important.

Moving the camera changes the position from which the player looks into the 3D world. The camera is implemented using the View property of the Effect, and we have in fact been using it, albeit without moving it, in all our 3D example projects.

In some ways, having a camera might seem unnecessary. After all, there wouldn't seem to be any visual difference between moving the camera toward an object and moving the object toward the camera. As soon as we start to build up complex multiobject scenes with lights, however, it becomes very much more convenient to be able to calculate the object and light positions without having to worry about moving them all to simulate camera movement.

Let's look at the way in which the position of the camera can be changed in XNA.

Camera Position and Orientation

To move the camera, we need to figure out exactly how to set the View matrix for the required camera position. Fortunately XNA takes care of this for us and provides a very useful function, CreateLookAt. This builds a view matrix such that the objects subsequently rendered will be positioned as if the camera had moved to the requested location.

The CreateLookAt function requires three pieces of information to be provided, all of which are Vector3 structures. The required values, in the order required by the function, are as follows:

- The current position of the camera as a coordinate in the 3D world (the *camera position*)

- A coordinate at which the camera is looking (the *target position*)

- A vector which tells XNA which way is up (the *up vector*)

The first two of these values are easy to understand. The view will be generated as it would be seen when looking from the camera position directly toward the target position. The specified target position will appear directly in the center of the rendered scene.

The up vector requires a little more explanation. In simple terms, it tells XNA which way is up (toward the top of the screen) relative to the camera position. In most cases, you can provide a vector that simply points along the positive y axis: (0, 1, 0). The up vector does not need to be perpendicular to the camera's direction of view.

There are two situations where a different value for the up vector might need to be used. The first is if we want to be able to *roll* the camera. Rolling the camera rotates it around its z axis so that its own view of which way is up deviates from the world's view of up (rolling the camera by 180 degrees would result in everything appearing upside down).

Figure 8–8 shows three views of the house object we imported earlier. In each of these, the house is identically positioned; it is only the camera's up vector that has changed. On the left is the view with the camera's up vector set (0, 1, 0), the default up vector. The middle image shows the view from a camera with an up vector of (0.5, 0.5, 0). The camera has rolled to the right so that its up vector is pointing between up and to the right (similar to tilting your head to the right). As a result, the house appears to have tilted to the left. In the final image, the camera's up vector is (1, 0, 0), so that up is along the positive x axis. The house now appears to have rotated 90 degrees to the left.

Figure 8–8. *Three views of a house displayed with different camera up vectors*

Rolling the camera might not be useful in all games, but for some it is extremely handy—any game that simulates the movement of an aircraft or spaceship, for example, will probably want to use it to allow the craft to bank to the sides as it flies.

The second situation where a different up vector is required is when the camera is looking directly along the y axis. If the camera were looking directly upward, we would be telling it that *forward* and *up* were both in exactly the same direction. This can't possibly be true, so XNA's transformation matrix results in nothing displaying at all.

In all other cases, XNA is very tolerant of the values provided for the up vector, and will cope fine with unnormalized vectors and vectors that are not perpendicular to the camera viewing angle.

Listing 8–4 shows a simple call to CreateLookAt that sets the camera so that it is located at position (0, 5, 5), is focused on position (0, 0, 0), and has an up vector of (0, 1, 0).

Listing 8–4. *Creating a view matrix using CreateLookAt*

```
Matrix view = Matrix.CreateLookAt(new Vector3(0, 5, 5),
                                  new Vector3(0, 0, 0),
                                  new Vector3(0, 1, 0));
```

This code can be made slightly more readable by using some of the static Vector3 properties, as shown in Listing 8–5.

Listing 8–5. Creating a view matrix using CreateLookAt and some of the static Vector3 properties

```
Matrix view = Matrix.CreateLookAt(new Vector3(0, 5, 5), Vector3.Zero, Vector3.Up);
```

■ **NOTE** Don't forget the near and far clip planes that have been defined for the viewing frustum. If you move the camera near enough to or far enough from an object that it falls outside these clip planes, it will disappear from view.

It is also possible to set the camera position using matrix manipulation, just as we do for the objects within our scenes. We will look at how to do this in the next section.

Integrating Camera Support into the Game Framework

Once again, we can simplify manipulation of the camera by integrating it into the game framework. Let's take a look at how it is implemented, and how we can use it in our game projects.

The Camera Class

In some ways, it is similar to the general game objects that we are using in our scenes: it has a transformation matrix, has a position, and can be transformed using the matrix transformation functions. For this reason, we will implement a camera class, derived from the MatrixObjectBase and named MatrixCameraObject. The class is concrete (nonabstract) and so can be used directly without needing to inherit a further class from it. The position of the camera class in the inheritance hierarchy can be seen in Figure 8–9.

However, there are some distinct differences between the camera and a standard game object:

- There can only be one camera active within the game at any time.

- Cameras don't have anything to draw, though they can still update their position like any other normal game object.

- The order that the camera position is updated and applied is significant within the 3D scene: if its position is altered halfway through a set of objects, some of the objects will appear relative to the old camera position and others to the new camera position, which could produce very odd-looking results.

- We need to know the location at which the camera is looking, and MatrixObjectBase class has no property to define it.

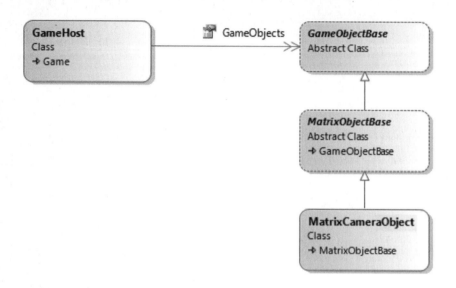

Figure 8–9. *The MatrixCameraObject class within the game framework class diagram*

The first of these points is addressed by adding a specific provision for a camera object directly into the GameHost class. Instead of adding the camera object to the GameObjects collection, the camera is set into the GameHost.Camera property. If a camera has been set, it will be processed during each call to Update and Draw. If no camera has been set, no camera-related processing will take place.

Although the second of the points is true (cameras don't have anything to draw), we will still take advantage of both the Update and Draw methods of the MatrixCameraObject class. In the Update method, we can set the camera position, just as we set the position for normal objects. In the Draw method, we will apply the camera position into the Effect object so that it is active for all subsequently rendered objects.

The third point is easily addressed by the game framework. It ensures that the camera is the very last object to be updated (in the GameHost.UpdateAll function) and the first to be drawn (in its DrawObjects function). Updating last ensures that, if the camera position is to be set relative to other objects in the scene (as we will demonstrate shortly), the target objects are always positioned before the camera so that the camera gets up-to-date information. Drawing first ensures that the camera position is active before any of the objects are rendered.

The fourth point is addressed by adding a new Vector3 property to the MatrixCameraObject class named LookAtTarget. This property can be used to specify the location toward which the camera is focused.

The default behavior for the camera class is to position itself at the location specified by its Position matrix, and look toward the location specified in its LookAtTarget vector. If additional positioning logic or a different implementation of the call to Matrix.CreateLookAt is required, the Update and/or Draw methods can be overridden in a derived class as required.

Camera Positioning

Although we clearly have a good deal of control over the camera simply by setting its Position and LookAtTarget, there is another camera position mechanism that we can take advantage of that will in some situations provide an easier way to put the camera where we want it. This mechanism is to use the matrix transformation approach that we are already using for our game objects.

If we use matrix transformations, we can once again provide a series of operations that the camera will follow through to determine its final position. For example, we might decide to translate the camera to a different position within the scene, rotate the camera's matrix around the y axis by a preset angle, and finally translate a little way along the camera's local z axis. As the rotation angle changes, the camera will orbit around the position defined within the first translation. This is much simpler to calculate than having to use trigonometry to calculate the circular path of the camera if we were simply setting its position vector.

Listing 8–6 shows an example of positioning the camera using this technique, taken from a derived camera class's Update method. It first rotates the camera; then translates along its new z axis and also along its y axis. The end result is that the camera gradually orbits around the scene.

Listing 8–6. Positioning a camera using matrix transformations

```
// Reset the position using the identity matrix
SetIdentity();
// Rotate the camera
ApplyTransformation(Matrix.CreateRotationY(AngleY));
// Translate the camera away from the origin
ApplyTransformation(Matrix.CreateTranslation(0, 5, -14));
```

Compare this approach with that shown in Listing 8–7, which generates exactly the same camera movement, but using trigonometry instead of matrix transformations. Assuming that you are comfortable with using matrix transformations, you will probably find Listing 8–6 much easier to read and understand. The difference between the two would be emphasized further if more complex camera position transformations were required.

Listing 8–7. Positioning a camera using the Position vector

```
// Reset the position using the identity matrix
SetIdentity();
// Calculate the camera position
Position = new Vector3((float)Math.Sin(AngleY) * 14, 5, (float)Math.Cos(AngleY) * 14);
// Apply the standard transformations to the object
ApplyStandardTransformations();
```

The Camera Object in Action

Accompanying this chapter is an example project named CameraMovement, which provides a simple example of using the camera within a game.

It creates a simple scene consisting of a square of ground on top of which a number of houses have been placed. The camera then rotates around the scene, allowing it to be seen from different angles. All the objects within the scene are completely stationary except for the camera. To allow the scene to better fit within the display, this project has been implemented to use landscape orientations, so you will need to rotate your device or the emulator accordingly. An image from the project can be seen in Figure 8–10.

***Figure 8–10.** The CameraMovement project*

The project's ResetGame function adds the objects for the ground and the houses into the GameObjects collection and then creates a camera object and sets this into the Camera property.

The camera object is implemented using a custom derived class named CameraObject in order to move the camera around the scene. Within its Update function, you will see two different blocks of code for positioning the camera: one using matrix transformations and the other directly setting the Position property. One of these is initially commented out, but try swapping out the two approaches and experiment with each to see how they work.

You can also try experimenting with the LookAtTarget property so that the camera looks in different directions as it moves around the scene.

Creating a Chase Cam

One type of camera that is very commonly used within computer games is the *chase cam*, a camera that follows along behind a key object (usually the player) to provide a first- or third-person view of what the object is able to see within the game world.

We already have many of the pieces in place to implement such a camera in our own games, but with a little enhancement to the game framework's camera class, we can make this absolute simplicity to implement within a game.

This section works through these changes and builds up a scene with a paper plane flying through the scene that we created in the last project. Once we have the plane moving (which will be an interesting task in itself), you will see how to attach the camera so that it automatically chases the plane and configure some different chase cam views.

All the code for this process can be found in the ChaseCam example project.

Adding the Paper Plane

The paper plane is a very simple 3D model created in SketchUp. It consists of just four triangles arranged to give the basic shape of a paper airplane. The model can be seen in SketchUp in Figure 8–11.

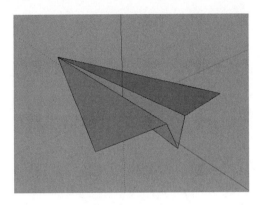

Figure 8–11. The paper plane model

This is positioned so that its center point is approximately on the origin point (0, 0, 0). This positioning will ensure that, when we rotate it, it rotates around its center point.

The object consists only of flat triangles, so in this case we need to ensure that it is exported so that the back faces of each triangle are included, too. Without this, the plane would be visible only from the top side of each triangle, disappearing entirely when viewed from underneath. The .x exporter has an option to export the back faces, too, so this option was used to create the model file.

The SketchUp model file can be found in the Resources folder along with the source code for this chapter.

The plane is then added to the game project as a standard MatrixModelObject-derived class, named PaperPlaneObject. Our goal for the plane is to make it fly smoothly between the houses, however, so we need to add some additional functionality to the class to achieve this.

Animating the Plane

Several of our previous projects have created objects that move smoothly around the screen in a variety of ways. They have all been based upon velocities that are applied to the objects' positions, however. In this case, we would get a much better flight path for the plane by allowing it to follow a series of movement points that are distributed throughout the 3D scene.

This works well for an example, but is probably not the kind of control mechanism that you would use in a game, which would be more likely to rely on user input to control the player's movement. Following a movement path is nevertheless a useful technique to know and does have a variety of applications in games, from *on rails* shooters (where the player controls aiming and firing a weapon but has no direct control over his movement) to computer-controlled characters in games.

The first thing that we will do is define a series of points along the movement path that the plane is to follow. They are declared as a static array of Vector3 structures at the beginning of the PaperPlaneObject class. We also store the array size to avoid having to requery it later. The point declaration is shown in Listing 8–8.

Listing 8–8. Movement points that define the path along which the plane will travel

```
// Points on the spline movement path
static Vector3[] _movementPath =
{
    new Vector3(-1, 1.5f, -2),
    new Vector3(-1.5f, 2.5f, 2),
    new Vector3(0, 1, 6),
    new Vector3(3, 0.5f, 6),
    new Vector3(4, 1, 2),
    new Vector3(0, 0.4f, 2),
    new Vector3(-4, 0.8f, 1),
    new Vector3(-5, 1.5f, 1),
    new Vector3(-4, 2.5f, -2),
    new Vector3(2, 2.0f, -4),
    new Vector3(4, 1.5f, -7),
    new Vector3(2, 1.0f, -7.2f),
    new Vector3(0, 0.5f, -6),
};
static int _movementPathLength = _movementPath.Length;
```

■ **TIP** These points were determined through a simple process of trial and error. In a game where lots of these points needed to be defined with a reasonable degree of accuracy, it would be well worth creating a simple designer utility to allow them to be positioned on the screen rather than entered by hand.

We could now move the plane between these positions, but the paths between them are undefined. The plane cannot simply jump from one position to another, and even if we calculated a straight line between the points and moved the plane along that line, its movement would look very angular and unnatural.

XNA provides another very useful tool that we can use to solve this problem: a function to calculate *splines*. A spline is a curved line that passes through a series of points such as those that we have defined. As well as asking for positions directly on the movement path points, we can also ask for points in between, and the spline will calculate a smooth curved transition from one point to the next. This calculated path is ideal for the movement of our plane.

The movement path generated from the spline for the set of movement path positions is shown in Figure 8–12, with a camera looking directly down on the scene. The images of the plane show the positions of the defined movement path points, and the lines between show the approximate spline paths.

There are various spline calculation functions, but the one we will call upon in XNA is called a *Catmull-Rom spline* (named after its creators, Edwin Catmull and Raphael Rom). It is very useful and simple to use, and ensures that the spline path passes exactly through all the defined positions (which not all splines do).

To generate the spline, the function needs to be passed four consecutive positions on the path along with a *weight* value between 0 and 1. As the weight increases between these two values, the spline returns positions further along the path.

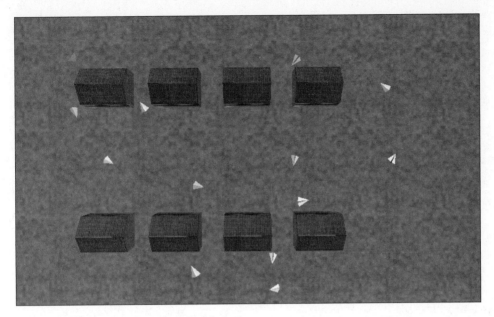

Figure 8–12. The paper plane's flight path

When a weight value of 0 is provided, the spline will return a position exactly on the second input position. When a weight value of 1 is provided, the spline will return a position exactly on the third input position. All four of the values are used in these calculations, however, to ensure a smooth path both between the second and third positions, and also onward into the next set of movement points.

This can be illustrated using the diagram in Figure 8–13. If the spline is calculated using points 0, 1, 2, and 3, and a weight of 0.0, the resulting position will be exactly on point 1. As the weight increases to 1.0, the spline positions travel along the line between points 1 and 2, reaching point 2 as the weight reaches 1.0. Note that from this set of points the spline positions never return values on the line toward point 0 or point 3, even though they are being passed to the spline function: these outside points are used just to calculate the angle of the curve between the central two points.

Once the weight has reached 1.0, the spline can move on to the next set of points, passing in points 1, 2, 3, and 4. The weight is then once again increased from 0.0 to 1.0, causing the calculated positions to travel along the line between points 2 and 3.

From this set of points, it is impossible to return spline positions between points 0 and 1, or between points 4 and 5 (shown in grey in the diagram) as there are insufficient outer points for these parts of the path to be processed.

By moving point by point through the movement path, a smooth curved line can be produced that passes through all the defined locations. And this all works perfectly well in three-dimensional space, too.

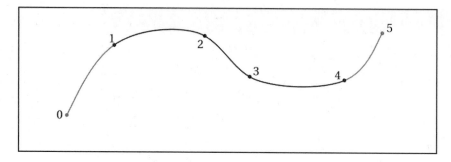

Figure 8–13. A series of points and the resulting spline path

■ **TIP** When defining a path, don't forget that it will take exactly the same amount of time to move between each consecutive pair of points along the path. You should therefore try to ensure that the points are approximately equally spaced. Points that have a larger gap than others will result in faster movement to traverse the increased distance within the fixed time interval, and points that are closer together will result in slower movements because less distance needs to be traveled.

In order to create a closed path, allowing the plane to loop seamlessly back to the beginning of its journey and start again, we need to ensure that the final three points of the spline are identical to the first three points. As the weight of these points reaches 1.0, the spline position will eventually land exactly back at the position of point 1 within the movement path, allowing the whole path to be traced from the beginning once again.

We implement this in the PaperPlaneObject code by storing two class-level variables, an int called _splineIndex, which defines the index of the first of the four points to use for spline calculation; and a float called _splineWeight, which allows us to traverse the path along the spline between the defined points.

In the Update function we add a small amount to the _splineWeight variable. If it reaches or exceeds 1.0, we subtract 1.0 from it and increment the _splineIndex. If _splineIndex passes the end of the movement path point array, it is reset back to the start. These updates move the plane along the spline and reset it back to the start when it reaches the end of its movement path.

With these updates made, we call a function named GetPlanePosition to perform the spline calculation and return the final plane coordinate. The function, which expects the spline index and spline weight values to be passed as parameters, is shown in Listing 8–9.

Listing 8–9. Calculating the position on the spline for a given spline index and spline weight

```
private Vector3 GetPlanePosition(int splineIndex, float splineWeight)
{
    Vector3 ret;

    // If the weight exceeds 1, reduce by 1 and move to the next index
    if (splineWeight > 1)
    {
        splineWeight -= 1;
```

```
        splineIndex += 1;
    }
    // Keep the spline index within the array bounds
    splineIndex = splineIndex % _movementPath.Length;

    // Calculate the spline position
    ret = Vector3.CatmullRom(_movementPath[splineIndex],
                            _movementPath[(splineIndex + 1) % _movementPathLength],
                            _movementPath[(splineIndex + 2) % _movementPathLength],
                            _movementPath[(splineIndex + 3) % _movementPathLength],
                            splineWeight);

    return ret;
}
```

The code first checks that the spline weight is not greater than 1. If it is, it subtracts 1 and shifts on to the next spline index (we'll see the reason for this in a moment). This is followed by a check that loops the spline index if it exceeds the bounds of the _movementPath array items.

The spline position is then calculated simply by passing in the four vertex positions and the spline weight to the Vector3.CatmullRom function. Note, however, that we are using the modulus operator on the spline index values because, if they exceed the array length, they loop back to the beginning. This operation allows us to implement our closed loop (requiring the first three points to be repeated) without actually having to repeat them in the array: they are simply reused from the beginning when the end of the array is reached.

With the ability to calculate the plane position in hand, we can now set the plane's position and smoothly move it along the path. This is a good start, but there is a very obvious visual problem when it is put in motion: the plane is always facing the same direction. It should, of course, always be facing in the direction that it is moving (paper planes as a rule don't fly sideways very well).

Fortunately it is very easy to make the plane look in the direction that it is flying. The first thing we need to do is calculate another position for the plane just a little farther along the path. We do this by calling GetPlanePosition a second time, this time adding 0.1 to the spline weight. This addition is the reason that GetPlanePosition checks whether the weight has exceeded 1.0 because this second call might cause this overflow to occur.

The second call allows us to see where the plane is now and where it will be in a second. The direction of the plane must be from the first of these points to the second because it is its path of movement. We therefore need a way to rotate the plane so that it is facing from the first position toward the second.

This rotation can be achieved using another of the very handy static Matrix functions: CreateWorld. The CreateWorld function creates a world matrix (which is ultimately what we are trying to do in each object's Update method) so that it is positioned at a particular location and facing in a particular direction. This is just what we need: the position is the first spline point we have calculated, and the direction is from there toward the second spline point.

The direction itself is calculated simply by subtracting the current position from the next position. The resulting vector is ready to be passed to CreateWorld.

Only one minor problem remains: the plane is now continuously flying sideways because it has been defined sideways within the SketchUp model. To correct this, we simply rotate it by 90 degrees after the matrix has been calculated.

The full code to calculate the position and orientation of the plane is shown in Listing 8–10.

Listing 8–10. Positioning the plane and ensuring that it faces in the direction of flight

```
// Calculate the current position and store in the Position property
Vector3 Position = GetPlanePosition(_splineIndex, _splineWeight);

// Calculate the next position too so we know which way we are moving
Vector3 nextPosition = GetPlanePosition(_splineIndex, _splineWeight + 0.1f);

// Find the movement direction
Vector3 delta = nextPosition - Position;

// Create the world matrix for the plane
Transformation = Matrix.CreateWorld(Position, delta, Vector3.Up);
// The plane needs to be rotated 90 degrees  so that it points
// forward, so apply a rotation
ApplyTransformation(Matrix.CreateRotationY(MathHelper.ToRadians(-90)));
```

The end result is that we have a plane that smoothly and realistically flies around the scene between the houses. You can see this in action by running the ChaseCam project—the initial view uses a camera that doesn't chase the plane, but instead slowly circles the scene, allowing the flight path to be easily seen.

Now that we have the plane moving, we are ready to set the camera to follow it.

Implementing the Chase Cam

To allow a game to easily use a chase cam, we will add a new property to the MatrixCameraObject class into which a reference to the target object can be placed. If this property, named ChaseObject, is left at its default (null) value, the camera will act exactly as it did before and just position itself according to its Position and LookAtTarget coordinates. If a game object is provided, however, the behavior of the camera will change so that it follows the object around the scene.

When operating in chase cam mode, the camera has two responsibilities that it must fulfill with each of its updates: it must position itself a little way behind the target object and it must look directly at the target object. Let's see how this can be implemented.

First, the Update code checks to see whether a ChaseObject has been provided. If not, it applies the default object transformation and returns without doing anything more, as shown in Listing 8–11.

Listing 8–11. Part of the camera's Update code: behavior for when no ChaseObject has been provided

```
base.Update(gameTime);

// Do we have a chase object?
if (ChaseObject == null)
{
    // No, so simply apply the identity matrix
    // Calculate and apply the standard camera transformations
    SetIdentity();
    ApplyStandardTransformations();
    return;
}
```

If a chase object *has* been provided, we need to first calculate the camera position. We do this by finding the distance between the current camera position and the object position. Initially the camera position might be nowhere near the object itself, but within a couple of frames it will be positioned behind it ready to chase.

The distance between the camera and the object is found by subtracting the object position from the camera position. The resulting value, named delta, is then normalized to provide a unit-length vector. This vector can then be scaled by the distance at which the camera is to chase in order to locate the camera position.

But what if the camera and the object are in exactly the same place? To deal with this circumstance, we always store the most recent of the distance vectors in a class-level variable, _lastChaseCamDelta, and will reuse this in case of a zero vector. This part of the Update code can be seen in Listing 8–12.

Listing 8–12. Part of the camera's Update code: finding the distance between the camera and the target object

```
// Find the vector between the current position and the chase object position
delta = Position - ChaseObject.Position;
// Normalize the delta vector
delta.Normalize();
// If the delta is zero (the camera position is already directly on the chase
// object, which will happen if the object stops moving) retain the last used delta
if (delta == Vector3.Zero)
{
    delta = _lastChaseCamDelta;
}
else
{
    // Store the delta for later use
    _lastChaseCamDelta = delta;
}
```

Having calculated the direction between the camera and the object, the code is now ready to build the camera's transformation matrix. It begins by translating exactly on top of the object. From here, it translates a little way back from the object so that we can see it from behind. The direction in which this translation is performed is the direction that we have calculated into the delta variable. This direction vector is scaled by the distance we want to keep between the camera and the plane.

The distance is defined in a public property named ChaseDistance. Setting it to positive values will position the camera behind the target object. It can also be set to negative values, however, which will put it in front of the object looking back at it (and generally traveling backward). This camera position can be useful in some situations but does mean that, if the player is in control of the object, he cannot see where he is going!

We also support a special value for ChaseDistance. If it is set to 0, we treat it as being in "first person" mode, which means we are looking directly from the point of view of the object rather than looking over its shoulder. Unfortunately, if we tell XNA to look at the same position as the camera location, it gets confused because it doesn't know which direction to actually point the camera. To work around this problem, we still subtract a small distance from the object position by multiplying delta by 0.01.

We also allow an elevation to be specified for the camera to raise it up a little from the object's location. Typically, you will provide a small elevation so that the camera is looking very slightly downward toward the object. This elevation is set into the ChaseElevation property.

Listing 8–13 shows all the transformations for the camera position.

Listing 8–13. Part of the camera's Update code: transforming the camera into position

```
// Transform the camera position to position it relative to the chase object
SetIdentity();
// Translate to the chase object's position
ApplyTransformation(Matrix.CreateTranslation(ChaseObject.Position));
// Apply the chase distance. Are we in first- or third-person view?
if (ChaseDistance != 0)
{
    // Third person view
    // Translate towards or away from the object based on the ChaseDistance
    ApplyTransformation(Matrix.CreateTranslation(delta * ChaseDistance));
    // Apply the vertical offset
    ApplyTransformation(Matrix.CreateTranslation(0, ChaseElevation, 0));
}
else
{
    // First person view
    // Translate a tiny distance back from the view point
    ApplyTransformation(Matrix.CreateTranslation(delta * 0.01f));
}
```

The camera is now positioned relative to the object as defined by the distance and elevation. The final couple of steps are to ensure that the camera is actually looking toward the object and then to update the camera position ready for the next update.

To set the direction that the camera is looking, we simply set the LookAtTarget property to contain the position of the chase object. When the camera's Draw method executes, it will use this value for its CreateLookAt matrix, ensuring that the chase object remains in the center of the screen.

The camera position is then updated by simply setting it to be exactly on top of the chase object. The next time Update is called, assuming that the object has moved, it will once again be able to determine the direction of movement of the object by comparing its new position with the camera position.

These last lines of the Update code are shown in Listing 8–14.

Listing 8–14. Part of the camera's Update code: setting the camera's direction and position

```
// Ensure that we are looking at the chase object
LookAtTarget = ChaseObject.Position;

// Set the camera position to exactly match the chase object position
// so that we can continue to follow it in the next update
Position = ChaseObject.Position;
```

Using the Chase Cam

You're ready to fly now, so let's make the last few small changes to the game and see how it looks.

The ResetGame function creates the paper plan object and stores it in a class-level variable called _plane for easy access later on. The camera is created but is initially left without a chase object. As a result, the camera position obeys the transformation that is manually provided rather than following the plane.

This initial configuration appears when the project is run. The houses and plane are visible, but the camera slowly circles the scene. This camera movement path is handled using simple rotation and translation matrices in the game's `CameraObject.Update` function.

When the player taps the screen, however, we then activate the chase cam. The game class's `Update` method checks for screen taps, and each time one is found it increments to the next of four camera configurations. The code required to activate the chase cam is shown in Listing 8–15.

Listing 8–15. Activating the chase cam

```
// Follow the plane from behind
Camera.ChaseObject = _plane;
Camera.ChaseDistance = 1;
Camera.ChaseElevation = 0.3f;
```

This is virtually all that is required to set the camera on its way. The only other change is required to our `CameraObject.Update` function: if it detects that a chase cam is active (the camera's `ChaseObject` is not equal to `null`), it simply calls into the base class and then returns. Any further transformations that the camera code made would either interfere with or entirely replace the camera's own chase cam transformations.

If you run the project and tap the screen once, you will see the chase cam in full effect. An image from the project running in this mode is shown in Figure 8–14.

Figure 8–14. In flight behind the paper plane

Tap the screen a second time, and the camera is repositioned in front of the plane, looking back. This is achieved simply by setting the camera's `ChaseDistance` to a negative value (-1 in this case). Remember that, although the plane knows its flight path and can calculate positions in its future, the camera knows nothing of its future positions, and yet it still positions itself correctly in front of the plane. Being able to set its position without knowledge of the future is important because, if the object were to be player-controlled, it would be impossible to predict its future movements.

Tap the screen a third time to activate the final mode, which displays a first-person camera, which is activated by setting `ChaseDistance` to 0. There is one further minor change we need to make in order for this to work well: putting the camera directly on the position of the plane results in a clipped image of the front half of the plane being rendered, which looks rather odd—for a first-person camera, we don't want to render the plane at all.

To resolve this first-person rendering problem, we make a small change to the PaperPlaneObject.Draw method. If it detects that it is the camera's ChaseObject and the camera's ChaseDistance is zero, it returns without drawing itself.

Just for fun, we can add some other planes into the scene too. You will find a small block of code inside ResetGame that does this, but it is initially commented out. Uncomment it and you will find a trail of planes happily circling around within the game world.

Adding Fog

A useful facility provided by XNA is the ability to add *fog* to a rendered scene, which provides a simple simulation of real-world fog, making objects that are further away from the camera gradually fade away until they are no longer visible.

Clearly there are limits to the amount of content that Windows Phone 7 devices can render to the screen, and if you have open environments that stretch off into the distance, you need to draw a line at some stage and tell XNA not to draw things that are too far away. This distance limit is generally achieved by setting an appropriate value for the far clip plane when setting up the projection matrix, as was discussed in Chapter 7.

The downside is that, as objects reach the far clip plane, they very visibly vanish. They often leave parts of themselves still visible as they edge past the clip plane, which can result in a very unnatural-looking scene.

You can use fog to help reduce the impact of the vanishing objects by allowing them to fade away before they disappear. This fading results in a much less jarring effect that will often go completely unnoticed by the player.

Fog is also useful as a game feature in its own right. It can make an environment feel much more enclosed and claustrophobic, and can also add atmosphere to a scene, taking away some of the clinical cleanliness that rendered graphics can often suffer from.

Figure 8–15 shows some examples of the scene from the earlier example projects rendered in XNA using fog. The image on the left has fog disabled, although the remaining two images show increasing levels of fog. The distant buildings in the image on the right have completely vanished into the background.

Figure 8–15. *A scene rendered with increasing levels of fog*

XNA implements fog by using a simple but effective trick. As it calculates the color and lighting for each vertex being rendered, it determines how far away the vertex is from the viewpoint. As the vertex becomes more distant and is therefore affected to a greater degree by the fog, XNA gradually fades the vertex color toward the defined fog color. If the object is sufficiently distant, its vertex colors will be fully set to the defined fog color, causing the object to fade completely away into the background. Just as with other vertex properties, the fog effect interpolates between the vertices of the triangles, causing them all to be appropriately affected by the fog.

Fog is very easy to use, requiring just a small number of parameters to be set. All these parameters are provided by the BasicEffect object, and so we can set them up alongside the rest of the Effect properties when our class-level Effect object is being initialized. The fog properties can, of course, be modified at any stage within the game (even between individual object renders), as required.

There are four properties available to set the behavior and appearance of fog, as follows:

- FogEnabled: this boolean value switches the fog feature on and off. It defaults to false.

- FogStart: sets the distance (in XNA units, from the camera viewpoint) at which the effects of the fog will begin to be applied. Vertices in front of this distance will not be affected by the fog at all.

- FogEnd: sets the distance at which the effects of the fog will end. At the end point, the fog is completely opaque, and all vertices at or beyond this distance will be colored entirely in the fog color.

- FogColor: the color of the fog. Generally when rendering with fog, a solid background color is used, and the fog color is set to match it.

An example of XNA's fog in action can be found in the Fog example project. The fog parameters are set in the FogGame.Initialize function. Feel free to play around with these parameters and experiment with the effect they have on the generated graphics.

A little care is required to produce a good foggy scene. Fog affects only rendered triangles, so the background is not altered by the presence of fog at all. It is therefore important to ensure that the fog color and background color are pretty much the same; otherwise, solid fog-colored structures appear in sharp contrast with the background color.

Using different fog and background colors can be useful, however: if the fog is configured so that the start and end values are both 0 (the whole scene is entirely full of fog), this configuration will produce a silhouette against the scene background in whatever fog color has been defined. The silhouette can be faded back into view by increasing the fog end and start values off into the distance.

It is also important to remember that fog within each triangle is calculated only by interpolation between its vertices. If very large triangles are used (such as the ground in our example), the fog might not always be applied in the way you expect, sometimes resulting in closer objects being affected more by the fog than those further away.

Adding a Skybox

Our 3D worlds are gradually beginning to look and feel more sophisticated, but they currently all suffer from one obvious visible shortcoming: they are all being presented against a blank background.

We created a background image for our sprite projects in Chapter 2 by simply drawing an image with the dimensions of the screen prior to rendering the sprites. This works well in 2D, but in 3D it falls apart: as the camera moves, the background needs to move, too, and we cannot make this happen with a static image.

There are various approaches that we can take to implement a working 3D background, and the one you will look at here is called a *skybox*. It is called this because it is implemented as a box (a cube) inside which the camera is placed. The camera is centralized within the box, and as its angle changes to look around the scene it also looks around inside the skybox. The result is a realistic-looking background with movement that is consistent with the camera and with the objects within the scene.

An example of a skybox working within our house scene, taken from the SkyBox example project, is shown in Figure 8–16.

Figure 8–16. Rendering a scene with a cloudy sky implemented using a skybox

Although this example uses a cloudy sky, the skybox technique can be used for all sorts of background effects, from city skylines to interstellar star fields.

The skybox is drawn before any other rendering takes place and switches off writing to the depth buffer. This ensures that the box is always present in the background, and that it has no effect on or interference with the objects drawn in the foreground of the scene. The box is actually fairly small, much smaller than the objects in the main scene in fact, but the rendering order ensures that this is not at all apparent to the end user.

To make the skybox look realistic, we need to move it in a particular way; or rather we need to prevent it from moving from the point of view of the camera. As the camera moves forward through the world, all the objects in the scene should get closer and larger, but the sky remains at a constant distance. This gives the impression that the sky is much larger and farther away than it really is.

We achieve this movement behavior for the sky by always setting the position of the skybox to exactly match that of the camera. As the camera moves around the scene, so too does the skybox. Relative to the camera, therefore, the skybox is not moving at all, resulting in its apparent constant position.

Only the camera's position is copied into the skybox, however: the skybox rotation and up vector are left unchanged. As a result, when the camera looks around in the world, it will look around inside the skybox, too.

An example project using a skybox can be found in the SkyBox example project.

Creating Skyboxes

In our example, the skybox is actually implemented as a square tube; it has no top or bottom face. This greatly simplifies the task of creating graphics for the skybox.

The effects of using a tube in this way have been hidden at the top of the skybox by ensuring that the top edge of the sky texture is the same color as the scene's background color, making it hard to see where the skybox ends and the background begins unless it is being directly looked at. At the bottom edge, we ensure that sufficient ground is drawn to hide away the lower edge of the texture. Instead, it simply disappears behind the contents of the scene.

If you are creating a game that needs to be able to look all around the skybox, including up and down, you need to enhance it to create a full cube instead of the tube shape that it is using at present. This is simply a matter of adding two additional faces at the top and bottom of the skybox, both pointing inward.

Generating skybox images can be something of a challenge, depending on what kind of environment you need. One option is to create the background texture yourself. This is how the texture in the example was created: I simply took a photo with a digital camera and then cropped it so that its width was four times its height. You can find the image in the SkyBoxContent project folder.

After cropping, the image just needed a little manual manipulation so that the left and right edges of the image tile properly without leaving a strip where the texture doesn't join together. This tiling effect was achieved using the "Seamless Tiling" effect in Corel's Paint Shop Pro application. If you don't have this or a similar application available, you can copy a strip from one side of the image, flip it around, and then blend it into the opposite side of the image so it is opaque where it touches the edge of the image and then fades to transparent after a short distance across the image.

The skybox image needs to be four times wider than it is tall because it wraps around the four sides of the cube horizontally. Many digital cameras have a *panorama* feature that allows a number of pictures to be taken and digitally stitched together to create an extra-wide image. This feature can be very handy for creating the required images.

Another option is to use a computer application to create the skybox image. One application that can help with this is Planetside Software's Terragen Classic application (see http://www.planetside.co.uk/content/view/16/28/ for details), which allows a variety of realistic-looking earth scenes to be created, including skies, terrain, and water. These scenes can then be rendered into images with the camera looking north, south, east, and west; and combined together to make an artificially generated skybox image. A good tutorial that explains how this can be achieved can be found at http://www.3drad.com/forum/index.php?topic=3002.0. After the images have been saved, they can be manually stitched together to create the sky scene.

Terragen Classic is free for noncommercial use, but any commercial application of the software will require an inexpensive license to be purchased. Details of how to buy this application are available on the Planetside Software web site.

Implementing the Skybox into the Game Framework

To make it as easy as possible to use skyboxes, we will integrate a special skybox class into the game framework, allowing us to ensure that it is rendered prior to any other content in the scene.

The skybox is created in a new game framework class: MatrixSkyboxObject. The class is derived from MatrixObjectBase and fits into the inheritance hierarchy as shown in Figure 8–17.

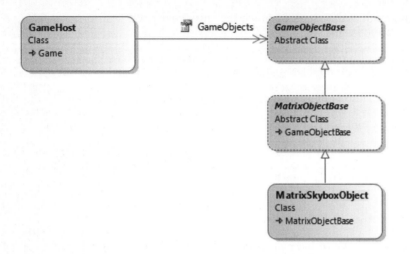

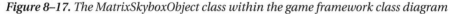

Figure 8–17. The MatrixSkyboxObject class within the game framework class diagram

Inside the class, the code creates a vertex buffer for the skybox consisting of the four side faces of a cube (excluding the top and bottom faces), all facing toward their interior. They are configured with texture coordinates that wrap the supplied texture around the inside of the box.

In the skybox class's Update method, the position of the camera is retrieved by reading its Transformation.Translation property and is set as the skybox's own position. Doing this ensures that the skybox always appears the same distance from the camera, regardless of where the camera is positioned within the scene. Reading the position from the camera's transformation matrix ensures that an accurate reading is retrieved regardless of how the camera has been positioned (the camera's Position property might not reflect its final position, depending on how the camera is being transformed). The Update function is shown in Listing 8–16.

Listing 8–16. Setting the position of the skybox

```
public override void Update(GameTime gameTime)
{
    base.Update(gameTime);

    // Calculate the transformation matrix
    SetIdentity();

    // Observe the camera's position if one is active
    if (Game.Camera != null)
    {
        // Read the camera's calculated position
        ApplyTransformation(
                    Matrix.CreateTranslation(Game.Camera.Transformation.Translation));
    }

    // Now apply the standard transformations
    ApplyStandardTransformations();
}
```

When the skybox is drawn, it first switches off any lighting that might be active and then disables the depth buffer. The lighting is important because we don't want light calculations to be applied to the sky—that's not how the real sky works. Disabling the depth buffer ensures that subsequently rendered objects will never appear behind the sky, an effect that would also look somewhat unrealistic.

With the rendering configured, the skybox is drawn. Once the drawing is complete, lighting and the depth buffer are set back to their previous states.

The code for the Draw function is shown in Listing 8–17.

Listing 8–17. Drawing the skybox

```
public override void Draw(Microsoft.Xna.Framework.GameTime gameTime, Effect effect)
{
    // Prepare the effect for drawing
    PrepareEffect(effect);

    // Disable lighting but remember whether it was switched on...
    bool lightingEnabled = ((BasicEffect)effect).LightingEnabled;
    ((BasicEffect)effect).LightingEnabled = false;
    // Disable the depth buffer
    DepthStencilState depthState = effect.GraphicsDevice.DepthStencilState;
    effect.GraphicsDevice.DepthStencilState = DepthStencilState.None;

    // Set the active vertex buffer
    effect.GraphicsDevice.SetVertexBuffer(_vertexBuffer);

    // Draw the object
    foreach (EffectPass pass in effect.CurrentTechnique.Passes)
    {
        // Apply the pass
        pass.Apply();
        // Draw the sky box
        effect.GraphicsDevice.DrawPrimitives(PrimitiveType.TriangleList,
                                                0, _vertices.Length / 3);
    }

    // Re-enable lighting and the depth buffer if required
    if (lightingEnabled) ((BasicEffect)effect).LightingEnabled = true;
    effect.GraphicsDevice.DepthStencilState = depthState;
}
```

For the skybox to draw correctly, it needs to be the very first thing that is drawn within the scene. So that we can ensure that this is the case, we treat the skybox as a special game within the GameHost object. In the same way that we added a Camera property to allow the camera to be processed at the appropriate points, so we will add a Skybox property, too. This new property can be set to an instance of the MatrixSkyboxObject class or any class that derives from it.

The GameHost.UpdateAll function updates the skybox object directly after the camera, so that the camera position can be retrieved by the skybox. The GameHost.DrawObjects function draws the skybox after the camera, but before any further objects are rendered. To make sure that the skybox is rendered only once per draw (even if DrawObjects is called multiple times), an internal class variable is used to track the drawing operation, preventing repeat draw operations from taking place.

Overall, this implementation provides a simple but effective skybox that will suffice for many games, particularly those that keep the camera so that it is primarily horizontally oriented. The class can be easily extended to provide full cube geometry if needed.

Particles

Another very useful technique that many games will benefit from is the use of *particles,* which are small, flat, textured rectangles that are drawn into the scene using transparency to create a variety of effects that can add a great deal of atmosphere to your game worlds.

In this section, you will look at how to use particles in a game and then discuss some specific examples.

How Particles are Implemented

Particles are added to the game just as any other objects would be, but with the following characteristics:

- They frequently use a technique known as *billboarding* to orient them so that they directly face the camera.

- They usually switch off writing to the depth buffer so that they do not occlude one another.

- They are often the last things to be rendered into the scene each update. Because they do not update the depth buffer, this rendering order prevents objects that are behind them from appearing in front.

- They are nearly always added in groups rather than individually.

You should already be familiar with everything here except for the billboarding technique, so let's look at that in a little more detail.

Billboarding

Billboards are simple quads (flat, square, or rectangular textured objects) rendered in the game world so they face directly toward the camera. As the camera moves around the world, so the billboard objects rotate so that they continue to face directly toward it.

Billboards have a number of potential uses other than for particles, including for rendering lens flares around bright points of light and basic trees rendered using a 2D image such that they always appear face-on to the camera.

For many types of rendered objects, applying a billboard in this way will give the appearance of depth, even though the object is actually completely flat. For example, imagine that you want to render an untextured and unlit spherical object in your game. Such a sphere looks exactly the same from all angles, so if we can simply render a flat drawing of a sphere and keep it angled directly toward the camera, it will be indistinguishable from an actual sphere but with considerably less computational power required to display it.

Billboard quads are very useful for particle systems. If we want to render a firework, we need to ensure that all the points of light that are rendered are actually visible. If we do not use billboarding, the quads that make up the firework could be drawn edge-on to the camera, causing them to become virtually invisible.

Quads rendered as billboards are still placed within the 3D scene, however. They will still retain their position within the game world, will observe the perspective transformation, and will be affected by the z-buffer just as any normal object would.

Figure 8–18 demonstrates the way in which quads are oriented in order for them to appear as billboards. The arrows show the direction in which they are facing. Notice that all the arrows are aligned directly toward the camera. As the camera moves, the quads rotate so that they are always facing toward it.

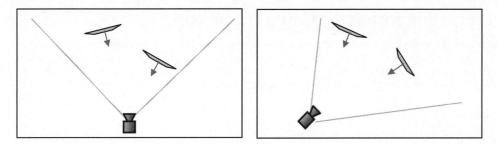

Figure 8–18. *A scene viewed from above with billboard quads rotated toward two different camera locations*

Getting quads to rotate in this way is actually fairly straightforward. Once again we can call another extremely useful static `Matrix` function, this time called `CreateBillboard`. When we call this function, passing it the position of the billboard object and details of the camera position and orientation, it will return a matrix that translates the object to the specified position and rotates the object directly toward the camera.

`CreateBillboard` expects the following parameters to be passed:

- `objectPosition`: the position of the billboard object.

- `cameraPosition`: the position of the camera, which can most easily be obtained by querying the `Camera.Transformation.Translation` property.

- `cameraUpVector`: the camera's up vector. Obtained from the `Camera.Transformation.Up` property.

- `cameraForwardVector`: a vector indicating the direction in which the camera is looking. Obtained from the `Camera.Transformation.Forward` property.

With the help of this matrix we ensure that the particles are always aligned to face directly toward the camera. Listing 8–18 shows a section of a particle class's `Update` code that uses this new function to transform itself ready for display. Notice that it rotates on the z axis after applying the billboard transformation: because the rotation is relative to the object's position, it rotates on the axis that is aligned toward the camera, regardless of how the camera is positioned within the world.

Listing 8–18. *Billboard transformations for a particle object*

```
// Calculate the transformation matrix
SetIdentity();
// Apply the billboard transformation
ApplyTransformation(Matrix.CreateBillboard(Position,
                                    Game.Camera.Transformation.Translation,
                                    Game.Camera.Transformation.Up,
                                    Game.Camera.Transformation.Forward));
// Rotate and scale
ApplyTransformation(Matrix.CreateRotationZ(AngleZ));
ApplyTransformation(Matrix.CreateScale(Scale));
```

Adding Particle Support to the Game Framework

The game framework provides some minor changes to more easily support the rendering of particles. It defines a new abstract base class, MatrixParticleObjectBase, from which particle object classes can be derived. The class is abstract, so it cannot be directly instantiated; instead just providing support for derived classes. Its position within the inheritance class hierarchy can be seen in Figure 8–19.

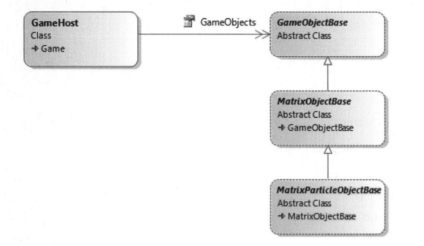

Figure 8–19. The MatrixParticleObjectBase class within the game framework inheritance hierarchy

The reason for having this class is that normally particles will be generated after all other objects within the scene, as we have already discussed. Making it possible to identify particle objects through the inheritance hierarchy in this way allows us to ignore them during the normal calls to GameHost.DrawObjects. To allow them to be rendered, the GameHost class provides a new function, DrawParticles, which can be called after all regular object rendering is complete. Just as with DrawObjects, two overloads are provided for DrawParticles: one draws all particles in the whole system, and the other only draws particles using a specified texture. This once again allows you to avoid unnecessary texture changes within the graphics hardware.

The only other functionality added to the particle base class is a public boolean property named IsActive. As particles are frequently created in large volumes and often have short lifespans, they can be put into a dormant state when no longer required rather than being destroyed. This saves unnecessary object instantiation, reducing the frequency of garbage collection. This property can be seen being put to work in the first of the particle example projects, so let's see some particles in action.

Creating Fire and Smoke

The example project FireAndSmoke uses two different particle classes to create a fire within the scene with smoke drifting away from it, as can be seen in Figure 8–20. Much of the code will be very familiar by now so we will just focus on the areas that relate to the particle effect.

Figure 8–20. Particle effects being used to create fire and smoke

The fire is managed through a class called `FireParticleObject`. Each instance manages a single particle within the fire. The particles are textured using a simple gray blob with an alpha channel applied so that the white areas of the texture are transparent and the darker areas are opaque. The texture is shown in Figure 8–21.

Figure 8–21. The texture used for the fire particles

When each particle is created, it generates a position that is randomized within the area of the fire, sets a random vertical velocity, and assigns a random color that is either somewhere between orange and yellow, or between yellow and white. The game creates 75 of these particles, all positioned within the same area.

The particles update themselves by adding their velocity to their `PositionY` value and then slowly increasing the velocity so that the particles accelerate upward. If they reach a preset height, they reset themselves back to the base of the fire so that the particles are continuously reused to keep the fire burning.

The particles also subtract a small amount from their `ObjectColor` alpha value, which causes the particles to fade away as they move upward, leaving the fire thinner nearer the top than at the bottom.

Finally, the transformation matrix is calculated, using the code shown back in Listing 8–18.

One further step is performed at the end of the Update function: initializing smoke particles. We'll look at this in more detail in a moment.

When it comes to drawing the particle, the code has a few preparatory steps to perform. First it switches off the lighting because it is unlikely to be useful when the objects are orientated toward the camera (and fire isn't affected by surrounding light, anyway). It then disables writing to the depth buffer and switches on alpha blending. The blend that we use for the fire is the built-in BlendState.Additive blending. As discussed in Chapter 6, this blend mode adds the colors being rendered to those already on the screen, pushing the colors toward white, resulting in a bright glowing effect that is perfect for the fire particles.

The particle is then rendered with a simple call to DrawPrimitives and then the lighting, depth buffer processing, and blend state are all restored to their original states. Restoring the state ensures that the particle rendering leaves the environment in a predictable state for subsequent rendering.

These steps are all that is required to render the fire.

The smoke is implemented by using a second particle class, SmokeParticleObject, which is very similar to the fire particle. Its movement behavior is a little different, but its largest visual difference is that it uses the BlendState.AlphaBlend blending mode instead. It blends the existing screen content directly toward the texture graphics, resulting in a darker effect that works well for smoke.

The smoke particles are managed in a different way from the fire particles. Instead of resetting themselves to their original position after they have expired, they set a property called IsActive to false. Each time the FireParticleObject code wants to add a new smoke particle to the game, it first scans the GameObjects list looking for existing smoke particles that have become inactive. If one is found, it is reset and reactivated, saving the need to create new objects. If no inactive objects are found, a new one is created. This is exactly the same approach that we used for the explosion particles in *Cosmic Rocks* in Chapter 3.

When the main FireAndSmokeGame class renders the scene's graphics, it draws the smoke particles first and then draws the fire particles. Rendering in this order displays the fire in front of the smoke, which produces a more natural-looking interaction between the two elements of the scene.

The resulting effect might not be photorealistic, but it is pleasing enough and sufficiently convincing for use within games. It is ideal for campfires, flaming torches, or (with a few tweaks to the particle movement) explosions.

Vapor and Smoke Trails

Another attractive effect, implemented along very similar lines to the smoke in the previous section, is the vapor or smoke trail. This effect can be applied to all sorts of vehicles, from cars to airplanes, and simulates the exhaust fumes or vapor trails that they leave behind as they travel along.

The effect can be seen in the VaporTrails example project, an image from which is shown in Figure 8–22. This is based on the paper plane scene set up in the ChaseCam project, but with the addition of a simple smoke particle class.

Figure 8–22. *Particles used to create vapor trails*

Every three updates, a smoke particle is added to the scene at the end of the
PaperPlaneObject.Update function. The function uses exactly the same particle-recycling technique
used for the smoke in the FireAndSmoke example, but this time passes the plane's position into the
particle's constructor and ResetParticle function. Each smoke particle is therefore positioned directly
on top of the plane.

The smoke particles do very little: they gradually increase in size and fade their alpha away
toward zero. When the alpha value hits zero, the object is made inactive. Because a new particle is
added every third update and they take 255 updates to fade away, this gives approximately 85 smoke
particles active in the scene at any time. Try changing the rate at which they are added by altering the
modulus operator at the end of the Update code; the trail looks even nicer with more objects, but of
course becomes more and more processor-intensive as a result.

The smoke particles in this example are rendered using additive blending rather than alpha
blending. Once again this pushes the rendered graphics toward white (particularly as the particles are
themselves rendered in white), resulting in a dense smoke trail.

Vapor trails can add a huge amount of energy to a rendered scene, and if processing power
permits are well worth considering if you have a use for them.

Fairy Dust

By now, you are probably getting the hang of particles, so this will be the final example, but it shows
another style of particle that once again can enhance the atmosphere of an otherwise simple scene.
The FairyDust example project, shown in Figure 8–23, creates a "fairy" particle that moves around the
scene, showering multicolored sparkling dust behind it.

Figure 8–23. *Fairy dust particles*

Much of the code in this project is just the same as in the earlier particle projects, so we'll just take a look at the specifics that create this effect. First there is the fairy. If you look carefully at it as it moves around the screen, you will see that it has a shimmering radiance around it formed from beams of light emanating from the center of the object. These moving light beams are created by overlaying two different particle objects in exactly the same location and rotating them in opposite directions. The texture contains the light beams, and as they rotate around one another they produce this shimmering effect. It is a lot less computationally expensive than it looks!

The dust particles are simply star-shaped textures created in random colors, and positioned on top of the fairy when they are initialized. They move in a random direction and gradually apply gravity by increasing the y axis velocity with each update.

Simple, but once again an effective tool for many types of games.

Using Effect Objects

When creating games for Windows or the Xbox 360, XNA offers up an additional graphics programming language called *High Level Shader Language (HLSL)*. This language is targeted very specifically to being able to process instructions relating to the objects drawn upon the screen, and programs written using the language are referred to as *shaders*.

There are two types of shaders: those that process vertices within rendered objects are known as *vertex shaders*, and those that work on individual pixels within the objects are *pixel shaders*. They allow a variety of very flexible effects to be created, including texture distortion, blurring, depth-of-field focus effects, and all kinds of other things.

The bad news is that Windows Phone 7 does not support these programmable shaders, which is something of a limitation compared to the desktop XNA implementation. To go some way to ease the loss of this graphical technique, XNA provides a series of *effect objects*.

Throughout all the matrix-based rendering, we have been using a class called BasicEffect as the gateway into rendering to the screen. We have defined this in a class-level variable named _effect at the top of each of our game classes. There are several other effects that can be used, however; the complete list is as follows:

- BasicEffect is a general-purpose effect with a large number of different configuration options.

- AlphaTestEffect is an effect that allows flexible depth buffer updates in response to alpha transparency.

- DualTextureEffect allows two textures to be rendered to geometry at the same time.

- EnvironmentMapEffect provides a simple way of simulation reflection of the surrounding environment on to an object.

- SkinnedEffect is a specialized effect that allows for animation of bones within an XNA model.

This section examines the properties and usage of some of these effects.

Effect Capabilities

Not all effects can use all the features that you have learned about up to this point. In fact, BasicEffect is the only effect that can use many of the features at all. Table 8–1 summarizes the effects and the features that are available for use within each. Those effects flagged as *Always* are always available and enabled ready for use; those marked *Optional* are available but must be specifically enabled before they have any effect; those marked *Not available* cannot be used by that effect at all.

Table 8–1. Effect Types and Capabilities

Feature	Basic	AlphaTest	EnvironmentMap	DualTexture	Skinned
Projection, view, and world matrix	Always	Always	Always	Always	Always
Diffuse color	Always	Always	Always	Always	Always
Alpha blending	Always	Always	Always	Always	Always
Fog	Optional	Optional	Optional	Optional	Optional
Vertex coloring	Optional	Optional	Not available	Optional	Not available
Texture mapping	Optional	Always	Always	Always	Always

Feature	Basic	AlphaTest	EnvironmentMap	DualTexture	Skinned
Ambient lighting	Optional	Nor available	Always	Not available	Always
Directional lighting	Optional	Not available	Always	Not available	Always
Specular lighting	Optional	Not available	Not available	Not available	Always
Per-pixel lighting	Optional	Not available	Not available	Not available	Optional
Emissive lighting	Optional	Not available	Always	Not available	Always
Special features	None	Alpha comparison function	Environment map control properties	Second texture property	Properties to set the transforms of the model's bones

Let's look at these effects in more detail.

AlphaTestEffect

The depth buffer is essential for proper rendering in 3D environments, but you can run into problems when you begin rendering transparent objects.

This is because the depth buffer can track only the depth of each pixel on the screen: it doesn't have any concept of transparency. If a semitransparent object is drawn on the screen, and then another opaque object is drawn behind it, how should XNA handle this? Should the object behind be rendered where it overlaps the transparent object (in which case it would incorrectly appear in front of it) or not (in which case the semitransparent object would in effect become opaque)?

The only solution for semitransparent objects is to change the order in which they are rendered to the screen. Objects should be rendered from those in the background first to those in the foreground last. This way, objects will always render on top of other objects that are behind them, allowing the alpha blending to work as required.

There is a special case exception, however, which XNA helps us handle more easily. When we render objects that are partly opaque and partly fully transparent, XNA offers us an *alpha test* feature that we can use to change the interaction with the depth buffer. Pixels within the texture that pass the alpha test will be rendered both to the screen and the depth buffer as opaque pixels; pixels that fail the alpha test will be considered as transparent, and the screen and depth buffer for that pixel will be left unchanged. Subsequent objects rendered behind the alpha-tested object will therefore show through the transparent areas while still being hidden by the opaque areas.

Just to restate the limitation with the alpha test, the comparison is a binary operation: pixels from the object will either be considered fully transparent or fully opaque. Semitransparent rendering is not supported by this effect.

Figure 8–24 shows an image in which three cubes have been rendered one in front of another using a BasicEffect. The cube is textured with an image that contains a lattice of opaque bars with fully transparent regions in between. To allow the inner faces of the box to be seen, culling has been switched off for this example. The background color is showing through the transparent areas of the texture, as would be expected.

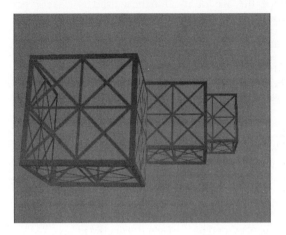

Figure 8–24. *Rendering transparent objects using BasicEffect*

Unwanted interactions between the alpha blending and the depth buffer are visible in two different areas, however. First, the distant cubes are being completely hidden by those in front, even though they are supposed to be transparent. Second, the inner surfaces of each cube are only partly displayed; on the left side of the frontmost box, the inner surface can be seen, but the top and back surfaces are hidden because the front face was drawn before the top and back faces, so the depth buffer thinks they are hidden.

Both of these problems can be cured by switching to use AlphaTestEffect instead of BasicEffect. The same scene is rendered again using AlphaTestEffect in Figure 8–25. You can see that all areas of the boxes that are supposed to be transparent now really are showing through both to their internal surfaces and also to the objects behind.

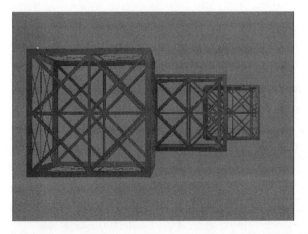

Figure 8–25. *Rendering transparent objects using AlphaTestEffect*

Switching over to use the AlphaTestEffect is easy, and all the code can be found in the AlphaTest example project. First of all, the _effect variable is changed to be of type AlphaTestEffect instead of BasicEffect, and is instantiated accordingly within the Initialize function.

Next, the effect properties are set. Some of the properties are identical to those used by BasicEffect (including the three matrix properties Projection, View, and World; the VertexColorEnabled property; fog; diffuse color; and alpha). Other properties are forced on by this effect (it always uses texturing and alpha blending, so there is no need to explicitly set them).

As shown in Table 8–1, however, some of the properties of BasicEffect do not exist within this new class. The most awkward of these are probably the lighting properties. Without lighting it can be difficult to mix alpha-tested objects in with other objects that are rendered using BasicEffect with lighting enabled. You will instead need to fall back to specifying vertex colors to provide a rough approximation of lighting.

Finally we get to the good stuff: the new properties offered by this effect. There are two such properties: AlphaFunction and ReferenceAlpha. Between them, these properties provide the mechanism whereby XNA determines whether each rendered pixel should be rendered or not.

Transparency is determined by comparing the alpha value of each pixel in the texture to a *reference alpha* value that we provide to the effect. The type of comparison performed depends upon the *alpha function* that we tell the effect to use. If we were to specify an alpha function of GreaterEqual and a reference alpha of 128, all pixels whose alpha value is 128 or more will be rendered as opaque, whereas all those with alpha less than 128 will be rendered transparent.

A number of different alpha functions are available, provided by the CompareFunction enumeration. These functions are Always (the pixel is always rendered as opaque regardless of their alpha values), Never (always rendered transparent, which makes the object entirely invisible), Less, LessEqual, Equal, GreaterEqual, Greater, and NotEqual. All these functions work just as you would expect.

The alpha reference is specified as an integer between 0 (pixels that are fully transparent) and 255 (pixels that are fully opaque).

The code required to instantiate and initialize the AlphaTestEffect is shown in Listing 8–19.

Listing 8–19. Creating and initializing an AlphaTestEffect

```
// Create and initialize the effect
_effect = new AlphaTestEffect(GraphicsDevice);
_effect.VertexColorEnabled = false;
_effect.Projection = projection;
_effect.View = view;
_effect.World = Matrix.Identity;
// Set the effect's alpha test parameters
_effect.AlphaFunction = CompareFunction.GreaterEqual;
_effect.ReferenceAlpha = 250;
```

The game framework also provides a modified version of MatrixObjectBase.PrepareEffect, which expects an AlphaTestEffect as its parameter. It sets only those properties that are relevant for this type of effect.

AlphaTestEffect and BasicEffect objects (and indeed, any of the effect objects) can be used together within the same rendered scene. This is achieved by creating two or more separate effect objects of the required types, and passing the appropriate object into the DrawObjects function from the game class's Draw method.

DualTextureEffect

Another useful rendering feature provided by XNA is the ability to combine two textures together when rendering each triangle.

All our textured objects so far have been given a texture coordinate for each vertex and it has been used by XNA to stretch the texture across the surface of the rendered object. When we use DualTextureEffect, we need to provide two texture coordinates for each vertex, and also two textures to blend together when displaying the object.

This additional texture presents a couple of initial problems to overcome. The first is easy to solve: our game framework objects can store only a reference to a single texture. We'll address this by simply adding a second texture property, ObjectTexture2, to the MatrixObjectBase class.

Then we come to the second problem, whose solution is a little less obvious. The vertex definition structures that we used for textured objects (one of VertexPositionTexture, VertexPositionNormalTexture, or VertexPositionColorTexture) all contain only a single property for specifying a texture. How therefore are we able to tell XNA the vertex coordinates of the second texture?

The answer lies in XNA's capability to work with *custom vertex formats*. Lots of different pieces of information can be encoded into a vertex format, and we have worked with positions, texture coordinates, colors, and normals throughout this and previous chapters. When working with HLSL, there are lots of other useful things that can be passed in as vertex data, but because Windows Phone 7 has no HLSL support, there are not many situations in which custom vertex formats are useful.

This is one situation where it is useful, however, because it allows us to create a custom vertex format containing a position and two texture coordinates, one for each of the dual textures. The format structure is named VertexPositionDualTexture to match XNA's naming scheme and to make it easily accessible to our games it has been added to the game framework inside the VertexDeclarations.cs source file. The code for the structure is not included here because it doesn't provide anything that we will build on and can simply be treated as a closed source structure, but if you are curious about its implementation, you can take a look in the game framework source code.

How then does XNA combine the two textures together when it is rendering? The calculation is very simple, but deserves a little exploration to understand its implications.

Each final rendered pixel color is calculated using the following formula (treating all red, green, and blue values as floats in the range of 0 to 1):

$$Red_{new} = (Red_1 \times Red_2) \times 2$$

$$Green_{new} = (Green_1 \times Green_2) \times 2$$

$$Blue_{new} = (Blue_1 \times Blue_2) \times 2$$

$$Alpha_{new} = (Alpha_1 \times Alpha_2) \times 2$$

In many cases, the easiest way to visualize this calculation in action is to consider the first texture as being the actual texture that is displayed upon the object and the second texture as *modulating* it by increasing or decreasing its brightness in each of the color components based upon its own color value.

Because each output pixel calculation multiplies the final value by 2, a color component value of 0.5 within one of the textures will have no effect at all on the color from the other texture (it will be multiplied by 0.5, halving it, and then multiplied by 2, restoring it to its original value). On the other hand, a value of 0.0 will remove all color from the other texture, and 1.0 will double the value from the other texture. As always, the colors are clamped, and resulting values above 1.0 will be treated as if they were 1.0.

The DualTexture example project shows two applications of this effect. The one that appears when the project is first launched has its first texture as a piece of rocky ground and its second texture as three white circles on a dark-gray background, as can be seen in Figure 8–26. The code changes the texture coordinates with each update, causing the two textures to gradually move across the face of the rendered square.

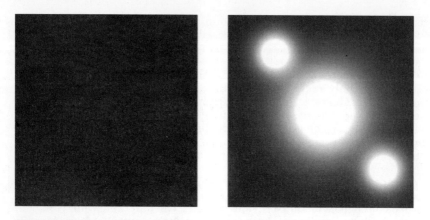

Figure 8–26. *The ground and lights textures used by the DualTexture example project*

The circles form an effective-looking spotlight effect on the ground. Their background color is darker than mid-gray, causing them to darken the ground texture, but the circles themselves are obviously very bright, illuminating the texture. The resulting image is shown in Figure 8–27—once again, it looks better in motion than in a still image.

Figure 8–27. *The ground and lights textures combined by DualTextureEffect*

The example project contains a second, much more colorful example, too. Edit the code and swap over the commenting of the two calls to GameObjects.Add in the DualTextureGame.ResetGame function so that the two moiré textures are passed instead of the ground and lights textures. These two new textures contain a series of concentric circles, as shown in Figure 8–28. Both textures contain the same pattern but in different colors.

Figure 8–28. The moiré pattern texture

These textures are combined using exactly the same code as before, but this time the concentrated patterns of bright and dark color interfere with each other to create a fantastic-looking interference pattern, which can be seen in Figure 8–29. And yes, this one looks better in motion, too!

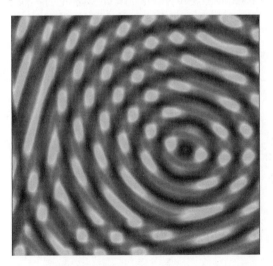

Figure 8–29. The effects of dual texturing the two moiré textures

Using DualTextureEffect is very simple. Create an instance of it in your game class and configure its properties as necessary. Once again it has a limited set of properties compared to BasicEffect, with no support for lighting.

When setting up your vertex buffers, declare them to be of type VertexPositionDualTexture, and set their texture coordinates using the two properties TexCoord0 and TexCoord1. The two textures are provided to the game objects in their ObjectTexture and ObjectTexture2 properties.

EnvironmentMapEffect

The next of the XNA effects is the EnvironmentMapEffect. We already saw some fairly shiny objects when we were experimenting with specular lighting in the previous chapter, but environment mapping allows us to take shiny surfaces to the next level.

Environment mapping is a technique that simulates the reflections of an object's surrounding onto the object itself. If your game is set in a forest, for example, you might want to reflect a forest image onto some of the objects in your game. Objects that use environment mapping in this way look like they are highly polished (which suits some objects more than others; for example, objects made of metal, glass, or polished wood will benefit from environment mapping, but objects with matte surfaces such as brick or plastic will probably look very strange).

It usually isn't important that the reflections being used for the environment map actually be accurate; as long as they fit in with the scene, users will be fooled into thinking they are seeing the real environment rather than a static image. Showing a reflection of a forest when the player is exploring a cave will, of course, be a little more jarring, so make sure the scene and the environment map match up.

In addition to allowing objects to reflect the environment, XNA's environment mapping also allows objects to have their own static textures, just like those used by the other effects. The effect of the object's own texture and its reflected environment leads to a very convincing illusion of reflectivity.

There are some minor challenges involved in setting up an environment map, but fortunately once you know how to do it, the process is very easy. And you will know exactly how to do it very soon! The code that we will look at in this section can be found in the EnvironmentMap project, and some images from it can be seen in Figure 8–30 (and yes, once again, this example also looks better in motion).

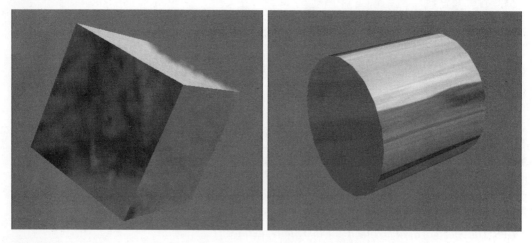

Figure 8–30. A cube and a cylinder reflecting a landscape environment

The EnvironmentMapEffect object is in many ways very similar to BasicEffect because it offers most of the same lighting properties and other effects. The only features that are absent, as compared with BasicEffect, are specular lighting and vertex coloring.

The effect needs a texture so that it can texture the object, and the `MatrixObjectBase.PrepareEffect` function will once again take care of providing this texture from each object's `ObjectTexture` property. A valid texture is a requirement of the `EnvironmentMapEffect` and setting its texture to `null` will result in a black silhouette of the object appearing. It is possible to render without applying a texture to the object, however, and we will look at how this can be achieved in a moment.

Preparing the Environment Map

The reflection functionality offered by this new effect is implemented by a new feature called an *environment map*. This map contains the texture that will be used for reflections on the rendered objects. However, we have a problem with setting the effect's `EnvironmentMap` property: its type is `TextureCube` rather than `Texture2D`, and this is a new type of object that we have not encountered before. How can we generate a `TextureCube` object?

A texture cube is similar in function to the skybox that we looked at earlier on: it is a set of six textures that can be applied to the front, back, left, right, top, and bottom faces of a cube such that when viewed from the inside they form a consistent seamless environment in all directions. XNA provides no built-in way to create texture cubes from an image, but one of the XNA sample projects that Microsoft released separately provides everything that is needed to very easily create a texture cube.

The sample project can be found at `http://create.msdn.com/en-US/education/catalog/sample/custom_model_effect`, and the relevant project from it is also included in this chapter's source code in the `CustomModelEffectPipeline` folder. It has been copied directly from the sample project without any modification.

The project contains an XNA game library, but it is one that we will use only as part of the compilation process; it doesn't get distributed along with your finished game. Instead it adds a custom content processor that the `Content` project can use to transform a simple PNG or JPG image into a texture cube.

To use the content processor, add the `CustomModelEffectPipeline` project to your solution. Then open the References branch of the `Content` project within Solution Explorer, right-click Add Reference, and select the `CustomModelEffectPipeline` item from the Add Reference window's Projects tab. When this is done, the project will appear as a reference alongside the other content processors provided by XNA, as shown in Figure 8–31.

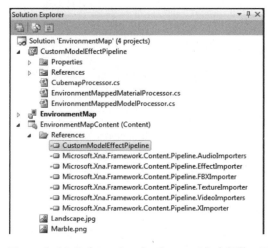

Figure 8–31. Referencing the CustomModelEffectPipeline from the game's Content project

Now that the Content project is aware of the custom content processor, it can be used to transform a graphic file into a TextureCube instead of a Texture2D object. To do this, add the image that you want to use for the environment map (Landscape.jpg in the example project) and edit its properties. The initial setting for the Content Processor property is Texture – XNA Framework. If you open the drop-down list for this property, you will find that some new processors have appeared, all of which are provided by the CustomModelEffectPipeline code. Select CubemapProcessor as the processor to use, as shown in Figure 8–32. When the project is compiled, this texture will now be created as a texture cube.

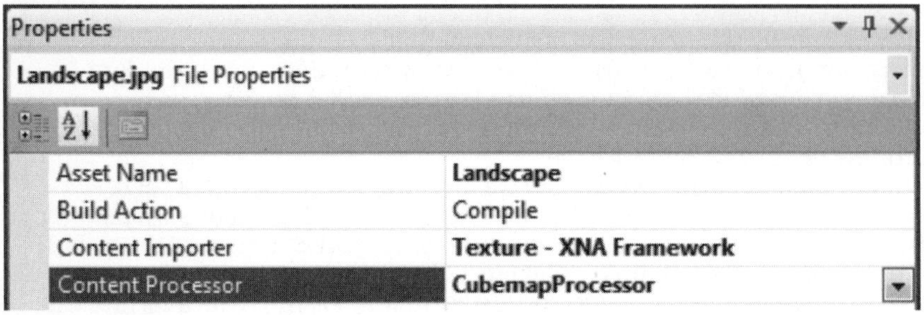

Properties	▾ ⇩ ✕
Landscape.jpg File Properties	▾
Asset Name	Landscape
Build Action	Compile
Content Importer	**Texture - XNA Framework**
Content Processor	**CubemapProcessor** ▾

Figure 8–32. A graphic file configured to be processed by the CubemapProcessor

■ **NOTE** There is no need to worry about making seamless wrapping graphic files before providing them to the CubemapProcessor: it will cleverly distort the image in a way that automatically wraps the image seamlessly around all the faces of the texture cube.

This configuration change is everything we need to prepare the TextureCube; now we simply need to activate it within the game. After instantiating and initializing the EnvironmentMapEffect, the TextureCube can be read from the Content object and set into the EnvironmentMap property. The code to do this, taken from the example project's LoadContent function, is shown in Listing 8–20.

Listing 8–20. Loading a TextureCube into the EnvironmentMapEffect object

```
// Load the environment cube map
_effect.EnvironmentMap = Content.Load<TextureCube>("Landscape");
```

■ **NOTE** We could easily add a new collection of TextureCube objects into the game framework, but because it is likely that only one will be used at a time, it is more straightforward to simply load it directly into the effect. Feel free to extend the game framework yourself to support a collection of texture cubes if you would find it useful.

Once the effect's environment map is set, all that is left is to simply render some objects. It is important that the objects have vertex normals configured correctly because the effect uses them (along with the vertex position) to determine which part of the environment map should reflect on each part of the object, but no further object configuration is required.

■ **TIP** Don't forget to configure the scene's lighting. Without it your objects will be entirely unlit but will still reflect their environment, which is probably not what you are expecting to see.

Environment Map Properties

Several additional effect properties are available to control the way in which the environment mapping is applied to your rendered objects.

First is the EnvironmentMapAmount property, which controls the strength of the blending effect between the environment texture and the object's own texture, in the range of 0 to 1. When set to 1 (its default value), the environment map will completely replace the object's texture; when set to 0, the environment map will be completely switched off. Values between will provide varying levels of subtlety to the strength of reflections.

Next is the EnvironmentMapSpecular property. If you encode additional data into your image's alpha channel, this property can be used to implement a cheap simulation of specular lighting on your objects. This effect works better when the object is highly curvy because large flat surfaces tend to break the illusion of the specular lighting. The EnvironmentMapSpecular property allows a color to be specified with which the alpha channel data will be tinted. It defaults to black, which disables this effect.

■ **TIP** Don't forget that JPG graphic files can't store alpha channel information, so this feature can be used only with PNG image files. Due to the way that the cubemap processor transforms the image into its texture cube, the resulting image sizes will not be hugely different because the images are recompressed in the same way regardless of the source image format.

The final property is the FresnelFactor. Another float property that ranges from 0 to 1, this property controls how the reflectivity of an object changes as relative to the viewing angle. With a FresnelFactor value of 1 (the default), object surfaces will stop reflecting the environment entirely when they are facing directly toward the camera, though they will increasingly reflect as they rotate away. A FresnelFactor of 0 disables this effect entirely so that the object reflectivity takes no account of the viewing angle. Values between make this effect more or less pronounced.

It is very useful to be able to experiment with these properties when setting up your environment-mapped objects. Highly reflective objects look very pretty, but are not necessarily all that realistic. Great results can be had from applying subtle environment mapping to your objects that the user is perhaps only subconsciously aware of.

To allow each of the objects within our games to have independent control over their environmental mapping settings, corresponding properties named EnvironmentMapAmount, EnvironmentMapSpecular, and FresnelFactor have been added to MatrixObjectBase in the game framework. They default to the values 1, Black, and 1, respectively, to match the defaults provided by XNA.

Rendering Untextured Objects with Environment Maps

It will sometimes be useful to draw objects that are entirely reflective and that have no texture of their own visible at all. This can be achieved by setting the EnvironmentMapAmount to 1, but it is still necessary to have a texture applied to the object itself, or else the object will appear completely black.

There are two things we can do to address this problem. The first is to create a 1-x-1-pixel white dummy texture and apply it to the objects in question. They will therefore be textured (in white), so the environment mapping will apply as required.

The only real downside is that the dummy texture needs to be loaded into the graphics hardware, replacing any other texture that might already be there. That other texture might then need to be subsequently reloaded, causing a performance hit.

The other alternative is to leave whatever texture is already in the graphics hardware active so that it will apply to the object being rendered. This texture might, of course, be entirely unsuitable for the new object, which probably hasn't been set up with any texture coordinates at all. To prevent it from causing unpredictable results, we can configure the environment mapping settings for the object to have an EnvironmentMapAmount of 1 and a FresnelFactor of 0. This will cause the environment map to completely overpower the object texture so that it has no visible effect whatsoever.

The game framework will set the environment map properties in this way if it detects that no texture has been set for the object being rendered. It is essential that there are other objects within the scene that do activate a texture within the EnvironmentMapEffect, however, so that a texture is set prior to the object being rendered. If this is not the case, a dummy texture will need to be applied as described previously.

SkinnedEffect

The final effect is the SkinnedEffect. This effect doesn't provide graphical effects in the way that the other effects have, but rather allows models that contain multiple bones to be controlled such that each bone can be moved around its joints to position complex models into different poses.

Creating models such as these is beyond the scope of this book, so we will not be going into any further detail about this particular effect. If you want to learn more and see the effect in action, take a look at the XNA Reach Graphics Demo, which can be found by pointing your web browser at http://create.msdn.com/en-US/education/catalog/sample/reach_graphics_demo and downloading the source code at the bottom of the page.

Mixing Sprite and Matrix Rendering

We have nearly finished our journey through XNA's matrix-based rendering now, but there is one final topic to cover: mixing rendering from sprites and from matrix-based graphics together at the same time.

There are obvious uses to rendering sprites and matrices together: 3D games will frequently need to display text, for example, and it is likely that 2D status overlays (energy bars, number of lives left, and so on) might be useful, too. XNA allows us to achieve this by rendering sprites and 3D objects together into the same scene.

Simply draw the 3D objects first and then draw the sprites afterward. Both will render exactly as you would expect, with the sprites appearing on top of any 3D objects that have already been rendered onscreen.

XNA's sprite renderer does, however, make some changes to the state of the rendering engine, and they will most likely need some minor additional changes to your code to compensate. When XNA begins rendering sprites, it reconfigures the environment as follows:

- GraphicsDevice.BlendState is set to BlendState.AlphaBlend. You will probably want to set it back to BlendState.Opaque, or whatever other blend state you require.

- GraphicsDevice.DepthStencilState is set to DepthStencilState.None, disabling the depth buffer (remember that sprites handle depth purely through the LayerDepth value on each rendered sprite). You will almost certainly need to set this back to DepthStencilState.Default.

- GraphicsDevice.RasterizerState is set to RasterizerState.CullCounterClockwise. This is its default value, anyway, so might not have any impact on your code.

- GraphicsDevice.SamplerState[0] is set to SamplerState.LinearClamp. This will prevent tiling of textures on your 3D objects, so you might want to revert this back to SamplerState.LinearWrap.

To simplify the management of these render states, two new functions have been added to the game framework's GameHost class: StoreStateBeforeSprites and RestoreStateAfterSprites. The StoreStateBeforeSprites function reads the current value for all four of these state properties and stores them away into private class variables within GameHost. This function should be called prior to calling the SpriteBatch.Begin method. The RestoreStateAfterSprites function retrieves these stored values and makes them current once again, and should be called after SpriteBatch.End. Storing and restoring the state in this way hides the state changes that the SpriteBatch makes, allowing the rest of the rendering code to continue unaffected.

Listing 8–21 shows the source code for these two functions.

Listing 8–21. Storing and restoring the graphics device state for before and after rendering sprites

```
protected void StoreStateBeforeSprites()
{
    _preSpriteBlendState = GraphicsDevice.BlendState;
    _preSpriteDepthStencilState = GraphicsDevice.DepthStencilState;
    _preSpriteRasterizerState = GraphicsDevice.RasterizerState;
    _preSpriteSamplerState = GraphicsDevice.SamplerStates[0];
}

protected void RestoreStateAfterSprites()
{
    GraphicsDevice.BlendState = _preSpriteBlendState;
    GraphicsDevice.DepthStencilState = _preSpriteDepthStencilState;
    GraphicsDevice.RasterizerState = _preSpriteRasterizerState;
    GraphicsDevice.SamplerStates[0] = _preSpriteSamplerState;
}
```

Listing 8–22 shows a Draw function that renders both 3D objects and sprites together, using the StoreStateBeforeSprites and RestoreStateAfterSprites functions to ensure that the rendering state is not modified by the sprites.

Listing 8–22. Drawing 3D objects and sprites together, storing and restoring the rendering state

```
protected override void Draw(GameTime gameTime)
{
    GraphicsDevice.Clear(Color.CornflowerBlue);

    // Draw all 3D objects
    DrawObjects(gameTime, _effect);
```

```
    // Draw all sprites and text...
    // First store the graphics device state
    StoreStateBeforeSprites();
    // Draw the sprites
    _spriteBatch.Begin(SpriteSortMode.BackToFront, BlendState.AlphaBlend);
    DrawSprites(gameTime, _spriteBatch);
    DrawText(gameTime, _spriteBatch);
    _spriteBatch.End();
    // Now restore the graphics device state
    RestoreStateAfterSprites();

    base.Draw(gameTime);
}
```

An example of using this technique can be found in the SpritesAndSolids example, from which Listing 8–22 was copied and from which an image is shown in Figure 8–33. You will see that it displays solid 3D objects, sprites, and text all on the screen at once. The two cubes intersect and can be clearly seen to still be observing and updating the depth buffer despite the SpriteBatch having disabled it. The semitransparent balloons show through to the 3D rendered content behind them.

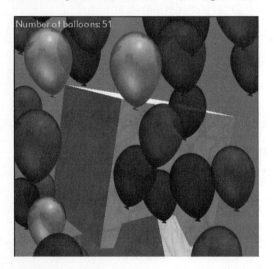

Figure 8–33. *A graphic file configured to be processed by the CubemapProcessor*

Because the sprites disable the depth buffer, they have no impact at all on any subsequent 3D objects that are rendered. It is, therefore, very easy to display sprites behind 3D objects, too: just render them first and the 3D objects second. If you want to create scenes that have some sprites behind the 3D objects and others in front, draw the background sprites first, then the 3D objects, and then the foreground sprites. Listing 8–23 shows a simple example of how this can be achieved.

Listing 8–23. *Drawing background and foreground sprites*

```
    // Draw background sprites
    StoreStateBeforeSprites();
    _spriteBatch.Begin(SpriteSortMode.BackToFront, BlendState.AlphaBlend);
```

```
DrawSprites(gameTime, _spriteBatch, Textures["BackgroundTexture"]);
_spriteBatch.End();
RestoreStateAfterSprites();

// Draw all 3D objects
DrawObjects(gameTime, _effect);

// Draw foreground sprites
StoreStateBeforeSprites();
_spriteBatch.Begin(SpriteSortMode.BackToFront, BlendState.AlphaBlend);
DrawSprites(gameTime, _spriteBatch, Textures["ForegroundTexture"]);
_spriteBatch.End();
RestoreStateAfterSprites();
```

A Universe of Possibilities

The gaming opportunities with 3D graphics are immense, and I hope that you now feel armed and prepared to go and conquer them. It is a complex environment to work with, and sometimes things won't work or look exactly the way you expect them to. Experimentation is key, however, so use the knowledge that you have gained to create test projects and try things out. With a little practice, you should find that things start to feel much more natural and manageable.

While we've covered a lot of XNA's functionality, it is a very rich and flexible environment and there's a great deal more that you can learn about it if you want to extend your knowledge further. The MSDN App Hub web site at http://create.msdn.com is probably the best learning resource.

The Education and Resources sections have enormous volumes of information that you can use to further your abilities, and the Community section has a highly active set of forums into which you can post for help if you need it. The community is always grateful for any help that you can provide, so please help to share your knowledge to others if you can!

The next chapter steps back from 3D rendering and looks at some useful functions that you can add to your games to enhance their features.

CHAPTER 9

■ ■ ■

Enhancing Your Game

There are many different styles and varieties of games, and they can be diverse in the ways that they play and function. Some game features are useful in many different games, though, and in this chapter, we'll examine a couple of useful pieces of functionality that fall into this category. These game enhancements will be created to be easily reusable so that they can be quickly and easily dropped into any game that would benefit from them.

The enhancements that we will create are as follows:

- A settings class, allowing us to easily set and retrieve configuration values, and save them to files so that they can be retrieved the next time the game is executed.

- A high score table, providing a very easy mechanism for adding and displaying scores that the player has achieved.

These features will be created within the game framework and can be easily accessed by calling into the methods of the appropriate class.

Along the way, we will also examine some other mechanisms that will be very useful within your games, such as handling the Back button, reading and writing data from and to isolated storage, and working with multiple sets of game objects.

Let's take a look at what each of these enhancements does in more detail, how they are used, and how they work internally. The internal workings are only discussed fairly briefly here as they are intended as end user components, but are described in case you want to make any changes to how they work or to lift any of the code out for use in other projects. The full source code is, of course, available in the GameFramework project for this chapter in the accompanying download.

Managing Game Settings

Most games and applications will want to offer the user control over how some of the features of the program function. In a game they will include things such as settings for the game (difficulty level, different game modes), settings for the game environment (sound effect and music volume levels, graphic options), or settings that are controlled by the application itself (such as remembering the date the game was last played or the name that the player last entered into a high score table).

There is nothing particularly difficult about managing this information, but as with everything else we have done with the game framework, our objective is to make this as simple to manage as possible. To look after all of this for us, we will add a new class, SettingsManager, to the GameFramework project. This class will allow us to easily set and query game settings, and to save them to the device and retrieve them once again.

There are a number of parts to this class, and also some things to consider when it comes to actually using it, so let's take a look at how it all fits together. All the code for this section is present in the Settings example project that accompanies this chapter and this chapter's updated GameFramework.

Class Structure

The SettingsManager class is declared as a public class, but with a constructor whose scope is internal. Setting the scope in this way prevents code outside of the game framework itself from being able to instantiate the class, and so we can ensure that just a single instance is created by the framework and used throughout the game. Limiting the class to a single instance ensures that all parts of the game see the same settings without having to pass an instance of the class around between functions.

The single object instance is accessed using the GameHost.SettingsManager property.

Setting and Retrieving Values

The main purpose of the SettingsManager class is to store values that we give to it, and to allow those values to be retrieved later. These two actions can be accomplished by calling the SetValue and GetValue methods.

A number of different overloads of these two functions are provided for different data types, with versions available for string, int, float, bool, and DateTime types. Internally they are all stored as strings, but the overloads ensure that the values are encoded and decoded properly so this internal storage mechanism is transparent to the calling code.

Whenever a value is retrieved using one of the GetValue methods, a defaultValue parameter is provided. This parameter serves two purposes. First, it allows for a sensible value to be returned if the requested setting is unknown and doesn't exist within the object. This simplifies the use of the class, as shown in Listing 9–1. If we try to retrieve the sound effects volume level and it hasn't already been set, we default it to 100 so that its initial setting is at full volume, even though no setting value actually exists within the object.

Listing 9–1. Retrieving a setting value from the SettingsManager Object

```
int volumeLevel;

// Retrieve the volume level from the game settings
volumeLevel = SettingsManager.GetValue("SoundEffectsVolume", 100);
```

The second role that the defaultValue parameter performs is identifying the expected return type of the GetValue function. If the defaultValue is passed as an int, the return value will be an int, too. This provides a convenient variable type mechanism, avoiding the need to cast and convert values to the appropriate types.

In addition to setting and getting values, the class also allows existing settings to be deleted. The DeleteValue function will remove a setting from the class, causing any subsequent calls to GetValue to return the provided default once again. To remove *all* the stored settings, the ClearValues function can be called. All the settings that have been previously written will be erased.

Inside the SettingsManager class, the values that are passed in to be set are routed into a single version of the SetValue function, which expects its value to be of type string. Within this function, the value is written into a special collection provided by the phone called ApplicationSettings, contained within the System.IO.IsolatedStorage namespace. ApplicationSettings is a dictionary collection, and every item added to the dictionary is immediately written away into *isolated storage*, a special data storage system used within the phone. We will look at the implications of isolated storage in more detail in the "Reading and Writing Files in Isolated Storage" section later in this chapter.

■ **Note** As of this writing, when running on the emulator, the isolated storage is reset every time the emulator is closed. This can be frustrating because stored data does not persist from one emulator session to the next, but can also be useful as it presents an opportunity to test your game in an environment that has no previously written files or settings.

The SetValue function's code to add the setting values to the settings dictionary is shown in Listing 9–2.

Listing 9–2. Writing settings values into the ApplicationSettings dictionary

```
public void SetValue(string settingName, string value)
{
    // Convert the setting name to lower case so that names are case-insensitive
    settingName = settingName.ToLower();

    // Does a setting with this name already exist?
    if (IsolatedStorageSettings.ApplicationSettings.Contains(settingName))
    {
        // Yes, so update its value
        IsolatedStorageSettings.ApplicationSettings[settingName] = value;
    }
    else
    {
        // No, so add it
        IsolatedStorageSettings.ApplicationSettings.Add(settingName, value);
    }
}
```

The function first converts the settingName parameter into lowercase. This makes the settings case-insensitive, which can help avoid obscure problems later on. Once this is done, the ApplicationSettings dictionary is checked to see whether a setting with the specified name already exists. If it does, it is updated with the new value; otherwise, a new dictionary item is added.

Reading the settings is equally straightforward. The GetValue function, shown in Listing 9–3, checks to see whether an item with the specified settingName exists. If it does, its value is returned; otherwise, the provided defaultValue is returned instead.

Listing 9–3. Reading settings values back from the ApplicationSettings dictionary

```
public string GetValue(string settingName, string defaultValue)
{
    // Convert the setting name to lower case so that names are case-insensitive
    settingName = settingName.ToLower();

    // Does a setting with this name exist?
    if (IsolatedStorageSettings.ApplicationSettings.Contains(settingName))
    {
        // Yes, so return it
        return IsolatedStorageSettings.ApplicationSettings[settingName].ToString();
    }
    else
```

```
        {
            // No, so return the default value
            return defaultValue;
        }
    }
```

We can now set, update, and interrogate the settings for our game, but then we come to the next question: how do we allow the player to view and change the settings?

Displaying a Settings Screen

XNA has no built-in graphical user interface components, but we can easily create a simple user interface for maintaining settings using simple text labels. We can represent them using the GameFramework.TextObject class and can use code that we have already written to detect when the user clicks them. Each click can cycle the setting on to its next value. This is primitive but workable; you can enhance this system in your own games to add more sophisticated user interaction if you need to.

The problem that presents itself with this approach is what to do with all the other game objects that are already active. If we have a spaceship and showers of aliens and missiles scattered all over the screen, how do we suddenly switch from this environment into an entirely different screen displaying game settings?

The answer is to allow multiple sets of game objects to be maintained at once. When we are ready to switch to the settings screen, we tell the game framework to suspend its list of game objects, allowing us to set up another list—one that displays the text for each of the settings. Once we have finished with the settings screen, we tell the game framework to restore the suspended game objects, reactivating them so that the game continues from exactly where we left it.

■ **Note** Use this technique only when you actually need to return to the set of suspended game objects. If your game has finished and there is no need to return to it, simply clear the GameObjects collection instead. This saves .NET from having to keep all the obsolete objects alive. The exception is if you are going to recycle the suspended objects, in which case suspending them can save the need to create more objects later.

This is implemented in the game framework by allowing a *stack* of suspended game objects to be maintained. If we want to suspend the current set of objects (for example, the game itself) so that we can temporarily display another set (the objects that form the settings screen), we can *push* the main game's list of objects onto the stack. This clears the GameObjects collection so that it is empty, ready for objects for the settings screen to be added. Once we are done with the settings screen, we *pop* the stack, discarding the current game objects list (containing the objects for the settings screen) and restoring those objects that were placed on the stack earlier.

In this way, we can interrupt the active objects as many times as we want and always return back to them later. It is similar in effect to clicking a link in a web browser to reach a second page and then clicking the Back button to return to the previous page.

.NET provides a generic Stack class, and we will use this to implement the game object stack. As the game objects are implemented as a list of GameObjectBase classes, the stack will be a stack of lists of GameObjectBase. Each item on the stack holds a complete collection of game objects, rather than the individual objects themselves. The declaration for the stack, taken from the top of the GameHost class, is shown in Listing 9–4.

Listing 9–4. The stack variable onto which collections of game objects will be pushed

```
// A stack of gameobjects lists so that we can work with multiple object sets
private Stack<List<GameObjectBase>> _gameObjectsStack;
```

To provide access to the stack, we provide two related methods inside GameHost. The first of these, PushGameObjects, places the current GameObjects list on to the top of the stack and creates a new list for the game to work with. The second, PopGameObjects, discards the current GameObjects list and replaces it with the list on the top of the stack. These methods can be seen in Listing 9–5.

Listing 9–5. Pushing and popping the game object list stack

```
public void PushGameObjects()
{
    // Push the current GameObjects list on to the stack
    _gameObjectsStack.Push(GameObjects);
    // Create a new empty list for the game to work with
    GameObjects = new List<GameObjectBase>();
}

public void PopGameObjects()
{
    // Pop the list from the top of the stack and set it as the GameObjects list
    GameObjects = _gameObjectsStack.Pop();
}
```

The tools for switching between sets of objects are now available, so our games need to know how to use them. Switching can be implemented by keeping track of what the game is currently doing. Is it playing, is it showing the settings, or is it doing something else (perhaps showing a title screen or high score table)? We can track this by creating an enumeration with an item for each of these modes, and updating it as the player moves from one mode to another.

The code required to manage this can be seen in the Settings example project. The enumeration and mode variables are declared at the top of the SettingsGame class and can be seen in Listing 9–6. The mode defaults to GameModes.Playing because this is the state in which the game begins.

Listing 9–6. Keeping track of the current game mode

```
// An enumeration containing the game modes that we can support
private enum GameModes
{
    Playing,
    Settings
};
// The active game mode
private GameModes _gameMode = GameModes.Playing;
```

The game is initialized and set up exactly as normal, remembering to load any existing settings but ignoring the presence of the settings mode. Within the Update and Draw methods, however, we execute a switch statement against the current mode, and call off to separate functions for each game mode. This allows us to clearly separate the functionality that each mode requires from each of the other modes.

When the game is playing, its update function (Update_Playing) waits for the user to touch the screen. When this happens, it calls into a function named EnterSettingsMode so that the settings screen can be initialized. EnterSettingsMode does three things: it pushes the game objects list on to the stack, updates the _gameMode variable to indicate that it is in Settings mode, and then adds its own game objects required for the settings page.

317

As soon as this happens, the game switches to displaying the settings. All drawing and updating of the original game objects is suspended as they are no longer present in the GameObjects list.

On the new screen, the user can now amend the settings as required. But how do they leave the settings page? The model used by Windows Phone 7 is to press the hardware Back button to leave a page and go back to the previous page, and so this is the mechanism that we will use.

This is very easy to implement. The whole time we have been working with XNA, the small piece of code shown in Listing 9–7 has been present at the beginning of our Update function. This monitors the Back button, and when it detects that it has been pressed, it exits the game.

Listing 9–7. Closing the game when the Back button is pressed

```
// Allows the game to exit
if (GamePad.GetState(PlayerIndex.One).Buttons.Back == ButtonState.Pressed)
{
    this.Exit();
}
```

It is essential that pressing the Back button from certain game screens does actually close the game, as without this the game will fail Microsoft's certification guidelines required for submission to the Windows Phone Marketplace (which we will discuss, along with more detail about Back button handling, in Chapter 15). If the user has navigated into a sub-screen such as the settings screen, however, we can use this button to allow backward navigation to the earlier screen—again, exactly like in a web browser.

We therefore check for this button within the Update_Settings function. When it is detected, instead of closing the game we call a function named LeaveSettingsMode. This function reads the user's new settings values back into the SettingsManager object, saves them to isolated storage, sets the game mode back to Playing, and pops the game objects from the stack. Everything is exactly back to how it was before the user entered the settings screen. This can be seen in Listing 9–8.

Listing 9–8. Handling the Back button when in Settings mode

```
// Allows the user to return to the main game
if (GamePad.GetState(PlayerIndex.One).Buttons.Back == ButtonState.Pressed)
{
    LeaveSettingsMode();
}
```

Creating the Settings User Interface

XNA offers a huge amount of functionality, but one of the things that it lacks is a user interface. Fortunately for the settings page we can keep things fairly simple and implement our own primitive user interface using TextObject instance.

Each instance will be configured with a position, a value, and a set of available values. Each time the object is tapped on the screen, it will cycle to the next available value, looping past the final value back to the beginning.

Clearly, this is not at all sophisticated and could be enhanced to support all sorts of other features, but this is left as an exercise for the reader. These simple classes will suffice for this example and also for many games.

So that the game framework can identify settings objects (as we will see in a moment), they are implemented as a new class in the game framework. SettingsItemObject inherits from TextObject, as shown in Figure 9–1.

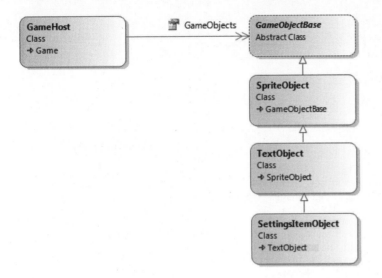

Figure 9–1. SettingsItemObject's position in the game framework object hierarchy

SettingsItemObject adds the following four public properties to those provided by the base TextObject:

- Name is the name of the setting as it will be stored in SettingsManager.

- Title is the display name for the setting.

- Values is an array of strings that form the permitted list of values for the setting.

- SelectedValue is the currently selected value.

All these properties are also required to be passed as parameters to the class constructor.

The class also exposes a new public method: SelectNextValue. Each time it is called, the object cycles to the next value within the Values array, looping back to the start once the final item is passed.

To use the settings screen, we need to add three new pieces of functionality to the game: one to initialize and display the settings screen, another to allow the user to tap the settings items to update them, and a final piece to save the settings and return to the game. Let's look at how they are implemented.

Opening the Settings Screen

For our example we will simply tap the screen to open the settings screen. This won't be good enough for a real game, but we could implement a menu system, as described shortly in "Planning a Game's Navigation Model" to provide a more realistic system of access.

When the game detects a tap on the screen (in the Update_Playing function), it calls into the EnterSettingsMode function, shown in Listing 9–9 (though the code shown here omits several of the items for brevity—the full list can be seen in the example project's SettingsGame class).

Listing 9–9. Entering Settings mode

```
private void EnterSettingsMode()
{
    // Push the game's objects onto the object stack
    PushGameObjects();

    // Add the title
    GameObjects.Add(new TextObject(this, Fonts["WascoSans"], new Vector2(10, 10),
                                                            "Game Settings"));

    // Add some settings
    GameObjects.Add(new SettingsItemObject(this, new Vector2(30, 90), Fonts["WascoSans"],
                        0.9f, SettingsManager, "Speed", "Speed",
                        "1", new string[] { "1", "2", "3" }));
    GameObjects.Add(new SettingsItemObject(this, new Vector2(30, 140), Fonts["WascoSans"],
                        0.9f, SettingsManager, "Difficulty", "Difficulty",
                        "Medium", new string[] { "Easy", "Medium", "Hard" }));
    GameObjects.Add(new SettingsItemObject(this, new Vector2(30, 190), Fonts["WascoSans"],
                        0.9f, SettingsManager, "MusicVolume", "Music volume",
                        "Medium", new string[] { "Off", "Quiet", "Medium", "Loud" }));

    // Set the new game mode
    _gameMode = GameModes.Settings;
}
```

As this code shows, there are several new `SettingsItemObject` instances created, and a number of parameters are passed into the class constructor each time. These parameters are as follows:

- `game` is the game's `GameHost` instance.

- `position` is the display position for the settings item.

- `font` is the font to use to display the text.

- `scale` is a scaling value to apply to the text.

- `settingsManager` is the game's `SettingsManager` instance. The value of the setting will be automatically retrieved from this object before the item is displayed.

- `name` is the name of the setting within the `SettingsManager`.

- `title` is the name for the item to display onscreen (note the difference between this and the item's name for the music volume setting).

- `defaultValue` is used if no existing setting value can be found in the `SettingsManager` object; this value will be used as an initial value for the setting.

- `values` is an array of string values that will be cycled through when the user taps the settings item.

The result of this function is that the running game objects are all placed on to the stack, and a new set of objects is created to display the settings screen. All the actual settings items are created as `SettingsItemObject` instances. The game mode is changed from `Playing` to `Settings` so that the game knows that the settings screen is now active. The `Update_Settings` and `Draw_Settings` functions are now called in the game class each cycle, resulting in the settings page appearing as shown in Figure 9–2.

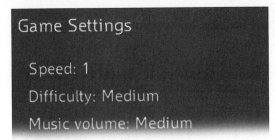

Figure 9–2. The Settings page

Updating the Settings Values

The user can change the value of any of the settings by simply tapping on its text onscreen. This is easily implemented by asking the GameHost to identify the selected object for each screen tap. If an object is found and is a SettingsItemObject, we can simply call its SelectNextValue method to move to the next available value.

The code to achieve this is performed in the Update_Settings function, shown in Listing 9–10.

Listing 9–10. Part of the Update_Settings function, allowing object values to be updated

```
GameObjectBase obj;
TouchCollection tc;

// Has the user touched the screen?
tc = TouchPanel.GetState();
if (tc.Count == 1 && tc[0].State == TouchLocationState.Pressed)
{
    // Find the object at the touch point
    obj = GetSpriteAtPoint(tc[0].Position);
    // Did we get a settings option object?
    if (obj is GameFramework.SettingsItemObject)
    {
        // Yes, so toggle it to the next value
        ((SettingsItemObject)obj).SelectNextValue();
    }
}
```

Nothing more is required to allow the objects to update themselves.

Leaving the Settings Screen

Once the settings screen is up and running, the player can change the settings as required and can then press the hardware Back button to leave the settings screen and return to the game. This is handled by calling the game's LeaveSettingsMode function, shown in Listing 9–11.

Listing 9–11. Leaving the Settings screen and returning to the game

```
private void LeaveSettingsMode()
{
    // Get and store the settings values
    SettingsManager.RetrieveValues();

    // Retrieve the previous game objects
    PopGameObjects();
    // Set the new game mode
    _gameMode = GameModes.Playing;

    // Update the speed of each ball
    foreach (GameObjectBase obj in GameObjects)
    {
        if (obj is BallObject)
        {
            ((BallObject)obj).Speed = SettingsManager.GetValue("Speed", 1);
        }
    }
}
```

The first thing that the function needs to do is retrieve the updated values back from the settings screen. This is easily achieved by calling the `SettingsManager.RetrieveValues` function. Each settings item is identifiable because it is of type (or is derived from type) `SettingsItemObject`, so `RetrieveValues` loops through the `GameObjects` collection looking for objects of this type. Each time it finds one, it reads out its setting name and value (both of which we provided as parameters to the object's constructor) and uses this to write the setting into the `SettingsManager` class.

Once this is done, the main game objects are then restored by calling `PopGameObjects`, and the game mode set back to `Playing`. The remainder of the code applies the modified Speed setting, updating the speed of all the balls in the game.

▨ **Note** Because this is just an example, the Speed setting is the only one that is actually observed by the project. In a real game, all the values would be considered and put into action in the `LeaveSettingsMode` function.

If you give the example project a try, you will see that the balls all observe whatever speed is selected in the settings screen. The settings are saved to storage when the game closes and automatically restored when it starts again. When you leave the settings screen, all the balls are present in exactly the positions they were in before the settings were displayed.

Planning a Game's Navigation Model

As has already been noted, tapping the main game screen is unlikely to be a satisfactory mechanism for entering the settings screen in a real game. Exactly how you structure navigation between different parts of the game is, of course, up to you and the needs of your game, but here is an approach that may work.

Open the game with a title page, displaying a welcome message and a game logo. Also on the page is a menu allowing the player to start the game, edit the settings, exit the game, and perhaps perform other tasks, too (such as viewing the high scores or the game's credits).

The player can select any of these items, and the game will react as requested. Wherever users end up, they can press the hardware Back button to return to the title page. They can then access settings and the other pages once again.

When returning to the title page from within an active game, the game should be suspended by pushing its objects on to the stack. Instead of a "start game" option, the menu should now offer "resume game" and "new game." This way, players can amend their settings and then return to the game, or can abandon the current game and start a new one.

Pressing the Back button while the title page is open will close the game and return the player to the phone's operating system pages.

This navigation model provides easy access to all areas of the game in a consistent and predictable fashion.

Adding a High Score Table

Another common requirement across many games is the ability to keep track of the highest scores that players have achieved. .NET provides some useful features to implement high scores (such as sortable collections into which we can place all our scores), but actually implementing the feature into a game requires a little effort, most of which is fairly unexciting—not what we want to be spending time addressing when we could be being creative instead.

To reduce the amount of work required, we can build support for high scores into the game framework. We won't make things too complicated, but our implementation will have the facility for keeping track of multiple tables at once if the game requires such a feature (for different difficulty levels, for example) and a very simple API so that the game doesn't require very much code to interact with the high scores.

The final feature that we will add is the ability to save the score tables to storage each time they are updated and load them back in each time the game is launched. Scores can therefore be stored indefinitely, providing a constant challenge to the player to better his or her earlier efforts.

All the code for maintaining and manipulating the high score table can be found in the GameFramework project for this chapter. Alongside this project is an example project named HighScores that demonstrates some user interaction with the high score table. A screenshot of a populated score table is shown in Figure 9–3.

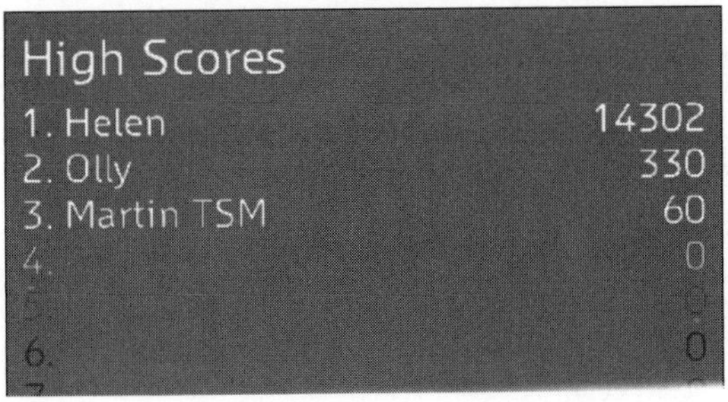

Figure 9–3. An example high score table display

Implementing the High Score Table

The high scores are implemented using three new classes in the game framework: HighScores, HighScoreTable and HighScoreEntry.

The first of these classes, HighScores, provides the top-level API for working with high scores. Its functions include loading and saving scores to and from storage, creating and obtaining individual high score tables, and a simple mechanism for displaying the scores from a table on the screen.

The HighScoreTable class represents a single table of scores (of which we may maintain several, as already mentioned). Its responsibilities are around maintaining the individual tables, allowing scores to be added and interrogated.

The final class, HighScoreEntry, represents a single score item within a high score table. It keeps track of the score and the player's name, as well as the date the score was achieved (the reason for which we will discuss shortly).

All three of these classes are declared with internal scope on their class constructors, preventing code outside the game framework from instantiating them. Instead, a single instance of HighScores can be accessed from the GameHost.HighScores property, and functions within this class and the HighScoreTable class allow instances of the other two objects to be created and manipulated. The relationships of the classes within the rest of the game framework can be seen in Figure 9–4.

Figure 9–4. *The high score classes within the game framework*

Defining Tables

Before the high score classes can be used for storing game scores, the tables within the high score environment must first be defined. This must be done before any scores are added, and also before scores are loaded from storage.

The tables are added by calling the HighScores.InitializeTable function. There are two overloads for this function: the first overload expects a table name to be supplied along with the number of score entries that it is to hold; the second overload also expects a description of the table.

If you decide to implement multiple tables for your game, each one must be given a different name. You may want to base these on your game's difficulty levels (for example, Easy, Normal, and Difficult) or on some other factor that is significant to the game. These values will be used as a key into a dictionary of HighScoreTable objects, so will need to be provided again later when you want to update or read one of the tables.

If you provide a description, it will be stored alongside the table for later retrieval.

Each table can store an arbitrary number of score entries, depending on the needs of your game. Many games will only store ten entries per table, but there is nothing stopping you from storing hundreds if you want.

References to the individual tables can be obtained by calling the HighScores.GetTable function, passing in the name of the table to be returned. This returns a HighScoreTable object, with which the scores inside the named table can be manipulated.

Working with High Score Tables

Having created a table and retrieved a reference to its object, the next set of functions is within the HighScoreTable class.

New scores can be added by calling the AddEntry function, passing in the name and the score. Providing the score is high enough to make it into the table, a new HighScoreEntry object will be added into the class's private _scoreEntries list, and the entry object returned back to the calling procedure. If the score is not good enough to qualify, the entry list is left alone, and the function returns null. The table will always be sorted by score, so there is no need for external code to sort the entries.

All high scores are date stamped, so if there is a collision between the new score and an existing score, the existing score will be given precedence and will appear higher in the list than the new entry.

Accompanying this function is another useful function, ScoreQualifies, which returns a boolean value that indicates whether the supplied score is good enough to make it on to the table. The return value from this function can be used to determine whether users should be prompted to enter their name or not.

A read-only collection of all the scores can be retrieved by querying the Entries property. The description of the table (if one was set when it was initialized) can be retrieved from the Description property.

High Score Entries

Each entry into the high score table is represented as an instance of the HighScoreEntry class. This class stores the name, score, and date for each entry, allowing the contents of the table to be read and displayed.

In addition to storing these properties, the class also implements the .NET IComparer interface. This interface is used to provide a simple mechanism for the HighScoreTable class to sort the entries in its table. The Compare method first sorts the items by score and then by date, ensuring that higher scores appear first, and for matching scores, older entries appear first.

Clearing Existing High Scores

If you decide that you want to clear the high scores (preferably at the user's request), you can call the Clear method of either the HighScores object (which will clear all entries from all tables) or an individual HighScoreTable object (which will clear that table alone).

Loading and Saving Scores

The final part of the HighScores data API is the ability to load and save the scores to and from the device so that they persist from one game session to the next. These functions are accessed using the LoadScores and SaveScores methods of the HighScores class.

Prior to calling either of these functions, however, the game can choose to set the file name within which the scores will be loaded and saved via the FileName property. If no file name is specified, the class defaults to using a name of Scores.dat. Being able to store high scores in different files allows for different sets of scores to be written should this be of benefit.

The high score data is written as an XML document, the structure of which is shown in Listing 9–12. A new <table> element is created for each defined table, and inside is an <entries> element containing an <entry> for each score within the table.

Listing 9–12. The content of a stored high scores file

```xml
<?xml version="1.0" encoding="utf-16"?>
<highscores>
    <table>
        <name>Normal</name>
        <entries>
            <entry>
                <score>14302</score>
                <name>Helen</name>
                <date>2010-09-21T21:27:46</date>
            </entry>
            <entry>
                <score>330</score>
                <name>Olly</name>
                <date>2010-09-21T21:27:46</date>
            </entry>
            <entry>
                <score>60</score>
                <name>Martin TSM</name>
                <date>2010-09-21T21:27:46</date>
            </entry>
        </entries>
    </table>
    <table>
        <name>Difficult</name>
        <entries />
    </table>
</highscores>
```

The code within SaveScores required to generate this XML is fairly straightforward, looping through the tables and the score entries, and adding the details of each into the XML output. The output is constructed with an XmlWriter object by the code shown in Listing 9–13.

Listing 9–13. Building the XML for the high score file

```csharp
        StringBuilder sb = new StringBuilder();
        XmlWriter xmlWriter = XmlWriter.Create(sb);
        HighScoreTable table;

        // Begin the document
        xmlWriter.WriteStartDocument();
        // Write the HighScores root element
        xmlWriter.WriteStartElement("highscores");

        // Loop for each table
        foreach (string tableName in _highscoreTables.Keys)
        {
            // Retrieve the table object for this table name
            table = _highscoreTables[tableName];

            // Write the Table element
            xmlWriter.WriteStartElement("table");
            // Write the table Name element
```

```
        xmlWriter.WriteStartElement("name");
        xmlWriter.WriteString(tableName);
        xmlWriter.WriteEndElement();      // name

        // Create the Entries element
        xmlWriter.WriteStartElement("entries");

        // Loop for each entry
        foreach (HighScoreEntry entry in table.Entries)
        {
            // Make sure the entry is not blank
            if (entry.Date != DateTime.MinValue)
            {
                // Write the Entry element
                xmlWriter.WriteStartElement("entry");
                // Write the score, name and date
                xmlWriter.WriteStartElement("score");
                xmlWriter.WriteString(entry.Score.ToString());
                xmlWriter.WriteEndElement();      // score
                xmlWriter.WriteStartElement("name");
                xmlWriter.WriteString(entry.Name);
                xmlWriter.WriteEndElement();      // name
                xmlWriter.WriteStartElement("date");
                xmlWriter.WriteString(entry.Date.ToString("yyyy-MM-ddTHH:mm:ss"));
                xmlWriter.WriteEndElement();      // date
                // End the Entry element
                xmlWriter.WriteEndElement();      // entry
            }
        }

        // End the Entries element
        xmlWriter.WriteEndElement();      // entries

        // End the Table element
        xmlWriter.WriteEndElement();      // table
    }

    // End the root element
    xmlWriter.WriteEndElement();      // highscores
    xmlWriter.WriteEndDocument();

    // Close the xml writer, which will put the finished document into the stringbuilder
    xmlWriter.Close();
```

■ **Tip** The comments present on each call to WriteEndElement help to clarify exactly which element is ending. Reading the code later on becomes much easier.

We will look at where the data is actually written to in a moment, but first let's take a quick look at the code that processes the XML after reading it back in. It uses the LINQ to XML functions to quickly and easily parse the content. LINQ to XML (LINQ being short for *Language INtegrated Query* and pronounced as *link*) allows the XML elements to be interrogated using a syntax similar in many ways to a database SQL statement, and it provides a simple mechanism for us to loop through each setting element and read out the name and value contained within.

The LINQ to XML code for loading the scores is shown in Listing 9–14. This code loops through all the entry elements so that we obtain an item in the result collection for each entry in the file. Besides reading out the details of the entry itself (from the name, score, and date elements), it also reads the entry's table name. This is achieved by looking at the parent node of the entry (the entries node), looking at its parent (the table node), and then retrieving the value of its name element. Once these these four values have been identified, the foreach loop that follows can easily add each score into the appropriate high score table.

Listing 9–14. Loading saved high score data from the stored XML document

```
// Parse the content XML that was loaded
XDocument xDoc = XDocument.Parse(fileContent);
// Create a query to read the score details from the xml
var result = from c in xDoc.Root.Descendants("entry")
                select new
                {
                    TableName = c.Parent.Parent.Element("name").Value,
                    Name = c.Element("name").Value,
                    Score = c.Element("score").Value,
                    Date = c.Element("date").Value
                };
// Loop through the resulting elements
foreach (var el in result)
{
    // Add the entry to the table.
    table = GetTable(el.TableName);
    if (table != null)
    {
        table.AddEntry(el.Name, int.Parse(el.Score), DateTime.Parse(el.Date));
    }
}
```

Reading and Writing Files in Isolated Storage

Everything is now present to create the high score file, parse the file, and retrieve its contents, but there is still the issue of actually reading from and writing to files on the device. Let's address that now.

Windows Phone 7, unlike Windows Mobile before it, has a *closed storage system*. Applications have access to multiple files and directories just like on a desktop PC, but they can access only files that they have created. Files from other applications or from the operating system are inaccessible.

This system is called *isolated storage*, and its purpose is to prevent applications from causing problems for one another or performing actions within the device that they are not permitted to perform. It is the same system that Silverlight uses when running on desktop PCs; isolated storage allows applications to save information that they need to disk, but prevents them from accessing the user's private files or any other information that may be stored on the computer.

In most cases, this storage mechanism won't present any problems for Windows Phone 7 games, but one significant implication is that the System.IO.File namespace that you might be familiar with using from programming .NET on the desktop cannot be used from the phone.

Instead, file access is performed using another class within the System.IO.IsolatedStorage namespace. The class is called IsolatedStorageFile, instances of which are obtained by calling the class's static GetUserStoreForApplication method.

Once an instance has been obtained, it can be used to perform the file-based operations that you would expect to be able to use: creating files, reading and writing files, checking whether files exist, creating directories, reading lists of file and directory names, and so on. The MSDN documentation contains plenty of information on this class if you want to learn more about it.

We will thus call on this class to read and write our high score XML data. Listing 9–15 shows the remainder of the SaveScores function, writing the constructed XML (in the StringBuilder object named sb) to the device's isolated storage.

Listing 9–15. Writing the settings XML document to isolated storage

```
// Get access to the isolated storage
using (IsolatedStorageFile store = IsolatedStorageFile.GetUserStoreForApplication())
{
    // Create a file and attach a streamwriter
    using (StreamWriter sw = new StreamWriter(store.CreateFile(FileName)))
    {
        // Write the XML string to the streamwriter
        sw.Write(sb.ToString());
    }
}
```

The code required to load the high score file from isolated storage is shown in Listing 9–16. This listing includes a simple check to see whether the file actually exists prior to loading it.

Listing 9–16. Checking for and loading the XML document from isolated storage

```
string settingsContent;

// Get access to the isolated storage
using (IsolatedStorageFile store = IsolatedStorageFile.GetUserStoreForApplication())
{
    if (!store.FileExists(FileName))
    {
        // The score file doesn't exist
        return;
    }
    // Read the contents of the file
    using (StreamReader sr = new StreamReader(
                                        store.OpenFile(FileName, FileMode.Open)))
    {
        fileContent = sr.ReadToEnd();
    }
}
```

We can now update, load, and save the high scores for our game. All we need to do now is actually use them, and this is what we will look into next.

Using the HighScore Classes in a Game

All the data structures are present and correct, but they still need to be actually wired up into a game. The HighScores example project shows how you can do this.

It begins by initializing the high score tables and loading any existing scores in its InitializeMethod, as shown in Listing 9–17.

Listing 9–17. Initializing the high score table

```
// Initialize and load the high scores
HighScores.InitializeTable("Normal", 20);
HighScores.InitializeTable("Difficult", 20);
HighScores.LoadScores();
```

Next, the game begins. The current game mode is managed using a class-level variable named _gameMode, exactly as we discussed with regard to the game settings screen earlier in this chapter. In our example, the game is fairly short-lived, however, and it immediately ends. A random score is assigned to the player to help you see how the high score table works.

Inside ResetGame, after creating the random score, the code adds some TextObject instances to the game to tell the player that the game is over and provide some information about the score. It calls into the HighScoreTable.GetScore function to determine whether the player's score is good enough, and displays an appropriate message onscreen.

The update loop then waits for the user to tap the screen before continuing. When Update_Playing detects this tap, it calls the EnterHighScoresMode function to prepare the game for displaying and updating the high score table.

EnterHighScoresMode, shown in Listing 9–18, first updates the game mode to indicate that we are now working with the high score table and then checks again to see whether the score qualifies for a new high score entry. If it does, it opens the text entry dialog, as described in the "Prompting the User to Enter Text" section in Chapter 4. The dialog is given some suitable captions and also reads the default text value from the game settings. We'll look at this again in a moment.

Alternatively, if the score isn't good enough, it calls into the ResetHighscoreTableDisplay function, which initializes the scores for display onscreen. You will see the code for this function shortly.

Listing 9–18. Preparing the game to display or update the high score table

```
private void EnterHighScoresMode()
{
    // Set the new game mode
    _gameMode = GameModes.HighScores;

    // Did the player's score qualify?
    if (HighScores.GetTable("Normal").ScoreQualifies(_score))
    {
        // Yes, so display the input dialog
        // Make sure the input dialog is not already visible
        if (!(Guide.IsVisible))
        {
            // Show the input dialog to get text from the user
            Guide.BeginShowKeyboardInput(PlayerIndex.One, "High score achieved",
                                "Please enter your name",
                                SettingsManager.GetValue("PlayerName", ""),
                                InputCallback, null);
        }
    }
}
```

```
        else
        {
            // Show the highscores now. No score added so nothing to highlight
            ResetHighscoreTableDisplay(null);
        }
    }
}
```

If the text entry dialog was displayed, it calls into the `InputCallback` function after text entry is complete, as shown in Listing 9–19. Assuming that a name was entered, the callback function adds the name to the high score table and retains the `HighScoreEntry` object that is returned before saving the updated scores. Once this is done, the `ResetHighscoreTableDisplay` function is called to show the high scores, passing the newly added entry as its parameter.

Listing 9–19. Responding to the completion of the text entry dialog

```
void InputCallback(IAsyncResult result)
{
    string sipContent = Guide.EndShowKeyboardInput(result);
    HighScoreEntry newEntry = null;

    // Did we get some input from the user?
    if (sipContent != null)
    {
        // Add the name to the highscore
        newEntry = HighScores.GetTable("Normal").AddEntry(sipContent, _score);
        // Save the scores
        HighScores.SaveScores();
        // Store the name for later use
        SettingsManager.SetValue("PlayerName", sipContent);          }
    // Show the highscores now and highlight the new entry if we have one
    ResetHighscoreTableDisplay(newEntry);
}
```

Notice that the name that was entered is stored into `SettingsManager` for later use. This is a nice little feature that allows players' names to be remembered between gaming sessions, saving them having to type it in again the next time they play. This is also an example of using `SettingsManager` for system settings that aren't directly altered by the player via a settings screen.

Finally, there is the `ResetHighscoreTableDisplay` function that was called twice in the previous listings. It sets up the `GameObjects` collection to show all the scores for the high score table. It uses a function named `CreateTextObjectsForTable` inside the `HighScores` class to assist with this. This function simply adds a series of text objects containing the score details, but it accepts among its parameters a start and end color (used for the first and last score items, with the items in between fading in color between the two); a highlight entry (when the player has just added a new score, pass its `HighScoreEntry` object here to highlight the entry within the table); and a highlight color. There is no requirement to use this function, and the high score classes can be used purely as a data manipulation structure if desired, but it can be a time saver if its functionality is sufficient for your game.

Listing 9–20. Responding to the completion of the text entry dialog

```
private void ResetHighscoreTableDisplay(HighScoreEntry highlightEntry)
{
    // Clear any existing game objects
    GameObjects.Clear();

    // Add the title
```

```
        GameObjects.Add(new TextObject(this, Fonts["WascoSans"],
                                        new Vector2(10, 10), "High Scores"));

        // Add the score objects
        HighScores.CreateTextObjectsForTable("Normal", Fonts["WascoSans"], 0.8f, 80, 30,
                            Color.White, Color.Blue, highlightEntry, Color.Yellow);
    }
```

Reusing Game Components

It is very easy to find yourself rewriting sections of code over and over again as you develop games, and each time you write things slightly differently or change how things work. Creating reusable components such as those in this chapter can save you the effort of reinventing these same concepts in each new project that you create.

Even though writing reusable components such as these may require a little extra work, you'll be pleased that you made the effort when you plug them into your future projects because the overall amount of development time will be decreased (plus you'll have consistency in the appearance and functionality of your games).

■ ■ ■

CHAPTER 10

The Application Life Cycle

This chapter deals with an area that you will almost certainly want to factor into your game in order for it to work as your users will expect. It covers what happens when your game loses focus on the device.

One of the more controversial decisions that Microsoft made about the Windows Phone 7 operating system is regarding its multitasking capabilities. Clearly, it is capable of multitasking, and some system applications run in the background the whole time, but third-party applications such as those that we can write are not permitted to multitask. When they lose focus, they completely stop executing.

The situation is slightly worse even than this; they don't simply stop executing, but they are actually closed. Managed applications written in .NET do not persist in the background at all. This clearly saves device resources and prevents unexpected battery drain, but it is a real nuisance in terms of maintaining the state of a game.

If people playing your game are interrupted by a phone call or have to quickly switch over to the calendar to set up an appointment, the chances are that they will want to return to where they were in your game and continue from where they left off. Unfortunately, the game was closed as soon as they navigated away from it. The onus is upon us to perform whatever steps are necessary to restore the game to its previous state once it is reactivated.

This state management requirement is a reasonably complex area of functionality, but is essential for consideration in your games. It is also something best implemented into your game as soon as possible so that it can be constantly tested during development. Trying to add this feature into a game that has already been written can be time-consuming at best, and nearly impossible at worse.

The Effects of Losing Focus

Let's start by understanding the problem. Load up the HighScores example project from the previous chapter and start it running (on the emulator or on a real device). Once it has launched, click the phone's hardware Back button and observe what happens. The phone returns to the home screen, and the Visual Studio IDE breaks out of run mode and returns to edit mode. Clearly, the game has stopped running. You can see, therefore, that clicking the Back button while in your game explicitly closes the application.

■ **Tip** If you are working in the emulator, you can use its keyboard shortcuts to activate the hardware buttons instead of clicking with the mouse. F1 clicks the Back button, F2 clicks the Windows button, and F3 clicks the Search button.

Now relaunch the project from the IDE. Once it is running and displaying the blue Game over screen, click the Windows hardware button. The phone once again returns to the home screen, but this time the IDE stays in run mode, even though the game looks like it has closed. Now click the hardware Back button. After a brief pause, the "Game Over" screen reappears.

But hold on. Didn't we just say that Windows Phone 7 applications always close when they lose the focus? This certainly isn't what appears to have just happened. Both the phone and Visual Studio appear to have indicated that the game was suspended and then restarted. What is happening?

The answer is that the game *was* closed. Visual Studio recognizes that the user has not explicitly closed it, and that it was closed because it lost focus. To help reconnect to the game when the user navigates back to it through the historical application stack on the device, it remains in run mode. When the user does navigate back, the application relaunches on the phone, and Visual Studio detects this and connects to the relaunched application. This gives the impression that it is the same application session that has been reconnected.

The important fact is that *the application was still closed*. When Visual Studio reconnects to the application on the device, it is connecting to an entirely new instance of the application. *All* data that was stored in the previous session is lost, and unless we do something to persist it, it cannot be recovered.

You can see this more clearly in the HighScores example project by tapping the screen when prompted and entering your name so that the orange Highscores screen is displayed. Now press the Windows button, and then the Back button. The game has clearly lost track of what it was doing because it has reset back to the blue Game over screen.

This procedure of deactivating and then restarting an application is known as *tombstoning*. When the user navigates away from the game, Windows Phone leaves a marker (a *tombstone*) behind to identify the game on the application stack. When the Back button is pressed so that the user navigates back through this application stack, Windows Phone 7 will find this marker and use it to determine that your game should be reactivated.

To allow the game to resume from where it left off, we need to get our code to save away any important state information inside this tombstone and then retrieve this data when the game relaunches. In this section, we will discuss the mechanisms around this goal and explore a strategy for achieving it.

■ **Note** In some games, it is not practical to completely maintain the state of all objects because their complexity might simply be too great to manage or they might contain internal data that is not accessible to your game code. Under these circumstances, the best that you can do is allow regular *checkpoints* (the game state is recorded at a point where it can be reasonably reconstructed). The player might lose a small amount of game progress as a result, but will still return to a recent known point within the game. Be aware of the potential for cheating that this might introduce, however: navigating away as soon as they lose a life and then returning to a prior checkpoint might make the game easier than you expected!

Life Cycle Events

Let's start by taking a close look at how we can hook into the four application life cycle events. These events cover the application starting up, closing down, deactivating, and reactivating. The code from this section can be found in the Tombstoning example project accompanying this chapter.

The Launching Event

When a game launches completely from scratch, the *launching* event will be triggered. This event can be used as an opportunity to load or initialize any data that is only required when the game is being started without any previous tombstoned session being present.

■ **Note** The launching event is fired after the `Initialize` and `LoadContent` methods have both been called, so you can safely refer to any data that those methods have initialized in your launching event code.

The Closing Event

The *closing* event fires when your game is closing down. This is in response to the game properly exiting because the user pressed the Back button while the game was playing, resulting in a call to the `Game.Exit` function (such as the call that is by default present at the beginning of the `Update` function within the main game class).

This event can be used to store away any persistent data that will be needed the next time the game is run.

■ **Caution** You cannot rely on the closing event always being called. It is possible for the user to navigate away from your game and for it to never be reactivated. Any essential data that needs to be retained should either be stored into isolated storage as soon as it changes (as we have done for both the `SettingsManager` and `HighScore` object data) or should be written by both the closing event and the deactivated event.

You might want to store the complete game state to isolated storage in this event so that it can be resumed the next time the player launches your game. Some types of games will benefit from this; others can happily restart in a default state with any previous game data discarded.

The Deactivated Event

When the user navigates away from your game (or is taken away by an external event, such as an incoming phone call), the *deactivated* event will fire. This event indicates that your game is about to be tombstoned and gives you an opportunity to prepare.

There are two ways in which data can be stored in this event, and you might want to use both of them.

The first storage mechanism is for *persistent data* that is shared between consecutive sessions of the game and that is written by your game code to isolated storage. Any data that needs to be retrieved later on, even if the game is never reactivated, should be stored in this way.

The second mechanism is for *transient data* (data that is required only by this particular instance of the game should it be reactivated). Instead of writing this data to isolated storage, it can be written into a *state* object, the contents of which can then be recovered if the game is reactivated (though there is no guarantee that it ever will be). There are restrictions around the type of data that can be placed into the state object, as you will see shortly.

However you store your data, the most important thing is to store it quickly when a game is deactivating. If your game takes too long, the operating system will kill it, even if it is still working. Deactivation is not the time to perform any calculations or other unnecessary tasks; the event code needs to focus solely on storing state and finishing as fast as it can.

There is no guarantee that a deactivated game will ever be reactivated again. The game can be relaunched from the start menu (in which case the deactivated game's tombstone would be discarded), or the user can navigate far enough away from the tombstone that it is considered too old and purged from memory.

The Activated Event

The final life cycle event is the *activated* event, which is triggered when the user returns to a previously deactivated game by pressing the Back button until the tombstoned game comes back into focus.

During this event, data can be read from isolated storage and/or from the state object in order to put the game back into a usable state ready to continue execution.

The activated event and the launching event are mutually exclusive; only one or the other will ever fire when your game is starting up.

▓ **Note** Under certain conditions, Windows Phone 7 may deactivate your game and then reactivate it without actually closing it in between. You should ensure that your game is written so that its activation will work even if the game state is still present.

Handling the Life Cycle Events

All four of these events can be intercepted by adding event handlers in your game code. The event handlers are added to the `Microsoft.Phone.Shell.PhoneApplicationService.Current` object, as shown in Listing 10–1, whose code is taken from the `TombstoneEvents` example project (unrelated code has been removed from this listing so that we can focus on just the event handling code).

Listing 10–1. Setting up the life cycle event handlers

```
using Microsoft.Phone.Shell;

namespace TombstoneEvents
{
    public class TombstoneEventsGame : GameHost
    {
        public TombstoneEventsGame()
        {
            // Set up application life cycle event handlers
            PhoneApplicationService.Current.Launching += GameLaunching;
            PhoneApplicationService.Current.Closing += GameClosing;
            PhoneApplicationService.Current.Deactivated += GameDeactivated;
            PhoneApplicationService.Current.Activated += GameActivated;
        }
```

```
        private void GameLaunching(object sender, LaunchingEventArgs e)
        {
            System.Diagnostics.Debug.WriteLine("Game launching");
        }

        private void GameClosing(object sender, ClosingEventArgs e)
        {
            System.Diagnostics.Debug.WriteLine("Game closing");
        }

        private void GameDeactivated(object sender, DeactivatedEventArgs e)
        {
            System.Diagnostics.Debug.WriteLine("Game deactivated");
        }

        private void GameActivated(object sender, ActivatedEventArgs e)
        {
            System.Diagnostics.Debug.WriteLine("Game activated");
        }
    }
}
```

■ **Note** In order to use the `Microsoft.Phone.Shell` classes, you will need to add a reference in your game project to both `Microsoft.Phone` and to `System.Windows`. Without these references, your code will not compile.

The event handlers are called each time one of the life cycle events is triggered. We will integrate some of this functionality into the game framework shortly and make it easier to respond to these events as a result, but the code in Listing 10–1 shows the underlying mechanism to access the events.

Seeing the Events in Action

Let's run up the `TombstoneEvents` example project and spend a little time experimenting with the sequence in which the life cycle events fire. Each event writes to the Visual Studio debug output stream, so it is easy to see what is happening.

The first time you launch the project, it displays the text Game launching as the launching event is fired. At this stage, you can click the Back button to exit the program; this time it displays Game closing to indicate that the game is shutting down rather than being tombstoned. Visual Studio returns to edit mode as the project stops running.

Now try running the project again, but this time press the Windows button after it starts up. Once again, the phone returns to the start page, but this time we navigated away from the game rather than closing it. The debug stream now shows Game deactivated instead of Game closing. The game has been tombstoned. It is not running (it was terminated just the same as before), but the tombstone marker has been left in the application stack.

■ **Caution** Notice that the Visual Studio IDE is still in run mode when the game is tombstoned. It is there to make it easier to reconnect to the game if and when it is reactivated. It does not mean that the game is still running (it is not; it was still closed completely and has lost all its state). Don't let the fact that the IDE continues in run mode confuse you into thinking that the game is running in the background.

To return to the tombstoned game, click the Back button. The phone navigates back through the application stack, finds the game's tombstone marker and reactivates the game. This time, the game shows Game activated instead of Game launching. The game has still started absolutely from scratch, though. Because the Activated event fired instead of the Launching event, it is our cue to read the tombstoned data back into the application, and you will see how this is done shortly.

One last thing to try is launching the game and tombstoning it once more by pressing the Windows button. This time, instead of pressing Back to return to the game, relaunch another instance of the game by clicking the circled arrow icon from the phone's start page and then clicking the game's icon in the application list, as shown in Figure 10–1.

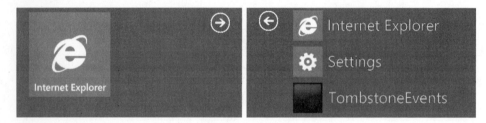

Figure 10–1. Starting a new instance of the tombstoned game

When a new instance launches like this, the existing tombstoned instance is completely discarded, and the new instance starts by firing its Launched event rather than its Activated event. Visual Studio returns to edit mode, and the tombstoned game instance cannot be reactivated by repeatedly using the Back button. This first instance is an example of a deactivated application that will never be reactivated.

Now that we have seen how the application life cycle works, let's look at how to use it to allow state to persist between sessions when the game is tombstoned.

Persisting Session State

So what can we do to allow our game to pick up where it left off after it is reactivated? Clearly we can hook into the Deactivate and Activate events and use them to store information about what our game is doing, but what is the best way to do this?

One option is to write all the information about our game to a file in isolated storage. When the game is activated, we could check for the presence of this file; if found, load it and read all the game data within it.

That process would certainly work, but there is another way: storing the game state in the PhoneApplicationService object. This second approach is recommended by Microsoft because it is faster to execute. Execution speed is important because if your game takes too long, the phone will decide that it isn't working and will abort the reactivation (and this problem will also cause your game to fail Microsoft's application certification guidelines required for entry into the Windows Phone Marketplace).

The PhoneApplicationService object (also found inside the Microsoft.Phone reference) contains a generic Dictionary, keyed by strings and storing objects, into which we can write values that are to be transferred from the deactivating session into the later activated session. And the good news is that we can simply drop objects into this dictionary in the Deactivate event, and then read them back in the Activate event. The bad news is that there are some important restrictions on the objects that can be placed within the dictionary, as we will see shortly.

Let's try this out first and see how it works. Inside the TombstoneEvents project, the Deactivated event contains a small amount of code that generates a random number into a variable named rand. It then puts the number into the PhoneApplicationService.Current.State dictionary. The code is shown in Listing 10–2.

Listing 10–2. Placing a randomly generated number into state storage in the Deactivated event

```
private void GameDeactivated(object sender, DeactivatedEventArgs e)
{
    System.Diagnostics.Debug.WriteLine("Game deactivated");

    // Generate a random number
    int rand = GameHelper.RandomNext(10000);
    // Write the number to the state object
    PhoneApplicationService.Current.State.Clear();
    PhoneApplicationService.Current.State.Add("RandomNumber", rand);
}
```

■ **Caution** Always remember to clear the State dictionary before you begin writing values to it, as shown in this listing. If an application is tombstoned for a second time, any content added from the first deactivation will still be present, resulting in key collisions or unexpected behavior.

Next to this data storage code is another piece of code inside the Activated event that reads the value back from the dictionary, as shown in Listing 10–3.

Listing 10–3. Reading a value back from state storage in the Activated event

```
private void GameActivated(object sender, ActivatedEventArgs e)
{
    System.Diagnostics.Debug.WriteLine("Game activated");

    // Recover the random number
    int rand = (int)PhoneApplicationService.Current.State["RandomNumber"];
}
```

Place breakpoints into these two functions so that you can trace through their execution and then start the project running. Once it opens, press the Windows button to navigate away from the game. The Deactivated event fires, and the random number is generated and added to the dictionary. Make a note of the number and then allow the project to continue running to completion.

On the phone, press the Back button to return to the tombstoned project. The breakpoint in the `Activated` event fires, and the value is retrieved back from the dictionary. The number that was generated is present and is restored back into the reactivated game.

This is the basis on which we will build our strategy for surviving being tombstoned.

The dictionary is not limited to numbers, of course: it can accept any object at all. However, only objects that are *serializable* can be added to the dictionary without errors occurring. Any non-serializable object will result in a failure to reactivate the game.

Objects can be serialized provided that

- they contain a public, parameterless constructor (though other constructors can be present, too).

- they only publicly expose fields and properties that use simple value types (including `structs` and enums) or other serializable objects.

Serialization recurses through all the public properties and fields within the object being serialized and then builds them all up into a representation that it can store away as a piece of data. When the data is later processed for deserialization, the object (and any subobjects it uses, and so on) is re-created just as it was before.

For many of the object properties that we use in our games, this will work very nicely: object positions, colors, vectors, matrices, and so on will serialize without any issues. However, all our game object classes have properties that contain objects that cannot be serialized (textures, fonts, and models); they all contain nonserializable data and will break if we try to add them to the state dictionary.

In order to be able to serialize these objects we need to overcome two problems: how to exclude the nonserializable elements from the serialization process and how to repopulate these nonserializable properties once the object is re-created. Let's see how these problems can be addressed.

Controlling Serialization

By default, objects that are placed into the state dictionary will have all their public fields and properties serialized. .NET provides a mechanism whereby instead of everything being included by the serialization operation, we can flag individual properties and fields that should be included. Those properties and fields that are not flagged will be excluded from serialization. By applying this mechanism to our classes, we can omit the flag from properties that return nonserializable objects such as textures, and the rest of the object will then be successfully persisted.

■ **Note** Fields and properties with `private` or `internal` scope are always ignored by the serialization process; only `public` fields and properties are included. Because it is usually a good idea to avoid public fields (it is impossible to later change them into public properties without breaking the binary interface), it is best practice to ensure that all values that need to be serialized are implemented using properties.

The inclusion and exclusion of properties within a class is enabled by applying the `DataContract` attribute to the class to be serialized. This attribute can be found within the `System.Runtime.Serialization` namespace, and to access it a reference must first be added to `System.Runtime.Serialization`, too.

Once this has been set up and the attribute applied to the class, the serialization process will only observe properties and fields that have had the DataMember attribute applied. Properties and fields that do not have this attribute will be excluded from serialization.

Listing 10–4 shows a very simple class definition that contains two public properties: a position vector and a Texture2D. The class has the DataContract attribute applied and the position has the DataMember attribute, but the texture property does not. This class can be serialized successfully, and will store the position away ready to be deserialized. The texture will not be serialized, and after deserialization will remain at its default null value.

Listing 10–4. Controlling which properties are included by the serialization process

```
[DataContract]
public class TestClass
{
    // Constructor
    public TestClass()
    {
    }

    // Public properties
    [DataMember]
    public Vector2 Position { get; set; }

    public Texture2D Texture { get; set; }
}
```

DataContracts and Inheritance

There are some important details about using the DataContract attribute with inheritance. If these details are incorrectly implemented in your game, you will find that serialization stops working properly, so it is important that you understand how .NET serializes classes under these conditions.

The DataContract attribute is not inheritable. If you apply it to a base class and then derive another class from that base class, the derived class will not have the DataContract attribute applied. Its default behavior therefore will be that all public properties defined within the derived class will be serialized, and all properties in the base class marked with the DataMember attribute will be serialized.

If you want the derived class to allow only some of its properties to be serialized, you must apply the DataContract to the derived class and then add the DataMember attribute to the appropriate properties. Specifying DataMember attributes without the class DataContract attribute will have no effect.

Derived classes cannot apply the DataContract attribute unless their base class also applies it.

And then there is one final complication that can cause all sorts of problems and confusion. If the class that is actually instantiated and serialized does not contain at least one serializable property (a public property marked for serialization and with a getter and a setter so that it can be both read and written), the object will not be serialized, even if its base classes do contain serializable properties. An override of a property from the base class does not count. Providing the derived class directly contains at least one serializable property of its own, it will then be fully serialized, including all the properties from the base classes.

If you create a derived game object class that doesn't have any properties that need to be serialized, you will need to add a dummy property so that the serialization process doesn't ignore the class. This process can be simple, as shown in Listing 10–5, but is essential for your objects to survive tombstoning.

Listing 10–5. Creating a dummy property to force serialization of a derived class with no other serializable properties

```
/// <summary>
/// A dummy property to force serialization of this class
/// </summary>
[DataMember]
public bool _SerializeDummy { get; set; }
```

If you are unsure as to whether your class is being serialized or not, put breakpoints on both the get and set parts of one of its serializable properties. If serialization is working, the get breakpoint will fire when the game is being deactivated, and the set breakpoint will fire when it is reactivated.

Also ensure that you have the Visual Studio IDE set to break on all exceptions because it can otherwise close your game during either of these events without an explanation. The IDE can be set in this way be selecting Debug/Exceptions from the main menu, and then checking the Common Language Runtime Exceptions Thrown box, as shown in Figure 10–2.

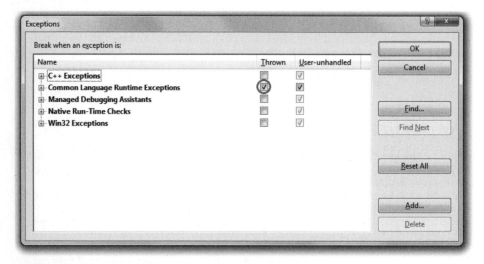

Figure 10–2. Setting the IDE to break on all thrown exceptions

Persisting Nonserializable Data

The DataContract attribute gets us past the problem of serializing the object, but we have lost the nonserializable data. When our object is restored, it will fail as soon as it tries to use the missing content.

We work around this by storing an identifier that represents the object rather than the object itself. For example, in the game framework, all the textures that we use are stored in the GameHost's Textures dictionary. Instead of serializing the texture, we can add an additional property that returns the *name* of the texture rather than the texture itself. The name will then be serialized, and will be provided to the deserialized object when the game is reactivated. Once the object knows the name, it can look it up in the dictionary and retrieve the actual texture object once again.

We're not quite there yet, however, because there is an additional complication: the deserialization process takes place before the game's Initialize or LoadContent methods fire. The game objects are therefore unable to read from the dictionaries because they haven't yet been populated. And in fact, the game object doesn't even have a reference to the GameHost object; this would normally be passed as a parameter to the class constructor, but because deserialization uses the parameterless constructor, this object is not available.

Instead we have to just store the content object name away as a string and retrieve the actual object later on once the game has had a chance to finish initializing itself.

Tombstoning in the Game Framework

There's a lot of complexity involved in getting a game to seamlessly resume after tombstoning, and unfortunately we can't really escape that. What we can do, though, is put as much of the complexity as possible into the game framework, allowing us to minimize the problem in our games.

The main task that the framework sets out to accomplish is the serialization of everything inside the GameObjects collection. A significant proportion of the game functionality is likely to be contained within these objects, so an easy and usable mechanism for persisting them will solve a large proportion of the problems that a game faces when it is tombstoned.

Allowing the game to become serializable in this way requires a number of changes to the game framework classes; most of them are fairly small, but some involve a little more complexity. Let's address each of the changes so that we can understand how the game framework helps to support this process.

All the code described in this section can be found in the Tombstoning example project.

Setting up the GameHost Event Handlers

To save us having to add event handlers for the four application lifecycle events, the GameHost does this for us. It provides four virtual functions that can be overridden in the game itself to respond to the events when necessary. This is a minor enhancement, but does simplify the event processing.

Listing 10–6 shows the overrides required to produce the same debug output functionality present in the earlier TombstoneEvents project.

Listing 10–6. Controlling which properties are included by the serialization process

```
protected override void GameLaunching()
{
    System.Diagnostics.Debug.WriteLine("Game launching");
    base.GameLaunching();
}
protected override void GameClosing()
{
    System.Diagnostics.Debug.WriteLine("Game closing");
    base.GameClosing();
}
protected override void GameDeactivated()
{
    System.Diagnostics.Debug.WriteLine("Game deactivated");
    base.GameDeactivated();
}
protected override void GameActivated()
{
    System.Diagnostics.Debug.WriteLine("Game activated");
    base.GameActivated();
}
```

Preparing the Classes for Serialization

For convenience, all the GameObjectBase-derived classes that we have created have used parameterized constructors into which various essential pieces of information have been passed. For the objects to be serialized, they must have a parameterless constructor, so such a constructor has been added to all the game object classes.

To provide control over which properties are serialized, GameObjectBase has the DataContract attribute set. Each of the derived object classes has the attribute set too. All the appropriate serializable properties are marked with the DataMember attribute. These include the UpdateCount property in GameObjectBase; the position, origin, scale, color, angle, and layer depth properties of SpriteObject; and so on through the other object classes. The properties that cannot be serialized (those that store textures, models, fonts, sound effects, and songs) do not have the DataMember attribute; we will look at how these are handled next.

With the classes configured in this way, instances are ready to be serialized and restored.

Persisting Content References

Next up, we need to deal with how content objects are persisted during tombstoning. As we have already discussed, although we cannot serialize the content itself, we can serialize its name. Taking SpriteObject as an example (though this approach is applied to all the objects that have content reference), we add a new SpriteTextureName property that accepts or returns a string value, and can therefore be easily serialized.

Unfortunately, there is nothing inside the sprite's Texture2D object that actually tells us its name. It does have a Name property, but it returns an empty string. We could set the name when the content object is loaded, but doing this has the potential to cause errors because if we should fail to set the object name, we would not be able later to identify the object.

Instead, we can interrogate the dictionaries and ask them to perform a reverse lookup—searching for the object that we are using and telling us its key. We can easily iterate through all the items in a dictionary by using a foreach loop, iterating a KeyValuePair object across the values.

The GameHost class contains a number of dictionaries, however, and they are all of different types. While we could set up a different function for each, we can save some repetitive coding by creating a generic dictionary scanning function instead. We can pass into this the dictionary to be scanned (e.g., the Textures dictionary) and the type of object it contains (Texture2D objects in this case) and it will return back the object's key.

The generic implementation of this function is shown in Listing 10–7.

Listing 10–7. Finding the key for an object inside any generic dictionary with a string-based key

```
public string GetContentObjectName<T>(Dictionary<string, T> objectDictionary,
                                                          T contentObject)
{
    // Loop for each key/value pair
    foreach (KeyValuePair<string, T> dictItem in objectDictionary)
    {
        // Is this item's value the object that we are searching for?
        if (EqualityComparer<T>.Default.Equals(dictItem.Value, contentObject))
        {
            return dictItem.Key;
        }
    }
    // Couldn't find the requested object
    return null;
}
```

The function is called as shown in Listing 10–8.

Listing 10–8. Finding the name of a sprite's texture object

```
textureName = Game.GetContentObjectName<Texture2D>(Game.Textures, SpriteTexture);
```

This gives us the ability to return a content object's name ready for serialization. That's the first part of the problem covered.

Next we need to be able to recover the name when the object is deserialized. .NET will pass the name string to the object, but the object cannot yet retrieve the actual content object because it has no reference to the GameHost object, and the content has not yet been loaded.

Instead, we simply store the name away in a private string variable. When the game has been fully initialized and is ready to actually use the texture, we will retrieve it from the GameHost object then.

The full implementation of the SpriteObject.SpriteTextureName property is in Listing 10–9.

Listing 10–9. Setting and returning the name of the sprite's texture object

```
/// <summary>
/// The name of the texture being used by this sprite
/// </summary>
private string _textureName;
/// <summary>
/// Sets or returns the sprite texture name.
/// This can be serialized when the game is tombstoned.
/// </summary>
[System.Runtime.Serialization.DataMember]
public virtual string SpriteTextureName
{
    get
    {
        // Return the texture name
        return _textureName;
    }
    set
    {
        // Is this texture name different to the one we are already using?
        if (_textureName != value)
        {
            // Store the new name
            _textureName = value;
            // Clear the stored texture so that the name is processed the name
            // time the SpriteTexture property is called
            _spriteTexture = null;
        }
    }
}
```

Each time the property is set to a new value, it removes any existing SpriteTexture object reference by setting the property's backing variable (_spriteTexture) to null. This ensures that the SpriteTexture property (whose modified definition we will look at next) will observe any changes to the SpriteTextureName that can be made during normal execution of the game at times other than deserialization. Without this, setting the name within our game code would have no effect on the texture actually being used.

The texture name can now be persisted through tombstoning and set back into the object when the game is reactivated. The final step is to get the object to actually restore the texture object when it needs it.

This step is achieved by adding some further code to the SpriteTexture property, shown in Listing 10–10. Whereas before this property was a simple automatically implemented property, we now need to expand it out with a little code and provide another private backing variable to store the actual texture object in.

Listing 10–10. The updated SpriteTexture property

```
/// <summary>
/// The underlying texture being used by this sprite
/// </summary>
private Texture2D _spriteTexture;
/// <summary>
/// A reference to the default texture used by this sprite
/// </summary>
public Texture2D SpriteTexture
{
    get
    {
        // Do we have a texture name but no actual texture?
        // This will be the case after recovering from being tombstoned.
        if (_spriteTexture == null && !String.IsNullOrEmpty(_textureName) && Game != null)
        {
            // Get the texture back from the Textures collection
            _spriteTexture = Game.Textures[_textureName];
        }
        // Return the sprite texture
        return _spriteTexture;
    }
    set
    {
        if (_spriteTexture != value)
        {
            // Set the sprite texture
            _spriteTexture = value;
            // Set the texture name
            _textureName = Game.GetContentObjectName<Texture2D>(Game.Textures, value);
        }
    }
}
```

Let's look at the set part of the property. Each time a new texture is set, the backing variable is updated and then the _textureName variable is updated with the name of the texture, which ensures that the texture name is always up to date. The _textureName variable is updated directly rather than through the SpriteTextureName property to avoid the SpriteTextureName set part clearing the _spriteTexture variable back to null again.

In the get part of the property, the code checks to see whether its _spriteTexture backing variable is null (which it will be after a tombstoned game is reactivated). If it is, and if the object has a non-blank texture name and a reference to the GameHost, it retrieves the texture from the Textures dictionary.

This is inescapably more complex than the implementation that we had for the SpriteTexture property. This implementation is able to survive tombstoning however, by always ensuring that it knows the texture name, and by retrieving the required texture if it finds that a name is set but the texture is not.

As complex as it is, all this functionality is packaged away inside the GameFramework.SpriteObject class and is therefore completely transparent to any derived classes or external code that is using the class. Any code that doesn't know the details of the internal implementation can use it just like the simple property that we implemented before.

This same property model is repeated for all the game framework classes that deal with content objects and allows them all to survive the tombstoning process.

Automatic Storage and Retrieval of Game Objects in the State Dictionary

The game objects are capable of being tombstoned, but we have a little more work still to do to ensure that they are actually added to the state dictionary during the Deactivated event and then retrieved in the Activated event. Once again we can simplify this work by moving the code into the game framework.

The first of the new functions is the GameHost.WriteGameObjectsToPhoneState function, shown in Listing 10–11. It first clears the existing state dictionary and then loops through all the items in the GameObjects list, adding each to the dictionary.

Listing 10–11. Adding the game objects into the state dictionary

```
protected void WriteGameObjectsToPhoneState()
{
    // Clear any previous state
    PhoneApplicationService.Current.State.Clear();

    // Track  the index so we can generate a unique dictionary key for each object
    int objectIndex = 0;
    foreach (GameObjectBase obj in GameObjects)
    {
        // Is this object interested in being added to the phone state?
        if (obj.WriteToPhoneState)
        {
            // Generate a name and add the object
            PhoneApplicationService.Current.State.Add("_obj" + objIndex.ToString(), obj);
            // Move to the next object index number
            objIndex += 1;
        }
    }
}
```

It might be that there are some game objects that do not need to be maintained when the game is deactivated. One example is particle objects. They are usually present purely for short-term visual effect, and if they were discarded during the tombstoning process they would have negligible effect on the game when it reawakens. Ignoring these objects can reduce the amount of data that needs to be serialized, speeding up the whole process.

To allow us to control which objects are serialized and which are not, a new property named WriteToPhoneState has been added to GameObjectBase. This is a virtual property with just a get part, and by default it simply returns true.

Classes that want to exclude some or all of their objects from serialization can override this property and return false instead. This is exactly what the MatrixParticleObjectBase class does, so by default all particle objects are excluded from serialization. If you have a particle object class that you do want to be included, you will need to override in your class and return true once again.

The WriteGameObjectsToPhoneState function can be simply called from your GameDeactivated function to put all the game objects into the state dictionary.

■ **Note** Always call `WriteGameObjectsToPhoneState` before adding any other items to the state dictionary because it clears the dictionary items before adding the game objects.

That's everything set up ready for deactivation, so how do we reactivate things when the game restarts? This is achieved by calling the `GameHost.ReadGameObjectsFromPhoneState` function. This function loops through all the objects in the state dictionary, pulling out every object that is derived from `GameObjectBase`. For each object that is found, it is given back its Game property reference to the `GameHost` and then added back into the `GameObjects` collection. The function is shown in Listing 10–12.

Listing 10–12. Reinstating objects that were stored in the state dictionary

```
protected void ReadGameObjectsFromPhoneState()
{
    GameObjectBase obj;
    // Loop for each state item key/value
    foreach (KeyValuePair<string, object> stateItem in
                                        PhoneApplicationService.Current.State)
    {
        // Is the value a game object?
        if (stateItem.Value is GameObjectBase)
        {
            // It is. Retrieve a reference to the object
            obj = (GameObjectBase)stateItem.Value;
            // Set its Game property so that it can see the GameHost
            obj.Game = this;
            // Add the object back into the GameObjects collection
            GameObjects.Add(obj);
        }
    }
}
```

This function is simply called from the `Activated` event and together with the changes in the "Persistent Content References" from the previous section will result in all the game objects being reinstated to their original condition.

Identifying Specific Objects After Tombstoning

The approach described so far repopulates the `GameObjects` collection after reactivation, but what if we had stored individual references to specific objects in class-level variables? We will frequently do this so that, for example, we know which game object is the player's object, or which object is displaying the player's score.

To provide a simple mechanism for reobtaining access to specific objects, we introduce another new property to `GameObjectBase`, this time named Tag. The Tag property can be set to contain any string value, and will be included in object serialization.

After the game has been reactivated, references to tagged objects can be obtained by calling `GameHost.GetObjectByTag`, passing in the tag string. If a matching object is found, it will be returned.

This can be seen in action inside the Tombstoning example project. Within the game class' `GameActivated`, the _scoreText object is repopulated by looking for the object tagged with the string _scoreText. This object tag is initially set when the text object is created inside `ResetGame`.

Game Initialization

In many of our examples, we have called in to the `ResetGame` function at the end of `LoadContent`. This has served us well in our simple examples, but is no longer adequate when tombstoning becomes a consideration.

`LoadContent` is called every time the game initializes, regardless of whether it is launching a new instance or activating a tombstoned instance. If we call `ResetGame` from the end of `LoadContent`, it will be called after reactivation, erasing all the game objects we have painstakingly restored and resetting the game back to its initial state. That's not quite the result we were looking for!

To make everything work as required, simply move the call to `ResetGame` into the `GameLaunching` function instead. This will then be called only when a new instance of the game is starting up.

One final detail to be aware of is that the first call to the game's `Update` might occur prior to the `Launching` or `Activated` events being called. If you have any code inside `Update` that expects the game to have been initialized, it might fail as a result. The simplest fix to this is to set a class-level boolean variable from the end of your `Launching` and `Activated` events, and return from any calls to `Update` if this variable has not yet been set.

Troubleshooting Serialization

You need to ensure that the derived game object classes you create in your game conform to the requirements for serialization in order for them to be able to survive tombstoning.

Here is a checklist of things to look for if your object serialization doesn't seem to be working:

- Ensure that the scope of your class is `public` (if no scope is specified, it will default to `private`).

- Ensure you have a public, parameterless constructor.

- Ensure that your class either has the `DataContract` attribute and that the appropriate properties within the class have the `DataMember` attribute, or that the class does not have the `DataContract` attribute and all the public properties in the class are serializable.

- Ensure that your class has at least one direct serializable public property (defined within the class itself, not inherited).

If any of these conditions is not met, your game will either throw an exception when its objects are being serialized (a potentially confusing `SecurityException` is one such possibility), your game will simply fail to relaunch when you navigate back to it, or some of your objects will be missing from the game when it is reactivated.

Tracking down and managing problems in this area can be a challenge, and this is one of the reasons why attending to tombstoning early on in your game's development process can save time and frustration later on.

Returning from the Grave

The `Tombstoning` project demonstrates everything that we have discussed in this section, including successful deserialization of several sprite and text objects, reobtaining a reference to a specific object, and also putting additional content (the player's score) into the state dictionary.

If you launch the game, press the Windows button, and then finally press the Back button, you will see that everything picks up exactly where it had left off.

A more complex example is in the `VaporTrailTS` project. This returns to the `VaporTrail` example from Chapter 8, and includes serialization and deserialization of a scene containing 3D objects, models, particles, a skybox, a custom camera, and a user-selectable view mode. Everything within the scene survives tombstoning except for the smoke particles, which are deliberately excluded.

A fair amount of effort is required within the game framework to support tombstoning, but the game itself can usually take advantage of this without too much extra work. In many cases, the end result will make the implementation of tombstoning support time well spent.

This chapter concludes our work with XNA. While we will refer back to it in the coming chapters (and even use some of its functionality), it is time to step across into a different technology now and examine the games that can be made using Silverlight.

PART 3

Silverlight

CHAPTER 11

■ ■ ■

Getting Started with Silverlight

For the next few chapters, we will explore the options for creating games using Windows Phone 7's other technology: Silverlight.

While XNA is focused specifically on creating games, Silverlight's objective is to allow applications in general to be created. This means that it doesn't provide many of the graphical technologies that we have found during our explanation of XNA. It doesn't, for example, offer support for rendering 3D objects.

Its graphical capabilities are still fairly comprehensive, however, allowing us to perform virtually everything that XNA's sprites can do, including scaling, rotation, transparency, and so on. They are very useful for game creation.

Silverlight also provides a very useful facility that is almost entirely missing from XNA: the ability to create a rich user interface. If your game needs to focus on detailed information displays and complex interaction from the user, you might find that Silverlight has the tools that can enable you to implement this quickly and easily.

In this chapter, we will begin to explore Silverlight: its capabilities and how we can develop with it. If you haven't used Silverlight before, you will gain a broad understanding of how to use it. This book's focus is on gaming rather than Silverlight itself, however, so we cannot hope to cover everything that Silverlight can do. Many other excellent books are available if you want to further your understanding beyond the information that is presented here.

If you are already familiar with Silverlight, much of this material might already be familiar to you. It might still be worth skimming the chapter, however, because there are differences that you might not expect in the way Silverlight operates on the phone as compared with in a browser.

A Brief History of Silverlight

Let's take a quick tour through the past and present of Silverlight so that we can understand its evolution into the product that we use today.

Windows Presentation Foundation

In the beginning, there was *Windows Presentation Foundation (WPF)*. This technology, introduced by Microsoft in 2006 as part of .NET 3.0, was for desktop PC development and introduced a new graphics API.

Prior to this, 2D rendering in Windows was generally performed using the aging *Graphics Device Interface (GDI)*. GDI has its strengths, but rendering games and fast-moving animated graphics are not among them. The majority of operations performed using GDI are driven by the processor rather than by the graphics hardware, limiting the performance of applications that use it.

WPF dramatically improves on these capabilities by offloading the graphics rendering onto the graphics hardware via the DirectX rendering system. As a result of this change, vastly improved levels of performance can be obtained with less load to the CPU itself, allowing the processor instead to focus on tasks such as data processing, game logic, and so on.

The sophisticated rendering abilities of the graphics hardware can also be taken advantage of by WPF, allowing for a much richer visual display. Graphics hardware can easily rotate, scale, perform alpha blending and transparency effects, and perform other visual transformations; so all this functionality becomes immediately available to the WPF user interface. 3D graphics rendering is also supported.

One of the important features of WPF is a layout engine that allows flexible and complex user interface designs to be specified. This engine uses a declarative language called *XAML* (short for *eXtensible Application Markup Language* and pronounced "zammal") to define the contents of the screens generated by WPF. We will be spending quite some time looking at XAML in this chapter.

Silverlight

A year after the release of the first version of WPF, Microsoft released the first version of *Silverlight*. Silverlight began as a web browser technology, based on WPF (and in fact was originally codenamed *WPF/E*, short for *Windows Presentation Foundation/Everywhere*). It took the central graphic presentation functionality present in WPF and allowed it to be used to deliver content within web pages using a small and reasonably unobtrusive browser plug-in. The 3D rendering element of WPF was not included in the transformation to Silverlight (and indeed is still not included today).

Silverlight 1.0 was useful and powerful in many ways, but was not as flexible as it might have been. It exposed a *Document Object Model (DOM)* that could be used to interact with and manipulate the content that it was presenting within the browser, but all interaction with this object model had to be performed using JavaScript. It also had no user interface controls built in to its runtime.

Silverlight 2, which was released in 2008, contained a large number of changes and enhancements. Possibly the most significant of these was the capability for it to be programmed using the .NET *Common Language Runtime (CLR)*. As a result of this enhancement, code could be created using any of the managed .NET languages, such as C# or Visual Basic.NET. This hugely increased the flexibility of the environment and opened it up as a usable platform to millions of existing .NET developers. Code embedded into Silverlight apps is known as *code behind* code because it sits behind the user-facing presentation layer. This is analogous to the code that is contained within a Form class in WinForms development.

Along with this change were numerous others, including the addition of flexible user interface controls (such as text boxes, combo boxes, check boxes, sliders, and many more), LINQ, data access functionality, and the capability for managed code within a Silverlight application to interact with the HTML on the page outside of the application itself. This resulted in a highly flexible and dynamic environment to work in.

In 2009, Silverlight 3 was released, bringing with it a number of additions such as new user interface controls, better audio and video decoding, and high-definition video streaming. Another very useful change in this new version is its capability to run outside of the browser. Instead of having to live inside a web page, a Silverlight application could now be installed on the PC as a stand-alone application, resulting in a very simple delivery and deployment experience.

The latest version of Silverlight is version 4, released in 2010. It contains another list of enhancements, though none on quite the same scale as seen in the earlier updates. New features include capabilities to work with printers and the clipboard; support for the right mouse button and mouse wheel; and the capability to use a web cam and microphone.

Silverlight on Windows Phone

Clearly, a Silverlight application running on a Windows Phone 7 device is working in a very different environment from one running in a web browser or on the desktop. Nevertheless, it still offers a huge amount of functionality and a great degree of flexibility for presenting data to and interacting with the user.

The version of Silverlight that runs on Windows Phone is version 3, not the more recent version 4. Because Silverlight on the phone is running in a known environment, however (unlike in a web browser that could be one of a number of browsers on one of a number of operating systems), it can take advantage of other facilities within the phone. As a result, it can safely use external libraries to provide accelerometer input, for example, or can hook into XNA for additional audio capabilities.

The binaries produced for Silverlight on the phone are identical to those produced for web-based or desktop applications. This means that third-party Silverlight libraries can theoretically be used by Windows Phone 7 applications. If you decide to try this, however, do bear in mind that desktop-targeted Silverlight libraries might require .NET namespaces and capabilities that are not available in Windows Phone 7; and might expect more processing power, memory, or available screen real estate than the phone can offer, so you will need to experiment with them to ensure their suitability.

In practice, you need to make some changes to your Silverlight games before they will run comfortably on off-phone platforms, but this is a definite possibility and a great way to advertise your game. We will explore this subject further in Chapter 16.

Creating Silverlight Projects for Windows Phone

To begin working with Silverlight, we must first create a Silverlight project. This is done by selecting the Silverlight for Windows Phone option within the project Templates panel of the New Project dialog, shown in Figure 11–1.

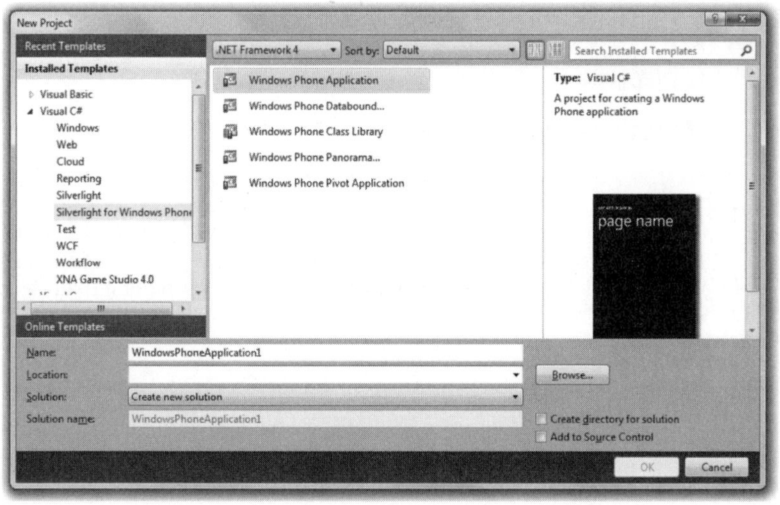

Figure 11–1. Creating a new Silverlight project

Try this now and create an empty Silverlight project to experiment with based on the Windows Phone Application template. Once again, you might find it beneficial to switch off the "Create directory for solution" option because it results in less directory nesting in the generated project.

The project opens within the IDE, showing a split view of the project's `MainPage.xaml` file, as discussed all the way back in Chapter 1.

Run the resulting project and allow it to be deployed to a device or to the emulator. The resulting application simply shows a black screen with an application name and a title at the top. The title initially displays the value page name. As this name suggests, the top-level design unit within Silverlight applications is called a *page* (analogous to the *form* in WinForms projects).

If you are running on a real device or the emulator with a fully supported graphics card in your PC, you should also see the *frame rate counter* displayed on the right edge of the screen. These counters show some useful performance indicators that can help identify how fast the application is running and rendering to the screen. We will explore these counters in more detail in the "Silverlight Performance" section in Chapter 13.

The initial page of the project, with the performance counters displayed, is shown in Figure 11–2.

Figure 11–2. The default display of a Silverlight Application project

Choosing a Project Template

As Figure 11–1 shows, the Windows Phone development environment comes with five project templates. Let's take a look at each of these templates and find out the types of projects that they are most likely to be useful for. Try creating a project using each of the templates and experimenting with their functionality as you work through this section.

Windows Phone Application Template

This is a general-purpose template that can be used as a basis for any type of application. It provides what essentially amounts to an empty but working environment, ready for further customization.

Most of the other project templates provide a starting point based around a particular user interface approach. There is a high probability that the games you create will not need to use these approaches, so the basic Windows Phone Application template is likely to be the most suitable starting point for game development.

Windows Phone Databound Application Template

The Databound Application template shows a simple example of creating a multi-item scrolling page with expandable detail behind each of the items. The default application shows a series of sample items (that are being built from a class elsewhere within the project). When one is selected, a detail page opens to provide more information on the item.

This template provides an example of one of the navigational models available within Silverlight. Selecting an item navigates forward into the detail of that item. The hardware Back button can then be pressed to return back to the item list page again. Pressing Back once again closes the application (because this is the root page) and returns to the phone's front page. This process feels similar to navigating backward through pages in a web browser and is consistent with the experience that we saw in XNA games when we covered tombstoning.

This template is less likely to be a useful starting point for game development.

Windows Phone Class Library Template

As you would expect, this template creates an empty class library project, ready to be populated and referenced from other Silverlight projects. Apart from some project references and a blank class file, projects created from this template are completely blank.

Windows Phone Panorama Application Template

This template creates a project based around one of the Metro user interface's new paradigms: the *Panorama*. Panoramic page layouts are to be found in many areas of the core phone operating system and many applications built on top of it.

The organization of the Panorama consists of an extra wide, horizontally scrolling page, inside of which are distinct columns of data. By swiping left or right, the user can navigate between these columns. The individual columns can be different in presentation and style, and will often include a vertical scrolling component to allow more content to be contained than can fit on the screen.

The vertical columns are sized so that the next column to the right is just visible, giving a visual clue to the user that more content is available than that presented on the screen. Further indications of this are contained within the Panorama title, which is displayed in a large font that usually stretches off the right edge of the screen.

This is an important configuration for many applications, but as with the databound application, it is less likely to be useful for us as a basis for writing games.

Windows Phone Pivot Application Template

The final template creates a project using a *Pivot* control. This is another Metro control type, and in many ways looks and feels similar to the Panorama, offering items grouped together under a series of headings.

In practice, the main difference between these two controls is down to presentation. It is also more common to find applications that dynamically add headings based on user configuration (for example, adding multiple cities to a weather forecasting application or different categories for a news reporting app). The headings within a Pivot control can be seen as analogous to tabs in a tab control in a desktop user interface.

This template is once again less likely to be used for game projects.

Working with Silverlight Projects

Getting comfortable with the Visual Studio IDE can take a little time when working with Silverlight projects. The main building blocks of the projects are the pages, which are represented by `.xaml` files.

Generally when working on pages, the IDE will be run using the "split" view, with the actual XAML code on one side of the screen and a preview of the page on the other. As changes are made to the XAML, they are immediately reflected in the preview, allowing the effect of code changes to be quickly and easily understood.

New in Visual Studio 2010 is the capability to actually interact with this preview. In Visual Studio 2008, the preview was just that: a read-only display of how the hand-crafted XAML would appear when the application was launched. Visual Studio 2010 turns the preview into a visual designer, just like the form designer that is available when developing WinForms applications.

Using the preview to visually design pages can be extremely useful and a great time-saving device. Controls can be visually added to and arranged within the preview, and the corresponding XAML code updates to reflect the changes that have been made. Clicking a control within the preview not only visually selects it within the designer, but also scrolls to and highlights the corresponding control in the XAML pane. Using these two panes together provides a very rich and powerful user interface design experience—once you've got the hang of it!

▓ **Note** As an additional or alternative method for editing page designs, Microsoft provides a comprehensive user interface design tool called Expression Blend. The idea behind this application is that designers, who don't necessarily have any programming experience, can use Expression Blend to create rich and attractive user interface frameworks, behind which the programmers can then slot in the required program code. Expression Blend 4 for Windows Phone is provided for free as part of the Windows Phone 7 software development kit and is well worth investigating if you find that you have large amounts of page design to do. This book will focus only on developing Silverlight applications within the main Visual Studio IDE, however.

Associated with each `.xaml` page file is a corresponding `.cs` code file, containing the "code behind" the page. This code file can be accessed either by clicking the View Code button in the Solution Explorer toolbar or by expanding the `.xaml` file within Solution Explorer's tree and double-clicking the `.cs` file that is revealed, as shown in Figure 11–3.

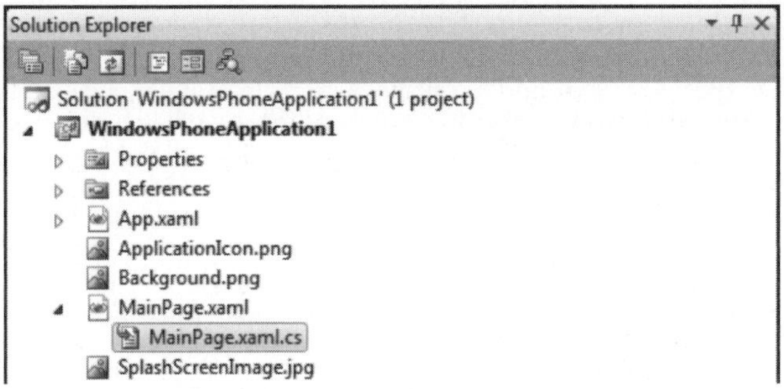

Figure 11–3. Accessing the code behind a Silverlight page

All these areas of the IDE are important for designing our game. The user interface and many of the game components will be created in the page and XAML designer, and the game logic and processing will be created in the C# code window just as in any other type of application.

Examining the Solution in More Detail

Let's take a more detailed look at the solution that Visual Studio creates for us when we ask it for a Silverlight application. These are the files created when the Windows Phone Application template is selected; other templates might result in additional files within the generated solution, but the core files detailed here are present in all the templates.

The Project Structure

Unlike new XNA solutions, the solution for a new Silverlight application consists of just one project. Any resources that we need to call on (such as graphic or sound files) are embedded directly into the main application rather than being provided by a separate Content project.

Project Images

The project contains three images: ApplicationIcon.png, Background.png, and SplashScreenImage.png, which are used to control the icons and start-up image used by the project.

The first of these images, ApplicationIcon.png, is a small 62-x-62-pixel icon that will be displayed within the application list on the device. Background.png is a larger icon at 173 x 173 pixels; it will be displayed on the main home page if the user decides to pin the application from the app list. Both of these images default to a white starburst shape on a black background. You will want to customize these images to allow your game to stand out. The two images should ideally be essentially the same except for their size so that the user doesn't get confused as to which icon the game uses.

The final image, SplashScreenImage.png, is a full-screen image measuring 480 x 800 pixels that is displayed when the game is initializing. When starting up the empty project applications, a small clock image appears briefly in the middle of the screen; this is the default splash screen image. It is perfectly acceptable to retain this default image, but you might want to add a little extra sparkle by customizing it. If you aren't sure what image to use, you can create a loading image based on a screenshot from within your game.

The App.xaml File

Alongside these images are two Silverlight page files: `App.xaml` and `MainPage.xaml`. The first file, `App.xaml`, contains a nonvisual XAML listing that sets up the application-wide environment for the project. Its default content is shown in Listing 11–1.

Listing 11–1. The XAML contained within App.xaml

```
<Application
    x:Class="WindowsPhoneApplication1.App"
    xmlns="http://schemas.microsoft.com/winfx/2006/xaml/presentation"
    xmlns:x="http://schemas.microsoft.com/winfx/2006/xaml"
    xmlns:phone="clr-namespace:Microsoft.Phone.Controls;assembly=Microsoft.Phone"
    xmlns:shell="clr-namespace:Microsoft.Phone.Shell;assembly=Microsoft.Phone">

    <!--Application Resources-->
    <Application.Resources>
    </Application.Resources>

    <Application.ApplicationLifetimeObjects>
        <!--Required object that handles lifetime events for the application-->
        <shell:PhoneApplicationService
            Launching="Application_Launching" Closing="Application_Closing"
            Activated="Application_Activated" Deactivated="Application_Deactivated"/>
    </Application.ApplicationLifetimeObjects>
</Application>
```

Don't worry too much about what is going on in here for the moment, but something you will be able to spot is the configuration of the application life cycle event handlers. Event functions are set up to process the launching, closing, activated, and deactivated events just as we set up in the Game Framework project for XNA. While the appearance and development styles of Silverlight and XNA might be very different, they are both running on the same underlying platform and have many internal similarities, such as this one.

The `App.xaml` file also has code behind it, which you can find by opening up the `App.xaml.cs` file, as described earlier. This file contains initialization code for the project. The majority of the code here is in scope for modification as per the needs of individual projects, so feel free to add or customize the content of this file. Open the file now in Visual Studio to take a look at its content.

At the beginning of the code is the declaration for a property named `RootFrame`. This can be accessed from anywhere within the project in order to gain access to the page that is currently open. We will see how to do this later on.

Following on from this is the class constructor. The main area of interest is a block of code that only executes when the Visual Studio debugger is attached. Inside, the class updates various properties that can help with debugging, so it makes sense only to use these properties when actually connected to the debugger—this approach minimizes the risk of debugging information being accidentally activated in production code.

The first updated property is the `EnableFrameRateCounter`, which we have already briefly discussed. If you ever want to turn the counter off, simply comment out this line of code. The rest of the block is commented out, but contains code to set two further properties named `EnableRedrawRegions` and `EnableCacheVisualization`. We will discuss these properties in the "Silverlight Performance" section in Chapter 13.

After the constructor you will find four functions that respond to the application life cycle events. Any processing code that you need to put into place when these events occur can be added here.

■ **Note** You won't find any C# code that wires up these functions to the corresponding events. The event handlers are actually set up by the XAML code shown in Listing 11–1. We will look into how event handlers are specified for events using XAML in the "Exploring XAML" section later in this chapter.

The final functions here allow the debugger to be triggered on two specific events that might occur within the application: an unhandled exception and a navigation failure (which will occur if there is a problem moving from one page to the next). Both of these event handlers are useful to have to help diagnose problems when developing applications.

The MainPage.xaml file

At last we reach the final file within the project: `MainPage.xaml`. As you have already seen, this file initially provides the XAML required to set up a simple outline page, ready for your custom content to be added inside. We will look at how the XAML fits together in a moment.

The class behind this page is essentially empty, ready to be populated with whatever additional code your game requires.

■ **Note** This blank page is identical to the one that you will get if you select to add a new `Page` item to your project.

The Hidden Source Files

Although not initially visible within Solution Explorer, there are three additional files included in the project. They can be found by expanding the `Properties` node in the project tree.

Inside you will find `AppManifest.xml`, which is essentially an empty XML document, and `AssemblyInfo.cs`, which provides all the details of the assembly (title, author, copyright details, and so on) that will be built into the binary when it is compiled.

The third file, `WMAppManifest.xml`, contains various application parameters that will be used to control how the application is deployed and launched. Of interest is the `DefaultTask` element, which specifies the initial Silverlight page that should be displayed when the application launches. If you add other pages and want to make one of them the start page, you can change this value to point to it as needed.

Referencing Other Projects

Just as with any other .NET environment, you can easily share and reuse functionality that your games require by building class libraries. If you want to create a class library based specifically around the Silverlight platform, use the Silverlight Class Library template detailed earlier in this chapter.

It is also possible to create class library projects that will work in both XNA and Silverlight. You can create the project from the Silverlight Class Library template or the XNA Game Library template, but remember that any code you write that needs to work in both environments should not specifically target features from the other platform. It is fine to create classes that manipulate basic datatypes, but once you start specifically referring to XNA or Silverlight classes, you will quickly find that problems occur when running in the other environment.

■ **Note** Silverlight and XNA can add binary (DLL) references to assemblies created in one another's environments, but Visual Studio does not like adding project references between the two different environments. You will therefore either need to add references by browsing to their DLL files or stick to keeping your assemblies focused on just one environment or the other.

Exploring XAML

Let's continue our journey into Silverlight by spending some time looking at XAML.

XAML is both intricate and complex, and although not a fully fledged programming language in its own right, it nonetheless contains all sorts of tricks and features and will take time to master. In this section, you will take a crash course in XAML and learn just the basics you need in order to set up a gaming environment.

While you will get a good idea of what XAML can do and a high-level understanding of how it works, providing a full and in-depth description of all its features is beyond the scope of this book. As and when you want to further your knowledge, there are many good books and online resources that will allow you to expand and deepen your knowledge. (Matthew MacDonald's *Pro Silverlight* series is one I can recommend.)

What Is XAML For?

XAML's primary purpose is to define the user interface layout of pages displayed within a Silverlight application.

Visual development environments have used text-based representations of form designs for a very long time. Starting back with the original pre-.NET versions of Visual Basic, forms were designed using a visual layout tool, and those designs were stored using a special syntax built purely around the need to define user interface elements and set the values of their properties. These designs were system-generated and only designed to be system-readable. They could be modified by hand, but to do so required the designer to explore the data files outside of the IDE and "hack" them. Such editing was not supported or recommended.

Things improved somewhat with the introduction of the .NET environment. The visual form designer continued to result in system-generated code, and it was by default still hidden away. The code it created was no longer in a special structure, however; it was plain C# or VB.NET, and it could be viewed and edited directly within the IDE if the developer wanted to do so. Generally it was still easier to simply use the form designer, however, not least of which because it generated reams and reams of verbose code.

The approach taken with WPF and Silverlight is somewhat different. The UI is marked up in XAML, and it is not only in plain view and editable but also editing is encouraged and recommended. In earlier versions of Visual Studio, manual editing of XAML was the only way to build it at all.

This open and structured approach to layout provides a number of benefits. It allows you to see exactly, without any ambiguity, what the structure and content of your user interface actually is. It lets you interact at a detailed level with its objects and properties without having to navigate through a complex visual interface. And with a little practice and experience, it also allows you to create your user interface more quickly than using the visual designer.

One of the things that made this approach less usable in the pre-WPF approach to form design was the verbosity of the UI construction code. Adding a text box to a form and setting its properties could require a dozen or more lines of code. XAML removes this problem by using a concise and targeted notation for specifying its content. User interface controls (or *elements*) are defined by simple XML elements, whose names correspond to the classes that they represent. Properties and events are defined by XML attributes (though support for complex properties that cannot be represented by a simple value is present, too).

When you compile your Silverlight project, the compiler processes all the XAML that has been defined and actually turns it into C# code. This code is then compiled as part of your project, just as any other C# code would be. Because of this, virtually everything that you can do in XAML could also be done by writing code instead.

Alongside all this, the XAML editor has a degree of predictive intelligence. While you are using it, the editor will do its best to insert the markup that you will need next (quotes around attribute values, closing elements, and so on), and Visual Studio's IntelliSense feature will provide suggestions for available attributes and property values. It can take a little time to learn to work with this feature rather than fight against it, but once you come to terms with it, you will find that it saves you a lot of time.

To begin with, feel free to use the visual designer to create your XAML for you. You can easily create and modify elements and their properties and more-or-less leave the XAML itself alone. But keep an eye on what is happening behind your page design and don't be afraid to make any changes to the markup directly in the editor. Before too long, you might find yourself more at home editing the XAML than using the designer.

The Silverlight Page Structure

Pages within Silverlight are structured in a conceptually similar way to pages in HTML. They are set up in a hierarchical system whereby elements are contained within other elements. If you add a panel and then want to add a text box inside that panel, the text box must be defined inside the panel's element within the XAML definition.

Silverlight elements can even have *styles* applied to them in a similar way to the way *cascading style sheets (CSS)* can be used for HTML documents. Silverlight styles are not as sophisticated as CSS but still can provide a method for updating elements within pages in a consistent manner.

Other similarities exist with the HTML world too. We have already seen that each Silverlight design is stored within a *page*, and when we want to take the user from one page to another, we do this by navigating to a page using a URI, just as we would in a web browser. The URIs are formed in a way that references content within the Silverlight application rather than actually looking on the Internet.

Parameter values can be passed between these pages by specifying them within the URI's *query string*, just as parameters are passed between pages within a web browser.

If you create an empty project based on the Windows Phone Databound Application template, you can see this application page navigation feature in use. Inside the MainPage.xaml.cs file is the code shown in Listing 11–2. The NavigationService.Navigate call is provided with the target page URI including the query string, which in this case indicates the index of the item within the list that has been touched by the user.

Listing 11–2. Navigating to the DetailsPage and passing it a parameter value

```
// Handle selection changed on ListBox
private void MainListBox_SelectionChanged(object sender, SelectionChangedEventArgs e)
{
    // If selected index is -1 (no selection) do nothing
    if (MainListBox.SelectedIndex == -1)
        return;
```

```
        // Navigate to the new page
        NavigationService.Navigate(new Uri("/DetailsPage.xaml?selectedItem=" +
                                    MainListBox.SelectedIndex, UriKind.Relative));

        // Reset selected index to -1 (no selection)
        MainListBox.SelectedIndex = -1;
    }
```

Don't forget that although we are using Silverlight to create stand-alone applications in the context of Windows Phone, the platform's origins are entirely web-based. This no doubt goes a long way to explain the similarities between the two environments.

XAML's Syntax

Let's take a more detailed look at some XAML code and break it down so that we can understand what it is doing. We'll examine this by taking a tour through some of the classes within a Silverlight project and will then summarize everything at the end.

Starting Off with App.xaml

The first example that we will look at is the App.xaml file from the default Windows Phone Application template, the beginning of which is reproduced in Listing 11–3.

Listing 11–3. The start of the App.xaml file

```
<Application
    x:Class="WindowsPhoneApplication1.App"
    xmlns="http://schemas.microsoft.com/winfx/2006/xaml/presentation"
    xmlns:x="http://schemas.microsoft.com/winfx/2006/xaml"
    xmlns:phone="clr-namespace:Microsoft.Phone.Controls;assembly=Microsoft.Phone"
    xmlns:shell="clr-namespace:Microsoft.Phone.Shell;assembly=Microsoft.Phone">
```

You might notice that this particular file doesn't display the visual editor when it is opened in Visual Studio; you will see the reason for that in a moment.

The very first line declares an XML element named Application. The name of the element defines the class from which this particular class inherits. The first line after this sets the x:Class attribute to have the value WindowsPhoneApplication1.App. It specifies the namespace inside which the class resides (WindowsPhoneApplication1) and the name of the class (App).

If you open the code behind the XAML, you will find that the class declaration begins with the code shown in Listing 11–4. This is exactly the same information, but written using the C# syntax.

Listing 11–4. The App class declaration in the C# code behind

```
namespace WindowsPhoneApplication1
{
    public partial class App : Application
    {
```

■ **Note** The XAML and the code for a class definition must agree on the details specified here; if the base class, namespace, or class name are inconsistent between the two, a compilation error will occur.

The next block of content within App.xaml defines four XML namespaces. These namespaces allow us to map elements within the following XAML back to specific DLLs or areas of functionality.

The first namespace that is defined references the URL http://schemas.microsoft.com/winfx/2006/xaml/presentation, which is the namespace used for Silverlight. No namespace prefix is specified for this, so all following elements within the document will default to this namespace unless another is explicitly specified.

Following this is the x namespace, refencing http://schemas.microsoft.com/winfx/2006/xaml. This namespace provides additional content specific to XAML, such as the x:Class attribute that was already discussed.

The remaining namespaces both reference .NET namespaces Microsoft.Phone.Controls and Microsoft.Phone.Shell. With these namespaces present, we can refer to items within these .NET namespaces by specifying the appropriate XML namespace (phone or shell). The editor will automatically create further namespace entries if controls from other assemblies are added to the page from the Toolbox.

Moving On to MainPage.xaml

Bearing all this in mind, let's now skip forward to another file: MainPage.xaml. The file begins as shown in Listing 11–5.

Listing 11–5. The beginning of MainPage.xaml

```
<phone:PhoneApplicationPage
    x:Class="WindowsPhoneApplication1.MainPage"
    xmlns="http://schemas.microsoft.com/winfx/2006/xaml/presentation"
    xmlns:x="http://schemas.microsoft.com/winfx/2006/xaml"
    xmlns:phone="clr-namespace:Microsoft.Phone.Controls;assembly=Microsoft.Phone"
    xmlns:shell="clr-namespace:Microsoft.Phone.Shell;assembly=Microsoft.Phone"
    xmlns:d="http://schemas.microsoft.com/expression/blend/2008"
    xmlns:mc="http://schemas.openxmlformats.org/markup-compatibility/2006"
```

This time, the root element is of type PhoneApplicationPage from the phone namespace. We already know that the phone namespace maps into the Microsoft.Phone.Controls .NET namespace, so this tells us that the type of class represented by this XAML is derived from Microsoft.Phone.Controls.PhoneApplicationPage. The second line names the class as MainPage within the WindowsPhoneApplication1 .NET namespace. Once again we can confirm this by viewing the code behind for the class and seeing that it reveals exactly the same information, as shown in Listing 11–6.

Listing 11–6. The code behind for the MainPage class declaration

```
namespace WindowsPhoneApplication1
{
    public partial class MainPage : PhoneApplicationPage
    {
```

Following the class name is another slightly larger list of XML namespaces. They are the same as in App.xaml, except for the addition of the d and mc namespaces. These namespaces are present primarily for the benefit of the visual designer (and for external designers such as Expression Blend), and we can safely ignore them from the perspective of managing our page designs.

A few lines farther down within the file you will see an element of type Grid being defined. The complete declaration for this and its content is shown in Listing 11–7.

Listing 11–7. The code behind for the MainPage class declaration

```
<!--LayoutRoot is the root grid where all page content is placed-->
<Grid x:Name="LayoutRoot" Background="Transparent">
    <Grid.RowDefinitions>
        <RowDefinition Height="Auto"/>
        <RowDefinition Height="*"/>
    </Grid.RowDefinitions>

    <!--TitlePanel contains the name of the application and page title-->
    <StackPanel x:Name="TitlePanel" Grid.Row="0" Margin="12,17,0,28">
        <TextBlock x:Name="ApplicationTitle" Text="MY APPLICATION"
                                        Style="{StaticResource PhoneTextNormalStyle}"/>
        <TextBlock x:Name="PageTitle" Text="page name"
                                        Margin="9,-7,0,0"
                                        Style="{StaticResource PhoneTextTitle1Style}"/>
    </StackPanel>

    <!--ContentPanel - place additional content here-->
    <Grid x:Name="ContentPanel" Grid.Row="1" Margin="12,0,12,0"></Grid>
</Grid>
```

This code declares a series of controls that are present within the page. Before we look in more detail at what the controls are for and how the XAML syntax is used to declare them, let's look at a visual representation of the controls within the page. Figure 11–4 shows the same controls within MainPage inside a Silverlight application. Other pages can be contained within the application, too (represented conceptually as Page2 and Page3 in this diagram).

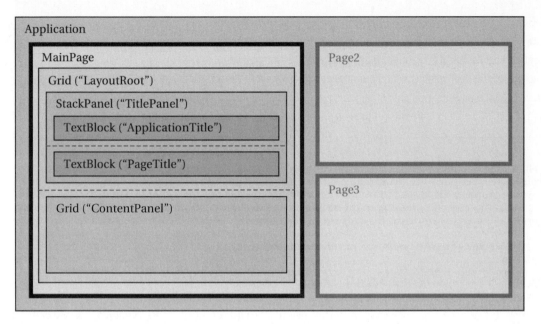

Figure 11–4. *The hierarchy of controls within MainPage.xaml*

Let's focus on the outermost Grid element first. Elements defined within the body of the XAML document represent objects that are being created. The name of the element specifies the name of the class to be used to create the object. Because the element's name is Grid, this element will create an instance of the Grid class. No namespace has been specified, so the default namespace will be used; as we know, this is the Silverlight namespace, and so the control will be taken from Silverlight's built-in classes, of which Grid is one.

The element declaration also specifies two attributes: x:Name and Background. When attributes are provided for an element, these attributes are used to set properties of the object that has been created. In other words, this XML element creates a Grid object, sets its Name to be LayoutRoot, and sets its Background to be Transparent. In addition, the grid is not simply floating within the page class; it is added as part of the collection of controls within the page.

This tiny piece of XAML creates an internal class variable, assigns to it a new instance of the Grid class, sets the grid's Background property, and adds the grid into the page's control collection. Clearly the corresponding C# required to do this would be a lot longer. Although XAML definitely needs an investment of time to learn, its capability to create content in a concise way is second to none.

More examples of creating and configuring objects can be seen in the TextBlock definitions inside the grid. TextBlock elements are similar to WinForms Label controls in many ways and can be used to simply place text onto the page. The "MY APPLICATION" and "page name" text items displayed at the top of the page are both implemented using the TextBlock element.

For each of the TextBlocks defined, three attributes are specified to set the element's name, text, and style. The text can be set to whatever is required; the style is configured to apply the standard presentation being used by the application.

■ **Note** Although all the elements we have examined so far have provided an x:Name attribute, there is no need for elements to specify this. If such an attribute is provided, an internal variable with the specified name will be created so that the defined object can be referenced from within the page's C# code. If the name is omitted, the object will be created as normal but without this internal variable, making it impossible to directly access the created object. You should therefore set the x:Name attribute on any objects that you need to refer to in your code.

There is an alternative syntax for specifying properties of the elements created within the XAML. Instead of specifying an attribute, we can create a child element and set its name to be the name of the class whose property it is to set, followed by a period, and then the property name. The XAML shown in Listing 11–8 is functionally identical to the first TextBlock declaration from Listing 11–7. Setting properties in this way is known as the *property-element syntax*.

Listing 11–8. Setting an element property using a child element

```
<TextBlock x:Name="ApplicationTitle" Style="{StaticResource PhoneTextNormalStyle}">
    <TextBlock.Text>MY APPLICATION</TextBlock.Text>
</TextBlock>
```

Why is this new syntax for setting properties useful? We can set more complex values than we can provide in a simple attribute string value. Many properties need to set other objects as their values, and we need a way to initialize those objects, too. The property-element syntax allows for those objects to be defined and have all their properties initialized in just the same way that the main elements are.

■ **Note** Property elements cannot have attributes of their own, and they cannot duplicate properties set by the parent element's attributes. Configuring the XAML in either of these ways will result in a compilation error.

We can see an example of this in Listing 11–9. The XAML here defines a Border element within the page. This new element provides a way of drawing a rectangular border around an object inside it, and we will examine it in more detail later in the next chapter. The object it contains is stored in a property named Child, and in this example the property is given another TextBlock object. Clearly we could not specify this child object just in an attribute string.

Listing 11–9. Setting an element property to be a complex object rather than a simple value

```
<Border BorderBrush="Yellow" BorderThickness="3">
    <Border.Child>
        <TextBlock Text="Bordered text" />
    </Border.Child>
</Border>
```

There are two simplifications that we can apply to the XAML in order to reduce the amount of code that is present—though they do also result in a degree of behavior that might appear to be "magic" at first glance, performing tasks that are not explicitly spelled out in the code.

First of all, each element provided by or for Silverlight can be defined with a `ContentProperty` attribute. This provides Silverlight with a default property to use if a child element is specified without first specifying a property of the parent.

As an example, look again at the XAML present in Listing 11–9. The `Border` object's `Child` property is set to contain a `TextBlock` object by explicitly providing the `Border.Child` element using property-element syntax. If we take a look at the definition for the `Border` class inside the IDE, we will find that it is declared as shown in Listing 11–10. The presence of the `ContentProperty` attribute tells us that by default, objects created for the `Border` will be assigned to its `Child` property if no explicit property assignment is made.

Listing 11–10. *The declaration of the Silverlight Border class*

```
[ContentProperty("Child", true)]
public sealed class Border : FrameworkElement
```

As a result of this, we can simplify the code from Listing 11–9 to that in Listing 11–11.

Listing 11–11. *Setting the Border.Child property based on its ContentProperty attribute*

```
<Border BorderBrush="Yellow" BorderThickness="3">
    <TextBlock Text="Bordered text" />
</Border>
```

This cut-down XAML can be a little harder to understand if you don't understand the way in which the objects have been configured in terms of their `ContentProperty` attributes, but generally these are set to the most obvious and sensible property, which can result in simpler and more readable code overall.

The second simplification in the XAML is with regard to collections. If the class to which child elements are being added is a list or dictionary class (i.e., it implements one of the generic `IList` or `IDictionary` interfaces), those elements will be added to the list or dictionary if they do not specify an explicit property name. This collection behavior takes precedence over the `ContentProperty` attribute.

Returning to App.xaml

Before we wrap up and summarize everything we've seen about XAML, let's quickly return back to `App.xaml` where we started, and look at the rest of the file. All the remaining content should make sense now.

After the opening of the `Application` XML element, the code shown in Listing 11–12 is present.

Listing 11–12. *The remainder of App.xaml*

```
<!--Application Resources-->
<Application.Resources>
</Application.Resources>

<Application.ApplicationLifetimeObjects>
    <!--Required object that handles lifetime events for the application-->
    <shell:PhoneApplicationService
        Launching="Application_Launching" Closing="Application_Closing"
        Activated="Application_Activated" Deactivated="Application_Deactivated"/>
</Application.ApplicationLifetimeObjects>
</Application>
```

The first element here sets the `Resources` property of the `Application` class. Because this element contains no embedded elements, its presence here has no effect, but creates a placeholder into which resources can be added later on should they be required.

The next element sets the `ApplicationLifetimeObjects` property of the `Application` class. This time, the element does contain some content and it creates an instance of the `Microsoft.Phone.Shell.PhoneApplicationService` class. Four attributes are specified for this new object for the `Launching`, `Closing`, `Activated`, and `Deactivated` properties.

These are, of course, the application life cycle events, and the values being provided for these attributes are the names of the event handlers within the code behind that will be used to handle the events. If you view the code behind, you will see the four event handlers. You can also access the code behind the page by right-clicking the function name inside the XAML and selecting Navigate to Event Handler.

So event handlers can be hooked into the XAML just as if they were property values, and .NET will automatically wire the event and the handler together.

The final question to answer is one that we asked earlier: why doesn't the page designer appear for this XAML file? The reason is because the class derives from `Application`, which is not recognized by Visual Studio as a class that requires a designer. If the class were instead deriving from a designable class such as `PhoneApplicationPage` (as `MainPage.xaml` does), the designer would appear.

XAML Syntax Summary

Here is a summary of the rules that we have explored for creating XAML code:

- The root element of the XAML specifies the class from which we are inheriting.

- The `x:Class` attribute defines the .NET Namespace and class name for the class being created.

- XML namespaces define names for .NET namespaces from which classes can be retrieved.

- Elements within the XAML document specify instances of objects, the class of which is defined by the element name.

- Element objects can be made accessible as internal fields by using the `x:Name` attribute, though there is no requirement to do so if access to the object through code is not necessary.

- Element attributes set properties of the object being created.

- Property-element syntax allows nested elements to set properties of their parent by specifying `[ParentClass].[PropertyName]` as their element name.

- If no parent property is specified for content contained within a parent element, it will either be added to a list or dictionary within the parent element, or will apply to the property specified as the parent's `ContentProperty`.

- Object event handlers can be set with attributes that contain the C# event handler function names.

This is not a complete list of XAML syntax rules, and we have glossed over certain areas of internal complexity, but it should be sufficient for us to keep moving forward into Silverlight game design.

Working with the Page Designer

Regardless of how dirty you want to get your hands in terms of manually crafting XAML, you will spend a lot of time working with the visual page designer displayed alongside the XAML window. Until you are comfortable crafting XAML directly, this designer is a great way to get started with adding new page elements and can often provide a way of updating the XAML that is more efficient than manual editing.

In this section, we will look at some of the options available for using the designer.

Adding and Positioning Elements

Controls can be added to the page designer in a very similar way to how controls are added to forms using the WinForms form designer. A control can be selected from the Toolbox and then drawn on to the page, or alternatively a control can be double-clicked in the Toolbox to add a new instance with a default size to the page.

An important thing to remember about the page is that it follows a hierarchical design, much more so than a WinForms form generally does. WinForms might place some controls inside panels or tabpanels, but the hierarchy inside a Silverlight page tends to be much deeper than this. The default MainPage provided when an empty project is created already contains the page itself, inside which is a Grid control that handles the separation of the headings and the main content, inside which is a further Grid handling the layout of the main page content.

When controls are added by being drawn onto the page, their container will be set based on the point at which the draw operation first begins. As the mouse cursor moves across the page design, Silverlight highlights the container that is effective at each position by putting a blue border around it, which makes it much easier to see where the control will be added before actually creating it.

When a control is added by double-clicking it in the Toolbox, it will be added to whichever container is currently selected within the designer. If the currently selected control is not a container, it will be added to that control's container.

Figure 11–5 shows a capture of the page designer with a new Rectangle control added and currently selected within the designer. The Rectangle is a very simple control that is very easy to see on the page, and so is handy for us to experiment with. It has had its Fill property set so that the region occupied by the rectangle is clearly visible.

Figure 11–5. A Rectangle control selected within the Silverlight page designer

Controls can be repositioned simply by dragging them. The designer will automatically snap the control's position to match the positions of other nearby controls within the page. This can be extremely useful for building a consistent layout, but if it gets the positioning wrong, the snapping can be temporarily disabled by holding down the Alt key.

Resizing controls is achieved by dragging one of the eight handles around the perimeter of the control until they reach the required dimensions. The designer will show a very handy measurement indicator alongside the control as it is resized that shows the control's new size.

It is also possible to drag a control into a new container. The control will be placed into whichever container is directly under the mouse cursor as it is being dragged. Once again, the designer highlights the target container with a blue outline as the control is dragged to clarify exactly where the control will be positioned within the container hierarchy when it is dropped.

■ **Tip** When you select controls within the page designer, the corresponding XAML element within the code window will be highlighted. Similarly, when you click a XAML element, the page designer will highlight the corresponding control. This can be a very useful way of understanding the relationship between the two views of the page, and of quickly reaching a relevant part of the code or the page design.

The Document Outline Window

Displayed by default alongside the page designer is a window called Document Outline. This displays a constantly updated map of the element hierarchy of the current page. This is synchronized with the page designer and the XAML view, and provides both a useful way of visualizing the structure of the elements within your page and a quick way of selecting one of the controls.

The Document Outline window is shown in Figure 11–6. If it is not open within your development environment, it can be opened from the View/Other Windows/Document Outline menu item. This window provides a simple view of the control structure similar in concept to the diagram that we used to visualize the page contents in Figure 11–4, but is interactive and always up to date.

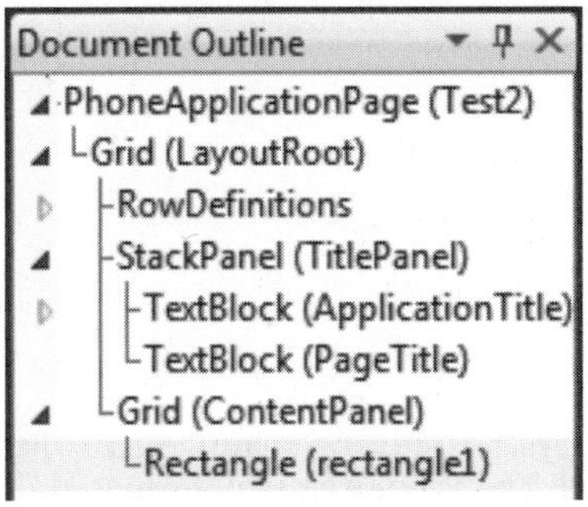

Figure 11–6. The Document Outline window

Hovering the mouse cursor over one of the items within the Document Outline window will display a pop-up preview of the element and all its contents. Note, however, that this is displayed with a white background, so controls with white content (the two TextBlock controls, for example) will appear to be blank.

Using the Properties Window

Just as in the WinForms designer, Silverlight's page designer provides a Properties window inside which all available properties of the selected control can be configured. As you would expect, it also supports multiple selection of controls, allowing many property values to be updated together. It can be a great time-saver compared with manually editing a series of properties in the XAML editor.

The Properties window has a number of useful enhancements compared with the WinForms designer. One of these is the capability to filter the displayed properties to just those containing a specific search string. Enter some text into the Search box above the property values, and the property list will be filtered as required, as shown in Figure 11–7.

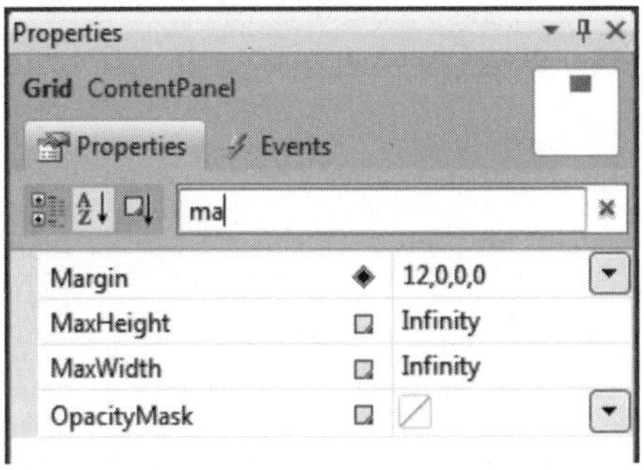

Figure 11–7. Filtering the property list

The control name display works a little differently in the WinForms designer. Because controls are not required to have a name, there is no drop-down-list at the top of the Properties window to allow named controls to be selected (the Document Outline window is the closest approximation). Instead, the control type is provided, along with the control's name if it has one, or the text <no name> if it does not. The name is editable here and can be modified, added, or removed by clicking into the name box, as shown in Figure 11–8.

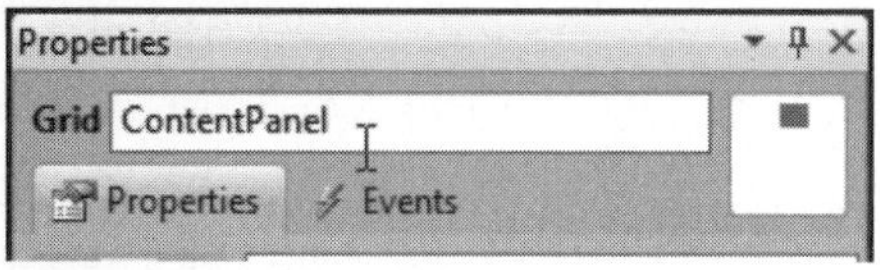

Figure 11–8. *Setting or editing a control's Name*

While many properties require simple values to be entered (numbers, strings, and so on), many others do not and instead require more complex objects to be specified. The Properties window has a particularly nice way of allowing such object values to be entered. Such properties have a small drop-down arrow displayed next to their values, which can be clicked to open a visual property editor appropriate for the type of data the property is storing. Figure 11–9 shows one of these editors, in this case for the Margin property.

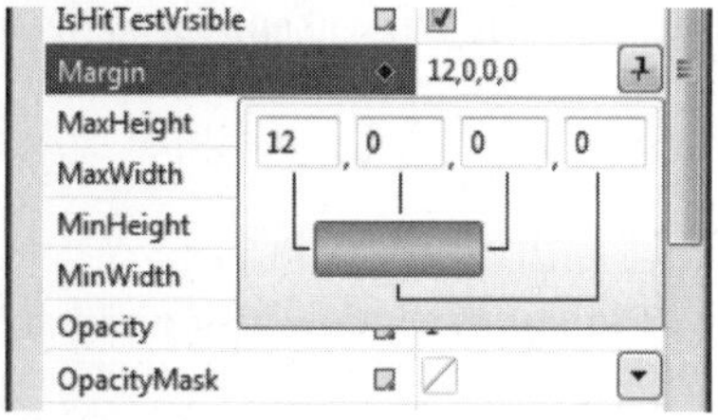

Figure 11–9. *Editing a complex property value*

Once the property editor has been dropped open, the drop-down array changes to a pushpin icon. Clicking this icon will pin the property editor into the Properties list so that it remains open, as shown in Figure 11–10. If you need to update a property repeatedly, pinning can be a real time saver.

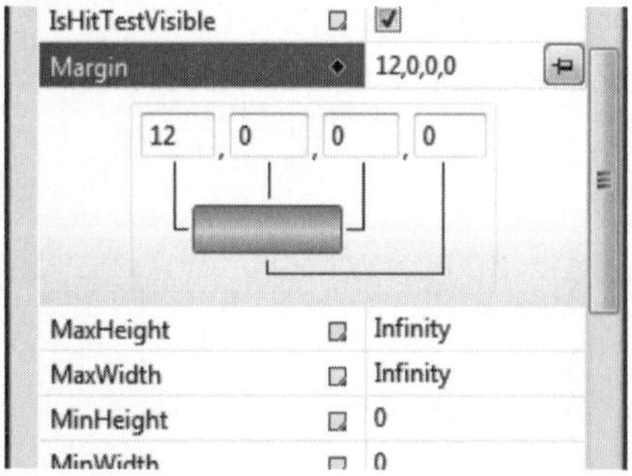

Figure 11–10. *Pinning open a complex property editor*

While many of these property editors are very useful, one worthy of particular note is the color editor. This editor is used by many control properties (the Fill property of the Rectangle control, for example), and can be seen in Figure 11–11.

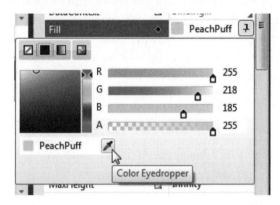

Figure 11–11. The color picker property editor

In addition to allowing colors to be entered by RGB value, the editor also permits selection from a color patch, from a drop-down list of named colors, or by using an *eyedropper*. After activating the eyedropper, any pixel on the entire screen can be clicked, and its color will be pulled into the property editor.

The color editor also can work with color gradients and images, and offers control over alpha levels so that objects can be made semitransparent.

The Properties window has another purpose, too: allowing event handlers for controls to be created. If you click the Events tab at the top of the window, it will display all possible events for the selected control. To create a handler for one of the events, simply double-click its name in the list, and Visual Studio will take care of the rest.

Double-clicking the MouseLeftButtonDown event (which might seem like a peculiar name for Windows Phone, but it is copied from the original browser-based Silverlight environment) will modify the Rectangle's XAML, as shown in Listing 11–13.

Listing 11–13. The Rectangle's XAML after the addition of an event handler

```
<Rectangle Stroke="Black" Margin="186,49,133,436" Fill="#FF8879C1"
        MouseLeftButtonDown="Rectangle_MouseLeftButtonDown" />
```

Visual Studio has created a handler function for the event named Rectangle_MouseLeftButtonDown, and it can be found in the code behind the page. The empty handler is shown in Listing 11–14.

Listing 11–14. The Rectangle's event handler function

```
private void Rectangle_MouseLeftButtonDown(object sender, MouseButtonEventArgs e)
{

}
```

▪ **Note** If Visual Studio is adding an event handler to a control with a name, it will name the handler as *controlname_eventname* (for example, `MyControl_MouseLeftButtonDown`). If the control does not have a name, it will prefix the handler with the control's class name instead (for example, `Rectangle_MouseLeftButtonDown`). If a handler already exists with this name, it will suffix it with a unique number (for example, `Rectangle_MouseLeftButtonDown_1`). It is a good idea, therefore, to name your controls before you begin adding event handlers to provide a more comprehensible set of event handler function names.

Configured values can be removed from properties and events by clicking the icon next to the property name and selecting Reset Value from the pop-up menu, as shown in Figure 11–12. This will remove the property value from the XAML, resetting it back to its default value.

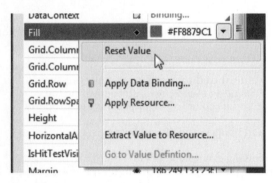

Figure 11–12. Resetting a property to its default value

Understanding Control Alignment

As Figure 11–5 shows, arrows are displayed to the top and left edges of the rectangle in the page designer, pointing toward the inner edges of its container (which have also been highlighted). These arrows help you to visualize the position of the control, the position of its container, and the way in which the control is *anchored* to the container.

Because the arrows are shown above and to the left, the control is anchored to the top and left edges of its container. If its container moves or changes size, the rectangle will always maintain the same distance from the top and left of its container.

The XAML for the control is shown in Listing 11–15. Notice that among its properties are `HorizontalAlignment` (set to `Left`) and `VerticalAlignment` (set to `Top`). These are the properties that control the anchoring of the element.

Listing 11–15. The XAML for the Rectangle control

```
<Rectangle Height="100" HorizontalAlignment="Left" Margin="76,58,0,0"
        Name="rectangle1" Stroke="Black" StrokeThickness="1" VerticalAlignment="Top"
        Width="200" Fill="CornflowerBlue" />
```

The position of the rectangle is not set using Left and Top coordinates, as it would be in a WinForms form, but instead by specifying a margin between itself and its container. The margin here specifies that it should be set 76 pixels away from its container's left edge and 58 pixels from the container's top (the four elements within the margin represent the left, top, right, and bottom margin sizes, respectively). Because the control has been given an explicit Width and Height, the right and bottom elements of the margin are ignored.

If we modify the HorizontalAlignment so that it is set to Right, the rectangle jumps all the way across so it is touching the right edge of its container. Now the margin's left distance is being ignored because the rectangle is no longer left-aligned. If we increase the right element of the margin (the third element), the rectangle sets itself to be this distance from the right edge of its container, moving back toward the left of the page. The designer now shows arrows from the rectangle to the top and right of its container, indicating that they are the edges to which it is anchored, as shown in Figure 11–13.

Figure 11–13. A Rectangle right-aligned within its container

You can see the right alignment working by resizing the Grid control inside which the rectangle is contained. This is most easily achieved by selecting the grid control and then dragging the arrow on its right edge, as shown in Figure 11–14. You will see that as the grid is resized, the rectangle maintains a constant distance from its right edge.

Figure 11–14. Resizing the Rectangle's containing Grid

Another available alignment value is Center. This mode doesn't actually center the element within its container as you might expect, but instead maintains the same relative distances on both of its sides, regardless of how large the container gets. In this mode, both horizontal arrows disappear from the rectangle to indicate that it is not anchored to either side of its container. Try setting this alignment mode and then resize the grid; the rectangle stays proportionally in the same position.

The final alignment mode is Stretch, which anchors to both sides of the container and displays arrows on either side to indicate it. However, there is a sizing conflict within the control at this stage: we are specifying both a width and also a left and right margin. When the control is so configured, the width takes precedence, so the stretch mode is actually ignored. Try editing the XAML and removing the Width attribute; the control will calculate its width based on its left and right margins. Set up like this, the control does indeed stretch and shrink when its container resizes.

This automatic sizing is another example of how Silverlight's layout behaves in many ways along the same lines of that of HTML. Whereas in a WinForms project you would have to put specific design effort into making the user interface resize (using the controls' Anchor properties), in Silverlight this behavior is pretty much automatic and requires a minimum of design effort.

Colors and Brushes

Before we move on to look at the available Silverlight controls, let's discuss how we specify colors and brushes in Silverlight.

Color Specifications

Silverlight understands XAML color specifications in several different formats. The first is via the standard set of named colors, as we have already used in XNA and as can be seen in Listing 11–16. Any known color name can be specified for one of the color properties within XAML or can be selected within the color list inside the color picker dialog.

Listing 11–16. Specifying a named color

```
<Rectangle Fill="Tomato" />
```

Alongside the normal list of named colors there is also the special color value `Transparent`. Setting this value causes the color to become completely invisible, showing through whatever is behind.

Alternatively, colors can be specified numerically as a hexadecimal number. The number is formed of three sets of two-digit values: the first two digits are the red intensity, the following two digits are the green intensity, and the final two digits are the blue intensity. The value `8000F0` therefore represents a color with half-intensity red (`80`), no green (`00`), and nearly full blue (`F0`). An example of using a color in this way is shown in Listing 11–17.

Listing 11–17. Specifying a color using hexadecimal notation

```
<Rectangle Fill="#8000F0" />
```

The hex notation can be extended to include an alpha component, too. The alpha component in Silverlight controls transparency just as it did in XNA. A control whose color is set to have full alpha will appear opaque, whereas those with their alpha value set to zero will be entirely invisible. Values in between will result in semitransparency. Transparency can be used all over the place in Silverlight that can allow for some very rich-looking graphical displays.

To specify an alpha component, add an additional two digits to the front of the hex value. If we want to specify the color in Listing 11–17 with a 25 percent alpha component, we can modify the color value to be `#408000F0`. If the alpha component is not included within the color specification, it is assumed to be set to its maximum value (`FF`).

Brushes

Although these color examples make it look like the `Rectangle`'s `Fill` property is a color property, it is in fact storing a *brush* rather than a color. In Silverlight, a brush allows us to specify how a solid region of the screen should be filled. Filling with a single color is clearly one of the brush options available, but there are several others. Let's take a look at these.

SolidColorBrush

When a color is specified for a control's property without any further brush information being provided, Silverlight defaults to creating an instance of the `SolidColorBrush` class. If we were to write the code from Listing 11–16 in full, instead of relying on the `ContentProperty` attributes, it would actually look like Listing 11–18.

Listing 11–18. Specifying a named color using the SolidColorBrush

```
<Rectangle>
    <Rectangle.Fill>
        <SolidColorBrush>
            <SolidColorBrush.Color>
                <Color>Red</Color>
            </SolidColorBrush.Color>
        </SolidColorBrush>
    </Rectangle.Fill>
</Rectangle>
```

While this code is clearly much more long-winded than it needs to be, it does clarify what is actually happening within the Silverlight objects' properties. The `Fill` property of the rectangle isn't being given just a color, but rather a `SolidColorBrush`, and it is this brush that is receiving the color.

The `Color` structure is being set here using a named color, but the hex notation can be used, too. When colors are set directly into their structure, they also support a third notation, in which we set the alpha, red, green, and blue intensity levels individually as properties of the color. Listing 11–19 shows how this notation can be used to set an opaque orange color. It also omits the `SolidColorBrush.Color` property specification because this is the defined content property for `SolidColorBrush`.

Listing 11–19. *Specifying a color using the Color structure's properties*

```
<Rectangle>
    <Rectangle.Fill>
        <SolidColorBrush>
            <Color A="255" R="255" G="127" B="0" />
        </SolidColorBrush>
    </Rectangle.Fill>
</Rectangle>
```

LinearGradientBrush

Silverlight can provide a much more attractive color filling than just solid color. It has two *gradient brushes* that provide color fades within the area being filled. The first of these is the `LinearGradientBrush`.

The first thing that this brush needs to know is a start point and end point within the area that it is filling. Each of these points is specified as a coordinate in the range of 0 to 1 along each axis (similar to the way we specified texture coordinates in XNA). The coordinate (0, 0) is on the top left of the area, while (1, 1) is the bottom right of the area.

Silverlight draws an imaginary line between these two points and places its first gradient fade color at the start point and the last gradient color at the end point. It then fades between these two points, extending the color out perpendicular to the imaginary line to fill the whole area.

For example, if we specify a start coordinate of (0, 0) (top-left) and an end coordinate of (0, 1) (bottom-left), the imaginary line will stretch down the entire left edge of the fill region. Because the line is vertical, the gradient fade will extend horizontally across the region. This fill effect is shown in Figure 11–15, which uses white as its start color and gray as its end color; the two coordinates and the imaginary line are shown to help clarify the effect, although they are not displayed by Silverlight.

Figure 11–15. *A linear gradient brush with a vertical linear path*

If the coordinates were changed to start at (0, 0) (top left) and end at (1, 0) (top right), the imaginary line would extend across the width of the area, so the gradient would fade across the area instead.

The coordinates need not be restricted to forming horizontal or vertical lines, of course. Figure 11–16 shows a linear gradient brush with coordinates (0,0) to (1,1) (top left to bottom right). The brush fades diagonally across the area of the fill.

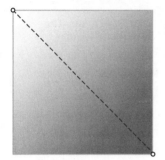

Figure 11–16. *Fading the linear gradient brush diagonally*

The XAML required to set up these gradient fades is really very simple. Listing 11–20 configures a Rectangle to use the gradient fill shown in Figure 11–16.

Listing 11–20. *Specifying a diagonal linear gradient fill*

```
<Rectangle>
    <Rectangle.Fill>
        <LinearGradientBrush EndPoint="1,1" StartPoint="0,0">
            <GradientStop Color="White" Offset="0" />
            <GradientStop Color="Gray" Offset="1" />
        </LinearGradientBrush>
    </Rectangle.Fill>
</Rectangle>
```

■ **Note** If you would rather set the StartPoint and EndPoint coordinates in pixels rather than as a proportion of the fill area, you can do it by setting the LinearGradientBrush's MappingMode property to Absolute. Both coordinates will then operate as pixel offsets from the top-left corner.

You will see in the XAML code that the two fade colors are specified by providing GradientStop structures, and that each also contains an Offset property as well as a color. This offset specifies the proportion across the imaginary gradient line at which this particular color should appear. Gradient fills are not limited to just two GradientStop items; we can use as many as we like, which allows more complex color fades to be achieved.

■ **Tip** You can also use the alpha component of the colors in your GradientStop items, which can result in gradients that fade between being transparent and opaque, in addition to or instead of fading colors.

Listing 11–21 shows another piece of XAML, this time containing four GradientStop items. The gradient fill begins in white and fades to black 25 percent of the way along. At 50 percent, it fades to white again, finally fading to gray at the end of the line.

Listing 11–21. Multiple GradientStop items within a gradient fill

```
<Rectangle>
    <Rectangle.Fill>
        <LinearGradientBrush EndPoint="0,1" StartPoint="0,0">
            <GradientStop Color="White" Offset="0" />
            <GradientStop Color="Black" Offset="0.25" />
            <GradientStop Color="White" Offset="0.5" />
            <GradientStop Color="Gray" Offset="1" />
        </LinearGradientBrush>
    </Rectangle.Fill>
</Rectangle>
```

The end result of this fill is shown in Figure 11–17. The four gradient stop points are displayed on the left edge of the figure for illustrative purposes.

Figure 11–17. Multiple GradientStop items within a gradient fill

■ **Tip** If you don't fancy creating the GradientStop items by hand, the color property editor contains comprehensive support for editing them. Stops can be easily added, colored, and positioned by moving colored sliders within the editor window. The editor can be accessed by selecting the property whose color is to be set— for example, the Fill property of the Rectangle control.

Another feature that the LinearGradientBrush can offer is the ability to place its start and end points so they do not completely cover the whole of the fill area. For example, if the start and end points were (0.333, 0) and (0.666, 0), respectively, the line would only cover the middle third of the fill area.

The brush has three different ways of handling such coordinate ranges, specified by the SpreadMethod property. If set to Pad (the default), the line will be extended in each direction until it fills the entire area, and all the additional area will be filled with the color specified nearest to that end of the line. (In simple terms, the line extension at its beginning will be filled with the color at offset 0, and the extension at its end will be filled with the color at offset 1.)

If SpreadMethod is set to Repeat, it will extend the line and repeat the original color range across the extension area at both ends. If it is set to Reflect, it will repeat the original color range once again, but will reverse it so that it mirrors the defined gradient stop colors.

These color spread methods can provide a useful and simple way of providing more complex fills than could be practically achieved by adding large numbers of repeating gradient stop items.

Figure 11–18 shows a horizontal white-to-gray gradient fill from coordinates (0.333, 0) to (0.666, 0) using each of the different SpreadMethod modes. On the left is Pad mode, in the middle is Repeat, and on the right is Reflect.

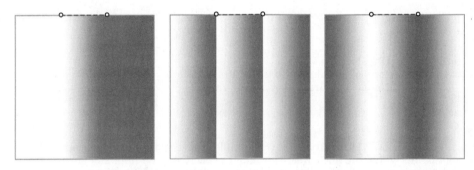

Figure 11–18. The three different SpreadMethod modes for the LinearGradientBrush

With very little effort, some very pleasing effects can be obtained from this brush. Consider using the brush with perhaps a fairly subtle fade for the background in your game screens—it can produce a much more pleasing result than a simple block of solid color.

RadialGradientBrush

The second gradient brush is the RadialGradientBrush, which provides similar functionality to the LinearGradientBrush but working with gradients that radiate out from an origin point. An example of this brush is shown in Figure 11–19, fading from white at its start point to gray at its end point.

Figure 11–19. A Rectangle filled with a RadialGradientBrush

The XAML required to achieve this fill is shown in Listing 11–22.

Listing 11–22. Filling an area with a RadialGradientBrush

```
<Rectangle>
    <Rectangle.Fill>
        <RadialGradientBrush>
            <GradientStop Color="White" Offset="0" />
            <GradientStop Color="Gray" Offset="1" />
        </RadialGradientBrush>
    </Rectangle.Fill>
</Rectangle>
```

Just like the linear brush, RadialGradientBrush allows multiple GradientStop items to be added to provide additional color points within the filled area. The Offset of each of these stops still ranges between 0 and 1, but now refers to the distance between the origin of the radial fill (with an offset of 0) to its outer edge (with an offset of 1).

The radial fill does not use start and end points as the linear fill does, but instead has two similar points called Center and GradientOrigin. Center specifies a point that will be the center of the outermost circle formed by the radial fill. GradientOrigin specifies a second point that is the focal point of the fill. Both of these points are specified with values in the range of 0 to 1 on each axis, where 0 is the left or top edge, and 1 is the right or bottom edge. Once again, the MappingMode property can be set to Absolute to change them to be interpreted as pixel offsets instead.

Alongside these properties are two values that define the size of the outermost circle. RadiusX and RadiusY both default to 0.5 to specify that the circle should be the same width and height as the area it fills. They can be decreased to focus the fill more tightly or increased to allow the circular area to expand so that it is greater than the fill area. Increasing the radius will allow the gradient to extend right into the corners of the area, which would otherwise be a solid color (as can be seen in Figure 11–19).

The RadialGradientBrush also supports the SpreadMethod property that we saw in the LinearGradientBrush. Setting it to Repeat or Reflect will cause the area outside of the defined circular region to be filled using this same behavior.

ImageBrush

The final type of brush we can use for filling areas is the ImageBrush. As its name suggests, this brush fills the area with an image.

The easiest way to insert an image into the brush is to open the color property editor and select the Image Brush item inside. This will present you with a Select Image button that can be used to browse for images on your computer, shown in Figure 11–20.

Figure 11–20. Setting an ImageBrush image using the color property editor

---

■ **Note** Just as in XNA, Silverlight supports BMP, JPG, and PNG images. GIF images are not supported and BMP images are not recommended!

When you select and add an image, Visual Studio creates a new folder within your project called Images and copies the selected image into it. The image is then added into the project with a Build Action of Resource. This embeds the image into your project so that it is accessible after deployment. If you change your mind about which images you want to use, remember to remove any unwanted images from the project because they will otherwise still be compiled in, wasting resources in your finished game.

The resulting XAML for the ImageBrush can be seen in Listing 11–23.

Listing 11–23. Filling an area with an ImageBrush

```
<ImageBrush ImageSource="/WindowsPhoneApplication1;component/Images/SmileyFace.png" />
```

By default, the selected image will appear at its actual size within the area that it is filling. There are four values available for the Stretch property that can be used to affect the size of the image within the brush.

The default stretch mode is None, which results in the behavior you have already seen. Setting it to Fill will stretch (or shrink) the image so that it completely fills the defined area. If the aspect ratio of the area does not match that of the image, the image will be distorted. We can avoid this by using either of the remaining modes: Uniform will stretch (or shrink) the image so that it is as large as it can possibly be while still fitting entirely inside the fill area without distorting, while UniformFill will entirely fill the area without distorting (possibly resulting in some of the image being clipped).

Examples of each of these modes can be seen in Figure 11–21. From left to right, the modes are None, Fill, Uniform, and UniformFill.

Figure 11–21. The four ImageBrush Stretch modes

The image can also be positioned within the fill area by setting the AlignmentX and AlignmentY properties. These properties allow the image to be aligned to the left or right, top or bottom, or remain vertically or horizontally centered as required.

Setting Colors in Code

It is very likely that you will want to set colors in C# code, too, and this can be easily accomplished. XAML's capability to hide the object structure away doesn't apply in C# code, however, so it is not possible to simply assign a color to a Fill property, for example. Listing 11–24 shows the code that is needed to create a new SolidColorBrush and put it into place inside the Fill property of a Rectangle. Of course, if the Rectangle were already configured with a brush at design time, and we simply wanted to change its color, we could update the existing brush rather than creating a new one.

Listing 11–24. Creating a SolidColorBrush for a Rectangle's Fill property

```
MyRectangle.Fill = new SolidColorBrush(Color.FromArgb(255, 255, 127, 0));
```

The ColorFade example project that accompanies this chapter provides a simple demonstration of updating the gradient stops in a RadialGradientBrush. The design time configuration for the page puts a radial brush into the large Rectangle occupying the main area of the page. Each time the rectangle is tapped, it removes the existing gradient stops and adds three new ones. The first two stops will have offset 0 and 1, respectively, while the last stop will have a randomized position between the two. All the stops are given a random color.

The XAML for the Rectangle is shown in Listing 11–25. Note that the brush has been given a name instead of the Rectangle because we don't need to access any of the Rectangle's other properties.

Listing 11–25. The Rectangle's XAML from the ColorFade example project

```
<Rectangle Height="562" Margin="0,0,0,0" Width="411"
                        MouseLeftButtonDown="rectangle1_MouseLeftButtonDown">
    <Rectangle.Fill>
        <RadialGradientBrush x:Name="FadeBrush">
            <GradientStop Color="Black" Offset="0" />
            <GradientStop Color="White" Offset="1" />
        </RadialGradientBrush>
    </Rectangle.Fill>
</Rectangle>
```

The code that updates the radial brush is implemented in the `rectangle1_MouseLeftButtonDown` event handler, shown in Listing 11–26. You can also see from this listing that the gradient stops do not need to be sorted into the order of their Offset values; Silverlight will take care of this automatically.

Listing 11–26. Randomizing the gradient stops within the RadialGradientBrush

```
private void rectangle1_MouseLeftButtonDown(object sender, MouseButtonEventArgs e)
{
    GradientStop gradStop;
    Random rand = new Random();

    // Clear the existing gradient stops
    FadeBrush.GradientStops.Clear();

    // Add a new stop with offset 0 (radial center)
    gradStop = new GradientStop();
    gradStop.Color = Color.FromArgb(255, (byte)rand.Next(256), (byte)rand.Next(256),
                                         (byte)rand.Next(256));
    gradStop.Offset = 0;
    FadeBrush.GradientStops.Add(gradStop);

    // Add a new stop with offset 1 (radial edge)
    gradStop = new GradientStop();
    gradStop.Color = Color.FromArgb(255, (byte)rand.Next(256), (byte)rand.Next(256),
                                         (byte)rand.Next(256));
    gradStop.Offset = 1;
    FadeBrush.GradientStops.Add(gradStop);

    // Add a new stop with a random offset
    gradStop = new GradientStop();
    gradStop.Color = Color.FromArgb(255, (byte)rand.Next(256), (byte)rand.Next(256),
                                         (byte)rand.Next(256));
    gradStop.Offset = rand.Next(100) / 100.0f;
    FadeBrush.GradientStops.Add(gradStop);
}
```

Using Brushes Together

More complex effects can be achieved by placing multiple objects together, each with different brushes. A simple (and rather garish) example of this can be seen in the MultipleGradientBrushes example project, an image from which is shown in Figure 11–22.

Figure 11–22. A Border and a TextBlock control with various brushes applied

This example creates a TextBlock control contained within a Border control. The Border has been filled with a linear red-white gradient background and also a linear gradient border, while the text has been given a radial gradient for its foreground color. You will find that these brushes can be used in a large variety of places throughout all the available Silverlight controls.

The thing that this example probably demonstrates best is that it is very easy to overuse these brushes. Used with a little more subtlety than they have been here, however, they can be a very effective way of adding interest to areas of the screen that would otherwise be dull and unexciting.

Exploring Silverlight

Silverlight is a rich and complex environment with many features and functions, many of which will not be obvious the first time you encounter them or find a need to call on them. This chapter has given you a rapid tour through some of the areas of functionality that Silverlight has to offer, but there is a huge amount more that we simply don't have the space to include within this book.

If you need help with using Silverlight or have questions about how to achieve things, the official Silverlight web site at www.silverlight.net is a great place to look for assistance. Among other things, the site contains some active discussion forums, including one that is specifically targeted at Silverlight development for Windows Phone 7.

Please spend some time experimenting and familiarizing yourself with Silverlight. In the next chapter, we will turn our attention to the various controls that can be used in Silverlight games and applications.

CHAPTER 12

Silverlight Controls and Pages

Now that you are hopefully feeling comfortable with the Silverlight design environment and with using XAML, it's time to spend some time getting familiar with the controls that are available to use in your Silverlight game projects, with ways to visually transform those controls, and with how the pages in your projects can be managed and manipulated. We will also cover topics including using different orientations within your game and how to run in full screen mode.

The Silverlight Controls

Let's take a tour through some of the controls that are available for use within your Silverlight pages. We won't cover them all, but will look at those that are most likely to be useful for your games and their user interfaces (UIs).

The controls can be broadly divided into three different groups: those that *display* information to the user, those that are *interactive* UI elements that the user can update as well as look at, and *layout* controls that help organize the presentation of the controls on the screen.

As you read through this section, please spend some time in Visual Studio and experiment with each of the controls—add and configure instances to a page in a test project, and then run them up in the emulator or on a phone to see how they look and how they can be interacted with. Having some basic experience with using the controls will be very beneficial when it comes to using them in your games because you will already have a feel for what each can achieve.

Display Controls

The controls that we will look at for the purposes of displaying information and content to the user are the TextBlock, Image, ProgressBar, Ellipse, Rectangle, Line, Polyline, and Polygon controls.

TextBlock Controls

One of the most frequently used controls is the TextBlock, whose responsibility is simply to display a piece of text within the page.

A number of properties are present to control the appearance and position of the text. Its font can be set using the FontFamily property, and its size using the FontSize property. Silverlight renders vector fonts rather than using bitmaps, so specifying a larger font size does not result in additional resource data as it did in XNA. As a result, all text rendered by Silverlight will appear sharp and focused regardless of how large it gets.

■ **Note** Silverlight, unlike XNA, renders the actual underlying font to the screen rather than building a bitmap representation of the font. It is important, therefore, to select a font that exists on the device, rather than on your PC. Selecting one of the fonts from the FontFamily property list will ensure that this is the case.

The font can also be italicized using the FontStyle property and set to be bold using the FontWeight property. If a specific bold version of the font exists (such as it does for the Segoe WP font), setting the FontWeight will have no effect; instead the appropriate version of the font must be selected for the FontFamily. The TextDecorations property can be left blank or set to Underline to underline the text.

The rendered text can be padded away from the boundaries of the TextBlock by setting the Padding property. It may be horizontally aligned using the TextAlignment property to one of Left, Center, or Right (though note that unfortunately the Justify option does not work and just displays an error message). The text can be configured to word wrap inside the TextBlock area by setting the TextWrapping property appropriately.

What is less obvious is that the control can display much more complex text formatting than the simple Text property would suggest. The Properties window does not offer any support for it, but the TextBlock has an alternative method for setting its text: the Inlines property. This new property is in fact the ContentProperty for the TextBlock, so any content entered directly inside the TextBlock's element will be assigned to it.

Besides simple text, a child element named Run can be added to the text. This can be used a little like a span in HTML, allowing custom formatting to be applied to a section of the text. Listing 12–1 shows how this can be used in XAML to highlight a word in a different color.

Listing 12–1. Using the Inlines property in a TextBlock

```
<TextBlock Height="147" FontSize="28" FontFamily="Arial" TextWrapping="Wrap">
    This is an example of using <Run Foreground="Blue">Inlines</Run> in a
    Silverlight TextBlock.
</TextBlock>
```

The resulting text shows with the word *Inlines* in blue text. Note, however, that it does not appear correctly within the Visual Studio page designer, failing to apply any spaces around the formatted text areas; this is just a preview error and it does appear normally when the application is running. Figure 12–1 shows the final output in a running application on the left, and on the right shows the appearance of the TextBlock within the Visual Studio preview.

Figure 12–1. The resulting TextBlock, running and in the Visual Studio preview

The text-formatting properties available for the Run element are FontFamily, FontSize, FontStretch, FontStyle, FontWeight, Foreground, and TextDecorations; and so any of them can be customized for the piece of text contained within the element. Note that Run elements cannot be nested, however.

Image Controls

To display a static image within the page, use an Image control. The image to be displayed is selected using its Source property, and can be added and addressed in exactly the same way as we saw with the ImageBrush earlier in Chapter 11.

The selected image can be stretched or shrunk using the Stretch property, which again behaves in the same way for each option as in the ImageBrush. If the displayed image is smaller than the control, it will always appear in the control's top-left corner.

ProgressBar Controls

Just as in the desktop world, the ProgressBar allows us to provide the user of our application with an indication of how far through a long-running process our code has progressed. This can be useful in gaming, whether it be for initializing a level, loading resources, or downloading content from the Internet. The Windows Phone 7 ProgressBar is space-optimized, allowing it to occupy very little vertical space within the page.

Its progress is set using three properties: Minimum, Maximum, and Value. The progress indication will be calculated by finding the proportion of the value between the minimum and maximum extents. By default, Minimum and Maximum have the values of 0 and 100, allowing Value to provide a percentage-based display. Figure 12–2 shows a progress bar using this default value range and with an actual Value setting of 25.

Figure 12–2. A ProgressBar showing 25 percent completion

There is an alternative way in which the control can be used, however, which is useful if you do not know how long your task will actually take to complete. If the IsIndeterminate property is set to be true, the Minimum, Maximum, and Value properties will be ignored, and instead a series of animated dots will appear (which will probably look very familiar to you!). These dots can be displayed while the task is running, and then hidden once the task is complete.

■ **Tip** The indeterminate ProgressBar is animated within the page designer at design time, too, which can be very distracting! It is, therefore, a good idea to leave IsIndeterminate set to false at design time and then switch it to true when your game is running and you are ready to display it. Additionally, an indeterminate progress bar consumes processor resources the entire time your application is running, even if it is invisible or offscreen. You should always, therefore, ensure that IsIndeterminate is set to false at runtime, too, unless you actually need it to be displayed onscreen.

Ellipse and Rectangle Controls

As you might expect, these controls allow ellipses, circles, rectangles, and squares to be placed inside your page. They can be filled (using all the available brushes) or transparent, and can have a border around them.

To create a circle or square, simply ensure that the ellipse or rectangle's Width and Height are set to the same value.

The interior of the shapes are filled using their Fill property, whereas their border is controlled using a series of properties whose names all begin with Stroke. The Stroke property itself sets the color, whereas the StrokeThickness sets the border width (though be aware that it starts at 0, making the border initially invisible).

The border offers up an extra feature that might be useful, however: it doesn't need to be a continuous line. One of the properties, StrokeDashArray, allows a dashed pattern to be configured for the border. This property cannot be edited via the Properties window, but can be directly entered into the XAML. Its value should be a list of numbers (separated by spaces) that define alternating length of filled and empty areas of the border.

For example, if this were set to a value of "1 1", the border would display dashes that were 1 unit long, followed by a gap that was also 1 unit long. Setting it to "3 1" would result in dashes 3 units long and gaps 1 unit long. More complex patterns can be formed by providing a larger pattern; "1 1 3 5" would result in a 1-unit dash, a 1-unit space, a 3-unit dash, and then a 5-unit space. Fractional numbers can be provided for any of these array elements, too.

The measurement unit that the border is using is the StrokeThickness. As this increases or decreases, so too do the lengths of the dashes.

Listing 12–2 shows how these properties can be used to create a filled ellipse with a dashed border.

Listing 12–2. Creating a filled ellipse with a dashed border

```
<Ellipse Height="250" Width="250" Stroke="SkyBlue" StrokeThickness="15"
                                    StrokeDashArray="3 3" Fill="Gray" />
```

The resulting ellipse is shown in Figure 12–3.

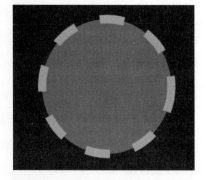

Figure 12–3. The resulting ellipse

Some additional options are available for the dashed border, too. The StrokeDashCap can be used to control the transition between the dashes and the empty space between. The default value for this property is Flat, but it can also be set to one of Square, Round, or Triangle. This difference can be seen in Figure 12–4, which uses the same ellipse as in Figure 12–3, but with each of the new dash cap values. Note that all these except for Flat will eat into the space allocated for the gaps, so if you want to use a dash cap while also retaining equal sizes of the dashes and gaps, you will need to manipulate the StrokeDashArray to accommodate the dash caps.

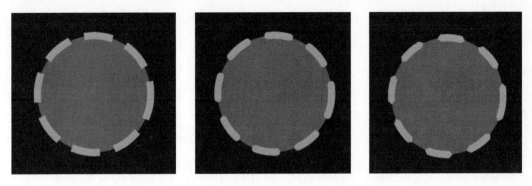

Figure 12–4. Dashed ellipses with Square, Round, and Triangle stroke dash caps

It is also possible to rotate the dashes around the ellipse by applying a StrokeDashOffset. This is measured in the same units as the StrokeDashArray is measured in, so if the total length of the stroke dashes is 6 units, the offset will produce identical results with a value of 0 or 6, but other values in between will change the positioning of the dashes. The StrokeDashOffset could be animated within a game to provide a simple implementation of a spinning outline box or disc—useful for highlighting selected game objects, for example.

The Rectangle offers a final pair of properties that might come in very handy: RadiusX and RadiusY. They allow rounded corners to be applied to the rectangle, and the elliptical rounding area will have its width and height defined by these two properties. Figure 12–5 shows a rectangle using a value of 15 for both of the corner radius properties.

Figure 12–5. A rectangle with rounded corners

Line, Polyline, and Polygon Controls

While we are discussing the Ellipse and Rectangle shape controls, it seems an appropriate time to also look at three additional shape-based controls. The Line control allows a simple straight line to be drawn within a page. Polyline controls allow a series of lines to be joined together. Finally, Polygon extends this further to create a solid shape from a number of lines and optionally fill its interior.

None of these controls is available from the Toolbox; instead, they must be manually created within the XAML editor. Once the control has been declared, all its properties can be viewed and modified in the Properties window as usual.

The Line requires two coordinates to be specified, for the start and end of the line. They are specified in pixels, relative to the top-left corner of their container. They also provide all the Stroke properties that we looked at for the Ellipse and Rectangle controls, allowing the line color, thickness, dashes, and so on to be configured.

Listing 12–3 shows the XAML required to create a line from coordinate (50, 50) to (200, 200).

Listing 12–3. Creating a Line

```
<Line Stroke="SkyBlue" StrokeThickness="15" X1="50" Y1="50" X2="200" Y2="200" />
```

Lines that have sufficient thickness will by default appear with flat ends. They can be changed by *capping* the line ends so that they have a different shape. This is controlled by the StrokeStartLineCap and StrokeEndLineCap properties, each of which can be set to one of Flat (the default), Square, Round, or Triangle.

The next shape is the Polyline, which allows a series of coordinates to be provided and joined together using a series of lines. The coordinates this time are specified as X,Y pairs using the shape's Points property. Listing 12–4 shows a Polyline that creates a zig-zag shape within its container.

Listing 12–4. Creating a Polyline

```
<Polyline Stroke="SkyBlue" StrokeThickness="15"
                          Points="100,50 200,100 100,150 200,200 100,250 " />
```

Besides simply joining between the points, the Polyline can provide additional flexibility around the corner points of the rendered lines. They are controlled using the StrokeLineJoin property, which can be set to one of Miter (the corners are extended into points), Bevel (the corners are flattened), or Round (the corners are rounded). Figure 12–6 shows the Polyline defined in Listing 12–4, but with each of the available StrokeLineJoin styles applied: Miter on the left, Bevel in the middle, and Round on the right.

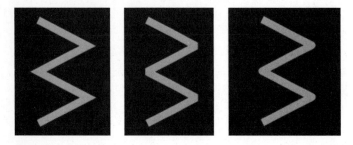

Figure 12–6. Polylines using each of the available StrokeLineJoin properties

Just like Lines, PolyLines also allow their start and end to be capped if needed.

The final shape is the Polygon, which is configured in exactly the same way as the Polyline, but it creates an enclosed region (the end point is automatically joined back to the start point). It supports all the same features as the Polyline, except for the stroke start and end line caps because the Polygon doesn't have any start or end point.

What it provides instead is the ability to set its Fill property, resulting in a solid interior to the rendered shape. Any of the available brushes can be used for this purpose.

Listing 12–5 shows the XAML for a filled Polygon.

Listing 12–5. Creating a Polygon

```
<Polygon Stroke="SkyBlue" StrokeThickness="15" Fill="Gold"
                          Points="100,50 200,100 150,150 200,200 100,250 " />
```

The resulting shape is shown in Figure 12–7.

Figure 12–7. The result of creating the filled Polygon

Interactive Controls

The controls that we will look at for the purposes of allowing user interaction and data entry are the TextBox, ListBox, ComboBox, CheckBox, RadioButton, Button, and ApplicationBar.

TextBox Controls

Silverlight's TextBox control provides a field within which the user can enter text, just like the TextBox control used in WinForms projects.

When the TextBox receives focus in a running application, Windows Phone will automatically display the onscreen keyboard (unless a hardware keyboard is currently open, in which case it will expect that to be used instead). If the onscreen keyboard would normally obscure the text box, the page will scroll to bring the text box back into view. Once focus is lost, the keyboard will disappear again.

Several properties are available to control the behavior of the control. Its font can be set using the same properties as for the TextBlock. The control can be locked to prevent text edits by setting the IsReadOnly property. The maximum number of characters that can be entered is controlled by the MaxLength property, defaulting to 0 for unlimited text.

The control can also support multiline text. If the AcceptsReturn property is set to True, pressing Enter on the keyboard will insert a line break. This can also be used with the TextWrapping property that will wrap text that is too long to fit on one line. The TextBox also offers properties named HorizontalScrollbar and VerticalScrollbar, which on the desktop implementation of Silverlight allow the displays of the field's scrollbars to be controlled, but unfortunately they have no effect on Windows Phone 7.

Useful events include GotFocus and LostFocus, KeyDown and KeyUp, and TextChanged.

ListBox Controls

ListBox controls in Silverlight are also very similar to their WinForms equivalent. They contain an Items collection into which any type of object can be added; the text displayed within the list will be obtained by calling the ToString method on each object. If the number of items exceeds the space available for them to be displayed, the user can scroll the items by dragging them up and down.

Additional functionality can be obtained, however, by adding ListBoxItem objects to the list instead of other objects. Each ListBoxItem offers a Content property (into which a text string can be placed or any other type of object just as if the object were being added directly to the ListBox). In addition, it also offers properties to allow the Background and Foreground colors to be changed, offers a selection of font properties, the IsEnabled property to allow individual items to be enabled or disabled, and

HorizontalAlignment and Visible properties, among others. These properties allow for very flexible control over the items within the list.

ListBoxItem objects can be added to the list either by entering them manually into the XAML as the content for the list or by clicking the ellipsis button against the ListBox's Items property in the Properties window.

Listing 12–6 shows a simple ListBox with some configuration applied to a few of the items.

Listing 12–6. *Setting up a ListBox and its items*

```
<ListBox Height="300" Width="300" BorderBrush="Gray" BorderThickness="1">
    <ListBoxItem Content="Item1" />
    <ListBoxItem Content="Item2" />
    <ListBoxItem Background="Navy" Content="Item3" />
    <ListBoxItem Content="Item4" />
    <ListBoxItem Content="Item5" IsEnabled="False" />
</ListBox>
```

The resulting ListBox is shown in Figure 12–8.

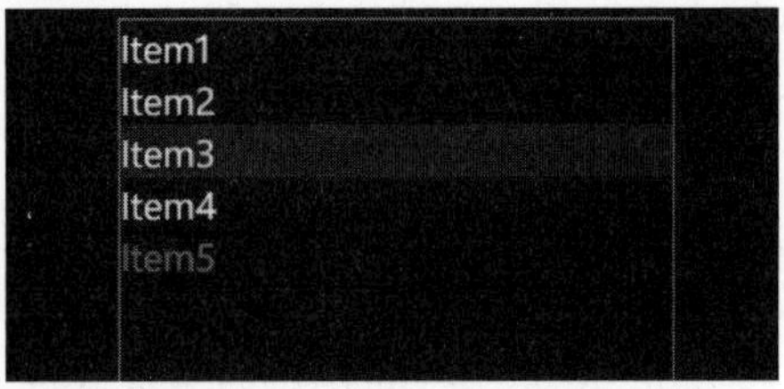

Figure 12–8. *The resulting ListBox control*

List items need not be limited just to displaying text strings, however. Other UI elements can be placed inside the list in order to create a very rich display of information. List items can therefore be formed from images, text boxes, and even other list boxes! Only a single control element can be placed inside each list item, but by using a Grid or StackPanel control (both of which we'll look at shortly), it is possible to nest multiple controls inside. By crafting your UI carefully, it is possible to create all sorts of ListBox display configurations, such as those used to display messages in the Windows Phone 7 e-mail application.

It is also possible to select multiple items within a ListBox. This feature can be activated by setting the SelectionMode property to Multiple. Once this has been done, tapping an item will toggle its selected state rather than deselecting the other items.

To track changes to the ListBox selection in your code, add a handler for the SelectionChanged event. Your event handler can use the ListBox's SelectedItem, SelectedItems (for multiselection) and SelectedIndex properties to query the items that are selected, but it can also use the handy AddedItems and RemovedItems collections provided by the event's SelectionChangedEventArgs property. This will contain the details of all items that were added to or removed from the SelectedItems collection as part of that event.

ComboBox Controls

You might have noticed the conspicuous absence of one of the most useful controls in the Toolbox: the ComboBox control. Unfortunately, official support for this control didn't make it into Silverlight for Windows Phone 7.

Although you can still use it, it must be created manually within the XAML rather than dragged from the Toolbox. There are also some severe presentational limitations that will make it appear different to your other controls, which is why the control is not properly supported.

The ComboBox will always appear with a shaded white background when closed and a similar background on the drop-down-list when it is opened by the user. Its default text color is also white, making the items virtually invisible. The background color cannot be changed (setting the ComboBox's Background property has no effect) but fortunately the Foreground property does work. Changing it to black (or some other color that shows up on a white background) will give you a usable control, even though it doesn't really fit in with the other controls around it.

Adding items to the ComboBox is very similar to the ListBox, except that ComboBoxItem objects are used in place of ListBoxItem objects. Once again, these item objects can be given a simple text value for their Content, or other UI elements can be used.

Listing 12–7 shows a simple ComboBox containing several items.

Listing 12–7. Setting up a ComboBox and its items

```
<ComboBox Width="200" Height="40" Foreground="Black" Background="Blue">
    <ComboBoxItem Content="Easy" />
    <ComboBoxItem Content="Medium" IsSelected="True" />
    <ComboBoxItem Content="Hard" />
</ComboBox>
```

The ComboBox created from this XAML can be seen in Figure 12–9. The image on the left shows the combo in its closed state; on the right, it is dropped open.

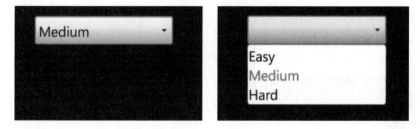

Figure 12–9. The resulting ComboBox control

Useful events for the ComboBox include the DropDownClosed and DropDownOpen events, as well as the SelectionChanged event. This latter event offers the AddedItems and RemovedItems collections just as are provided to the ListBox, but because there is no multiselection option in the ComboBox, these collections will always simply identify the previously selected item (if there was one) and the newly selected item. The ComboBox's SelectedItem and SelectedIndex properties are also available for interrogating the selection within the control.

■ **Note** As an alternative to the unsupported ComboBox control, try the ListPicker control that is supplied as part of the very useful Silverlight Toolkit package. Visit http://silverlight.codeplex.com to download this. A number of other very useful controls are included within the toolkit too, as detailed on the site.

CheckBox Controls

A simple but useful control, the CheckBox allows simple boolean values to be gathered from the user. When the control's value is true, it displays a check mark within the control; when it is false, the box is shown empty.

The caption displayed next to the CheckBox is part of the control itself rather than being implemented as a separate control, so tapping on either the actual displayed box or its caption will cause the state of the box to be toggled.

The caption is provided using the CheckBox control's Content property, and is not limited to being just a simple string: other controls can be placed into the content to provide additional formatting options.

A few useful properties that we might want to use are offered by the control. Among them are the IsChecked property, which allows the initial state of the CheckBox to be set (and which can, of course, also be set or queried in code to update or read the state of the control).

Another potentially useful property is the IsThreeState property. When this property is set to true, the CheckBox will cycle through three different states when it is tapped: checked, unchecked, and *indeterminate*. This final state can be used when the CheckBox is at an unknown state or when its value cannot currently be represented as a simple boolean value. When the control's value is indeterminate, the IsChecked property in code will return null. To set this in XAML, the special value {x:Null} must be provided for the property (though this can be picked from the Properties window).

Listing 12–8 shows the XAML for three CheckBox controls, each with a different initial state.

Listing 12–8. *Several CheckBox controls*

```
<CheckBox Height="70" Width="215" Margin="50,100" VerticalAlignment="Top"
                              Content="Unchecked" />
<CheckBox Height="70" Width="215" Margin="50,160" VerticalAlignment="Top"
                              Content="Checked" IsChecked="True" />
<CheckBox Height="70" Width="215" Margin="50,220" VerticalAlignment="Top"
                              Content="Indeterminate" IsChecked="{x:Null}" />
```

The resulting controls are shown in Figure 12–10.

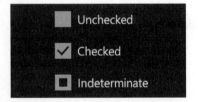

Figure 12–10. *The resulting CheckBox controls*

The CheckBox offers two different ways of responding to its state changing. The first is to add a handler for its Click event that will fire every time the control is tapped by the user, allowing the IsChecked property to be queried to determine the control's new value.

Alternatively. you might add handlers to any or all of the Checked, Unchecked, or Indeterminate events. These handlers will fire when the CheckBox is updated to the corresponding state. If they are used as well as the Click event, the Click event will fire after the approriate state-based event.

■ **Note** A useful feature of the Checked, Unchecked, and Indeterminate events is that they fire when the page first loads, allowing for any initial processing that is required based on the CheckBox state to be performed. The Click event only fires when the user actually interacts with the control.

RadioButton Controls

RadioButton controls offer similar functionality to the CheckBox, except that they are formed into mutually exclusive groups from which only a single RadioButton at a time can be selected. The properties and events used by the RadioButton are virtually identical to those of the CheckBox.

An additional property, called GroupName, is available, however. It is not set by default, and will result in the radio buttons being set as a group according to the container that they are placed in (only one of the radio buttons in the container can be selected). In many cases, this will be the desirable behavior, but if you want to have radio buttons that span across multiple containers or if you want to create separate groups of radio buttons within the same container, set the GroupName to a consistent value for all the controls within each group. Silverlight will look after everything else.

Button Controls

The next of the interactive controls that we will look at is also one of the simplest. Button controls simply display some content within a rectangular frame on the screen and respond to being clicked by raising their Click event.

The Button's text is specified within its Content property, but once again the property is not limited only to strings. Other UI elements can be placed within the button to facilitate buttons with images or other content.

ApplicationBar Controls

The ApplicationBar is responsible for displaying the small toolbars that are often seen at the bottom of the screen. It can hold up to a maximum of four image-based application buttons, and also a potentially unlimited number of menu items. These can be used to offer access to common features within your game (getting help, showing the scores, starting a new game, and so on).

An example project named ApplicationBarExample can be found in the download accompanying this chapter. It can be used for experimenting with the ApplicationBar, its buttons, and its menus.

The ApplicationBar is not added to the page from the Toolbox, but rather it already exists as a property of the PhoneApplicationPage object that forms the basis for all the pages within Silverlight. To add an ApplicationBar, we therefore need to set the PhoneApplicationPage.ApplicationBar property to a new instance of the ApplicationBar class.

This can be achieved using code along the lines of that shown in Listing 12–9. This should be added to the XAML at the very end of the code, just before the closure of the root phone:PhoneApplicationPage element.

Listing 12–9. A template for an ApplicationBar

```
<phone:PhoneApplicationPage.ApplicationBar>
   <shell:ApplicationBar>
     <shell:ApplicationBarIconButton IconUri="/Images/AppBarButton1.png" Text="Button 1"/>
     <shell:ApplicationBarIconButton IconUri="/Images/AppBarButton2.png" Text="Button 2"/>
     <shell:ApplicationBar.MenuItems>
        <shell:ApplicationBarMenuItem Text="MenuItem 1"/>
```

```
        <shell:ApplicationBarMenuItem Text="MenuItem 2"/>
    </shell:ApplicationBar.MenuItems>
  </shell:ApplicationBar>
</phone:PhoneApplicationPage.ApplicationBar>
```

This code produces an `ApplicationBar` that in its default state looks like the one shown in Figure 12–11.

Figure 12–11. *The ApplicationBar in its default closed state*

Tapping the ellipsis button on the right edge of the `ApplicationBar` will cause it to open, revealing the text for each of the buttons and the menu items hidden beneath (see Figure 12–12). Note that Silverlight has automatically set the text for the buttons and menu items into lowercase; this is the standard behavior across all Windows Phone 7 application bars and cannot be changed.

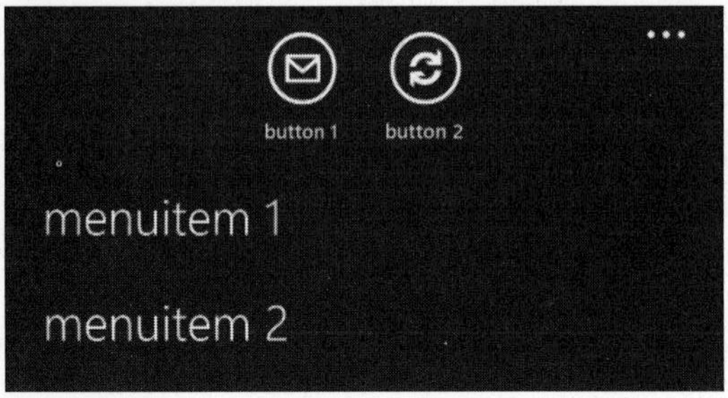

Figure 12–12. *The ApplicationBar in its open state*

To add more buttons, simply add additional instances if the `ApplicationBarIconButton` class (or indeed, remove the instances that are already there to show less buttons).

The `IconUri` property of each button is shown referencing an image file within the `Images` folder. These image paths must be entered manually because there is no Properties window editor to help you to select them.

■ **Note** When adding `ApplicationBar` icon images to your project, it is essential that their `Build Action` be set to `Content`. If they are left with the more usual (and default) `Resource`, they will simply appear as broken image icons when your project is run.

Images should be created at 48 x 48 pixels and should be created so that they have a white foreground on a transparent background (using the alpha channel to enforce the transparency). The circle that can be seen displayed around the icons is added automatically and should not be part of the image. To allow for this circular outline, the icon should be restricted to the 26 x 26 pixel region in the centre of the provided image.

■ **Tip** Microsoft helpfully provides a small library of useful image files as part of the Windows Phone 7 SDK. You can find them in your `Program Files` directory (or `Program Files (x86)` on 64-bit installations of Windows) inside the `Microsoft SDKs\Windows Phone\v7.0\Icons\dark` directory.

Buttons can be enabled or disabled using their `IsEnabled` property. When the user taps one of the buttons, its `Click` event will be fired.

Menu items can be added or removed as required by providing an appropriate number of `ApplicationBarMenuItem` objects. Microsoft recommends a maximum of five menu items to prevent the user having to scroll, but more than this can be added if required. Each menu item also has an `IsEnabled` property and a `Click` event.

The `ApplicationBar` also has several properties that can be used to control its appearance and function. The most useful of these are the `IsVisible` and `Opacity` properties.

Setting `IsVisible` to `false` will fairly predictably cause the menu to disappear.

The `Opacity` property has some more subtle behavior, however. When set to `1` (its default), it reserves some space from the page for itself, pushing the content above up and out of the way. Setting to any lower value than this will cause its background (though not the buttons themselves) to become less and less opaque, but will also cause it to stop reserving space within the page. The bar will therefore appear in front of any other page content that occupies the bottom area of the screen.

■ **Caution** With an `Opacity` less than 1, the `ApplicationBar` will be placed in front of any other content in the bottom of the page, but will still receive all screen taps in that area even with an `Opacity` of 0. Ensure that there is never anything behind the `ApplicationBar` that the user will want to interact with because they will be unable to do so.

Figure 12–13 shows three pictures of an `ApplicationBar`. It is contained on a page that has a large `Image` control aligned to its bottom. The picture on the left has the `Opacity` property set to 1. Notice that it has pushed the `Image` up and out of the way. The pictures in the middle and on the right have `Opacity` values of `0.5` and `0`, respectively. The background transparency has clearly changed, but you can also see that the `Image` is now appearing behind the `ApplicationBar` rather than above it.

Figure 12–13. ApplicationBars with varying levels of Opacity

Layout Controls

Along with the controls we have seen for the presentation of content and user interaction, a final set of controls exists whose purpose is to facilitate the flexible and predictable layout of control elements on each page. In this section, we will explore some of these controls, covering the Grid, StackPanel, ScrollViewer, Border, and Canvas controls.

Grid Controls

One of the most flexible of the layout controls is the Grid control. This control can seem somewhat puzzling to developers who encounter it in Silverlight after having worked with grid controls in WinForms development because the expectation is that it will offer functionality along the lines of a data grid, presenting tables of data to the user. That is not the Grid's purpose, however; instead it is used to allow the organization of other controls into consistent rows or columns.

A reasonable approximation of the Grid is perhaps the HTML table element, which also defines a layout of rows and columns, and allows content to be placed within them. Just like HTML tables, Grids allow row and column sizes to be set, arbitrary content to appear within each cell, and their content to span across multiple rows or columns.

For an example of a useful application for a grid, imagine that we are creating a Settings page for a game that we are writing. The page can be divided into two columns. For each setting, the first column will contain a TextBlock providing the name of the setting, while the second column will contain a control allowing the value of the setting to be entered or modified. With the columns configured in this way, we can then add as many rows as we need to accommodate each of the available settings.

When a Grid control is first added to the page, it is completely empty and does not define any rows or columns. This empty configuration results in a default row and a default column, providing a single empty cell ready for use. In order to turn the control into an actual grid, we need to tell it how many rows and how many columns we want to display.

There are two ways to achieve this. The first is through the page designer. If you hover the mouse cursor over the top or left edge of a selected Grid control, you will see that it displays a split point at the cursor position. Clicking the left mouse button will create a new column or row boundary at that position. This process can be repeated for each of the rows and columns that are required, as shown in Figure 12–14.

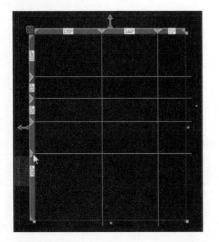

Figure 12–14. Inserting rows and columns into a Grid control

The second approach is to create the rows and columns within the XAML. When configuring the grid in this way, we do not necessarily need to specify the size of each of the rows or columns. Instead we can simply state that there is a row or column and let Silverlight automatically manage the size based on the content that we subsequently provide.

Listing 12–10 shows a Grid defined in XAML with two columns and three rows, with no sizes specified at all.

Listing 12–10. Declaring rows and columns for a Grid in XAML

```
<Grid Name="grid1">
    <Grid.ColumnDefinitions>
        <ColumnDefinition />
        <ColumnDefinition />
    </Grid.ColumnDefinitions>
    <Grid.RowDefinitions>
        <RowDefinition />
        <RowDefinition />
        <RowDefinition />
    </Grid.RowDefinitions>
</Grid>
```

If you declare a grid in this way and then view it in the designer preview, you will see that the row and column headings, which were showing the row or column size in pixels in Figure 12–14, display something that might be unexpected. All the sizes are now displayed as 1* instead of a pixel width. Alongside this displayed value, the rows and columns are evenly distributed across the height and width of the grid.

The reason for this behavior is that we actually have a variety of methods for specifying the sizes of rows and columns:

- *Fixed size*: We specify a size in pixels, and the grid uses exactly this size for the row or column.

- *Weighted size*: We specify a proportion of the grid by weighting each column, and the grid retains these weights as the grid.

- *Automatic size*: The row or column size will be set to match the largest item that it contains. If there is nothing contained within the row or column at all, it will collapse to have a size of 0.

Fixed-size rows and columns are declared by just giving them a size value. Weighted sizes are specified by providing a weight value followed by an asterisk. The size will be calculated by comparing the weight of each row or column to the total weights of all the rows or columns. For example, if two columns are present with widths of 2* and 1*, the first column will occupy two-thirds of the width, and the second column will occupy the remaining one-third. A weight of 1 can be specified just by using an asterisk character without a numeric prefix. Automatic sizes are specified by providing the keyword Auto as the size.

The grid defined by the code in Listing 12–11 uses all three of these sizing methods for the three columns that it declares.

Listing 12–11. Declaring rows and columns for a Grid in XAML

```
<Grid Name="grid1">
    <Grid.RowDefinitions>
        <RowDefinition Height="50" />
        <RowDefinition Height="2*" />
        <RowDefinition Height="Auto" />
    </Grid.RowDefinitions>
</Grid>
```

Although the page designer clearly shows the lines that separate the grid cells, they are only there as a guide. When the application runs, the grid lines are completely invisible. To aid in developing against grids, Silverlight allows the lines to be displayed at runtime, too. This display is only intended as a development and debugging aid, however, so there is no control provided for configuring the appearance of the grid lines. The lines can be switched on by using the Grid's ShowGridLines property.

So once we have defined the structure for the grid, how then do we tell Silverlight which cell to use for each of the controls that we want to place inside the grid? As is becoming very common, there are two ways to do this.

The first way is to add the new control by selecting a control in the Toolbox and drawing it into the page designer. Visual Studio will indicate the cell into which it is being added by shading the other cells in gray.

The second way is to add the control directly via the XAML editor. Controls added in this way should be placed inside the Grid element, but not inside the RowDefinitions or ColumnDefinitions elements. The target cell is then specified by setting a property of the grid as part of the new control's declaration. For example, the code in Listing 12–12 places a Button into the third row and the second column of the grid. If either the grid row or column is unspecified, it will be assumed to be the Grid's first row or column.

Listing 12–12. Specifying the target Grid cell for a TextBlock

```
<Grid Name="grid1">
    <Grid.ColumnDefinitions>
        <ColumnDefinition />
        <ColumnDefinition />
    </Grid.ColumnDefinitions>
    <Grid.RowDefinitions>
        <RowDefinition />
        <RowDefinition />
        <RowDefinition />
    </Grid.RowDefinitions>
    <Button Content="Button" Grid.Column="1" Grid.Row="2" />
</Grid>
```

The resulting output from this XAML is shown in Figure 12–15.

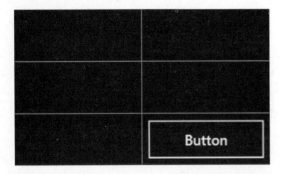

Figure 12–15. The Button in the page designer, positioned in row 2, column 1

To span content across multiple rows or columns, the contained control should set the Grid's RowSpan and/or ColumnSpan properties. These properties should indicate how many rows or columns should be included in the space (and both default to 1 if not specified).

We can modify the button in the previous listing to span across the second and third rows by changing the XAML, as shown in Listing 12–13.

Listing 12–13. Spanning a contained control across multiple grid rows

```
<Grid Name="grid1" Margin="0,0,0,333" ShowGridLines="True">
    <Grid.ColumnDefinitions>
        <ColumnDefinition />
        <ColumnDefinition />
    </Grid.ColumnDefinitions>
    <Grid.RowDefinitions>
        <RowDefinition />
        <RowDefinition />
        <RowDefinition />
    </Grid.RowDefinitions>
    <Button Content="Button" Grid.Column="1" Grid.Row="1" Grid.RowSpan="2" />
</Grid>
```

The resulting layout from this listing is shown in Figure 12–16.

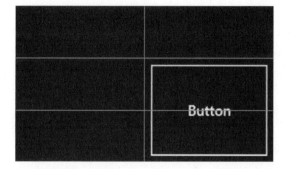

Figure 12–16. The Button in the page designer, spanned across rows 1 and 2

Using the Grid control, you can get a high degree of control over the placement of controls within your page. Another use for the Grid control is to provide a host for complex layouts inside locations that do not directly permit them. For example, inside the ListBoxItem elements that we looked at earlier we saw that only a single UI element can be placed as the content for each list item. If we were to make that single UI element a Grid, however, we could then place as many controls inside that Grid as we wanted.

StackPanel Controls

While Grid controls provide an open and flexible container inside which controls can be placed in virtually any way required, StackPanel controls take a different approach to organizing their contained controls. Instead of allowing controls to be placed in arbitrary arrangements, they instead allow an ordered series of controls to be arranged in a single row or column. If a control is added to the middle of this list of controls, all subsequent controls will be pushed out of the way to make space. If a stacked control's visibility is toggled or its size is changed, all the subsequent controls will be pushed or pulled around to fill the available space.

This control can be useful for creating pages or areas that consist of repeating items placed either one above or next to each other. Another useful example is for placement within a ListBoxItem object: if you want to have images displayed as part of each list item, or if you need each item to have an associated check box, you can create a horizontally orientated StackPanel as the Content for each list item, and place the Image, CheckBox, and TextBlock controls inside to facilitate the required functionality.

As always, you can add controls to the StackPanel either by drawing them from the Toolbox or by adding them directly in the XAML editor. If you use the Toolbox, the page designer will display a horizontal or vertical bar above, below, or between the existing items to indicate to you where your new control will be inserted. This can be seen in Figure 12–17, where a control at the mouse cursor's current location will be added between the first and second buttons. The same indicator appears if a control is dragged over a StackPanel, indicating what its position would be if it were dropped at that location.

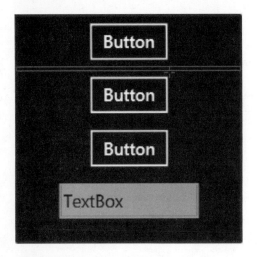

Figure 12–17. Drawing a new control into an existing StackPanel

Controls can be added directly as XAML elements, too. The order in which the controls are present in the XAML dictates the order in which they will be stacked on the page.

The only significant new property offered by the StackPanel is its Orientation. When set to its default value of Vertical, the controls will be stacked one above another, as in Figure 12–17. If the value is changed to Horizontal, the controls will stack from left to right instead.

Canvas Controls

The next layout control that we will look at is the Canvas control. The purpose of this container control is to allow objects placed within it to be positioned absolutely using a simple (x, y) coordinate system. Whereas the other containers we have looked at have taken control alignment and margins into consideration, all controls placed within a Canvas need to know is where they are positioned relative to the top-left corner of the Canvas itself.

Just as controls placed into a Grid can set the Grid.Row and Grid.Column properties as part of their own element declaration, so controls placed into a Canvas can set its Canvas.Left and Canvas.Top properties to specify their positions. They will then appear at exactly the requested location, sized per their own Width and Height properties.

This is a very useful container for games, as you will see in the next chapter, because clearly for any game we need to be able to position graphics on the screen at precise coordinates.

One other detail to be aware of with the Canvas control is that, unlike other container controls, objects that do not properly fit into the Canvas will "overflow" outside of the Canvas area. The control acts like this for performance reasons; because it is frequently used to contain animated and moving objects, it is quicker for it to simply render all its content rather than to have to clip them into its own area.

If this should present an issue, you can work around it by using the Canvas control's Clip property. By applying a rectangular clipping area that exactly matches the size of the Canvas, anything that falls outside of that area will be clipped and obscured from view. Listing 12–14 shows an example. The Canvas contains a Rectangle control that is partly outside of its own area. The Canvas.Clip property is set to prevent the overflowing parts of the Rectangle from being displayed. Remember, though, that you will get better performance with clipping disabled.

Listing 12–14. Clipping the contents of a Canvas

```
<Canvas Width="300" Height="200" Background="Gray">
    <Canvas.Clip>
        <RectangleGeometry Rect="0 0 300 200" />
    </Canvas.Clip>
    <Rectangle Canvas.Left="250" Canvas.Top="150" Height="100" Width="100"
                                                    Fill="OrangeRed" />
</Canvas>
```

Figure 12–18 shows the results both without the clipping region on the left, and with it on the right. In both cases, the Canvas itself is shown with a light gray background, and the rectangle is shown with a dark gray background.

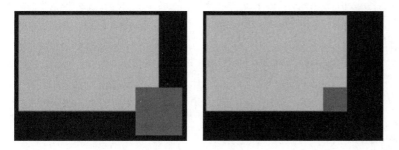

Figure 12–18. A Canvas control with no clipping on the left and with clipping on the right

ScrollViewer Controls

ListBox controls provide a very useful way of scrolling up and down through a list of items. Sometimes you will want a layout that is more flexible than the ListBox, but that is still too large to display all at once and requires the ability to scroll. None of the container controls that we have seen so far has any scrolling capability at all because it is provided instead by the ScrollViewer control.

ScrollViewer controls will take into account the size of the control that is placed inside them, and if it is larger than the ScrollViewer, then automatic scrolling facilities will be made available to allow the user to access the parts of the contained control that would otherwise be out of view. Only a single control can be directly contained within a ScrollViewer, but by using a Grid, StackPanel, or Canvas as that control, we can then place additional child controls indirectly into the ScrollViewer, too.

The ScrollViewerExample project that accompanies this chapter shows an example of this control in action. The ScrollViewer contains a StackPanel whose Width and Height have both been set to Auto so that they automatically expand to match the sizes of the controls contained within. Eight Button controls have then been placed into the StackPanel, causing it to grow much larger than the ScrollViewer that contains it.

When the project is launched, the first five buttons are visible because they fit within the area defined for the ScrollViewer. The remaining buttons are still accessible, however, by dragging the area inside the ScrollViewer. It is actually very tolerant of where we initiate the drag: even if you start dragging within one of the buttons, it will still understand the gesture and begin scrolling its contents.

Figure 12–19 shows the ScrollViewerExample project with its StackPanel partly scrolled. The scrollbar on the right indicates the position through the overall extent of the StackPanel.

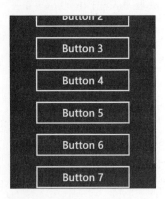

Figure 12–19. Scrolling through the contents of a ScrollViewer

The ScrollViewer can be controlled using its HorizontalScrollBarVisible and VerticalScrollBarVisible properties. Each of these can be set to Disabled, Auto, Hidden, or Visible; and by default it is set to Auto for vertical scrolling and Disabled for horizontal scrolling.

Setting one of these properties to Auto or Visible will enable scrolling in that particular direction. On desktop Silverlight apps, Auto will cause the scrollbar to appear only when it is actually needed, whereas Visible will display it all the time; but in Windows Phone 7, the scrollbar always appears just when it is actually being scrolled. If the scrollbar is set to Disabled, scrolling in that direction will be switched off, even if the content is large enough to allow scrolling. Finally, Hidden scrollbars allow scrolling, but don't display a scrollbar.

Border Controls

The final control that we will look at is a simple one. Many of the other controls we have seen support a background color or a border, but they are not supported in all instances. The TextBlock, for example, offers neither of these properties. Any time we find a need for a background or border, but the control we need it for does not provide it, we can place that control into a Border.

Border controls allow a single child control to be placed inside them and can then set a background color behind it and a border around it.

The border thickness can be set independently for each of its four edges. The BorderThickness property can be given a single number (which it will use for all edges), two numbers (the first will apply to the left and right edge; the second applies to the top and bottom) or four numbers (for the left, top, right, and bottom edges), separated by spaces or commas.

The control can also display rounded corners using the CornerRadius property.

While the Border can be defined with a Width and Height if you want, it is also possible to omit both of these properties from its definition. When the control is configured in this way, it will exactly match itself to the control that is contained within it.

User Interface Design

Clearly there is an enormous amount of complexity and flexibility in the Silverlight page designs. Because Silverlight's original environment was inside a web browser, some of those functions are not appropriate or do not function properly on Windows Phone 7 devices. The vast majority performs exactly as expected, however, providing enormous potential for flexible UIs and game configurations.

If you are unsure about how a control should be presented or what its features are, Microsoft has released a User Interface Design and Interaction Guide document that might well provide answers or inspiration. You can visit http://go.microsoft.com/?linkid=9713252 to download it as a PDF file.

Now that you are familiar with all the controls it uses, you should be able to look again at the default MainPage.xaml file that is created in an empty Windows Phone Application project. All the structure of the page should make a lot more sense now than it did when we first began exploring it at the beginning of the previous chapter!

Using Control Transforms and Projections

Fortunately for game developers, Silverlight is perfectly capable when it comes to graphical effects such as rotating and scaling. In fact, it uses matrix-based transformations to accomplish these tasks, along exactly the same lines as the transformations that we used in XNA.

The transforms available to Silverlight are as follows:

- RotateTransform: Rotates an object by a specified angle.

- ScaleTransform: Scales an object to make it smaller or larger.

- SkewTransform: Skews an object.

- TranslateTransform: Translates an object to a different location within its container.

Options are also available for combining multiple transforms into a single group or composite transformation.

We can also use a very useful *projection* feature that allows us to simulate rotating an object around any 3D axis with perspective. This feature does not really provide proper 3D rendering, but it does allow for nice animated transitions and visual effects.

All the transforms and projections are made available in Silverlight by the UIElement class, which is part of the base class hierarchy from which all the visual controls are derived. This means that transforms can be applied to virtually any control in the whole of the Silverlight environment.

Better yet, transforms applied to container objects cause the entire container and all its contents to be affected. This transformation behavior includes interactive UI elements, meaning that you can create sideways-orientated text boxes, perspective-rotated control panels, grids that expand when you touch them and shrink when you touch elsewhere on the screen, and all sorts of other effects.

Using RotateTransform

Control transforms are applied by setting the RenderTransform property of the appropriate control. This is set using the appropriate transformation class for the transform that we want to use. To rotate a control, we apply the RotateTransform.

The RotateTransform class offers us three properties that we can use to control its effects. The first of these is the Angle property. This property is set in degrees (not radians as you might have expected—Silverlight is clearly targeted at designers as much as programmers!) and rotates clockwise with 0 degrees representing the normal way up. Fractional angles, negative angles, and angles greater than 360 degrees are all permitted and work as you would expect.

Alongside the rotation angle are two additional properties, CenterX and CenterY, which control the point around which the rotation will take place. To rotate an object around its own center point, CenterX and CenterY will need to be set to be half the control's width and height, respectively.

Listing 12–15 shows the XAML code to display an image that has been rotated by 22 degrees.

Listing 12–15. Rotating an image

```
<Image Height="150" Stretch="Fill" Width="150"
                Source="/WindowsPhoneApplication1;component/Images/SmileyFace.png">
    <Image.RenderTransform>
        <RotateTransform Angle="22" CenterX="75" CenterY="75" />
    </Image.RenderTransform>
</Image>
```

The resulting image, shown here in the page designer, can be seen in Figure 12–20. As you can see, the designer updates to show the object in its transformed position.

Figure 12–20. The rotated image

Having the designer update to show the transformed layout is useful in most cases, but if you are applying transforms to any large objects, or to containers that you subsequently want to draw other controls inside, it can be quite awkward using a page designer full of rotated objects. In these situations, it might be better to apply the transform using code instead. This can be achieved by ensuring that your control has a name (image1 in this example) and then executing code in the PhoneApplicationPage_Loaded event handler, as shown in Listing 12–16.

Listing 12–16. Applying a RotateTransform at runtime using C# code behind

```
private void PhoneApplicationPage_Loaded(object sender, RoutedEventArgs e)
{
    image1.RenderTransform = new RotateTransform()
            { Angle = 22, CenterX = image1.Width / 2, CenterY = image1.Height / 2 };
}
```

In addition to setting the angle, this code also programmatically calculates the center point of the image from its width and height, something that we cannot perform in XAML markup.

Using ScaleTransform

UI elements can be scaled by applying a ScaleTransform, which allows a nonuniform scale transformation to be applied using the properties ScaleX and ScaleY to define the scale on each axis. Either of these properties can be omitted from the XAML to avoid scaling on that axis. Just as in XNA, a scale value of 1 keeps the size unchanged; setting a value of 0 will scale the object to have no size on that axis, causing it to vanish.

Like RotateTransform, the ScaleTransform object also has CenterX and CenterY properties, so you can define the point around which the element will scale.

Listing 12–17 shows the XAML required to scale an image to double its normal width and 1.5 times its height. No center point is specified, so it will scale from its local coordinate (0, 0); in other words, its top-left corner.

Listing 12–17. Applying a ScaleTransform to an image control

```
<Image x:Name="image1" Height="150" Stretch="Fill" Width="150"
                Source="/WindowsPhoneApplication1;component/Images/SmileyFace.png">
    <Image.RenderTransform>
        <ScaleTransform ScaleX="2" ScaleY="1.5" />
    </Image.RenderTransform>
</Image>
```

■ **Note** As the name of the RenderTransform property suggests, these transformations are applied purely to the rendering of the control objects. They don't affect the design-time layout of the control. If you set a scaled control to have its HorizontalAlignment property set to Center, for example, the centering will be based on the defined control size, not its scaled size.

Using SkewTransform

A *skew* is a transformation that you have not yet encountered in this book. A skew, also known as a *shear*, distorts the rectangular region that is being transformed by essentially slanting it along the x or y axis. This is easier to describe visually: Figure 12–21 shows a box on the left that has been skewed horizontally in the middle image and vertically in the right image. The skewed images both show an outline of the original box for reference.

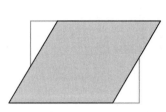

Figure 12–21. Skewing a box horizontally and vertically

Skewing is implemented using the SkewTransform object, which provides four properties: AngleX and AngleY define the skew angle on the x and y axes, and CenterX and CenterY once again specify the position around which the skew will take place.

The behavior of the skew when just one of other axis is specified is fairly predictable. Setting AngleX to 22, for example, will cause the shape to be skewed horizontally until its vertical axis is at a 22-degree angle (see the left side of Figure 12–22). The behavior when using both skew axes together might not at first be so obvious, but it is still very simple; on the right of Figure 12–22 is another shape that has been skewed by 20 degrees on the x axis and 35 degrees on the y axis.

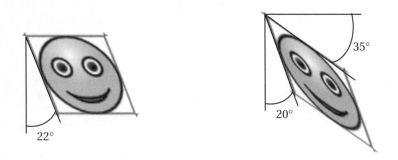

Figure 12–22. Skewing angles on one or both axes

Using TranslateTransform

The final simple transformation class is TranslateTransform, which, as you might expect, can be used to translate an object relative to its defined position. The transformation class accepts just two properties, X and Y, which define the movement distance along each axis.

The effects of this transformation can be easily replicated by just changing the object position. There are some applications of the transform, however, that result in slightly simpler code than changing the object position properties. One such use is creating a drop-shadow for text. Figure 12–23 shows such an effect created using two TextBlock controls, both at exactly the same location, but one with a TranslateTransform applied to shift it slightly down and to the right.

Figure 12–23. Translating a TextBlock to create a shadow effect

The TranslateTransform also has a benefit when used inside a TransformGroup, as you will see next.

Using TransformGroups

The UIElement.RenderTransform property allows us to transform the Silverlight controls in a variety of ways, but it has a limitation: it allows only a single transformation to take place. If we try to rotate and scale the same control by specifying both of the required transform objects for a control's RenderTransform, we get a compilation error—clearly we cannot set a property to two different values at the same time.

As you learned when we were exploring XNA, however, transformation matrices can be multiplied together to create a single resulting matrix that contains the effects of both of the transformations. Silverlight allows us to use exactly the same technique.

This is achieved using another transformation class, TransformGroup. Instead of expecting simple numeric parameters as all the other transformation objects have, TransformGroup expects a list of transformation objects to be provided. We can therefore specify as many transforms as we need, and it will multiply them all together to create a single resulting transformation matrix, as required by UIElement. Any of the transformation objects can be specified—even more TransformGroups if you need them!

Remember that the order in which matrices are multiplied is significant. Rotating before a translation will cause the translation to move along the rotated axes rather than along the page's own x and y axes (and indeed, this is the benefit that TranslateTransform offers that cannot be replicated simply by changing the control's position on the screen). If you use the transformation visualization method that I described back in Chapter 6, you need to be aware that the transformation at the *end* of the list will apply first, working from there backward toward the start of the list.

Listing 12–18 shows a TransformGroup that rotates an image by 45 degrees and translates 100 pixels along the rotated axis.

Listing 12–18. Applying a ScaleTransform to an image control

```
<Image Height="150" Stretch="Fill" Width="150"
                    Source="/WindowsPhoneApplication1;component/Images/SmileyFace.png">
    <Image.RenderTransform>
        <TransformGroup>
            <TranslateTransform X="100" />
            <RotateTransform Angle="45" />
        </TransformGroup>
    </Image.RenderTransform>
</Image>
```

Using CompositeTransform

There is one final transformation class that Silverlight offers: CompositeTransform. This class is like a simplified version of TransformGroup: it allows multiple transformations to be applied together, but they must consist of exactly one rotation, one scale, one skew, and one translation. Any of these individual transformations can, of course, be omitted by leaving their values at their defaults.

The order in which the transformations are multiplied together is as follows:

- *Scale*: Using the ScaleX and ScaleY properties

- *Skew*: Using the SkewX and SkewY properties

- *Rotate*: Using the Rotation property

- *Translate*: Using the TranslateX and TranslateY properties

To clarify, if you use the transform to both translate and rotate, it will translate along the unrotated page axes and then apply the rotation in the translated position. If this order is not suitable for your needs, a TransformGroup will need to be used instead.

One other difference between CompositeTransform and TransformGroup is that CompositeTransform has just a single origin point (specified with the CenterX and CenterY properties as usual), which is used for all the transformations that it applies. TransformGroup, however, can use a separate origin for each of the transformations that it combines.

Using Projection

All the transformations that you have looked at are locked purely into the two-dimensional geometry of the page. While Silverlight does not offer any true 3D rendering capabilities, it does allow us to simulate the perspective projection of objects using another UIElement property: Projection.

The Projection property allows any object that derives from the Projection class to be assigned. There are two such classes within Silverlight: PlaneProjection (which allows rotation around the x, y, and z axes) and MatrixProjection (which allows an arbitrary projection matrix to be provided). This book discusses only the PlaneProjection class.

A number of properties are available to this class. First are the three rotation angle properties: RotationX, RotationY, and RotationZ. These properties specify the rotation angle, in degrees, about which the control is to be rotated for each axis.

Listing 12–19 shows the XAML for an image that has been rotated by 80 degrees around the y axis.

Listing 12–19. Rotating a control using the Projection property

```
<Image Height="150" Stretch="Fill" Width="150"
                    Source="/WindowsPhoneApplication1;component/Images/Box.png">
    <Image.Projection>
        <PlaneProjection RotationY="80" />
    </Image.Projection>
</Image>
```

The resulting image is shown in Figure 12–24.

Figure 12–24. A projection-rotated control

■ **Note** You might notice that the designer does not reflect the projection; it is only visible at runtime. This is to prevent the need to have to edit controls that have projections applied or that are in projected containers, which can quickly become very difficult to interact with.

The next set of properties is the CenterOfRotationX, CenterOfRotationY, and CenterOfRotationZ properties. They define a point within the shape around which the rotation will take place. They are not defined in pixel coordinates, but rather in the range 0 to 1 relative to the size of the control being rotated.

For the x and y axes, 0 relates to the left or top of the control, 1 to the right or bottom, and 0.5 (the default) to the center point of the control on that axis. For the z axis, values above 0 corresponding to coordinates coming out the front of the screen, values below zero to coordinates into the screen, and 0 (the default) to the screen itself. None of these properties is bound into any range, and can be set as high or low as is required.

Figure 12–25 shows two images of projections of the same set of controls. On the left, the rotation center has been left at its default, so the rotation takes place around the center point of the shape. On the right, the CenterOfRotationX property for each shape has been set to 0, so rotation takes place around the shapes' left edges.

Figure 12–25. *Sets of rotated images with differing centers of rotation*

Finally, we have some *offset* properties, which allow us to apply translation to the projection. There are two sets of these properties. The first set is GlobalOffsetX, GlobalOffsetY, and GlobalOffsetZ. These properties specify translation distances relative to the global coordinate system—in other words, relative to the page itself. They simply move the shape around the screen—but don't forget that we are applying a perspective projection, so GlobalOffsetZ moves the object in or out of the screen by making it appear larger or smaller.

In contrast, the LocalOffsetX, LocalOffsetY, and LocalOffsetZ properties translate the control in its local coordinate system after its rotations have been applied. If a control were to be rotated by 45 degrees around the y axis and then translated by increasing its LocalOffsetX property, it would appear to move to the right and out of the screen because this is the direction in which its local x axis now points.

■ **Note** Silverlight will try its best to automatically depth sort the objects that you project. Objects with higher z values will appear in front of objects with lower z values, but Silverlight implements this just by setting the rendering order. It does not have a depth buffer like XNA does, and so cannot manage to properly display objects that intersect on the z axis.

Although the effect that projection offers is primitive compared with the true 3D rendering offered by XNA, it is still a very useful feature to have. In fact, Windows Phone 7 makes heavy use of this feature throughout the whole of its UI: many of the page and content transitions that take place throughout the operating system are based on projecting sections of content to add interest to what would otherwise be unremarkable onscreen operations.

As this internal usage indicates, projection can be applied to containers just as transformations can. This opens up all sorts of possibilities for perspective-projected input forms, but practicality should always be considered before presentation in these instances! While actually interacting with rotated UIs might not be too enjoyable, the ability to rotate UI containers does offer possibilities such as rotating an information panel onto the screen from within the distance and then sliding it out of the front of the screen once the user has finished interacting with it.

Orientation

Silverlight provides flexible support for multiple orientations within your games and applications just as XNA does. Silverlight defaults to portrait-only apps, but it takes very little effort to support landscape-only, or both landscape and portrait, depending on the needs of your code.

Orientation is controlled individually for each Silverlight page, and as such is set using properties provided by the `PhoneApplicationPage` class. You can see these properties in the opening XAML element at the beginning of each page. Listing 12–20 shows the required properties in the initial page.

Listing 12–20. Rotating a control using the Projection property

```
SupportedOrientations="Portrait"
Orientation="Portrait"
```

The first of these properties, `SupportedOrientations`, allows you to specify the orientations that the application can adopt when it is running. The available options are `Portrait`, `Landscape`, and `PortraitOrLandscape`. The `Landscape` option supports both left- and right-landscape mode; `PortraitOrLandscape` support all three orientations.

Because the initial layout of the page is based entirely around containers and controls that automatically expand and contract to fit their surroundings, the page will adjust to changes in orientation without any code being required. As long as you configure your page controls in this way, using margins and alignment rather than absolute widths, they also will behave in this way.

If you are working on a game or application whose primary orientation is landscape, however, it is very much easier to set things up if you view the page designer in landscape mode, too. This is achieved using the `Orientation` property. This property can only be set at design time, and its value applies just to the page designer and not to the running application. You can also switch the page designer between portrait and landscape mode by right-clicking it and selecting Switch To Portrait or Switch To Landscape. Figure 12–26 shows the page designer in landscape mode.

Figure 12–26. Designing a page using landscape orientation

If you switch the designer to an orientation that is not currently supported by that page, the designer will display a warning at the top of the window warning you about this configuration. Clicking this warning will set the page to use the PortraitOrLandscape orientation.

While the page layout might be able to look after itself in many cases, it is still very likely that you will want to be able to detect when the orientation has changed. This is achieved using the PhoneApplicationPage's OrientationChanged event. The OrientationChangedEventArgs property provided to the event will indicate the new orientation. This event will also fire when the page first opens if the current orientation is anything other than portrait; when the page loads in a portrait orientation, the event does not fire.

The current orientation can also be queried at any time by reading the page's Orientation property.

Running in Full Screen Mode

By default, Silverlight pages leave the *system tray* visible at the top of the screen. This normally displays the clock, battery level, cellular signal levels, and so on, and is often a very useful thing to be able to see.

If you want to take control of this space for your own purposes, you can easily do so by hiding the system tray when your page loads. You should consider carefully whether you really want to do this: it gives you some extra screen space and can increase the sense of immersion in your game, but at the cost of hiding useful information that the user might want to glance at while playing. It is often a nice touch to allow the user to show or hide the system tray as a game setting, setting it to be visible by default.

If you do decide to hide the system tray, simply set the Shell.SystemTray.IsVisible property as required. Listing 12–21 hides the system tray in a page's Loaded event, ensuring that it is hidden at the moment the page is displayed.

Listing 12–21. Hiding the system tray when the page loads

```
private void PhoneApplicationPage_Loaded(object sender, RoutedEventArgs e)
{
    // Hide the system tray so that we display using the full screen
    Microsoft.Phone.Shell.SystemTray.IsVisible = false;
}
```

Multipage Projects

Most Silverlight projects need to display more than one page of information. In a game, such pages can include a title page, game menu, the game itself, high scores, settings, an About page, and possibly many more.

These pages could be accommodated by placing lots of hidden controls into a single XAML page definition, but Silverlight offers a much smarter way to implement this requirement. Just as a web site can offer multiple pages that a browser can navigate through, so Silverlight offers multiple pages that the application can navigate through.

All the projects we have used in the examples so far have been built around a single page: the default MainPage.xaml. We can add as many pages as we need to our projects and then ask Silverlight to move between them. Parameters can be passed from one page to the next, allowing easy transfer of data between pages. And perhaps best of all, Silverlight keeps track of where we have navigated from and to, so pressing the phone's hardware Back button will automatically navigate back to the previous page in the page stack without us having to code anything to handle this at all.

The MultiplePages example project that accompanies this chapter contains the code that we will look at in this section. This project shows a simple main page design, containing a text field into which users can enter their names, and two buttons: Save (which simulates saving the users' names into the application) and About (which shows a simple information page).

Adding New Pages to a Project

To add a new page to your project, right-click the project in Solution Explorer and then select Add/New Item. The Add New Item page will appear, allowing you to select the name and type of item to add to the project, as shown in Figure 12–27.

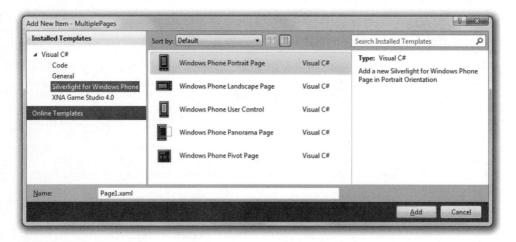

***Figure 12–27.** The available types of Silverlight items that can be added to a project*

The usual options are available for adding classes, interfaces, and so on, but we also have a small selection of Silverlight item types that can be added:

- *Windows Phone Portrait Page*: A standard page layout (exactly like the default `MainPage.aspx`) initially using portrait orientation.

- *Windows Phone Landscape Page*: Another standard page layout, but this time initially using landscape orientation.

- *Windows Phone User Control*: Silverlight allows reusable user controls to be created along the same lines as WinForms does, and this option will place an empty Silverlight user control into your project ready for customization.

- *Windows Phone Panorama Page*: Adds a simple page based around the `Panorama` control.

- *Windows Phone Pivot Page*: Adds a simple page based around the `Pivot` control.

To add another page, select either of the first two page options. The page will initially look exactly like the original `MainPage` and can then be modified as required for whichever purpose you want it to perform.

Navigating Between Pages

Moving from one page to another is very easy; we call upon the page's `NavigationService` object and tell it which page we want to navigate to.

Navigation is URI-based, so instead of creating an instance of a page and showing it (as we would in the WinForms world) we simply tell Silverlight the page within our application of the page to display.

This code required for such navigation can be seen in Listing 12–22, which contains the code from the About button in the example project.

Listing 12–22. Navigating to AboutPage.xaml

```
private void buttonAbout_Click(object sender, RoutedEventArgs e)
{
    NavigationService.Navigate(new Uri("/AboutPage.xaml", UriKind.Relative));
}
```

Note the way that the code specifies the page to navigate to by specifying its path. If you run the project and click the About button, you will find that the AboutPage is displayed just as you would expect.

■ **Note** Each time you navigate to a page, a new instance of that page is created. Any content that might be present on an existing instance of the page will be retained by the previous instance only.

Having navigated to this page, try pressing the hardware Back button; instead of closing the application down, Silverlight navigates back to the main page. This provides an intuitive and consistent navigation experience for the user.

It is possible to programmatically navigate backward (and forward, too). An event handler has been set up in the About page's `MouseLeftButtonDown` event, and it contains the code shown in Listing 12–23.

Listing 12–23. Navigating backward using code

```
private void PhoneApplicationPage_MouseLeftButtonDown(object sender,
                                                      MouseButtonEventArgs e)
{
    // Can we navigate backward?
    if (NavigationService.CanGoBack)
    {
        // Yes, so go there now
        NavigationService.GoBack();
    }
}
```

Tapping the screen when the About page is open triggers this code, which has exactly the same effect as pressing the Back button, navigating back through the page stack. Note that this is different from navigating forward to the main page by using the `Navigate` method, which would add a new entry to the page stack rather than working back to the previous entry.

Passing Values When Navigating

So moving between pages is useful, but chances are you will need to pass data to the page that you are navigating to. There are two methods that we can use to accomplish this; let's take a look at them now.

Adding URI Query String Elements

Because we use using URIs to navigate, we can take advantage of their *query string* capabilities and pass additional data as part of the URI itself.

These work using exactly the same technique as query strings in a URL in a web browser. The beginning of the query string is indicated by adding a question mark to the URI; it is then followed by any number of name/value pairs formatted as the name, then an equals sign, and then the value. If multiple parameters are being passed, an ampersand is used to separate them. For example, to pass a name and a score to a page named Scores.xaml, we could construct a URI as follows:

```
Scores.xaml?Name=Player name&Score=12345
```

Those of you familiar with using query strings for web navigation will be aware of the need to *encode* values that are passed in query strings. If the user entered the name as "Adam & Joe", the resulting query string would be as follows:

```
Scores.xaml?Name=Adam & Joe&Score=12345
```

In this case, the ampersand in the name will confuse the query string. It will consider the name to be "Adam " (with a trailing space); it will then find an unexpected keyword that it doesn't know how to handle (" Joe", with a leading space), and then finally it will find the score (which it will process correctly). The result of this is that retrieving the name from this query string will return just "Adam "; the rest of the name will be lost.

This is easily solved by using a Silverlight function that will encode strings for inclusion into URLs and URIs. The HttpUtility.UrlEncode function does this perfectly. The resulting URI, once the name has been encoded, is the following:

```
Scores.xaml?Name=Adam+%26+Joe&Score=12345
```

The + characters will be interpreted by the navigation engine as spaces, and %26 will be decoded to the character whose ASCII value is identified from the hexadecimal number 26 (which results in an ampersand). None of these characters causes any problem when Silverlight parses the query string, however, so the value passes through navigation undamaged.

Listing 12–24 shows the code from the Hello button in the example project. It navigates to the NamePage, passing whatever name the user has entered as a parameter. The name is encoded to ensure that it doesn't cause any problems in the query string.

Listing 12–24. Navigating to a new page and passing a parameter

```
private void buttonSave_Click(object sender, RoutedEventArgs e)
{
    // Navigate to the Name page
    NavigationService.Navigate(
            new Uri("/NamePage.xaml?YourName=" + HttpUtility.UrlEncode(textName.Text),
            UriKind.Relative));
}
```

This passes the value into NamePage, but we need to be able to receive and process the value as well. This is also very easily achieved. The NamePage's C# code overrides the OnNavigatedTo event in order to locate the data that has been passed to the page. It looks for the data by calling the

NavigationContext.QueryString.TryGetValue method. If a value with the specified name exists, it is passed back in an output parameter, and the function returns true; if no value can be found, the function returns false.

The good news is that we don't need to do anything at all to decode query string values that have been encoded prior to navigation. Silverlight will take care of decoding automatically, giving us back the string that we actually need to process.

Listing 12–25 shows the OnNavigatedTo event for NamePage. It reads out the provided name and displays it inside a TextBlock for the user to see.

Listing 12–25. Receiving values on navigating to a new page

```
protected override void OnNavigatedTo(System.Windows.Navigation.NavigationEventArgs e)
{
    base.OnNavigatedTo(e);

    string yourName = "";
    // See if we can retrieve the passed name
    if (NavigationContext.QueryString.TryGetValue("YourName", out yourName))
    {
        // Display the name
        textblockName.Text = "Hello, " + yourName + "!";
    }
    else
    {
        // Couldn't locate a name
        textblockName.Text = "Couldn't find your name, sorry!";
    }
}
```

Passing Values with the DataContext Object

Using the query string to pass data is simple and flexible, but only allows simple values to be passed; if a value cannot be represented as a string, there is no way to add it to the URI.

Silverlight provides another internal mechanism for storing data in a way in which it can be accessed by all pages within the entire application. The App class exposes a property called RootFrame, which returns a reference to the topmost element within the Silverlight element hierarchy (it is the element that actually contains the pages that are being displayed). The object returned by RootFrame has a DataContext property, into which any object can be set or retrieved. One page can therefore place an item into the DataContext property before navigating to another page, and the second page can read the value back out.

Game On...

As you can see, there is plenty of potential within the Silverlight environment for creating games, and the rest of our exploration of this environment will focus specifically on how it can be used for this task. In the next chapter, you will create a control that allows you to use the same functionality as XNA's sprites, and will then use it to begin building a simple but working game project.

CHAPTER 13

Gaming with Silverlight

Now that we know our way around Silverlight, it's time to start using it to create some games. In this chapter, we will look at the options for gaming and will develop some of the environment that we need for games.

Topics that we will cover include creating and using a simple sprite implementation, game timing, automating simple animation, performance considerations, and user interaction. At the end of the chapter, we will put together a simple game example using all the features that we have discussed along the way.

Let's begin by exploring how to simplify the task of using sprites within our games.

Creating Sprites

We saw all the way back at the beginning of the book how effective sprites are as a concept for creating 2D games in XNA. XNA's sprites are implemented by issuing drawing instructions, specifying the position and other information that the sprite should use for rendering, and the result is that an image appears on the screen.

In Silverlight, we have to approach this in a slightly different way. Whereas XNA expects everything to be redrawn entirely each time it updates the screen, the Silverlight environment is quite different. We don't tell Silverlight to draw anything at all; instead, we provide it with user interface elements and tell it how to position them on the screen, and it takes care of the drawing for us automatically.

Sprites could be implemented in Silverlight by simply adding Image controls to a page and moving them around. This is, in fact, the basis that we will use in this chapter to create sprites, but we will add a little extra flexibility to expand the sprite feature set and also to reduce the amount of work involved in applying transformations (rotation or scaling, for example) to the sprites on our pages.

All the code discussed in this section can be found in the Sprites example project that accompanies this chapter.

Sprite User Control

So that we can easily reuse the enhanced sprite functionality, we will implement it as a Silverlight *user control*. User controls are custom control types defined within our code, and they can be used in exactly the same way as the built-in control types such as the TextArea, Button, and so on. If you have created or worked with user controls in WinForms development, you should find yourself feeling at home with Silverlight user controls because they work along exactly the same lines.

Before creating the user control, we need somewhere to put it. When we were working with XNA, we placed all the utility code into a separate project, called GameFramework. This is the same approach that we will take in Silverlight.

The project is named SLGameFramework to help distinguish it from the original XNA GameFramework project. This project (or its resulting DLL) can then be referenced in any of our Silverlight games to reuse the functionality that we create inside it.

User controls are created by adding a new element to an existing project and selecting the Silverlight Windows Phone User Control template, as shown in Figure 13–1.

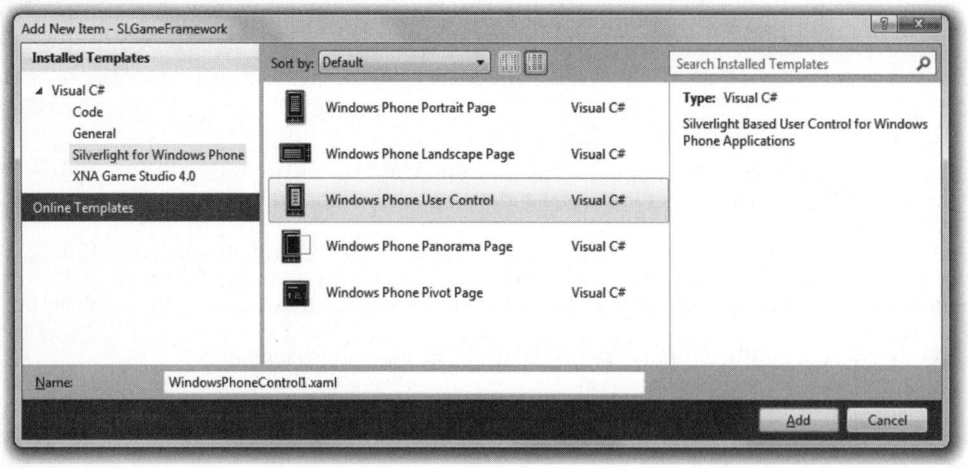

Figure 13–1. *Creating a new Silverlight user control*

Just like Silverlight pages, user controls are implemented as a XAML file with C# code behind. When a new user control is created, the initial XAML is as shown in Listing 13–1. The code behind is essentially empty, containing just a default class constructor.

Listing 13–1. *The default XAML for a new user control*

```
<UserControl x:Class="SLGameFramework.WindowsPhoneControl1"
    xmlns="http://schemas.microsoft.com/winfx/2006/xaml/presentation"
    xmlns:x="http://schemas.microsoft.com/winfx/2006/xaml"
    xmlns:d="http://schemas.microsoft.com/expression/blend/2008"
    xmlns:mc="http://schemas.openxmlformats.org/markup-compatibility/2006"
    mc:Ignorable="d"
    FontFamily="{StaticResource PhoneFontFamilyNormal}"
    FontSize="{StaticResource PhoneFontSizeNormal}"
    Foreground="{StaticResource PhoneForegroundBrush}"
    d:DesignHeight="480" d:DesignWidth="480">

    <Grid x:Name="LayoutRoot" Background="{StaticResource PhoneChromeBrush}">

    </Grid>
</UserControl>
```

The initial XAML defines the new user control class, derived from Silverlight's UserControl class, and initially provides a Grid element inside which we can put our content. It also sets various font-related attributes. This is the initial basis from which the Sprite user control will be defined.

Sprite Image Handling

One of the features that we might want to use in our sprites is the ability to show a subsection of the overall source image. We have already seen how this can be used to create frame-based animation in XNA, by providing a series of related images within the same texture and cycling between them each time the sprite is drawn. The Image control has no way to reproduce this effect; it always shows the entire image that has been assigned to it.

With a little preparation, this effect can be easily re-created in Silverlight, however. The image can be *clipped* so that only a portion of it is displayed within the sprite. This clipping can be achieved by placing the image within a Canvas control, whose size is smaller than that of the image, and then moving the image around so that sections of the graphic come into view.

Figure 13–2 illustrates how the sprite clipping works. The sprite has been defined so that it is the full height of its image (which contains three different smiley graphics) but only one-third of its width. At any time, two-thirds of the image falls outside the defined size of the Canvas.

Figure 13–2. Moving the sprite image to allow different sections of the image to be revealed.

In this example, the size of the underlying image is 300 x 100 pixels. The Canvas element, shown as a thick gray box, is sized at 100 x 100 pixels. The top part of the figure shows the image with a Canvas.Left value of 0: the left side of the image is in view, and the remaining image content is clipped (shown faded in the figure). The middle part of the figure shows the underlying image moved to the left—its Canvas.Left property is now set to -100. This position results in the second of the smiley images that comes into view. The bottom part shows the image's Canvas.Left property set to -200, revealing the final of the three smileys.

Besides frame-based animation, this technique offers other useful benefits, too. For example, we could create tile images that contain lots of different subimages and then position the image within the canvas to reveal images that we want to display. We could create a world map in the image and move it around to correspond to the player's position in the world, allowing them to see the map of the area around them. The clipped image has lots of potential applications.

The Canvas and the Image are implemented inside the user control with the XAML code shown in Listing 13–2.

Listing 13–2. The basic XAML for the Sprite user control

```
<UserControl x:Class="SLGameFramework.Sprite"
    xmlns="http://schemas.microsoft.com/winfx/2006/xaml/presentation"
    xmlns:x="http://schemas.microsoft.com/winfx/2006/xaml"
    xmlns:d="http://schemas.microsoft.com/expression/blend/2008"
    xmlns:mc="http://schemas.openxmlformats.org/markup-compatibility/2006"
    mc:Ignorable="d"
    d:DesignHeight="100" d:DesignWidth="100">

    <!-- The Canvas inside which the sprite's image is contained -->
    <Canvas x:Name="spriteCanvas" SizeChanged="spriteCanvas_SizeChanged">
        <!-- The canvas is clipped to prevent the image showing outside its area -->
        <Canvas.Clip>
            <RectangleGeometry x:Name="canvasRect"/>
        </Canvas.Clip>
        <!-- The image to display within the sprite -->
        <Image Name="spriteImage" Height="Auto" Stretch="Fill" Width="Auto" />
    </Canvas>
</UserControl>
```

■ **Note** If you take a look at the Sprite user control in the SLGameFramework project, you will find that there is some more content than is shown in Listing 13–2. This can be ignored for now because we will continue to build this up through the course of this chapter.

The Canvas does not specify any dimensions, and as a result it will automatically expand to fill the size of the user control. It is therefore the user control size that dictates how much of the underlying image is displayed. The Canvas does, however, have an event handler set up for its SizeChanged event and also an object set into its Clip property.

You might recall, however, from when we discussed Canvas controls in Chapter 11 that objects they contain are not actually clipped to the Canvas area: they appear in full, breaking outside the boundaries of the canvas. Clearly this defeats the objective of using the Canvas because we want these overflowing areas of the image to be hidden. This is addressed using the Canvas's Clip property.

The Clip property is available to all the Silverlight controls because it is defined as part of the base UIElement class. It allows the controls to define an area within which their contents will be displayed. Anything that falls outside that area will be clipped and not displayed on the screen.

To specify the region inside which content should be displayed, we set into the property a RectangleGeometry class instance. This class defines a simple rectangular region, and anything that falls outside of it will be clipped. The geometry object is named canvasRect in the Sprite XAML, but you will see that it has no size defined. This is because we do not know at design time how large the sprite will actually be, and so there is no sensible value that we can set. Instead we need to use some C# code to configure the clipping rectangle size, and this is the reason for the spriteCanvas_SizeChanged event handler specified against the Canvas itself.

■ **Note** Clipping regions do not need to be limited to rectangular spaces, though this is all we will need to use for our sprite example. It is quite possible to create clipping regions based on ellipses, polygons, and even combinations of simple geometric shapes. You can find out more by visiting `http://tinyurl.com/slgeometry` and reading the MSDN Geometry Class overview.

As you can probably guess, the SizeChanged event fires every time the related object's size changes, including when the control is being first initialized when the page is initially displayed. We can hook into this event and use it to set the size of the clipping rectangle. The event handler is shown in Listing 13–3.

Listing 13–3. Setting the size of the Canvas clipping rectangle

```
private void spriteCanvas_SizeChanged(object sender, SizeChangedEventArgs e)
{
    // Set the clipping rectangle to match the size of the Canvas
    canvasRect.Rect = new Rect(0, 0, e.NewSize.Width, e.NewSize.Height);
}
```

Because the Canvas is automatically matching the size of the user control, this event code ensures that the image is always clipped exactly to the size of the user control itself.

To allow the user to set the position of the image within the canvas, we provide two properties in the code behind the user control. The properties are called ImageOffsetX and ImageOffsetY, and setting either will cause the image position to be updated. This leads us to a question we have not yet encountered before. The position of an object inside a Canvas is set using property-element syntax, an example of which can be seen in Listing 13–4. How do we access these property values from C# code?

Listing 13–4. The Image object position set using property-element syntax

```
<Canvas x:Name="spriteCanvas" SizeChanged="spriteCanvas_SizeChanged">
    <Image Name="spriteImage" Canvas.Left="100" Canvas.Top="50" />
</Canvas>
```

The Left and Top properties do not exist within the Image control because they are properties of the Canvas; but they don't exist on the Canvas, either, because they relate to the specific control that is using them—the Image in this case.

There are actually two ways in which properties such as these can be accessed. The first approach is to ask the containing property class (Canvas in this case) to return the value for a property as used by a specific control. Listing 13–5 shows how to both get and set the value of the Left and Top properties for the Image in our user control using this approach. The GetLeft and GetTop methods are static methods and are therefore called on the Canvas class, rather than a specific instance. Similar methods are available for all property-element properties of all control classes.

Listing 13–5. Getting and setting the Canvas Left and Top properties for the contained Image control

```
// Read the Canvas.Left and Canvas.Top properties for the image
double left = Canvas.GetLeft(spriteImage);
double top = Canvas.GetTop(spriteImage);

// Set the Canvas.Left and Canvas.Top properties for the image
Canvas.SetLeft(spriteImage, left);
Canvas.SetTop(spriteImage, left);
```

The alternative way to interact with these properties is to access them via the contained control (the Image in this case), rather than via the container. When we use this approach, the property that we want to get or set is provided as a parameter to a single GetValue or SetValue function. This can be advantageous in some cases because the property to access can be set dynamically, but the disadvantage is that the return value when reading a property is always of type object and needs to be cast to the required type. Code for getting and setting the same value using this approach is shown in Listing 13–6; this is functionally identical to Listing 13–5.

Listing 13–6. Getting and setting the Canvas Left and Top properties using GetValue and SetValue

```
// Read the Canvas.Left and Canvas.Top properties for the image
double left = (double)spriteImage.GetValue(Canvas.LeftProperty);
double top = (double)spriteImage.GetValue(Canvas.TopProperty);
// Set the Canvas.Left and Canvas.Top properties for the image
spriteImage.SetValue(Canvas.LeftProperty, left);
spriteImage.SetValue(Canvas.TopProperty, left);
```

In general, the first of these two approaches results in code that is cleaner and more concise, so this is the approach that we will use for our sprite image.

As Figure 13–2 showed, to view areas to the right of the image we need to provide a negative value for the Canvas.Left property. This can be confusing to visualize: it's much easier to control it by specifying the coordinate within the image that is to appear at the top-left corner of the sprite. We will therefore facilitate this by negating the values provided so that when we specify a value of 100, the corresponding negative value -100 will instead be used to position the image.

The properties used to implement these offsets are called ImageOffsetX and ImageOffsetY, and their code is shown in Listing 13–7. Note that they store and retrieve their value directly within the canvas, and negate the value both when setting and reading it. From the outside this will therefore always be presented as a positive value, but internally it is always negative.

Listing 13–7. Properties to set the top-left offset into the image for display inside the sprite

```
/// <summary>
/// The horizontal offset across the sprite image
/// </summary>
public double ImageOffsetX
{
    get { return -Canvas.GetLeft(spriteImage); }
    set { Canvas.SetLeft(spriteImage, -value); }
}

/// <summary>
/// The vertical offset across the sprite image
/// </summary>
public double ImageOffsetY
{
    get { return -Canvas.GetTop(spriteImage); }
    set { Canvas.SetTop(spriteImage, -value); }
}
```

Another very useful feature of a sprite is the ability to set the size of the image that it is showing, independently of the sprite size itself. By default, the sprite graphic is shown at its actual size, with each pixel within the image mapping to a pixel on the screen. Some simple properties within the user control will allow some alternative sizing options, however: setting the width to a fixed amount and allowing the height to scale proportionally, setting the height to a fixed amount and allowing the width to scale proportionally, or setting both the width and height explicitly and allowing the image to be stretched as required.

Silverlight makes these configurations very easy to implement. If you look back at Listing 13–2, you will see that the Image control's Width and Height are both specified as Auto. This configuration will display the image at its normal size.

If just one of these properties is set to a fixed amount while the other is left set to Auto, the specified dimension will be sized as requested and will automatically scale the other dimension to match. If, for example, we continue to use the smiley face image from earlier in this section (which is 300 x 100 pixels) and set the Width to 150 and the Height to Auto, Silverlight will display the image so that it occupies 150 x 50 pixels—it scales the width by 50 percent, as we specified, and scales the height proportionally to match.

For the final option, directly specifying the overall image size, we can set both the Width and Height properties to the required values, and the image will stretch to match.

Control over this image sizing is provided using two additional properties: ImageWidth and ImageHeight. These are both of type double, which is the underlying type of the spriteImage object's Width and Height properties. How then is the value Auto represented as a double?

Silverlight will treat the special value double.NaN (short for *Not a Number*) as representing Auto. To avoid our properties showing the word NaN in the Properties window, we will use the value 0 to represent automatic width or height. We therefore translate NaN into 0 when getting the value, and 0 back to NaN when setting the property. The properties are implemented as shown in Listing 13–8.

Listing 13–8. Properties to set the image display width and height

```
/// <summary>
/// The height of the sprite's image. Set to 0 for auto
/// </summary>
public double ImageHeight
{
    get { return (double.IsNaN(spriteImage.Height) ? 0 : spriteImage.Height); }
    set { spriteImage.Height = (value == 0 ? double.NaN : value); }
}

/// <summary>
/// The width of the sprite's image. Set to 0 for auto
/// </summary>
public double ImageWidth
{
    get { return (double.IsNaN(spriteImage.Width) ? 0 : spriteImage.Width); }
    set { spriteImage.Width = (value == 0 ? double.NaN : value); }
}
```

The final image-related property is, of course, the most important of all: the ability to actually set a graphic image into the sprite. The Image control contained within the user control is where we want the graphic to go, but unless we expose a property from the user control, our users won't be able to get the picture in.

The property we will add for this is called Source, to match that of the Image control itself. Its code is shown in Listing 13–9. The property type is ImageSource, which not only matches the Image's Source property type but also results in the same image-selector property editor appearing in the Properties window, which allows the user to very easily pick the image for the sprite.

Listing 13–9. The sprite's Source property

```
/// <summary>
/// The image to use to display the sprite
/// </summary>
public ImageSource Source
```

```
{
    get { return spriteImage.Source; }
    set { spriteImage.Source = value; }
}
```

These properties together provide everything that the user needs to display a sprite graphic on the screen.

Positioning the Sprite

While the Sprite control can be used in any type of container, the most likely container will be a Canvas control because it allows the greatest flexibility for positioning the sprite within the page. The sprite position will normally be set using the property-element syntax, specifically the Canvas.Left and Canvas.Top properties. Due to the nature of sprites, however, they are likely to need to be moved around the screen, and to simplify this we provide a couple of extra properties to control the position.

These properties, named Left and Top, simply wrap around the Canvas.Left and Canvas.Top properties, providing that the control's container is a Canvas (if it is not, the properties always return zero and setting them has no effect). This allows the properties to be used just like the Left and Top properties of a control in a WinForms environment would be used, positioning the sprite within its containing Canvas at whatever position is required.

The properties are implemented as shown in Listing 13–10.

Listing 13–10. The sprite's Left and Top properties

```
public double Left
{
    get
    {
        // Make sure the parent actually is a Canvas. If so, return the position
        if (Parent is Canvas) return Canvas.GetLeft(this);
        // Not in a Canvas, so return 0
        return 0;
    }
    set
    {
        // Make sure the parent actually is a Canvas.
        if (Parent is Canvas) Canvas.SetLeft(this, value);
    }
}

public double Top
{
    get
    {
        // Make sure the parent actually is a Canvas. If so, return the position
        if (Parent is Canvas) return Canvas.GetTop(this);
        // Not in a Canvas, so return 0
        return 0;
    }
    set
    {
        // Make sure the parent actually is a Canvas.
        if (Parent is Canvas) Canvas.SetTop(this, value);
    }
}
```

These properties are just present for convenience and their use is not mandatory. The property-element syntax still works, and the position of the sprite controls can be updated without using these properties if that is more convenient for the game.

Sprite Transformations

Another very likely set of requirements for a sprite is the need to transform it, most commonly applying translation, scaling, and rotation transformations. These processes can be performed against the sprite itself when it has been added to a page by using the `Sprite.RenderTransform` property, but to simplify these tasks we once again provide native properties that will operate on the sprite's internal `Canvas`.

The transformations are provided by five new properties: `TranslationX`, `TranslationY`, `ScaleX`, `ScaleY`, and `Rotation`. All these operate exactly as you would expect. The scale properties default to a value of 1, and the remaining properties default to 0.

■ **Note** If the transformation results in the sprite image being positioned outside the bounds of the `Sprite` control itself, the image will not be clipped and will remain entirely visible. If this is not the desired behavior, the `Clip` property of the `Sprite` can be set in exactly the same way as we set it for the `Canvas` earlier in this chapter.

Because these transformations are provided inside the sprite rather than to the sprite itself, they can coexist with transformations performed on the sprite control. For example, the sprite's `Rotation` property might be set to 90 to rotate the sprite a quarter turn clockwise, but the sprite itself might then be rotated by -90 degrees, rotating it a quarter turn counterclockwise. These two rotations will cancel each other out, leaving the sprite without any visible rotation.

The transformations are implemented within the sprite as a single `CompositeTransform`, and the interaction between the different transformation types will therefore be as they were when we discussed this transform object in the last chapter. If other transformation behavior is required, it will need to be performed against the `Sprite` control.

Two final transformation properties are provided to allow the transformation center to be specified. `TransformCenterX` and `TransformCenterY` facilitate this, both defaulting to 0.

Adding Sprites to a Silverlight Page

Being the flexible environment that it is, Silverlight makes no special provision for its built-in controls, and allows user controls to be added and manipulated in the page designer just as easily as any other control.

Before the Sprite control can be used, the game project must first add a reference to the `SLGameFramework` project. Once this has been added, the `Sprite` control will appear in the Toolbox, as shown in Figure 13–3. Selecting this control and painting a control on to the page designer will add a new instance of the `Sprite` to the page.

Figure 13–3. Selecting the Sprite control within the page designer Toolbox

When the control is added, Visual Studio does two things within the XAML code. First, it adds a new XML namespace that references the SLGameFramework project. This gets put at the end of the PhoneApplicationPage property list, rather than alongside the other existing namespaces. So it can be a bit tricky to spot, but it will be there, as shown in bold text in Listing 13–11.

Listing 13–11. The new namespace referring to the SLGameFramework project

```
<phone:PhoneApplicationPage
    x:Class="Sprites.MainPage"
    xmlns="http://schemas.microsoft.com/winfx/2006/xaml/presentation"
    xmlns:x="http://schemas.microsoft.com/winfx/2006/xaml"
    xmlns:phone="clr-namespace:Microsoft.Phone.Controls;assembly=Microsoft.Phone"
    xmlns:shell="clr-namespace:Microsoft.Phone.Shell;assembly=Microsoft.Phone"
    xmlns:d="http://schemas.microsoft.com/expression/blend/2008"
    xmlns:mc="http://schemas.openxmlformats.org/markup-compatibility/2006"
    mc:Ignorable="d" d:DesignWidth="480" d:DesignHeight="768"
    FontFamily="{StaticResource PhoneFontFamilyNormal}"
    FontSize="{StaticResource PhoneFontSizeNormal}"
    Foreground="{StaticResource PhoneForegroundBrush}"
    SupportedOrientations="Portrait" Orientation="Portrait"
    xmlns:my="clr-namespace:SLGameFramework;assembly=SLGameFramework">
```

By default, Visual Studio uses the name my for this namespace, though you can change it to something else if you prefer.

Visual Studio also adds the my:Sprite element to the XAML for the sprite control itself. The initial content of this is shown in Listing 13–12 (in this case, it has been created inside a Canvas).

Listing 13–12. The Sprite control definition within the page XAML

```
<Canvas x:Name="GameCanvas" Grid.Row="1" Margin="0,0,0,0" Background="Beige">
    <my:Sprite Canvas.Left="150" Canvas.Top="246" Height="89" Name="sprite1" Width="90" />
</Canvas>
```

These changes can be performed manually if you prefer, but it is often useful to add the first control to the page using the page designer simply so that the namespace is set up correctly. Once this is done, the control can be deleted and readded to the XAML editor if you wish.

With the sprite present on the page, all its properties are accessible just as they would be for any other control and can be set both directly in the XAML editor and via the Properties window. Figure 13–4 shows the Properties window for a sprite, including several of the custom properties that you have seen in this section.

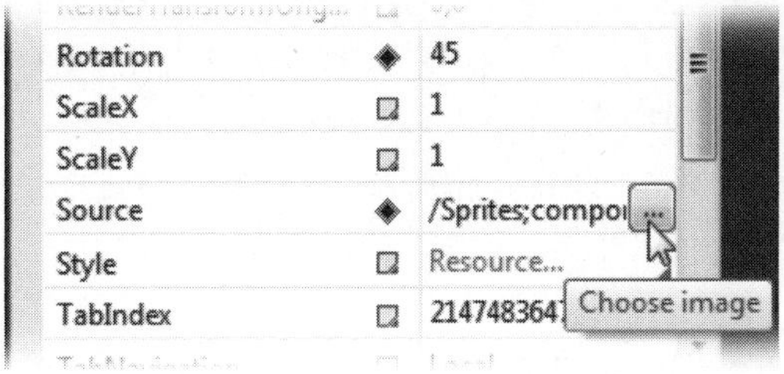

Figure 13–4. *A Sprite control's properties within the Properties window*

Observe that the properties all have an immediate effect on the sprite within the page designer. Setting the sprite Source, scaling, and rotation: all these changes are shown in the designer as soon as they are modified. Also observe how modifying the Left and Top properties that we created have an immediate effect on the position of the sprite within the page designer (and vice versa).

Creating Sprites at Runtime

Adding sprites at design time is useful, but many times we will actually need to create the sprites at runtime instead—either because we need to create sprites dynamically or because the number of sprites is simply impractical to create through tedious design-time updates.

Runtime sprite creation is easily achieved and simply requires an instance of the Sprite user control to be created, initialized, and then added to the Children collection of the container that will host it (usually a Canvas control).

The only potential point of complexity arises when setting the sprite's Source property. So far, we have always set this using the XAML editor or the Properties window, but neither of these are available at runtime, so we will have to find the equivalent approach to set this using C# code.

The easiest way to place a picture into the sprite is by adding the picture into the project with a Build Action of Content. It can then be set into the sprite by providing its URI to a new BitmapImage object, as shown in Listing 13–13.

Listing 13–13. *Obtaining a reference to a picture added to the project as Content*

```
// Create and initialize the sprite
Sprite runtimeSprite = new Sprite();
GameCanvas.Children.Add(runtimeSprite);
runtimeSprite.Source = new BitmapImage(
                        new Uri("Images/SmileyFace.png", UriKind.Relative));
runtimeSprite.Width = 100;
runtimeSprite.Height = 100;
runtimeSprite.Left = 20;
runtimeSprite.Top = 20;
```

This works fine for the new sprite, but it has a drawback: if you try to use the same image when setting the sprite's Source property at design time, the picture will not appear because the design-time configuration of the image requires the image to be added with its Build Action set to Resource.

If we change the Build Action to Resource, the design time sprite appears correctly, but the image disappears from the runtime-created sprite. Resources cannot be accessed by simply passing their URI to the BitmapImage constructor. Instead we must obtain a data stream for the resource, and use it to create the bitmap.

The code required to do this is not very much more complex and is shown in Listing 13–14.

Listing 13–14. Loading an image from an embedded resource

```
// Load the sprite image from the application resources
StreamResourceInfo sr = Application.GetResourceStream(
            new Uri("Sprites;component/Images/SmileyFace.png", UriKind.Relative));
BitmapImage spriteImage = new BitmapImage();
spriteImage.SetSource(sr.Stream);

// Create and initialize the sprite
Sprite runtimeSprite = new Sprite();
GameCanvas.Children.Add(runtimeSprite);
runtimeSprite.Source = spriteImage;
runtimeSprite.Width = 100;
runtimeSprite.Height = 100;
runtimeSprite.Left = 20;
runtimeSprite.Top = 20;
```

■ **Tip** If you are unsure about which URI to use, simply add a `Sprite` or an `Image` control to the page and browse to the required graphic using the `Source` property editor in the Properties window. The full URI for the selected image will be displayed in the image chooser window's `Path` field.

This resource-based approach allows the same embedded graphic file to be used for sprites created both at design time and at runtime. If you only need to use the graphic for runtime objects, you might choose to add it as `Content` and use the simpler code shown in Listing 13–13.

■ **Note** The `BitmapImage` class referenced in these listings is contained within the `System.Windows.Media.Imaging` namespace, and the `StreamResourceInfo` class is contained within `System.Windows.Resources`. To use these unqualified as they are here, add these two namespaces to the source file with the `using` keyword.

Sprite Examples

The `Sprites` example project shows a number of different sprite configurations based on all the features that we have discussed in this section. A screenshot from the project is shown in Figure 13–5.

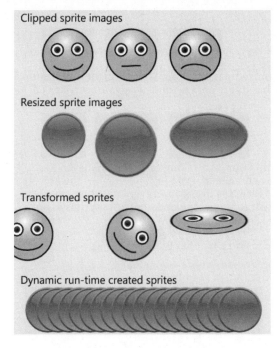

Figure 13–5. The graphics generated by the Sprites example project

The "Clipped sprite images" row contains three separate Sprite controls, all of which use the same underlying graphic file (SmileyFaces.png). The control size has been set to 100 x 100 pixels, which exactly matches the height and width of the individual smiley graphics within the file. By setting the ImageOffsetX property to the values 0, 100, and 200, respectively, each of the three smileys can be displayed.

The "Resized sprite images" row shows three additional sprites that demonstrate the different graphic sizing options offered by the sprite. The ball is shown on the left at its actual size, with the sprite's ImageWidth and ImageHeight properties set to 0. In the middle, the sprite has had its ImageWidth set to 120 and its ImageHeight left at zero. This causes it to scale uniformly until the specified width is reached. The sprite on the right has nonzero values set for both its ImageWidth and ImageHeight, resulting in a nonuniform stretch.

The "Transformed sprites" row shows some transformations being performed within the sprite. On the left, the TranslateX property has been used to move the sprite away from its normal position (its actual Left value is the same as that for the first clipped sprite image). The second sprite has had its Rotation property set, while the third has customized values for ScaleX and ScaleY. Note that none of these effects has been obtained by transforming the sprite; they are all obtained by setting the sprite's properties.

The final row contains a series of sprites created at runtime using code similar to that in Listing 13–14. Clearly it would be tedious to create these sprites within the page designer, but it is very little effort to write the code to generate them dynamically. Each of the generated sprites is still a Sprite control instance, however, just like those created at design time.

Sprite Movement

Having a screen full of sprites is of little use for gaming if they cannot move, so this section will look at different methods for moving the sprites around the page.

There are two approaches that we can use for this: procedural movement based on the application's rendering event or *storyboard* animation. Each of these has its advantages and disadvantages, so let's take a look and see how they work and what they do.

Procedural Animation

We can provide programmatic updates to the sprites within our game along very similar lines to the approach used in XNA. While Silverlight doesn't have any concept of updating and drawing the objects that it wants to display, it does provide an event named Rendering that is fired every time the scene is ready to be redrawn. We can hook into this event and use it to trigger the updates to the sprites in our game. There is no need to explicitly draw them, of course, because Silverlight automatically draws all controls within its current page.

Listing 13–15 shows the code required within a page to add a handler to the Rendering event and respond to it when it fires.

Listing 13–15. Responding to the Rendering event

```
public MainPage()
{
    InitializeComponent();

    // Add the Rendering event handler
    CompositionTarget.Rendering += new EventHandler(CompositionTarget_Rendering);
}

/// <summary>
/// Update the scene each time it is ready to render
/// </summary>
void CompositionTarget_Rendering(object sender, EventArgs e)
{
    // Update code goes here
}
```

An example of this technique can be found in the ProceduralAnimation project that accompanies this chapter. This example displays a series of raindrops that fall down the screen at varying speeds.

To provide some autonomy to each raindrop sprite, the project implements a Raindrop class, which allows us to store information and behavior about each sprite, along similar lines to the approach we used in XNA. The Raindrop code is responsible for creating and configuring its own Sprite object, and this takes place in its constructor. The code for this initialization is shown in Listing 13–16, along with the class-level variables used to support the raindrops.

Listing 13–16. Initializing the raindrop sprite

```
// The raindrop image. Static so only one instance is created per application,
// rather than one per object.
static BitmapImage _raindropBitmap;

private Canvas _gameCanvas; // The canvas into which the sprite has been added
private Sprite _sprite;     // The Sprite control instance used by this object
```

```
private double _speed;        // The movement speed for this object's raindrop

public Raindrop(Canvas gameCanvas)
{
    // Store the reference to the canvas
    _gameCanvas = gameCanvas;

    // Generate a random speed
    _speed = GameHelper.RandomNext(2.0, 5.0);

    // Load the sprite image from the application resources if not already loaded
    if (_raindropBitmap == null)
    {
        StreamResourceInfo sr = Application.GetResourceStream(
                            new Uri("ProceduralAnimation;component/Images/Raindrop.png",
                            UriKind.Relative));
        _raindropBitmap = new BitmapImage();
        _raindropBitmap.SetSource(sr.Stream);
    }

    // Create and add the sprite at a random position
    _sprite = new Sprite();
    _gameCanvas.Children.Add(_sprite);
    _sprite.Source = _raindropBitmap;
    _sprite.Width = _raindropBitmap.PixelWidth;
    _sprite.Height = _raindropBitmap.PixelHeight;
    _sprite.Left = GameHelper.RandomNext(0, _gameCanvas.ActualWidth);
    _sprite.Top = GameHelper.RandomNext(0, _gameCanvas.ActualHeight);
    _sprite.ScaleX = GameHelper.RandomNext(0.5, 1.0);
    _sprite.ScaleY = _sprite.ScaleX;
}
```

All the code here should be familiar and expected by now. Note that just as we did with our Model objects in XNA, we store a static reference to the sprite's BitmapImage object so that the same object can be shared by all instances of the sprite.

The only other code required within the Raindrop class is a simple method named Update. This will be called each time the Rendering event fires and updates the position of the sprite within the page. Its code is shown in Listing 13–17.

Listing 13–17. Updating the position of the raindrop sprite

```
public void Update()
{
    // Add the speed to the sprite position
    _sprite.Top += _speed;
    // If we leave the bottom of the canvas, reset back to the top
    if (_sprite.Top > _gameCanvas.ActualHeight) _sprite.Top =
                                                    -_raindropBitmap.PixelHeight;
}
```

All that is left to get the sprites moving is to add each Raindrop into a List within the code behind MainPage and call each object's Update method within the Rendering event.

This nice simple example gets the raindrops moving down the screen and demonstrates that the Sprite control forms a solid foundation on which we can begin to build games.

There is one other detail that needs to be discussed before we move on, however. By default, images and controls in Silverlight are not accelerated by the graphics hardware; the phone's CPU has to perform all the rendering. For user interfaces and page content that is static there are few problems, but the sprites are likely to be moving all around the screen, so hardware acceleration is an important consideration.

■ **Note** You will find out how to determine whether graphics are being hardware-accelerated or not in the Silverlight Performance section later in this chapter.

Fortunately, Silverlight makes it very easy to switch hardware acceleration on for controls. To enable acceleration of our procedurally animated objects, we need to tell Silverlight to *cache* the object graphics. When we do this, it takes an internal snapshot of the control's visuals and uses it for future rendering, which can then be performed by the graphics hardware instead of in software.

Caching is enabled by simply creating a BitmapCache object and setting it into any control's CacheMode property. We can enable this in the Sprite class via a simple boolean property named UseBitmapCache. The property is shown in Listing 13–18.

Listing 13–18. The implementation of the UseBitmapCache property

```
public bool UseBitmapCache
{
    get { return this.CacheMode != null; }
    set
    {
        // If set to true and no cache already in place...
        if (value == true && this.CacheMode == null)
        {
            // ...create a cache now
            this.CacheMode = new BitmapCache();
        }
        else if (value == false)
        {
            // Clear the cache
            this.CacheMode = null;
        }
    }
}
```

In the majority of cases, this property will provide a performance boost to your sprites, and for this reason it is set to true by default within the Sprite constructor. There are a couple of potential drawbacks of using caching, however. The memory requirements of your game will be increased, which could have an impact on performance; scaling the object so that it is substantially larger than its original size can result in performance degradation; interleaving cached and uncached UI elements can create extra work for the compositor because it has to mix the hardware- and software-based rendering, creating implicit surfaces as a result. If you find that performance drops unexpectedly when using your sprites, you can try disabling the cache, but in most cases it will be a benefit.

Storyboard Animation

An alternative method for animating sprites within a game is by using a *storyboard*.

Storyboards provide a simple mechanism for updating the properties of objects within a Silverlight application over time. They contain a series of relevant timestamps at which the values of the object properties to be updated are set. When the storyboards are executed, they set the object properties as specified, but also interpolate between the specified values when the time is between the timestamps, or *key frames*.

This is illustrated in Figure 13–6, which shows a graph of the movement of an object controlled by a storyboard. The vertical axis represents the y axis position of a sprite that the storyboard is controlling, and the horizontal axis represents time, with each tick-mark representing one second of elapsed time.

Key frames have been inserted at 0, 9, 12, 18, and 21 seconds, each providing a different value for the sprite. As the storyboard plays out, the position of the sprite is as shown by the black line, smoothly moving from between the positions defined for each of the key frames.

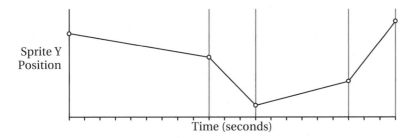

Figure 13–6. *The effects of animating a sprite's y axis position using a storyboard*

This approach to animation is typically applied to noninteractive animation because it allows complex movements to be obtained with just a small amount of input data. This can be a useful technique to use in Silverlight applications, and indeed Expression Blend has areas of its user interface set up specifically to deal with storyboard animation in this way.

For games, this approach to moving objects is generally far too rigid. We can, however, use storyboards in a slightly different way to animate sprites within our games. Sometimes animating with storyboards will be easier than the "traditional" approach and will result in greater movement flexibility with less code. At other times, storyboards will be completely unworkable because they will not be able to provide the required complexity of movement, in which case procedural animation will be required instead. Usually storyboards fall somewhere between the two.

▪ **Note** Hardware acceleration is automatically applied to objects that are animated using storyboards, regardless of whether they have bitmap caches set up.

To animate a sprite using a storyboard, we apply a single transition to one or more of its properties over a defined duration. For example, we might ask a sprite to "translate from point A to point B over the next five seconds," or "rotate to an angle of 90 degrees during the next 0.3 seconds." Given one of these instructions, the sprite will automatically perform the movement asynchronously, without requiring any additional interaction from our code.

Clearly this is quite a different approach to how we have animated things in the past, but it doesn't need to be too dissimilar in practice. For example, the class representing a sprite might decide to calculate a new sprite position twice per second and generate a continuing series of half-second storyboards. The final screen positions would all be calculated by the storyboard, but the start and end points of each storyboard would be finely controlled by the game code.

Storyboard Features

In addition to simply transitioning properties between a start and an end value, storyboards offer a number of additional features that can be very useful in your games.

The first of these is a feature called *easing*. Figure 13–6 shows that the transitions between the defined values all use *linear interpolation*—they are joined by straight lines. Easing allows the storyboard to gently introduce the transition at the beginning of the movement or to gently fade it away at the end (or both). As a result, objects can appear to accelerate into movement rather than immediately jump into motion. Other easing functions allow for more dramatic movement, such as bouncing to a stop at the end of the storyboard.

All the easing functions can operate in three different modes. EaseIn mode applies the easing effect to the beginning of the storyboard, but has no effect on the end. EaseOut mode applies the easing to the end of the storyboard, but has no effect on the beginning. EaseInOut applies the easing effect to both the beginning and end of the storyboard. It is not possible to begin a storyboard with one easing function and end it with another: this will instead require two storyboards to be used back-to-back.

Silverlight provides 11 different easing functions: BackEase, BounceEase, CircleEase, CubicEase, ElasticEase, ExponentialEase, PowerEase, QuadraticEase, QuarticEase, QuinticEase and SineEase. Each function is implemented as its own class (and these function names are in fact the names of the easing classes), and some offer additional properties to allow the easing to be configured.

In practice many of these are very similar to one another, but some of the more useful are as follows:

- BackEase: Causes the object property to move back a little from its initial position before beginning its forward motion (or, when used in EaseOut mode, causes the object to slightly overshoot its target before falling back to its final value). The BackEase class offers a property named Amplitude, which can be used to define how strong the pullback or overshoot effect is, defaulting to a value of 1.

  The animation effect of BackEase for each of the three easing modes is as follows:

  In: Out: Both:

  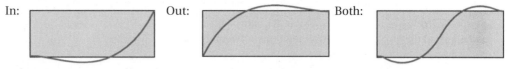

- BounceEase: Creates a bouncing effect at the beginning or end of the property animation. To specify that a storyboard object should bounce to a stop, use this function in EaseOut mode. Class properties are Bounces (how many times the property should bounce, defaulting to 2) and Bounciness (the speed at which the bounces fall off, also defaulting to 2).

  The animation effect of BounceEase is as follows:

  In: Out: Both:

  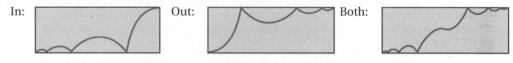

- ElasticEase: Causes the object property to oscillate around its start or end point as if it were suspended on a piece of elastic. Class properties are Oscillations (how many times the property should oscillate around its start or end point) and Springiness (how quickly the strength of the oscillations decrease or increase).

  The animation effect of ElasticEase is as follows:

  In: 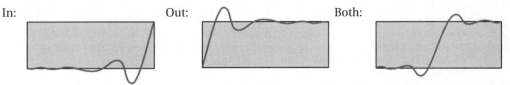 Out: Both:

- CircleEase: Accelerates or decelerates the property using a circular formula, which is good for gradually increasing or decreasing the speed of property movement.

  The animation effect of CircleEase is as follows:

  In: 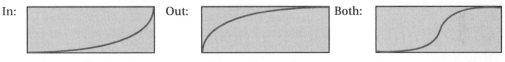 Out: Both:

- SineEase: Accelerates or decelerates the property based on a sine wave.

  The animation effect of SineEase is as follows:

  In:  Out:  Both:

- PowerEase: Accelerates or decelerates the property based on the formula value = time^{power}, where value is the resulting interpolated position, time is the proportion of the time through the storyboard (so 0 is the beginning and 1 is the end), and power is the value provided to the class's Power property, which defaults to 2.

  The animation effect of PowerEase is as follows:

  In: Out: Both:

Using these easing functions, you can often achieve complex-looking movement patterns with very little effort. If you want to experiment with them in a more practical way, you can visit http://tinyurl.com/easingfunctions to see an interactive demonstration of each of the functions from the Microsoft MSDN documentation library.

Storyboards can be applied across any duration that you need; it is also possible to get a storyboard to begin partway through its animation sequence if this is required.

Besides simply playing through from start to finish, storyboards can repeat their animation instructions in various ways. Each time they repeat, they reset their property values back to their start positions and animate toward their end positions once again. They can be instructed to repeat forever, for a set number of repeat loops, or for a set period of time.

Storyboards can also be instructed to autoreverse once they reach their end point, effectively rewinding the transition from its end point back to its start point. This can be very useful for in-place animation. For example, consider using a storyboard to update the scaling of a sprite from a start value of 0.8 to an end value of 1.2, repeating forever with autoreverse applied. This would cause the sprite to continuously grow and shrink in size, which can be a great way to highlight a selected object within a game.

Each time a storyboard fully completes its animation (taking into account repeats and autoreversing), it fires an event to indicate that the animation has finished. We can hook into this so that additional processing can be performed each time an animation completes, and also use it to update a property indicating whether an animation is currently in progress or not.

Taking all these capabilities together, it should be clear that using storyboards can present benefits that cannot be easily replicated using procedural updates. With some thought and planning it is possible to obtain some very sophisticated-looking visual effects.

Using Storyboards

Adding and using a storyboard within a Silverlight page or user control is very straightforward. Let's take a look at how this is achieved. The code described in this section can be found in the Storyboards example project.

▓ **Note** While you might well want to implement your own storyboards, we will simplify the task for many uses within our Sprite user control by building storyboard support directly into the control itself. As a result, there is often no need to manually create storyboards when working with the Sprite control. This integration is detailed in the next section.

To get started, we need to create s Storyboard object instance. You could create this in code, but it is probably easier to use XAML for this. Storyboard objects are not controls, however, so we cannot place them directly inside the content of a Silverlight PhoneApplicationPage. Instead we access the PhoneApplicationPage's Resources property, a dictionary that allows arbitrary objects to be added to a page and put the Storyboard object in here. Because this is a dictionary, it is essential that objects contained within it have a name. Listing 13–19 shows the declaration of the Storyboard so far.

Listing 13–19. Beginning the declaration of the Storyboard object

```
<phone:PhoneApplicationPage.Resources>
    <!-- The storyboard that we will use for our example -->
    <Storyboard x:Name="TestStoryboard">
    </Storyboard>
</phone:PhoneApplicationPage.Resources>
```

This code creates an empty storyboard, but it doesn't yet have any information about what it is supposed to be doing. We address this by adding one of a number of different *animation classes* to the storyboard. Different classes exist depending on the type of property that is to be updated. These classes include DoubleAnimation (for updating properties of type double), ColorAnimation, PointAnimation, and RectAnimation. The one that is generally the most useful is DoubleAnimation because a huge number of Silverlight object properties (including all those used for transformations) are implemented as double parameters.

All the animation classes expect a set of parameters to be provided to tell them how the animation should operate. These properties include the following:

- Storyboard.TargetName: Identifies the name of the object whose properties are to be updated.

- Storyboard.TargetProperty: Specifies the actual property to update.

- Duration: Specifies how long the storyboard should take to complete. This is specified in XAML as "*hours*:*minutes*:*seconds*.*fractions-of-a-second*," so to specify that a storyboard should last for 7.5 seconds, use the value 0:0:7.5.

- From: Specifies the value to apply to the property at the beginning of the storyboard

- To: Specifies the value to apply at the end of the storyboard. The storyboard will interpolate between the From and To values.

Listing 13–20 shows the Storyboard object with a DoubleAnimation added inside. The animation is set to update the TextblockRotation object's Angle property from an initial value of 0 through to a final value of 360.

Listing 13–20. *A complete Storyboard definition*

```
<phone:PhoneApplicationPage.Resources>
    <!-- The storyboard that we will use for our example -->
    <Storyboard x:Name="TestStoryboard">
        <DoubleAnimation
            Storyboard.TargetName="TextblockRotation"
            Storyboard.TargetProperty="Angle"
            Duration="0:0:5"
            From="0"
            To="360"/>
    </Storyboard>
</phone:PhoneApplicationPage.Resources>

<Grid x:Name="ContentPanel" Grid.Row="1" Margin="12,0,12,0">
    <TextBlock Height="57" HorizontalAlignment="Left" Margin="156,237,0,0"
                Text="storyboards" VerticalAlignment="Top" Width="209" FontSize="36">
        <TextBlock.RenderTransform>
            <RotateTransform x:Name="TextblockRotation" Angle="0" />
        </TextBlock.RenderTransform>
    </TextBlock>
</Grid>
```

■ **Tip** This particular Storyboard contains a single DoubleAnimation object, but you can place as many animation objects into the same storyboard as you like. You can even queue them up by setting their BeginTime property. Multiple animations within a single Storyboard cannot target the same object property, however.

The storyboard is ready to go but it doesn't start animating on its own; it needs something to start it. The easiest way to start it running is to call its Begin method from code. Listing 13–21 shows the handler for the page's Loaded event, where this call takes place.

Listing 13–21. The code required to begin the Storyboard animation

```
private void PhoneApplicationPage_Loaded(object sender, RoutedEventArgs e)
{
    // Start the storyboard
    TestStoryboard.Begin();
}
```

If you run the project, you will see that the text on the screen swings through a 360-degree rotation, circling around to where it started.

Contained within the DoubleAnimation in the example project is an easing function declaration, too, initially commented out. Try uncommenting this and see the effect that it has on the rotation. Spend a little time getting familiar with the storyboard, its properties, and the various easing options that are available. There's a good chance that you'll find lots of uses for storyboard animation in your games, so it's good to be familiar with its capabilities.

Don't forget that storyboards aren't limited just to the RenderTransform properties; they can be applied to all sorts of control properties. In fact, it is a combination of storyboards and the Projection property that is used to animate many of the transition pages that Windows Phone 7 displays as you move around the Start menu and launch applications.

Integrating Storyboard Support into the Sprite Control

Because storyboard animation of our sprites is likely to be a common requirement, we can build this behavior directly into the sprite user control. Just as the translation, scaling, and rotation properties cause the internal control objects to be manipulated, so the storyboard functions will update the internal objects, too.

The heart of the storyboard integration will be provided by three functions in the Sprite class: BeginTranslate, BeginScale, and BeginRotate. So that varying levels of functionality can be passed to these functions, a number of overloads are provided, each expecting more parameters than the last. Internally the overloads all call into one another until the final overload (with the most parameters) actually performs the work.

The parameters passed to the three functions are essentially the same. The most complex version of BeginTranslate requires the following parameters to be passed:

- fromX is the x offset from which translation will begin.

- toX is the x offset at which translation will end.

- fromY is the beginning y offset.

- toY is the ending y offset.

- duration is the amount of time the storyboard animation should run for, specified in seconds.

- startTime is a time offset through the duration at which the animation will begin (for example, if duration is passed as 10 seconds and startTime as 5 seconds, the animation will commence halfway through its animation).

- easingFunction is an easing function object to apply to the animation.

- repeatBehavior specifies a RepeatBehavior object to apply to the animation. Pass the static RepeatBehavior.RepeatForever object to repeat forever.

- autoReverse indicates whether the animation should autoreverse at its end point.

■ **Caution** Remember that the translation affects the distance from the sprite position, not the sprite position itself! Translating with `fromX` and `fromY` values of 0 will cause the sprite to begin moving from the sprite's defined location, not from the top-left corner of the containing `Canvas`.

The parameters for `BeginScale` are identical, except that the `fromX`, `toX`, `fromY`, and `toY` parameters represent scaling rather than translation values. The parameters for `BeginRotate` are identical except from `fromX`, `toX`, `fromY`, and `toY` are replaced with `fromAngle` and `toAngle`.

Having these functions available means that the games using the `Sprite` control can initiate an animation in a single call and then just leave them to run their course.

Some additional information about the translation is provided by the user control. Three new properties are present: `IsTranslating`, `IsScaling`, and `IsRotating`. They can be queried at any time to determine whether the corresponding transformation storyboard is currently running. The properties can be used alongside a `Rendering` event so that a storyboard can be initialized, and the `Rendering` loop then monitors these properties to determine when it has finished. Once the storyboard completes, another update can be performed on the sprite as needed.

Along similar lines, the `Sprite` user control also offers three events that indicate when each of these transformation storyboards completes. The event names are `TranslateCompleted`, `ScaleCompleted`, and `RotateCompleted`. Classes that derive from `Sprite` can also override the corresponding virtual functions `OnTranslateCompleted`, `OnScaleCompleted`, and `OnRotateCompleted`.

■ **Note** These events only fire when the storyboard has completely finished its animation. If a transformation is initiated with repeat-forever behavior, the event for that transformation will never fire.

Finally, three corresponding functions are present to halt any transformation storyboard that might be active: `StopRotate`, `StopScale`, and `StopRotate`.

The `StoryboardSprites` example project shows various configurations of storyboard-animated sprites on the screen together. The first row contains two sprites performing a simple nonrepeating translation and rotation; the second row has a translating sprite that repeats forever and applies a `BounceEase` easing function. On the third row is another translating sprite, this time with autoreverse switched on. The final row combines translation and rotation within the same sprite to make it appear to be rolling across the screen.

If you take a look at the code behind the page, you will see how these sprites are configured, once again in the page's `Loaded` event. Note that after the sprites are initialized, there is no code running within the application at all, and the `Rendering` event is completely unused. The sprite animation is being driven entirely by the storyboards contained within the sprite controls.

Storyboard Raindrops

We started looking at storyboards after creating a project that displayed a series of falling raindrops, moved using procedural animation. Let's revisit the raindrops project, but rewrite it this time using storyboard animation.

The implementation for this animation can be found in the StoryboardAnimation project. If you run it, you will see that it looks essentially identical to the previous project. The internal implementation is quite different, however, as you will see if you look in the code behind MainPage.

Instead of relying on the Rendering event for moving the sprites, each sprite is now moved simply by making a call to BeginTranslate after it is created inside the Raindrop class constructor. Each sprite is given a random position, is given a random translation duration, and is set to use the CircleEase easing function and to repeat its translation forever.

One other point of interest here is the use of the BeginTranslate function's startTime parameter. Without this parameter, all the storyboards would start at exactly the same moment, resulting in all the drops appearing to begin together at the top of the page. By providing a random start time between 0 and the overall duration, each sprite begins at a random position through its translation, providing a much better initial distribution of sprites.

Silverlight Performance

When running on a mobile platform, device performance is always a critical factor. If too much content is rendered, the game can begin to stutter and slow down, and can put users off or even alienate them entirely. It is important, therefore, to keep an eye on performance while you are developing and understand the causes of any degradation that starts to appear during development.

The first crucial component in this area is to make sure you regularly test your game on a real phone. The emulator is fantastic in its ability to function like a real device, but it tends to massively outperform a real phone, which can lead to nasty surprises if you have spent your entire development cycle running in the emulator.

There are some other things that you can do to ensure that your game is running as fast as it can, and in this chapter you will look at the tools at your disposal to make sure everything is working as it should be.

■ **Note** All the features discussed in this section will only work in the emulator if you have a DirectX 10 and WDDM 1.1–compliant graphics card. They will, however, work on a real device regardless of your PC hardware. Also be aware that enabling these features will have a negative performance impact, so make sure you switch them off when trying to ascertain how a game is visually performing.

Reading the Frame Rate Counters

You will no doubt by now be familiar with the frame rate counters that Silverlight displays by default when your game is running in the Visual Studio debugger. We briefly discussed these in Chapter 11, and saw how they are switched on in the code behind App.xaml.

The frame rate counters are displayed vertically along the right edge of the screen. The reason for displaying them here rather than at the top of the screen is to stop them from colliding with the system tray, which would make them both very difficult to read. Figure 13–7 shows a typical reading from the frame rate counters (rotated back to a horizontal orientation to save some space!).

Figure 13-7. *The values from the Silverlight frame rate counters*

The six values displayed here, from left to right, are as follows:

- *Compositor thread frame rate*: The compositor is the part of Silverlight responsible for creating graphical output on the screen.

- *User interface thread frame rate*: The UI thread is responsible primary for user input. If this value falls too low, the game will begin to become unresponsive to user input.

- *Texture memory usage*: Displays the amount of memory allocated for graphics textures. If lots of textures are being used together, this value will increase.

- *The Number of GPU surfaces*: Shows how many surfaces are being rendered by the graphics hardware.

- *The Number of implicit surfaces*: Implicit surfaces are created when other surfaces interact to maintain the depth ordering of controls.

- *The Fill rate counter*: Displays how many pixels of graphical data are being rendered by the GPU each frame, and is measured in *screens* (in other words, a value of 1 indicates that the number of pixels being rendered are sufficient to fill a 480 x 800 pixel screen). Low values are better; values in excess of 2 will begin to show visible degradation of the frame rate.

The counters that are of particular interest are the compositor thread frame rate (the first value), the number of GPU surfaces (the fourth value), and the fill rate counter (the final value). Let's explore these in a little more detail.

Compositor Thread Frame Rate

This is the graphics output frame rate, and therefore provides the best *frames per second* reading for your game. Ideally, it should be kept as close to 60 as possible. Note that if the graphics on the screen are completely stationary, this rate will fall to zero because no compositing is required at all.

The easiest way to measure how your game is performing when the graphics load increases is to monitor this value. If it falls too low, the device is struggling to cope with the demands being made of it. As already mentioned, keep checking this on a real device to see how it is coping as your game develops.

GPU Surface Count

All the rendering that is passed to the graphics hardware will be drawn to the screen using surfaces based on triangular primitives, exactly same as those we used directly back in the XNA chapters. This figure tells us how many accelerated surfaces are being rendered by each update.

We can clearly see the effect of this by running the ProceduralAnimation project. Ensure that the RaindropCount constant is set back to 20 and then run the project and take a look at the GPU Surface Count reading.

The value displayed is 021. This figure is formed from an internal surface that Silverlight uses within all of its pages, plus 20 raindrop surfaces—one for each raindrop being displayed.

Now stop the project and locate the constructor for the Raindrop class. The very last line is commented out, but sets the sprite's UseBitmapCache property to false. Uncomment this line so that bitmap caching is disabled for all the raindrops and then run the project again.

Now the GPU surface count shows 001. Only the internal surface is being rendered by the GPU; all the sprites are being handled in the much slower software renderer instead.

Clearly the GPU is being used for sprites that have bitmap caching enabled, and it is also used for sprites that are transformed using storyboards. Keeping an eye on this figure is useful, but there is in fact an even easier way of visualizing hardware-accelerated graphics, as you will see in a moment.

Fill Rate Counter

The volume of rendered pixels is a useful thing to be able to track; if we are rendering content on top of other content, this figure can increase without a corresponding increase in actual modified pixels on the screen. If it gets too high, we can monitor it to try to understand which objects being drawn are the most expensive in terms of processing power.

You will notice in the StoryboardAnimation and ProceduralAnimation projects (with bitmap caching enabled) that this figure fluctuates between around 0.98 and 1.0. That seems like quite a lot—we are only drawing a handful of raindrops after all!

In fact, it is not the raindrops that make up the bulk of this figure, but the Canvas inside which they are being drawn. It has been set with a colored background and it occupies about 80 percent of the screen. Even with the RaindropCount constant set to zero, the fill rate counter still shows a value of 0.93.

If you modify the Canvas element within MainPage so that it has no background defined, the fill rate counter drops to virtually zero. The colored Canvas therefore has a relatively high cost in terms of fill rate, even though it is completely static.

Increased fill rates such as the one seen here do not necessarily cause problems; it is, after all, the actual rendered frames per second that dictates the performance and appearance of your game. When things to begin to slow down, however, the fill rate can be a useful tool to determine which elements of the game are requiring the most attention from the graphics hardware.

Using Cache Visualization

As promised, there is an easier way to determine which graphic updates are taking advantage of the graphics hardware and which are not. While the frame rate counters are extremely useful when it comes to understanding the load that your game is placing on the graphics hardware, there is nothing that helps identify accelerated and unaccelerated graphics as clearly as having them individually highlighted on the screen.

That is exactly the function of the *cache visualization* feature. It draws an overlay around every single update drawn to the screen. If the overlay is dull, the update is not hardware-accelerated; if it is colored, the update is accelerated. This allows you to very clearly and easily identify which areas of the game are not taking advantage of the GPU.

To activate the visualization, open the code behind the App.xaml file and find the App class constructor. Inside is a commented-out line of code that sets the EnableCacheVisualizations property to true. Uncomment this line so that the property is set and then run your project.

If you try this with the ProceduralAnimation example project, you should see a blue highlight around all the raindrops. Graphics that are highlighted in this way are being rendered by the GPU and are therefore taking advantage of hardware acceleration. If you modify the constructor of the Raindrop class so that the `Sprite`'s `UseBitmapCache` property is set to `false`, the highlights disappear from the raindrops, indicating that they are not being accelerated by the GPU.

■ **Note** If you have used the browser-based version of Silverlight, it is important to be aware that the shading has the opposite meaning on Windows Phone 7. Silverlight in a browser highlights the graphics that are *not* being rendered by the GPU.

Viewing Redraw Regions

The final performance assistance tool that Silverlight offers is the ability to highlight *redraw regions*. These are graphics that are being drawn from scratch when displayed to the screen, rather than being rendered from cached textures by the graphics hardware.

When a region of the screen is drawn in software in this way, it is given a colored background. Each subsequent redraw is colored in a different color, identifying the fact that the redraw has taken place. If when you use this feature you find that areas of the screen are flickering in different colors, that is a sure sign that the region is being redrawn in software each update rather than being drawn by a cached texture. All the graphics will be colored (because they do all need to be drawn from scratch at least once), but those colors should be stable and not flashing.

To view the redraw regions, visit the `App.xaml.cs` source file once again; this time, uncomment the line of code that sets the `EnableRedrawRegions` property to `true`. Try running the `ProceduralAnimation` project again with the `Sprite.UseBitmapCache` property in both states and see the results. With the cache enabled, the shading is stable, indicating that the raindrops are being rendered from the cache; with the cache disabled, the screen flickers fiercely, showing the areas that are being redrawn.

■ **Note** Enabling cache visualization and redraw regions together will result in a display that is very hard to interpret. It is best to use only one of these features at a time.

User Input

Let's now move away from graphical output and spend some time working instead with user input, an essential part of any game.

In this section, we will look at how to use input in Silverlight from control events, raw touch input, gestures, and the accelerometer.

Control Events

Unlike in XNA, the graphical objects we are presenting on the screen in our Silverlight games are implemented as controls, rather than being simply painted onto a canvas; as a result, Silverlight knows where everything is on the page, how large it is, its rotation angle, and so on.

We can take advantage of this by using the control events to tell us when the user is interacting with one of our controls. All controls, including those implemented by our `Sprite` class, provide a number of events that can be used to tell when touch has been established with the control, how it is being moved while touched, and when touch is released.

■ **Note** Sprites will still fire the expected events when clicked, even if they have been translated, scaled, or rotated. Silverlight takes these render transformations into account when determining whether or not the sprite has been touched.

Mouse Events

The simplest of the events are provided by the MouseLeftButtonDown, MouseMove, and MouseLeftButtonUp events. They are all named in this way so that they remain compatible with the browser version of Silverlight, but really relate to touch contact with the screen.

When contact is made with a control, its MouseLeftButtonDown event will be fired. If touch is maintained and the touch point moved, MouseMove events will fire—but only within the boundary of the control; when the touch point leaves the control's area, these events will stop. Finally when the touch point is released, the MouseLeftButtonUp event will fire, but once again this only fires if the touch point is released inside the control's area. It is highly likely, therefore, that you will receive MouseLeftButtonDown events with no corresponding MouseLeftButtonUp event.

All three of these events have a GetPosition method that can be called on their respective EventArgs objects in order to find the location of the touch point. The methods expect a UIElement to be passed and will return the position relative to the top-left corner of that element (you can alternatively pass null and get a position relative to the top left of the screen). Listing 13–22 shows a simple example of a MouseLeftButtonDown handler that writes to the Output window the touch position relative to the page and relative to the top left of the sprite that was touched.

Listing 13–22. Determining relative touch positions

```
private void sprite1_MouseLeftButtonDown(object sender, MouseButtonEventArgs e)
{
    System.Diagnostics.Debug.WriteLine("Coordinate within page: "
                                    + e.GetPosition(null).ToString());
    System.Diagnostics.Debug.WriteLine("Coordinate within sprite: "
                                    + e.GetPosition(sprite1).ToString());
}
```

These elements are probably best suited for simple click processing rather than for more sophisticated object movement. Silverlight provides another set of events, however, that allows much greater control and understanding of movement that is being requested by the user, discussed next.

Manipulation Events

Silverlight's other set of control events consists of the ManipulationStarted, ManipulationDelta, and ManipulationCompleted events, which are triggered at broadly the same points as the MouseLeftButtonDown, MouseMove, and MouseLeftButtonUp events, respectively. The manipulation events continue to fire when the touch point is moved outside of the control boundary, however, and will therefore always fire a ManipulationCompleted for every ManipulationStarted that takes place.

These events provide other useful information, too. First, the ManipulationStarted event offers the ManipulationOrigin property from its ManipulationStartedEventArgs object. This property returns a Point structure indicating the coordinate of the touch point relative to the top-left corner of the control that is being touched.

The ManipulationDelta event allows the distance that the touch point has moved to be easily obtained. This distance can be accessed via the ManipulationDeltaEventArgs.DeltaManipulation property. The returned object has two very useful properties: Translation (which indicates the distance that the object has moved since the last manipulation event) and Scale (which indicates how the object has been scaled since the last manipulation event).

Scaling will always return values of 0 if a single touch point has been established, but if two touch points are present, it will contain the multiplier for the increase or decrease between the two points on each axis. This can be used to make the object being manipulated larger or smaller if you want to allow such manipulation by multiplying the current width or height by the multiplier—but do ensure that it is nonzero first.

Listing 13–23 shows how this event can be used to allow a sprite to be dragged around its containing Canvas, and stretched and compressed by using multitouch.

Listing 13–23. Translating and scaling a sprite using the ManipulationDelta event

```
private void image1_ManipulationDelta(object sender, ManipulationDeltaEventArgs e)
{
    // Add the delta translation
    sprite1.Left += e.DeltaManipulation.Translation.X;
    sprite1.Top += e.DeltaManipulation.Translation.Y;

    // Apply the delta scaling
    if (e.DeltaManipulation.Scale.X != 0)
    {
        smileySprite.Width *= e.DeltaManipulation.Scale.X;
    }
    if (e.DeltaManipulation.Scale.Y != 0)
    {
        smileySprite.Height *= e.DeltaManipulation.Scale.Y;
    }
    // Set the image to match the sprite size
    sprite1.ImageWidth = sprite1.Width;
    sprite1.ImageHeight = sprite1.Height;
}
```

The handling of all these events can be seen in the InputEvents example project. The project displays two sprites: a ball and a smiley face. The ball sprite has handlers set up for its left mouse button properties, which display in the text within the page the event names as they fire and the positions provided to the events relative to the top-left corner of the sprite itself. The sprite simply reports the events and does not move.

The smiley face sprite is set up to have its manipulation events handled. It also displays the touch point origin on the screen when contact is established, but shows the translation and scale delta values when the touch point(s) move, and the total translation and scale values when the manipulation is completed. This sprite also moves and resizes in response to the translation and scale delta values, allowing it to be manipulated and moved around the screen.

Spend a little time with this example to become familiar with the way these events work. They might be relatively simple, but they will often be quite sufficient for a game's requirements.

Event Bubbling

There is one other subtle feature of both these sets of events that might not at first be obvious. In the world of WinForms development, when the user interacts with a control using the mouse, that control receives the appropriate event and handles it if it needs to, and that is the end of the matter. Nothing else within the form is notified about the click.

This is not the case in Silverlight. When any of the mouse or manipulation events we have discussed above are triggered for a control, the control's event handler can process it as normal. Once this processing is finished, however, the event will be fired again for the element that contains the clicked control. Then it will be fired for that control's container too, and so on all the way up to the top-level container (the PhoneApplicationPage). The event *bubbles up* through all the parent controls of the one that initially received the event. All these controls can respond to their events, all triggered by the same single user interaction;

■ **Note** This *bubbling* of events up through the controls is based only on the control container hierarchy within the page. Whether controls are physically overlapping one another is of no significance.

Event bubbling can be very useful. For example, if you have a Button control inside which you have placed a TextBlock and an Image, it will most likely be one of these contained controls that directly receives any interaction events from the user, rather than the button. The event bubbling ensures that the button receives the event as well as its child controls.

Sometimes however you might wish to consume an event so that it does not bubble up any further. All the events we have discussed here except for MouseMove offer a property on their EventArgs objects called Handled. Setting this to true before returning from the event handler will indicate to Silverlight that the event has been dealt with and no additional processing is necessary. Once this is done, the event will not bubble up the control hierarchy any further.

MouseMove events do bubble up, but they unfortunately have no Handled property. If this presents a problem, the best way to work around it is simply to use the manipulation events for mouse movement instead.

Any of the events involved in bubbling can retrieve a reference to the control that actually initiated the event by querying the OriginalSource property from the EventArgs object. This will always return the lowest-level control possible however; for example, when tapping on an instance of the Sprite control that we have created, the OriginalSource will not return a reference to the Sprite itself, but rather to the Image control contained inside the sprite, because it is this that actually received the interaction.

Touch Events

If the control events are not suitable for your requirements, you can use the low-level *touch events* to receive data from the touch screen. These are provided by Silverlight's Touch object, work along very similar lines to the TouchPanel object that we used for XNA input back in Chapter 4. The primary difference is the use of events as opposed to polling the object in the way we did in XNA.

To subscribe to events from the Touch object, add a handler to its FrameReported event. An example of an event handler set to receive these events is shown in Listing 13–24.

Listing 13–24. Setting up an event handler for the Touch.FrameReported event

```
public MainPage()
{
    InitializeComponent();

    Touch.FrameReported += new TouchFrameEventHandler(Touch_FrameReported);
}

void Touch_FrameReported(object sender, TouchFrameEventArgs e)
{
    // Event handler code goes here
}
```

The event will fire every time a new touch point is established, each time one of the touch points moves, and each time a touch point is released.

Single-Touch Input

You can retrieve details of the interaction from the FrameReported event's TouchFrameEventArgs object. The simplest way to obtain the data is to call its GetPrimaryTouchPoint function. This function requires a relativeTo parameter just as the GetPosition function did in the mouse events earlier, and will return the touch point relative to the top-left corner of the specified element. Once again, null can be passed to get the position as a screen coordinate.

There will always be a primary touch point when this event is fired, because the event is only triggered in response to a touch interaction of some description.

The object that is returned from this function is a TouchPoint object, which contains various read-only properties that we can use to find out about the touch. The first of these is the Action property, which will contain one of the values Down (for a new touch point), Move (for an existing touch point) or Up (for a released touch point).

The next property is the Position property, which returns a Point structure inside which the touch coordinate is contained, relative to the control specified in the call to GetPrimaryTouchPoint.

Finally we have the TouchDevice property. This returns another object to us, from which we can query the Id of the touch point, and also the frontmost control underneath the touch point from the DirectlyOver property.

The DirectlyOver property returns a UIElement object if the touch point is over a control on the page, or null if it is not. An example of a null return value is when the user drags a touch point up to the top of the screen and into the system tray. Don't therefore assume that DirectlyOver will always return a valid object reference.

We will cover the Id property in the "MultiTouch Input" section in a moment.

The InputTouchEvents project that accompanies this chapter shows a simple example of using the FrameReported event. It shows a series of controls on the screen and provides reports about all touch actions, coordinates (relative to the screen), and details of which control is under the touch point at any time.

The code for the project's FrameReported event is shown in Listing 13–25. This code builds several pieces of information up into a StringBuilder each time the event fires, including the touch point's Action, its Position, its DirectlyOver control (if there is one), and the total number of active touch points. Try tapping and dragging your finger (or mouse cursor) around with the project running and take a look at the values that are displayed in response.

Listing 13–25. Reporting touch point information from the FrameReported event

```
void Touch_FrameReported(object sender, TouchFrameEventArgs e)
{
    System.Text.StringBuilder status = new System.Text.StringBuilder();

    // Get a reference to the primary touch point
    TouchPoint primary = e.GetPrimaryTouchPoint(null);
    // Report on its status
    status.AppendLine("Touch status: " + primary.Action.ToString() + " @ " +
                                            primary.Position.ToString());

    // Report on the control underneath the primary touch point
    UIElement overControl = primary.TouchDevice.DirectlyOver;
    if (overControl != null)
    {
        status.AppendLine(" Over control '" + overControl.GetValue(NameProperty) + "'");
    }
    else
    {
        status.AppendLine(" Not over any control");
    }

    // Report on the total number of touch points
    status.AppendLine(" Touch point count: " + e.GetTouchPoints(null).Count.ToString());

    // Put the status into the textblock
    touchText.Text = status.ToString();
}
```

Multitouch Input

The final piece of information displayed in the example project code has probably given you a clue about how multitouch input is retrieved.

Instead of calling the GetPrimaryTouchPoint function, you can instead call GetTouchPoints. Once again, this expects a relativeTo control (or null), but this time a collection of TouchPoint objects is returned instead of a single primary TouchPoint object. Each TouchPoint object in the collection corresponds to one of the contact points that has been made, moved, or released. The number of returned objects will vary as contact points are established and released, but will always contain at least one touch point.

Working with multitouch is where the TouchPoint.Id property comes in handy because it allows you to distinguish each point from the others. Just as in XNA, each touch point's Id will be unique within the current set of touch points and will be maintained for the duration of the touch.

Gestures

When we explored input in XNA, another type of touch-based input was available to us: gestures. These provided a series of high-level input forms including double-tapping, dragging and flicking.

The bad news is that these gestures are not replicated in Silverlight. The good news is that with a little clever trickery we can borrow the XNA gestures feature and use it directly within our Silverlight games.

■ **Note** If you have forgotten the details of using gestures in XNA, take a quick trip back to Chapter 4 to refresh your memory.

The gesture mechanism is wrapped up inside XNA's TouchPanel class, which is defined within the Microsoft.Xna.Framework.Input.Touch assembly. By adding a reference to this assembly, the TouchPanel class becomes available in Silverlight, too. We also need to add a reference to Microsoft.Xna.Framework because it contains the Vector2 structure required to read touch coordinates from the TouchPanel.

Having done this, we can set up the gestures that we are interested in exactly as we did in XNA. Listing 13–26 shows the beginning of a class declaration (including some using statements to simplify the XNA class references) that enables the gestures in this way.

Listing 13–26. Initializing the TouchPanel gestures

```
using Microsoft.Xna.Framework;
using Microsoft.Xna.Framework.Input.Touch;

namespace InputGestures
{
    public partial class MainPage : PhoneApplicationPage
    {
        // Constructor
        public MainPage()
        {
            InitializeComponent();

            TouchPanel.EnabledGestures = GestureType.Tap | GestureType.DoubleTap |
                                        GestureType.FreeDrag | GestureType.Flick;
        }
    }
}
```

The next problem is how to read the gesture details. In XNA, we were in a constantly running game loop, so we could simply poll the TouchPanel.IsGestureAvailable property during each update. In Silverlight, our code only runs in response to events.

If you are using the CompositionTarget.Rendering event, as described in the "Procedural Animation" section earlier in this chapter, you can indeed continue to use this method. Check for new gestures each time the event fires and handle them as appropriate.

If you prefer not to use this event, there is another way that gets you access to *nearly* all the available gestures. Each time users perform a gesture, they must by definition also set up a series of manipulation events as they establish and move their screen contact point. We can, therefore, hook into the ManipulationDelta and ManipulationCompleted events and use them as triggers to check the gesture queue.

This approach provides access to everything except for the Hold gesture. Hold is unusual because unlike all the other gestures, it is triggered by a period of *inactivity*, and so we have nothing to indicate that it has taken place. The only way to interact with this gesture from Silverlight is by polling with the CompositionTarget.Rendering event.

Listing 13–27 shows the remainder of the class that was started in Listing 13–26. This uses the two manipulation event handlers for the top-level PhoneApplicationPage to track and report on all the gestures that occur within the application. The full source code for this example can be found in the InputGestures example project. Give this a try and see how it responds to the gestures that you make.

Listing 13–27. Detecting and processing gestures

```
private void PhoneApplicationPage_ManipulationDelta(object sender,
                                          ManipulationDeltaEventArgs e)
{
    // See if there are any gestures waiting to be processed
    ProcessGestures();
}

private void PhoneApplicationPage_ManipulationCompleted(object sender,
                                          ManipulationCompletedEventArgs e)
{
    // See if there are any gestures waiting to be processed
    ProcessGestures();
}

private void ProcessGestures()
{
    // Are there any gestures queued?
    while (TouchPanel.IsGestureAvailable)
    {
        // Yes, so read the gesture
        GestureSample gesture = TouchPanel.ReadGesture();

        // Display information on the screen
        gestureText.Text = "Gesture status: " + gesture.GestureType.ToString() +
                              " @ " + gesture.Position.ToString();
    }
}
```

The best way to use gestures in Silverlight is likely to be to mix them with the manipulation events; use manipulation events to determine the touch position, and the gestures to track more complex interactions such as flicking and double-tapping.

Accelerometer

Our final stop in this section is with the accelerometer. We looked at this in the context of XNA back in Chapter 4, and using it in Silverlight is very similar—in fact, we use exactly the same object to access its properties in Silverlight as we did in XNA.

First, we need to add a reference to the `Microsoft.Devices.Sensors` assembly, which contains the accelerometer functionality. With this done, we can create an instance of its `Accelerometer` class and assign a handler to the `ReadingChanged` event. Data will then be received from the accelerometer after we call the `Start` method. Listing 13–28 shows a section of code from a class that sets this all up.

Listing 13–28. Initializing, starting, and handling the accelerometer sensor events

```
using Microsoft.Devices.Sensors;

namespace InputAccelerometer
{
    public partial class MainPage : PhoneApplicationPage
    {
```

```
        // The accelerometer object
        private Accelerometer _accelerometer = new Accelerometer();

        // Constructor
        public MainPage()
        {
            InitializeComponent();
        }

        private void PhoneApplicationPage_Loaded(object sender, RoutedEventArgs e)
        {
            // Add an event handler and start processing the events
            _accelerometer.ReadingChanged += Accelerometer_ReadingChanged;
            _accelerometer.Start();
        }

        void Accelerometer_ReadingChanged(object sender, AccelerometerReadingEventArgs e)
        {
            // Process the accelerometer data here
        }
    }
}
```

■ **Note** For a refresher on the accelerometer and the data that it returns, refer to its section in Chapter 4.

This looks like it is all we need, but there is a problem lurking within the Accelerometer object: its event is fired on a different thread from that used by Silverlight's user interface, and so we cannot update any UI objects from within the event handler. If we try to do so, an exception will be thrown.

There are various ways to deal with this problem, but the easiest is simply to store the accelerometer's X, Y, and Z values during the event and do nothing else. The values can then be picked up by the page's Rendering event, or through whatever other update mechanism your game is using. Because the accelerometer's ReadingChanged event fires continuously, anyway, there is no particular significance to the timing of its updates.

The InputAccelerometer example project provides a simple demonstration of using the accelerometer to move a ball around the page.

Game in Focus: Diamond Lines, Part I

We will conclude this chapter by presenting another example game. The game, called *Diamond Lines*, is a simple example of the popular "match three" genre. An image from the game is shown in Figure 13–8.

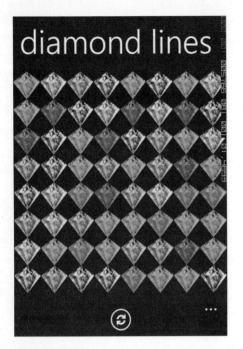

Figure 13–8. *The output from the Diamond Lines example game*

The game displays an 8 x 8 matrix of colored diamonds and allows adjacent diamonds to be swapped. Each swap must result in a horizontal or vertical line of three or more matching diamonds; if this is not the case, the swap is reversed to put the diamonds back into their original positions.

When a line of diamonds is formed, it is removed from the board. The space that is left is filled by allowing the diamonds above to fall down into the space, filling the board at the top with new randomly generated diamonds. If these falling diamonds result in more lines forming, they are removed, too, which can result in a chain reaction of lines being created by the falling diamonds.

The game continues until the player can no longer form any more lines.

So that we can focus on its mechanics and implementation, we will skip a few features that the completed game would need to support. For example, there is no "game over" detection, so the game will carry on until the player chooses to close it or to begin a new game. Enhancing the game with features such as game over detection, scoring, and so on, is left as an exercise for the reader (but before you start, don't miss the second part of this game in the next chapter).

In this text, we concentrate primarily on the way the game is put together rather than the detail of how the internal game functions are implemented. The code is well commented and not particularly lengthy, so you should be able to explore it within Visual Studio to pull apart all its inner workings.

Sprite Configuration

The diamonds are implemented as a series of sprites, all of which use the same underlying image. The image contains six different color variations of the diamond graphic placed next to each other; it can be seen in Figure 13–9.

Figure 13–9. The diamond sprite graphic

The diamonds graphic file measures 360 x 60 pixels, and the individual diamonds within are exactly 60 x 60 pixels. A width of 60 pixels also allows us to fit exactly eight sprites across the screen, so the diamond graphics can be shown at their native size without needing to be scaled.

To select one of the colors to be displayed, we can simply set the sprite's ImageOffsetX property. Setting this to 0 will show the first diamond color, setting it to 60 (the width of the individual diamond images) will show the second diamond, and so on.

The diamonds are managed by a class named Diamond. The class constructor expects to be passed three parameters: a reference back to MainPage inside which the game is being displayed, and an x and y position within the game board. These are board coordinates in the range 0 to 7, not screen coordinates. The screen coordinates can be derived however by multiplying the board coordinates by the width or height of the diamond graphic.

After storing these pieces of information away, the class constructor loads the Diamonds.png graphic file and then creates a Sprite control to represent this diamond. All the sprites are created programmatically in this way; none of them is present at design time. The sprite's image, size, diamond color, and position are all configured so that the sprite is displayed onscreen. Finally, a handler is added for the sprite's MouseLeftButtonDown event so that the game can tell when the player touches one of the sprites.

Back in the MainPage code, the ResetGame function has the responsibility of creating all these Diamond objects. It loops across the width and height of the board, creating the objects and storing them in an 8 x 8 element class-level array of Diamond objects named _gameBoard. This array will be used throughout the game to read and update the content of the board.

It is highly likely that lines of three or more diamonds will be formed during the random generation of the initial board. We want the board to start in a state where the first line must be formed by the player, so the ResetGame function calls repeatedly into another function named FindLines, which identifies and removes any lines within the game board. We will look at the FindLines function shortly. Once FindLines returns false, indicating that no lines were found, the loop exits and the game is ready to play.

Game Flow

The game is driven forward using the page's Rendering event, but all the sprite animation is performed using storyboards, and all the user input is provided by control events.

What we use the Rendering event for is to switch the game between different *states*. These states are defined in the GameStates enumeration, and the current state is stored in the _gameState variable. The known states are as follows:

- Idle: Indicates that nothing is currently happening, and we are waiting for input from the player.

- Swapping: Indicates that we are swapping two diamonds that the player has selected.

- SwappingBack: Indicates that a swap completed but no lines were formed, so the diamonds are reverting to their original positions.

- Dropping: Used when diamonds are falling to fill the space left by a line that was removed from the board.

Each time the Rendering event is called, it first checks to see whether any diamonds are currently in motion. This is checked using the DiamondsAreMoving function, which simply examines the IsTranslating property of each sprite in the game, returning true if it finds any that are moving.

Assuming no diamonds are moving, it checks the state that has just finished animating, and determines which state to switch to next.

If the finished state is Swapping, the code checks to see whether any lines have been formed. If they have, the FindLines function returns true, and the Rendering event switches into the Dropping state, in which it will stay until all the dropping diamonds complete their translations. If FindLines returns false, the swap that just completed was not valid, so it switches to the SwappingBack state to revert back to their original positions.

If the finished state is SwappingBack, the game has no additional animations to perform, so it switches into Idle mode ready for the user to make another move.

If the finished state is Dropping, all the diamonds are now dropped into their new positions. However, there might be new lines formed by the diamonds, so once again the code calls into FindLines. If more lines are found, the state switches back to Dropping so that these new lines can be removed and refilled; otherwise, the diamond-dropping cycle is complete, and the game returns to Idle mode.

This straightforward set of behaviors is responsible for ensuring that the game continues to flow from one stage to the next the whole time the user is playing.

Input Processing

How then do we allow the user to interact with the game and tell it what to do? This is all handled via the sprites' MouseLeftButtonDown event, a handler for which is present in the Diamond class. Each time a diamond is touched, it calls into the MainPage.ActivateDiamond function, passing in the x and y position within the board so that the game knows which diamond has been pressed.

ActivateDiamond then needs to work out what to do in response to this action. When the user touches a diamond, it becomes *selected* and fades in and out to indicate this. The options then available to the player are the following:

- Touch the same diamond again to cancel its selection.

- Touch an adjacent diamond to initiate a swap of the selected and the touched diamond.

- Touch a nonadjacent diamond to select it instead of the currently selected diamond.

The code first checks to see whether the touched diamond is already selected. If so, the selection is cancelled, and the function returns without doing any additional work.

If the code detects that the touched diamond is adjacent to the selected diamond, it calls the SwapDiamonds function to initiate swapping. We will look at this function in just a moment.

If neither of these checks has evaluated to true, the touched diamond cannot be adjacent to any existing selected diamond, so it becomes the selected diamond, replacing any previous selection. A storyboard named Fader, defined within MainPage, is attached to the sprite to fade its Opacity between 1 and 0, using AutoReverse and repeating forever. This is how the selection is displayed to the player.

That is, in fact, all the input processing that is needed for this game. A useful enhancement would be to allow a diamond to be dragged from its current position to an adjacent position, but this is also left as an exercise for the reader.

Sprite Animation

There are two functions within the game that can result in movement of the diamonds to be initiated: SwapDiamonds and FindLines. The former swaps the positions of two adjacent diamonds; the latter removes all lines and can result in potentially large numbers of diamonds moving into new positions within the board.

In actual fact, the way the movement of diamonds is handled is cheating somewhat. The effect is invisible to the player, but simplifies the internal processing required to move the diamonds around the screen. The cheat is that none of the sprites ever changes position within the game board; the sprite in the top-left corner, for example, is always the same Sprite control, even though it appears to fall down the screen when diamonds below it are removed.

Let's look at an example to explain how this works. If we take a scenario where the player has just removed a horizontal line of diamonds within the middle of the board, the effect is that the diamonds above need to fall down into their new positions. Figure 13–10 shows the steps required to update a single column of diamonds that are affected by this update.

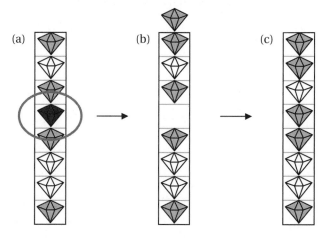

Figure 13–10. Removing a diamond from a column of diamonds

Figure 13–10 (a) shows the dark-colored diamond that is being removed from the board. Figure 13–10 (b) shows the diamonds with the dark diamond removed and a new diamond replacing it at the top of the column. It would appear that a new diamond sprite has been inserted at the top of the column, but the diamond positions have all been updated at this point. The actual positions of the diamonds are as shown in Figure 13–10 (c), which have been achieved simply by changing the colors of the existing sprites. None of the sprites has been moved within the game board at all, nor have any been allocated new x or y positions.

The reason why the sprites *appear* to have moved in Figure 13–10 (b) is because the topmost four diamonds have been given a negative TranslationY value. Because they are translated upward at the exact same moment that they are given the color of the diamond above, they appear not to have moved at all. The "new" diamond sprite that has appeared at the top of the column is in fact the sprite that was already present at the top of the column, simply translated up a little.

Once the diamonds have been recolored and translated in this way, their translation storyboard is activated to slide them back to their actual positions, providing the illusion of dropping into place.

Swapping diamonds is achieved in the same way. The two sprites that are apparently being swapped actually just exchange colors and set their offsets so that they appear to remain in their original locations. Their storyboards are then activated to animate them into their new positions. The BackEase

461

easing mode is applied to this translation to make the swap a little more interesting; this is an example of how storyboards make animation much easier than manually updating the offsets each time the diamonds need to change position.

This discussion should give you a feel for how all the elements we have explored can be wired together into a working game. It is worth spending a little time working through the *Diamond Lines* code and getting comfortable with how the sprites are set up and displayed, how the game state is maintained, and how the animation is performed. The rest of the code is quite specific to this particular game, but these are features that many games will need to encompass, so please feel free to use this example as inspiration for how you can wire together your own games.

Using Silverlight for Game Development

While Silverlight is clearly not as directly targeted at gaming as XNA is, it nevertheless contains a significant set of highly useful features that can allow attractive and dynamic games to be written. Among the advantages of using XNA are a highly flexible user interface and the potential of porting your game into the browser-based version of Silverlight for use outside of Windows Phone 7.

The next chapter will look at a number of enhancements that you can add to your Silverlight games to provide a richer experience for your players.

■ ■ ■

CHAPTER 14

Enhancing Your Silverlight Games

With some experience and practice with getting games written in Silverlight, there will be various features that you might want to add to provide additional functionality and polish. We will examine some of these features in this chapter.

The areas covered will include setting up a game navigation structure, music and sound effects, creating high score tables, saving and retrieving game settings, and handling tombstoning in Silverlight. Some of these features are very similar to features that we have already explored in the context of XNA, so there shouldn't be too much here that is new or unfamiliar.

Game Navigation

In a finished game you will almost certainly need to have multiple Silverlight pages in your project, allowing the user to move between them in an appropriate manner. Pages will likely be required for a title page, the game itself, an "about" screen, high scores, and so on.

Silverlight allows movement between different pages of content in a much more straightforward manner than XNA, as each page is entirely self-contained and can coexist with other pages that the application needs to use.

Actually structuring the game in a way that acts intuitively, allows flexible navigation from any page to any other page, and also meets Microsoft's requirements for navigation is a little trickier, however.

There are several issues that need to be addressed. First is the navigation history. When a Silverlight application launches, it displays its initial page (MainPage by default) that we can use to display a menu with options such as to start a new game, show the settings, and so on. The user can navigate from here to another page, say the game play page, and the initial MainPage will be added to the navigation history. If the user presses the Back button, they return to the MainPage and can access the menu again.

All good so far, but what happens if the game wants to take the player from the game play page into a high score page? It can navigate to the high score page easily enough, but then when users click the Back button they will return not to the MainPage menu as they might expect, but instead to the finished game play page. We somehow need to be able to manipulate the page history so that we can always get to the menu when the Back button is pressed, but can still navigate from any page to any other page.

This is compounded by one of Microsoft's Marketplace publication requirements. It states that:

- Pressing Back from the game's first screen must exit the game.

- Pressing Back while playing the game must display an in-game menu, and pressing Back while this is displayed must exit the game.

- Outside of game play (such as when looking at settings or high scores), pressing Back must return to the previous page or menu.

The final complication is that there is no way to cleanly exit a Silverlight application on demand. In XNA we have access to the Game.Exit method, which immediately closes the game, but there is no equivalent in Silverlight. The only methods of closing a Silverlight app are for the user to navigate back when viewing the first page in the navigation history, or for the app to throw an unhandled exception. Personally I can't stomach the latter of the two options, so we need to find a way to get the first option to work.

Defining the Navigation Flow

The basic flow of navigation that we will aim for will be along the lines of that shown in Figure 14–1.

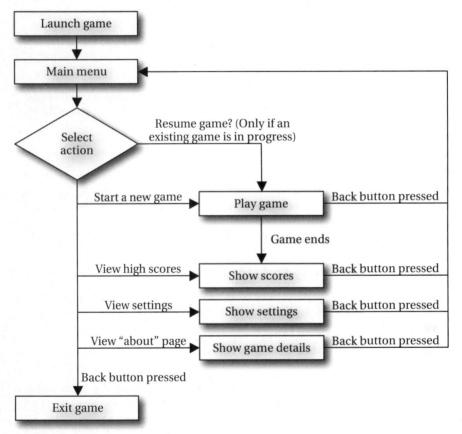

Figure 14–1. The game navigation flow

■ **Note** The game need not be limited to the pages defined here, but for the purpose of this book we will use this as a reasonable model of how the game pages can fit together.

With the exception of the Play Game page, all the navigation flows already fit within both the technical limitations of the Silverlight application, and Microsoft's publication requirements. By always forcing the player back to the main menu when they want to reach another part of the game (the Settings page, for example), the navigation model is kept very simple, while also ensuring that a menu is displayed when Back is pressed during a game. From any of the pages, pressing Back twice will exit the game.

It is important, however, that the game in progress is not lost when navigating back while playing. The users have no choice but to access the Main Menu page to gain access to other pages, and will not be very pleased if their game is discarded when they navigate in this way.

To avoid this problem, we make a note of the fact that a game is in progress when navigating back from the Play Game page, which allows the Main Menu page to add an additional option to resume the current game. This is one of the key features of this relatively simple navigation model.

There is one final problem within the defined model. When the Play Game page reaches a state where the game has ended, it shows a flow directly to the Show Scores page. It's very nice to take users to the high score page after a game finishes, both to see their own score added to the table if it was good enough, and to see what other scores are there for them to beat. The problem with this is that the navigation stack would end up including the Play Game page, so pressing Back from the Show Scores page would navigate back there rather than to the menu. How can we get the Back button to go back to the menu in this situation?

The answer is to use *redirection*.

Redirecting Navigation

In fact, the only way to get from the Play Game page to the Show Scores page while having just the Main Menu in the navigation history is to not actually navigate directly from Play Game to Show Scores at all. Instead, we add a little extra code into the Main Menu page, which allows one page to redirect the navigation into another page via the menu itself.

When the Play Game page wants to transfer the player into the Show Scores page, instead of navigating there itself, it instead sets a property on the Main Menu page, indicating where it wants to go and then navigates *back* instead. Silverlight therefore ends back on the Main Menu page, but detecting the request to move elsewhere, the menu page immediately navigates on to the new destination, opening the Show Scores page. The result is that the only page in the navigation history is still the Main Menu page.

Let's clarify that by viewing it as a diagram. Figure 14–2 shows the processes that the game undergoes and the navigation stack at each stage. The dark-shaded item on the stack is the page that is on display at each stage, and the writing between the stages shows the point at which one stage moves to the next.

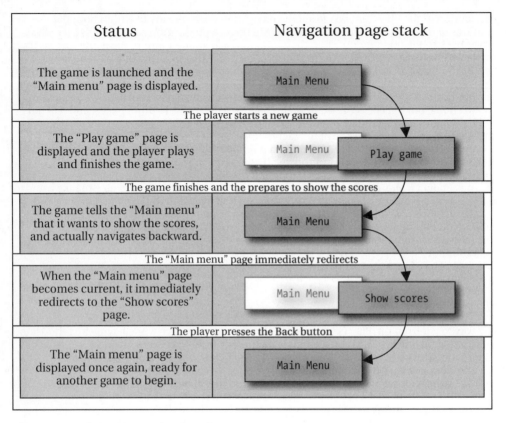

Figure 14–2. *The navigation stack as the game progresses*

As this diagram clarifies, the navigation stack will always have the Main Menu page as its first item and will only ever have one other page after the menu in the stack. When one page wants to navigate to another, it does so by navigating back to the menu, ensuring that the stack never gets any deeper than this.

Implementing the Navigation Flow

So that's the theory; now it's time to look at how we implement this in a game project. All the code for this section can be found in the GameNavigation example project that accompanies this chapter. It is set up to use exactly the same pages and navigation, as described in Figure 14–1.

Nearly all the required code is present in MainPage, which is the page that implements our main menu. The first thing we need to add is an enumeration containing the details of all the pages within the project. Each enumeration item must exactly match the name of the page it represents. Listing 14–1 shows the enumeration defined for the example project.

Listing 14–1. The GamePages enumeration defining each of the pages available to the game

```
internal enum GamePages
{
    MainPage = 0,
    GamePage,
    SettingsPage,
    HighScorePage,
    AboutPage,
}
```

■ **Note** The enumeration as configured here will launch the game at the MainPage page. If you wanted to begin with a different page, perhaps a title page, this can be achieved by placing it at the start of the enumeration with the value 0; whichever enumeration item gets the value 0 will be initially displayed when the game launches.

Next a static property called TargetGamePage is created with which a non-menu page can request navigation to a different page (for example, the game page requesting navigation to the high score page). Being static, other pages can set this property without needing access to an instance of the MainPage class. We will look at an example of how a page can use this shortly. A corresponding property to allow navigation parameters, TargetGamePageParameters, is provided, too. The property declarations are shown in Listing 14–2.

Listing 14–2. Declaring the static TargetGamePage and TargetGamePageParameters properties

```
/// <summary>
/// The page that should next be opened when the menu page is navigated to
/// </summary>
static internal GamePages TargetGamePage { get; set; }
static internal string TargetGamePageParameters { get; set; }
```

Now we need a function to actually perform the navigation from the menu page. This is the NavigateToPage function, and it exists in two versions: one that requires just a GamePages enumeration value to indicate where to navigate to, and another that also accepts a parameter string to append to the navigation URI. Listing 14–3 contains the code for both versions of the function.

Listing 14–3. The two overloaded versions of the NavigateToPage function

```
/// <summary>
/// Navigate to the specified page
/// </summary>
private void NavigateToPage(GamePages toPage)
{
    NavigateToPage(toPage, null);
}
/// <summary>
/// Navigate to the specified page, passing the provided parameters
/// </summary>
private void NavigateToPage(GamePages toPage, string parameters)
{
```

```
        string uriString;

        // Are we navigating to the menu page?
        if (toPage == GamePages.MainPage)
        {
            // We are already on the menu page, no navigation required
            // Show the menu so that it is displayed within the page
            this.Visibility = System.Windows.Visibility.Visible;
            return;
        }

        // Build the URI for navigation
        uriString = "/" + toPage.ToString() + ".xaml";
        // Include parameters if there are any
        if (!string.IsNullOrEmpty(parameters))
        {
            uriString += "?" + parameters;
        }

        // Navigate to the specified page
        NavigationService.Navigate(new Uri(uriString, UriKind.Relative));

        // Hide the page content so that it doesn't briefly appear when navigating
        // directly between other pages
        this.Visibility = System.Windows.Visibility.Collapsed;
    }
```

Let's take a quick look at some of the details of this piece of code. The function will only ever be called when the MainPage itself is on top of the navigation stack, so the first thing it does is check to see whether MainPage is the navigation target. If so, no further navigation is required as we are already displaying the required page. The code can therefore return without doing anything more—though before doing so, it makes the page visible; we will discuss the reason for this in a moment.

For any other page, a URI is constructed containing the name of the page, taking from the enumeration value name with a leading slash and the trailing .xaml suffix. If any parameters were provided, they are added to the URI, too. The function then navigates to the requested page.

After navigating the menu page content is made invisible; we already saw it being made visible again when navigating to the menu page itself. Why is this necessary?

The reason is that when one page (such as the GamePage) navigates directly to another page (such as the HighScorePage) via the menu page, the menu page is very briefly displayed on the screen. This results in the menu appearing unexpectedly for a moment, which looks very odd. We stop it from being displayed by simply making the content of the menu page invisible when navigating away from MainPage. When the game navigates back to actually display MainPage, the page content is made visible once again.

The final piece of code required to wire this all together is present in the MainPage class' OnNavigatedTo override. This will be called every time the game navigates to MainPage, including when the game is first launched. All the function needs to do is call into NavigateToPage, passing in the value from the static TargetGamePage and TargetGamePageParameters properties. This ensures that if another page sets these properties before navigating back to MainPage, the MainPage code will immediately navigate onto the requested target page.

Once the navigation has been processed, the two properties are set back to navigate by default to MainPage itself. This way, if the user presses Back in any other page, the application will return to MainPage rather than to whichever page was most recently set into the TargetGamePage property.

Listing 14–4 shows the MainPage.OnNavigatedTo function.

Listing 14–4. Navigating to whichever page is required when MainPage becomes active

```
protected override void OnNavigatedTo(System.Windows.Navigation.NavigationEventArgs e)
{
    base.OnNavigatedTo(e);

    // Navigate to whichever page has been set to be opened next
    NavigateToPage(TargetGamePage, TargetGamePageParameters);
    // Reset the target page and parameters to be the menu so that by default
    // when other pages navigate back, they return to the menu
    TargetGamePage = GamePages.MainPage;
    TargetGamePageParameters = null;
}
```

Navigating Between Pages

Everything is now in place to allow our pages to navigate in whatever way they need with minimal code. MainPage itself can navigate to any other page by calling the NavigateToPage function directly. Listing 14–5, for example, shows the code for the New Game button, which navigates to GamePage.

Listing 14–5. Processing a click on the New Game button within MainPage

```
private void newGameButton_Click(object sender, RoutedEventArgs e)
{
    // Begin a new game
    NavigateToPage(GamePages.GamePage);
}
```

Parameters can be passed to the target page, as shown in Listing 14–6. This also navigates to GamePage, but this time includes a parameter to indicate that an existing game in progress should be resumed. We will look at how games are resumed in a moment.

Listing 14–6. Passing parameters when navigating from the Resume Game button within MainPage

```
private void resumeButton_Click(object sender, RoutedEventArgs e)
{
    // Resume the game
    NavigateToPage(GamePages.GamePage, "GameState=Resume");
}
```

Other pages that want to allow the user to return to the menu by pressing the Back button do not need any extra code to be added to facilitate this. As the menu is already on the navigation stack, pressing Back will naturally navigate back to the menu.

If other pages want to provide another mechanism for returning to the menu (clicking a button, for example), they simply need to call the NavigationService.GoBack function to emulate a press of the Back button.

The final requirement is for one non-menu page to be able to take the player directly into another non-menu page—the game page taking the player to the high score page in our example. A very simple demonstration of this is present in the example project: start a game and then click the End Game button on the game page to simulate the game finishing, and the high score page appears straight away.

All that a non-menu page needs to do to implement this is to set the static MainPage.TargetGamePage property and then call NavigationService.GoBack. This will return to MainPage, which will detect the value in the TargetGamePage property and navigate immediately on to this page. Listing 14–7 shows the code behind the End Game button.

Listing 14–7. Taking the player directly from the game page to the high score page

```
private void endGameButton_Click(object sender, RoutedEventArgs e)
{
    // Go directly to the high score page
    MainPage.TargetGamePage = MainPage.GamePages.HighScorePage;
    NavigationService.GoBack();
}
```

Have a play with the example project and see how it works. Some specific scenarios to try are as follows:

- Navigating back and forth between the pages by selecting them in the menu and pressing the Back button

- Ending a game and pressing Back from the high score page, which returns to the menu and not to the game

- Pressing Back from the menu page, which always closes the application

There is, in fact, a little more navigation work to do when it comes to tombstoning and the application life cycle, but we will consider these details in the "Application Life Cycle" section later in this chapter.

Maintaining Game State

Other than support for tombstoning, it looks like we're finished with navigation. Unfortunately, however, there is one final area that we need to cover, which is how we maintain the stage of our game from one page to the next.

In Silverlight games on Windows Phone, navigating back to an existing page will return to the existing instance of the page that was put on the navigation stack; the page is cached and reused. Navigating forward, however, always creates a *new* instance of the page being displayed, and its content will therefore never be cached.

This might sound like a nuisance, particularly as the page *could* be cached if we navigated backward instead of forward. The truth is that we will need to be able to rebuild the game page from stored state in order to recover from tombstoning anyway, so using the same approach for navigation does not really introduce any additional effort.

If we want to allow the players to resume their game after navigating back to the menu, we therefore need to be able to restore all the game state so that the game picks up exactly where it left off. The game state needs to encompass *everything* the game needs to resume in a new game page instance: the positions and types of all objects within the game, the player's score, health and number of lives, and any other details that the game needs to function.

In practice, this is not really too difficult to achieve. What we need to do is remove all this information from the game page and place it into another class—we will call this the GameState class. The game will create a single instance of this class when it launches, and it can then be accessed by all the pages within the application.

As well as allowing the game to resume by rebuilding the game page from the stored state, having the state stored also allows us to implement some other nice features, such as the automatic addition or removal of the Resume Game button on the game menu, and the ability to warn the players that they will lose their game if they select Start New Game while a game is in progress. If you tried out the project, you will probably have seen all these features in action.

The GameNavigation example project implements just the framework of a game, but we will track two pieces of information in the GameState object:

- The IsGameActive property identifies whether a game is currently in progress. This is set to true when the game is initialized, and is set back to false when the game ends (when the player clicks the End Game button in our example).

- The Score property contains the player's current score. It is set to a random value each time a new game begins, but not when a game is resumed. This will allow us to see during our experimentation when a new game starts (because its value will have changed), and when a game is resumed (because its value will remain unchanged).

GameState also contains a function named ResetGame, which can be used to set the game to its initial state, ready to play. In the example project, this function simply sets up the random score value. It is also responsible for setting IsGameActive to true to show that a game is in progress.

An instance of the GameState class is provided by GamePage via a static property, also named GameState. When this is first queried, the underlying private _gameState backing field will be null, and so a new instance of the class is created. After this, the same object instance will be returned every time the property is called. It can be accessed from within GamePage or from within any other page in the application.

Listing 14–8 shows the code from GamePage that implements the GameState property.

Listing 14–8. The GamePage class' GameState property

```
private static GameState _gameState;
/// <summary>
/// Returns a reference to the game's GameState object
/// </summary>
internal static GameState GameState
{
    get
    {
        if (_gameState == null) _gameState = new GameState();
        return _gameState;
    }
    set
    {
        _gameState = value;
    }
}
```

The state of the game can now be tracked, so all that is left is to actually use the object within the pages of the application.

The first place this is used is when the Start New Game button is clicked on the menu page. Before navigating to the game page, it calls into the GameState.ResetGame function to prepare the game ready to be played.

■ **Note** It may seem odd to handle the initialization of the game in this button click, rather than in one of the functions or events inside GamePage. There is an important reason for calling the reset function from here, however, as we will see in the "Application Life Cycle" section later in this chapter.

The next place the GameState object is used is in GamePage.OnNavigatedTo, shown in Listing 14–9. This function will be invoked by Silverlight each time GamePage is displayed, as a result of clicking either the Start New Game or the Resume Game button on the game menu. As we saw back in Listing 14–5 and Listing 14–6, these two buttons both navigate to the game page, but one passes the URI parameter string GameState=Resume, and the other does not. The code, therefore, checks for this parameter and displays a corresponding message within the page.

Listing 14–9. Handling the OnNavigatedTo event inside GamePage

```
protected override void OnNavigatedTo(System.Windows.Navigation.NavigationEventArgs e)
{
    base.OnNavigatedTo(e);

    // See if we can find a resume mode specified in the querystring
    string resumeMode;
    NavigationContext.QueryString.TryGetValue("GameState", out resumeMode);
    if (resumeMode == "Resume")
    {
        gameStateText.Text = "Game state: resuming an existing game.";
    }
    else
    {
        gameStateText.Text = "Game state: starting a new game.";
    }

    // Display the player's score
    scoreText.Text = "Score: " + GameState.Score.ToString();
}
```

The only other uses of the GameState within the example are inside MenuPage. The GameState.IsGameActive property is used to determine whether the Resume button should be displayed or hidden (in the MainPage.OnNavigatedTo function), and also to see whether a confirmation message should be displayed (in the MainPage.newGameButton_Click event handler) to warn the player that they will lose their existing game if they proceed.

We will need to work more with the GameState object when we deal with tombstoning, but until then the use of the object within the project is really very straightforward.

Putting these pieces of functionality into the foundation of your games results in a consistent and predictable navigation model that should serve most, if not all, of the games that you create.

Game Settings

Many games will want to offer a choice of game settings to the user, and just as we did in XNA, we can easily store and retrieve them in Silverlight.

The method of actually storing the settings is identical to the approach we used in XNA back in Chapter 9, so have a look there if you have forgotten how the storage works. The SettingsManager class from the XNA GameFramework has been added to this chapter's version of the SLGameFramework project and is virtually identical. The main changes are that the class has been made static so no instance is required, and the RetrieveValues function (which was used to read settings from XNA game objects) has been removed.

The SLGameFramework.SettingsManager class can be seen in action in the SettingsExample project that accompanies this chapter. It builds on the navigation project from the previous section and implements the Settings page. The example implements four simple settings, as shown in Figure 14–3.

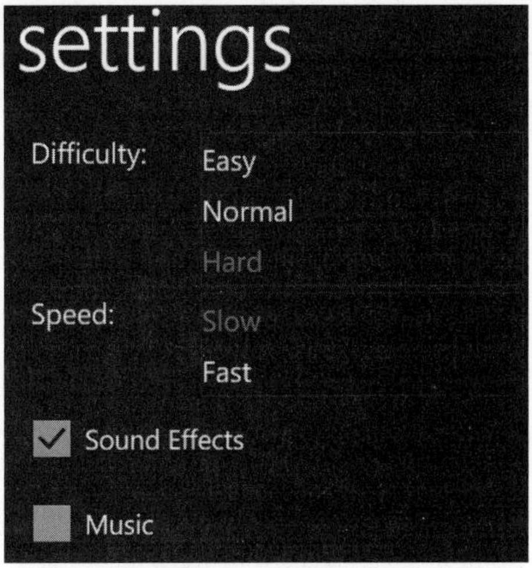

Figure 14–3. The Settings page in the SettingsExample project

There is, in fact, very little to do to implement this functionality. Silverlight's rich user interface hugely simplifies the task of displaying the settings options to users and allowing them to interact with these settings. All we really need to do for the Settings page is display the appropriate values when it opens and store any modified values when it closes.

The first of these tasks is handled by overriding the page's OnNavigatedTo function, which is called each time the page appears on the top of the navigation stack. In here we can read out all the existing settings and ensure that they are displayed in the page. Listing 14–10 shows all the code required for this.

Listing 14–10. Putting the current game settings into the Settings page

```
protected override void OnNavigatedTo(System.Windows.Navigation.NavigationEventArgs e)
{
    base.OnNavigatedTo(e);

    // Put the current settings values into the form controls
    SelectListItem(difficultyList, SettingsManager.GetValue("Difficulty", "Normal"));
    SelectListItem(speedList, SettingsManager.GetValue("Speed", "Slow"));
    musicCheckbox.IsChecked = SettingsManager.GetValue("Music", true);
    soundCheckbox.IsChecked = SettingsManager.GetValue("Sound", true);
}
```

■ **Note** The SelectListItem function shown here is a little helper function also contained within the SettingsPage code that makes it easy to select an item in a ListBox control by its item text. Another function in the class, GetListItemText, allows the text of an item to be retrieved.

This piece of code displays all the current game settings, ready to be updated by the user. When users finish, they simply press the Back button to return to the game menu. This will cause the

OnNavigatingFrom function to be called, so we can override it and use it as a trigger to write the values back into the SettingsManager class. Listing 14–11 shows the code.

Listing 14–11. Putting the game settings back into SettingsManager

```
protected override void OnNavigatingFrom(NavigatingCancelEventArgs e)
{
    base.OnNavigatingFrom(e);

    // Save each setting
    SettingsManager.SetValue("Difficulty", GetListItemText(difficultyList.SelectedItem));
    SettingsManager.SetValue("Speed", GetListItemText(speedList.SelectedItem));
    SettingsManager.SetValue("Music", musicCheckbox.IsChecked.Value);
    SettingsManager.SetValue("Sound", soundCheckbox.IsChecked.Value);
}
```

■ **Note** OnNavigatingFrom will be called even if the user navigates away by pressing the Windows button. This ensures that the settings are saved even when the game is about to be tombstoned.

From the code side of the page, this is all we need to do to maintain the game settings. Other parts of the game can query the settings by simply calling into the SettingsManager.GetValue function.

Before we move on, though, let's just quickly look at the design of the page's user interface. The various controls used by the form have been placed into a Grid control, with one control per grid cell, as this provides a simple and flexible layout mechanism.

The grid itself has been placed inside a ScrollViewer control is to allow the settings to still be accessed if the game is running in a landscape orientation. Without this, the settings further down the page could easily run off the bottom of the screen and become accessible. The same approach can be useful in portrait mode, too, if there are more settings than can be comfortably contained within the visible page.

Creating a High Score Table

Following on from the high score placeholder in the previous sections, we will now implement a working high score table into the project.

This functionality will be based entirely on the high score table code that we added to XNA back in Chapter 9, so please refer to that chapter for details on the class structure and its internal workings. The main changes described here will revolve around transferring the code into the SLGameFramework project, updating its presentational functions to work with Silverlight and XNA, and seeing how to integrate it into the navigation structure.

All the code in this section can be found in the HighScoresExample project that accompanies this chapter.

The High Score Table Classes

Of the three classes used in the XNA GameFramework project (HighScores, HighScoreTable, and HighScoreEntry), two are essentially identical in the Silverlight implementation; the only class needing code changes of note being the HighScores class. These changes primarily revolve around the presentation of the scores.

In XNA we created a series of TextObjects to present the scores, and its HighScores class offers a function named CreateTextObjectsForTable that can build these TextObject instances for display on the screen, saving the games that use this class the effort of having to create these objects themselves. While this particular function implementation is not relevant for Silverlight, we will provide an equivalent function to simplify display of the scores onscreen, and for Silverlight it is simply named ShowScores.

Silverlight offers several controls that we could potentially use to host the display of scores, but the one that best meets our requirements is the Grid control. This is the control that provides the simplest method for presenting a three-column data display (the columns being for the position within the high score table, the name, and the score) while allowing us to control the alignment of text in the individual columns and also allowing the columns to expand or contract as needed to fit the text that it contains.

The ShowScores function expects a Grid to be passed as one of its parameters, and will fully configure and populate the grid with all the scores. There are several parts to this. First of all, the grid configuration is set up. Any existing content is removed, and the grid columns are set so that the first and third columns (the position and score columns) automatically adjust to their content, while the second column (the name column) expands to fill as much space as it can. We have seen all these settings before in XAML, but not yet looked at the equivalent C# code. Listing 14–12 shows how this is set up.

Listing 14–12. Configuring the Grid read for the display of scores

```
//Clear any controls contained in the grid
scoresGrid.Children.Clear();

// Reset the grid columns
scoresGrid.ColumnDefinitions.Clear();
scoresGrid.ColumnDefinitions.Add(new ColumnDefinition() { Width = GridLength.Auto });
scoresGrid.ColumnDefinitions.Add(new ColumnDefinition()
                                    { Width = new GridLength(1, GridUnitType.Star) });
scoresGrid.ColumnDefinitions.Add(new ColumnDefinition() { Width = GridLength.Auto });

// Reset the grid rows
scoresGrid.RowDefinitions.Clear();
```

Once the grid is ready to display its data, the code loops through each high score entry, adding TextBlock controls to the cells of the grid so that the position, name and score are displayed.

ShowScores also allows a highlightIndex parameter to be provided. If this value is available, the score at the specified index will be displayed in bold text and will fade its opacity to highlight the player's new score. As the code loops through adding the score entries, it looks for the entry matching this index; if the index is found, a reference to that row's name TextBlock is stored in the highlightedName variable.

Once all the names have been added, the code sets up a Storyboard for the highlightedName TextBlock, if one was found, so that its Opacity can be faded. We have seen how to set Storyboard objects up in XAML, but not in code. Listing 14–13 shows how this is achieved.

Listing 14–13. Preparing and activating a Storyboard using C#

```
// Did we find a name to highlight?
if (highlightedName != null)
{
    // Yes, so create a storyboard and a double animation to fade its opacity
    Storyboard scoreFader = new Storyboard();
    DoubleAnimation faderAnim = new DoubleAnimation();

    // Set the target object and target property of the fader animation
```

```
Storyboard.SetTarget(faderAnim, highlightedName);
Storyboard.SetTargetProperty(faderAnim, new PropertyPath("Opacity"));
// Set the other animation parameters
faderAnim.Duration = new Duration(new TimeSpan(0, 0, 1));
faderAnim.RepeatBehavior = RepeatBehavior.Forever;
faderAnim.AutoReverse = true;
faderAnim.From = 1;
faderAnim.To = 0;
// Add the fader to the storyboard
scoreFader.Children.Add(faderAnim);
// Add the storyboard to the grid
scoresGrid.Resources.Add("scorefader", scoreFader);
// Begin the storyboard
scoreFader.Begin();
}
```

We will see how and when this function is called in a moment.

Instantiating the HighScores Object

So the game can gain access to the high score tables, we must first create an instance of the HighScores object. To allow the whole game access to the high score data, this instance is implemented as a static property inside HighScorePage.

When the property is first queried, the HighScores object instance is created and initialized with each of the high score tables that the game needs. All subsequent calls to the property are returned this same object instance, ensuring that the whole game sees an up-to-date set of scores.

Listing 14–14 shows the implementation of this property. In our example we use a single table, named Default, and set it to contain a maximum of 20 entries.

Listing 14–14. The HighScorePage.HighScores property

```
private static HighScores _highScores;
/// <summary>
/// Returns a reference to the game's GameState object
/// </summary>
internal static HighScores HighScores
{
    get
    {
        // Do we already have a highscore instance?
        if (_highScores == null)
        {
            // No, so create one
            _highScores = new HighScores();
            // Add the tables
            _highScores.InitializeTable("Default", 20);
            // Load any existing scores
            _highScores.LoadScores();
        }
        return _highScores;
    }
}
```

■ **Note** The Silverlight implementation of the high score classes support multiple score tables, just as they did in the XNA implementation. In this example, we only use the Default table, but you can easily add multiple tables based on game difficulty or some other variable if you wanted to.

Adding New Score Entries

When each game finishes, we need to check whether the score the player has achieved is good enough to add to the high score table, and if so, prompt the player to enter their name.

The first part of this is handled in the game over sequence inside the game page. In our example, this is handled by the End Game button inside GamePage. The code behind the button is shown in Listing 14–15.

Listing 14–15. Checking to see whether a high score was achieved and navigating accordingly

```
private void endGameButton_Click(object sender, RoutedEventArgs e)
{
    // Indicate that the game has finished
    GameState.IsGameActive = false;

    // Was the score good enough for the high score table?
    if (HighScorePage.HighScores.GetTable("Default").ScoreQualifies(GameState.Score))
    {
        // Yes, so go to the "enter your name" page
        MainPage.TargetGamePage = MainPage.GamePages.HighScoreNamePage;
    }
    else
    {
        // No, so go to the high score page
        MainPage.TargetGamePage = MainPage.GamePages.HighScorePage;
    }
    // Either way, navigate back to the menu so that it can redirect for us
    NavigationService.GoBack();
}
```

The HighScoreTable's ScoreQualifies function is used to find out whether the player's score is good enough for the high score table. If the score is not good enough, the code navigates to the existing HighScorePage to show the player the scores to beat—we will take a look at the contents of that page in a moment. On the other hand, if the score is good enough to make it in to the high scores, the game navigates to a new page: HighScoreNamePage.

HighScoreNamePage simply allows the players to enter their name for inclusion in the high score table. At its heart, the page consists of little more than a TextBox, but there are several nice touches that we can add to the page to make it a little nicer to use.

One such touch is to automatically save the player's name to the game settings whenever a high score is achieved. The saved name can then be restored the next time the page is displayed, saving users from having to enter their names again. The page also automatically focuses on the player's name field and selects the existing text so that if a new name is entered it automatically overwrites the name that is present.

The page also offers an ApplicationBar that can be used to signal addition of the entered name, and handles pressing of the Enter key (either from a hardware keyboard on from the SIP) for the same purpose.

Once the player's name is entered and submitted, the page's AddName function is called to process it. This function accesses the high score table object via the HighScorePage.HighScores property, adds the new name, and saves the score.

It then redirects off to HighScorePage to display the score. If a name was actually entered by the player, the MainPage.TargetGamePageParameters property is used to pass the index of the new score entry. This can then be used by HighScorePage to highlight the addition, as we will see in a moment.

The code of the AddName function can be seen in Listing 14–16.

Listing 14–16. Processing the submission of a new high score name

```
private void AddName()
{
    // Do we have a name?
    if (nameText.Text.Length > 0)
    {
        // Store the name into the game Settings
        SettingsManager.SetValue("HighscoreName", nameText.Text);
        // Add to the high score table and retrieve the index of the new position
        int newScoreIndex = HighScorePage.HighScores.GetTable("Default").AddEntry(
                                    nameText.Text, GamePage.GameState.Score);
        // Save the updated scores
        HighScorePage.HighScores.SaveScores();
        // Pass the new score index to the highscore page so we can highlight it
        MainPage.TargetGamePageParameters = "HighlightIndex=" + newScoreIndex.ToString();
    }
    // We need to navigate to the high score page...
    MainPage.TargetGamePage = MainPage.GamePages.HighScorePage;
    // Go back to the menu and allow it to redirect for us
    NavigationService.GoBack();
}
```

Displaying the Scores

All we have left to do is to display the high score table on the screen. We have already covered most of the code required for this, and we now just need to actually set up a Grid control to receive the score text.

The presentation of the high score table will be enhanced, particularly if there are lots of entries within it, by allowing the user to scroll up and down. With scrolling enabled, you can have potentially hundreds of entries, and the user will be able to access them all with a simple swipe of a finger.

Making the grid scrollable is simply a matter of placing it inside a ScrollViewer control. This control will automatically allow the player scroll to the full height of the grid, allowing all the scores to be brought into display.

The entire XAML code for the ContentPanel within HighScorePage is shown in Listing 14–17.

Listing 14–17. The user interface markup for the high score table

```
<!--ContentPanel-->
<Grid x:Name="ContentPanel" Grid.Row="1" Margin="12,10,12,0">
    <ScrollViewer FontSize="28">
        <Grid Name="scoresGrid" Margin="10 0 10 0" />
    </ScrollViewer>
```

```
</Grid>
```

Omitting any size information for the ScrollViewer will result in it expanding to fill its container, the ContentPanel. The same applies to the scoresGrid, which will fill the ScrollViewer completely except for a 10-pixel margin on the left and right edges, as specified by the Margin attribute.

The C# code required to display the scores within this Grid is little more complex than the XAML, and is shown in Listing 14–18. It looks for a new score entry index in the navigation query string (as will be passed by HighScoreNamePage), and then calls the HighScores.ShowScores method to populate the high score grid.

Listing 14–18. Getting the high scores displayed on the screen

```
private void PhoneApplicationPage_Loaded(object sender, RoutedEventArgs e)
{
    string paramValue;
    int newScoreIndex;

    // Are we highlighting an entry?
    NavigationContext.QueryString.TryGetValue("HighlightIndex", out paramValue);
    if (!int.TryParse(paramValue, out newScoreIndex))
    {
        // Nothing found or not numeric, so don't highlight anything
        newScoreIndex = -1;
    }

    // Get the HighScores class to show the scores inside the scoresGrid control
    HighScores.ShowScores(scoresGrid, "Default", newScoreIndex);
}
```

The score display is not especially interesting to look at, so there are lots of presentation enhancements that could be applied to make the page a little more visually exciting, but in terms of functionality, this is all that we need to do!

Playing Music and Sound Effects

Sound was the subject of Chapter 5, where we looked at how to play music and sound effects in XNA games. In this section, we will find out how to achieve the same things in Silverlight.

In actual fact, Silverlight on Windows Phone 7 does not have any direct audio capabilities. This is not a problem, though, as we can hook into XNA's audio library and get it to do the work for us. We will therefore be using exactly the same audio classes as we did back in Chapter 5: SoundEffect, SoundEffectInstance, Song, and MediaPlayer. If you need to jog your memory about these classes, this would be a good opportunity to do so!

There are two main differences with the way these classes are used in Silverlight as compared with XNA. The first is the need for a timer to be set up to process XNA's updates; without this, any attempt to play sound will fail with an error. The second difference revolves around loading sound and music data, as there is no Content project in Silverlight projects.

Let's take a look at the details. All the code for this section can be found in the MusicAndSounds example project that accompanies this chapter.

Accessing the XNA Audio Library

Before we can use XNA's audio features, we must first reference its audio assembly. To directly access the audio classes, a reference is needed to the `Microsoft.Xna.Framework` assembly, inside which the `Audio` namespace contains all the classes that we are interested in working with.

As you will see in a moment, we will actually wrap up all the access to the audio classes inside a new class within the `SLGameFramework`, so in many cases your game can use the functions offered by this class without actually having to add the XNA assembly reference itself.

Initializing the XNA Dispatch Timer

You saw when we worked with sound effects and music in XNA that it is very easy to set up a music file or a sound effect and tell it to play. It then plays asynchronously in the background until it finishes. We can optionally instruct it to loop when it repeats, and all this happens entirely automatically.

The reason this background playback can work is because XNA is constantly attending to the playing sound, ensuring that it continues to play and that it loops at the appropriate point. This happens automatically as part of XNA's internal update/draw cycle.

When sounds are played in Silverlight, the XNA audio library still needs to attend to the playing sound, but it cannot do so in the update/draw cycle because there is no such thing in Silverlight applications. For the audio processing to be carried out, we must manually create a timer for XNA and allow it to call into its internal `Update` method on a regular and frequent basis.

If we forget to do this, XNA's audio library will throw an exception as soon as we attempt to play a sound, so it will come to our attention fairly quickly. We can add some code to the `SLGameFramework` project, however, which will simplify the task of initializing this timer as far as is possible, taking away the nuisance factor of setting it up in each of your games.

The timer is initialized in a class inside `SLGameFramework` called `XNAAsyncDispatcher`. The code for the class is wrapped up in a series of private functions, and the class constructor is private, too, so it cannot be instantiated. Instead, it offers some static members that can be called from your game.

To initialize the timer, simply call the static `XNAAsyncDispatcher.Start` method. Nothing more is required, but this call *must* be made from your Silverlight application's `App` class constructor. If you call if after that, it will fail to initialize. If you don't know when your app starts whether you will need sound or not, initialize the timer anyway—you can always ignore it if you later decide that it is not required. You can check whether the timer has been initialized by querying the static `XNAAsyncDispatcher.IsStarted` property.

Listing 14–19 shows a simple `App` class constructor that is configured to initialize the XNA dispatcher.

Listing 14–19. Initializing the XNAAsyncDispatcher timer

```
/// <summary>
/// Constructor for the Application object.
/// </summary>
public App()
{
    // Global handler for uncaught exceptions.
    UnhandledException += Application_UnhandledException;

    // Standard Silverlight initialization
    InitializeComponent();

    // Phone-specific initialization
    InitializePhoneApplication();
```

```
    // Start the XNA Async Dispatcher so that we can play music and sound effects
    SLGameFramework.XNAAsyncDispatcher.Start();
}
```

The code inside the XNAAsyncDispatcher class is not especially interesting; essentially it configures a timer that calls into an XNA Update method every 1/20 of a second. Feel free to take a look in the class if you would like to see its content in more detail.

Playing Sound Effects

The main thing we need to overcome to play sound effects in Silverlight is the lack of the Content project. Fortunately, this is not too much of a problem, as we can initialize a SoundEffect object from a Stream. XNA provides a simple way of obtaining such a Stream via its TitleContainer function, which we can use to open a sound file contained within our project.

Listing 14–20 shows a simple example of using these objects and methods to create a sound and start it playing.

Listing 14–20. Loading and playing a sound file

```
using System.IO;
using Microsoft.Xna.Framework;
using Microsoft.Xna.Framework.Audio;

[...]

    private void PlaySound()
    {
        // Create and load the SoundEffect
        SoundEffect mySound;
        mySound = SoundEffect.FromStream(TitleContainer.OpenStream("Sounds/Piano.wav"));
        // Play the sound
        mySound.Play();
    }
```

The sounds that are to be played are added into the project, just as we added images for our sprites. They can be placed into a folder (as they are in this example, in the Sounds folder) to keep them separate from other files and resources, and must be in .wav format. Their Build Action property must be set to Content.

A new Stream is created each time the code in Listing 14–20 is executed, and as we are likely to want to play the same sound effect hundreds or thousands of times within a game, it makes sense to cache the sound data instead of needing to repeatedly reload the same sound multiple times.

We can, in fact, cache the SoundEffect object because it is all we need to initiate playback of the sound as many times as we want.

To simplify the initialization and caching of sounds, a new class named AudioPlayer is added to the SLGameFramework project. This will take care of as much of the work of dealing with sounds as it can, providing a simple API for our games to use. The class is static, so it can be used without first having to create an instance.

The class first declares a class-level dictionary of SoundEffect objects named _soundEffects. It will be keyed by the path and file name of the sound being played, allowing it to easily identify whether a particular sound has already been loaded or is being played for the first time.

To populate the dictionary, a private function named GetSoundEffect is used. Passed the path and file name of a sound, it will check to see whether it has already been cached; if not, it will be loaded and added to the dictionary. Either way, the sound (newly loaded or cached) is returned to the calling procedure.

This is then used by a public function named PlaySoundEffect. Provided with the path and file name of the sound and the playback parameters (volume, pitch, and pan values), this function performs two tasks: it checks that the XNA dispatcher timer has been started (by calling into the XNAAsyncDispatcher class); assuming that it has, it retrieves the SoundEffect object and calls its Play method.

A further overload of PlaySoundEffect accepts just a sound path and file name, and uses the default playback parameters (maximum volume, normal pitch, no panning) for when they do not need to be adjusted.

Listing 14–21 shows all the SLGameFramework.AudioPlayer functions described so far.

Listing 14–21. Loading and playing sound files in the AudioPlayer class

```
private static Dictionary<string, SoundEffect> _soundEffects =
                                        new Dictionary<string,SoundEffect>();

// Plays the sound effect at the specified content path and filename
public static void PlaySoundEffect(string soundPath)
{
    PlaySoundEffect(soundPath, 1, 0, 0);
}

// Plays the sound effect at the specified content path and filename
public static void PlaySoundEffect(string soundPath, float volume, float pitch,
                                                                    float pan)
{
    // Check that the XNAAsyncDispatcher has been started
    XNAAsyncDispatcher.CheckIsStarted();

    // If we have no volume then there is nothing to play
    if (volume * SoundEffectMasterVolume == 0) return;

    // Get and play the sound effect
    GetSoundEffect(soundPath).Play(volume * SoundEffectMasterVolume, pitch, pan);
}

// Checks if the specified sound is cached (and loads and caches it if not),
// then returns its SoundEffect object.
private static SoundEffect GetSoundEffect(string soundPath)
{
    // Convert the path to lowercase so that it is case-insensitive
    soundPath = soundPath.ToLower();

    // Do we already have this sound loaded?
    if (!_soundEffects.ContainsKey(soundPath))
    {
        // No, so load it now and add it to the dictionary
        _soundEffects.Add(soundPath,
                        SoundEffect.FromStream(TitleContainer.OpenStream(soundPath)));
    }

    // Return the sound
    return _soundEffects[soundPath];
}
```

Playing a sound from a Silverlight game is now as easy as simply calling the
AudioPlayer.PlaySoundEffect function. Listing 14–22 shows the code behind the Piano button in the
MusicAndSounds example project. This single line of code is now all we need to load, cache, and play the
specified sound.

Listing 14–22. Loading and playing sound files in the AudioPlayer class

```
private void pianoButton_Click(object sender, RoutedEventArgs e)
{
    // Play the Piano sound effect
    AudioPlayer.PlaySoundEffect("Sounds/Piano.wav");
}
```

Sound effect instances can be used in Silverlight, too, allowing the sound to be controlled after its
playback has started using the SoundEffectInstance class' IsLooped, Pan, Pitch, and Volume properties
along with its Pause, Play, Resume, and Stop methods.

To allow instances to be created, the CreateSoundEffectInstance function shown in Listing 14–23 is
added to the AudioPlayer class.

Listing 14–23. Initializing and returning SoundEffectInstance objects

```
public static SoundEffectInstance CreateSoundEffectInstance(string soundPath)
{
    SoundEffectInstance instance;

    XNAAsyncDispatcher.CheckIsStarted();

    instance = GetSoundEffect(soundPath).CreateInstance();
    instance.Volume = SoundEffectMasterVolume;
    return instance;
}
```

Listing 14–24 shows a simple example of using a sound effect instance, taken from the Motorbike
button in the MusicAndSounds project. This example doesn't actually use the sound instance for anything
that could not have been achieved with a simple call to PlaySoundEffect, but it does show how instances
can be obtained and used.

Listing 14–24. Obtaining and playing a SoundEffectInstance

```
private void motorbikeButton_Click(object sender, RoutedEventArgs e)
{
    // Play the Motorbike sound effect using a SoundEffectInstance
    SoundEffectInstance sound =
                        AudioPlayer.CreateSoundEffectInstance("Sounds/Motorbike.wav");
    // Set a random pitch
    sound.Pitch = GameHelper.RandomNext(-1.0f, 1.0f);
    sound.Play();
}
```

As you may have spotted in the code listings, the class also provides a property named
SoundEffectMasterVolume that allows the volume level for all played sounds to be controlled. It is a
simple float property, whose value is multiplied by the volume levels provided for each call to the sound
effect functions. Volume levels specified in calls to PlaySoundEffect are, therefore, proportional up to a
maximum of the specified master volume level.

This property provides a great way of allowing the overall volume level of your game to be set in a Settings page. If the volume level is set to 0, the class will actually skip playing sounds altogether to save processor resources.

■ **Note** The master volume will not have any effect on sounds that are already playing when its value is modified. If you have any existing sound instances that need to be modified, particularly those that are looped, you will need to adjust their volume levels manually in your game code.

You can experiment with the effect of the master volume by altering the value of the slider in the example project.

Playing Music

To allow MP3 and WMA music files to be played, the XNA Song class is at our disposal. Just to be awkward, music files are loaded into Song objects in a different way from SoundEffect objects; we simply call the static Song.FromUri function, passing in the path to the music file, and its data will be loaded ready for playback.

However, as you may recall from when we explored this subject in Chapter 5, Microsoft has some specific requirements about when a game is allowed to play music. If the phone's media player is currently playing music, a game must respect the existing playback and not begin playback of its own music. The same restriction applies in Silverlight games.

We can package up the process of checking for playback permission, loading, caching (using the same approach as for SoundEffects), and finally playing a song in the AudioPlayer class once again. This is handled by the PlaySong function, shown in Listing 14–25.

Listing 14–25. Initialing and playing a Song from an MP3 or WMA file

```
public static void PlaySong(string songPath,  bool autoRepeat)
{
    // Make sure we are in control of the media player
    if (MediaPlayer.GameHasControl)
    {
        // Convert the songPath to lower case so it is case-insensitive
        songPath = songPath.ToLower();
        // Is the song cached?
        if (!_songs.ContainsKey(songPath))
        {
            // Load the song
            _songs.Add(songPath,
                        Song.FromUri(songPath, new Uri(songPath, UriKind.Relative)));
        }
        // Get a reference to the song
        Song song = _songs[songPath];
        // Set media player parameters
        MediaPlayer.IsRepeating = autoRepeat;
        MediaPlayer.Volume = MusicMasterVolume;
        // Start playing
        MediaPlayer.Play(song);
    }
}
```

Alongside this function the `AudioPlayer` class provides a series of related methods and properties: `StopSong`, `PauseSong`, and `ResumeSong` can be used to control playback; `SongState` returns a value indicating whether the song is stopped, playing, or paused; `SongPosition` returns a `TimeSpan` that shows how far through the playback of the song has progressed; and finally the `GameHasControl` property tells us whether we are actually allowed to play music at the current time.

Listing 14–26 shows the code for the example project's Music button, which loads and plays a piece of music when first clicked. Subsequent clicks toggle its state between paused and playing.

Listing 14–26. Playing, pausing, and resuming a piece of music

```
private void musicButton_Click(object sender, RoutedEventArgs e)
{
    // Start, pause or resume the song
    switch (AudioPlayer.SongState)
    {
        case MediaState.Stopped:
            AudioPlayer.PlaySong("Sounds/JoshWoodward-Breadcrumbs-NoVox-02-2020.mp3");
            break;
        case MediaState.Paused:
            AudioPlayer.ResumeSong();
            break;
        case MediaState.Playing:
            AudioPlayer.PauseSong();
            break;
    }
}
```

Music files also need to be added to the project with a `Build Action` of `Content`, exactly the same as for sound effect files.

Along similar lines to the `SoundEffectMasterVolume` property, another property named `SongMasterVolume` is available for controlling the Song playback volume. This is actually just a wrapper around the `MediaPlayer.Volume` property, but is provided for convenience and consistency. Changing the volume using this property will affect songs that are already being played.

Unlike sound effects, Song playback will still be initiated even if the volume is zero because the volume could later be increased, and to ensure that the expected output is achieved, the Song needs to be initiated when requested by the calling code.

Application Life Cycle

The next subject area is the application life cycle and how to handle your game being deactivated and reactived by the operating system.

Silverlight applications do not escape the need to handle the application life cycle, tombstoning, and saving and restoring game state. The requirements for Silverlight are very similar to those for XNA, which was covered back in Chapter 10, but as usual there are some differences.

One difference is that Silverlight does provide a *little* more assistance in the task than XNA did (that is to say, more than none, which is about how much help XNA provided!).

If the user navigates away from your game by pressing the Windows key, or if the game is interrupted in some other way such as the arrival of an incoming phone call, the application will be tombstoned as with our XNA games. This results in the application being terminated (though it will give the appearance of still running in Visual Studio to allow the IDE to reconnect to the application when it is reactivated), and nearly all content of the game will be lost.

The help we get from Silverlight is that it remembers *some* of what our application was doing. This amounts to automatic storage of the navigation stack, including the full URI of each page within the stack.

When the user returns to the application, it will open to the page that was last being used before it was tombstoned. Any query string values that were passed to that page via its URI will be present and can be read out once again. Other than this, though, it is an entirely new page.

The same goes for the other pages on the navigation stack; Silverlight may have retained their URIs, but not the actual page instances. Each page will be reinstantiated as the user navigates back to it.

This assistance certainly saves us some work, but it doesn't remove the need for your games to save their state to either isolated storage or the `PhoneApplicationService.Current.State` dictionary each time the game is deactivated, and then retrieve it again when it is subsequently reactivated.

Exploring Tombstoning Behavior in Silverlight

Let's explore this automatic storage of the navigation stack by experimenting briefly with the `HighScoresExample` project that we worked on earlier in this chapter. Run the project and with its main menu displayed, press the Windows button and then the Back button. Silverlight remembers that we were on the menu page and restores it to the top of the navigation stack.

Repeat this with the About page open. When the game is reactivated, the About page automatically displays once again. Pressing Back again returns to the main menu, and pressing it a final time closes the application. Clearly all the page navigation is working exactly as we need.

Now try deactivating the game while the Game page is displayed—but make a note of the displayed score before you do. When the game is reactivated, it redisplays the correct page, but the score has been lost and set to 0; it was not persisted.

This is all just as you would probably expect, but here are a couple of things you might *not* expect. First of all, end a game and enter your name so that it appears in the high score table. With the high score table displayed and your name highlighted, press the Windows button and then the Back button. The game returns to the high score page as expected, but your name continues to be highlighted. How did it survive the tombstoning process?

The answer is that the highlight index is part of the query string used to navigate to the high score page. You can see this being set up using the `MainPage.TargetGamePageParameters` property back in Listing 14–16. When you navigate back to the game, the high score page is being completely reconstructed from scratch, but the `HighlightIndex` query string element is still on the navigation stack, so it is picked up once again and used to highlight the same table entry.

The other behavior you may not expect is on the Settings page. Navigate your way there and change one or two of the options; then press the Windows button and then the Back button. The modified options all survive the tombstoning process.

This behavior is in fact because there is code in the `SettingsPage` class managing the storage of the settings for us. You may recall that all the settings are persisted in the page's `OnNavigatingFrom` function, as shown back in Listing 14–11. As well as being called when the user navigates away within the application, this function is also called when navigating out of the application, so it is storing the values for us.

Hopefully this clarifies what does get automatically stored by Silverlight and what does not. For the substantial part of the data that does not, we need to make arrangements for our code to look after itself.

Storing and Restoring State

The four life cycle events are handled in Silverlight projects by the `App` class. Their event handlers, `Application_Launching`, `Application_Closing`, `Application_Activated`, and `Application_Deactivated`, are all provided automatically when a new project is created, and can be filled in with whatever code is required. We will use them to store away the values that our game needs when it is deactivated and recover them when it is reactivated. The code required for this state storage can be found in the Tombstoning example project.

Our simple example game needs to store only two pieces of information: the player's score, and whether or not the game is currently active. We could simply write each of these values into the PhoneApplicationService.Current.State dictionary individually when the game is deactivated, and that is a perfectly valid and workable way to store the game data. However, there is an easier way: store the GameState object itself.

As you may recall from Chapter 10, we can place any object we want into the State dictionary, providing it can be serialized. The GameState object in the example project can certainly be serialized: its scope is public, it has a default constructor (which is public and has no parameters), and all its properties are serializable.

■ **Note** If your GameState object contained properties that could not be directly serialized, they would need to be controlled via the use of the DataContract and DataMember attributes. The "Controlling Serialization" section in Chapter 10 contains everything you need to know to get these attributes working in your game.

To store our game state when it is deactivated and to restore it when it is activated again, all we need is the code shown in Listing 14–27.

Listing 14–27. Storing and restoring game state before and after being tombstoned

```
// Code to execute when the application is deactivated (sent to background)
private void Application_Deactivated(object sender, DeactivatedEventArgs e)
{
    // Write the game state to the state object
    PhoneApplicationService.Current.State.Clear();
    PhoneApplicationService.Current.State.Add("GameState", GamePage.GameState);
}

// Code to execute when the application is activated (brought to foreground)
private void Application_Activated(object sender, ActivatedEventArgs e)
{
    // Restore the game state from the state object
    GamePage.GameState = (GameState)PhoneApplicationService.Current.State["GameState"];
}
```

■ **Tip** When you restore a real-time game, a nice touch is to automatically put the game into pause mode so that players have a chance to work out where the game has got to before they are thrown back into the action.

That is all there is to it, but don't forget that all the pages will be re-created after the state has been restored. This means that all the pages' constructors, Loaded events, and OnNavigatedTo functions will be called again when the pages are next navigated to. It is important therefore not to put anything into these procedures that will disrupt the restoration of the existing game.

This behavior is why the example projects call into GameState.ResetGame inside the Start New Game button click event handler rather than inside GamePage; putting the call into the GamePage's Loaded event would result in it being called again after the application reactivated, wiping out the restored data.

■ **Tip** For data that you always want to persist between sessions, you should try to ensure that the data is stored every time it is updated rather than just in the life cycle events. For example, we save the high scores every time they are changed rather than just when the game deactivates. This helps to ensure that unexpected closure of the application does not result in lost data.

Game in Focus: Diamond Lines, Part II

Let's wrap up by putting some of the things we have covered in this chapter into the *Diamond Lines* example game. Specifically, we will add page navigation, a GameState class, support for tombstoning, some game settings, and sound effects. All the changes can be found in the DiamondLinesPartII project.

Adding Game Navigation

The navigation is added using the technique described in the "Game Navigation" section at the beginning of this chapter. No implementation changes were required.

The supported pages are MainPage (displaying the game menu), GamePage (into which all the game content has been placed), SettingsPage, and AboutPage. As the game does not currently have any "game over" checking, or indeed any scoring, there is no high score functionality included.

Maintaining Game State

The area of the game that has changed the most since the first version of this code was presented in the last chapter is around the control of game state. Just as in the example project we looked at in the last section, *Diamond Lines* uses an object called GameState to store the information about the game.

The state of the game is really very simple; we just need to know whether it is active and the colors of the diamonds in the game grid. None of the other information that the game uses is of significance, as it all revolves around animation and updating the game board.

For data storage, the GameState class therefore simply requires two properties: IsGameActive to track whether a game is in progress or not, and DiamondColors to store an array of the diamond colors in play.

■ **Note** Due to a limitation of the way serialization works, the DiamondColors array is stored in a slightly unusual way. We will examine this in more detail in the "Tombstoning Support" section in a moment.

Alongside these properties, GameState also offers a ResetGame function that randomizes all the diamond colors, and two additional functions named GetDiamondColor and SetDiamondColor that allow the color for an individual game cell to be queried or updated.

When the game is actually playing, the diamond colors are stored inside the corresponding Diamond objects rather than being stored in the GameState object. This is very convenient as it allows the Diamond class to completely look after its own state and content. It doesn't lend itself well to serialization, however; ideally we want to get all that data moved across into the GameState class.

This data transfer could have been achieved by getting the Diamond class to work with the data in the GameState class each time it needs to read or set a color, but there is an easier way to handle the state. There are, in fact, only two points within the game at which the GameState actually needs to be valid and up to date: when the game is being resumed and GamePage is opening, and when GamePage is closing due to the user navigating away or the game being tombstoned.

We can respond to GamePage opening by ensuring that when it initializes all the Diamond objects, it simply reads out all the colors from the GameState object. That will ensure that anything placed into GameState will be restored into the board when GamePage is next activated. Listing 14–28 shows the InitializeDiamonds function, called when the page is first loaded, performs this task.

Listing 14–28. Restoring game state into the Diamond objects

```
/// <summary>
/// Initialise the sprites ready for the game to be displayed
/// </summary>
private void InitializeDiamonds()
{
    // Stop the fader animation if it is activated
    Fader.Stop();

    // Remove all existing sprites from the canvas
    GameCanvas.Children.Clear();

    // Add a new set of random diamonds
    for (int x = 0; x < BoardWidth; x++)
    {
        for (int y = 0; y < BoardHeight; y++)
        {
            // Create the diamond sprite
            _gameBoard[x, y] = new Diamond(this, x, y);
            // Set its color from the colors in GameState
            _gameBoard[x, y].Color = GameState.GetDiamondColor(x, y);
        }
    }

    // All the time there are lines left on the board, remove them
    while (FindLines(false));

    // Switch to idle state
    MovementState = MovementStates.Idle;
}
```

Putting the diamond colors back into GameState is handled by the OnNavigatingFrom override, which simply loops through each Diamond object, transferring the color value across to the state object. This update ensures that when the page closes, for whatever reason, the GameState always contains the data of the game in play. Listing 14–29 shows how this is achieved.

Listing 14–29. Putting the diamond colors back into GameState

```
protected override void OnNavigatingFrom(
                                System.Windows.Navigation.NavigatingCancelEventArgs e)
{
    base.OnNavigatingFrom(e);

    // Loop for each diamond, copying the colors back to the GameState object
    for (int x = 0; x < GamePage.BoardWidth; x++)
    {
        for (int y = 0; y < GamePage.BoardWidth; y++)
        {
            GameState.SetDiamondColor(x, y, _gameBoard[x, y].Color);
        }
    }
}
```

Transferring data from and to the GameState object in this way is a convenient mechanism of allowing complex in-game data to be stored away and retrieved when needed. Just be sure to keep the execution of the OnNavigatingFrom code as fast as possible so that it doesn't get terminated prematurely during tombstoning.

Tombstoning Support

Most of the work for supporting tombstoning is already done by this stage, and in theory the only thing left to do is to add and retrieve the GameState object to and from the PhoneApplicationService.Current dictionary each time the application deactivates and reactivates. The code required is just as shown in the "Application Life Cycle" section earlier in this chapter.

However, using this in *Diamond Lines* reveals a limitation with the .NET serializer: it is unable to serialize multi-dimensional arrays. The normal way to store the diamond colors inside GameState would be as a two-dimensional array, but attempting to put GameState into storage in this way results in an exception.

There are several ways to manipulate the array so that it can store the game data without needing to be multidimensional, but the approach I decided to use was to change it into an array of arrays. Each item in the *outer* array will represent a column across the x axis and will contain an *inner* array full of the actual colors for that column. The declaration of this array inside the GameState class is shown in Listing 14–30.

Listing 14–30. Declaring the GameState color array without using multiple dimensions

```
/// <summary>
/// The array of colors of the diamonds in play
/// </summary>
/// <remarks>.NET is unable to serialize multi-dimensional arrays, but it is
/// able to serialize arrays of arrays. This is therefore implemented as an
/// array of arrays: the outer array is for the x axis, the inner arrays for
/// the y axis.</remarks>
public int[][] DiamondColors { get; set; }
```

One of the downsides to this structure is that the array cannot be dimensioned within a single call. The outer array can be set up easily enough, but the inner arrays must be created individually. This is handled in the GameState constructor, as can be seen in Listing 14–31.

Listing 14–31. Creating the empty DiamondColors array

```
public GameState()
{
    // Create all the required space in the DiamondColors array.
    // First create the outer array
    DiamondColors = new int[GamePage.BoardWidth][];
    // Now create the inner arrays at each outer array index
    for (int x = 0; x < GamePage.BoardWidth; x++)
    {
        DiamondColors[x] = new int[GamePage.BoardHeight];
    }
}
```

Finally, to simplify reading and writing from and to the array, the GetDiamondColor and SetDiamondColor functions are provided, as shown in Listing 14–32.

Listing 14–32. Utility functions to get and set diamond colors for specific array items

```
public int GetDiamondColor(int x, int y)
{
    return DiamondColors[x][y];
}
public void SetDiamondColor(int x, int y, int color)
{
    DiamondColors[x][y] = color;
}
```

Once the GameState class has been set up in this way, it is quite happy to be serialized when the game is deactivated.

There is another handy feature that we can add to the game too, which will preserve the game state not only when the game is tombstoned but also when it actually closed. This allows the player to leave the game alone for an extended period of time or to back out of it, and the next time they launch it the game that they were playing will still be present.

This is achieved simply by placing the object into the IsolatedStorageSettings.ApplicationSettings dictionary, the same location we are storing game settings. The SLGameFramework.SettingsManager class can look after this for us using the SetObjectValue and GetObjectValue methods; they are the same as SetValue and GetValue, but specifically work with object types.

Implementing this feature starts by checking for a stored GameState object when the Launching event, recovering it if one is found. After restoration it is removed from storage so that old game states cannot be recovered later on. Listing 14–33 shows the code for this.

Listing 14–33. Restoring persisted game state when the game launches

```
private void Application_Launching(object sender, LaunchingEventArgs e)
{
    // Do we have a stored game state from a previous game session?
    if (SettingsManager.GetObjectValue("StoredGameState", null) != null)
    {
        // Yes, read it out so that it can be restored
        GamePage.GameState =
                (GameState)SettingsManager.GetObjectValue("StoredGameState", null);
        // Remove the game state from storage
        SettingsManager.DeleteValue("StoredGameState");
```

```
        }
    }
```

Placing the game state into storage is very easy, too, but there is one detail to remember: just because a game is deactivated, there is no guarantee that it will ever be reactivated again. To ensure the player really does not lose their game, deactivation should place the game state into storage in both the Deactivated and the Closing event, as shown in Listing 14–34.

Listing 14–34. Persisting the game into permanent storage for retrieval in later sessions

```
private void Application_Deactivated(object sender, DeactivatedEventArgs e)
{
    // Write the game state to the state object
    PhoneApplicationService.Current.State.Clear();
    PhoneApplicationService.Current.State.Add("GameState", GamePage.GameState);
    // Is a game currently active?
    if (GamePage.GameState.IsGameActive)
    {
        // Yes, so place the GameState object into the ApplicationSettings in case we
        // never reactivate
        SettingsManager.SetObjectValue("StoredGameState", GamePage.GameState);
    }
}

// Code to execute when the application is closing (eg, user hit Back)
// This code will not execute when the application is deactivated
private void Application_Closing(object sender, ClosingEventArgs e)
{
    // We can place the game state into isolated storage ready to be retrieved next
    // time the game begins. Is a game currently active?
    if (GamePage.GameState.IsGameActive)
    {
        // Yes, so place the GameState object into ApplicationSettings
        SettingsManager.SetObjectValue("StoredGameState", GamePage.GameState);
    }
}
```

Give the game a try and experiment with tombstoning it and with completely closing it. The game state survives all these operations, always allowing the players to carry on exactly where they left off.

Adding Game Settings

The *Diamond Lines* settings are very simple, allowing the player to choose the speed at which the diamonds animate ("normal" or "fast") and to turn sound effects on and off. SettingsPage is implemented exactly as described in the "Game Settings" section earlier in this chapter.

Actually using the settings is a very easy task, too. The animation speed is observed inside the Diamond class' BeginTranslate method. When this is called, the calling code will already have set the TranslateDuration property as appropriate, but we can make it faster by simply scaling it down. In our code, we multiple the value by 0.4 if the animation speed is "fast," reducing the time by 60 percent, as shown in Listing 14–35.

Listing 14–35. Applying the animation speed setting

```
internal void BeginTranslate()
{
    double animSpeed = 1;

    // Reduce the translation duration if in fast animation mode
    if (SettingsManager.GetValue("AnimSpeed", "Normal") == "Fast") animSpeed = 0.4;

    // Is there any translation to do?
    if (XOffset != 0 || YOffset != 0)
    {
        _diamondSprite.BeginTranslate(XOffset, YOffset, 0, 0,
                            TranslateDuration * animSpeed, 0, TranslateEasing);
    }
}
```

The sound effect control is handled in the GamePage's Loaded event. It simply sets the
AudioPlayer.SoundEffectMasterVolume property to 1 if sound effects are enabled or 0 if they are disabled.
No further processing for this setting is needed. Listing 14–36 shows this piece of code.

Listing 14–36. Switching sound effects on or off

```
private void GameCanvas_Loaded(object sender, RoutedEventArgs e)
{
    // Now that the page has loaded, reset the game so that we have some diamonds to
    // display
    InitializeDiamonds();

    // Add an event handler for the CompositionTarget's Rendering event so that
    // we can keep the game moving
    CompositionTarget.Rendering += new EventHandler(compositionTarget_Rendering);

    // Set the sound effect volume level
    AudioPlayer.SoundEffectMasterVolume = (SettingsManager.GetValue("Sound", true) ? 1 : 0);
}
```

Implementing the Sound Effects

Our final enhancement is to add in the sound effects. Three different effects are provided: a "whoosh"
sound when diamonds swap position, a sound for each time a line of diamonds is formed, and a quiet
high-pitched ringing sound to represent the diamonds landing within the board.

The first two of these sounds are easily implemented by simply calling the
AudioPlayer.PlaySoundEffect function at the appropriate points: within the SwapDiamonds function and
the FindLines function. When removing lines, the game now keeps track of "chain reactions" (lines
formed after other diamonds fall) and increases the pitch of each subsequent chain reaction to increase
the sense of excitement.

The final sound is played each time a diamond completes its fall within the game board. We don't
initially have an appropriate point to trigger that sound, but we can add one by handling the Sprite
control's TranslateCompleted event inside the Diamond class. As each diamond finishes moving, it will fire
this event and allow the sound to be played.

Any of the movement modes could be active when this event fires however, so we must first check that the game is in Dropping mode. Only then is the sound effect played. A random pitch is applied to vary the sound. Listing 14–37 shows the implementation.

Listing 14–37. Playing the DiamondDrop sound effect each time a diamond falls into a new location

```
void _diamondSprite_TranslateCompleted(object sender, EventArgs e)
{
    // Are the diamonds currently dropping?
    if (_gamePage.MovementState == GamePage.MovementStates.Dropping)
    {
        // Yes, so this diamond has just landed. Play a drop sound effect.
        AudioPlayer.PlaySoundEffect("Sounds/DiamondDrop.wav", 1,
                                        GameHelper.RandomNext(0.0f, 0.5f), 0);
    }
}
```

That covers all the new functionality that we will add to this example game. Its presentation is undeniably basic, but the fundamental parts of a complete working game are here (and the addictive nature of the game content clearly shows through, as I have found many times while "testing"!)

Gaming with Silverlight

While XNA will be the choice for many games on Windows Phone 7, Silverlight still offers a rich and capable set of functions for gaming and will sometimes prove to be the better option of the two technologies. XNA excels with flexible, accelerated graphics displays and 3D graphics, but falls far behind in terms of user interface. Silverlight may not have quite the same level of power and flexibility for graphical rendering, but is much more capable when complex user interfaces are required and can hold its head high in terms of animation effects.

Deciding which of these technologies to use will be one of the first decisions you make when writing a game, as they are fundamentally different in the ways that they work. Both have their strengths, however, so consider carefully which one better suits the type of game that you are planning to write.

At this stage we conclude our exploration of Silverlight, and in fact this is pretty much the end of designing and developing games altogether. I very much hope you have enjoyed the journey so far!

For the last two chapters we will explore some other aspects of working with games, starting with a very important topic that will inevitably follow on from your game programming: how to distribute your game to your audience.

■■■

PART 4

Distribution

CHAPTER 15

■ ■ ■

Distributing Your Game

So your masterpiece is complete. The graphics are drawn and animating, the game logic is working, everything is sounding great, navigation around the different sections of the game is all done, and you have all sorts of extras such as high scores, tombstoning support, and information pages. Now it is time to share your creation with the rest of the world.

The actual process of sharing is pretty straightforward: you submit your game to the Windows Phone 7 Marketplace. Microsoft will check that the game meets its submission requirements, and (assuming Microsoft is satisfied with the way the game works), it appears in the Marketplace within a few days, ready for others to download.

Using the Marketplace is the only way to distribute your games and applications for Windows Phone 7. Unlike Windows Mobile, which preceded it, local installation (or *side loading* as it is often known) is not supported for Windows Phone 7.

It is possible (and advisable!) to offer a *trial mode* for your game if you are selling it, so that potential customers can download it and try a limited version prior to purchase. This is a great way to win over your audience, as it takes the risk out of purchasing.

In this chapter we will examine the things you need to do to get prepare and release your game to the rest of the world. In theory, this need not be a complex or time-consuming task, but there are various things you can do to attempt to simplify things and reduce problems during the submission process. Unless otherwise specified, everything in this chapter applies to both XNA and Silverlight games.

Testing Your Game

It might be obvious, but its importance cannot be overstated: the first thing you need to do is test your game. Test it until you are sick of looking at it. Get your friends, family, and neighbors to test it. Find and fill every hole that anyone can find.

Besides the obvious reasons for testing, you should be aware of a couple of testing requirements that are specific to Windows Phone 7 development rather than to programming in general.

The first requirement is in relation to the emulator. It is a fantastic tool for development, allowing you to quickly and easily access a device environment without needing to actually plug anything in to your PC, and to keep everything your program does on your PC screen where your source code is.

Overall, the emulator provides an extremely good representation of how a game or application will work on a real device, but there are certain elements that let it down. Multitouch support (unless you are lucky enough to have a multitouch–capable PC monitor) and the accelerometer are two obvious areas in which the emulator cannot satisfactorily stand in for a real device. Less obvious (but equally significant) is the area of performance.

As we have discussed a couple of times during the course of this book, the emulator runs as fast as your computer hardware allows it to. It is, therefore, highly likely that it will greatly outperform a real phone. You need to make sure that this is not a problem before it hits the Marketplace.

Test on a real device as frequently as you can, and especially before releasing to the public. As of this writing, all the available devices have essentially identical specifications in turns of processing and graphical power, so testing on multiple devices is unlikely to provide much additional benefit. As the platform evolves, however, and newer devices with faster processors appear, you should test on the most limited Windows Phone 7 hardware you can get access to. If performance is poor, find out the reasons why and either optimize the problems away or reduce the complexity of the game until the performance is acceptable.

Another Windows Phone 7–specific check to make if your game has been developed using Silverlight is to verify that your game still appears with both a light- and dark-colored background. Real devices and the emulator default to a dark background, but can be switched to a light background by opening the Settings page, choosing to change the Theme, and then changing the background to Light, as shown in Figure 15–1.

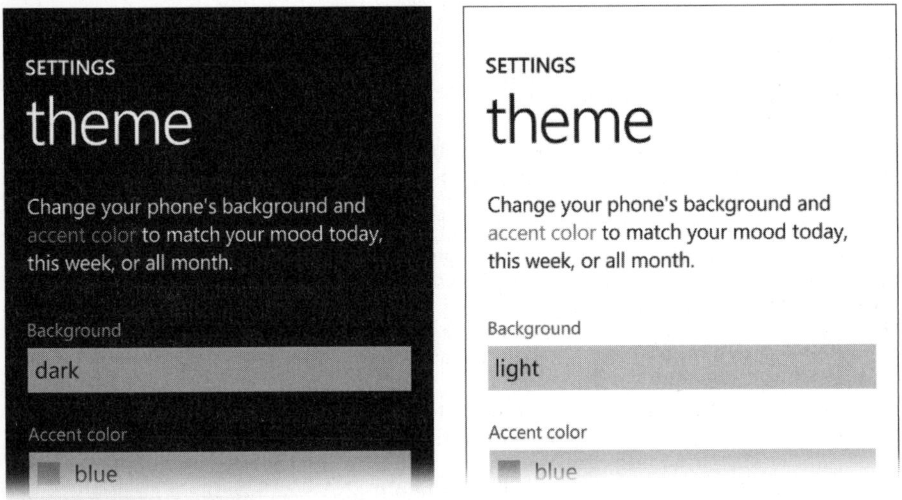

Figure 15–1. Setting the dark or light background color

With the background changed, run your game again and check every single page, graphic, and piece of text that it can display. If you have specifically designed anything in a light color and are displaying it on the default background color, it might be hard to see or even be invisible. Also make sure to pay attention to the appearance of ApplicationBar buttons. Windows Phone 7 will automatically invert their colors, but if you have used anything other than simple monochrome buttons with transparency, the inversion might not always produce the result you expect.

One of the primary reasons for ensuring that you have tested everything as much as possible is that once your game is accepted into the Marketplace, it can take up to a week for a new version to be submitted and accepted. During this whole time, your game will potentially be building up poor reviews and low scores just because of silly bugs; there is nothing you can do to prevent them. Don't let the reputation of your game be ruined before you have even finished working on it!

Trial Mode

Windows Phone 7's Marketplace has integral support for an extremely useful feature: trial mode. This is not mandatory, but I strongly recommend you use it in all applications that you intend to sell. It allows people to download your game free of charge and evaluate it in a restricted form prior to actually spending any money purchasing the game.

When you decide to support trial mode, an additional button will appear next to your game in the Marketplace: the Try button. Pressing this button *will install the full application* on the user's device, but will set a flag within the .NET environment indicating that the game is in trial mode. Your code must check for this and limit the game in some way.

Using trial mode simplifies the development and submission of your games. You do not need to create and submit two versions, one for the user to try for free and the other to buy in full. The user, having discovered your game, does not have to hunt around trying to determine whether a free trial version exists. Everything is integrated into a single package, quick and easy to use. Better still, it is easy to send the user back to the Marketplace from your trial game so that they can quickly and easily purchase the full version.

Exactly how you decide to limit your game is entirely up to you. You might limit the number of levels that are available, restrict or remove certain features of the game, put a limit on the experience levels that the player can gain, disable the game's scoring, put a time limit in place, show ads, nag users periodically to upgrade and avoid the reminder messages, or any combination of these. The Marketplace doesn't tell you how to work in trial mode; it simply tells you that the game is running in that mode.

One limitation is a timed evaluation period. It is common in many applications to allow the game to work without any restrictions at all for a period of time (perhaps a week or a month) and then to stop working entirely. It is easy enough to monitor the installation date of your game, but when the trial elapses the user can simply uninstall and reinstall. Uninstallation removes all the isolated storage data from the game, so it is unable to tell after reinstallation that it had ever been installed before.

Of course, you can simply view the fact that the user has to uninstall and reinstall as being sufficiently irritating that they will eventually decide to pay to avoid the repeated annoyance.

However you do decide to limit your game, try to ensure that a representative sample is offered so that your potential customers can decide whether the game appeals to them.

While you should not hide the trial status from your user, it is often a good idea to prompt the user to purchase at an opportune moment—perhaps at a cliffhanger point in the game or just as an exciting new feature is introduced. When the player is itching for more, the likelihood of buying the game is increased.

Detecting Trial Mode

Two mechanisms exist to determine whether your game is running in trial mode. The first is to query the `Microsoft.Phone.Marketplace.LicenseInformation.IsTrial` property. The second is to use the `Microsoft.XNA.Framework.GamerServices.Guide.IsTrialMode` property, provided by XNA but easily usable in Silverlight by simply adding a reference to the `Microsoft.Xna.Framework` and `Microsoft.Xna.Framework.GamerServices` assemblies.

The two properties are very similar and essentially return the same information, but there are differences between the two:

- The `GamerServices.Guide.IsTrialMode` property is static, so no object instance needs to be created before it can be queried. `LicenseInformation.IsTrial` is not static, requiring an instance of the `LicenseInformation` class to be created first.

- `GamerServices.Guide.IsTrialMode` offers a very simple and useful way to simulate trial mode in your game. `LicenseInformation.IsTrial` has no equivalent simulation facility, requiring you to create additional code in your game to implement its own trial simulation alongside the actual value returned from the property.

For both these reasons, we will focus primarily on the `GamerServices.Guide.IsTrialMode` property in this section.

By default, both of the properties return `false` when in development mode to indicate that it is the full version of the game that is running. When using the `GamerServices.Guide.IsTrialMode` property, we can simulate trial mode by setting the `GamerServices.Guide.SimulateTrialMode` property to `true` in the constructor of the main class (the App class in a Silverlight game or the main game class in XNA). Once this has been set, `GamerServices.Guide.IsTrialMode` will then return `true` (though `LicenseInformation.IsTrial` will ignore the simulation request and continue to return `false`).

There are several very important details to bear in mind when setting up your application's trial mode functionality. Please check and double-check them in your games as getting them wrong could be very costly!

- *Important detail number 1*: The `SimulateTrialMode` property will have the same effect in a game actually released to the Marketplace as it will in your development environment. This will result in customers that have actually purchased the game finding that it still runs in trial mode, which very quickly leads to unhappy customers.

  You can avoid this problem by only activating the trial simulation if the debugger is attached, as this can only be the case when you are developing. Listing 15–1 shows a simple piece of code that performs this check before activating the trial simulation.

Listing 15–1. Simulating trial mode

```
// Only simulate trial mode if we are running inside the Visual Studio IDE
if (System.Diagnostics.Debugger.IsAttached)
{
    // Simulate trial mode
    Microsoft.Xna.Framework.GamerServices.Guide.SimulateTrialMode = true;
}
```

For double safety, comment out the simulation mode code before building your final version of the game. This removes all possibility of it being accidentally activated.

- *Important detail number 2*: When running an actual Marketplace-downloaded game, it takes a little time to execute a call to either of the trial mode properties—in the range of 60 milliseconds. This delay *does not occur when running in the development environment*. You should, therefore, make sure that you do not query the property in your game loop as it will have a noticeable impact on the performance of your game.

  If you need to know all the time whether the game is in trial mode, check it once and cache the result (and don't miss the third important detail coming up!). If you need to know this information only at certain stages of the game (for example, as each new level commences), it is fine to query it on demand as this call will be made only at infrequent intervals.

- *Important detail number 3*: If you are reading and caching the `IsTrialMode` property, you should do so in response to both the game's `Launching` and `Activated` events. The value cannot be reliably retrieved in the App class constructor. Don't overlook that it might be either of these events that is actually called when the game begins, depending on whether it is being launched from scratch or restored from tombstoning. If your trial player can simply leave the game and then return to it to unlock the full functionality, the incentive to purchase is somewhat reduced.

The TrialMode example project that accompanies this chapter demonstrates the use of the IsTrialMode and SimulateTrialMode properties. Both of them are interacted with in the App class code, and the static App.IsTrialMode property is set with the cached value. This can then be queried wherever the game needs to know the trial state. The relevant portions of the App code are shown in Listing 15–2.

Listing 15–2. Simulating, detecting, and publishing trial mode information within the App class

```
public App()
{
    // Global handler for uncaught exceptions.
    UnhandledException += Application_UnhandledException;

    // Simulate trial mode if in the debugger
    if (System.Diagnostics.Debugger.IsAttached)
    {
        Microsoft.Xna.Framework.GamerServices.Guide.SimulateTrialMode = true;
    }

    // Standard Silverlight initialization
    InitializeComponent();

    // Phone-specific initialization
    InitializePhoneApplication();
}


private void Application_Launching(object sender, LaunchingEventArgs e)
{
    // Set the static App.IsTrialMode property as appropriate
    RefreshTrialModeProperty();
}

private void Application_Activated(object sender, ActivatedEventArgs e)
{
    // Set the static App.IsTrialMode property as appropriate
    RefreshTrialModeProperty()
}


/// <summary>
/// Update the IsTrialMode property with the current trial mode state
/// </summary>
internal static void RefreshTrialModeProperty()
{
    IsTrialMode = Microsoft.Xna.Framework.GamerServices.Guide.IsTrialMode;
}

/// <summary>
/// Property to identify whether the app is in trial mode or not
/// </summary>
public static bool IsTrialMode { get; set; }
```

The example project's MainPage uses the App.IsTrialMode property in its Loaded event to configure the display of controls. If it detects that the game is in trial mode, an information message is displayed explaining this to the player, and a Buy Full Game button appears (the function of which we will discuss in a moment). When not in trial mode, the message and buy button are hidden.

Try running the project to see how it behaves—the initial code is set to simulate trial mode. Also try commenting out the code that sets the SimulateTrialMode property in the App class constructor and see how the project's behavior changes.

Purchasing the Full Version

If the players like your game, hopefully they will decide to buy the full version. They could do this by navigating their way back through the Marketplace, but it would be very easy for them to get lost or distracted along the way, or to somehow fail to locate your game—possibly resulting in a lost sale.

It is in your interest to be able to get players back to your game's page in the Marketplace as quickly and easily as you can. Microsoft recognized this requirement and provided a very easy way to achieve this objective: with a single line of code, you can deliver the user directly back to the game's page in the Marketplace.

The required code is shown in Listing 15–3, and is also behind the Buy Full Game button in the TrialMode example project.

Listing 15–3. Taking the player to the Marketplace to buy a full version of your game

```
// Show the Marketplace
Microsoft.Xna.Framework.GamerServices.Guide.ShowMarketplace(
                              Microsoft.Xna.Framework.PlayerIndex.One);
```

If you click this button on an application that is not actually in the Marketplace, the function does something rather useful: it displays a message box that allows you to simulate the purchase of your app, as can be seen in Figure 15–2.

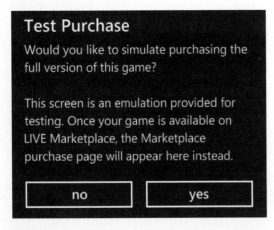

Figure 15–2. Simulating an application purchase

Clicking Yes in this dialog will cause the GamerServices.Guide.IsTrialMode property to be set back to false, indicating that the game is now the full version. This is extremely useful, but there are a couple of things to be aware of when using this dialog.

The most important is that the dialog runs within your game's process, whereas actually navigating to the Marketplace results in your game being tombstoned. The path back into your code is therefore very different: a real visit to the Marketplace would result in your game's `Activated` event being fired, whereas a visit to this dialog results in no such code path being followed. If you want your game to actually simulate being purchased, you might therefore need to provide additional code to update the existing user interface that the finished game would not require.

Second, the dialog is asynchronous, and the code that calls it carries on executing immediately instead of waiting for you to click one of the dialog buttons. This is irritating, particularly as there is no event that reliably fires after the completion of the dialog; the page's `GotFocus` event works most of the time, but occasionally is triggered before the `GamerServices.Guide.IsTrialMode` property is actually updated.

You should call `App.RefreshTrialModeProperty` and perform any UI updates that are required in the button click handler (as well as in `GotFocus`, if you like) so that a subsequent click on the button after requesting simulation of the full game purchase does actually update the game state accordingly.

In the `TrialMode` example, you will see that the code to switch to refresh the `App.IsTrialMode` property and update the UI for the full version of the game is present in both the button click handler and the page's `GotFocus` event. Neither of these pieces of code should have any effect in the real game when downloaded from the Marketplace.

Offering Promotional Upgrades

At the time of writing, there is no facility within the Marketplace to offer a promotional upgrade or gift to friends, reviewers, competition winners, and so on, to whom you might want to give a free version of the full game. It is entirely possible that such a feature might be added in the future, but then again it might not.

If you want to be able to provide such a feature, you will need to create your own implementation. The full implementation of such a system is beyond the scope of this chapter and requires web site capabilities that not everyone will have access to, but here is an approach that you could adopt to allow this kind of function within your game.

When you want to provide free access to your game, generate a single use activation code. Add an Enter Promotional Code button to your game that prompts the user to enter the activation code, and then sends a request to your web site including the name of the game and the activation code as part of the URL. For example, it might send a request to a URL like this one:
`http://www.mydomain.com/CheckActivationCode?Game=MyGame&Code=1234567890`

You can manually or programmatically generate the codes and then store them in a database on your web site. When a request such as this is received, the web server should look for the code in the database and return a value to indicate whether it was found. If it is found, *it should be removed from the database*. This will stop people from distributing the code and allowing it to be used repeatedly (which amounts to pirating your game).

If the game receives a positive response from the web server, it can store the details of this in a file in isolated storage and use it in subsequent executions of the game to indicate that it is no longer in trial mode. If we were to implement this into the `TrialMode` example project, the isolated storage file would be checked in the `App.RefreshTrialModeProperty`, allowing the game to respond to the promotional upgrade without needing any other changes.

If the user later uninstalls the game, the isolated storage file will be lost and they will be unable to return to the full version of the game unless they obtain another promotional code. This is potentially a nuisance, but is still better than being unable to offer this functionality at all.

Submission Requirements

Before your game is accepted into the Marketplace, Microsoft will perform a series of tests on it to ensure that it meets all the submission requirements. If any of these tests should fail, the game will fail the submission process and will need to be fixed and resubmitted.

The full list of requirements can be obtained from the http://create.msdn.com web site (look for the "Windows Phone 7 Application Certification Requirements" document) and you should review this in detail before submitting. The document might change in the future, and additional requirements might be added or existing requirements relaxed, so don't assume that you know its contents even if you have read through it before. The document contains a Change History section at the end to help clarify any sections that have been modified.

In this section we will briefly review some of the areas that might be relevant to your games.

Content Policies

Your application will fail the submission process if it contains any unlicensed or unpermitted third-party content such as logos, music, sound files, and so on. If this type of content is present, it must be clearly marked as being used with permission.

Any form of illegal, obscene, indecent, threatening, or "adult" content will result in submission failure, as will excessive use of profanity.

The "Violence" section is worth checking carefully if you are creating a game of a violent nature; it lists a series of types of content that will result in submission failure.

Application Requirements

Your game must consist entirely of managed .NET code. Any attempt to use P/Invoke ("API calls") or COM interop will result in the submission failing.

If your game is a Silverlight game, it must not reference the Microsoft.Xna.Framework.Game or Microsoft.Xna. Framework.Graphics assemblies: using either of these will result in a submission failure. Other XNA assemblies are permitted, however.

Localization

When you submit your game to the Marketplace, you can choose which geographical areas of the world it is actually offered to, and you might, of course, include localization support so that the game is presented in different languages.

This is all good and to be encouraged, but Microsoft require that at least one of the supported languages must be English, French, Italian, German, or Spanish. If none of these languages is supported, the submission will fail.

Application Features

The submitted application must be able to run on all current Windows Phone 7 devices and must not rely on hardware that is present only in a subset of devices.

As the base set of hardware features for Windows Phone 7 is very standard, you are unlikely to run into any serious problems in this area, but one thing that you will need to watch out for is any requirement for the user to have a hardware keyboard. It is fine to take advantage of a hardware keyboard if one is present, but not to the exclusion of other devices.

Reliability and Performance

Your game must not cause any unhandled exceptions to be thrown, or it will fail the verification process.

In Silverlight, you can use the App class's `Application_UnhandledException` function to handle all exceptions and display them as an informational message to the user instead of causing the application to close. The game should continue to function after an exception has occurred.

The application should always remain responsive to user input. When a long-running operation is taking place (generating level data or downloading content from the Internet, for example), a progress indicator must be displayed so that users are aware of what is happening and how much longer they will need to wait. A "cancel" option must also be made available to abort the process, and it must be responsive within a reasonable time frame.

Your game must present its first screen within five seconds of being launched. If it is a Silverlight game, the first screen is actually presented by the game itself and does not count the `SplashScreenImage.jpg` that is automatically displayed by the Silverlight environment.

The time between launching and the game first accepting input must not exceed 20 seconds.

These launch time requirements also apply when the game is being reactivated after having been tombstoned. In this environment, if they take longer than 10 seconds to reawaken, the process might be killed by the operating system.

Handling the Back button comes in for some specific attention. The requirements are as follows:

- Pressing Back on the game's first screen must exit the game.

- Pressing Back anywhere else within a game must return the player either to the previous screen or to an in-game pause menu. Pressing Back again while such a menu is open should close the menu and return to the game. You should therefore offer an Exit Game option within the menu.

- Whenever Back is pressed while a context menu or dialog is open, the menu or dialog should close without any additional navigation taking place.

The handling of the Back button is a common reason for submission failure, so ensure that it behaves appropriately within all game modes and screens.

Technical Information

Your game must include easy access to its name, version number, and contact details for technical support. Using an About screen is an ideal way to present this. We will look at a simple way to retrieve the version number in the "Preparing for Distribution" section later in this chapter.

Music and Sound

As discussed in the earlier sections covering music playback, it is not permitted for any application to stop, pause, resume, or change any music that the user is playing without first asking for consent (including changing the volume level). This restriction does not apply to sound effects, which can play alongside existing background music.

If the game does provide its own background music, the user must also be provided with the ability to disable it. It's a very good idea to allow the same facility for the sound effects, too, so that the game can be played in a quiet environment without disturbing anyone.

Preparing for Distribution

When you are happy that the game is ready to be distributed, there are just a few final things that you need to attend to prior to submitting it to the Marketplace. These are mostly very straightforward, but might involve a little graphical work.

This section lists the final steps you need to do to prepare for game release. As a quick checklist for future reference, the things to ensure are up to date are as follows:

- Set your game details inside the Assembly Information window.

- Update your application version number in the Assembly Information window.

- Set the Assembly Project Properties.

- Update the WMAppManifest.xml file.

- Provide graphic and icon files for the game.

- Compile in release mode ready for distribution.

Setting the Assembly Information

Each .NET assembly stores a series of values that provide information about the assembly such as its title, description, copyright information, and so on. When preparing your game for release, you need to provide appropriate content for each of these fields.

There are two different ways in which you can enter the information into the assembly. The first is through a Visual Studio properties window, which is accessed by first opening the project properties and then clicking the Assembly Information button, shown in Figure 15–3.

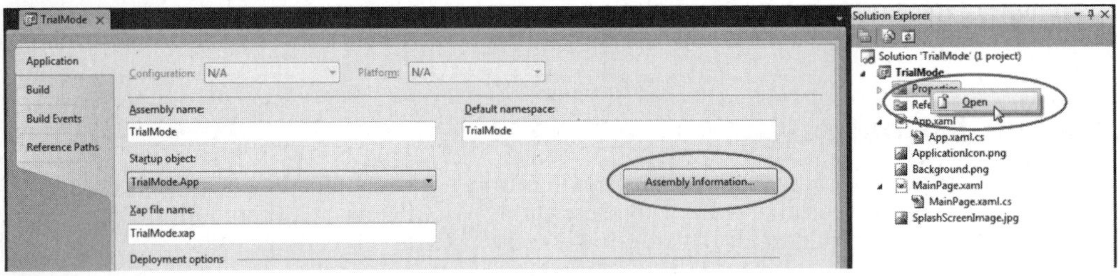

Figure 15–3. *Accessing the Assembly Information window*

The Assembly Information window then appears, as shown in Figure 15–4. As a minimum, you should complete the Title, Description, Company, Product, and Copyright values. We will discuss the version number fields in the next section.

Figure 15–4. Setting the Assembly Information

If you prefer, you can also edit these values in the Visual Studio source code editor. Inside the Properties node of the project within Solution Explorer, shown in Figure 15–5, is a file called AssemblyInfo.cs, and it is this file that actually contains all the information about the assembly. You can modify it directly and bypass the need to use the Assembly Information window.

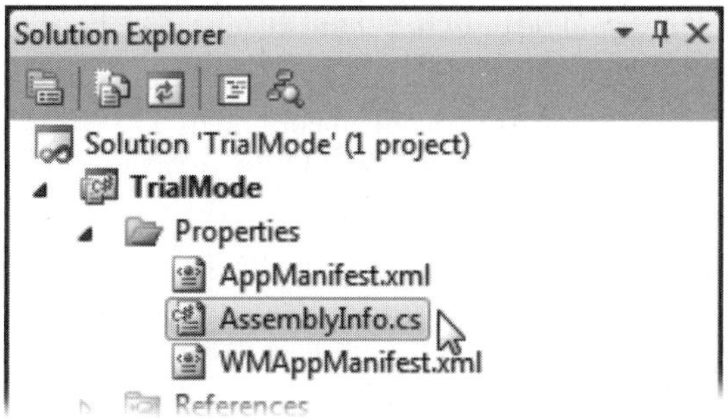

Figure 15–5. Accessing the AssemblyInfo.cs source file

Once you have set these values up once for your project, it is unlikely that you will need to change them again, but don't forget to set them before you release the first version of your game.

Setting the Assembly Version

It is essential to adopt a version numbering scheme for your game so that you and your users know exactly which version of a game they have installed. The version number is one of the pieces of information that you will be required to provide during the upload to the Marketplace, and you must ensure that the version number you provide matches the version number in your game.

The assembly version is also accessed via either the Assembly Information window or the `AssemblyInfo.cs` code file. There are two version numbers defined: the Assembly version and the File version. For Windows Phone 7 assemblies, these should both be set to the same value.

Version numbers are formed by four numeric values separated by periods. For example, 1.0.0.0 might be the first version of a released executable. The four parts of the version number, from left to right, are:

- Major version

- Minor version

- Build number

- Revision

Each of them can contain a value in the range of 0 to 65535. When you submit to the Marketplace, you will be prompted only for the major and minor elements of the version number, and the range of acceptable values is much more limited: 0 to 9 for the major version and 0 to 25 for the minor version.

Exactly how you use these version number elements is really up to you, but here is a suggested strategy:

- The major version is incremented each time a whole new version of a product is released (e.g., it has been rewritten or is substantially different from a previous version). You will also need to increment the major version if you "run out" of minor versions (i.e., exceed a minor version of 25).

- The minor version is incremented each time a new version of an application is released, but the application is still the same basic product as the previous release. This would be incremented when new features have been added to a product, but the product has not been rewritten or substantially modified so that the major version would be increased. The minor version would be reset to 0 if the major version number increases.

- The build number and revision are unlikely to be of any use outside of your own needs, so you could either leave them set to 0 or use them to store an internal build count or something similar.

■ **Note** It is important to remember that the periods here are just field separators, not decimal separators. Incrementing the revision of a version string set to 1.9.0.0 results in a version string of 1.10.0.0, not 2.0.0.0.

It is a requirement of the Marketplace (and also a very useful thing to have, anyway) that the application be able to report its version number from inside the game. You could certainly hard-code the version number into your About page, but then you have to remember to update it with each new release of your game. This could be easily overlooked, resulting in confusion for your users and a potential submission failure.

To remove this possibility, we can write a few lines of code to retrieve the project's version number from the Assembly Information. Listing 15–4 shows how this can be achieved; in this case, placing the assembly version number into a Silverlight `TextBlock` control.

Listing 15–4. Reading the assembly's version number

```
using System.Reflection;
[...]

        // Get the assembly name
        string name = Assembly.GetExecutingAssembly().FullName;
        // Use this to obtain its version
        Version version = new AssemblyName(name).Version;
        // Display the version on the page
        versionText.Text = "Version " + version.ToString();
```

The VersionNumber example project accompanying this chapter has been set up to display the version number using this piece of code. Try changing the project's version number, and you will find that the display is updated accordingly.

Setting the Project Properties

The Application tab of the project properties window contains several fields that you might want to amend for your game. Most of them will be set correctly by default when your project is created, but you might want to update the Deployment options Title field and the Tile options Title field.

The Deployment options Title field provides the title that appears for your game in the Games hub. You can add spaces or make other minor alterations to this, but it must still clearly identify itself as your game.

■ **Note** This field is handled a little differently for XNA games: these projects do not have a Deployment options Title field in their Project properties, and instead use the Title from the Assembly Information window for this purpose.

The Tile options Title field provides the title that appears alongside your game icon if the user pins it to the Start menu. Once again this should clearly identify itself as your game, so limit the changes to little more than simply adding punctuation if needed.

■ **Note** For XNA projects, this field is contained within the XNA Game Studio tab, and is named Tile title.

Microsoft suggests that title lengths should be a maximum of 11 to 15 characters; and should be catchy, memorable, and representative of your game.

Setting the Manifest Properties

The final file of project settings that needs to be attended to is the WMAppManifest.xml file. It is also contained inside the Properties node in Solution Explorer, next to AssemblyInfo.cs, as shown in Figure 15–5.

Most of the content in this section can be left alone as it will be regenerated by Microsoft as part of the submission process. You should ensure that the following elements within the App element are up to date, however:

- Title: the title of your game, the same as in the Title field of the Assembly Information
- Version: The version number of your game
- Genre: For games, this should be set to apps.game
- Author: The name of the game author
- Description: A brief description of the game, per the Assembly Information Description field
- Publisher: The name of the publisher of the game

■ **Note** If you change the Genre to apps.game, the icon for the game will then appear under the Games hub instead of on the main applications list. This is not too much of an issue on a real device, but on the emulator it presents a problem as the Games hub is not accessible. If you need to be able to launch your game from within the emulator, leave the genre set to apps.normal until you are ready to release.

Be aware that if you modify the Project properties, the WMAppManifest.xml file will be rewritten, so you should ensure that you set your Project properties as you need them prior to editing this file.

Providing Graphics Files

We are getting close to being able to submit a game, but we're not quite there yet. The next things needed are some graphics files that present the game to the user in the Marketplace and on the phone.

All the images must be in PNG format.

The following graphic images need to be compiled into your project when it is created:

- *An application icon (Silverlight only)*: This is a 62 x 62 pixel image that is used for the application when it is in the application list. A placeholder image will be present in each new Silverlight project with the name ApplicationIcon.png.

- *A game thumbnail icon (XNA only)*: This is a 64 x 64 pixel image that is used for the game in the application list. A placeholder image will be present in each new XNA project with the name GameThumbnail.png.

- *An application tile icon*: A 173 x 173 pixel image used when your game is pinned to the start menu. Silverlight and XNA projects will both be created with a placeholder image called Background.png.

Alongside these images, more are required when actually submitting the project to the Marketplace. The additional requirements are:

- *Small and large application icons for use in the Marketplace catalog when displayed on the phone*: The small icon must measure 99 x 99 pixels, and the large icon must be 173 x 173 pixels.

- *A large icon used to display the application in the Marketplace catalog when it is viewed on a desktop PC*: This must be 200 x 200 pixels in size.

- *Panoramic background art*: This file is optional, but if present will be displayed in the background behind your game when it is viewed in the Marketplace. Supply the image with full contrast: it will appear faded when displayed so that the application text is clearly visible in front of it.

- *One or more screenshots of the game, measuring 480 x 800 pixels, to display in the Marketplace catalog*: Up to a maximum of eight screenshots can be provided. If your game runs in landscape mode, the images should still be saved in portrait orientation. The screenshots should be direct screen captures and cannot be enhanced or modified.

All the icon graphic files must contain essentially the same image; if you use a different image between the icons, it will fail the Marketplace submission process.

Compiling the Game

The final step (really!) is to compile the game. Ensure that all the steps have been followed and then make one last final check before hitting the compile button: ensure that you compile in Release configuration, not Debug configuration in the Visual Studio toolbar, as shown in Figure 15–6.

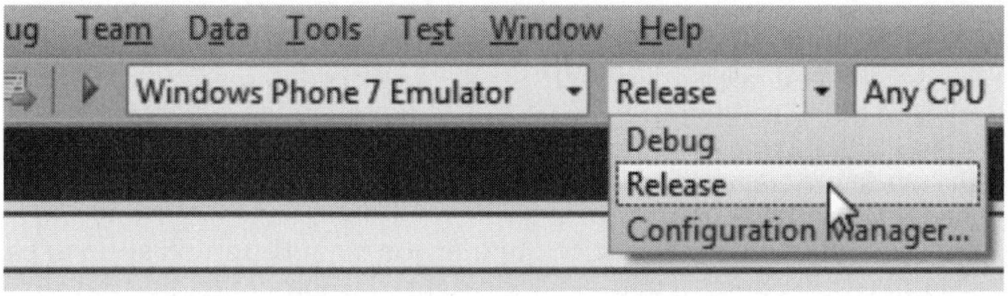

Figure 15–6. Compiling the game in Release mode

Each different configuration has its own set of compilation options, so it is a good idea to perform one final set of testing after selecting this mode, just to make sure everything is still working as expected.

Once you are happy, take a deep breath; it's time to upload to the Marketplace.

Selling or Giving Your Game for Free

One of the decisions you will need to make is whether your game will be sold or can be downloaded for free. Free applications can be great promotional tools, or you might simply decide that you want to maximize your audience (many people will give something a try if it's free!).

If you decide to sell your game, you will need to decide on the selling price. This can vary between about US$1 and US$500. Microsoft will keep 30 percent of all sales revenue, and you will receive the remaining 70 percent, subject to taxes and other applicable deductions.

Be aware that if you are not a U.S. citizen, the Internal Revenue Service will deduct 30 percent of your earnings as tax unless you have an American tax number (called an *Individual Tax Identification Number*, or ITIN). These numbers can be applied for in many (but not all) countries. For additional information, speak to your tax advisor or post questions to the Taxes forum on the Microsoft App Hub community forums (see http://forums.create.msdn.com/forums/ for details).

Payment will be made directly into your bank account once per month after you have accrued a minimum of US$200.

You can submit as many paid applications as you want, but only a maximum of five free applications per year. If you want to submit more free applications than this, a small submission fee (currently US$20) will be applied for each additional application.

Submitting Your Game to the Marketplace

Before you can use the Marketplace, you will need to have your Windows Live account set up, have applied to join the Marketplace, and have had your identify verified. All these steps were required just to deploy your games to a real phone, however, and we covered them back in Chapter 1, so hopefully they should all be long taken care of by now.

To begin the process, visit http://create.msdn.com in your browser and open the Windows Phone dashboard. One of the links in the dashboard will invite you to submit a new app. Click this to get started.

You will now be guided through a series of pages that allow you to upload the game itself and its graphic files, and to provide information about the game and how it should be made available.

The Windows Phone App Hub provides a detailed and informative step-by-step guide to everything that is involved with submitting your application to the Marketplace, so instead of repeating its content here it is more sensible for you to take a look at the guide itself—you can find it here: http://tinyurl.com/wp7appsubmission

The first page of the guide contains a submission checklist that is well worth reviewing just to double-check that you have done everything you need. It is much quicker to fix problems at this stage than to find later on that your submission failed validation.

Among the steps that you will follow will be one that allows you to specify which markets your game will be available in, how much it will cost (if anything), and whether a trial mode exists within the application. Be sure to enter all the values carefully.

The final option within the submission allows you to specify whether you want the application to be automatically published to the Marketplace as soon as it passes verification or whether you want to publish it manually. Normally automatic publication is preferable, but if you need to time the release to coincide with some external event, you can elect to publish it as and when you are ready.

My overriding advice for submitting to the Marketplace is to *take your time*. If you make any mistakes in the process, change your mind about the graphics, decide that the description is wrong, spot glaring spelling mistakes, or find any other fault with the data you have provided, there is no option to modify the existing application, and you will need to begin the submission process all over again.

Once the submission process is complete, the next step is to wait patiently for a few days. Microsoft's stated verification goal is around five days, so hopefully the wait won't be too long. The submission status will be updated as it works its way through each of Microsoft's test areas, and will eventually reach a state of having passed or failed the submission process.

If your application passes verification: congratulations! Your first game is now available for download through the Marketplace. If it fails, don't be discouraged; you should receive a detailed failure report that tells you *exactly* what was wrong, and if you correct everything that the report identifies, it should pass verification the next time you submit. Fingers crossed!

Games and applications that have been successfully submitted to the Marketplace will continue to show in your dashboard and can be managed from here, too. When you are ready to release a new version of your game, you can submit it through the dashboard, too. It will need to pass the same certification process as the original version. Once it passes and is ready for distribution, existing users of the game will be notified so that they can obtain the update.

Promoting Your Game

Just because the Marketplace is the only way to distribute your game, that doesn't mean that it's the only way to publicize it. Take advantage of every opportunity to tell the world about your project: add information to your blog or web site, shout about it in social networking sites, and add details to your signature.

Among the most powerful publicity options are showing screenshots and video captures of the game running. It is very easy to obtain screenshots by simply capturing the screen while your game is running in the emulator. An even better way to demonstrate the awesomeness of your game, though, is to create a video of it in action, running inside the emulator. You can then upload this to sites such as YouTube for the entire world to see.

Capturing Your Game in Motion

There are lots of applications that you can use to capture video, but one that is both free to use and able to produce very good quality results is part of Microsoft's Expression Encoder 4 application, which you can find by visiting http://www.microsoft.com/expression/try-it/Default.aspx and clicking the Download button for Expression Encoder 4.

This product is actually a component of the Expression Studio 4 application suite, but this feature-limited version of the Encoder application is available separately for free. It can capture video and sound from your PC and perform video processing on the results, but is limited to a maximum of ten minutes per video. This is likely to be more than enough to capture your game in action.

After installing the application, launch the Expression Encoder 4 Screen Capture application. It will display a small tool window, as shown in Figure 15–7.

Figure 15–7. The Expression Encoder 4 Screen Capture tool window

From here, the first place you should visit is the Options window, accessed by clicking the cog-wheel button. In the window that appears, set the desired frame rate (30 or 60 frames per second will result in a smoother animation than the default of 15) and choose whether you want the mouse pointer to be displayed (generally for Windows Phone 7 games it is better to hide it, but it is up to you).

The other tabs inside the Options window are worth visiting, too; they allow you to set up hotkeys to begin and end recording, to define your audio input options (select Speakers to record the audio that your game produces), and various other options.

After closing the Options window, click the Capture Manager button. The window will increase in height, allowing you to select an output folder. Browse to a convenient location on your hard drive into which the captures will be saved.

Once you have everything configured, start the Windows Phone 7 emulator. In the Expression Encoder 4 Screen Capture window, click the Record button, and the Select Region panel will appear, as shown in Figure 15–8. It allows a specific area of the screen to be used for recording.

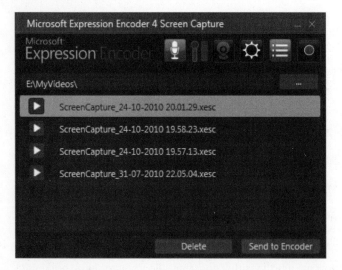

Figure 15–8. Selecting the Expression Encoder 4 Screen Capture capture region

Once the Select Region window is displayed, bring the emulator to the foreground. Click the Define Capture Area button in the Select Region window (the leftmost button) and then move the mouse cursor over the main screen area of the emulator. A thick red border should appear around the edge of the emulated screen to indicate that this is the area that will be captured. Click the screen to set it as the activate capture area.

Once you have defined the area to capture, simply click the Record button in the Select Region window to actually begin recording. Then take your game for a drive! Make sure you show off the core elements of the game—the features that will make your viewers think that they need to give the game a try. It might take a lot of time and repeat recordings to do this to your satisfaction, but don't rush it; you might only get one chance to win people over.

When your recording is complete, click the Stop Capture button on the Expression Encoder 4 window, and the recording will appear back in the main Expression Encoder 4 Screen Capture window, as shown in Figure 15–9.

Figure 15–9. A list of captured video sessions

Click the Play button to the left of each capture to view it and see how it looks. Once you have a video that you are happy with, click the Send to Encoder button to open the capture in the main Expression Encoder 4 application.

Editing Your Video Clip

Expression Encoder 4 is a video editing application that you can use to set up the final video that you want to produce, and encode it to a stand-alone video file ready for uploading to the Internet. The full feature set of the application is far beyond the scope of this book, but we will briefly discuss some of the features that you can use to enhance your video clip.

At the bottom of the screen is the Media Content window, which should initially contain the clip that you have recorded. Click the Play button just above this window to see the video clip that is loaded. You can add additional video clips into the project by using the various Insert Media buttons displayed alongside the Play button and can therefore build up a series of different scenes into one single video file. Figure 15–10 shows the Media content window and the various controls described here, circled in the image.

Figure 15–10. Playing and manipulating the captured video in Expression Encoder 4

The initial volume setting for the capture is very low. It can be increased by clicking the Enhance tab that is displayed along the right edge of the screen and dragging the volume level up to 10, as shown in Figure 15–11.

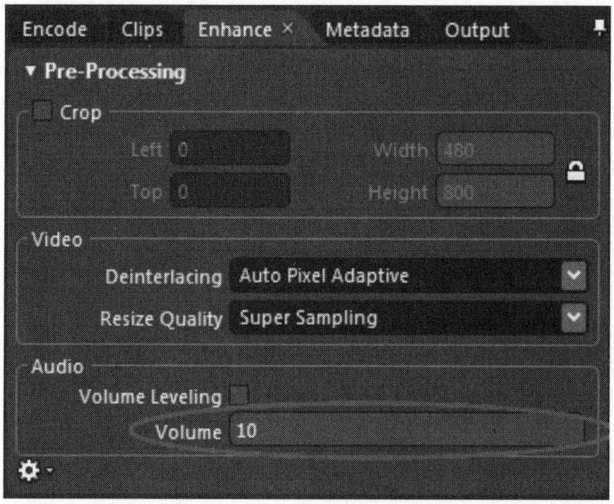

Figure 15–11. Setting the volume level for the captured video

Also within the Enhance tab you can select a piece a separate audio track that will be played over the top of your captured video. This is a great way to add interest to the video, but be careful not to get in trouble over music copyright issues when using this feature. To add an audio track, check the Add Audio

Overlay check box at the bottom of the Enhance tab and then browse to the audio file that you want to use. Once again, the volume can be set here as appropriate.

When you have all your video clips assembled in sequence and your audio settings all configured the way you want them, you are finally ready to produce the finished video file. In the Encode tab (to the left of the Enhance tab) you can set the Output Format as required. For uploading to YouTube or similar video services, use Windows Media (which will produce a .wmv file) or MP4. Then click the Encode button at the bottom of the screen. The resulting file will appear in the output directory that you used to capture the original video file.

Video previews are a great way of allowing people to quickly and easily see what your game has to offer. You can embed the video player directly into your web site along with the other product information, allowing people to view the clip without even leaving your site.

Go Create!

The only thing you need to add to your toolset now is your imagination. There are huge opportunities for gaming on Windows Phone 7, so let your creativity run free! I look forward to seeing many of your games appearing in the Windows Phone 7 Marketplace.

We are just about done with our journey through gaming on Windows Phone 7 now, and I really hope you have enjoyed the ride. Before we finish, though, there is one subject left to explore. Both of the Windows Phone 7 application environments, XNA and Silverlight, can operate on other platforms too: XNA games can run on Windows PCs and also on the Xbox360, while Silverlight projects can be run inside a desktop PC's web browser. In the next chapter, we will briefly explore the options for converting your projects to run on these alternative platforms.

■ ■ ■

CHAPTER 16

Running on Other Platforms

I hope that during the course of this book you have learned a lot about programming XNA and Silverlight for Windows Phone 7. There is an additional bonus from having gained all this experience: You have also learned a substantial amount of information about creating XNA games for Windows and the Xbox 360, and about creating Silverlight games and applications for the full browser-based version of Silverlight.

Both of these technologies have differences when run on Windows Phone 7 compared with the other platforms, but the fundamentals are the exactly the same. XNA games can be ported to run in Windows very easily; while Silverlight games take a little more time, they are still quite portable with some effort.

This chapter examines both XNA and Silverlight, and you will learn what is involved in transferring projects from Windows Phone 7 onto the desktop. The chapter won't include any in-depth learning of the PC versions of the environments, but will be enough to get you started. If you decide you need to know more at the end, there are plenty of online references and other books that you can use to extend your knowledge in these areas.

The example projects that accompany this chapter are all copies taken from previous chapters and modified to work in the new target environment. Each of them will be covered in more detail in the appropriate section of the chapter.

Before we start, it is important to clarify that the free Express version of Visual Studio can create Windows and Xbox 360 versions of XNA games, but it does not have the ability to create desktop versions of Silverlight applications: the full Visual Studio Professional application is required for this.

Running XNA Projects in Windows

Let's begin then with XNA. XNA supports two different *profiles*—sets of features that are supported by the underlying API. The first profile, *Reach*, limits the features to those that are available for Windows Phone 7, Windows, and the Xbox 360. The second profile is the *HiDef* profile, which provides additional functionality that is not available to Windows Phone 7 (programmable vertex and pixel shaders for advanced graphics techniques, for example).

The active profile can be selected by opening the Project Properties page for your XNA game. For Windows Phone 7 projects, this will be locked into the Reach profile; once we have transferred projects across to Windows, they will default to HiDef. You can switch the Windows project profile back to Reach if you want to reduce the chance of adding any functionality that the phone is unable to support.

Because the HiDef profile is a superset of Reach, the majority of the core API that we have been using can be converted directly over to Windows. A few features are different or missing, including these:

- The TouchPanel object and high level Gestures support

- Isolated storage (Windows can use the normal file system instead)

- Tombstoning support (there is no such thing in Windows as it offers full multitasking)

Nearly everything else is identical, however, and can be transferred across to Windows without too much effort.

■ **Note** This chapter will focus on transferring content to run in Windows rather than on the Xbox 360. Getting things up and running on the Xbox 360 involves a very similar process, however, so you should be able to make a good start with Xbox 360 project translation if you need to after reading this chapter. The Xbox 360 supports the HiDef profile, just like Windows.

Porting Projects to Windows

Fortunately for us, Microsoft has simplified this process about as much as it could have. Once you have developed your Windows Phone 7 XNA project, the Visual Studio will create a Windows version with just a couple of mouse clicks.

Let's walk through the steps needed to accomplish this; we will start with something simple. All the way back in Chapter 2 we used an example project called FirstXNAProject, which simply displayed a smiley-face sprite that gradually moved down the screen. We will use this as the basis for our for Windows XNA project conversion.

Reopen the project in Visual Studio (or, if you prefer, make a copy and open that so that the original project is not disturbed). Once it has opened, right-click the main game project and select Create Copy of Project for Windows from the context menu, as shown in Figure 16–1.

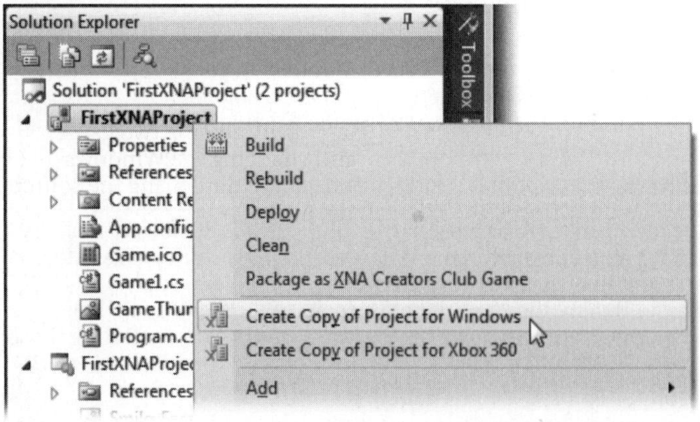

Figure 16–1. Creating a copy of the project for Windows

The result of this operation will be that a new project appears in your solution, named `Windows Copy of FirstXNAProject`. To run the project, right-click it and select Set as StartUp Project from the context menu; the project title will become bold to indicate that it is the project that will run when you begin debugging. Start the project running, and after a few seconds the project will appear, but this time running directly inside a Windows window, rather than in the emulator. Figure 16–2 shows the results.

Figure 16–2. Running the FirstXNAProject example in Windows

■ **Note** If the Windows Phone 7 emulator is not running when you launch the project, you might find that it opens, even though you are not running the phone version of the game. You can simply minimize it to get it out of the way.

There—that was easy! There is a little more to it than this once we start to get into more complex projects, but that is the heart of the conversion process. You can switch back and forward between the two target platforms just by setting the appropriate startup project in Solution Explorer.

At this stage, you have three projects in your solution: the main game project for Windows Phone 7, the main game project for Windows, and the Content project. There is a lot of sharing going on between these projects. The more obvious sharing is of the Content project, which is used by both of the game projects.

Less obvious is the fact that the copy of the project created for Windows is really only a copy of the project file. The source code files within are not copied and are being shared between the two game projects. If you begin making changes to the Windows version, you are also changing the Windows Phone 7 version, as they are using the same source code files. Don't spend a lot of time fixing the source code for one platform only to find that you have destroyed the code for the other!

■ **Tip** If you want to temporarily remove one of the two projects from your solution with a view to adding it back in later on, right-click the project and select Unload Project from the context menu. The project will remain inside Solution Explorer marked as Unavailable, but will otherwise be completely ignored. To restore it later on, right-click it again and select Reload Project.

Before spending any more time working on projects that have been converted in this way, you should decide whether you want to try to maintain a single source code base that works for both platforms (which is entirely feasible, as discussed in a moment), or whether you want to branch the source code and create two completely separate projects, each with its own independent source code. This decision will be dictated by how much additional development you intend to do on your game; it would be counterproductive to have to make every change twice if this can be avoided.

Using Conditional Compilation

If you do decide to try to get the same source code working on both platforms, you will need to use a handy feature of the C# compiler called *conditional compilation*. By adding special compiler directives to your source code, you can instruct the compiler to build sections of your code only if certain conditions are met, and to completely ignore it if they are not met.

This allows us to very easily create alternative code paths for the Windows Phone 7 and Windows versions of the project, even though they share the same source files. The Windows Phone 7 project file declares a compilation constant named WINDOWS_PHONE, while the Windows project instead declares a constant named WINDOWS. By checking for one or other of these, the compiler can include code that is relevant just to the appropriate project type.

Listing 16–1 shows how this is used. The #if directive begins a block of code that will only be compiled if the WINDOWS_PHONE constant is defined. The block is terminated with a corresponding #endif. This example contains an alternative code path for non-Windows Phone 7 platforms.

Listing 16–1. Conditional compilation for Windows Phone 7 or other platforms

```
#if WINDOWS_PHONE
        // Execute code for Windows Phone 7
        DoWP7Stuff();
#else
        // Execute code for non-Windows Phone 7
        DoNonWP7Stuff();
#endif
```

In addition to #if and #endif, the #elif operator can be used for "else/if" logic. Listing 16–2 shows separate code paths for Windows Phone 7, Windows. and Xbox 360.

Listing 16–2. Multiple alternate compilation code paths

```
#if WINDOWS_PHONE
        // Execute code for Windows Phone 7
        DoWP7Stuff();
#elif WINDOWS
        // Execute code for Windows
        DoWindowsStuff();
#elif XBOX
        // Execute code for Xbox 360
        DoXboxStuff();
#endif
```

■ **Note** Visual Studio will automatically gray out conditional code that will not be included by the current project. Switching between the same source file in the various projects will change this highlighting, but each source file can only be opened from within one project at a time, so the existing source code window will need to be closed before it can be reopened in another project.

Clearly this conditional compilation approach introduces an increased level of code volume and complexity, and this complexity is one of the things that should be factored into your decision about whether to maintain a single code base for multiple platforms.

In this chapter, we will focus on using a single code base with conditional compilation so that the source code can run on both the phone and on Windows.

Project Differences

When running XNA games on Windows Phone 7, the runtime environment always looked for a class within the project that derived from `Microsoft.Framework.Xna.Game`. When one was found, this class would be used to host the game.

In Windows, the program launches in a different way. The runtime looks for a static class named `Program` and calls its `Main` method to initiate the game. This class by default uses conditional compilation so that it is entirely omitted when running under Windows Phone 7, but it is an integral part of the game in Windows.

If you have renamed your main game class from the default name `Game1`, you will find that the class does not compile in the Windows environment. This is because it is still referring to the game class using its original name. The two references to `Game1` within the class will need to be modified to use the actual game class name for compilation to succeed.

Display Differences

There are several adjustments that need to be made in terms of the display when moving a project from Windows Phone 7 to Windows. Clearly, the two platforms have very different display devices and capabilities and you will need to make provision for these in order for your game to integrate nicely into both environments.

Setting the Window Size

The Windows version of the project runs in a tall, thin window; a window whose client area has a width of 480 pixels and a height of 800 pixels—exactly the size of the Windows Phone 7 screen.

The window is sized in this way because these are the dimensions specified for the `graphics.PreferredBackBufferWidth` and `graphics.PreferredBackBufferHeight` properties in the `Game1` class constructor. By setting these dimensions to different values for the Windows version of the game, we can get a more appropriate window size. Listing 16–3 includes code for both Windows Phone 7 and Windows, using a 1024 x 768 pixel window for the latter. You can find this code in the `FirstXNAProject` example accompanying this chapter.

Listing 16–3. Setting up different window sizes for each platform

```
        // Set backbuffer size and orientation
#if WINDOWS_PHONE
        _graphics.PreferredBackBufferWidth = 480;
        _graphics.PreferredBackBufferHeight = 800;
#else
        _graphics.PreferredBackBufferWidth = 1024;
        _graphics.PreferredBackBufferHeight = 768;
#endif
```

This size feels much more comfortable in Windows now, but has resulted in a differently sized window, which is therefore able to display fractionally less content on the y axis, and considerably more on the x axis than the original portrait-oriented Windows Phone 7 display.

You will almost certainly have to make adjustments to your game to compensate for these differences if you use this phone orientation. If nothing else, you will want to center the graphics horizontally to stop them from appearing along the left edge of the window.

In games using matrix rendering rather than sprites, the impact of this change might not be as great because the abstract coordinate system will adjust to match the new window size. There will still be considerably more space available at each side of the window, though, which might result in unexpected graphics appearing.

If your Windows Phone 7 game uses landscape orientation, the effect of the new window size will be much less significant as the Windows monitor is very likely to be using the same orientation. A window that is 800 x 480 pixels feels much more comfortable in Windows than one that is 480 x 800 pixels.

Using Full Screen Mode

A very common feature of Windows games is the ability to run in *full screen mode*, where the game takes over the entire display rather than running inside a floating window. Full screen mode is handled in Windows in the same way as the phone—by setting the graphics.IsFullScreen property to true in the class constructor.

You will find this instruction inside this chapter's FirstXNAProject example, commented out. You can uncomment it to see its effects, but *before you do*, note that when the game is running in full screen mode, there is no Close Window button to use to leave the game and return to Windows. The keyboard shortcut Alt+F4 is the answer here because it closes the active window; use it when the game is running to close its window down.

■ **Caution** Be very careful when using breakpoints in a game running in full screen mode. The breakpoint will fire, but the game window will continue to display over the whole screen, making it difficult to proceed. It is strongly advisable to run the game in windowed mode when you are debugging it.

Once your game is running, if you decide to switch between full screen and windowed mode, you can just call the graphics.ToggleFullScreen method and XNA will take care of everything for you.

When the game runs in full screen mode, Windows will automatically stretch it to fill the whole monitor. This can be very useful, but can also result in the graphics being stretched if the aspect ratio of the monitor doesn't match that of the window.

Something you might want to do is to run the game at the native screen resolution being used by Windows. At the time the game class constructor is running, nothing is available to provide this information, but we can defer the setting of the resolution until a moment later, by which time the desktop width and height can be retrieved.

This is achieved instead by setting up an event handler for the _graphics object's PreparingDeviceSettings event. When that event fires, the back buffer size can be set to match the size of the current display mode, as shown in Listing 16–4.

Listing 16–4. Setting the window size to match the size of the desktop

```
public Game1()
{
    _graphics = new GraphicsDeviceManager(this);
    Content.RootDirectory = "Content";

    // Frame rate is 30 fps by default for Windows Phone.
    TargetElapsedTime = TimeSpan.FromSeconds(1.0f / 30);

    // Set backbuffer size and orientation
#if WINDOWS_PHONE
    _graphics.PreferredBackBufferWidth = 480;
    _graphics.PreferredBackBufferHeight = 800;
#else
    // Instead of setting a fixed size, use the size of the Windows desktop
    _graphics.PreparingDeviceSettings += new
        EventHandler<PreparingDeviceSettingsEventArgs>(_graphics_PreparingDeviceSettings);
#endif

    // Switch to full screen mode
    _graphics.IsFullScreen = true;
}

// Set the window size to match the desktop resolution
void _graphics_PreparingDeviceSettings(object sender, PreparingDeviceSettingsEventArgs e)
{
    e.GraphicsDeviceInformation.PresentationParameters.BackBufferHeight =
                    e.GraphicsDeviceInformation.Adapter.CurrentDisplayMode.Height;
    e.GraphicsDeviceInformation.PresentationParameters.BackBufferWidth =
                    e.GraphicsDeviceInformation.Adapter.CurrentDisplayMode.Width;
}
```

Be aware when setting the resolution in this way that you have no idea what size your window will actually end up being. You will need to ensure that your rendering code is resolution-independent to ensure that the game continues to be playable on all different screen modes.

In a finished game, it is worth considering providing options to give the user a choice of window sizes and control over whether the game will display in full screen mode or not.

Showing and Hiding the Mouse Cursor

XNA's default behavior in Windows is to hide the mouse cursor when it is over the game window. This might be what you want in full screen mode (though it also might not), but in windowed mode it can be quite distracting—when the user moves the cursor across the window to click the window's Close button, the cursor suddenly vanishes!

Its behavior is easy controlled using the `IsMouseVisible` property provided by the XNA `Game` class. You can therefore simply change this property in your constructor or elsewhere in your game to control the cursor visibility, as shown in Listing 16–5.

Listing 16–5. *Showing the mouse cursor*

```
this.IsMouseVisible = true;
```

Input Differences

The majority of Windows users will not have access to a touch screen, but the mouse can be used to provide most of the interaction that the touch screen can provide. The loss of multitouch input is offset by having multiple mouse buttons, and the mouse wheel available to most users.

On the other hand, all your users will have keyboards, whereas only a minority of Windows Phone 7 users will have this hardware available.

This section explores the differences in input methods between the two environments.

Mouse Input

When we wanted to read raw touch input from the screen in our Windows Phone 7 projects, we used the `TouchPanel` class (refer to Chapter 4 if you need to refresh your memory on this subject). The `TouchPanel` class is available when running on Windows so the code still compiles, but unless you have a capable touch-screen monitor running under Windows 7, it reports a `MaximumTouchCount` of 0 and never returns anything from its `GetState` function.

Assuming that we decide to use mouse input as an alternative to touch input, the best way to obtain this data in a Windows game is by using the `Mouse` class.

This class contains a static method named `GetState` that returns a `MouseState` object containing all sorts of details about the mouse. These include the following:

- The mouse position relative to the window, using the `X` and `Y` properties. This will be available regardless of which mouse buttons are pressed, and at all times, even if the mouse cursor is outside the game window.

- The state of the `LeftButton`, `MiddleButton`, and `RightButton`. The available state values are `Released` when the button is up, and `Pressed` when it is down.

- Support for the state of two additional mouse buttons via the `XButton1` and `XButton2` properties (though many mice will not have sufficient buttons to support this, and exactly which buttons they correspond to will vary from one mouse to the next).

- A `ScrollWheelValue` that contains the cumulative distance that the mouse wheel has been scrolled. This is not incremented or decremented by values of 1, but uses larger values (typically 120 for each unit that the wheel is scrolled).

The capabilities are very different from the multitouch values that the `TouchPanel` class provides, and if your game is doing anything more complex than simple single-point interaction, you might need to invest some thought and time into remapping the control mechanism into the Windows environment.

The `Mouse` class is available and functional inside the Windows Phone 7 environment, too, so if its capabilities are suitable, you might be able to use the same code in both places. Windows Phone 7 treats the primary contact point as if it were the left mouse button.

There are several useful TouchPanel features that you will lose as a result of using Mouse on the device, however, as they are not offered by the MouseState class. They include the ability to tell whether the touch state is Pressed, Moved, or Released; and the TryGetPreviousLocation method. Also note that the X and Y position properties will always return the last known position unless contact is currently being made with the phone's screen.

The TouchPanel example project that accompanies this chapter has been copied from the project with the same name in Chapter 4 and modified to additionally support Windows. As you will see if you look through the source code, the touch processing code in the TouchPanelGame.Update method needed to be completely rewritten to support the use of the Mouse class.

■ **Note** This project uses a Windows version of the GameFramework project that we built up through the XNA chapters. We will cover the conversion of this project to the Windows environment shortly, so just ignore it for the time being.

Gestures

The high-level TouchPanel gestures are not supported in the Windows environment. The code will compile and run without any problems, but no gestures will be returned by the IsGestureAvailable or ReadGesture class members.

Keyboard Input

Now for a little good news: keyboard input is handled exactly the same way in Windows as it is in Windows Phone 7. The Keyboard.GetState function is used to return information about keys that are pressed, and the data is formatted just the same as on the phone.

GamePad Input

Windows games have an input mechanism that Windows Phone 7 does not, however, and that is the ability to use Xbox 360 game controllers for input. Input from these controllers is provided using the GamePad class.

Data is obtained by calling the static GamePad.GetState function, which is called passing in the index of the player whose gamepad values are to be returned. For single-player games, just pass PlayerIndex.One. The function returns a GamePadState object.

The first thing you need to do with this returned object is check whether it is actually receiving data from a connected gamepad. Its IsConnected property will return this piece of information; if it returns false, the rest of the state object will be entirely empty and another input mechanism must be sought.

If the device is connected, it offers a wealth of controller information:

- The Buttons property returns a GamePadButtons object, which in turn has properties to allow the state of each individual button to be checked. These button properties are A, B, Back, BigButton, LeftShoulder, LeftStick, RightShoulder, RightStick, Start, X, and Y. That should be enough buttons for anyone.

- The DPad property returns a GamePadDPad object, with properties to query the state of the directional pad: Down, Left, Right, and Up.

- The ThumbSticks property returns a GamePadThumbSticks object, with properties for the controller's thumb sticks. Two properties are available, Left and Right, corresponding to the left and right stick. They each return a Vector2, allowing proportional values to be read rather than simple pressed or released values.

- The Triggers property returns a GamePadTriggers object, allowing the state of the trigger buttons to be read. They are obtained from the Left and Right properties, and are once again proportional values, returned as a float.

The class also offers two methods, IsButtonDown and IsButtonUp, which allow a specific button's state to be checked. This will sometimes be more useful than the GamePadButtons properties, as passing the button as a parameter allows it to be easily reassigned by the player.

■ **Note** The GamePad class will compile in the Windows Phone 7 environment, and in fact is used in all XNA projects to check for the state of the Back button. This is the only button that will return any values on the device, however.

Isolated Storage

Unlike Windows Phone 7, Windows is an open operating system and allows full access to its underlying file system. There is therefore no concept of isolated storage when running in Windows.

File access is instead performed using the normal System.IO namespace, exactly as it would be in another game.

XNA games in Windows also have no access to the IsolatedStorageSettings class that we used in the game framework to save and reload our game settings. This was a very useful class to have around, and we will need to replicate its behavior when running in Windows – this issue will be addressed in a moment.

Application Life Cycle

Windows is a fully multitasking operating system with none of the memory or processing constraints that the phone has to work within, so it does not have any concept similar to that of tombstoning.

When a Windows application is put into the background, it continues running exactly as it would have in the foreground. There is no need to maintain application state when the game deactivates or to perform any other similar processing.

Converting the Game Framework to Run on Windows

Most of the example projects that we created during the course of the XNA section of this book relied on the GameFramework project, which provides a useful set of additional features in addition to those offered natively by XNA. To get our projects running both on the phone and on Windows, we will need to create a version of this library that works in Windows, too.

This turns out to be a simple process for the most part, and allows us to transfer the phone's projects into Windows without too much effort.

In this section we will look at the steps involved in getting GameFramework working in both environments.

Storing and Retrieving Game Settings

As mentioned in the "Isolated Storage" section a moment ago, there is no IsolatedStorageSettings class in the Windows version of XNA, so we will need to find an alternative method for Windows to use for storing settings in the GameFramework.SettingsManager class.

This functionality is not too tricky to replicate. First of all, when compiling for Windows, the class will provide a dictionary into which string values can be written. Two new functions are then provided that allow the contents of this dictionary to be translated into an XML document and written to disk, or to be read back from the XML and placed back into the dictionary.

The API for the class can remain identical across the two platforms, removing any need for the games using the class to have to cater separately for each target environment.

First there is the settings dictionary. This dictionary is declared as a class-level variable, as shown in Listing 16–6, set to compile only under Windows. Alongside it we declare a file name to use when reading and writing the settings. No path is specified, so this will be created in the same directory as the game's executable.

Listing 16–6. Creating a Dictionary to store the game's settings

```
#if WINDOWS
    // Declare a dictionary into which all of our settings will be written
    private Dictionary<string, string> _settings = new Dictionary<string, string>();
    // The name of the file in which the settings will be stored
    private const string FileName = "Settings.dat";
#endif
```

Following on from this is a minor change to the class constructor. So that any previously stored settings are available as soon as the class is queried, they must be reloaded. The constructor handles it to ensure that values are always available to the class. Listing 16–7 shows the new constructor; we will look at the LoadSettings function shortly.

Listing 16–7. The modified SettingsManager class constructor

```
    internal SettingsManager(GameHost game)
    {
        // Store the game reference
        _game = game;

#if WINDOWS
        // Load any existing stored settings
        LoadSettings();
#endif
    }
```

The next change that the class needs relates to putting values into the dictionary and getting them back out again. Although there are multiple overloads of SetValue and GetValue, only one overload for each function actually interacts with the settings, so this is the only one that we need to modify.

SetValue is enhanced as shown in Listing 16–8 so that it will work for both Windows Phone 7 games and Windows games. The Windows code is virtually identical to that of Windows Phone 7, except that it uses the class's _settings dictionary instead of IsolatedStorageSettings.

Listing 16–8. Creating or updating settings values

```
    public void SetValue(string settingName, string value)
    {
        // Convert the setting name to lower case so that names are case-insensitive
        settingName = settingName.ToLower();
#if WINDOWS_PHONE
        // Does a setting with this name already exist?
        if (IsolatedStorageSettings.ApplicationSettings.Contains(settingName))
        {
            // Yes, so update its value
            IsolatedStorageSettings.ApplicationSettings[settingName] = value;
        }
        else
        {
            // No, so add it
            IsolatedStorageSettings.ApplicationSettings.Add(settingName, value);
        }
#else
        // Does this setting already exist in the dictionary?
        if (_settings.ContainsKey(settingName))
        {
            // Update the setting's value
            _settings[settingName] = value;
        }
        else
        {
            // Add the value
            _settings.Add(settingName, value);
        }
        // Save the settings
        SaveSettings();
#endif
    }
```

One final change is present in this piece of code in addition to the change of dictionary, however: it makes a call to SaveSettings each time a value is updated. This ensures that the settings are always retained from the moment they are modified, mirroring the behavior on the phone. We will look at the SaveSettings function shortly.

The code for GetValue is similarly modified, reading from either the _settings dictionary or IsolatedStorageSettings as appropriate. This is repeated, too, for the ClearValues and DeleteValue functions, both of which also call SaveSettings to ensure that their changes are immediately reflected to the data file on disk.

Finally we arrive at SaveSettings and LoadSettings, whose responsibilities are to ensure that the data is stored for later use, and then read back in for subsequent interrogation. They operate using an XML file, into which all the defined values are placed.

The code within these functions is not particularly interesting, using exactly the same techniques that we used for saving and restoring the high scores inside the HighScores class, so please take a look in the project's source code if you want to see how they are implemented.

With these changes in place, the class operates identically (from the client's perspective) under both environments. If you scan through the code for the class, the conditional compilation statements scattered throughout do make the code harder to read, but the overall functionality is worth that increase in complexity if you want to be able to target both platforms.

Application Life Cycle Events

Although in Windows Phone 7 we need to deal with the Launching, Closing, Deactivated, and Activated events, in Windows, we don't particularly need to worry about any of these as there is no application life cycle as such.

It is likely that you will have taken advantage of the Launching event to initialize your game, however, so it is important that its event still fires when running under Windows so that the initialization still completes properly.

Instead of setting up the event handlers, the GameHost class constructor simply calls into the virtual GameLaunching function when running under Windows. This is the same path that a newly launched game would take on the phone, resulting in the same startup behavior.

All the rest of the life cycle code can be excluded from this class as it is not needed in Windows.

High Scores

A small and simple change is required to the HighScores class to instruct it to read and write its score data to a file using the System.IO namespace instead of using isolated storage. As the class already stores its content in an XML document, no additional modifications are necessary.

Everything Else

There are no other changes required to the game framework. The rest of the project works identically in both environments.

The biggest changes that you will find you need to make when getting your games running for Windows will almost certainly be in the area of the organization of your display (taking the Windows display orientation and screen resolutions into account) and input (using Mouse and Keyboard instead of TouchPanel). You should find that the rest of your game will work as expected without any changes being required.

Trial Mode

XNA's trial mode does not function in Windows so it cannot be used to allow the player to switch between an evaluation or full copy of the game. You will need to implement this functionality yourself.

The easiest way to do this by far is to create two different versions of the game: one a trial version (with whichever features are being excluded completely removed from the game), and the second a full version with all the missing features restored. Your users can then evaluate the trial version before purchasing, at which point you provide them with the full version.

Without the Windows Phone Marketplace, you will need to implement your own purchase system. One simple option is to use an online credit card–processing service such as PayPal and to send out full versions of the game each time you are notified of a purchase.

Distribution

The lack of a Windows Phone Marketplace equivalent for Windows also means that you have no centralized channel through which to distribute your game. Instead, you will need to create your own channels via a web site or online software portal, for example.

One advantage of being in control of the distribution yourself, however, is that you do not have to undergo any kind of submission process before you can release your software. When you decide that it is ready, you can distribute it immediately.

Revisiting Some Example Projects

Two of the more complex example projects have been re-created for Windows to show how little effort is generally required in getting them up and running.

Let's see what was involved in converting these projects across. Both of the example projects can be found set up to run in Windows in this chapter's accompanying downloads.

The FireAndSmoke Project

FireAndSmoke was a project that we used back in Chapter 8 to demonstrate particle effects. It runs in landscape orientation, so it should convert fairly easily to the default Windows landscape screen orientation; and has no interaction at all, removing the need to change any input processing code.

Only one change was required during the conversion of the project: to simply set a more appropriate default screen resolution—1024 x 768 pixels instead of the phone's 800 x 480.

With this change made, the project runs very nicely under both Windows and Windows Phone 7.

The VaporTrailTS project

This project was developed in Chapter 8 and then updated in Chapter 10 to add tombstoning support. We will leave all this in place in the conversion to Windows so that the functionality remains when compiling for the phone.

Three changes were required during the conversion of the project. The first was to set a more appropriate default screen resolution, just as we did for the FireAndSmoke project.

The second change, the only one of any substance, was to the way the camera mode is changed. On the phone, the TouchPanel class is used to detect taps to the screen, but in Windows we need to use the Mouse class instead. However, the Mouse class only tells us whether the button is up or down, and doesn't directly provide a way to tell whether the button has been pressed down since the last update. As a result, simply checking the left button state would cause the camera to constantly and rapidly cycle through all the different modes when the button was held down, making it very difficult for the user to simply move to the next mode.

We can replicate the "just pressed" behavior by storing the state of the mouse from the previous update and comparing it with the state for the current update. If it was up previously but is down now, it has just been pressed, and we can move to the next camera mode; otherwise, the camera mode is not altered.

Listing 16–9 shows the first part of this modification. It declares a class-level variable to hold the mouse state from the previous update. We begin by setting the current state into it, so there is always a valid set of data contained within the variable even during the first call to Update.

Listing 16–9. Storing the previous state of the mouse

```
#if WINDOWS
    // Track the previous mouse state so we can tell when the button pressed state changes
    private MouseState lastMouseState = Mouse.GetState();
#endif
```

The remainder of the code is shown in Listing 16–10. It checks the current state of the left mouse button and compares it with the previous state, indicating that the camera should be updated only if the button has just been pressed.

Listing 16–10. Checking to see whether the camera mode should be updated

```
        bool toggleCamera = false;

#if WINDOWS_PHONE
        // Has the user touched the screen?
        TouchCollection tc = TouchPanel.GetState();
        if (tc.Count == 1 && tc[0].State == TouchLocationState.Pressed) toggleCamera = true;
#else
        // Was the mouse up last time, but is down now?
        MouseState thisMouseState = Mouse.GetState();
        if (lastMouseState.LeftButton == ButtonState.Released &&
                                    thisMouseState.LeftButton == ButtonState.Pressed)
        {
            // Yes, so change camera
            toggleCamera = true;
        }
        // Store the new mouse state for next time
        lastMouseState = thisMouseState;
#endif
```

The final change to the project is a cosmetic one that is present only to make the project look better. When we ran on the phone, we instructed the PaperPlaneObject class to add a new vapor particle only every three updates. This provided a reasonable balance between display complexity and performance; adding more particles caused the game to slow down when running on the device.

Windows PCs tend to have significantly more graphical power than the phone, so we can happily add a particle every update. This results in a much thicker and more voluminous vapor trail.

Everything else works as required without needing to be changed.

Developing Games for Windows Phone 7 and Windows

If you decide that you want to target both platforms, you know now that it is a feasible goal. The primary piece of advice that I can offer is to simply test your game in both environments as often as you can throughout its development. The sooner you try things out, the quicker you can spot problems and correct them before you build too much additional complexity on top of them.

Running Silverlight Projects in the Browser

The conversion of a Silverlight project from Windows Phone 7 into the general Silverlight environment is unfortunately not quite as straightforward as it is for XNA. Although a fair bit more effort is required, however, it is still possible to get your project moved across relatively unscathed.

Browser-based conversions can provide a great way of demonstrating your game. What better way to tell people about it than to actually allow them to play it? You might also choose to develop the Silverlight version as a game in its own right, separate from the Windows Phone 7 version.

Because the assembly references and classes used by Silverlight in the browser are a bit different from the phone, it is not really possible to get a single source code base running in both environments. Instead you will need to create a new project and import the functionality in from the original source files, modifying them as you go for the new environment.

You will take a brief tour through the process required to transfer your Windows Phone 7 Silverlight games into the browser using Visual Studio 2010 Professional or above. We will only focus on this specific area; for additional information about how to package up and deploy your Silverlight game to a web site or details about additional Silverlight features, please look online or refer to a source of information dedicated to this subject.

We will transfer in three projects from the Silverlight section of this book: the ColorFade project from Chapter 11, the GameNavigation project from Chapter 13, and the DiamondLines project from Chapter 12. All use the SLGameFramework project, which we will transfer, too. (The converted projects can be found in the download for this chapter.)

Differences between Silverlight and Silverlight for Windows Phone

Both versions of Silverlight are based on the same principles and (for the most part) the same underlying API and feature sets.

Silverlight on Windows Phone uses the Silverlight 3 runtime, but has various additions not present in Silverlight 3 for the browser. One such example is the CompositeTransform class that we have been using to manipulate our sprites in the SLGameFramework project. For this reason, it is advisable to create your Silverlight projects for the browser using Silverlight 4 instead of Silverlight 3 so that these features are available in both environments.

To help identify the exact discrepancies between the two environments, Microsoft has published a document covering all the differences in detail. You can visit http://tinyurl.com/sldifferences to read it.

Converting Projects from Windows Phone 7

Generally the easiest way to begin converting your Windows Phone 7 project is to create a brand new Silverlight project and copy the source code and data files in. Initiating your project in this way ensures that the project is configured properly for browser use, including all the necessary references. It also allows a web project to be created, inside which your game will be hosted, ready to be displayed by the browser.

In this section you will walk through the steps required to create a new application and then import the ColorFade project that you first looked at in Chapter 11 so that it runs in the browser. Feel free to follow along with these steps if you like, or just take a look at the ColorFade project that accompanies this chapter to see the end result.

Creating a New Silverlight Project

To create a new project, use the Silverlight Application template, as shown in Figure 16–3. Use the same name for your application as you used for the Windows Phone 7 application. In this case, we will use the name ColorFade.

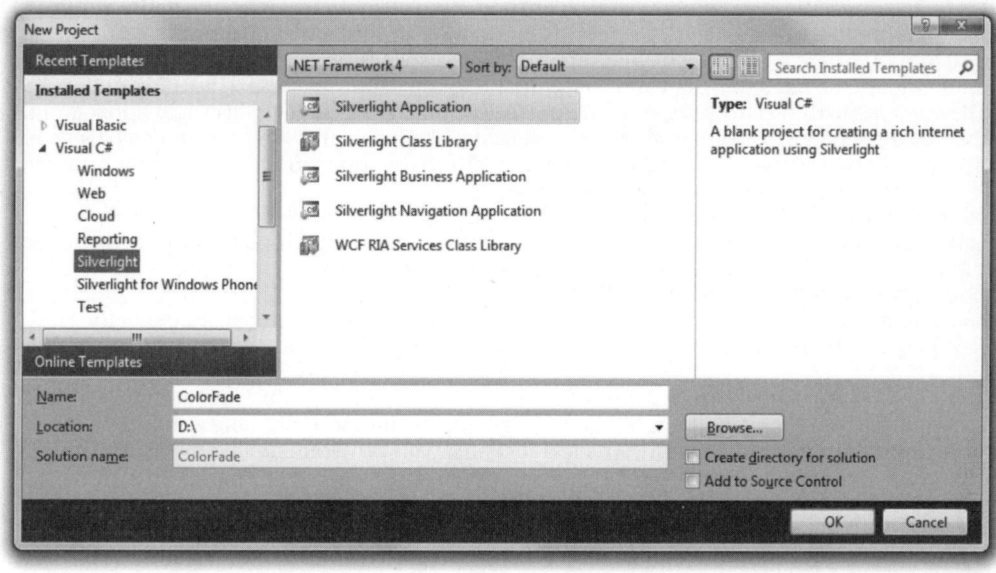

Figure 16–3. Creating a new Silverlight application project

Once you have selected a location for your project and clicked the OK button, the New Silverlight Application window will appear, shown in Figure 16–4. It can be used to set the parameters for the project that you are creating.

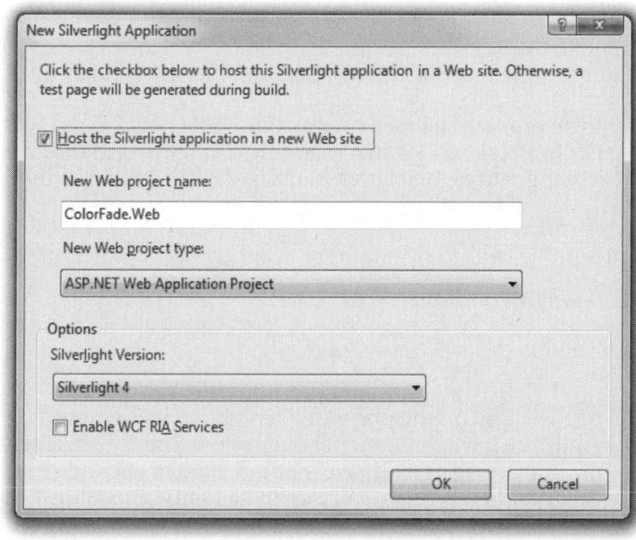

Figure 16–4. Setting the configuration of the new Silverlight application project

Unless you have specific requirements to the contrary, keep all the options set as shown in the screenshot. This will create a Silverlight 4 project (as mentioned earlier) and will host it in the ASP.NET Development Server. This is a lightweight web server designed specifically for hosting .NET debug sessions, and removes the need to install and configure IIS for development and debugging.

The IDE will open with two projects in the new solution: one for the actual Silverlight application, and the other for the ASP.NET Development Server web site. The latter of these projects can be ignored for our purposes as it is already configured to launch the Silverlight application in the default browser. We will concentrate instead on the main application project.

This project contains a similar set of source files to those we saw when developing for the phone, and they have very similar initial content, too. App.cs contains the code required to start up the project, and MainPage.xaml contains an empty page—though it is actually *completely* empty this time, whereas on the phone we were given a simple control layout by default.

We could run the project at this stage to see how it looks in the browser, but all it does at the moment is display a white rectangle on a white background. This makes it kind of hard to see whether it is working!

To resolve this issue, click into the main area of the MainPage.xaml page designer and set a color for the Background property of the Grid that is filling the page—any color will do as long as it's not white. With this done, start the project running. After a few seconds, your browser should appear, and it will then display your colored rectangle. Success!

The rectangle will, however, be displayed so that it completely fills the entire browser client area. This is because the Width and Height properties of the page have both been set to Auto. This can be very useful as it allows the content and the user interface to automatically adapt to the available space, but for the purposes of our games it would be much more useful to fix the page to the same screen area that the phone uses.

Try changing the Width property of the page (not the Grid) value to 480 and the Height to 800, and then run the project again. Now the colored rectangle appears at the defined size, ready for us to start putting some content inside it.

Silverlight Navigation Model

Silverlight in the browser uses a different method to display multiple pages of data. If you look carefully at the MainPage code that has been created in our sample project, you will find that it is not actually a page at all, but instead a UserControl.

Silverlight in the browser can display one single top-level element at any time. This is called the *root visual*, and is set into the application's App object. If you take a look in App.xaml.cs, you will find the code from Listing 16–11. It is this piece of code that actually causes the contents of MainPage to appear in the browser.

Listing 16–11. *Setting the Silverlight root visual*

```
private void Application_Startup(object sender, StartupEventArgs e)
{
    this.RootVisual = new MainPage();
}
```

This approach is clearly different from the one we used on the phone. Silverlight offers a control class named Frame, however, which provides exactly the navigation model that we used on the phone. It can navigate to a Page contained within the application using its Navigate method, has GoBack and GoForward methods, and has CanGoBack and CanGoForward properties—all exactly the same as the NavigationService object on the phone.

To take advantage of these navigation functions, we will place a Frame control onto MainPage. All our application pages will then be displayed inside this page, avoiding the need to change any structures of our converted projects.

Delete the existing `Grid` control from `MainPage`, and then add a new `Frame` control from the Toolbox. Right-click the `Frame` and select Reset Layout/All from the context menu, as shown in Figure 16–5. It will remove all configuration from the `Frame` so that it completely fills its container: the `MainPage` user control.

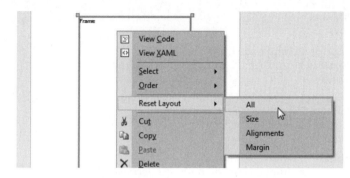

Figure 16–5. *Resetting the layout of the Frame control*

Change the `Frame`'s name so that it is called `mainFrame` instead of the default `frame1`. This is all we need within the XAML to host our content.

We have a slight naming issue to deal with next. The page we have been working on is called `MainPage`, but we have also been using a class with this name in our Windows Phone 7 projects to actually store the content of the main page. To resolve this naming collision, we will rename the `MainPage` class in the new Silverlight project to `HostPage` instead. This then clearly has the role of hosting the pages rather than providing the content for one.

The class can be renamed by first right-clicking the `MainPage.xaml` file in Solution Explorer and selecting Rename from the context menu. Enter the new name, `HostPage.xaml`, and the `.xaml` file itself and the `.xaml.cs` code file will both be renamed accordingly.

This procedure has only affected the file names, however, not the name of the class defined in the code. To complete the rename operation, open the code behind the page, right-click the name MainPage in the class declaration, and select Refactor/Rename, as shown in Figure 16–6. Enter the new name, `HostPage`, and click OK to complete the renaming of the class.

```
public partial class MainPage : UserControl
{
    public MainPage()
    {
        InitializeComponent(
    }
}
```

🖼 View Designer	Shift+F7	
Refactor ▶		ab✓ Rename...
Organize Usings ▶		🔧 Extract Method...
📋 Create Unit Tests...		🔧 Encapsulate Field...
📋 Insert Snippet...	Ctrl+K, Ctrl+X	🔧 Extract Interface...
📋 Surround With...	Ctrl+K, Ctrl+S	a,x Remove Parameters...
🔧 Go To Definition	Shift+F2	a,b Reorder Parameters...

Figure 16–6. *Renaming the MainPage class*

Our project now contains a single `UserControl` named `HostPage`, inside which an empty `Frame` resides. The next step is to add the source files from our Windows Phone 7 project.

Adding the Project Pages

The only page in the original ColorFade project is MainPage, so we copy across the MainPage.xaml and MainPage.xaml.cs files, putting them into the new project's directory along with the existing source files. MainPage.xaml can then be added into the project.

Several compilation errors appear at this stage due to differences between the two Silverlight environments. We can fix them up as follows:

1. In MainPage.xaml, change the type of the root node from phone:PhoneApplicationPage to navigation:Page (don't forget to change the element terminator at the end of the file, too).

2. Add the navigation namespace to the root node. This is most easily obtained by adding a new item to the project of type Silverlight Page and then copying the line that begins xmlns:navigation from the new page back into MainPage. The new page can then be deleted.

3. Remove the SupportedOrientations, Orientation, and shell:SystemTray.IsVisible attributes from the XAML root node because they are only supported in Windows Phone 7.

4. Remove the xmlns:phone and xmlns:shell namespace declarations from the root node.

5. Remove the FontFamily, FontSize, and Foreground attributes from the root node.

6. Remove the two Style attributes from the TextBlock controls within the page.

7. In the code behind, remove the using Microsoft.Phone.Controls statement.

8. Modify the class declaration in the code behind so that the class derives from Page instead of PhoneApplicationPage.

This is quite a lot of effort for a single simple page and clarifies why a single code base for both Silverlight environments is not practical. After completing these steps, your project should compile without errors, though it still shows nothing when run because we just get to see the empty frame.

To actually display MainPage, we simply need to tell the frame to navigate there. Modify the HostPage class constructor to contain the code shown in Listing 16–12.

Listing 16–12. Instructing the Frame to navigate to MainPage

```
public HostPage()
{
    InitializeComponent();

    // Navigate to MainPage
    hostFrame.Navigate(new Uri("/MainPage.xaml", UriKind.Relative));
}
```

Now when you run the application, the browser window appears and displays the contents of MainPage.

These are the basic steps that need to be performed to transfer your pages across to Silverlight from the phone. Once you have followed these steps, the majority of the XAML layout and the code behind the page should work with little or no modification (unless you are calling in to any Windows Phone 7 libraries, in which case they will need to be redesigned or refactored).

The amount of effort involved is great enough that you will not want to have to repeat the steps on a regular basis. For this reason, a sensible strategy for putting a demonstration game into Silverlight is to focus just on the main game content and leave all the navigation, high scores, and so on behind. This results in a much simpler task.

Another strategy that is worth adopting if you plan to target both environments is to put as little content into the game's Page classes as possible. Simple non-page classes will copy in to the Silverlight environment with little or no modification required at all, so getting as much content into such classes as possible will reduce the overall amount of effort, particularly if you want to regularly update the browser-based Silverlight application to match changes you have made to the Windows Phone 7 version.

Example Projects

As promised, here are two more simple conversions of Windows Phone 7 Silverlight examples that we created earlier. Neither of these has had any presentation attention lavished upon them, so they look extremely basic, but they demonstrate the direct conversion results that are achieved when converting into the browser-based Silverlight environment.

Both of the example projects can be found in the download that accompanies this chapter.

Navigation

The Navigation project demonstrates how navigation within a Frame control works when running in the browser. When you launch the project, the simple game framework menu will appear just as it did on the phone. Clicking the buttons will navigate between the different pages.

Note that each time you click a button, the browser's navigation history is updated. This allows you to use the browser's Back button to return to the previous page, just like on the phone. Also observe that the stack is manipulated in exactly the same way as on the phone when navigating between non-menu pages; click the End Game button in the "Game" page and you will be sent to the "High scores" page, but clicking Back here returns you to the menu, not to the "Game" page.

Also note that state is maintained between the pages in exactly the same way as on the phone. If you click the Back button from the game page, the menu offers the Resume Game button, and clicking it will return you to the game. The state is maintained despite the browser navigation that is taking place.

If you click to start a new game while an existing game is active, you will notice that the MessageBox call works perfectly well in the browser-based Silverlight, too.

In practice, including navigation in a game that you are converting to the browser might be more than you really need, especially if you simply want to give the player an idea of what the game has to offer. It might be more sensible to launch straight into the game and not worry about including the overheads of high score tables and so on. Once you have convinced the players that your game is worth further investigation, they can take advantage of all these features in the full version on the phone.

Apart from the changes described for converting project pages from the Windows Phone 7 Silverlight environment into the browser environment, there are no code changes to this project at all.

Diamond Lines

To demonstrate getting a game up and running, let's convert the DiamondLines example from Chapter 12. This demonstrates the use of the SLGameFramework, Sprite control, storyboards and animation, user interaction, and (of course) results in a playable game at the end (even if it is very basic).

As you will see if you open and launch the project, it performs very nicely in the browser. The higher specification of a PC results in a very smooth experience. The storyboard animation really helps as it allows the graphics to move as quickly as the PC can animate them, but still ensure that they move at the correct speed, resulting in predictable and very smooth animation.

Figure 16–7 shows a screenshot of the game running inside Mozilla Firefox.

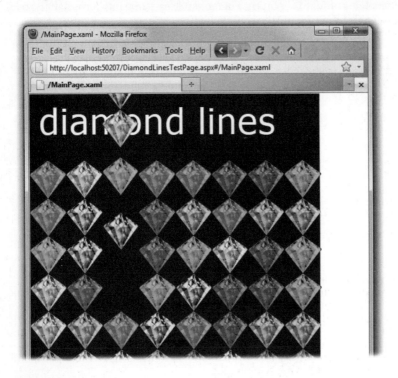

Figure 16–7. Playing Diamond Lines inside a web browser

Once again, the changes required to get this running were no more than described for converting pages earlier on. Despite the game using just a single page (MainPage, in which the game is displayed) we still use the HostPage approach here, both because it simplifies the import of the existing page and because it allows us to more easily add in navigation support later should we want to.

Let's Play…

This brings us to the end of this chapter and to the end of the book. I sincerely hope that you have found it useful and informative, but more than anything I hope that it inspires you to open Visual Studio, plug in your phone, and get started creating your own games.

Windows Phone 7 is an exciting and powerful environment for gaming, with massive potential for creating original and inventive styles of gameplay. Let your imagination run free. Who knows where it will take you? I wish you many happy days of writing games for Windows Phone 7 devices!

Please do let me know about the games that you create. I would also love to hear any feedback that you have about this book. You can contact me by sending e-mail to adam@adamdawes.com.

Index

■ ■ ■

■ C

■ J

■ K

■ L

You Need the Companion eBook

Your purchase of this book entitles you to buy the companion PDF-version eBook for only $10. Take the weightless companion with you anywhere.

We believe this Apress title will prove so indispensable that you'll want to carry it with you everywhere, which is why we are offering the companion eBook (in PDF format) for $10 to customers who purchase this book now. Convenient and fully searchable, the PDF version of any content-rich, page-heavy Apress book makes a valuable addition to your programming library. You can easily find and copy code—or perform examples by quickly toggling between instructions and the application. Even simultaneously tackling a donut, diet soda, and complex code becomes simplified with hands-free eBooks!

Once you purchase your book, getting the $10 companion eBook is simple:

1. Visit **www.apress.com/promo/tendollars/**.

2. Complete a basic registration form to receive a randomly generated question about this title.

3. Answer the question correctly in 60 seconds, and you will receive a promotional code to redeem for the $10.00 eBook.

233 Spring Street, New York, NY 10013

Offer valid through 6/11.